A NEW COMMENTARY
ON THE POEMS OF
W. B. YEATS

A NEW COMMENTARY
ON THE POEMS OF
W. B. YEATS

A. Norman Jeffares

Stanford University Press
Stanford, California
1984

TO ADÈLE CROWDER

Stanford University Press
Stanford, California

© 1968, 1984 A. Norman Jeffares

Originating publisher: The Macmillan Press Ltd, London

First published in the U.S.A. by Stanford University Press in 1984

Printed in Hong Kong

ISBN 0-8047-1221-2

LC 83-40105

Contents

Preface

'I don't want them', Yeats once remarked to his wife, 'to know all about everything.' Scholarly and critical work, however, continues apace, and specialised studies (based upon an increased amount of material now available to scholars in various libraries and collections) add to our knowledge of the poet's life, of his thought and technique. Much, however, still remains uncertain and at times obscure (and in certain biographical details will probably continue to do so), a situation to which Yeats himself might not have been averse.

This new Commentary is intended to provide readers with information which will help them to assess the effect of Yeats's sources - his wide and varied reading - and some of the events of his life; to understand some of the sources for the factual meanings of the poems; and to recognise the circumstances in which some of them were written.

The Commentary attempts to date the composition of poems where this is possible, and to give the place of their first publication. Yeats's prose has been quoted where it throws light on the meaning of particular poems, and these passages of prose have been annotated where this has seemed likely to be useful. Passages from the poet's notes to early editions are included as well as passages from his autobiographical, critical or journalistic writings. Abbreviations of titles of works cited are given in a list on pp. xii-xv. An appendix gives his views on the pronunciation and spelling of Gaelic names, and maps are supplied.

This Commentary is intended to assist the reader of either Yeats's *Collected Poems* (page references to the second edition (1950) are given in italic type in the margins) or *The Poems: A New Edition* (the numbers given to the poems by the editor of this edition (1984) are placed before the titles of the poems in the Commentary in bold type). *The Contents of The Poems: A New Edition* (pp. xxii-xxxv) gives the titles of the poems, and their numbers; for convenience the page numbers of *Collected Poems* are also given (in italic type) in this contents list. Where necessary, poems which were not included in *Collected Poems*, but which are included in *The Poems: A New Edition*, have earlier places of publication given beside their titles in the Commentary upon them.

The bibliographical material given in the Commentary can be supplemented by consultation of the essential *Variorum Edition of the Poems of W. B. Yeats* (ed. Peter Allt and Russell K. Alspach, 1957) and *The Variorum Edition of the Plays of W. B. Yeats* (ed. Russell K. Alspach, assisted by Catherine C. Alspach, 1966). *A Concordance to the Poems of W. B. Yeats* (ed. Stephen Maxfield Parish, 1963) and *A Concordance to the Plays of W. B. Yeats* (ed. Eric Domville, 1972) provide quick means of comparing images and symbols used by Yeats.

This commentary inevitably owes much to the work of others (my previous *Commentary on the Collected Poems* (1968) was revised in four subsequent printings in the light of fresh information) and I have tried to acknowledge my debts to them by citing them, where apposite, as sources for my information. In the earlier Commentary, I paid tribute to the helpfulness of Mrs W. B. Yeats in allowing me access to the poet's library, correspondence and manuscripts, in providing me with information about the composition of poems, plays and prose, and in indicating actual and possible sources for images and ideas. Over the years scholars and critics owed much to her generosity, her concern to preserve Yeats's books and papers, to help in establishing the meaning of poems. She was herself a discerning critic (with a sharp sense of humour, a nice appreciation of the ridiculous), a learned woman who wore her learning lightly. I am particularly indebted to Professor Brendan Kennelly for help in annotating material relating to literature in Irish and to the work of the late Sheelah Kirby, author of *The Yeats Country* (1962), and to Mr James P. McGarry, whose *Place Names in the Writings of William Butler Yeats* (1976) is an invaluable work, drawing upon oral as well as written sources.

It is a matter of regret to me that *The Poems: A New Edition* (1983) does not adopt the chronological ordering of the poems in the first volume of the 'Definitive Edition' of 1949, *The Poems of W. B. Yeats*, but follows instead the division made in *The Collected Poems of W. B. Yeats* (1933, 2nd ed. 1950) between lyrical poems and narrative and dramatic poems. The different ordering exists because Yeats and his publishers saw different purposes being served by the chronological arrangement of poems which culminated in *The Poems of W. B. Yeats* (1949) and the arrangement adopted in the *Collected Poems* (1933). The history of these editions is complicated, but it has to be considered when a reader ponders which ordering is to be preferred and for what purposes. The account begins with the economic situation at the end of 1920. Yeats wrote to Macmillan, in a letter of 23 December 1920, that he thought it unlikely 'with book producing at its present expensiveness' that Macmillan would want to publish a six-volume edition of his collected work (as arranged in his original Agreement with the firm in 1916), but he wondered whether they 'might not do something short of it with profit'. This suggestion led to the uniform edition issued from 1922 onwards, which was obviously regarded as adequate for a period of financial difficulty. An Edition de Luxe, however, of seven volumes of Yeats's work began to be planned in 1930, the contents of which were agreed by Yeats and Harold Macmillan in 1931. This was to be a 'new, collected, limited edition' of all his work. It was to be sold (and possibly subscribed) in an edition of 375 copies, each to have a signed numbered title page inserted in the first volume.

The problems which beset this edition (some of the proofs of which Yeats corrected, some of which were revised and had fresh copy added) are well described in the introduction to *The Secret Rose, Stories by W. B. Yeats: a Variorum Edition*, edited by Philip L. Marcus, Warwick Gould and Michael J. Sidnell (1981) xvii–xxvii. In a letter of 11 August 1932 (British Library Add MS 55731 ff405-7) Harold Macmillan told Yeats that economic conditions were so bad that he was 'not particularly anxious to hurry on the production, as I think it would hardly be in our interest to do so'. Ideas of publishing the Edition de Luxe were to remain in abeyance until Yeats's death in 1939. The Edition de Luxe was to be regarded as 'delayed but by no means abandoned'.

The *Collected Poems* arose out of a meeting in London on 19 October 1932 when Yeats, en route to America, made 'a new proposal' to Harold Macmillan that a one volume *Collected Poems* should be issued which would keep his poems before the public. The firm suggested to Yeats (in a letter of 30 March 1933) a different order of poems from that of the first volume of the Edition de Luxe (which was already in proof; a request from Harold Macmillan that Yeats should sign 390 title pages was sent on 29 March 1933, even though the Edition de Luxe was 'temporarily held up, pending better times'). This suggestion of a change in the order of the poems 'from the arrangement of the Edition de Luxe volume' was that the narrative and dramatic poems might be 'moved to the end of the volume, where they would make a group more or less related in style, subject and length'. The suggestion was made as a 'quite tentative one', the argument being that Macmillan thought it

> possible that the book would be more attractive to the potential purchaser who glances through it in a bookshop if what first caught his eye were the shorter lyrical poems contained in 'Crossways', 'The Rose', 'The Wind among the Reeds' etc, rather than a lengthy work like 'The Wanderings of Oisin'. Our impression is that we might move the longer narrative and dramatic pieces to the end of the volume, where they would make a group more or less related in style, subject and length. . . . (British Library Add MS 55738 460-62)

Yeats wrote on 2 April 1933 to say that he was 'delighted with your suggestion to put long poems in a section at the end', suggesting the division should be into 'longer poems' and 'shorter poems' or 'narrative and dramatic poetry' and 'lyrical poetry' (British Library Add MS 55003 f141). The rights to the earlier poetry held by T. Fisher Unwin and subsequently by Ernest Benn were to lapse in 1933; neither Yeats nor Macmillan wished to renew the agreement, and there was a good deal of discussion between Harold Macmillan, A. P. Watt (Yeats's agent) and Benn (see British Library Add MS 55733 ff424 and 589, also 54902 f4) before all was settled by February 1933 (see British Library Add MS 55737 f291). The *Collected Poems* duly appeared in November 1933, was reprinted in 1934, reissued in April 1934, reprinted in October 1935, April 1937, October 1938 and posthumously. The second edition 'with later poems added' was first published in 1950.

The *Collected Poems* was a commercially viable (and successful) edition aimed at 'the potential purchaser'; the Edition de Luxe was kept in proof and new poems were added to it. The poems in it were arranged in chronological order and thus 'The Wanderings of Oisin' began the volume, 'The Old Age of Queen Maeve' and 'Baile and Aillinn' preceded *In The Seven Woods*, and *The Shadowy Waters* was placed before *From The Green Helmet and Other Poems* while *Responsibilities* contained 'The Two Kings' and *The Tower* 'The Gift of Harun Al-Rashid'. All of these poems were placed in the 'Narrative and Dramatic' section at the end of *Collected Poems*. There were, in fact, two orderings of the poems, one for the Edition de Luxe, one for the *Collected Poems*, both of which Yeats approved. There is no evidence to suggest that he contemplated any change in the order of the poems in the Edition de Luxe – and we know that Macmillan did not. And neither did Mrs Yeats (who discussed *The Poems of W. B. Yeats* (1949) with me) nor did Thomas Mark, the Macmillan editor and director who dealt with Yeats's work, and with whom Mrs Yeats worked closely after Yeats's death on 25 January 1939. Mark and she were then involved in the plans for the Edition de Luxe which had been 'delayed but by no means abandoned'. Mrs Yeats, in answer to a query from Harold Macmillan, in a letter of 28 February 1939 (British Library Add MS 55820 ff203-5), suggested that the Edition de Luxe should be called the 'Coole Edition' (on the lines of the Macmillan Mellstock edition of Hardy, Sussex edition of Kipling, and New York edition of James). It was now to be of eleven volumes, containing the poems in two volumes; but the war put a stop to Macmillan's plans to publish the edition in September 1939. 'It has to wait for better times', Mark wrote to Mrs Yeats in October 1939.

Yeats had agreed to the order of the poems in *Collected Poems* (1933); a quickly published edition for the 'ordinary reader', to use Harold Macmillan's description of the companion *Collected Plays* (1934). When Scribner's proposed, in 1935, to produce another Edition de Luxe in the United States – the Dublin Edition – he was also agreeable to Macmillan retaining the 'special features' of their Edition de Luxe: the more divergence between the Macmillan Edition de Luxe and the proposed Scribner's edition the better for the Macmillan edition, Harold Macmillan thought, which the firm wanted to make 'a very fine piece of work'; he suggested that in their edition Scribner's should follow the text of the *Collected Poems* and *Collected Plays* and the Uniform edition for the prose work (British Library Add MS 55787 ff444-45). To this suggestion Yeats's agent, A. P. Watt, agreed. In the event Scribner's did not proceed with their projected edition, though Yeats prepared copy for it using the editions that Macmillan (cleverly from the point of view of making their Edition de Luxe unique) had suggested.

We can see from Yeats's treatment of the arrangement of the *Collected Plays* (British Library Add MS 55003 f160) that he regarded this one volume edition 'intended for the ordinary reader' as different from 'the other editions' in the Edition de Luxe. And this was like his attitude to the *Collected Poems*. Both single volume editions were popular, non-definitive editions. Yeats obviously liked the idea of the Edition de Luxe, he had great faith in the taste and ability of Thomas Mark as an editor, and, according to Mrs Yeats, he realised that Macmillan would only bring it out after his death. Macmillan, for their part, obviously realised that he would be writing – and revising – to the end and that no edition would be definitive until then. (For instance, in a letter of 13 August 1933 he wrote that 'the Edition de Luxe will not lack new work for I am constantly writing essays and poems & what I write will be added at the end of the various volumes' (British Library Add MS 55003 f145).) They did, however, discuss with Yeats the contents of the poems to be included in the Edition de Luxe in a nine page document of 5 June 1937, replied to on 11 June 1937. Nothing was then mentioned by Yeats about departing from the chronological order of the poems (and Yeats indicated in reply to a query of Mark's that the chronological order was to be observed in the first volume of plays in the Edition de Luxe).

In an interview in August 1980 with Mr Warwick Gould (to whom I am deeply indebted for guidance through some of the minutiae of this complex history) Harold Macmillan described the project of the Edition de Luxe as 'canonical', designed 'not to be read' but to be 'a memorial'. He remembered the suggestion (made by Thomas Mark) of altering the chronological order of poems in the Edition de Luxe for the *Collected Poems* but thought that this suggestion was for a book which was to be sold while the canonical edition was in progress, to aid sales to 'the potential purchaser'. Yeats had greatly enjoyed the publication of his sumptuous *Collected Works* in the earlier 1908 edition; but he always knew the commercial advantage of cheaper editions too, and he, with the idea of the Edition de Luxe in the background, could benefit from other editions (as Harold Macmillan put it to A. P. Watt, Yeats stood to make a 'substantial profit' out of the Scribner's edition). In *PNE* the editor remarks in the 'Textual Notes' that Yeats's supplying material and corrections for the projected Scribner's edition supports his own argument that Yeats's 'preference' was for the *Collected Poems* divisions of 'Lyrical' and 'Narrative and Dramatic'. This view, however, does not seem to take into account Yeats's eminently practical attitude, his wanting his work available in both profitable and canonical arrangements. He always found it hard to resist correcting or altering his text when opportunities to do so – such as that afforded by the Scribner's edition – occurred; but the idea of a canonical, definitive edition obviously greatly appealed to him and while apparently parallel projects – the Edition de Luxe, the *Collected Poems*, the abortive Scribner's Dublin edition – intertwine in a complex way, the question of the order of the poems (the matter of the actual texts of the poems is another matter altogether) in the Edition de Luxe was (as Mr Gould has well put it in a latter to me of 7 September 1982) 'never reopened or queried, between poet and publishers, or between poet's widow, publisher's reader and publisher, while its memorial status grew and grew'.

The reason for preferring the chronological order is that it gives the reader a more effective picture of Yeats's development as a poet. Putting *The Wanderings of Oisin* in its chronological position forcibly reminds us of what a remarkable work he had achieved, at the age of twenty-three, while the longer narrative poems, *The Old Age of Queen Maeve* and *Baile and Aillinn*, show even more clearly than the shorter lyric poems of *In the Seven Woods* how Yeats was changing his attitudes and his style as he emerged from the Celtic Twilight. The more we know about Yeats and his work, the more we piece together our own personal informed critical judgements, the more likely it is that our appreciation of his achievement will deepen: he was an impressive, indeed a great poet.

Stirling   A. NORMAN JEFFARES

Acknowledgement

THE quotations from the work of W. B. Yeats are reprinted by kind permission of Mr Michael Butler Yeats.

Abbreviations

BOOKS BY YEATS

A	*Autobiographies* (1955)
AV (A)	*A Vision* (1925)
AV (B)	*A Vision* (1937)
BS	*The Bounty of Sweden* (1925)
CK	*The Countess Kathleen and Various Legends and Lyrics* (1892). (In *Poems* (1895) and subsequent printings the spelling *Countess Cathleen* was used)
CP	*Collected Poems* (1933; 2nd edn, with later poems added, 1950). References are to the second edition unless otherwise stated
CPl	*Collected Plays* (1934; 2nd edn, with additional plays, 1952)
CT	*The Celtic Twilight* (1893)
CW	*Collected Works* (1908)
DP	*Dramatis Personae* (Dublin, 1935; London, 1936). The latter edition includes *Estrangement, The Death of Synge* and *The Bounty of Sweden*
DWL	*Letters on Poetry from W. B. Yeats to Dorothy Wellesley* (1940; reissued 1964). References are to the 1964 reissue
E	*Explorations* (1962)
E & I	*Essays and Introductions* (1961)
FFT	*Fairy and Folk Tales of the Irish Peasantry* (1888)
FMM	*A Full Moon in March* (1935)
GH	*The Green Helmet and Other Poems* (1910)
ISW	*In the Seven Woods* (1903)
KGCT	*The King of the Great Clock Tower* (1934)
L	*Letters*, ed. Allan Wade (1954)
LKT	*Letters to Katharine Tynan*, ed. Roger McHugh (1953)
M	*Mythologies* (1959)
MRD	*Michael Robartes and the Dancer* (1921)
MS	*Memoirs*, ed. Denis Donoghue (1972)
NP	*New Poems* (1938)
OB	*October Blast* (1927)
OTB	*On the Boiler* (1939)
P (1895)	*Poems* (1895)
PASL	*Per Amica Silentia Lunae* (1918)
PMLA	*Publications of the Modern Language Association*
PNE	*The Poems: A New Edition*, ed. Richard J. Finneran (1984)
PPV	*Plays in Prose and Verse* (1922)

PW	*Poetical Works*, 2 vols (1906; 1907)
PWD	*Poems Written in Discouragement* (1913)
PY	*The Poems of W. B. Yeats* (1949)
RIT	*Representative Irish Tales*
RPP	*Responsibilities: Poems and a Play* (1914)
SP	*Selected Poems* (1929)
SPF	*Seven Poems and a Fragment* (1922)
SSY	*The Senate Speeches of W. B. Yeats*, ed. Donald R. Pearce (1960)
TSR	*The Secret Rose* (1897)
UP	*Uncollected Prose by W. B. Yeats*, I, ed. John P. Frayne (1970); II, ed. John P. Frayne and Colton Johnson (1975)
VE	*The Variorum Edition of the Poems of W. B. Yeats*, ed. Peter Allt and Russell K. Alspach (1957)
VPl	*The Variorum Edition of the Plays of W. B. Yeats*, ed. Russell K. Alspach (1966)
W & B	*Wheels and Butterflies* (1934)
WPM	*Words for Music Perhaps and Other Poems* (1932)
WO	*The Wanderings of Oisin and Other Poems* (1889)
WR	*The Wind Among the Reeds* (1899)
WS	*The Winding Stair and Other Poems* (1933)
WSC	*The Wild Swans at Coole* (1917)
WWP	*The Words upon the Window-pane* (1934)
Y & TSM	*W. B. Yeats and T. Sturge Moore. Their Correspondence 1901–1937*, ed. Ursula Bridge (1953)

OTHER BOOKS

AB	*A Broad Sheet* (1902)
ACE	Hugh Kenner, *A Colder Eye. The Modern Irish Writers* (1983)
B	*A Bibliography of the Writings of W. B. Yeats*, ed. Allan Wade, 2nd edn (1958)
BL	J. Stallworthy, *Between the Lines* (1963)
ED	Richard Ellmann, *Eminent Domain* (1967)
HG	*An Honoured Guest*, ed. Denis Donoghue and J. R. Mulryne (1965)
HI	Edmund Curtis, *A History of Ireland* (1936)
HS	C. M. Bowra, *The Heritage of Symbolism* (1943)
ICL	Birgit Bjersby, *The Interpretation of the Cuchulain Legend in the Works of W. B. Yeats* (1950)
IER	*In Excited Reverie*, ed. A. Norman Jeffares and K. G. W. Cross (1965)
IP	D. J. Gordon, *W. B. Yeats, Images of a Poet* (1961)
IY	Richard Ellmann, *The Identity of Yeats* (1954)
LCH	John Rhys, *Lectures on the Origin and Growth of Religion as Illustrated by Celtic Heathendom* (1888)
LT	T. R. Henn, *The Lonely Tower* (1950; rev. edn 1965). References are to the 1965 edition

LTHS   John Butler Yeats, *Letters to his Son W. B. Yeats and others* (1944)
McG   James McGarry, *Place Names in the Writings of William Butler Yeats* (1976)

MGLE   Nancy Cardozo, *Maud Gonne Lucky Eyes and a High Heart* (1979)
MLD   John Rees Moore, *Masks of Love and Death* (1971)
PYP   George Brandon Saul, *Prolegomena to the Study of Yeats's Poems* (1957)

RG   John Unterecker, *A Reader's Guide to W. B. Yeats* (1959)
RI   Frank Kermode, *Romantic Image* (1957)
S & S   Thomas R. Whitaker, *Swan and Shadow: Yeats's Dialogue with History* (1964)

SQ   Maud Gonne MacBride, *A Servant of the Queen* (1938)
TCA   A. Norman Jeffares, *The Circus Animals. Essays on W. B. Yeats* (1970)

TD   Leonard E. Nathan, *The Tragic Drama of W. B. Yeats* (1965)
TM   Peter Ure, *Towards a Mythology* (1946)
WBY   J. M. Hone, *W. B. Yeats 1865-1939* (1942; rev. edn 1962). References are to the 1962 edition

WMA   Giorgio Melchiori, *The Whole Mystery of Art* (1960)
Y   Harold Bloom, *Yeats* (1970)
Y & GI   Donald T. Torchiana, *Yeats and Georgian Ireland* (1966)
Y & T   F. A. C. Wilson, *W. B. Yeats and Tradition* (1958)
YASAC   David R. Clark, *Yeats at Songs and Choruses* (1983)
YCE   *W. B. Yeats 1865-1939 Centenary Essays,* ed. D. E. S. Maxwell and S. B. Bushrui (1965)

YCI   B. Rajan, *W. B. Yeats. A Critical Introduction* (1965)
YI   F. A. C. Wilson, *Yeats's Iconography* (1960)
Y:M & M   Richard Ellmann, *Yeats: the Man and the Masks* (1948; rev. edn 1961). References are to the 1948 edition
Y:M & P   A. Norman Jeffares, *Yeats: Man and Poet* (1949, rev. edn 1962). References are to the 1962 edition

YP & T   A. G. Stock, *W. B. Yeats His Poetry and Thought* (1961, rev. edn 1964). References are to the 1964 edition
YTLP   Thomas Parkinson, *W. B. Yeats: the Later Poetry* (1964)
YTDR   David R. Clark, *W. B. Yeats and the Theatre of Desolate Reality* (1965)

YTP   Peter Ure, *Yeats the Playwright* (1963)
YUIT   Sheila O'Sullivan, 'W. B. Yeats's Use of Irish Oral and Literary Tradition', *Heritage: Essays and Studies* presented to Seumas O'Duilearga, ed. Bo Almqvist and others (1975) pp. 266-79. Also included in *Béaloideas* [Journal of the Folklore of Ireland Society] 39-41, 1971-3 [1975] pp. 266-79

YV   Helen Hennessy Vendler, *Yeats's Vision and the Later Plays* (1963)
YVP   S. B. Bushrui, *Yeats's Verse-Plays: The Revisions 1900-1910* (1965)
YW   Curtis Bradford, *Yeats at Work* (1965)

JOURNALS

BR	*British Review*
D	*The Dome*
DM	*Dublin Magazine*
DUR	*Dublin University Review*
ER	*English Review*
IM	*Irish Monthly*
IR	*Irish Review*
LM	*London Mercury*
LR	*London Review*
N	*The Nation*
NO	*National Observer*
NR	*New Review*
P(Ch)	*Poetry* (Chicago)
RES	*Review of English Studies*
S	*The Savoy*
SO	*Scots Observer*
SR	*Saturday Review*
TB	*The Bookman*
TS	*The Shanachie*
UI	*United Ireland*

Chronology of Yeats's Life

1865   William Butler Yeats, the son of John Butler Yeats and his wife, Susan (*née* Pollexfen), born at 1 George's Ville, Sandymount Avenue, Dublin, 13 June.

1867   John Butler Yeats moves with his family to 23 Fitzroy Road, Regent's Park, London. Robert (d. 1873), John Butler (Jack), Elizabeth Corbet (Lolly) were born here. Susan Mary (Lily), the elder daughter, was born at Enniscrone. Frequent visits were made to Sligo to Mrs Yeats's parents, the Pollexfens.

1874   The family moves to 14 Edith Villas, West Kensington.

1876   The family moves to 8 Woodstock Road, Bedford Park.

1877   Yeats goes to the Godolphin School, Hammersmith. Holidays spent in Sligo.

1880   John Butler Yeats's income decreases because of Land War and decline in economy.

1881   Family returns to Ireland, is lent Balscadden Cottage, Howth, Dublin. W. B. Yeats goes to High School, Harcourt Street, Dublin (until 1883).

1882   Family moves to Island View, small house overlooking Howth Harbour. Yeats thinks himself in love with his cousin Laura Armstrong.

1884   W. B. Yeats enters School of Art, Dublin.

1885   Family moves to 10 Ashfield Terrace, off Harold's Cross Road, Dublin. First published poems (and Charles Johnston's article on esoteric Buddhism) appear in *Dublin University Review*. Founder member of Dublin Hermetic Society. Becomes friend of Katharine Tynan and John O'Leary.

1886   First experience of séance. Attacks Anglo-Irish, begins to read Irish poets who wrote in English and translations of Gaelic sagas.

1887   Family moves to 58 Eardley Crescent, Earls Court, London. Mrs Yeats has two strokes. W. B. Yeats visits William Morris at Kelmscott House. Joins London Lodge of Theosophists.

1888   Family installed in 3 Blenheim Road, Bedford Park (J. B. Yeats's home till 1902). Last of Yeats family land sold in accordance with Ashbourne Act (1888). Contributions to American journals. Visits Oxford to work in Bodleian. Joins esoteric section of Theosophists.

1889   Mild collapse. Prepares selections for Walter Scott. *The Wanderings of Oisin and Other Poems*. Visits W. E. Henley, meets Oscar Wilde, John Todhunter, York Powell, John Nettleship, and Edwin Ellis (with whom he decides to edit Blake's poems). Edits *Fairy and Folk Tales of the Irish Peasantry*. Maud Gonne visits Bedford Park; he falls in love with her; offers to write *The Countess Cathleen* for her.

1890   'The Lake Isle of Innisfree.' Asked to resign from Theosophists. Meets Florence Farr, who was acting in John Todhunter's *A Sicilian Idyll*. Initiated into the Order of the Golden Dawn.

1891   *Representative Irish Tales. John Sherman and Dhoya.* The Rhymers' Club founded in London. Friendship with Johnson and Dowson. Asks Maud Gonne to marry him. She goes to France. He meets her on her return on ship with Parnell's body. Writes poem on Parnell. Founds London-Irish Literary Society with T. W. Rolleston. Founds National Literary Society in Dublin with John O'Leary as President.

1892   *The Countess Kathleen and Various Legends and Lyrics. Irish Fairy Tales.*

1893   *The Celtic Twilight. The Works of William Blake* (ed. Ellis and Yeats, 3 vols).

1894   First visit to Paris; stays with MacGregor Mathers and proposes to Maud Gonne again. Sees *Axel*. Meets 'Diana Vernon'. Revises *The Countess Cathleen* in Sligo while staying with George Pollexfen and conducting experiments with symbols. *The Land of Heart's Desire* produced. Visits Gore-Booths at Lissadell.

1895   *Poems*. Not on good terms with Dowden and Mahaffy. Lionel Johnson drinking heavily. Shares rooms in the Temple with Arthur Symons for a few months (between 1895 and 1896, date uncertain).

1896   Takes rooms in Woburn Buildings; affair with 'Diana Vernon' lasts a year. Visits Edward Martyn with Arthur Symons, meets Lady Gregory, visits Aran Islands. Meets Synge in Paris, when there to found order of Celtic Mysteries. Member of Irish Republican Brotherhood; forms idea of uniting Irish political parties.

1897   *The Adoration of the Magi. The Secret Rose.* Disturbed by effects of Jubilee Riots in Dublin. Visits Coole; collects folklore there with Lady Gregory; writing *The Speckled Bird* (unpublished novel).

1898   Accompanies Maud Gonne on tour of Irish in England and Scotland. Forms idea of creating Irish Theatre with Lady Gregory and Edward Martyn. 'Spiritual marriage' with Maud Gonne.

1899   *The Wind Among the Reeds.* In Paris, again proposes marriage to Maud Gonne. *The Countess Cathleen* and Martyn's *Heather Field* produced in Antient Concert Rooms, Dublin, as programme of Irish Literary Theatre.

1900   Proposes marriage to Maud Gonne in London. Leaves IRB (probably in
        1900). Forms new order of Golden Dawn after trouble with Mathers and
        Aleister Crowley. Helps George Moore to rewrite Martyn's *The Tale of
        a Town*, which became *The Bending of the Bough*.

1901   Proposes marriage to Maud Gonne again.

1902   Lectures on the psalteries. *Diarmuid and Grania* written in collaboration
        with George Moore. Becomes President of Irish National Dramatic
        Society. *Cathleen ni Houlihan* performed in Dublin with Maud Gonne in
        title role.

1903   Maud Gonne marries John MacBride. *The Countess Cathleen, The Pot of
        Broth* and *The Hour Glass* produced in visit of Irish National Dramatic
        Company to London. First lecture tour in U.S., arranged by John Quinn.

1904   Abbey Theatre opens with Yeats as producer-manager. *The King's
        Theshold* and *On Baile's Strand*.

1905   Limited company replaces National Theatre. Co-director with Lady
        Gregory and Synge. *Stories of Red Hanrahan* (dated 1904).

1906   *Poems 1895–1905*.

1907   Crisis over Synge's *The Playboy of the Western World*. Visits Italy with
        Lady Gregory and her son. Works on *The Player Queen*. Father goes to
        New York.

1908   *Collected Works* (in 8 vols). Stays with Maud Gonne in Paris. Meets Ezra
        Pound.

1910   Resigns managership. Crisis in affair with Mabel Dickinson. *The Green
        Helmet and other poems*.

1911   Accompanies Abbey players to U.S. Meets Georgie Hyde-Lees.

1912   Stays with Maud Gonne in Normandy.

1913   Receives Civil List pension of £150 p.a. *Poems Written in
        Discouragement* (dealing with Lane Gallery controversy). Stays at Stone
        Cottage, Coleman's Hatch, Sussex, in autumn with Ezra Pound.

1914   Visits U.S. (January). Returns for Ezra Pound's marriage to Mrs
        Shakespeare's daughter. Investigates miracle at Mirebeau with Maud
        Gonne MacBride and the Hon. Everard Feilding (May). *Responsibilities:
        poems and a play*. Becomes interested in family history; finishes *Reveries*
        (first part of *Autobiographies*).

1915   Hugh Lane goes down with *Lusitania*. Refuses knighthood.

1916   With Ezra Pound (winter). First of *Plays for Dancers* produced in Lady
        Cunard's house, London (March). Easter Rising (leaders, including
        MacBride, executed), writes 'Easter 1916'. In Normandy proposes
        marriage to Maud Gonne. Reads French poets with Iseult Gonne.

1917   Buys Castle at Ballylee. Proposes to Iseult Gonne. Marries Georgie Hyde-Lees on 20 October. *The Wild Swans at Coole.*

1918   They stay at Oxford, then Glendalough, then visit Sligo; stay at Coole (and supervise restoration of tower), later at 73 St Stephen's Green (Maud Gonne's house) until December. *Per Amica Silentia Lunae.*

1919   Anne Butler Yeats born (26 February) in Dublin. Summer at Ballylee. Winter spent in Oxford in Broad Street.

1920   American lecture tour until May. Yeats in Ireland in autumn.

1921   Michael Butler Yeats born (22 August). *Michael Robartes and the Dancer. Four Plays for Dancers.*

1922   Buys Georgian house, 82 Merrion Square, Dublin. J. B. Yeats dies in New York. D.Litt. of Dublin University. Spends summer at Ballylee. *The Trembling of the Veil. Later Poems. The Player Queen.* Becomes Senator of Irish Free State.

1923   Nobel Prize for Poetry. Visits Stockholm in December for award of Nobel Prize.

1924   *Essays. The Cat and the Moon and certain poems.* Year mainly spent in final work on *A Vision.* Reading history and philosophy. High blood pressure. Visits Sicily (November).

1925   Visits Capri, Rome, Milan (February). May at Ballylee. Reading Burke and Berkeley. Speech on divorce in Senate. *A Vision* (dated 1925, published January 1926).

1926   *Estrangement.* Chairman of Coinage Committee in Senate. Visits St Otteran's School in Waterford ('Among School Children').

1927   Ballylee in summer. *October Blast.* Congestion of lungs (October). Algeciras, Seville (lung bleeding). Cannes.

1928   Cannes (till February). *The Tower.* Rapallo (April). Dublin house sold. Ballylee (June). Furnished house at Howth (July). Last Senate Speech (July).

1929   Rapallo (winter). Summer in Ireland, in flat (Fitzwilliam Square, Dublin), at Coole and Ballylee, then at Howth. *A Packet for Ezra Pound* (August). *The Winding Stair* (October). Rapallo. Malta fever (December). Ezra Pound and George Antheil at Rapallo.

1930   Portofino (April). Writes 'Byzantium'. Renvyle, Connemara (June). Coole. *Words upon the Window-pane* produced at Abbey Theatre (November). Visits Masefield at Boar's Hill, Oxford, thirtieth anniversary of their first meeting. Spends winter in Dublin, in furnished house on Killiney Hill.

1931   Writes 'The Seven Sages'. D.Litt. at Oxford (May). Writes much verse at

Coole in summer. Broadcast BBC Belfast (September). Spends winter at Coole, reading Balzac; Lady Gregory dying.

1932 Works on 'Coole Park and Ballylee 1931'. Winter and spring at Coole. Lady Gregory dies. Foundation of Irish Academy of Letters (September). Last American tour (October). *Words for Music Perhaps and other poems* (November). Leases Riversdale, Rathfarnham, Co. Dublin.

1933 Interested in O'Duffy's blueshirt movement. *The Winding Stair and other poems* (September), *Collected Poems* (November).

1934 Steinach operation. Rapallo (June). Rome (autumn). *Wheels and Butterflies. Collected Plays. The King of the Great Clock Tower.*

1935 Majorca (winter). Shri Purohit Swami collaborates in translation of *Upanishads* there. *Dramatis Personae. A Full Moon in March* (November).

1936 Seriously ill; heart missing beat (January); nephritis. Returns to Riversdale. Broadcasts on modern poetry, BBC London (summer). *Oxford Book of Modern Verse (1892-1935).*

1937 Elected member Athenaeum. Broadcasts BBC London (April, July, September). *A Speech and Two Poems* (August). Visits Lady Gerald Wellesley. *A Vision* (October). Mentone (winter). *Essays 1931-1936* (December).

1938 *The Herne's Egg* (January). Visits Sussex, stays with Lady Gerald Wellesley, and with Edith Shackleton Heald. *New Poems* (May). Sussex (June). Last public appearance at Abbey Theatre for performance of *Purgatory* (August). Maud Gonne visits him at Riversdale (late summer). Sussex (September).

1939 Dies 28 January, buried at Roquebrune. *Last Poems and Two Plays* (June). *On the Boiler.*

1948 Body reinterred at Drumcliffe Churchyard, Sligo.

Contents and Order of the Commentary

The contents and order of the *Commentary* follow the arrangements in *PNE* which gives each poem a number. The first 304 poems in *PNE* are the same as those in *CP*. *PNE* removes 'Three Songs to the Same Tune' (*CP* 320) to place it in *Part Two: Additional Poems* as A101, then continues with the poems in *CP*, in the same order, from poem 305 'Alternative Song for the Severed Head in *The King of the Great Clock Tower*' (*CP* 324) up to poem 355 'Are You Content?' (*CP* 370). The heading adopted in *PNE* for the poems from poem 321 'The Gyres' (*CP* 337) to poem 355 'Are You Content?' (*CP* 370) is that of the Cuala Press edition *New Poems* (1938); the order of the poems in *PNE* beginning with poem 356 'Under Ben Bulben' (*CP* 397) is that of [*Last Poems*]. *PNE* here follows the argument put forward by the late Professor Curtis Bradford, in 'Yeats's *Last Poems* again' (see below, p. 359), arranging the poems of the Cuala Press edition *Last Poems and Two Plays* (1939) in the order Yeats intended. The contents and order of the Macmillan edition of *Last Poems and Two Plays* (1940), included in *CP* as *Last Poems*, are different.

The provenance (in other easily accessible editions) of the 125 poems in *PNE*'s *Part Two: Additional Poems* is given. Of the 125 poems there, 4 are included in *CP* and 64 in *CPl*. Of those not included in *CP* and *CPl*, 39 are included in *VE* and 6 in *VPl*. The remainder can be found thus: 4 in *W & B*, 3 in *M*, 1 in *SPF*, 1 in *TB*, 1 in *AB*, and 1 in *TS*.

In the text of the *Commentary* bold figures in the margin are the numbers given to the poems in *PNE*, while figures in italics denote page numbers in *CP*.

The Contents of 'The Poems: A New Edition'

In this contents list the numbers of the poems in *The Poems: A New Edition* (1984) are given in **bold** type before the titles of all the poems. Page numbers in *italic* type following the titles in Part One are those of *The Collected Poems of W. B. Yeats* (2nd edn 1950 and subsequent printings); those page numbers following the titles in Part Two are prefaced by abbreviated titles in initials showing (with the exception of four poems) the location of the poems in *CP*, *CPI*, *VE*, *VPI*, *M* or *W & B*. Page references of poems in this Commentary are given in ordinary type in the extreme right hand column.

PART ONE

LYRICAL

Contents of 'The Poems: A New Edition'

Contents of 'The Poems: A New Edition'

xxv

Contents of 'The Poems: A New Edition'

Michael Robartes and the Dancer (1921)

The Tower (1928)

Contents of 'The Poems: A New Edition'

Words for Music Perhaps:

A Woman Young and Old:

NARRATIVE AND DRAMATIC

Contents of 'The Poems: A New Edition'

Contents of 'The Poems: A New Edition'

Ballylee (*W. B. Yeats*)
Sandymount (*Yeats's birthplace*)
Rathfarnham (*Yeats's last Irish residence*)
Aran Islands (*J. M. Synge*)
Coole Park (*Lady Gregory*)
French Park (*Douglas Hyde*)

Tulira (*Edward Martyn*)
Lissoy (*? The Deserted Village*)
Moore Hall (*George Moore*)
Elphin (*Oliver Goldsmith*)
Cloyne (*Bishop Berkeley*)
Ballyshannon (*Wm. Allingham*)

YEATS'S IRELAND

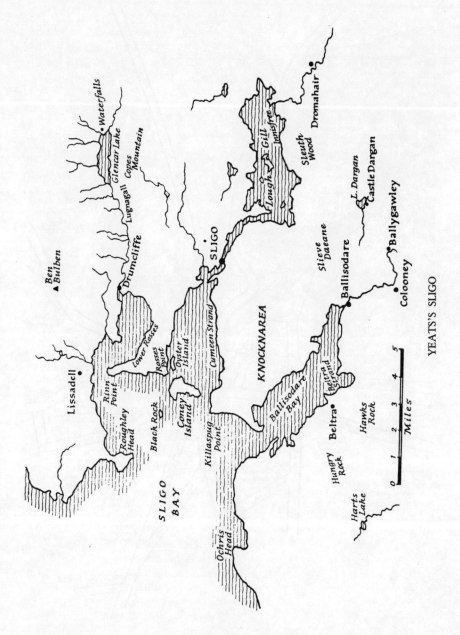

Waterfalls

Glencar Lake
Copes Mountain
Lugnagall

Ben Bulben

Drumcliffe

Lissadell

Rinn Point
Roughley Head
Black Rock
Lower Rosses
Rosses Point
Oyster Island
Coney Island
Killaspug Point
Cumeen Strand

Ochris Head

SLIGO BAY

Sleuth Wood
Dromahair

Lough Gill
Innisfree

SLIGO

Castle Dargan
L. Dargan

Ballygawley

Slieve Daeane

Colooney

Ballisodare

KNOCKNAREA

Ballisodare Bay
Beltra Strand

Hungry Rock
Beltra
Hawks Rock

Harts Lake

0   1   2   3   4   5
Miles

YEATS'S SLIGO

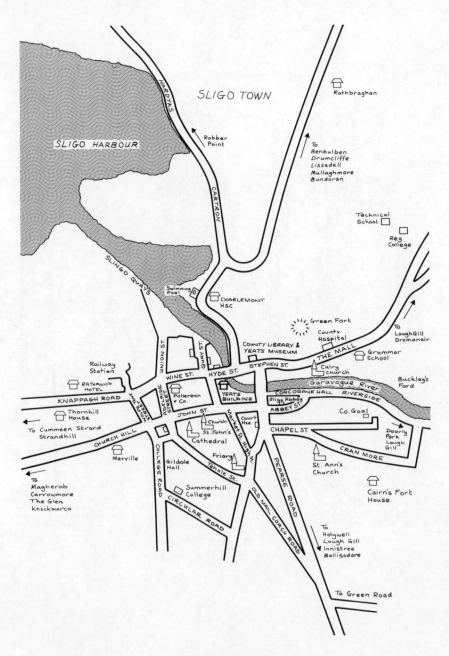

YEATS'S SLIGO TOWN

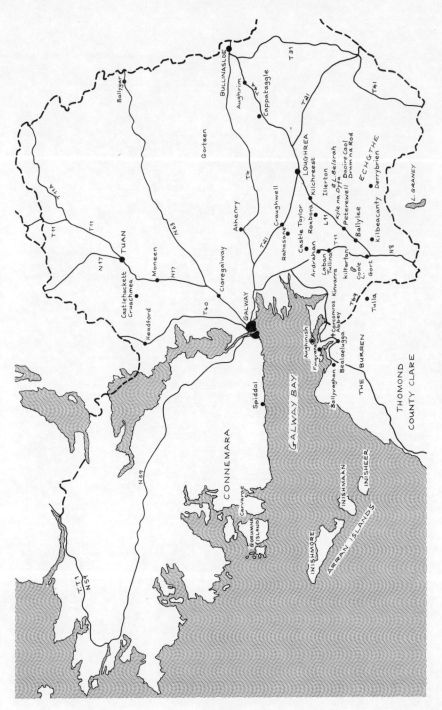

YEATS'S CO. GALWAY

PART ONE

LYRICAL

This heading was used in *CP* (1933) to include the poems up to p. 315. The next section begins in *CP* (1950) with 'From *A Full Moon in March*' (1935) followed by *Last Poems* (1936-1939). The *Narrative and Dramatic* sections then follows (from p. 403) as in *CP* (1933). For the re-arrangement in *PNE* see p. xxi above

Note: bold figures in the margins are poem numbers in *PNE*, while italicised figures denote page numbers in *CP*.

Crossways was a heading first given by Yeats to a group of poems in *P* (1895), most of which were taken from an earlier volume (*WO*), with the exception of two ballads, 'The Ballad of Father O'Hart' and 'The Ballad of the Foxhunter', which, as Yeats wrote in the Preface to *P* (1895), were 'written at the same time, though published later', in *CK*. The title *Crossways* was adopted because in these poems he 'tried many pathways' (*P* (1895)). Yeats commented, in a note dated 1925, that

> Many of the poems in *Crossways*, certainly those upon Indian subjects or upon shepherds and fauns, must have been written before I was twenty, for from the moment I began *The Wanderings of Oisin*, which I did at that age, I believe, my subject matter became Irish.   (*CP*)

DEDICATION

AE, the pen name (shortened from Aeon) of George William Russell (1867–   *5*
1935), Yeats's friend, the mystic, poet, painter and editor of the *Irish Statesman*.

EPIGRAPH

From Blake's 'Night the Ninth being The Last Judgement', *Vala, or the Four*   *4*
Zoas. (See *Poetry and Prose of William Blake* ed. Geoffrey Keynes (1939) 365.)
In *The Works of William Blake* ed. E. J. Ellis and W. B. Yeats (1893) III, 131,
the line reads 'And all the Nations were threshed out, & the stars thresh'd from
their husks.'

THE SONG OF THE HAPPY SHEPHERD   **1**

This poem was written in 1885 and first appeared in *DUR* (Oct. 1885). It was   *7*
entitled 'An Epilogue. To "The Island of Statues" and "The Seeker". *Spoken*
by a Satyr, carrying a sea-shell'. Later, it was entitled 'Song of the Last Arcadian
(*He carries a sea-shell*)' in *WO*.

1   *Arcady*: from Arcadia in the Peloponnesus, a pastoral paradise in Greek
literature. Yeats commented: 'When I first wrote I went here and there for my

subjects as my reading led me, and preferred to all other countries Arcadia and the India of Romance.'   (*CW* 1). His Arcadian ideas probably came from Edmund Spenser (?1552-99).

4   *Grey Truth*: in his teens Yeats began

> occasionally telling people that one should believe whatever had been believed in all countries and periods, and only reject any part of it after much evidence, instead of starting all over afresh and only believing what one could prove. (*A* 78)

He had grown to hate science 'with a monkish hate' (*A* 82). He had made himself a new religion:

> almost an infallible Church of poetic tradition, of a fardel of stories, and of personages, and of emotions, inseparable from their first expression, passed on from generation to generation by poets and painters with some help from philosophers and theologians . . . I had even created a dogma: 'Because those imaginary people are created out of the deepest instinct of man, to be his measure and his norm, whatever I can imagine those mouths speaking may be the nearest I can go to truth'.   (*A* 116)

9   *Chronos*: Kronos or Cronos, one of the Titans, a son of Uranus and Ge, who conspired against his father with his brothers and sisters. He succeeded Uranus as ruler of the Universe and was himself overthrown by his own son, Zeus. The Roman god Saturn was identified with Kronos: he was thought to have been an early king at Rome, his rule so benign that his reign was known as the Golden Age. It is possible Yeats had Milton's *Paradise Lost*, I, 510-21, in mind (see note on line 29 of this poem), which connects Saturn with Mount Ida, Olympus, Delphi, Dodona and the Celtic isles. The Greek word Χρόνος means time; but Kronos was only later interpreted as Χρόνος.

10   *Words alone*: A. G. Stock (*YP & T* 10-11) compares these lines to Spenser's *The Ruines of Time*, 400-6, where deeds are described as dying:

> But wise wordes taught in numbers for to runne,
> Recorded by the Muses, live for ay.

12   *Word be-mockers*: the warring kings who are men of action: their memory lives on in the words of the dreaming poets. In the first version of the poem this line was included after line 13 'They were of no wordy mood'.

the Rood: the cross on which Jesus Christ was crucified

16   *entangled story*: the first version reads 'In the verse of Attic story'.

8   29   *optic glass*: an echo of John Milton's (1608-74) description in *Paradise Lost* (1667; 1674), I 286-91, of Galileo's use of the telescope:

4

                    the moon, whose orb
Through optic glass the Tuscan artist views
At evening from the top of Fesole
Or in Valdarno, to descry new lands,
Rivers or mountains, in her spotty globe.

31 *sooth*: truth

36 *shell*: cf. lines 18-25 'The Sad Shepherd' (*PNE* 2). The happy shepherd's fretful words are reworded by the shell. The sad shepherd's words were changed to an inarticulate moan.

39 *Rewarding*: probably an uncorrected misprint of 'rewording'. See *VE* 66.

56 *poppies*: the juice of poppies possesses narcotic properties.

THE SAD SHEPHERD   2

This poem was written in 1885 and first appeared in *DUR* (Oct. 1886). It was
then entitled 'Miserrimus'. This was also the title of a Godwinian tale of a fiend,   9
dedicated to Godwin by E. M. Reynolds and published in 1832.

18 *a shell*: cf. 'The Song of the Happy Shepherd' (*PNE* 1). See note on line 36
of that poem.

26 *sad dweller*: the shell

THE CLOAK, THE BOAT, AND THE SHOES   3

The original title was 'Voices' in *DUR* (March 1885). The poem was untitled in   10
the play *The Island of Statues*, where it opens Act II, scene iii, and untitled also in
WO. Yeats described *The Island of Statues* as 'an Arcadian play in imitation of
Edmund Spenser'; he read it aloud 'to a gathering of critics who were to decide
whether it was worthy of publication in the College magazine' (*A* 92). The text is
included in *VE*, which gives details of its printings on p. 644. In the early
printings the song is sung by six voices in turn, the lines divided thus: 1; 2-5; 6;
7-10; 11; 12-15. The voices are described by the enchantress as being 'the
flowers' guardian sprights'.

ANASHUYA AND VIJAYA   4

This poem first appeared in *WO*; its original title was 'Jealousy'. In *P* (1895) it is   10
dated 1887. Yeats commented, in a note dated 1925, that the

little Indian dramatic scene was meant to be the first scene of a play about a man loved by two women, who had the one soul between them, the one woman waking when the other slept, and knowing but daylight as the other only night. It came into my head when I saw a man at Rosses Point (in Sligo) carrying two salmon. 'One man with two souls,' I said, and added, 'O no, two people with one soul.' I am now once more in *A Vision* [(1925); published January 1926] busy with that thought, the antithesis of day and night and of moon and sun. (*CP*)

F. F. Farag, 'Oriental and Celtic Elements in the Poetry of W. B. Yeats', in *YCE*, remarks that Yeats has evidently taken the name 'Anashuya' from Kalidasa's play *Sakuntala* which he read in the translation of Monier Williams.

11   14   *Brahma*: the supreme God of Hindu mythology

12   26   *Kama*: Yeats's footnote reads 'The Indian Cupid' in *WO* and his note in *P* (1895) reads '*The Indian Eros*', Kama being a Hindu god of love.

13   66-75   *the parents of the gods*: Richard Ellmann (*Y:M & M* 71) comments that these lines celebrate the Tibetan adepts Koot-Hoomi and Morya, the masters of Madame Blavatsky whom Yeats saw on her door in poorly drawn pictures supposed to have been telepathically projected. (See *A* 176.) Madame Blavatsky (Helena Petrovna Blavatsky, 1831–91) was born in Russia, married General Blavatsky, founded the Theosophical Society with Colonel Olcott in 1875 and wrote several books about theology, *Isis Unveiled* (1877) and *The Secret Doctrine* (1888–97) being perhaps the best known. Yeats's schoolfriend Charles Johnston read books by A. P. Sinnett (1840–1921), *The Occult World* (1881) and *Esoteric Buddhism* (1883), and then read a paper on Theosophy at the Dublin Hermetic Society in 1885, which Yeats heard. Johnston was indignant when Madame Blavatsky was denounced as a charlatan before the Society for Psychical Research in London in 1885, and he founded a Dublin Lodge in 1886. Yeats and George Russell refused to join, but when Yeats's family moved to London in May 1887 Yeats was impressed by Madame Blavatsky and joined the London Lodge. He joined the Esoteric Section of the Lodge in 1888 (about December), but was asked to resign (probably in the autumn) in 1890, as he 'was causing discussion and disturbance'. He hated all abstraction and had begun a series of experiments in his search for some kind of certainty. Yeats found support in the Society for his opposition to materialism, the 'grey truth' of 'The Sad Shepherd' (*PNE* 2) and he wrote a lively account of Madame Blavatsky in *A* 173–82.

   PNE suggests Kasyapa as the progenitor of the gods (he and Aditi were the parents of Agni, son of Heaven and of Earth). Here Yeats may also have drawn upon Kalidasa's Sanskrit drama *Sakuntala*. (See comment on Anashuya above) Monier Williams thought Kalidasa lived early in the third century AD. The Golden Peak is Hermakuta, a sacred mountain to the north of the Himalayas, sometimes identified with the mountain Kailasa. See note on 'Meru' (*PNE* 320).

THE INDIAN UPON GOD

This poem was written in 1886 and first appeared in *DUR* (Oct. 1886). Its   *14*
original title was 'From the Book of Kauri the Indian – Section V. On the Nature
of God.' In *WO* the title is 'Kanva, the Indian, on God'. *P* (1895) gives the date
of the poem as 1886. It is possible that this poem and 'The Indian to his Love'
(*PNE* 6) were inspired by the Brahmin Theosophist Mohini M. Chatterjee, who
visited Dublin in 1885 and gave a lecture to the Hermetic Society, a group of
young men who had taken a room in York Street, Dublin, as their headquarters.
They included A E (George Russell, 1867–1935), a poet, essayist, painter and
mystic, an active member of the Irish literary renaissance and the Home Rule
movement, and a founder of the Abbey Theatre. He worked with Sir Horace
Plunkett in the foundation of the Irish Cooperative Movement, and edited the
Irish Statesman. Yeats first met him when he was a pupil at the School of Art in
Dublin. Another member was Charles Johnston, son of the M.P. for Ballykilbeg,
Northern Ireland, a brilliant fellow pupil of Yeats's at the High School, Dublin,
who married Madame Blavatsky's niece. Claude Wright and Charles Weekes were
also members of the group. Their purpose was to study Eastern philosophy. A
poem 'Kanva on Himself', included in *WO*, puts into verse a saying of the
Brahmin in reply to a query as to whether one should pray:

> No, one should say before sleeping: 'I have lived many lives, I have been a slave
> and a prince. Many a beloved has sat upon my knees and I have sat upon the
> knees of many a beloved. Everything that has been shall be again.'

> Now wherefore hast thou tears innumerous?
>   Hast thou not known all sorrow and delight
> Wanderings of yore in forests rumorous,
>   Beneath the flaming eyeballs of the night,
>
> And as a slave been wakeful in the halls
>   Of Rajas and Mahrajas beyond number?
> Hast thou not ruled among the gilded walls?
>   Hast thou not known a Raja's dreamless slumber?
>
> Hast thou not sat of yore upon the knees
>   Of myriads of beloveds, and on thine
> Have not a myriad swayed below strange trees
>   In other lives? Hast thou not quaffed old wine
>
> By tables that were fallen into dust
>   Ere yonder palm commenced his thousand years?
> Is not thy body but the garnered rust
>   Of ancient passions and of ancient fears?
>
> Then wherefore fear the usury of Time,
>   Or Death that cometh with the next life-key?
> Nay, rise and flatter her with golden rhyme
>   For as things were so shall things ever be.

This poem's theme is recaptured in 'Mohini Chatterjee' (*PNE* 259), written in
February 1929, where it is far better handled. F. F. Farag (*YCE* 40) points out
that Mohini meant that one 'should realise the permanence of the soul in the

7

eternal essence amidst all the transient forms through which it has passed'. Other poems dealing with reincarnation are 'Fergus and the Druid' (*PNE* 18), 'He mourns for the Change that has come upon him and his Beloved' (*PNE* 52), and 'Broken Dreams' (*PNE* 167). See also the note on 'Ephemera' (*PNE* 8).

6   THE INDIAN TO HIS LOVE

15   This poem was written in 1886 and first appeared in *DUR* (Dec. 1886).

3   *The peahens dance*: Yeats replied (to a critic's objections that peahens do not dance) that they 'dance throughout the whole of Indian poetry. If I had *Kalidasa* by me I could find many such dancings. As to the poultry yards, with them I have no concern. The wild peahen dances or all Indian poets lie' (*L* 109, quoted by F. F. Farag, *YCE* 38-9). See note on 'Anashuya and Vijaya' (*PNE* 4); Kalidasa (? early 3rd century AD) was the Indian poet and dramatist, author of the play *Sakuntala*.

7   THE FALLING OF THE LEAVES

16   This poem first appeared in *WO*. Its original title was 'Falling of the Leaves'. In 1907 Yeats wrote in 'Speaking to the Psaltery':

> Sometimes one composes to a remembered air. I wrote and I will speak the verses that begin 'Autumn is over the long leaves that love us' to some traditional air, though I could not tell that air or any other on another's lips ... (*E & I* 21)

Yeats was tone-deaf; he often composed by repeating the words aloud in a form of chant. He described the process clearly in *BS*:

> Every now and then, when something has stirred my imagination, I begin talking to myself. I speak in my own person and dramatise myself, very much as I have seen a mad old woman do upon the Dublin quays, and sometimes detect myself speaking and moving as if I were still young, or walking perhaps like an old man with fumbling steps. Occasionally, I write out what I have said in verse, and generally for no better reason than because I remember that I have written no verse for a long time. I do not think of my soliloquies as having different literary qualities. They stir my interest, by their appropriateness to the men I imagine myself to be, or by their accurate description of some emotional circumstance, more than by any aesthetic value. When I begin to write I have no object but to find for them some natural speech, rhythm and syntax, and to set it out in some pattern, so seeming old that it may seem all men's speech, and though the labour is very great, I seem to have used no faculty peculiar to myself, certainly no special gift. I print the poem and never hear about it again, until I find the book years after with a page dog-eared by some young man, or marked by some girl with a violet, and when I have seen that, I am a little ashamed, as though somebody were to attribute to me a delicacy of feeling I should but do not possess. What came so easily at first, and amidst so much

drama, and was written so laboriously at the last, cannot be counted among my possessions.   (*A* 532-3)

J. M. Hone quotes Cecil Salkeld's description of Yeats composing:

> Coming down to breakfast, Madame Gonne MacBride smiled at me and said: 'Willie is booming and buzzing like a bumble bee . . . that means he is writing something. . . .' To my great surprise, Yeats, who appeared shortly, obviously preoccupied and absent-minded, asked me if I would walk up the glen with him. We walked, treading our way among boulders and small stones along the river bank for nearly half an hour in silence. By that I mean no word was spoken; but, all the while Yeats kept up a persistent murmur – under his breath, as it were. Suddenly, he pulled up short at a big stone and said: 'Do you realise that eternity is not a long time but a *short* time . . . ?' I just said, I didn't quite understand. 'Eternity,' Yeats said, 'Eternity is in the glitter on the beetle's wing . . . it is something infinitely short. . . .'   (*WBY* 326-7)

EPHEMERA   8

This poem was written in 1884. It was originally entitled 'Ephemera. An   16
Autumn Idyl', and first appeared in *WO*.

21   *other loves*: Yeats frequently used the idea of reincarnation in his poetry.   17
Some of his interest in it was derived from George Russell and some from Mohini
M. Chatterjee. But his belief in reincarnation was at the mercy of his sceptical
intelligence. He wrote: 'Ought I not to say ''The whole doctrine of the
reincarnation of the soul is hypothetic; it is the most plausible of the explanations
of the world but can we say more than that?'' ' (unpublished Autobiography).

THE MADNESS OF KING GOLL   9

This poem was written in 1884 and it first appeared in *The Leisure Hour* (Sept.   17
1887) entitled 'King Goll, An Irish Legend'. Subsequent titles were in *Poems
and Ballads of Young Ireland* (1888), 'King Goll (*Third Century*)', and in *WO*
'King Goll (Third Century)'. The poem was altered extensively and *VE* 81-6
should be consulted for the changes. Yeats's note reads 'In the legend King Goll
hid himself in a valley near Cork where it is said all the madmen in Ireland would
gather were they free, so mighty a spell did he cast over that valley' (*P* (1895)).
Goll means one-eyed in Irish, and the name appears in the Fenian and
mythological cycles.

Yeats's note of 1887 refers to and quotes Eugene O'Curry, *Lectures on the
Manuscript Materials of Ancient Irish History* (2nd edn, 1878) 316, where Gall
is a son of the king of Ulster. O'Curry's source was an eighteenth or nineteenth-
century version of 'The Battle of Ventry'. In the fifteenth-century version of this
tale Gall dies bravely in battle. *PNE* suggests that the element of madness is
introduced from tales of Mad Sweeney, the king who fled into the woods in a state

of frenzy after the battle of Moira in 637; he composed poems, collected in 'Sweeney's Frenzy'.

2   *Ith*: possibly Ith (*Irish* magh itha) the plain of corn, a plain near Raphoe, Co. Donegal. Ith was one of the Milesian invaders; see *McG* 56.

Emain: Yeats glossed this as 'the capital of the Red branch kings (*P* (1895)), and their 'chief town' (*P* (1895; rev. 1899)). The 'Red Branch' cycle of Irish tales was probably transmitted orally early in the Christian period, written down by monks in the seventh or eighth century and incorporated in late manuscripts between the eleventh and fifteenth centuries. The ruins of Emain Macha (the twins of the horse goddess Macha) are still to be seen some miles south-west of Armagh. Warriors came there each summer for training at Conchubar (or Conor) MacNessa's court, he being King of Ulster.

3   *Inver Amergin*: The mouth of the Avoca river in Co. Wicklow, named after the druid and poet Amergin. He was one of Conchubar's druids in the Red Branch stories and tutor to Cuchulain. See Lady Gregory, *Cuchulain of Muirthemne* (1970 edn), 24. *McG* 56 identifies Amergin as one of the sons of Milesius by Scota. He is alleged to have compiled a history of earlier inhabitants of Ireland and written the first poem in Ireland. The Milesians were traditionally thought to have come from Spain about the time of Alexander the Great. Mileadh's three sons, Heber, Heremon ['the ancestors of the merely human inhabitants of Ireland' (*P* (1895)) 'according to mythology' (*P* (1895; rev. 1899))] and Ir conquered the Tuatha de Danaan, or tribes of the goddess Dana, who were traditionally divine masters of magic. Yeats described them as follows:

> Tuath De Danaan means the Race of the Gods of Dana. Dana was the mother of all the ancient Gods of Ireland. They were the powers of light and life and warmth, and did battle with the Fomoroh, or powers of night and death and cold. Robbed of offerings and honour, they have gradually dwindled in the popular imagination until they have become the Faeries.   (*P* (1895))

Elsewhere he calls them 'Gods of Danu. They were . . . become Faeries' (*P* 1895; rev. 1899)).

The other inhabitants were the Firbolgs, a short dark plebeian people, described by Yeats as 'an early race who warred vainly upon the Fomorians, or Fomoroh before the coming of the Tuath de Danaan'. Certain Firbolg kings, killed at Southern Moytura, are supposed to be buried at Ballisodare, Co. Sligo. It is by their graves that Usheen and his companions rode; 'Usheen was the poet of the Fenian cycle of legend as Fergus was the poet of the Red Branch Cycle' (*P* 1895)). The Fianna are thought to have been a body of infantry, although horsemen are mentioned in the cycle. They were particularly prominent in the reign of Cormac MacArt, whose supposed son-in-law Finn MacCumhall was their leader; and are thought to have been put down in the Battle of Gabhra (AD 297). MS. evidence suggests twelfth-century composition for the tales and ballads, though some may have been composed in the eighth century.

Yeats explained Fomoroh as meaning

from under the sea, and is the name of the gods of night and death and cold. The Fomoroh were misshapen and had now the heads of goats and bulls, and now but one leg, and one arm that came out of the middle of their breasts. They were the ancestors of the evil faeries and, according to one Gaelic writer, of all misshapen persons. The giants and the leprechauns are expressly mentioned as of the Fomoroh.   (*P* (1895))

4   *the world-troubling seamen*: G. B. Saul (*PYP* 46) speculates that these are the Milesians, but they are more likely Fomorians.

9   *Ollave*: an Irish poet, of the highest grade of the order of Filidh who were the hereditary keepers of the lore and learning of Ireland (*HI* 2-3)

11   *Northern cold*: Yeats comments, 'The Fomoroh, the powers of death and darkness and cold and evil, came from the north.' (*P* (1895)). Douglas Hyde may have translated this name for Yeats, *PNE* suggests, drawing attention to Hyde's *A Literary History of Ireland* (1899) 282, and Whitley Stokes's translation of *The Book of the Dun Cow* in 'Mythological Notes', *Revue Celtique*, I, 1870-2, 257.

45   *The grey wolf*: the last wolf in Ireland was reputed to have been killed in the   *19* eighteenth century.

49   *a little town*: reminiscent of Allingham's 'The Winding Banks of Erne'

55   *tympan*: kettle-drum, in original version of poem a harp

62   *Orchil*: a Fomorian sorceress (*P* (1895)). Describing her as a 'Fomoroh and a sorceress', Yeats wrote, 'I forget whatever I may have once known about her' (*P* (1895; rev. 1899)). See Standish O'Grady, *The Coming of Cuchulain: A Romance of the Heroic Age* (1894) 62 and 109, where she is described as a queen or ruler of the underworld and a great sorceress.

68   *ulalu*: an Irish exclamation, usually of mourning but also of wonder or amazement

THE STOLEN CHILD   **10**

This poem first appeared in *IM* (Dec. 1886). Yeats's note read: *20*

The places mentioned are round about Sligo. Further Rosses is a very noted fairy locality. There is here a little point of rocks where, if anyone falls asleep, there is danger of their waking silly, the fairies having carried off their souls.   (*FFT*)

2   *Sleuth Wood*: this wood lies between Lough Gill and Dromahair. Yeats described it in 'The Heart of the Spring': 'Sleuth Wood [*Irish* sliv, a slope] away to the south looked as though cut out of green beryl, and the waters that mirrored

it shone like pale opal' (*M* 175). It is locally known as Slesh or Slish Wood (*Irish* slis/slios, sloped): and Yeats also uses Slish as a name for it. See *A* 72 and *McG* 82–3.

9–12   *Come away, O human child*: Yeats wrote to Katharine Tynan, on 14 March 1888, that in the process of correcting his poems he had noticed things about his poetry he had not known before, that it was

> almost all a flight into fairyland from the real world. . . . The Chorus to the 'Stolen Child' sums it up – that it is not the poetry of insight and knowledge but of longing and complaint – the cry of the heart against necessity. I hope some day to alter that and write poetry of insight and knowledge.   (*L* 63)

This poem probably marks the shift from Arcadian and Indian scenes to Irish – Yeats wrote later that for such reasons as those in 'Ireland and the arts' (*E & I* 203) he convinced himself that he should never 'go for the scenery of a poem to any country but my own, and I think that I shall hold to that conviction to the end' (*CW* 1).

15   *Rosses*: Rosses Point, a seaside village in Co. Sligo, to the north-west of Sligo town. Yeats described the area as 'a little sea-dividing, sandy plain, covered with short grass, like a green tablecloth and lying in the foam midway between the round cairn-headed Knocknarea and "Ben Bulben" ' (*M* 88). It had its supernatural aspects:

> At the northern corner of Rosses is a little promontory of sand and rocks and grass: a mournful, haunted place. Few countrymen would fall asleep under its low cliff, for he who sleeps here may wake 'silly', the Sidhe having carried off his soul. There is no more ready short-cut to the dim kingdom than this plovery headland, for, covered and smothered now from sight by mounds of sand, a long cave goes thither 'full of gold and silver, and the most beautiful parlours and drawing-rooms'. Once, before the sand covered it, a dog strayed in, and was heard yelping helplessly deep underground in a fort far inland. These forts or raths, made before modern history had begun, cover all Rosses and all Columcille. The one where the dog yelped has, like most others, an underground beehive chamber in the midst. Once when I was poking about there, an unusually intelligent and 'reading' countryman who had come with me, and waited outside, knelt down by the opening, and whispered in a timid voice, 'Are you all right, sir?' I had been some little while underground, and he feared I had been carried off like the dog.   (*M* 88–9)

29   *Glen-Car*: Glencar (from *Irish* Gleann an Chairthe, the Glen of the standing or monumental stone) Lake, in the north-east of Co. Sligo. Cf. note on 'Towards Break of Day' (*PNE* 198) and *M* 158.

11   TO AN ISLE IN THE WATER

22   This poem first appeared in *WO*.

DOWN BY THE SALLEY GARDENS

This poem first appeared in *WO*. Its original title was 'An Old Song Re-sung' and
Yeats's footnote explained that 'This is an attempt to reconstruct an old song from
three lines imperfectly remembered by an old peasant woman in the village of
Ballysodare, Sligo, who often sings them to herself' (*P* (1895)). He later called it
'an extension of three lines sung by an old woman at Ballisodare' and a letter to
Katharine Tynan, written after 6 September 1888, suggests that the lines were
'Old Irish verse' (*L* 86). A letter to Dorothy Wellesley of 25 September 1935
commented that the Irish Free State army marched to a tune called 'Down by the
Salley Garden' without knowing that the march was 'first published with words of
mine, words that are now folklore' (*DWL* 29). The source of the poem has been
given by H. E. Shields, 'Yeats and the "salley gardens"', *Hermathena*, C1
(Autumn 1965), 22–6. He argues that it is not 'Going to Mass last Sunday' (as
stated by Colin O'Lochlainn, *Anglo-Irish Song-Writers* (1950), 17) but 'The
Rambling Boys of Pleasure', an Anglo-Irish broadside ballad, the text of which is
in the National Library, Dublin. Mr Shields gives several versions and says it was
written to the Irish metre of, for example, An beinnsín luachra; he obtained his
source from Mr Paddy Tunney.

I

You rambling boys of pleasure, give ear unto these words I write
For I own I am a rover and in rambling I take great delight.
I've set my heart on a fair young girl though oftentimes she does me slight
But my mind is never easy but when my own girl is in my sight.

II

Down by yon flowery garden my love and I we first did meet.
I took her in my arms and to her I gave kisses sweet.
She bade me take life easy just as the leaves fall from the tree
But I being young and foolish with my own darling did not agree.

III

The second time I met my love I vowed her heart was surely mine
But as the weather changes my darling girl she changed her mind.
Gold is the root of evil although it wears a glittering hue:
Causes many a lad and lass to part though their hearts like mine be e'er so true.

IV

I wish I was in Americay and my true love along with me,
Money in my pocket to keep us in good company,
Liquor to be plenty, a flowing bowl on every side
Hard fortune ne'er would daunt me for I am young and the world is wide.

Mr Shields quotes two other stanzas and remarks that Yeats would probably not
have liked the rest of the ballad and 'retained only the most strikingly poetic
lines'. But see Michael B. Yeats, 'W. B. Yeats and Irish Folk Song', *Southern
Folklore Quarterly* 30, 2 (June 1966) 158 for the text of a manuscript in the P. J.
McCall Ballad Collection, National Library of Ireland. The third stanza of this
was not used by Yeats but the 'snowy-white feet' and the 'leaves' of the first

stanza and the river field, the shoulder, and the weirs of the second stanza are echoed in his version:

> Down by the Sally Gardens my own true love and I did meet;
> She passed the Sally Gardens, a tripping with her snow white feet.
> She bid me take life easy just as leaves fall from each tree;
> But I being young and foolish with my true love would not agree.
>
> In a field by the river my lovely girl and I did stand
> And leaning on her shoulder I pressed her burning hand,
> She bid me take life easy, just as the stream flows o'er the weirs
> But I being young and foolish I parted her that day in tears
>
> I wish I was in Banagher and my fine girl on my knee
> And I with money plenty to keep her in good company.
> I'd call for a liquor of the best with flowing bowls on every side
> Kind fortune ne'er daunt me, I am young and the world's wide.

1   *salley*: willow. See *McG* 79 for location of the salley gardens on the bank of the Ballysadare river between the Ballina road and the mills; thatched houses there had gardens to provide scollops for their thatched roofs.

13   THE MEDITATION OF THE OLD FISHERMAN

23   This poem was written in June 1886 and first appeared in *IM* (Oct. 1886). Yeats commented that 'This poem is founded upon some things a fisherman said to me when out fishing in Sligo Bay' (*P* (1895)). He is elsewhere described as 'a not very old fisherman at Rosses Point' (*CW* 1).

6   *creel*: wicker basket for fish, or in Ireland, for turf (peat)

14   THE BALLAD OF FATHER O'HART

23   This poem first appeared in *Irish Minstrelsy* (ed. H. Halliday Sparling, 1888); it was then entitled 'The Priest of Coloony'. 'Father O'Hart' was the title used in *CK*. Yeats appended to the text of the poem a brief note which reads:

> Coloony is a few miles south of the town of Sligo. Father O'Hart lived there in the last century, and was greatly beloved. These lines accurately record the tradition. No one who has held the stolen land has prospered. It has changed owners many times.   (*FFT* 220)

This comment was expanded in the notes:

> Father O'Rorke is the priest of the parishes of Ballysadare and Kilvarnet and it is from his learnedly and faithfully and sympathetically written history of these parishes [T. F. O'Rorke, *History, Antiquities and Present State of the Parishes of Ballysodare and Kilvarnet, in the County of Sligo* (1878, IV, Section 2)] that I have taken the story of Father John, who had been priest of these parishes, dying in the year 1739. Coloony is a village in Kilvarnet.

Some sayings of Father John's have come down. Once when he was sorrowing greatly for the death of his brother, the people said to him, 'Why do you sorrow so for your brother when you forbid us to keen?' 'Nature', he answered, 'forces me, but ye force nature.' His memory and influence survives, in the fact that to the present day there has been no keening in Coloony.

He was a friend of the celebrated poet and physician, Carolan. [Turlough Carolan (1670–1738) lost his sight at fourteen but, apprenticed to a harper by Mrs MacDermott Roe, became famous for his poems and songs.] (*FFT* 324)

In a later volume Yeats further glossed the poem:

The robbery of the lands of Father O'Hart was one of those incidents which occurred sometimes, though but rarely, during the time of the penal laws. Catholics, who were forbidden to own landed property, evaded the law by giving some honest Protestant nominal possession of their estates. There are instances on record in which poor men were nominal owners of unnumbered acres. (*CK*)

See *McG* 94, for details of Father O'Hart's moving from Cloonamahon near Colloney to Killaser on the Annaghmore estate of the O'Haras after being dispossessed. The 'Coloony' spelling was retained in editions up to and including *CP* (1933). The spelling 'Colloney' is used in *McG*.

2 *penal days*: Penal laws against Roman Catholics existed in Ireland after the 1560 Parliament but 'the amount of persecuting statutes in Ireland was actually small compared to England' (*HI* 224). Yeats, however, is referring to a series of measures enacted against Catholics by the Irish parliament after William of Orange's victories; they were enacted from 1695 to 1727, and were a violation of the spirit and letter of the Treaty of Limerick of 1691. They were not repealed until 1829.

3 *shoneen*: Yeats's footnote read 'upstart'; his note was longer:

Shoneen is the diminutive of shone (*Irish* Séon). There are two Irish names for John – one is *Shone*, the other is *Shawn* (*Irish* Séaghan). Shone is the 'grandest' of the two, and is applied to the gentry. Hence *Shoneen* means 'a little gentry John', and is applied to upstarts and 'big' farmers, who ape the rank of gentleman. (*FFT*)

Shoneen means a person who affects English ways, after the Irish *Seon* for an Englishman; Shawn is the Irish for Sean, Séaghan being an archaic form of the word.

6 *Sleiveens*: Yeats's footnote read 'mean fellow'; his note was longer: 24

Sleiveen, not to be found in the dictionaries, is a comical Irish word (at least in Connaught) for a rogue. It probably comes from *sliabh*, a mountain, meaning primarily a mountaineer, and in a secondary sense, on the principle that mountaineers are worse than anybody else, a rogue. I am indebted to Mr Douglas Hyde for these details, as for many others. (*FFT*)

A sleiveen means a sly, tricky person, not from (*Irish*) sliabh, a mountain, but from (*Irish*) sli, a means, a way.

15

13   *only*: except

22   *keeners*: professional mourners who utter the keen for the dead at wakes and funerals in Ireland. From (*Irish*) caoinim, I wail

27   *Colooney*: Yeats commented: 'a few miles south of the town of Sligo'. See *McG* 33, and *M* 234, 238 and 240.

30   *Knocknarea*: 'round cairn-headed Knocknarea', the 'hill of the executions', a mountain overlooking Sligo, where Queen Maeve is supposed to be buried. She was a Queen of Connaught who invaded Ulster in the Cattle Raid of Cooley, the central story of the Red Branch cycle told in the *Taín Bó Cuálgne*.
It is also called the Hill of the King, and Eoghan Bel, the last pagan King of Connaught, was buried upright there, with his spear, and while he remained the northerners could never defeat Connaught. He was disinterred later by the Ui Neill and buried face downwards at Lough Gill (*McG* 62-3). Maeve was buried at the capital of Connaught, Cruachan in Co. Roscommon, named after her mother Cruacha, according to MS tradition (See *McG* 38). See Yeats's note on 'The Hosting of the Sidhe' (*PNE* 40) and his comments (quoted in note on *The Wanderings of Oisin* (*PNE* 375)); see also 'Red Hanrahan's Song about Ireland' (*PNE* 84).

31   *Knocknashee*: this may be Knocknashee Common or a round hill in the parish of Achonry in the Barony of Leyny, Co. Sligo. There is a Knocknashee in Boyle, Co. Roscommon. Knocknashee (*Irish* Cnoc na Sidhe), the hill of the fairy palace.

25   35   *Tiraragh*: this may be Teeraree (*Irish* Tir a rig), a townland in the parish of Kilmorgan, Co. Sligo. See *McG* 85, who states that it is named after Fiachra Ealgach, the son of Dathi, king of Ireland (*Irish* Tir Fhiachrach or Fiachra's district).

36   *Ballinafad*: a village in the parish of Aughanagh, on the Sligo road near Boyle. The name means (*Irish* Bel-an-atha-fada) the mouth of the long ford.

37   *Inishmurray*: an island in the Atlantic, now uninhabited. This island, off the Sligo coast near Streedagh Point, is named after St Muireadhach, Bishop of Killala (*McG* 55).

15   THE BALLAD OF MOLL MAGEE

25   This poem first appeared in *WO*, but Katharine Tynan told Allan Wade she thought it appeared in *The Gael* (1887). See *B* 20. It was derived from a sermon preached in the chapel at Howth [then a fishing village, now a suburb on the northern side of the headland and peninsula which forms the northern arm of

Dublin Bay (*PW* 11). John Butler Yeats and his family lived there from 1881–83].

6   *say*: sea

7-9   *saltin' herrings . . . saltin' shed*: Howth herrings were supplied by a local fishing fleet and the salting sheds lined one of the piers of the harbour.

24   *Kinsale*: fishing port in Co. Cork (*Irish* Cionn Tsaile, the head of the sea)   *26*

32   *boreen*: (*Irish*) lane

48   *keenin'*: see note on line 22 'The Ballad of Father O'Hart' (*PNE* 14).

49   *she*: Saul (*PYP* 50) comments that this refers to the dead child.

THE BALLAD OF THE FOXHUNTER   16

The original title was 'The Ballad of the Old Fox-hunter' in the first published   *27* version, in *East and West* (Nov. 1889). The second printing, in *UI* (28 May 1892), added 'An incident from Kickham's ''Knocknagow'' ' and Yeats's note remarked that the ballad founded on this incident from *Knocknagow* was probably in its turn a transcript from Tipperary tradition. C. J. Kickham (1826–82) author and journalist, member of Young Ireland movement 1848, joined the Fenian movement 1860, was condemned to fourteen years penal servitude in 1865, and released after four years. He wrote ballads as well as the novel *Knocknagow* (1879). Yeats read *Knocknagow* when he was collecting material for *RIT* and included items from it in that volume. He also used material from it in *WO*. The following pages are the source for the poem.

Dr. Kiely was astonished to find his patient in a chair on the lawn, propped up with pillows. His son, a tall, cadaverous-looking man with grizzled hair and beard, stood on one side of the chair, and a saintly looking though somewhat spruce young clergyman at the other. Two graceful young ladies stood a little apart, looking very sad and interesting, but not altogether oblivious of the handsome young clergyman's presence.

'Blow, Rody, blow,' muttered the poor old invalid. And the horn sounded, and the woods gave back the echo.

'O sweet Woodlands, must I leave you?' exclaimed the old foxhunter in tones of the deepest grief.

'You're going to a better place,' said the clergyman, impressively.

'Yoix! Tallyho!' cried the invalid, faintly. 'Blow, Rody, blow.'

'Don't ax me, sir,' returned the huntsman, after putting the horn to his lips and taking it away again; 'my heart is ready to burst.'

'O sweet Woodlands, must I leave you?' his master exclaimed again.

'My dear sir,' the clergyman repeated, stooping over him and placing his gloved hand gently upon his shoulder, 'my dear sir, you are going to a better place.'

The invalid turned round and looked earnestly into the young clergyman's face, as if he had until then been unconscious of his presence.

'You're going to a better place; trust me, you're going to a better place,' the clergyman repeated fervently.

'Ah!' replied the old foxhunter, with a sorrowful shake of his head, and looking earnestly into the parson's face – 'ah! by G——, I doubt you!'

The parson's look of consternation brought a grim smile into the hard features of Mr. Sam Somerfield, as he adjusted his father's nightcap, which was displaced by the effort to turn round to look at his spiritual director.

The dying foxhunter seemed to drop suddenly into a doze, from which a low fretful whine from one of the hounds caused him to awake with a start. 'Poor Bluebell; poor Bluebell,' he murmured. The hound named wagged her tail, and coming close to him, looked wistfully into his face. The whole pack followed Bluebell, waving their tails, and with their trustful eyes appeared to claim recognition, too, from their old master. But his head drooped, and he seemed falling asleep again. He roused himself, however, and gazed once more upon the fine landscape before him, and again called upon the huntsman to sound the horn. The huntsman put it to his lips, and his chest heaved as he laboured for breath; but no sound awoke the echoes again.

'God knows I can't, sir,' he cried at last, bursting into tears. The huntsman's emotion moved the two young ladies to tears, and they came nearer to their grandfather's chair, and looked anxiously into his face. Dr. Kiely laid his finger on the old man's wrist, and turned to whisper something to his son, who was still standing by the chair. But the doctor drew back, as if the eye of a murderer were upon him. Mr. Sam Somerfield's face was ashy pale and his lips vivid, while a baleful light glared from under his shaggy brows, which were dragged together in puckered folds. His daughters, too, were terrified, and wondered what could have brought that shocking expression into their father's face. But guided by his eyes they turned round and saw that Mr. Lowe was standing near them: then they understood that terrible look.

The young girls gazed upon the woods and groves and undulating meadows, just as their grandfather had done. And the expression in the bright eye of youth and in the dimmed eye of age was the same.

'Ah,' said the younger girl, as her sister's eyes met hers, 'it is a sweet place.'

Turn round, young ladies, and look through that arched gateway to yon sloping hillside, speckled with white sheep, upon which the sun shines so brightly. There were many happy homes along that green slope not many years ago. There is not one now. You remember the last of them – the old farmhouse in the trees, with its cluster of cornstacks; and the square orchard, that looked so pretty in the spring-time; and the narrow boreen leading to the road between tangled wild roses and woodbines? You remember the children who peered shyly at you from under their brown arms when you rode by upon your pretty ponies? You remember what a rage your papa was in when the man who lived there refused to give up the old lease; and how he swore when the old lease had expired, and the 'scoundrel' – that was the word – refused to go until the sheriff and police and military drove him away?

To be sure, his father, and grandfather, and great-grandfather had lived there before him. He paid your papa fifty gold guineas every year, and was willing to pay half as many more if he were allowed to toil on there to the end of his days; though old people remembered when that productive little farm was covered with furze and briers, with patches of green rushes here and there in the

18

marshy places. Well, he should go; and the children – but what do you care for such things? We merely meant to remind you that, to that poor man and his wife and children, their place, too, was 'a sweet place.'

'I suppose,' thought Mr. Sam Somerfield, 'he came here purposely to watch till the breath is out of him, in order that I may be hunted without an hour's delay.' Then fixing his eyes upon the old man with a look in which pity and hatred seemed blended, he continued, 'What right had he to take such a lease? He cared only for himself. Why wasn't it *my* life he got it for? He might have died, and died an old man, twenty years ago. And I wish to heaven he did die twenty years ago, before my heart was rooted in it.'

An old blind hound, lying on a mat near the door, raised his head, and uttered a long dismal howl. The whole pack took up the cry; and, as it passed like a wail of sorrow over the hills, the old foxhunter fell back in his chair – dead!

The huntsman threw himself from his horse; and, with the help of two or three other servants, carried his old master into the house.

'O papa, poor grandpapa is gone!' the young girls exclaimed, flinging their arms round their father's neck.

He bent down as they clung to him, looking quite helpless and stupefied. But, when he saw the horse from which the huntsman had dismounted, walk to a square stone near the end of the house, and stand quietly beside it, and thought that 'old Somerfield' would never mount his hunter from that stone again, the tears ran down his hard, yellow cheeks, and fell upon his children's hair.

(*Knocknagow*, 491–4)

7   *Lollard*: the name of the horse; in other versions of the poem he is called Brown Dermot (see *VE*); he is not named in the novel.

10   *Rody*: the huntsman in *Knocknagow*

The Rose

The Rose was a heading used first by Yeats in *P* (1895) for a group of some shorter poems taken from *CK*. Yeats wrote in 1925 that on reading the poems in *The Rose* for the first time for several years he noticed that the quality symbolised as The Rose differed from the Intellectual Beauty of Shelley and of Spenser (references, presumably to the 'Hymn to Intellectual Beauty' by Percy Bysshe Shelley (1799-1822) and the 'Foure Hymnes' of Edmund Spenser (? 1552-99)), in that he had imagined it as suffering with man and not as something pursued and seen from afar.

It must have been a thought of my generation, for I remember the mystical painter Horton [W. T. Horton (1864-1919), a black-and-white artist of a mystic nature, whose *A Book of Images* (1898) contained an Introduction by Yeats; he is described in 'All Souls Night', see note, *PNE* 239] whose work had little of his personal charm and real strangeness, writing me these words, 'I met your beloved in Russell Square and she was weeping', by which he meant that he had seen a vision of my neglected soul. (*CP*)

Horton wrote to Yeats (who was then living at 18 Woburn Buildings, near Russell Square, London) on 6 May 1896:

It is night.
Yeats – naked and gaunt, with long black dishevelled hair falling partly over the face of a deathly whiteness, with eyes that flame yet have within them depths of unutterable sadness. He is wearily going on his way following many lights that dance in front and at side of him. Behind, follows with outstretched arms a lovely girl in long trailing white garments, weeping. Within Yeats, a knocking is heard & a Voice 'My son, my son, open thou unto me & I will give thee light'.

See George Mills Harper, *W. B. Yeats and W. T. Horton: The Record of an Occult Friendship* (1980) 13, 101.

The poems in the section named *The Rose* were printed because in them 'he has found, he believes, the only pathway whereon he can hope to see with his own eyes the Eternal Rose of Beauty and of Peace' (*P* (1895)). 'Who goes with Fergus?' (*PNE* 32) was added to the section in *Poems* (1912).

EPIGRAPH

From St Augustine, *Confessions*, x, 27: 'Too late I loved you Beauty so old and so new. Too late I loved you'.

The Rose

DEDICATION:

Lionel Johnson (1867–1902), English poet and critic, who published two books of verse, *Poems* (1895) and *Ireland* (1897). Yeats and he were friends and fellow members of the Rhymers' Club; he is described in *A* 164f.

TO THE ROSE UPON THE ROOD OF TIME

This poem first appeared in *CK*.

17

1   *Red Rose*: Yeats used roses decoratively in very early poems, but by 1891 he had begun to use the rose as an increasingly complex symbol. In doing so he was influenced by current English poetic practice and by the work of Irish poets in whose work it had stood for Ireland: 'It has given a name to more than one poem, both Gaelic and English, and is used, not merely in love poems but in addresses to Ireland, as in De Vere's line, "The little black rose shall be red at last", and in Mangan's "Dark Rosaleen". I do not of course, use it in this latter sense' (*CK*). Rose was the name of a girl with black hair in Irish patriotic poetry; she was Róisín Dubh, Dark Rosaleen, and personified Ireland.

35

The poets Yeats mentions are Aubrey De Vere (1788–1846) and James Clarence Mangan (1803–49); see Zimmermann's note on De Vere's poem (quoted on p. 194) and note on Mangan, 'To Ireland in the Coming Times' (*PNE* 39). Yeats also alluded to the use of the Rose symbol in religious poems 'like the old Gaelic which speaks of "the Rose of Friday" meaning the Rose of Austerity' (*P* (1895)). He added that he had written a good deal on it in the notes to *WR* and these notes are included in this volume's comments on 'The Poet pleads with the Elemental Powers' (*PNE* 72), 'He thinks of his Past Greatness . . .' (*PNE* 75), 'He hears the Cry of the Sedge' (*PNE* 64). The Rose symbolises spiritual and eternal beauty. Its meaning as a symbol was intensified by Yeats's membership of the Golden Dawn, an occult society or Rosicrucian order (See note on 'The Mountain Tomb' (*PNE* 130)) into which he was initiated by MacGregor Mathers, the author of *The Kabbalah Unveiled*, on 7 March 1890. See note on 'All Souls' Night' (*PNE* 239). From him and from the rituals of the Golden Dawn (which included Egyptian, Kabbalist and Christian imagery) Yeats learned of a series of geometric symbols that he could classify according to the four elements, and what the ancients called the fifth element and sub-divisions of these. In his unpublished Autobiography he wrote: 'I allowed my mind to drift from image to image and these images began to affect my writing, making it more sensuous and vivid.' In the Rosicrucian symbolism a conjunction of rose (with four leaves) and cross forms a fifth element – a mystic marriage – the rose possessing feminine sexual elements, the cross masculine; the rose being the flower that blooms upon the sacrifice of the cross. The Rose was a central symbol in the Order of the Golden Dawn, and Ellmann (*Y:M & M* 97), quotes Stanislas de Guaïta (who founded in Paris in 1888 a Kabbalistic Order of the Rosy Cross) who wrote in *Rosa Mystica*:

The Rose that I invite you to pluck – sympathetic friend who turns these pages – does not flower on the shores of far-away countries; and we shall take, if you please, neither the express train nor the transatlantic steamer.

21

Are you susceptible to a deep emotion of the intellect? and do your favourite thoughts so haunt you as to give you at times the illusion of being real? . . . You are then a magician, and the mystic Rose will go of her own accord, however little you desire it, to bloom in your garden.

Yeats wrote to Ernest Boyd in February 1915 that his interest in mystic symbolism did not come from Arthur Symons or any other contemporary writers but from his own study of the mystic tradition which dated from 1887; he had found in writers such as Valentin Andrea authority for his use of the Rose (*L* 592). Wade commented that Yeats probably read Johannes Valentine Andreae or Andreas (1586-1654) the German theologican and mystic, in Foxcroft's translation of *The Hermetic Romance or the Chymical Wedding* (1690) originally written in High Dutch by C[hristian] R[osenkreuz]; this was reprinted in A. E. Waite, *The Real History of the Rosicrucians* (1887). In July 1892 Yeats wrote to John O'Leary that he could not have written his Blake book nor *The Countess Cathleen* had he not made magic his constant study – 'The mystical life is the centre of all that I do and all that I think and all that I write.' The study of magic was 'next to my poetry, the most important pursuit of my life' (*L* 210).

The Rose symbolism had other elements: physical and spiritual, pagan and Christian, and Yeats described them in an autobiographical passage:

I planned a mystical Order . . . and for ten years to come my most impassioned thought was a vain attempt to find philosophy and to create ritual for that Order. I had an unshakable conviction, arising how or whence I cannot tell, that invisible gates would open as they opened for Blake [see note on 'The Rose of Peace' (*PNE* 21). 'The Blessed' (*PNE* 66) has his association of holiness with passion, an idea also contained in 'The Secret Rose' (*PNE* 67), where the Rose symbolises spiritual beauty], as they opened for Swedenborg, as they opened for Boehme [Jacob Boehme, or Böhme, or Bohm (1575-1624), the German mystic], and that this philosophy would find its manuals of devotion in all imaginative literature and set before Irishmen for special manual an Irish literature which, though made by many minds, would seem the work of a single mind, and turn our places of beauty or legendary association into holy symbols. I did not think this philosophy would be altogether pagan, for it was plain that its symbols must be selected from all those things that had moved men most during many, mainly Christian, centuries.

I thought for a time I could rhyme of love, calling it *The Rose* because of the Rose's double meaning; of a fisherman who had 'never a crack' in his heart; of an old woman complaining of the idleness of the young, or of some cheerful fiddler, all those things that 'popular poets' write of, but that I must some day – on that day when the gates began to open – become difficult or obscure. With a rhythm that still echoed Morris I prayed to the Red Rose, to Intellectual Beauty. [He then quoted from the second stanza of 'To the Rose upon the Rood of Time'.] (*A* 253)

The 'mystical Order' was to include Maud Gonne (1866-1953); Yeats's uncle George Pollexfen and MacGregor Mathers were helpful but the idea was his own, and in the 1890s he envisaged the order centring on an empty castle on the Castle Rock (see *McG* 28) in Lough Key, near Boyle, Co. Roscommon, which he had seen when visiting Douglas Hyde:

There is a small island entirely covered and still [indecipherable] empty castle. The last man who lived there had been Dr Hyde's father who when a young man had lived there for a few weeks. All round it were the wooded and hilly shores – a place of great beauty. I believed that this castle could be hired for little money and I had long dreamed of a king, an Irish Eleusis [a Greek city in Attica where mysteries were celebrated in honour of Demeter and Persephone] or Samothrace [an island in the north-west Aegean sea which had a mystery cult of its twin gods, the Cabiri]. An obsession more constant than anything but my love itself was the need of mystical writing a retired system of evocation and meditation – to reunite the perception of the spirit, of the divine with natural beauty. I believed that instead of thinking of Judaea as holy we should [believe] our own land holy and most holy when most beautiful. Commerce and manufacture have made the world ugly. The death of pagan nature worship had robbed visible beauty of its inviolable sanctity and I was convinced that all lonely and lovely places were crowded with invisible beings and that it would be possible to communicate with them. I meant to interest young men and women in the worship which would unite the radical truths of Christianity with those of a more ancient world, and to use the Castle Rock for these occasional retirements from the world. For years to come I was in my thoughts as in much of my writing to seek alone to bring again imaginative life in the old sacred places [? in] Slieve Knocknarea all that old reverence that hung above all conspicuous hills. But I wished by writing and thought of the school I founded . . . I believed we were about to have a revelation. Maud Gonne entirely shared this idea and I did not doubt that in carrying this out I should win her for myself. Politics were merely a means of meeting her but this was a link so perfect that would restore at once even in a quarrel the sense of intimacy. At every moment of leisure we obtained in visions long lists of various symbols that corresponded to the cardinal points and all the old gods and heroes took place gradually in the symbolic fabric that had for its centre the four tales bringing the Tuatha de Danaan the sword the stone the pen and the cauldron which related themselves in my mind to the Irish of the Tarot cards. (Unpublished MS., cf. *A* 253)

This Order of Celtic mysteries was regarded by Yeats as a means of escaping from active life and politics as well as a means of gaining Maud Gonne's love. He wrote to George Russell (AE) on 23 January 1898:

I am deep in 'Celtic Mysticism', the whole thing is forming an elaborate vision. Maud Gonne and myself are going for a week or two perhaps to some country place in Ireland to get as you do the forms of gods and spirits and to get some sacred earth for evocation. Perhaps we can arrange to go somewhere where you are so that we can all work together. Maud Gonne has seen a vision of a little temple of the heroes which she proposes to build somewhere in Ireland when '98 is over [celebrations to commemorate Wolfe Tone and the Rebellion of 1798] and to make the centre of our mystical and literary movements. (*L* 295)

The Rose also symbolises Maud Gonne, who told the present editor that Yeats intended to allude to her by the symbol, and through her to Ireland. In 'The Rose upon the Rood of Time' the Rose is eternal beauty and something of its meaning is indicated in his remark that Timon of Athens and Cleopatra sorrow for all men's fate. 'Tragic joy' was a quality Yeats appreciated and he wrote of it:

23

That shaping joy has kept the sorrow pure, as it had kept it were the emotion love or hate, for the nobleness of the arts is in the mingling of contraries, the extremity of sorrow, the extremity of joy, perfection of personality, the perfection of its surrender, overflowing turbulent energy, and marmorean stillness; and its red rose opens at the meeting of the two beams of the cross, and at the trysting-place of mortal and immortal, time and eternity. (*E & I* 255)

See also Yeats's note quoted below.

Title   the rood: see note on 'The Song of the Happy Shepherd' (*PNE* 1).

3   *Cuchulain*: the 'Hound of Culain', the hero of the Red Branch (or Ulster, or Conorian) cycle of tales. In *The Tragical Death of Conlaech* the hero kills his own son. Yeats also spelt the name Cuhoollin and Cuchullin, and commented that it is pronounced Cuhoolin (see Appendix: Gaelic Names) and remarks that his poem is founded on a West of Ireland legend given by Curtin in *Myths and Folk-Lore in Ireland* (1890) adding that the bardic tale of the death of Cuchulain is very different (*CK*). See also 'Cuchulain's Fight with the Sea' (*PNE* 19) and the plays *On Baile's Strand* and *The Only Jealousy of Emer*. Birgit Bjersby (*ICL*) gives a useful account, and Brendan Kennelly, 'The heroic ideals in Yeats's Cuchulain plays', *Hermathena*, CI (Autumn 1965), 13–21, is also stimulating.

4   *Druid*: druids were priests, seers and healers in Gaelic Ireland. See Yeats's note on 'The Secret Rose' (*PNE* 67).

5   *Fergus*: Fergus MacRoy, also from the Red Branch cycle, was King of Ulster; he was tricked out of his crown by Ness the mother of Conchubar. The story is told in the Book of Leinster, translated by Whitley Stokes, *Eriu*, IV, 22. Yeats remarked that he was the poet of the cycle and that he gave up his throne that he might live at peace hunting in the woods (*P* (1895)).

20   *the bright hearts*: Yeats wrote 'I do not remember what I meant by "the bright hearts" but a little later I wrote of spirits "with mirrors in their hearts" ' (*A* 255).

23   *Eire*, Irish for Ireland, originally a name of a queen of the tribes of the goddess Dana, subsequently the Tuatha de Danaan. The *Book of Invasions* called them earlier inhabitants of Ireland.

18   FERGUS AND THE DRUID

36   This poem first appeared in *NO* (21 May 1892).

1   *Fergus*: see note on 'To the Rose upon the Rood of Time' (*PNE* 17). Yeats suggested that his source for the legend was Sir Samuel Ferguson (1810–86; see note on 'To Ireland in the Coming Times' (*PNE* 39), *P* (1895; rev. 1899)). He

commented that 'the proud dreaming king' of 'The Secret Rose' (*PNE* 67) was founded upon Fergus, the son of Roigh, the legendary poet of 'the quest of the bull of Cualg[n]e' as he was in the ancient story of Deirdre and in modern poems by Sir Samuel Ferguson [The Abdication of Fergus Mac Roy]. Fergus married Ness (or Nessa) and Ferguson 'makes him tell how she took him "captive in a single look" ':

> I am but an empty shade,
> Far from life and passion laid;
> Yet does sweet remembrance thrill
> And my shadowy being still.

Presently, because of his great love, he gave up his throne to Conchobar, her son by another, and lived out his days feasting, and fighting, and hunting. His promise never to refuse a feast from a certain comrade, and the mischief that came by his promise, and the vengeance he took afterwards, are a principal theme of the poets.   (*WR*)

In the *Taín Bó Cualgne* he is the lover of Maeve, Queen of Connaught.

8   *Druid*: cf. line 4 'To the Rose upon the Rood of Time' (*PNE* 17)

Red Branch kings: the Red Branch heroes served Conchubar King of Ulster at his court Emain Macha.

10   *Conchubar*: Yeats also spelt the name Conhor, Conchobar and Concobar and described him as king of all Ireland in the time of the Red Branch kings (*P* (1895)). He is the central figure in the saga *The Fate of the Children of Usna* from which Yeats and Synge among other Irish writers quarried their Deirdre plays. He succeeded Fergus, who was his step-father, his mother Ness having tricked Fergus into giving up the Kingship of Ulster.

35   *quern*: apparatus for grinding corn, usually consisting of two circular stones, *37* the upper turned by hand

40   *slate-coloured thing*: the little bag of dreams of line 29, described in early versions as a 'small slate-coloured bag of dreams'

CUCHULAIN'S FIGHT WITH THE SEA   19

This poem first appeared in *UI* (11 June 1892) with the title 'The Death of *37* Cuchulain'; it was extensively revised and *VE* 105 should be consulted. The last version is strengthened.

2   *Emer*: Emer of Borda, spelt Emir in the original version, the daughter of Forgael, was Cuchulain's wife. His wooing is told in *The Wooing of Emer* in the *Book of the Dun Cow*. This poem derives from J. Curtin, *Myths and Folk-Lore of Ireland* (1890) (*CK*), from oral tradition, and from a ninth-century tale in *The*

Yellow Book of Lecan where Cuchulain's son (Conlaech) is by Aoife (with whom the hero had an affair when he was having advanced training in arms with Scathach, an Amazon) not by Emer. Other tales concerning their married life are *The Sickbed of Cuchulain* (in which Emer has her only jealousy of another woman, Fand, the wife of Manannan MacLir), and *Bricriu's Feast* (which deals with questions of precedence between Cuchulain and two other warriors and their wives). Bjersby, (*ICL* 23-7), discusses other possible sources, among them Sir Samuel Ferguson. In this poem Yeats may have confused Emer and Aoife.

raddling: this can mean either to dye with red ochre, or to weave or intertwine: 'dyeing cloth' was originally intended as the first three lines read:

> A man came slowly from the setting sun,
> To Emer of Borda, in her clay-piled dun
> And found her dyeing cloth with subtle care . . .

dun: fortress

3   *that swineherd*: the original version included the line 'I am Aileel, the swineherd, whom you bid' and Aileel was spelt Aleel in later versions.

6   *web*: woven stuff

7   *raddled*: red with dye

38   16   *one sweet-throated*: Eithne Inguba, Cuchulain's young mistress

18   *her son*: Finmole in early versions (see note on line 68)

21   *herd*: herdsman

33   *The Red Branch*: Conchubar and his army

39   *Cuchulain*: see note on 'To the Rose upon the Rood of Time' (*PNE* 17).

39   40   *young sweetheart*: Eithne Inguba

45   *Conchubar*: see note on 'Fergus and the Druid' (*PNE* 18).

40   68   *Cuchulain I*: the original version read 'I am Finmole mighty Cuchulain's son'.

72   *sweet-throated maid*: Eithne Inguba

20   THE ROSE OF THE WORLD

41   This poem first appeared in *NO* (2 Jan. 1892) entitled 'Rosa Mundi'.

4   *Troy*: this poem was written to Maud Gonne, later (*c.* 1903–14) frequently identified with Helen of Troy, and with Deirdre. At the time Yeats was full of John Todhunter's play *Helen of Troy*.

Troy was the Trojan city destroyed by the Greeks after a ten-year siege, brought about by the abduction of Helen (wife of Menelaus, King of Sparta) by Paris, son of Priam, King of Troy.

5   *Usna's children*: Deirdre, the daughter of King Conchubar's storyteller, prophesied she would bring great suffering upon Ulster. Conchubar prevented her death at the hands of the Ulstermen by saying she was to be brought up to be his future queen. Despite isolation with a nurse, Lavarcam, she fell in love with Naoise, one of the Red Branch heroes. He escaped with her to Scotland (along with his brothers, the other sons of Usna, who were Ainle and Ardan) where they lived happily for some years. Conchubar then sent Fergus to offer a peaceful return. Deirdre opposed the return, but Naoise insisted and they were separated from Fergus (for whom it was *geasa* – an equivalent to *tabu* – not to be able to refuse an invitation to a feast). See notes on 'Fergus and the Druid' (*PNE* 18). Conchubar then had the sons of Usna beheaded, contrary to the promise he had made to Cathbad the Druid, who had used spells to bring about their capture. Yeats referred (*P* (1895)) to Deirdre's beautiful lament over the bodies of the children of Usna which had been finely translated by Sir Samuel Ferguson. Ferguson's poem was 'Deirdra's Lament for the Sons of Usnach', *Lays of the Western Gael and Other Poems* (1864). Cathbad cursed Conchubar and Emania, and this curse was worked out in the legend of the *Tain Bó Cualgne*. Deirdre, in one version of the legend, stabbed herself; in another was forced to live a year with Conchubar, who intended to hand her on to Owen (who killed Naoise, her husband), but killed herself by leaping from a chariot in which both men were travelling with her. Yeats's note reads: 'the quality symbolised in such poems . . . differs from the intellectual beauty of Shelley and of Spenser in that it is imagined as suffering, with man and not as something pursued from afar'. See *McG* 88, on Usna (*Irish* Uisneach, place of fawns) in Co. Westmeath. See Ferguson, *Lays of the Red Branch* (1897) pp. 89–91. See also Yeats's quotation of a version of the poem (not in the standard editions of Ferguson but included in Justice O'Hagan's *The Poetry of Sir Samuel Ferguson* (1887) in his second article 'The Poetry of Samuel Ferguson', *DUR*, November 1886.

13   *Weary and kind*: the poem was first composed of two stanzas. Yeats recited it to George Russell (AE) and some friends in this original form after he and Maud Gonne had returned from walking a long distance in the Dublin mountains. Yeats was worried because she had been exhausted by walking on the rough mountain roads, and added the third stanza, much to George Russell's disapproval. The latter told Professor E. R. Dodds (to whom the present editor is indebted for this information) that he disliked these lines for their sentimentality and especially for the incongruity of the words 'weary and kind'. He thought the word 'kind' meaningless in its context and explained that it was there because Maud Gonne, though tired and footsore, was in a gentler mood than usual after the long walk. He also thought it ridiculous to call the world of human experience 'a grassy road'

and told the story to illustrate how fine poetry can be ruined by the intrusion of the transient and incidental.

21   THE ROSE OF PEACE

41   The poem first appeared in *NO* (13 Feb. 1892). Its original title was 'The Peace of the Rose'.

1   *Michael*: the archangel who overcomes Satan

4   *deeds*: in the war between God and Satan, of which Yeats read in *Paradise Lost*

16   *Heaven with Hell*: Swedenborgian but also reminiscent of Blake's juxtapositions though not the 'paradoxical violence' of *The Marriage of Heaven and Hell*. Cf. *E* 44.

22   THE ROSE OF BATTLE

42   This poem first appeared in *CK*; its title then was 'They went forth to the Battle but they always Fell'.

23   A FAERY SONG

43   *Sung by the people of Faery over Diarmuid and Grania,*
in their bridal sleep under a cromlech

This poem first appeared in *NO* (12 Sept. 1891).

Subtitle: The earlier versions state the song was sung by 'the good people' over the author Michael Dwyer and his bride, who had escaped into the mountains. (Michael Dwyer was a rebel leader in the 1798 rebellion who operated in the Wicklow mountains.) *The Pursuit of Diarmuid and Grania* is one of the Fenian cycle of tales. The Fianna (Yeats described the Fenians as 'a great military order of which Finn was chief' in *P* (1895; rev. 1899)) are generally supposed to have been a body of infantry (though there is some mention of horsemen in the cycle) who were particularly prominent in the reign of Cormac Mac Art, whose supposed son-in-law Finn MacCumhall (Yeats spelt his name Fion) was their leader. Their power was supposed to have been broken in the Battle of Gabhra, AD 297 (Yeats spelt it Gavra). MS. evidence points to twelfth-century composition for the tales and ballads, though some of them may have been composed in the eighth century. In the tale Finn, an ageing widower, decided to marry Grania (Grainne) the daughter of Cormac Mac Art, but she preferred a younger man and offered herself, after she had drugged the other banqueters at her betrothal feast, to Diarmuid and Oisin. Both refused, but she put Diarmuid under *geasa* to elope with her that night, which he did unwillingly. Finn pursued them with the Fianna, who tried to protect Diarmuid and Grania from him, but he eventually killed Diarmuid by treachery and Grania transferred her attentions back to him. Yeats described her as a beautiful woman

> who fled with Dermot to escape from the love of aged Finn. She fled from place to place over Ireland, but at last Dermot was killed at Sligo upon the seaward point of Benbulben, and Finn won her love and brought her, leaning upon his neck, into the assembly of the Fenians, who burst into inextinguishable laughter. (*P*(1895))

Cromlech: a prehistoric stone construction usually consisting of one large stone laid upon several upright stones; they are sometimes known in Ireland as the beds of Diarmuid and Grainne, used by them in their flight from Finn.

5 *these children*: the lovers Diarmuid and Grania. See also Yeats's story 'Hanrahan's Vision' (*M* 246-52). The return of Grania to Finn comes from Standish Hayes O'Grady's (1832-1915) version of the story, *Transactions of the Ossianic Society*, 3 (1857).

THE LAKE ISLE OF INNISFREE   24

This poem was written in 1890 and first appeared in *NO* (13 Dec. 1890). It was   44
written in Bedford Park, a London suburb, and a passage in 'Ganconagh's'[1]
[Yeats's] novel *John Sherman* (1891) gives an insight into the personal feelings
underlying the poem:

> Delayed by a crush in the Strand, he heard a faint trickling of water near by; it came from a shop window where a little water-jet balanced a wooden ball upon its point. The sound suggested a cataract with a long Gaelic name, that leaped crying into the gate of the winds at Ballagh. . . . He was set dreaming a whole day by walking down one Sunday morning to the borders of the Thames a few hundred yards from his house – and looking at the osier-covered Chiswick eyot. It made him remember an old day-dream of his. The source of the river that passed his garden at home was a certain wood-bordered and islanded lake, whither in childhood he had often gone blackberrying. At the further end was a little islet called Innisfree. Its rocky centre, covered with many bushes, rose some forty feet above the lake. Often when life and its difficulties had seemed to him like the lessons of some elder boy given to a younger by mistake, it had seemed good to dream of going away to that islet and building a wooden hut there and burning a few years out rowing to and fro fishing, or lying on the island slopes by day, and listening at night to the ripple of the water and the quivering of the bushes – full always of unknown creatures – and going out at morning to see the island's edge marked by the feet of birds.

Yeats described himself as 'very homesick in London' when he made the poem, in

[1] Yeats annotated the word in *FFT* 323-4, pointing out that it was not to be found in dictionaries and meant a 'love-talker'. He quoted O'Kearney for the description 'another diminutive being of the same tribe as the Lepracaun but, unlike him, he personated love and idleness, and always appeared with a dudeen [clay pipe] in his jaw in lonesome valleys, and it was his custom to make love to shepherdesses and milkmaids. It was considered very unlucky to meet him . . .'

a letter of 30 November 1922, replying to schoolgirls who had asked if Innisfree was a real island (*WBY* 39), and is explicit elsewhere:

> I had still the ambition, formed in Sligo in my teens, of living in imitation of Thoreau on Innisfree, a little island in Lough Gill [(*Irish*) Loch Gile, the bright lake. See *M* 101, 171], and when walking through Fleet Street very homesick I heard a little tinkle of water and saw a fountain in a shop-window which balanced a little ball upon its jet, and began to remember lake water. From the sudden remembrance came my poem *Innisfree* my first lyric with anything in its rhythm of my own music. I had begun to loosen rhythm as an escape from rhetoric and from that emotion of the crowd rhetoric brings, but I only understood vaguely and occasionally that I must for my special purpose use nothing but the common syntax. A couple of years later I would not have written that first line with its conventional archaism – 'Arise and go' – nor the inversion in the last stanza. (*A* 153)

Elsewhere Yeats suggested that Thoreau might have had some influence on the desire for solitary life expressed by the poems and linked the island again with the local legends:

> My father had read to me some passage out of *Walden*, and I planned to live some day in a cottage on a little island called Innisfree, and Innisfree was opposite Slish Wood. . . . I thought that having conquered bodily desire and the inclination of my mind toward women and love, I should live, as Thoreau lived, seeking wisdom. There was a story in the county history [William Gregory Wood-Martin, *History of Sligo* (1882)] of a tree that had once grown upon that island guarded by some terrible monster and borne the food of the gods. A young girl pined for the fruit and told her lover to kill the monster and carry the fruit away. He did as he had been told, but tasted the fruit; and when he reached the mainland where she waited for him, he was dying of its powerful virtue. And from sorrow and remorse she too ate of it and died. I do not remember whether I chose the island because of its beauty or for the story's sake, but I was twenty-two or three before I gave up the dream. (*A* 71-2)

Katharine Tynan probably discussed Thoreau with him; she included a poem 'Thoreau at Walden' in her *Louise de la Vallière and other Poems* (1885), and on 21 December 1888 Yeats wrote to her enclosing 'two verses I made the other day' – an early version of the first two stanzas of the poem about the little rocky island with a legended past: 'In my story [*John Sherman*] I make one of the characters whenever he is in trouble long to go away and live alone on that Island – an old day dream of my own' (*L* 99). The island (mentioned in the *Four Masters* under AD 1244) attracted Yeats because of its association with Irish legend and folk-lore. These are discussed by Russell K. Alspach, *Yeats and Innisfree* (1965). A poem 'The Danaan Quicken Tree' printed in *TB* (May 1893) had a note after the title explaining these associations which runs:

> It is said that an enchanted tree grew once on the little lake-island of Innisfree, and that its berries were, according to one legend, poisonous to mortals, and according to another, able to endow them with more than mortal powers. Both legends say that the berries were the food of the *Tuatha de Danaan*, or faeries. Quicken is the old Irish name for the mountain ash. The Dark Joan mentioned in the last verse is a famous faery who often goes about

the roads disguised as a clutch of chickens. Niamh is the famous and beautiful faery who carried Oisin into Faeryland. *Aslauga Shee* means faery host.

1   *I will arise*: cf. the parable of the prodigal son, Luke XV. 18: 'I will arise and go to my father.'

Innisfree: (*Irish* Inis Fraoigh) Heather Island

9   *night and day*: cf. the cleansing of the unclean spirits, Mark V. 5: 'And always, night and day, he was in the mountains.'

12   *heart's core*: perhaps an echo of Shelley's *Adonais*, line 192, 'thy heart's core'

A CRADLE SONG   25

This poem first appeared in *SO* (19 April 1890). Early versions had an epigraph: *45*

> *'Cloth yani nu von gilli beg,*
> *'N heur ve thu more a creena'*

'*Cloth*' was altered to 'Coth' in *CK*. Early versions (*VE* 118) show how Yeats's rewriting strengthened the poem. It was altered by W. E. Henley (1849-1903), the editor of *SO*, in its early state.

7   *The Sailing Seven*: the planets. *PNE* suggests as an alternative the seven stars of the Pleiades.

11-12   *That I shall miss you when you have grown*: Yeats wrote to Katharine Tynan that the last two lines were suggested by a Gaelic song quoted in Gerald Griffin's novel *The Collegians* (*L* 148). Gerald Griffin (1803-40) was an Irish novelist, poet and dramatist.

THE PITY OF LOVE   26

This poem first appeared in *CK*.   *45*

THE SORROW OF LOVE   27

This poem was written in October 1891 and first appeared in *CK*. Yeats described   *45* it as one of several altogether new poems produced by rewriting (*Early Poems and Stories* (1925)). *VE* 119 gives different versions of the poem; it is one of the best known examples of Yeats's rewriting of his earlier work.

5   *A girl arose*: presumably Helen of Troy, but the poem also relates to Maud Gonne's beauty. Yeats first met her and fell in love with her in 1889.

6   *Odysseus*: son of Laertes, king of the Island of Ithaca, a suitor of Helen and married to Penelope. He took part in the Greek expedition to recover Helen from Troy where Paris took her from Sparta. He took nearly ten years to return home to Ithaca after the sack of Troy, his adventures being recounted in Homer's *Odyssey*.

7   *Priam*: Son of Laomedon, was the last king of Troy and father of many children, among whom were Hector, Paris, and Cassandra; he was killed by Neoptolemus, the son of Achilles, after the fall of Troy.

28   WHEN YOU ARE OLD

46   This poem was written on 21 October 1891 and first appeared in *CK*. It was written to Maud Gonne, and is founded upon, but is not a translation of, Ronsard's 'Quand Vous Serez Bien Vieille', *Sonnets pour Hélène*, II (1578).

29   THE WHITE BIRDS

46   This poem first appeared in *NO* (7 May 1892). The title in this printing had a note after it which read '(*The birds of fairyland are said to be white as snow. The Danaan Islands are the islands of the fairies.*)' 'The Danaan Shore is, of course, *Tier-nan-Oge*, or fairy-land.' (*CK*). Tir na nOg was a name, 'the Land of the Young', given to the land where mortals could share the everlasting youth of the fairies. See Yeats's note, *FFT* 323.
         Madame MacBride (to whom, as Maud Gonne, the poem was written) told the present author that she and Yeats had been walking on the cliffs at Howth one afternoon (the day after Yeats had first proposed to her and been rejected) and were resting when two seagulls flew over their heads and on out to sea. She had said that if she was to have the choice of being any bird she would choose to be a seagull above all, a commonplace remark, but 'in three days he sent me the poem with its gentle theme, ''I would that we were my beloved, white birds on the foam of the sea''.'

2   *meteor*: because meteors do not last long in the sight of the onlooker

47   3   *blue star of twilight*: Venus

5   *the lily and rose*: the lily is a masculine symbol, the rose feminine.

9   *Danaan*: fairy. See Yeats's note on 'The Hosting of the Sidhe' (*PNE* 40).

A DREAM OF DEATH   30

This poem first appeared in *NO* (12 Dec. 1891), the title being 'An Epitaph'.   *47*

1   *one*: Maud Gonne, who had gone to France to recover from fatigue caused by
her aiding victims of evictions in Donegal, where there was a famine. She had a
tendency to tuberculosis. Her comment on the poem was, 'I was getting steadily
better and was greatly amused when Willie Yeats sent me a poem, my epitaph he
had written with much feeling' (*SQ* 147). Cf. 'He wishes his Beloved were Dead'
(*PNE* 73).

strange place: the south of France where Maud Gonne was convalescing

11   *thy first love*: perhaps Laura Armstrong, a red-headed cousin with whom   *48*
Yeats fell in love when the Yeatses lived at Howth:

   . . . I saw a great deal of her and was soon in love. I did not tell her I was in love,
   however, because she was engaged. She had chosen me for her confidant and I
   learned all about her quarrels with her lover. Several times he broke the
   engagement off, and she fell ill, and friends had to make peace. . . . I wrote her
   some bad poems and had more than one sleepless night through anger with her
   betrothed.   (*A* 76)

THE COUNTESS CATHLEEN IN PARADISE   31

This poem first appeared in *NO* (31 Oct. 1891) with the title 'Kathleen'. This   *48*
was altered to 'Song' in *CK*. This song was from scene V of *The Countess
Cathleen*; the title used in *P* (1895) was 'A Dream of a Blessed Spirit'. The poem
was renamed 'The Countess Cathleen in Paradise' because, as Yeats commented
in 1926, he had rewritten it so much (see *VE* 124), that it was 'almost a new
poem' (*P* (1895; rev. 1927)). See also a letter to Olivia Shakespear, written in
October 1927, stating he had rewritten 'a poor threadbare poem of his youth . . .
it is almost a poem for children . . . I like the last verse, the dancer Cathleen has
become heaven itself.' (*L* 731). Yeats initially wrote *The Countess Cathleen* to
convince Maud Gonne that he could write for a public audience; the play
illustrates Cathleen's 'sad resolve' to aid the famine-crazed folk (which was like
Maud Gonne's desire to help the Donegal peasants). His play was founded on
'The Countess Kathleen O'Shea', *FFT*, 232–35, which was 'quoted in a London-
Irish newspaper'.
   The poet in the play, Kevin (Aleel), in his relationship to Cathleen, is not
unlike Yeats *vis-à-vis* Maud Gonne, despairing of persuading her to marry him
and to give up the politics that were, he thought, swamping her noble qualities: he
is tired of his soul, but he tries to stop Cathleen selling hers. In old age Yeats
records this in 'The Circus Animals' Desertion' (*PNE* 373):

>   And then a counter-truth filled out its play,
>   *The Countess Cathleen* was the name I gave it;
>   She, pity-crazed, had given her soul away,

But masterful Heaven had intervened to save it.
I thought my dear must her own soul destroy,
So did fanaticism and hate enslave it,
And this brought forth a dream and soon enough
This dream itself had all my thought and love.

He wrote in his Preface that the chief poem was an attempt to mingle personal thought and feeling with the beliefs and customs of Christian Ireland, whereas his earlier book *The Wanderings of Oisin* had tried to record the effect on his imagination of the pre-Christian cycle of legends. He hoped Ireland, having a huge body of tradition behind her in the depths of time, would draw inspiration from the double fountainhead of the Christian and Pagan cycles, and make for herself 'a great distinctive poetic literature'. She already had many moving songs and ballads which are quite her own, and *The Countess Cathleen*, like *The Wanderings of Oisin*, was an attempt to write a more ample method to feeling 'not less national, Celtic and distinctive' (*CK*).

7   *mournful*: an alteration from the first version of the line ('For she needs not her sad beauty'), the adjective used in line 5 of 'The Sorrow of Love' (*PNE* 27)

9   *Mother Mary*: the Virgin Mary, mother of Jesus Christ

13   *angels seven*: the detail is reminiscent of Rossetti, the original version of the line reading, 'And her guides are angels seven'.

32   WHO GOES WITH FERGUS?

48   This poem first appeared in *CK* and is a lyric in the second scene of the play *The Countess Cathleen.*

1   *Fergus*: see note on 'Fergus and the Druid' (*PNE* 18)

49   9   *rules the brazen cars*: Fergus uses chariots for his peaceful, poetic pursuits, and the wood is presumably a place in which the cares of life could be escaped.

33   THE MAN WHO DREAMED OF FAERYLAND

49   This poem first appeared in *NO* (7 Feb. 1891).

1   *Drumahair*: a village in Co. Leitrim (*Irish* Dromdha-Eithiar, the ridge of the two demons), on the river Bonnet which flows into Lough Gill. See *M* 5, 70; *McG* 42–3. It is spelt Dromahair in *CP* (1950).

8   *world-forgotten isle*: akin to the first of the four paradises to which Niamh brings Oisin in 'The Wanderings of Oisin', II, 193–357. Cf. George Mills Harper, *Yeats's Quest for Eden* (1965), 302–5.

13   *Lissadell*: Yeats mentions the barony of Lissadell in Co. Sligo in *P* 1896 (*Irish* Lis-a-Doill means the fort of the blind man); Lissadell has been the home of the Gore-Booth family since the early 18th century. See note on 'In Memory of Eva Gore-Booth and Con Markievicz' (*PNE* 240); the present house was built in 1832–4.

14   *money cares and fears*: as a young man Yeats spent many summers in Sligo through lack of funds, sometimes staying with his mother's family, later with his uncle George Pollexfen.

16   *hill*: the hill of Lugnagall; see line 37.

21   *the golden or the silver skies*: solar and lunar principles when fused are an *50* alchemical emblem of perfection (see *Y & T* 219). Yeats distinguished between solar meaning, according to what he learned from MacGregor Mathers (see note on 'All Souls' Night' (*PNE* 239)) 'elaborate, full of artifice, rich, all that resembles the work of a goldsmith, whereas . . . lunar . . . is simple, popular, traditional, emotional' (*A* 371).
  The poem displays Yeats's symbolist technique developing in richness; the gold and silver of the first stanza are blended in the second with its dancer and its golden and silver skies and the sun and moon. The symbols gradually attain their power by repetition and the idea of blessedness, of perfection, is created. Poems like this and 'The Song of Wandering Aengus' (*PNE* 48) with 'The silver apples of the Moon, the golden apples of the Sun'; 'He wishes for the Cloths of Heaven' (*PNE* 74) with its cloths 'Enwrought with golden and silver light'; and 'The Happy Townland' (*PNE* 90) with its 'golden and silver wood', are later caught up in the fuller symbolism of poems like 'Under the Round Tower' (*PNE* 148) with its 'sun and moon', its 'golden king and silver lady'; 'The Tower' (*PNE* 205) where the sunlight and moonlight seem 'one inextricable beam' of perfection, and 'Those Dancing Days are Gone' (*PNE* 286) with '. . . *the sun in a golden cup, The moon in a silver bag.*'

22   *a dancer*: represents fairyland and blessedness. Cf. line 45, where the symbols represent Innocence by the dreamless wave, an idea recaptured later in 'To a Child dancing in the Wind' (*PNE* 131). It becomes more important in poems like 'The Double Vision of Michael Robartes' (*PNE* 188), 'Among School Children' (*PNE* 222), and even in the ironic fusion of 'News for the Delphic Oracle' (*PNE* 363) with its 'golden codgers' and 'all the silver dew'.

23   *sun and moon*: see note on line 21.

25   *Scanavin*: Padraic Colum has informed the editor that Scanavin, Knockfefin and Crevroe are three small townlands in Co. Sligo. See notes on line 179 'The Wanderings of Oisin', III (*PNE* 375). There is a well at Scanavin (*Irish* Tober Sceanmhan, the well of fine shingle) a mile from Colloney, Co. Sligo (*McG* 80).

33   *silver fret the gold*: cf. note on line 21.

35   *lover there by lover*: cf. the 'lover by lover' of 'The Wild Swans at Coole' (*PNE* 143).

37   *the hill of Lugnagall*: 'The Curse of the Fires and of the Shadows' is a story of the death of five Puritan troopers who attacked an Abbey and were subsequently led by a (fairy?) piper to their deaths. Their route led them in pursuit of two rebels along 'the road between Ben Bulben and the great mountain spur that is called Cashel-na-Gael' (*M* 182). Their guide led them to

> the brink of the abyss that is now called Lugnagall, or in English the Steep Place of the Strangers. [It should be 'Hollow of the Strangers' (*McG* 68).] The six horses sprang forward, and five screams went up into the air, and a moment later five men and five horses fell with a dull crash upon the green slopes at the foot of the rocks.   (*M* 183)

Lugnagall is a townland in the Glencar Valley in Co. Sligo.

41   *spired*: a use which anticipates the later 'spiring' in 'Demon and Beast' (*PNE* 199)

47   *God burn Nature*: this idea of God burning time was used in 'He tells of the Perfect Beauty' (*PNE* 63); the idea of the world burning out 'like a candle that is spent' was also used in 'The Death of Hanrahan' (*M* 260), and in 'In Memory of Eva Gore-Booth and Con Markiewicz' (*PNE* 240), '. . . strike a match, And strike another till time catch'.

34   THE DEDICATION TO A BOOK OF STORIES SELECTED FROM THE IRISH NOVELISTS

51   This poem first appeared in *RIT*. Yeats called it, even in its rewritten form, 'a sheaf of wild oats' (*Irish Statesman* (8 Nov. 1924)). It was originally entitled 'Dedication'.

1   *green branch*: *bell-branch* Yeats explained as a legendary branch whose shaking cast all men into a gentle sleep (*P* (1895)). See line 12.

2   *Eire*: Eire, spelt Eri in early version, see note on line 23 'The Rose upon the Rood of Time' (*PNE* 17)

24   *Munster . . . Connemara*: Munster, the southern province of Ireland's four provinces; Connemara, an area in Co. Galway, with its western border on the Atlantic (*McG*, 36, *A* 361, *M* 226, *E & I* 350, *CPl* 443). Connemara is derived from Conmaicne-Mara, the hound son of the sea, descendants of Conmac, a son of Maeve and Fergus MacRoy.

THE LAMENTATION OF THE OLD PENSIONER

This poem first appeared in *SO* (15 Nov. 1890) entitled 'The Old Pensioner'. It   *52*
is another drastically rewritten poem. The original version runs as follows:

> I had a chair at every hearth
> When no one turned to see,
> With 'Look at the old fellow there;
> And who may he be?'
> And therefore do I wander on,
> And the fret lies on me.
>
> The road-side trees keep murmuring.
> Ah, wherefore murmur ye,
> As in the old days long gone by,
> Green oak and poplar tree?
> The well-known faces are all gone,
> And the fret lies on me.

Of this Yeats said it was 'little more than a translation into verse of the very words
of an old Wicklow peasant' (*CK*). Yeats used the experience in *CT* also:

A winter or two ago he spent much of the night walking up and down upon
the mountain talking to an old peasant who, dumb to most men, poured out his
cares for him. Both were unhappy: X because he had then first decided that art
and poetry were not for him, and the old peasant because his life was ebbing out
with no achievement remaining and no hope left him. Both how Celtic! How
full of striving after a something never to be completely expressed in word or
deed. The peasant was wandering in his mind with prolonged sorrow. Once he
burst out with, 'God possesses the heavens but He covets the earth' and once
he lamented that his old neighbours were gone and that all had forgotten him:
they used to draw a chair to the fire for him in every cabin, and now they said
'Who is that old fellow there?' 'The fret (Irish for doom) is over me,' he
repeated, and then went on to talk once more of God and Heaven. More than
once he said, waving his arm towards the mountain, 'Only myself knows what
happened under the thorn-tree forty years ago'; and as he said it the tears upon
his face glistened in the moonlight. This old man always rises before me when I
think of X. Both seek – one in wandering sentences, the other in symbolic
pictures and subtle allegoric poetry – to express something that lies beyond the
range of expression; and both, if X will forgive me, have within them the vast
and vague extravagance that lies at the bottom of the Celtic heart. The peasant
visionaries that are, the landlord duellists that were, and the whole hurly burly
of legends – Cuchullin fighting the sea for two days until the waves pass over
him and he dies, Caolte storming the palace of the Gods, Oisin seeking in vain
for three hundred years, to appease his insatiable heart with all the pleasures of
faeryland, these two mystics walking up and down upon the mountain uttering
the central dream of their souls in no less dream-laden sentences, and this mind
that finds X so interesting – all are a portion of that great Celtic phantasmagoria
whose meaning no man has discovered nor any angel revealed (*CT* 23. A
different version is given in *M* 13 ff.)

X is George Russell (AE), and another note places the conversation as occurring on the Two Rock Mountain, south-west of Dublin. See also 'My friend's Book' (*E & I* 412–13) for AE's meditating there.

36   THE BALLAD OF FATHER GILLIGAN

52   This poem first appeared in *SO* (5 July 1890) with the title 'Father Gilligan/A Legend told by the people of Castleisland, Kerry'.

Yeats commented that the ballad was written to a modification of the air *A Fine Old English Gentleman* (*E & I* 21).

53   25   *Mavrone*: (*Irish* mo bhron) cry of grief. In *The Book of the Rhymers' Club* (1892) this appears as 'Ochone, ochone!', a similar cry.

37   THE TWO TREES

54   This poem first appeared in *CK*.

2   *The holy tree*: the Sephirotic tree of the Kabbalah and the tree of knowledge. Two other early poems deal with the tree of life, 'He thinks of his Past Greatness when a Part of the Constellations of Heaven' (*PNE* 75) and 'He hears the Cry of the Sedge' (*PNE* 64). Ellmann (*IY* 76) comments:

> The Kabbalah is helpful in interpreting his poem 'The Two Trees', because the Sephirotic tree has two aspects, one benign, the reverse side malign. On one side are the *Sephiroth*, on the other the dead *Qlippoth*. Since the Kabbalists consider man to be a microcosm, the double-natured tree is a picture both of the universe and of the human mind, whose faculties, even the lowest, can work for good or ill. Yeats can therefore write,

> > Beloved, gaze in thine own heart,
> > The holy tree is growing there . . .

> and at the same time warn her not to look in 'the bitter glass', where the tree appears in its reverse aspect:

> > For there a fatal image grows,
> > With broken boughs and blackened leaves,
> > And roots half-hidden under snows
> > Driven by a storm that ever grieves.

Although the poem is comprehensible without the esoteric source, the source helps to explain how it came to be written. F. Kermode (*RI* 96) suggests Blake as a source:

> Love and harmony combine,
> And around our souls entwine,
> While thy branches mix with mine,
> And our roots together join.

Joys upon our branches sit,
Chirping loud, and singing sweet;
Like gentle streams beneath our feet
Innocence and virtue meet.

Thou the golden fruit dost bear,
I am clad in flowers fair;
Thy sweet boughs perfume the air,
And the turtle buildeth there.

There she sits and feeds her young,
Sweet I hear her mournful song;
And thy lovely leaves among,
There is love; I hear his tongue.

There his charming nest doth lay,
There he sleeps the night away;
There he sports along the day,
And doth among our branches play.

He regards this tree (in a poem of innocence) as the Tree of Life, and thinks Yeats drew upon Blake's later 'Art is the Tree of Life . . . Science is the Tree of Death', trying to incorporate in 'The Two Trees' the ideas in 'Blake's illustrations to Dante', that the good tree is desire and divine energy, the bad is morality and nature, the fallen world, selfhood and abstraction. Yeats wrote:

> The kingdom that was passing was, he held, the kingdom of the Tree of Knowledge; the kingdom that was coming was the kingdom of the Tree of Life: men who ate from the Tree of Knowledge wasted their days in anger against one another, and in taking one another captive in great nets; men who sought their food among the green leaves of the Tree of Life condemned none but the unimaginative and the idle, and those who forget that even love and death and old age are an imaginative art. (*E & I* 130)

Kermode explains as the Tree of Life or Imagination 'the holy tree' of the poem, inhabited by love, growing in the heart of a beautiful woman who does not think. If she does so she is breaking her beauty by an act of homage to the abstract, bartering beauty for argument, for the Tree of the Fall. This is depicted in the lines which follow 'Gaze no more in the bitter glass . . .'. Kermode thinks the poem one of the few improved by revision because Yeats only emphasised the difference between the anti-intellectual tree and the 'dead rottenness' of the second tree.

In an essay on Magic (*E & I* 28–52) Yeats described how he saw a young Irishwoman cast into trance who thought in her waking state the apple of Eve the kind bought in a grocer's shop, but in trance saw the Tree of Life with ever-sighing souls moving in its branches instead of sap, and all the fowls of the air among its leaves with a white fowl on its highest bough wearing a crown. When Yeats returned home he took from the shelf a translation [by MacGregor Mathers in *The Kabbalah Unveiled*] of *The Book of Concealed Mystery*, an old Jewish book, 'and cutting the pages came upon this passage, which I cannot think I had ever read: ''The Tree . . . is the Tree of the Knowledge of Good and Evil . . . in its branches the birds lodge and build their nests, the souls and the angels have their place'' ' (*E & I* 44).

55   13   *circle*: Yeats elsewhere described the Tree of Life as a geometrical figure made up of ten circles or spheres called Sephiroth joined by straight lines, and added that once men must have thought of it as 'like some great tree covered with its fruit and its foliage', but he thought at some period it had lost its natural form (*A* 375).

13–18   The original version reads:

> There, through bewildered branches, go
> Winged Loves borne on in gentle strife
> Tossing and tossing to and fro
> The flaming circle of our life.
> When looking on their shaken hair
> And dreaming how they dance and dart . . .

16   *ignorant*: is here a virtue compared to the 'unresting thought' of line 34

22   *the demons*: perhaps of abstract thought. The soul was likely to be ambushed on its road to truth. 'Abstract thought' which devoured the freedom and pride of life and hunger for miracles were listed in Yeats's opening address to the Hermetic Society of June 1885. See *Y: M & M* 43.

25   *a fatal image*: this is the Tree of Knowledge as opposed to the Tree of Life. See Yeats's comment on Blake, quoted earlier.

38   TO SOME I HAVE TALKED WITH BY THE FIRE

56   This poem first appeared in *TB* (May 1895) with a sub-title *The Dedication of a new book of verse*.

1   *Danaan*: see note on line 9 'The White Birds' (*PNE* 29) and Yeats's note on 'The Hosting of the Sidhe' (*PNE* 40).

39   TO IRELAND IN THE COMING TIMES

56   This poem first appeared in *CK*. The title then read 'Apologia addressed to Ireland in the coming days'. This poem is in part a defence of the obscurity caused by 'a passion for the symbolism of the mystical rose which has saddened my friends', in part an explanation of Yeats's attitude to the role of literature in the struggle for Irish independence, in part a love poem to Maud Gonne. He argued that his patriotism was to be considered as being no less than that of the Young Irelanders and patriotic writers of the past.

4   *rann*: a verse of a poem in Irish, not the whole poem

18   *Davis, Mangan, Ferguson*: Yeats discussed the part played by these writers in a letter in *UI* (10 Sept. 1892). Thomas Osborne Davis (1814-45) founded *N* in 1842, and was leader of the Young Ireland party. He wrote poems and prose of a popular, patriotic kind. James Clarence Mangan (1803-49), was a romantic Irish poet and essayist, who wrote prolifically for the magazines and journals of his period, sometimes translating, sometimes adapting Irish material and German. Sir Samuel Ferguson (1810-86) was an Irish lawyer, poet and antiquary who translated the Gaelic legends in a masculine manner truer to the originals than Yeats's twilight style.

20   *more than their rhyming tell*: Yeats wanted to recreate the old mythology by infusing new life into it, to reach beyond nationality into universality. His interest in the occult and in symbolism added a new dimension to the material he was handling and gave the touch of mystery he required. See note on *WR* in the following section.

The Wind Among the Reeds

YEATS introduced this volume (first published as a separate volume in 1899) in *CW* 1 in 1906 with the comment that he had so meditated on the images that had come to him in writing 'Ballads and Lyrics', 'The Rose' and 'The Wanderings of Oisin' and other images from Irish folklore that they had become true symbols. He had when awake, but more often in sleep, moments of vision; 'a state very unlike dreaming, when these images took upon themselves what seemed an independent life and became a part of a mystic language, which seemed always as if it would bring me some strange revelation.' Being troubled by what was thought to be reckless obscurity he tried to explain himself in lengthy notes into which he put 'all the little learning I had, and more wilful phantasy than I now think admirable, though what is most mystical still seems to me the most true'.

40 THE HOSTING OF THE SIDHE

61 This poem was written on 29 August 1893, and first appeared in *NO* (7 Oct. 1893) with the title 'The Faery Host'. Yeats's note covers the following words: Sidhe, Knocknarea, Clooth-na-Bare, Caolite and Niamh, and is quoted in full:

> The powerful and wealthy called the gods of ancient Ireland the Tuatha De Danaan, or the Tribes of the goddess Danu [the mother of the gods], but the poor called them, and still sometimes call them, the Sidhe, from Aes Sidhe or Sluagh Sidhe, the people of the Faery Hills, as these words are usually explained. Sidhe is also Gaelic for wind, and certainly the Sidhe have much to do with the wind. They journey in whirling winds, the winds that were called the dance of the daughters of Herodias in the Middle Ages, Herodias doubtless taking the place of some old goddess. [*PNE* cites Reginald Scot, *The Discoverie of Witchcraft* (1584), III, 16, for women who 'seduced by the illusions of divels, beleeve and professe, that in the night times they ride abroad with Diana, the goddesse of the Pagans or else with Herodias with an innumerable multitude'. See also note on 'Nineteen Hundred and Nineteen', VI (*PNE* 213).] When the country people see the leaves whirling on the road they bless themselves, because they believe the Sidhe to be passing by. They are almost always said to wear no covering upon their heads, and to let their hair stream out; and the great among them, for they have great and simple, go much on horseback. If any one becomes too much interested in them, and sees them over much, he loses all interest in ordinary things. I shall write a great deal elsewhere about such enchanted persons, and can give but an example or two now. [*PNE* points out that Yeats was writing six articles on Irish folklore from

1897-1902. See *UP*, II, 54-70, 74-87, 94-108, 167-83, 219-36, and 267-82.]

A woman near Gort, in Galway, says: 'There is a boy, now, of the Cloran's; but I wouldn't for the world let them think I spoke of him; it's two years since he came from America, and since that time he never went to Mass, or to Church, or to fairs, or to market, or to stand on the cross roads, or to hurling, or to nothing. And if anyone comes into the house, it's into the room he'll slip, not to see them; and as to work, he has the garden dug to bits, and the whole place smeared with cow dung; and such a crop as was never seen; and the alders all plaited till they look grand. One day he went as far as the chapel; but as soon as he got to the door he turned straight round again, as if he hadn't power to pass it. I wonder he wouldn't get the priest to read a Mass for him, or something; but the crop he has is grand, and you may know well he has some to help him.' One hears many stories of the kind; and a man whose son is believed to go out riding among them at night tells me that he is careless about everything, and lies in bed until it is late in the day. A doctor believes this boy to be mad. Those that are at times 'away', as it is called, know all things, but are afraid to speak [Cf. *UP*, II, 267-8]. A countryman at Kiltartan says, 'There was one of the Lydons – John – was away for seven years, lying in his bed, but brought away at nights, and he knew everything; and one, Kearney, up in the mountains, a cousin of his own, lost two hoggets, and came and told him, and he knew the very spot where they were, and told him, and he got them back again. But *they* were vexed at that, and took away the power, so that he never knew anything again, no more than another.' [Cf. *UP*, II, 267-8]. This wisdom is the wisdom of the fools of the Celtic stories, that was above all the wisdom of the wise. Lomna, the fool of Fiann, had so great wisdom that his head, cut from his body, was still able to sing and prophesy [*PNE* suggests as source John Rhys, *LCH* (2nd edn, 1892) 98-9]; and a writer in the 'Encyclopaedia Britannica' writes that Tristram, in the oldest form of the tale of Tristram and Iseult, drank wisdom, and madness the shadow of wisdom, and not love, out of the magic cup. [*PNE* suggests as source instead of this, Edward Tyrrel Leith, *On the Legend of Tristan: Its Origin in Myth and its Development in Romance* (1868), 10 and 23n.]

The great of the old times are among the Tribes of Danu, and are kings and queens among them. Caolte was a companion of Fiann; and years after his death he appeared to a king in a forest, and was a flaming man, that he might lead him in the darkness. When the king asked him who he was, he said, 'I am your candlestick.' I do not remember where I have read this story, and I have, maybe, half forgotten it. [Sheila O'Sullivan suggests (*YUIT* 271) the source was Standish James O'Grady, *History of Ireland: Critical and Philosophical* (1881) 354. O'Grady gives no reference but Sheila O'Sullivan thinks that he was quoting *The Dean of Lismore's Book*, ed. Rev. Thomas M'Lauchlan (1862), 62-72. Caolte's 'burning hair' in the poem may, she suggests, come from Blake's application of 'flaming' to hair.] Niam was a beautiful woman of the Tribes of Danu, that led Oisin to the Country of the Young, as their country is called; I have written about her in *The Wandering[s] of Usheen*; and he came back, at last, to bitterness and weariness.

Knocknarea is in Sligo, and the country people say that Maeve, still a great queen of the western Sidhe, is buried in the cairn of stones upon it. [In the Ulster cycle of tales she was Queen of Connaught and began the war described in the *Taín Bó Cualgne*.] I have written of Clooth-na-Bare in *The Celtic Twilight*. She 'went all over the world, seeking a lake deep enough to drown

43

her faery life, of which she had grown weary, leaping from hill to hill, and setting up a cairn of stones wherever her feet lighted, until, at last, she found the deepest water in the world in little Lough Ia [(*Irish* Loch Da Ghe, the lake of the two geese. See *M* 79], on the top of the bird mountain, in Sligo.' I forget, now, where I heard this story, but it may have been from a priest at Collooney. [*PNE* draws attention to W. G. Wood-Martin, *History of Sligo, County and Town* (1882–92), III, 354, and his *Pagan Ireland: An Archaeological Sketch* (1895) 126, as sources for the priest's information.] Clooth-na-Bare would mean the old woman of Bare, but is evidently a corruption of Cailleac Bare, the old woman Bare, who, under the names Bare, and Berah, and Beri, and Verah, and Dera, and Dhira, appears in the legends of many places. [The Veiled Woman or Hag of Beare, in Co. Cork, is the speaker in a nineteenth-century poem; she laments her lost youth, her present decay and decrepitude; the poem can be taken as an old nun's lament or as a symbol of Christian Ireland remembering her pagan past.] Mr O'Grady found her haunting Lough Liath high up on the top of a mountain of the Fews [in Co. Armagh], the Slieve Fuadh, or Slieve G-Cullain of old times, under the name of the Cailleac Buillia. He describes Lough Liath as a desolate moon-shaped lake, with made wells and sunken passages upon its borders, and beset by marsh and heather and gray boulders, and closes his 'Flight of the Eagle' [(1897); see pp. 255–7 and 296–7] with a long rhapsody upon mountain and lake, because of the heroic tales and beautiful old myths that have hung about them always. He identifies the Cailleac Buillia with that Meluchra who persuaded Fionn to go to her amid the waters of Lough Liath, and so changed him with her enchantments, that, though she had to free him because of the threats of the Fiana, his hair was ever afterwards as white as snow. To this day, the Tribes of the Goddess Danu that are in the waters beckon to men, and drown them in the waters; and Bare, or Dhira, or Meluchra, or whatever name one likes the best, is, doubtless, the name of a mistress among them. Meluchra was daughter of Cullain; and Cullain Mr O'Grady calls, upon I know not what authority, a form of Lir, the master of waters. The people of the waters have been in all ages beautiful and changeable and lascivious, or beautiful and wise and lonely, for water is everywhere the signature of the fruitfulness of the body and of the fruitfulness of dreams. The white hair of Fionn may be but another of the troubles of those that come to unearthly wisdom and earthly trouble, and the threats and violence of the Fiana against her, a different form of the threats and violence the country people use, to make the Tribes of Danu give up those that are 'away'. Bare is now often called an ugly old woman; but Dr Joyce says that one of her old names was Aebhin, which means beautiful. Aebhen was the goddess of the tribes of northern Leinster; and the lover she had made immortal, and who loved her perfectly, left her, and put on mortality, to fight among them against the stranger, and died on the strand of Clontarf. (*WR*)

3 *Caoilte*: cf. Yeats's note on 'The Secret Rose' (*PNE* 67), and his note on this poem quoted above. Though Yeats described him there as a companion of Fiann, he was also a comrade of Oisin, the son of Finn. He was the swiftest runner of the Fianna.

4 *Niamh*: cf. 'The Wanderings of Oisin' (*PNE* 375 ff.) and 'News for the Delphic Oracle' (*PNE* 363), where she is described as 'Man-picker'; and 'The Circus Animals' Desertion' (*PNE* 373) where she is the 'faery bride'. In the

Fenian tale, *Oisin in the Land of the Young*, Niamh, who is extremely beautiful, spirits Oisin off to the land of the Young for three hundred years.

11-12 *between him and the deed . . . and the hope*: a passage in Yeats's *Pages from a Diary written in 1930* seems to link this poem and these lines with 'The Everlasting Voices' (*PNE* 41), and 'To his Heart, bidding it have no Fear' (*PNE* 58). In it Yeats suggested that his conceptions, one of reality as a congeries of beings, another of reality as a single being, alternate in emotion and history and cannot be reconciled by human reason because it is always subject to one or the other. He saw himself as driven to a moment 'which is the realisation of myself as unique and free, or to a moment which is the surrender to God of all that I am'. He thought there were historical cycles in which one or the other predominated, and that a cycle was approaching where all would be as particular and concrete as human intensity would permit. He had tried again and again

> to sing that approach – *The Hosting of the Sidhe*, 'O Sweet Everlasting Voices' and those lines about 'The lonely, majestical multitude' – and have almost understood my intention. Again and again with remorse, a sense of defeat, I have failed when I would write of God, written coldly and conventionally. Could those two impulses, one as much a part of the truth as the other, be reconciled, or if one or the other could prevail, all life would cease. (*E* 305)

THE EVERLASTING VOICES   41

This poem was written on 29 August 1895 and first appeared in *NR* (Jan. 1896)   *61* with the title 'Everlasting Voices'.

1 *everlasting Voices, be still*: In one of Yeats's stories, Hanrahan, when he is dying, hears 'faint joyful voices' and he asks who they are, to receive the reply, 'I am one of the lasting people, of the lasting unwearied Voices, that make my dwelling in the broken and the dying and those that have lost their wits; and I came looking for you, and you are mine until the whole world is burned out like a candle that is spent . . .' (*M* 260). Another essay, 'The Golden Age', refers to Yeats seeming to hear a voice of lamentation of the Golden Age. It told him that humans were imperfect and incomplete, that the world was once perfect and kindly and that the kindly and perfect world still existed but 'buried like a mass of roses under many spadefuls of earth'. The fairies and more innocent spirits dwelt within it and lamented over the fallen world of humanity 'in the lamentation of the wind-tossed reeds' in the song of birds, the moan of waves, and the cry of the fiddle. It is said that 'if only they who live in the Golden Age could die we might be happy, for the sad voices would be still; but they must sing and we must weep until the eternal gates swing open'. (*M* 104-5)

62   This poem first appeared in *TB* (Aug. 1893). Yeats's essay on 'The Moods', dated 1895, provides a prose gloss upon the poem. It reads:

> Literature differs from explanatory and scientific writing in being wrought about a mood, or a community of moods, as the body is wrought about an invisible soul; and if it uses argument, theory, erudition, observation, and seems to grow hot in assertion or denial, it does so merely to make us partakers at the banquet of the moods. It seems to me that these moods are the labourers and messengers of the Ruler of All, the gods of ancient days still dwelling on their secret Olympus, the angels of more modern days ascending and descending upon their shining ladder; and that argument, theory, erudition, observation, are merely what Blake called 'little devils who fight for themselves,' illusions of our visible passing life, who must be made serve the moods, or we have no part in eternity. Everything that can be seen, touched, measured, explained, understood, argued over, is to the imaginative artist nothing more than a means, for he belongs to the invisible life, and delivers its ever new and ever ancient revelation. We hear much of his need for the restraints of reason, but the only restraint he can obey is the mysterious instinct that has made him an artist, and that teaches him to discover immortal moods in mortal desires, an undecaying hope in our trivial ambitions, a divine love in sexual passion.   (*E & I* 195)

3   *mountains and woods*: these lines are close to a passage in 'The Death of Hanrahan':

> I am young, I am young; look upon me, mountains; look upon me, perishing woods, for my body will be shining like the white waters when you have been hurried away. You and the whole race of men, and the race of the beasts, and the race of the fish, and the winged race, are dropping like a candle that is nearly burned out . . .   (*M* 254)

4   *have their day*: a passage in the essay 'Rosa Alchemica' illustrates these lines with the picture given to six students in a book of alchemical doctrines. If they were to imagine the semblance of a living being it was at once possessed by a wandering soul which went hither and thither working good or evil, until the moment of its death had come:

> If you would give forms to the evil powers, it went on, you were to make them ugly, thrusting out a lip with the thirsts of life, or breaking the proportions of a body with the burdens of life; but the divine powers would only appear in beautiful shapes, which are but, as it were, shapes trembling out of existence, folding up into a timeless ecstasy, drifting with half-shut eyes into a sleepy stillness. The bodiless souls who descended into these forms were what men called the moods; and worked all great changes in the world; for just as the magician or the artist could call them when he would, so, they could call out of the mind of the magician or the artist, or if they were demons, out of the mind of the mad or the ignoble, what shape they would, and through its voice and its gestures pour themselves out upon the world. In this way all great events were accomplished; a mood, a divinity or a demon, first descending like a faint sigh into men's minds and then changing their thoughts and their actions until hair

that was yellow had grown black, or hair that was black had grown yellow, and empires moved their border, as though they were but drifts of leaves. (*M* 285)

6   *fire-born moods*: Yeats wrote in 'Anima Mundi' 'in the condition of fire is all music and all rest' (*M* 357) when he distinguished between terrestrial reality and the condition of fire.

7   *fallen away*: The essay 'Anima Mundi' continued:

All power is from the terrestrial condition, for there all opposites meet and there only is the extreme of choice possible, full freedom. And there the heterogeneous is, and evil, for evil is the strain one upon another of opposites; but in the condition of fire is all music and all rest. Between is the condition of air where images have but a borrowed life, that of memory or that reflected upon them when they symbolise colours and intensities of fire: the place of shades who are 'in the whirl of those who are fading. . . .'
After so many rhythmic beats the soul must cease to desire its images, and can, as it were, close its eyes.
When all sequence comes to an end, time comes to an end and the soul puts on the rhythmic or spiritual body or luminous body and contemplates all the events of its memory [cf. 'Man and the Echo' (*PNE* 372), where Yeats contemplates events in his life, arranges all in one clear view, 'Then stands in judgment on his soul'] and every possible impulse in an eternal possession of itself in one single moment. That condition is alone animate, all the rest is fantasy, and from thence come all the passions and, some have held, the very heat of the body.   (*M* 356-7)

He then quoted the present poem, but 'A Meditation in Time of War' (*PNE* 202) gives a similar idea. Cf. also *AV* (B) 225 ff.

THE LOVER TELLS OF THE ROSE IN HIS HEART   43

This poem first appeared in *NO* (12 Nov. 1892) with the title 'The Rose in my   62
Heart'. In *WR* the title was 'Aedh tells of the Rose in his Heart'. Yeats's note in that volume explained that 'Aedh' (Aodh), 'Hanrahan,' and 'Michael Robartes' were personages in the stories of *TSR* but that with the exception of some of Hanrahan's and one of Aedh's poems, the poems were not from that book. He was using these personages more as principles of the mind than as actual personages. He thought it likely that only students of the magical tradition would understand him when he said that Michael Robartes was fire reflected in water, that Aedh, whose name is not only the Irish for Hugh but also for fire, was fire burning by itself:

To put it in a different way, Hanrahan is the simplicity of an imagination too changeable to gather permanent possessions, or the adoration of the shepherds; and Michael Robartes is the pride of the imagination brooding upon the greatness of its possessions, or the adoration of the Magi; while Aedh is the myrrh and frankincense that the imagination offers continually before all that it loves.   (*WR*)

4   *your image*: Maud Gonne's

6   *green knoll*: this may refer to his dream of creating a Celtic order of mysteries, centring on the island in Lough Key. See note on 'To the Rose upon the Rood of Time' (*PNE* 17).

44   THE HOST OF THE AIR

63   This poem first appeared in *TB* (Nov. 1893), dated 1 October 1893, with the title 'The Stolen Bride'. Yeats's note after the title read:

> I heard the story on which this ballad is founded from an old woman at Balesodare, Sligo. She repeated me a Gaelic poem on the subject, and then translated it to me. I have always regretted not having taken down her words, and as some amends for not having done so, have made this ballad. Any one who tastes fairy food or drink is glamoured and stolen by the fairies. This is why Bridget sets O'Driscoll to play cards. 'The folk of the air' is a Gaelic name for the fairies.

4   *Hart Lake*: a lake high up in the Ox Mountains, six or seven miles west of Ballisodare in Co. Sligo

8   *Bridget his bride*: In the story 'Kidnappers' Yeats used the same story (a footnote to the story pointed out that he had used the theme in a ballad in *WR*), and told how a young man going at nightfall to his house and his just married bride, met on his way a jolly company and with them his bride:

> They were faeries and had stolen her as a wife for the chief of their band. To him they seemed only a company of merry mortals. His bride, when she saw her old love, bade him welcome, but was most fearful lest he should eat the faery food, and so be glamoured out of the earth into that bloodless dim nation, wherefore she set him down to play cards with three of the cavalcade; and he played on, realising nothing until he saw the chief of the band carrying his bride away in his arms. Immediately he started up, and knew that they were faeries, for all that jolly company melted into shadow and night. He hurried to his house, and as he drew near he heard the cry of the keeners [the original version of the poem included the following lines, placed after the present line 40 (which was altered from the original version):

> > He knew now the folk of the air,
> > And his heart was blackened by dread,
> > And he ran to the door of his house;
> > Old women were keening the dead.

In *Later Poems* (1924) Yeats commented, in a note dated 1899, that the poem was founded in an old Gaelic ballad, but in the ballad the husband found the keeners (see note on line 22 'The Ballad of Father O'Hart' (*PNE* 14)) keening his wife when he got to his house] and knew that his wife was dead. Some noteless Gaelic poet had made this into a forgotten ballad, some old verses of which my white-capped friend remembered and sang for me.   (*M* 73 ff.)

Yeats's note reads:

Some writers distinguish between the Sluagh Gaoith [*PNE* points out that this should be Gaoithe], the host of the air, and Sluagh Sidhe, the host of the Sidhe, and describe the host of the air of a peculiar malignancy. Dr Joyce says, 'of all the different kinds of goblins . . . air demons were most dreaded by the people. They lived among clouds, and mists, and rocks, and hated the human race with the utmost malignity.' ['Fergus O'Mara and the Demons', *Good and Pleasant Reading* (1892) which Yeats included in *Irish Fairy Tales* (1892).] A very old Arann charm, which contains the words 'Send God, by his strength, between us and the host of the Sidhe, between us and the host of the air', seems also to distinguish among them. I am inclined, however, to think that the distinction came in with Christianity and its belief about the prince of the air [Satan], for the host of the Sidhe, as I have already explained, are closely associated with the wind. [See Yeats's note on 'The Hosting of the Sidhe' (*PNE* 40).]

They are said to steal brides just after their marriage, and sometimes in a blast of wind. A man in Galway says, 'At Aughanish [a promontory, north-west of Kinvarra, Co. Clare. See also *CPl* 370, 437] there were two couples came to the shore to be married, and one of the newly married women was in the boat with the priest, and they going back to the island; and a sudden blast of wind came, and the priest said some blessed words that were able to save himself, but the girl was swept.' [See *UP*, II, 80.]

This woman was drowned; but more often the persons who are taken 'get the touch', as it is called, and fall into a half dream, and grow indifferent to all things, for their true life has gone out of the world, and is among the hills and the forts of the Sidhe. A faery doctor has told me that his wife 'got the touch' at her marriage because there was one of them wanted her; and the way he knew for certain was, that when he took a pitchfork out of the rafters, and told her it was a broom, she said, 'It is a broom.' [See *UP*, II, 228-9.] She was, the truth is, in the magical sleep to which people have given a new name lately [hypnosis], that makes the imagination so passive that it can be moulded by any voice in any world into any shape. A mere likeness of some old woman, or even old animal, some one or some thing the Sidhe have no longer a use for, is believed to be left instead of the person who is 'away'; this some one or some thing can, it is thought, be driven away by threats, or by violence (though I have heard country women say that violence is wrong), which perhaps awakes the soul out of the magical sleep. The story in the poem is founded on an old Gaelic ballad that was sung and translated for me by a woman at Ballisodare in County Sligo; but in the ballad the husband found the keeners keening his wife when he got to his house. She was 'swept' at once; but the Sidhe are said to value those the most whom they but cast into a half dream, which may last for years, for they need the help of a living person in most of the things they do. There are many stories of people who seem to die and be buried – though the country people will tell you it is but some one or some thing put in their place that dies and is buried – and yet are brought back afterwards. These tales are perhaps memories of true awakenings out of the magical sleep, moulded by the imagination, under the influence of a mystical doctrine which it understands too literally, into the shape of some well-known traditional tale. One does not hear them as one hears the others, from the persons who are 'away', or from their wives or husbands; and one old man, who had often seen the Sidhe, began one of them with 'Maybe it is all vanity.'

Here is a tale that a friend of mine [Lady Gregory] heard in the Burren hills [a rocky district in Co. Clare. See *McG* 24, and *M* 58, *E & I* 209, 211], and it is a type of all:

'There was a girl to be married, and she didn't like the man, and she cried when the day was coming, and said she wouldn't go along with him. And the mother said, ''Get into the bed, then, and I'll say that you're sick.'' And so she did. And when the man came the mother said to him, ''You can't get her, she's sick in the bed.'' And he looked in and said, ''That's not my wife that's in the bed, it's some old hag.'' And the mother began to cry and to roar. And he went out and got two hampers of turf and made a fire, that they thought he was going to burn the house down. And when the fire was kindled, ''Come out now,'' says he, ''and we'll see who you are, when I'll put you on the fire.'' And when she heard that, she gave one leap, and was out of the house, and they saw, then, it was an old hag she was. Well, the man asked the advice of an old woman, and she bid him go to a faery-bush that was near, and he might get some word of her. So he went there at night, and saw all sorts of grand people, and they in carriages or riding on horses, and among them he could see the girl he came to look for. So he went again to the old woman, and she said, ''If you can get the three bits of blackthorn out of her hair, you'll get her again.'' So that night he went back again, and that time he only got hold of a bit of her hair. But the old woman told him that he was no use, and that he was put back now, and it might be twelve nights before he'd get her. But on the fourth night he got the third bit of blackthorn, and he took her, and she came away with him. He never told the mother he had got her; but one day she saw her at a fair, and, says she, ''That's my daughter; I know her by the smile and by the laugh of her,'' and she with a shawl about her head. So the husband said, ''You're right there, and hard I worked to get her.'' She spoke often of the grand things she saw underground, and how she used to have wine to drink, and to drive out in a carriage with four horses every night. And she used to be able to see her husband when he came to look for her, and she was greatly afraid he'd get a drop of the wine, for then he would have come underground and never left it again. And she was glad herself to come to earth again, and not to be left there.'

The old Gaelic literature is full of the appeals of the Tribes of the goddess Danu to mortals whom they would bring into their country; but the song of Midher to the beautiful Etain, the wife of the king who was called Echaid the ploughman, is the type of all. [See notes on 'The Harp of Aengus' (*PNE* 379) and 'The Two Kings' (*PNE* 381).]

'O beautiful woman, come with me to the marvellous land where one listens to a sweet music, where one has spring flowers in one's hair, where the body is like snow from head to foot, where no one is sad or silent, where teeth are white and eyebrows are black . . . cheeks red like foxglove in flower . . . Ireland is beautiful, but not so beautiful as the Great Plain I call you to. The beer of Ireland is heady, but the beer of the Great Plain is much more heady. How marvellous is the country I am speaking of! Youth does not grow old there. Streams with warm flood flow there; sometimes mead, sometimes wine. Men are charming and without a blot there, and love is not forbidden there. O woman, when you come into my powerful country you will wear a crown of gold upon your head. I will give you the flesh of swine, and you will have beer and milk to drink. O beautiful woman. O beautiful woman, come with me!' (*WR*)

[*PNE* suggests Yeats was using as source Kuno Meyer's and Alfred Nutt's version of the song in *The Voyage of Bran* (1895–7, I, 176).]

THE FISH 45

This poem first appeared in the *Cornish Magazine* (Dec. 1898) with the title 64 'Bressel the Fisherman'. 'Bressel' became 'Breasel' in *WR*. The poem was written to Maud Gonne.

6 *the little silver cords*: cf. 'their little silver heads', line 6 'The Man who dreamed of Faeryland' (*PNE* 33), and 'a little silver trout', line 8 'The Song of Wandering Aengus' (*PNE* 48)

THE UNAPPEASABLE HOST 46

This poem first appeared in *S* (April 1896) under the title 'Two Poems 65 concerning Peasant Visionaries'. (The other poem was 'The Valley of the Black Pig' (*PNE* 60).) In *WR* it was entitled 'A Cradle Song'.

1 *Danaan children*: the Danaan children stand for the Tuatha de Danaan, the race of the gods of Dana, the mother of the ancient gods of Ireland, hence, in the popular imagination, fairies. See note on line 3 'The Madness of King Goll' (*PNE* 9).

3 *the North*: presumably wind. The original version's third line ran: 'For winds will bear them gently when the eagle flies', and the second version published in *The Senate* (Nov. 1896) had 'For they will ride the winds when the gier-eagle flies'. Yeats's note reads:

I use the wind as a symbol of vague desires and hopes, not merely because the Sidhe are in the wind, or because the wind bloweth as it listeth, but because wind and spirit and vague desire have been associated everywhere. A highland scholar tells me that his country people use the wind in their talk and their proverbs as I use it in my poem.   (*WR*)

In the same volume he associated the North with night and sleep.

3 *ger-eagle*: geier-eagle, used (as gier eagle) in Authorised Version of the Bible to translate Hebrew *raham*, a kind of vulture. Cf. Lev. xi. 18 and Deut. xiv. 17

8 *flaming West*: Yeats associated the West, the place of sunset, with fading and dreaming things (*WR*).

12 *Mother Mary*: see note on line 9 'The Countess Cathleen in Paradise' (*PNE* 31).

47   INTO THE TWILIGHT

65   This poem was written on 31 June (1893?) and first appeared in *NO* (29 July
1893) with the title 'The Celtic Twilight'. It was published as the last item with
the title 'Into the Twilight' in *CT*.

    5   *Eire*: see note on line 23 'To the Rose upon the Rood of Time' (*PNE* 17).

48   THE SONG OF WANDERING AENGUS

66   This poem was written on 31 January (1893?) and first appeared in *The Sketch*
(4 Aug. 1897) with the title 'A Mad Song'; it appeared without a title in the
story 'Red Hanrahan's Vision' in *McClure's Magazine* (March 1905). Yeats's
note reads:

> The Tribes of the goddess Danu [see note on line 1, 'The Unappeasable
> Host' (*PNE* 46)] can take all shapes, and those that are in the waters take often
> the shape of fish. A woman of Burren, in Galway, says, 'There are more of
> them in the sea than on the land, and they sometimes try to come over the side
> of the boat in the form of fishes, for they can take their choice shape.' At other
> times they are beautiful women; and another Galway woman says, 'Surely
> those things are in the sea as well as on land. My father was out fishing one
> night off Tyrone. And something came beside the boat that had eyes shining
> like candles. And then a wave came in, and a storm rose all in a minute, and
> whatever was in the wave, the weight of it had like to sink the boat. And then
> they saw that it was a woman in the sea that had the shining eyes. So my father
> went to the priest, and he bid him always to take a drop of holy water and a
> pinch of salt out in the boat with him, and nothing could harm him.'
> The poem was suggested to me by a Greek folk song; but the folk belief of
> Greece is very like that of Ireland, and I certainly thought, when I wrote it, of
> Ireland, and of the spirits that are in Ireland. An old man who was cutting a
> quickset hedge near Gort, in Galway, said, only the other day, 'One time I was
> cutting timber over in Inchy, and about eight o'clock one morning, when I got
> there, I saw a girl picking nuts, with her hair hanging down over her shoulders;
> brown hair; and she had a good clean face, and she was tall, and nothing on her
> head, and her dress no way gaudy, but simple. And when she felt me coming
> she gathered herself up, and was gone, as if the earth had swallowed her up.
> And I followed her, and looked for her, but I never could see her again from
> that day to this, never again.'
> The county Galway people use the word 'clean' in its old sense of fresh and
> comely. (*WR*)

R. K. Alspach, 'Two Songs of Yeats', *Modern Language Notes*, lxi, 395–400,
considers that Yeats's note that the poem was suggested by a Greek folk song
leads us to Lucy Garnett, 'The Three Fishes', *Greek Folk Poesy* (1896) which
Yeats reviewed in *TB* (Oct. 1896). Alspach also suggests as a source Samuel
Lover's 'The White Trout' which was included in Yeats' *FFT*.

1   *I*: Yeats's note on 'He mourns for the Change that has come upon Him and
his Beloved, and longs for the End of the World' (*PNE* 52) explains that the 'man

with a hazel wand' of that poem 'may well have been Angus, Master of Love', described by Yeats as the God of Youth, beauty and poetry, who reigned in Tir-nan-Oge, the country of the Young (*P* (1895)). He spelt the name Angus and Aengus.

hazel wood: Sheila O'Sullivan suggests (*YUIT* 268) that the imagery of the first stanza comes from Standish Hayes O'Grady's edition of the story of Diarmuid and Grainne in *Transactions of the Ossianic Society*, III (1857) 78-81. A wandering youth tells the fleeing lovers that he is Muadhan and is seeking a lord to serve. In reality he is Aengus, the god of love; he provides them with food:

> He himself went into the next wood to him, and plucked in it a straight long rod, and put a holly berry upon the hook, and went (and stood) over the stream, and took a fish that cast.

2   *a fire was in my head*: Ellmann (*IY* 298) compares Symons's 'The Broken Tryst', 'That day a fire was in my blood'. The likely source for this stanza is Samuel Lover, 'The White Trout – A Legend of Cong', *Legends and Stories of Ireland* (n.d.) 23-31. Sheila O'Sullivan suggests (*YUIT* 269) that there is also a memory of 'The Story of the Fisherman' in *The Arabian Nights' Entertainment* (See the translation by E. W. Lane (n.d.) 32) where the fisherman catches four strangely coloured fish. When the Sultan's servant proceeds to cook them the walls of the kitchen 'clove asunder, and there came forth a damsel of tall stature, beautiful in countenance.' She addressed the fish who then 'raised their heads from the frying pan' and spoke.

3   *hazel wand*: elsewhere Yeats commented that the hazel tree was the Irish tree of Life or of Knowledge, and in Ireland it was doubtless, as elsewhere, the tree of the heavens (*D* (Oct. 1898)).

13   *glimmering girl*: an image of Maud Gonne with whom Yeats associated apple blossom. His account of his first meeting with her in 1889 includes the image:

> How important it all seemed to me. How much would I have given so that she might think exactly right on all these great questions. And today all is faint to me beside a moment when she passed before a window dressed white and re-arranged a spray of flowers in a vase. Twelve years after I put this impression into verse ('She pulled down the pale blossoms') I felt in the presence of a great generosity and courage and a mind without rest, and when she and all the singing birds had gone, my melancholy was not the mere melancholy of love. I had what I thought was a clairvoyant perception (of some immediate disaster) but was I can see now but an obvious deduction of an immediate waiting disaster. . . . I was in love but had not spoken of love and never meant to speak of love as the months passed I gained a mastery of myself again. What wife would she make, I thought, what share could she have in the life of a student? (Unpublished Autobiography)

Another description of this meeting was published:

> Her complexion was luminous, like that of apple-blossom through which the

53

light falls, and I remember her standing that first day by a great heap of such blossoms in the window.   (*A* 123)

Sheila O'Sullivan has suggested (*YUIT* 270) as a possible source for the image a book which Yeats reviewed in 1890 for the *Scots Observer*, Lady Wilde's *Ancient Cures, Charms and Usages* (1890) 101–2:

> Mayday in old times was the period of greatest rejoicing in Ireland, a festival of dances and garlands to celebrate the Resurrection of Nature, as November was a time of solemn gloom and mourning for the dying sun; for the year was divided into these two epochs, symbolizing death and resurrection, and the year itself was expressed by a word meaning 'the circle of the sun', the symbol of which was a hoop, always carried in the popular procession, wreathed with the rowan and the marsh marigold, and bearing suspended within it, two balls to represent the sun and the moon, sometimes covered with gold and silver paper.

67   23–4   *The silver apples ... The golden apples*: see note on 'The Man who dreamed of Faeryland' (*PNE* 33).

49   THE SONG OF THE OLD MOTHER

67   This poem first appeared in *TB* (April 1894) and was described as 'an old woman complaining of the idleness of the young', one of the poems that 'popular poets' write (*A* 254).

2   *seed of the fire*: Yeats's note after the title in the original explained this as 'the Irish phrase for the little fragment of burning turf [peat] and hot ashes which remains in the hearth from the day before.'

50   THE HEART OF THE WOMAN

67   This poem was written in 1894 and first appeared in *The Speaker* (21 July 1894). It was untitled, and was included in the story, 'Those Who Live in the Storm' which was reprinted with the title 'The Rose of Shadow' in *TSR*.

4   *breast lies upon his breast*: cf. line 9 'He hears the Cry of the Sedge' (*PNE* 64), line 4 'He wishes his Beloved were Dead' (*PNE* 73), line 9 'He thinks of his Past Greatness when a Part of the Constellations of Heaven' (*PNE* 75).

51   THE LOVER MOURNS FOR THE LOSS OF LOVE

68   This poem first appeared in *D* (May 1898) with the title 'Aodh to Dectora. Three Songs'. The others were 'He hears the Cry of the Sedge' (*PNE* 64) and 'He thinks of Those who have spoken Evil of his Beloved' (*PNE* 65).

2   *beautiful friend*: 'Diana Vernon' [the name presumably came from the heroine of Scott's *Rob Roy*], Mrs Olivia Shakespear, with whom Yeats had his first affair in 1896. The story is told in Yeats's unpublished Autobiography. See *Y:M & P* 100-3. See note on her on 'Friends' (*PNE* 135). The identification of Diana Vernon and Mrs Shakespear is made explicit in *PYP* 66-7. Cf. note on 'The Empty Cup' (*PNE* 231).

6   *Your image*: Maud Gonne's. Cf. *Y:M & P* 102.

HE MOURNS FOR THE CHANGE THAT HAS COME UPON HIM AND HIS   52
BELOVED, AND LONGS FOR THE END OF THE WORLD

This poem first appeared in *D* (June 1897) dated 'Sligo, June 1897' with the title   68
'The Desire of Man and Woman'. 'Mongan laments the Change that has come upon Him and His Beloved . . .' was the title given in *WR*. In his original note to 'He [in the first version, Mongan] thinks of his Past Greatness when a Part of the Constellations of Heaven' (*PNE* 75), Yeats wrote: 'Mongan, in the old Celtic poetry, is a famous wizard and king who remembers his passed lives.' (*D* Oct. 1898).

In the original version the following note was printed after the title:

In the old Irish story of Usheen's journey to the Islands of the Young, Usheen sees amid the waters a hound with one red ear, following a deer with no horns; and other persons in other old Celtic stories see the like images of the desire of the man, and of the desire of the woman 'which is for the desire of the man', and of all desires that are as these. The man with the wand of hazel may well have been Angus, Master of Love; and the boar without bristles is the ancient Celtic image of the darkness which will at last destroy the world, as it destroys the sun at nightfall in the west.

A fuller note in *WR* read:

My deer and hound are properly related to the deer and hound that flicker in and out of the various tellings of the Arthurian legends, leading different knights upon adventures, and to the hounds and to the hornless deer at the beginning of, I think, all tellings of Oisin's journey to the country of the young. The hound is certainly related to the Hounds of Annwvyn or of Hades, who are white, and have red ears, and were heard, and are, perhaps, still heard by Welsh peasants, following some flying thing in the night winds [this is derived from Lady Charlotte Guest's edition of *The Mabinogion* (1877) 363]; and is probably related to the hounds that Irish country people believe will awake and seize the souls of the dead if you lament them too loudly or too soon. An old woman told a friend and myself that she saw what she thought were white birds, flying over an enchanted place, but found, when she got near, that they had dogs' heads; and I do not doubt that my hound and these dog-headed birds are of the same family. I got my hound and deer out of a last-century Gaelic poem [see note on Bryan O'Looney's translation of 'The Lay of Oisin in the Land of Youth' as source for *The Wanderings of Oisin* (*PNE* 375), lines 139-145, and see note below on line 1] about Oisin's journey to the country of the young. After the hunting of the hornless deer, that leads him to the seashore, and while he is riding over the sea with Niamh, he sees amid the waters – I have not the Gaelic poem by me, and describe it from memory – a young man following a girl who has a golden apple, and afterwards a hound with one red ear following a deer with no horns. This hound and this deer seem plain images of the desire of the man 'which is for the woman,' and 'the desire of the woman which is for the desire of the man' [*PNE* suggests as source Samuel Taylor Coleridge's (1772–1834) *Table Talk of Samuel Taylor Coleridge and the Rime of the Ancient Mariner, Christabel &c.*, Introd. Henry Morley (n.d.) 65] and of all desires that are as these. I have read them in this way in *The Wanderings of Oisin*, and have made my lover sigh because he has seen in their faces 'the immortal desire of immortals.'

The man in my poem who has a hazel wand may have been Aengus, Master of Love; and I have made the boar without bristles come out of the West, because the place of sunset was in Ireland, as in other countries, a place of symbolic darkness and death. – 1899.   (*CW* 1)

white deer with no horns: cf. *The Wanderings of Oisin* (*PNE* 375) where the Land of Youth is described:

> We galloped; now a hornless deer
> Passed by us, chased by a phantom hound
> All pearly white, save one red ear . . .

The source for the image is probably Brian O'Looney's translation of Michael Comyn's *The Lay of Oisin in the Land of Youth* (the Gaelic poem of the last century mentioned in Yeats's Notes):

> We saw also, by our sides
> A hornless fawn leaping nimbly,
> And a red-eared white dog,
> Urging it boldly in the chase.

(See Russell K. Alspach, 'Some Sources of Yeats's ''The Wanderings of Oisin'' ', *PMLA* (Sept. 1943).)

10   *the Boar*: cf. 'The Valley of the Black Pig' (*PNE* 60)

the West: see note on 'The Unappeasable Host' (*PNE* 46), and cf. line 5 'He bids his Beloved be at Peace' (*PNE* 53), 'He reproves the Curlew' (*PNE* 54) and 'He wishes his Beloved were Dead' (*PNE* 73).

53   HE BIDS HIS BELOVED BE AT PEACE

69   This poem was written on 24 September 1895 and first appeared in *S* (Jan. 1896), its title being '[Two Love Poems. The Shadowy Horses] Michael Robartes bids his Beloved be at Peace'. For Michael Robartes see note on 'The Lover tells of the Rose in his Heart' (*PNE* 43). Yeats's note to this poem read:

November, the old beginning of winter, or of the victory of the Fomor [see note on 'The Madness of King Goll' (*PNE* 9)], or powers of death, and dismay, and cold, and darkness, is associated by the Irish people with the horse-shaped Púcas [See *FFT* 94 for a description of púcas as solitary faeries and of their shapes], who are now mischievous spirits, but were once Fomorian divinities. I think that they may have some connection with the horses of Mannannan [God of the sea], who reigned over the country of the dead, where the Fomorian Tethra [a king of the Fomorians whom older stories make a ruler of Tir-na-nOg] reigned also; and the horses of Mannannan, though they could cross the land as easily as the sea, are constantly associated with the waves. Some neo-platonist, I forget who [*PNE* suggests Thomas Taylor (1758–1835) writing of the sea in *A Dissertation on the Eleusinian and Bacchic Mysteries* (1790, p. 165) as perpetually rolling without admitting any period of repose], describes the sea as a symbol of the drifting indefinite bitterness of life, and I believe there is like symbolism intended in the many Irish voyages to the islands of enchantment, or that there was, at any rate, in the mythology out of which these stories have been shaped. I follow much Irish and other mythology, and the magical tradition, in associating the North with night and sleep, and the East, the place of sunrise, with hope, and the South, the place of the sun when at its height, with passion and desire, and the West, the place of sunset, with fading and dreaming things.   (*WR*)

3   *The North*: the Fomoroh, the gods of night and death and cold, the word meaning from under the sea, were of the north and winter, according to Yeats's note in *P* (1895).

9   *Beloved*: the poem was written to 'Diana Vernon'. See note on 'The Lover mourns for the Loss of Love' (*PNE* 51).

10   *your hair fall over my breast*: cf. line 6 'The Travail of Passion' (*PNE* 69) also written to 'Diana Vernon'.

HE REPROVES THE CURLEW   54

This poem first appeared in *S* (Nov. 1896) with the title 'Windlestraws I.   69
O'Sullivan Rua to the Curlew [and II. Out of the Old Days]'. The poem was entitled 'Hanrahan reproves the Curlew' in *WR*.

2   *water in the West*: see note on 'The Unappeasable Host' (*PNE* 46). Perhaps there is an echo here of the Neoplatonist who 'describes the sea as a symbol of the drifting indefinite bitterness of life' in Yeats's note to 'He bids his Beloved be at Peace' (*PNE* 53). The West is the region 'of fading and dreaming things'.

5   *breast*: see note on line 10 'He bids his Beloved be at Peace' (*PNE* 53)

6   *wind*: a symbol of vague desires, hopes

HE REMEMBERS FORGOTTEN BEAUTY   55

This poem first appeared in *S* (July 1896) with the title 'O'Sullivan Rua to Mary   69

Lavell'; in *WR* this became 'Michael Robartes remembers Forgotten Beauty'. For Michael Robartes see note on 'The Lover tells of the Rose in his Heart' (*PNE* 43).

56   A POET TO HIS BELOVED

70   This poem was written in 1895 and first appeared in *The Senate* (March 1896) with the title 'O'Sullivan the Red to Mary Lavell II [and was accompanied by another poem, later entitled 'Aedh tells of the Perfect Beauty', but printed under the title 'O'Sullivan the Red to Mary Lavell I' in *The Senate*]. 'A Poet to his Beloved' was used as title in *WR*.

57   HE GIVES HIS BELOVED CERTAIN RHYMES

71   This poem was written in 1895 and first appeared in a story, 'The Binding of the Hair', in *S* (Jan. 1896) and was untitled. In *WR* it was entitled 'Aedh [see note on 'The Lover tells of the Rose in his Heart' (*PNE* 43)] gives his Beloved certain Rhymes'. Yeats's note on *KGCT* comments that:

> In the first edition of *The Secret Rose* there is a story based on some old Gaelic legend. A certain man swears to sing the praise of a certain woman, his head is cut off and the head sings [somewhat parallel to the story of the horse Fallada in Grimm's Tales]. A poem of mine called 'He Gives His Beloved Certain Rhymes' was the song of the head.

Hone (*WBY* 123) comments that this poem was written to 'Diana Vernon', but it seems more likely – in view of lines 3-6 – to have been written to Maud Gonne.

58   TO HIS HEART, BIDDING IT HAVE NO FEAR

71   This poem first appeard in *S* (Nov. 1896) with the title 'Windlestraws II. Out of the Old Days' [the companion poem was 'He reproves the Curlew']. The present title was used in *WR*.

5   *the flame and the flood*: a phrase from the initiation ritual of the Golden Dawn. See note on line 7 'He hears the Cry of the Sedge' (*PNE* 64).

59   THE CAP AND BELLS

71   This poem was written in 1893 and first appeared in *NO* (17 March 1894) with the title 'Cap and Bell'. The present title was used in *WR*. Yeats's note reads:

> I dreamed this story exactly as I have written it, and dreamed another long dream after it, trying to make out its meaning, and whether I was to write it in

prose or verse. The first dream was more a vision than a dream, for it was beautiful and coherent, and gave me the sense of illumination and exaltation that one gets from visions, while the second dream was confused and meaningless. The poem has always meant a great deal to me, though, as is the way with symbolic poems, it has not always meant quite the same thing. Blake would have said 'The authors are in eternity' [Blake's letter of 6 July 1803 to Thomas Butts about his *Milton* . . . 'I dare not pretend to be any other than the secretary; the authors are in eternity'; cf. *The Works of William Blake* ed. E. J. Ellis and W. B. Yeats (1893) I, vii. The letter is in Alexander Gilchrist, *Life of William Blake* (1880) I, 187] and I am quite sure they can only be questioned in dreams. (*WR*)

3   *his soul*: the Jester offers the lady his soul and his heart (line 13) but she is not affected by either offering but by his cap and bells (line 21). Yeats regarded this poem as the way to win a lady, but 'He wishes for the Cloths of Heaven' as the way to lose one. See *WBY* 152.

21   *cap and bells*: Yeats wrote in 1901 that he knew a man who was trying to   72 bring an image of Angus, the Irish god of love, ecstasy and poetry, before his mind's eye: 'who changed four of his kisses into birds, and suddenly the image of a man with cap and bells rushed before his mind's eye, and grew vivid and spoke and called itself 'Aengus' Messenger' (*M* 115).

THE VALLEY OF THE BLACK PIG   60

This poem first appeared in *S* (April 1896) with the title 'Two Poems concerning   73 Peasant Visionaries The Valley of the Black Pig' (the companion poem was 'A Cradle Song', later 'The Unappeasable Host' (*PNE* 46)). A note after the title read:

> The Irish peasantry have for generations comforted themselves, in their misfortunes, with visions of a great battle, to be fought in a mysterious valley called, 'The Valley of the Black Pig', and to break at last the power of their enemies. A few years ago, in the barony of Lisadell, in Country Sligo, an old man would fall entranced upon the ground from time to time, and rave out a description of the battle; and I have myself heard [it] said that the girths shall rot from the bellies of the horses, because of the few men that shall come alive out of the valley.

See *McG*, 89, for three possible locations of the valley. A longer note in *WR* read:

> All over Ireland there are prophecies of the coming rout of the enemies of Ireland, in a certain Valley of the Black Pig, and these prophecies are, no doubt, now, as they were in the Fenian days [probably a reference to the period of the Fenian rising of 1867. The Fenian movement was founded by James Stephens (1824-1901) in 1858; it believed in the use of force], a political force. I have heard of one man who would not give any money to the Land League [formed in 1879 by Michael Davitt (1846-1906); it was suppressed in 1881. Its aims were to protect tenants and win possession of the land for the people of Ireland], because the Battle could not be until the close of the century; but, as a rule,

periods of trouble bring prophecies of its near coming. A few years before my time, an old man who lived at Lisadell, in Sligo, used to fall down in a fit and rave out descriptions of the Battle; and a man in Sligo has told me that it will be so great a battle that the horses shall go up to their fetlocks in blood, and that their girths, when it is over, will rot from their bellies for lack of a hand to unbuckle them. The battle is a mythological battle, and the black pig is one with the bristleless boar, that killed Dearmod, in November, upon the western end of Ben Bulben; Misroide MacDatha's son, whose [an errata slip in the first printing of *WR* read 'Misroide MacDatha's sow, whose'] carving brought on so great a battle; 'the croppy black sow,' and 'the cutty black sow' of Welsh November rhymes (*Celtic Heathendom*, 509–516); the boar that killed Adonis; the bear that killed Attis; and the pig embodiment of Typhon (*Golden Bough*, II. 26, 31). The pig seems to have been originally a genius of the corn, and seemingly because the too great power of their divinity makes divine things dangerous to mortals, its flesh was forbidden to many eastern nations; but as the meaning of the prohibition was forgotten, abhorrence took the place of reverence, pigs and boars grew into types of evil, and were described as the enemies of the very gods they once typified (*Golden Bough*, II. 26–31, 56–7). The Pig would, therefore, become the Black Pig, a type of cold and of winter that awake in November, the old beginning of winter, to do battle with the summer, and with the fruit and leaves, and finally, as I suggest; and as I believe, for the purposes of poetry; of the darkness that will at last destroy the gods and the world. The country people say there is no shape for a spirit to take so dangerous as the shape of a pig; and a Galway blacksmith – and blacksmiths are thought to be especially protected – says he would be afraid to meet a pig on the road at night; and another Galway man tells this story: 'There was a man coming the road from Gort to Garryland one night, and he had a drop taken; and before him, on the road, he saw a pig walking; and having a drop in, he gave a shout, and made a kick at it, and bid it get out of that. And by the time he got home, his arm was swelled from the shoulder to be as big as a bag, and he couldn't use his hand with the pain of it. And his wife brought him, after a few days, to a woman that used to do cures at Rahasane. And on the road all she could do would hardly keep him from lying down to sleep on the grass. And when they got to the woman she knew all that happened; and, says she, it's well for you that your wife didn't let you fall asleep on the grass, for if you had done that but even for one instant, you'd be a lost man.'

It is possible that bristles were associated with fertility, as the tail certainly was, for a pig's tail is stuck into the ground in Courland, that the corn may grow abundantly, and the tails of pigs, and other animal embodiments of the corn genius, are dragged over the ground to make it fertile in different countries. Professor Rhys, who considers the bristleless boar a symbol of darkness and cold, rather than of winter and cold, thinks it was without bristles because the darkness is shorn away by the sun. It may have had different meanings, just as the scourging of the man god has had different though not contradictory meanings in different epochs of the world. [The note in *CW* reads: If one reads Professor Rhys' *Celtic Heathendom* by the light of Professor Frazer's *Golden Bough*, and puts together what one finds there about the boar that killed Diarmuid, and other old Celtic boars and sows, one sees that the Battle is mythological, and that the Pig it is named from must be a type of cold and winter doing battle with the summer, or of death battling with life. For the purposes of poetry, at any rate, I think it a symbol of the darkness that will destroy the world. . . .]

The Battle should, I believe, be compared with three other battles; a battle the Sidhe are said to fight when a person is being taken away by them; a battle they are said to fight in November for the harvest; the great battle the Tribes of the goddess Danu fought, according to the Gaelic chroniclers, with the Fomor at Moy Tura, or the Towery Plain [overlooking Lough Arrow, Co. Sligo].

I have heard of the battle over the dying both in County Galway and in the Isles of Arann, an old Arann fisherman having told me that it was fought over two of his children, and that he found blood in a box he had for keeping fish, when it was over; and I have written about it, and given examples elsewhere. A faery doctor, on the borders of Galway and Clare, explained it as a battle between the friends and enemies of the dying, the one party trying to take them, the other trying to save them from being taken. It may once, when the land of the Sidhe was the only other world, and when every man who died was carried thither, have always accompanied death. I suggest that the battle between the Tribes of the goddess Danu, the powers of light, and warmth, and fruitfulness, and goodness, and the Fomor, the powers of darkness, and cold, and barrenness, and badness upon the Towery Plain, was the establishment of the habitable world, the rout of the ancestral darkness; that the battle among the Sidhe for the harvest is the annual battle of summer and winter; that the battle among the Sidhe at a man's death is the battle between the manifest world and the ancestral darkness at the end of all things; and that all these battles are one, the battle of all things with shadowy decay. Once a symbolism has possessed the imagination of large numbers of men, it becomes, as I believe, an embodiment of disembodied powers, and repeats itself in dreams and visions, age after age.   (*WR*)

Yeats commented in 'The Tragic Generation' that it must have been 'some talk of MacGregor Mathers' (see note on 'All Souls' Night' *PNE* 239) that made him write the poem. Mathers had announced in 1893 or 1894 the imminence of immense wars (*A* 336). Yeats also, in 1902, wrote that when he was discussing the Battle of the Black Pig with a Sligo countrywoman this seemed to her a battle between Ireland and England but to him an Armageddon which would quench all things in Ancestral Darkness again (*M* 111). He may have read 'The Chase of the Enchanted Pigs of Aenghus an Bhrogha', *Fenian Poems, Transactions of the Ossianic Society* (1861) 6, 143, where a note refers to the Valley of the Black Pig in Ulster (see *McG* 89).

5   *cromlech*: see note on 'A Faery Song' (*PNE* 23).

6   *grey cairn*: this may refer to Maeve's grave, the Cairn on Knocknarea, Sligo.

THE LOVER ASKS FORGIVENESS BECAUSE OF HIS MANY MOODS   61

This poem was written on 23 August 1895 and first appeared in *SR* (2 Nov.   73
1895) with the title 'The Twilight of Forgiveness', which was altered to 'Michael Robartes [see note on 'The Lover tells of the Rose in his Heart' (*PNE* 43)] asks Forgiveness because of his Many Moods'.

7   *O Winds*: Yeats's note read:

> I use the wind as a symbol of vague desires and hopes, not merely because the Sidhe are in the wind, or because the wind bloweth as it listeth, but because wind and spirit and vague desire have been associated everywhere. A highland scholar tells me that his country people use the wind in their talk as I use it in my poem.

9   *tabors*: small drums

74   13   *Niamh*: the beautiful immortal who spirited Oisin away to the Land of the Young. Tir na nOg, for three hundred years. Yeats used the Fenian tale *Oisin in the Land of the Young* as a source for his own *The Wanderings of Oisin (PNE* 375). See note on 'The Hosting of the Sidhe' *(PNE* 40).

16   *Phoenix*: a mythical bird, fabled to be the only one of its kind, which lived five or six hundred years in the Arabian desert. It burnt itself to death on a funeral pyre but emerged with renewed youth to live another cycle.

62   HE TELLS OF A VALLEY FULL OF LOVERS

74   This poem first appeared in *SR* (9 Jan. 1897) with the title 'The Valley of Lovers' altered in *WR* to 'Aedh [see note on 'The Lover tells of the Rose in his Heart' *(PNE* 43)] tells of a Valley full of Lovers'.

63   HE TELLS OF THE PERFECT BEAUTY

74   This poem was written in December 1895 and first appeared in *The Senate* (March 1896) and twice (because proof sheets miscarried and Yeats found the first reprint 'got a good deal on his nerves') in *UI* (4 and 11 April 1896). The poem was originally Stanza 1 of 'O'Sullivan the Red to Mary Lavell' but in *WR* this became 'Aedh [see note on 'The Lover tells of the Rose in his Heart' *(PNE* 43)] tells of the Perfect Beauty'.

5   *brood of the skies*: the stars

7   *God burn time*: see note on line 47 'The Man who dreamed of Faeryland' *(PNE* 33).

64   HE HEARS THE CRY OF THE SEDGE

75   This poem first appeared in *D* (May 1898) with the title 'Aodh to Dectora. Three Songs 1' [the companion poems were '2', later 'The Lover mourns for the Loss of Love' *(PNE* 51) and '3', later 'He thinks of those who have spoken Evil of his

Beloved' (*PNE* 65)]. The title was altered to 'Aedh [see note on 'The Lover tells of the Rose in his Heart' (*PNE* 43)] hears the Cry of The Sedge'. Yeats's note, which also covers 'The Poet pleads with the Elemental Powers' (*PNE* 72) and 'He thinks of his Past Greatness when a Part of the Constellations of Heaven' (*PNE* 75), reads:

The Rose has been for many centuries a symbol of spiritual love and supreme beauty. The Count Goblet D'Alviella thinks [see his *The Migration of Symbols* (1894), 150] that it was once a symbol of the sun, – itself a principal symbol of the divine nature, and the symbolic heart of things. The lotus was in some Eastern countries imagined blossoming upon the Tree of Life, as the Flower of Life, and is thus represented in Assyrian bas-reliefs. Because the Rose, the flower sacred to the Virgin Mary, and the flower that Apuleius' adventurer ate when he was changed out of the ass's shape and received into the fellowship of Isis [an incident in Lucius Apuleius (b.c. AD 114), *The Golden Ass*, a supposed satirical autobiography], is the western Flower of Life, I have imagined it growing upon the Tree of Life. I once stood beside a man in Ireland when he saw it growing there in a vision, that seemed to have rapt him out of his body. He saw the garden of Eden walled about, and in the top of a high mountain, as in certain mediaeval diagrams, and after passing the Tree of Knowledge, on which grew fruit full of troubled faces, and through whose branches flowed, he was told, sap that was human souls, he came to a tall, dark tree, with little bitter fruits, and was shown a kind of stair or ladder going up through the tree, and told to go up; and near the top of the tree, a beautiful woman, like the Goddess of Life associated with the tree in Assyria, gave him a rose that seemed to have been growing upon the tree. One finds the Rose in the Irish poets, sometimes as a religious symbol, as in the phrase, 'the Rose of Friday,' meaning the Rose of austerity, in a Gaelic poem in Dr Hyde's *Religious Songs of Connacht* [see *PNE* for comment on Hyde's translation], and, I think, was a symbol of woman's beauty in the Gaelic song, 'Roseen Dubh' [an anonymous seventeenth-century Irish poem]; and a symbol of Ireland in Mangan's adaptation of 'Roseen Dubh,' 'My Dark Rosaleen,' and in Mr Aubrey de Vere's 'The Little Black Rose.' I do not know any evidence to prove whether this symbol came to Ireland with medieval Christianity, or whether it has come down from Celtic times. I have read somewhere [see *PNE* for suggestion that Yeats is misremembering John Rhys *LCH*, 58] that a stone engraved with a Celtic god, who holds what looks like a rose in one hand, has been found somewhere in England; but I cannot find the reference, though I certainly made a note of it. If the Rose was really a symbol of Ireland among the Gaelic poets, and if 'Roseen Dubh' is really a political poem, as some think, one may feel pretty certain that the ancient Celts associated the Rose with Eire, or Fotla, or Banba – goddesses [of the Tuatha de Danaan] who gave their names to Ireland [see *McG*, 56. In the *Book of Invasions* each asked the Milesian invaders to name the country after her] – or with some principal god or goddess, for such symbols are not suddenly adopted or invented, but come out of mythology.

I have made the Seven Lights, the constellation of the Bear, lament for the theft of the Rose, and I have made the Dragon, the constellation Draco, the guardian of the Rose, because these constellations move about the pole of the heavens [an imaginary line around which the heavens were thought to revolve], the ancient Tree of Life in many countries, and are often associated with the Tree of Life in mythology. It is this Tree of Life that I have put into the 'Song of

Mongan' under its common Irish form of a hazel; and, because it had sometimes the stars for fruit, I have hung upon it 'The Crooked Plough' and the 'Pilot star,' as Gaelic-speaking Irishmen sometimes call the Bear and the North star. I have made it an axle-tree in 'Aedh hears the Cry of the Sedge', for this was another ancient way of representing it.   (*WR*)

This poem was written to Maud Gonne in a time of great strain and sorrow. Yeats wrote:

> Since my mistress had left me no other woman had come into my life and for nearly seven years none did. I was tortured with sexual desire and disappointed love. Often as I walked in the woods at Coole it would have been a relief to have screamed aloud.   (unpublished Autobiography)

2   *lake*: perhaps the lake at Coole Park, Lady Gregory's house in Co. Galway

3   *sedge*: the echo of Keats's 'La Belle Dame sans Merci' ('The sedge is withered from the lake') is perhaps not unintentional.

7   *banners of East and West*: this line may relate to the initiation ceremony of The Order of the Golden Dawn. See V. Moore, *The Unicorn* (1954) 139.

65   HE THINKS OF THOSE WHO HAVE SPOKEN EVIL OF HIS BELOVED

75   This poem first appeared in *D* (May 1898) under the title 'Aodh to Dectora. Three Songs 3' [the companion poems being 1 & 2, later entitled 'The Lover mourns for the Loss of Love' (*PNE* 51) and 'He hears the Cry of the Sedge' (*PNE* 64)]. The title became 'Aedh [see note on 'The Lover tells of the Rose in his Heart' (*PNE* 43)] thinks of those who have spoken Evil of his Beloved' in *WR*.

5   *a mouthful of air*: the phrase was used by Yeats to describe faeries, 'nations of gay creatures, having no souls; nothing in their bright bodies but a mouthful of sweet air' ('Tales from the Twilight', *SO* (1 March 1890)). See *IY* 325. The phrase was used in Ganconagh's [Yeats's] novel *John Sherman* (1891): for 'what have we in this life but a mouthful of air' (see *PYP* 72) and in the lyric at the end of *At the Hawk's Well* as well as in the play *KGCT*, 'O, what is life but a mouthful of air?'

66   THE BLESSED

75   This poem first appeared in *The Yellow Book* (April 1897).

1   *Cumhal*: he appears as 'Cumhal the King' in the early versions of the poem; there is another Cumhal, the son of Cormac, who is crucified by monks in 'The Crucifixion of the Outcast' (*M* 147ff.).

2   *Dathi*: 'Dathi the Blessed' in the early versions of the poem. The Dathi

mentioned in 'The Crucifixion of the Outcast' is, *PNE* suggests, the last King of pagan Ireland, who succeeded Niall of the Nine Hostages in AD 405:

> 'I would', mutters Cumhal, 'that the red wind of the Druids had withered in his cradle the soldier of Dathi who brought the tree of death out of barbarous lands, or that the lightning, when it smote Dathi at the foot of the mountain [Dathi was killed by lightning at the foot of the Alps], had smitten him also. . . .' (*M* 147).

36   *The Incorruptible Rose*: see notes on 'To the Rose upon the Rood of Time'   77 (*PNE* 17), and 'He hears the Cry of the Sedge' (*PNE* 43). Yeats regarded it as symbol of the highest spiritual ideal.

THE SECRET ROSE   67

This poem first appeared in *S* (Sept. 1896) with the title 'O'Sullivan Rua to the   77 Secret Rose'; it was entitled 'To the Secret Rose' in *TSR*, 'The Secret Rose' in *WR*. Yeats's note reads:

> I find that I have unintentionally changed the old story of Conchobar's death. [Conchubar was king of Ulster in the Red Branch (Ulster) cycle of tales.] He did not see the crucifix in a vision, but was told about it. He had been struck by a ball, made of the dried brain of a dead enemy, and hurled out of a sling; and this ball had been left in his head, and his head had been mended, the Book of Leinster [The Book of Leinster, now in Trinity College Dublin, is part of a manuscript miscellany (of nearly 1000 pieces of different kinds). Yeats may have read this part of it in Eugene O'Curry, *Lectures on the Manuscript Material of Ancient Ireland* (1879) 637–43] says, with thread of gold because his hair was like gold. Keating, a writer of the time of Elizabeth [Geoffrey Keating (*c.* 1570–1650), author of the *History of Ireland*, begun *c.*1620, completed 1634], says: 'In that state did he remain seven years, until the Friday on which Christ was crucified, according to some historians; and when he saw the unusual changes of the creation and the eclipse of the sun and the moon at its full, he asked of Bucrach, a Leinster Druid, who was long with him, what was it that brought that unusual change upon the planets of Heaven and Earth. "Jesus Christ, the son of God," said the Druid, "who is now being crucified by the Jews." "That is a pity," said Conchobar; "were I in his presence I would kill those who were putting him to death." And with that he brought out his sword, and rushed at a woody grove which was convenient to him, and began to cut and fell it; and what he said was, that if he were among the Jews that was the usage he would give them, and from the excessiveness of his fury which seized upon him, the ball started out of his head, and some of the brain came after it, and in that way he died. The wood of Lanshraigh, in Feara Rois, is the name by which that shrubby wood is called.' [The source for the story is the Irish Texts Society edition of Keating's *History of Ireland* (1902–14) II, 203.]
> I have imagined Cuchullain [see note on 'To the Rose upon the Rood of Time' (*PNE* 17)] meeting Fand 'walking among flaming dew.' [Yeats's source was Standish O'Grady, *History of Ireland* (1879–80) II, 73, or his *History of Ireland: Critical and Philosophical* (1881) 107.] The story of their love is one of the most beautiful of our old tales.

Two birds, bound one to another with a chain of gold, came to a lake side where Cuchullain and the host of Uladh was encamped, and sang so sweetly that all the host fell into a magic sleep. Presently they took the shape of two beautiful women, and cast a magical weakness upon Cuchullain, in which he lay for a year. At the year's end an Aengus, who was probably Aengus the master of love, one of the greatest of the children of the goddess Danu, came and sat upon his bedside, and sang how Fand, the wife of Mannannan, the master of the sea, and of the islands of the dead, loved him; and that if he would come into the country of the gods, where there was wine and gold and silver, Fand, and Laban her sister, would heal him of his magical weakness. [In 'Mortal Help' Cuchullain 'won the goddess Fand for a while by helping her married sister and her sister's husband to overthrow another nation of the Land of Promise' (*M* 9).] Cuchullain went to the country of the gods, and, after being for a month the lover of Fand, made her a promise to meet her at a place called 'the Yew at the Strand's End,' and came back to the earth. Emer, his mortal wife, won his love again, and Mannannan came to 'the Yew at the Strand's End,' and carried Fand away. When Cuchullain saw her going, his love for her fell upon him again, and he went mad, and wandered among the mountains without food or drink, until he was at last cured by a Druid drink of forgetfulness.

I have founded the man 'who drove the gods out of their Liss,' or fort, upon something I have read about Caolte after the battle of Gabra, when almost all his companions were killed, driving the gods out of their Liss, either at Osraighe, now Ossory, or at Eas Ruaidh, now Asseroe, a waterfall at Ballyshannon, where Ilbreac, one of the children of the goddess Danu, had a Liss. [Yeats probably derived his knowledge of Caolte MacRonan from Standish O'Grady, *History of Ireland: Critical and Philosophical* (1881) 324-5 and 353, and from Eugene O'Curry's commentary on 'The Fate of the Children of Tuireann', *Atlantis* (1863) 4, 231, and his *On the Manners and Customs of the Ancient Irish* (1873) III, 366.] I am writing away from most of my books, and have not been able to find the passage; but I certainly read it somewhere. [But maybe I only read it in Mr Standish O'Grady, who has a fine imagination, for I find no such story in Lady Gregory's book. <See notes on 'Fergus and the Druid' (*PNE* 18). Yeats had also used Standish O'Grady, *History of Ireland*, II, 249-50 as a source for Fergus.> (*CW* 1).

I have founded 'the proud dreaming king' upon Fergus, the son of Roigh, the legendary poet of 'the quest of the bull of Cualg[n]e,' as he is in the ancient story of Deirdre, and in modern poems by Ferguson. ['The Abdication of Fergus Mac Roy', *Lays of the Western Gael, and Other Poems* (1864).] He married Nessa, and Ferguson makes him tell how she took him 'captive in a single look.'

> 'I am but an empty shade,
> Far from life and passion laid;
> Yet does sweet remembrance thrill
> All my shadowy being still.'

Presently, because of his great love, he gave up his throne to Conchobar, her son by another, and lived out his days feasting, and fighting, and hunting. [In the Irish legend Fergus agreed to give up his throne for a year to Conchubar, the son of Ness; she so influenced the chiefs that they refused to allow Fergus to reclaim the kingship when the year was up.] His promise never to refuse a feast from a certain comrade, and the mischief that came by his promise, and the vengeance he took afterwards, are a principal theme of the poets. I have explained my imagination of him in 'Fergus and the Druid,' and in a little song in the second act of 'The Countess Kathleen'.

I have founded him 'who sold tillage, and house, and goods,' upon something in 'The Red Pony,' a folk tale in Mr Larmine's *West Irish Folk Tales [and Romances* (1893) 212 ff.]. A young man 'saw a light before him on the high road. When he came as far, there was an open box on the road, and a light coming up out of it. He took up the box. There was a lock of hair in it. Presently he had to go to become the servant of a king for his living. There were eleven boys. When they were going out into the stable at ten o'clock, each of them took a light but he. He took no candle at all with him. Each of them went into his own stable. When he went into his stable he opened the box. He left it in a hole in the wall. The light was great. It was twice as much as in the other stables.' The king hears of it, and makes him show him the box. The king says, 'You must go and bring me the woman to whom the hair belongs.' In the end, the young man, and not the king, marries the woman. *(WR)*

3   *the Holy Sepulchre*: Christ's tomb in Jerusalem

7   *great leaves*: the Rosicrucian emblem of the four-leaved rose. Yeats's half-belief in the possibility of some revelation was bound up with his proposed Order of Celtic Mysteries, and with it the hope of complete understanding between himself and Maud Gonne. Cf. the passage from *A*, which begins 'I had an unshakable conviction . . .' quoted below, note on line 28.

9   *the Magi*: the three wise men who came from the East to attend Christ's birth, bringing gifts of gold and frankincense and myrrh

13   *Fand*: wife of Manannan MacLir, god of the sea

15   *Emer*: Cuchulain's wife

16   *liss*: (*Irish* lios) a mound inhabited by supernatural beings, also an enclosed space

19   *proud . . . king*: Fergus MacRoigh (MacRoy), Conchubar's predecessor

25   *so shining loveliness*: the poem was written to Maud Gonne.   78

28   *thy great wind*: this is probably a reference to the end of the world. Cf. 'He mourns for the Change that has come upon Him . . . and longs for the End of the World' (*PNE* 52).

I had an unshakable conviction, arising how or whence I cannot tell, that invisible gates would open as they opened for Blake, as they opened for Swedenborg, as they opened for Boehme, and that this philosophy would find its manuals of devotion in all imaginative literature and set before Irishmen for special manual an Irish literature which, though made by many minds, would seem the work of a single mind, and turn our places of beauty or legendary association into holy symbols. I did not think this philosophy would be altogether pagan, for it was plain that its symbols must be selected from all those things that have moved men most during many, mainly Christian, centuries.

I thought for a time I could rhyme of love, calling it *The Rose*, because of the Rose's double meaning; of a fisherman who had 'never a crack' in his heart; of an old woman complaining of the idleness of the young, or of some cheerful fiddler, all those things that 'popular poets' write of, but that I must some day – on that day when the gates began to open – become difficult or obscure. With a rhythm that still echoed Morris I prayed to the Red Rose, to Intellectual Beauty. . . . (*A* 254)

68 MAID QUIET

78 This poem first appeared, untitled, in the story 'The Twisting of the Rope', in *NO* (24 Dec. 1892). It was entitled 'O'Sullivan the Red upon his Wanderings' in *NR* (Aug. 1897) and 'Hanrahan laments because of his Wanderings' in *WR*, altered to 'The Lover mourns because of his Wanderings' in *PW 1*. The poem was reduced from twelve lines to eight and entitled 'Maid Quiet' in *CW 1*. Yeats wrote of Hanrahan in John Quinn's copy of *Stories of Red Hanrahan*: 'Red Hanrahan is an imaginary name – I saw it over a shop, or rather part of it over a shop in a Galway village – but there were many poets like him in the eighteenth century in Ireland.' See (*B* 72). His note after the title in the first published version read:

'Gulleon's place of pride' [part of a line included in the original version] is the mountain now called 'The Fews', and once called 'Sleive Fua'. It is fabled to be his (Hanrahan's) tomb, and was doubtless the place of his worship, for Gulleon was Cullain, a god of the underworld. The 'pale deer' ['I would the pale deer had come' was a line from the original version] were certain deer hunted once by Cuchullain in his battle fury, and, as I understand them, symbols of night and shadow.

In his note on 'He mourns for the Change that has come upon Him and his Beloved, and longs for the End of the World' (*PNE* 52) Yeats comments on this poem:

He [a solar mythologist] could certainly, I think, say that when Cuchullain, whom Professor Rhys calls a solar hero, hunted the enchanted deer of Slieve Fuadh because the battle fury was still on him, he was the sun pursuing clouds, or cold, or darkness. I have understood them in this sense in 'Hanrahan laments because of his wandering' and made Hanrahan long for the day when they, fragments of ancestral darkness, will overthrow the world. The desire of the woman, the flying darkness, it is all one! The image – a cross, a man preaching in the wilderness, a dancing Salome, a lily in a girl's hand, a flame leaping, a globe with wings, a pale sunset over still waters – is an eternal act; but our understandings are temporal and understand but a little at a time. (*WR*)

THE TRAVAIL OF PASSION 69

This poem first appeared in *S* (Jan. 1896) under the title 'Two Love Poems. The 78 Travail of Passion' (the companion poem was 'The Shadowy Horses', later 'Michael Robartes (still later 'He') bids his Beloved be at Peace' (*PNE* 53)). This poem was written to 'Diana Vernon', see note on 'The Lover mourns for the Loss of Love' (*PNE* 51).

5 *Kedron*: spelt Kidron in early versions, the brook flowing between Jerusalem 79 and the Mount of Olives. Biblical imagery is also evident in the echoes of the crucifixion – the plaited thorns; the *via dolorosa*, the way crowded with bitter faces; the wounds; the sponge filled with vinegar; and the brook Kedron suggesting the Mount of Olives.

THE LOVER PLEADS WITH HIS FRIEND FOR OLD FRIENDS 70

This poem first appeared in *SR* (24 July 1897) entitled 'The Poet pleads with his 79 friend for old friends'.

1 *your shining days*: probably a reference to Maud Gonne's political work. Her power over crowds was at its height, and Yeats travelled to many public meetings with her in 1897 and 1898 in the cause of the '98 Association (of which he was President) which was formed to commemorate the 1798 Rebellion and its leader Wolfe Tone. Cf. 'Fallen Majesty' (*PNE* 134), '. . . crowds gathered once if she but showed her face/And even old men's eyes grew dim'.

8 *all eyes but these eyes*: these lines were prophetic, in that after Maud Gonne married and she and her husband separated, she was deserted by the mob. Cf. 'Fallen Majesty' again:

> '. . . this hand alone
> Like some last courtier at a gypsy camping-place
> Babbling of fallen majesty, records what's gone.'

Other poems recorded her power over others. Cf. 'Her Praise' (*PNE* 163), 'The People' (*PNE* 164) and 'Broken Dreams' (*PNE* 167).

THE LOVER SPEAKS TO THE HEARERS OF HIS SONGS IN COMING DAYS 71

This poem was written in November 1895 and first appeared untitled, in the 79 story 'The Vision of O'Sullivan the Red' in *NR* (April 1896). It was entitled 'Hanrahan [see note on 'The Lover tells of the Rose in his Heart' (*PNE* 42) and 'Maid Quiet' (*PNE* 68)] speaks to the Lovers of his Songs in coming Days' in *WR*.

6 *Attorney for Lost Souls*: the Virgin Mary. The original version had 'Till Maurya ['Mary' in later versions] of the wounded heart cry out'.

72 THE POET PLEADS WITH THE ELEMENTAL POWERS

80 This poem first appeared in *TB* (Oct. 1892) entitled 'A Mystical Prayer to the Masters of the Elements, Michael, Gabriel, and Raphael'. In *The Second Book of the Rhymers' Club* (1894) 'Finvarra' replaced Michael, 'Feacra' Gabriel, and 'Caolte' Gabriel. The title became 'Aodh (Aedh) [see 'The Lover tells of the Rose in his Heart' (*PNE* 42)] pleads with the Elemental Powers' in *WR*. Yeats's note after the title read:

> The Seven Lights are the seven stars of the Great Bear, and the Dragon is the constellation of the Dragon, and these, in certain old mythologies, encircle the Tree of Life, on which is here imagined the Rose of the Ideal Beauty growing before it was cast into the world. Three or four lines are taken from a poem of the author's on the same subject in 'The Second Book of the Rhymers' Club'.

1 *The Powers*: various conjectures have been made as to their identity. W. Y. Tindall, *Forces in Modern British Literature* (1947), 243 suggested Madame Blavatsky's elemental spirits; Saul (*PYP* 75) referred to the 'Heart of the Spring' (*M* 171) which described the beings who dwell 'in the waters and among the hazels and oak trees'. Henn (*LT* 252) saw stanza 1 as a Rosicrucian or Hermetic image. But the title suggests some correspondence between the three 'Masters of the Elements' and the Powers of wave and wind and fire, cf. line 7.

2 *the Immortal Rose*: partially the Rosicrucian symbol, but in Yeats's words the 'Rose of Ideal Beauty'.

3 *Seven lights*: the seven stars of the Great Bear

4 *The Polar Dragon*: the constellation of the Dragon. The 'Dragon of the Hesperides' is suggested by Wilson (*YI* 249). Ellmann (*IY* 78) remarks that if we look at the cover of *TSR* we find the serpent's folds encircling the trunk of the tree of life as if it were indeed the 'Guardian of the Rose'. He continues:

> In Kabbalism this serpent is the serpent of nature in its benign aspects, and the occultist is said to follow the serpent's winding path upwards through many initiations, corresponding to each of the *Sephiroth*, until he reaches the top of the tree. Since in the poem the polar dragon sleeps, like earth in the 'Introduction' to Blake's *Songs of Experience*, the meaning seems to be that the natural world has become uncoiled or detached from beauty.

For the tree of life see notes on 'The Two Trees' (*PNE* 37).

9 *her I love*: Maud Gonne

73 HE WISHES HIS BELOVED WERE DEAD

80 This poem first appeared in *The Sketch* (9 Feb. 1898) with the title 'Aodh [see 'The Lover tells of the Rose in his Heart' (*PNE* 43)] to Dectora', altered to 'Aedh to Dectora' in *WR*. This poem develops an idea in 'A Dream of Death' (*PNE* 30) written when Maud Gonne was in France in 1891 convalescing from an illness. There is a passage in *CK* (where Kevin the poet is a projection of Yeats) which indicates the death imagery which came to him in moments of intense stress:

> Sometimes he [Kevin] laid his head upon the ground.
> They say he hears the Sherogues down below
> Nailing four boards . . .
> For love has made him crazy
> And loneliness and famine dwell with him.

HE WISHES FOR THE CLOTHS OF HEAVEN 74

This poem first appeared in *WR* entitled 'Aedh [see note on 'The Lover tells of 81 the Rose in his Heart' (*PNE* 43)] wishes for the Cloths of Heaven'. Yeats remarked of this defeatist pre-Raphaelite poem that it was the way to lose a lady. See note on 'The Cap and Bells' (*PNE* 59).

HE THINKS OF HIS PAST GREATNESS WHEN A PART OF THE CONSTELLATIONS 75
OF HEAVEN

This poem first appeared in *D* (Oct. 1898) entitled 'Song of Mongan'. In *WR* it 81 was entitled 'Mongan thinks of his Past Greatness'. Yeats's note after the title reads:

> Mongan, in the old Celtic poetry, is a famous wizard and king who remembers his passed lives. 'The Country of the Young' is a name in the Celtic poetry for the country of the gods and of the happy dead. The hazel tree was the Irish tree of Life or of Knowledge, and in Ireland it was doubtless, as elsewhere, the tree of the heavens. The Crooked Plough and the Pilot Star are translations of the Gaelic names of the Plough and the Pole star.

See Yeats's note on 'He hears the Cry of the Sedge' (*PNE* 64).

THE FIDDLER OF DOONEY 76

This poem first appeared in *TB* (Dec. 1892) dated November 1892. *82*

1 *Dooney*: Dooney Rock (*Irish* Dun Aodh, Hugh's Port) on the shore of Lough Gill, Co. Sligo. See *McG* 41.

3 *Kilvarnet*: originally 'My brother is priest of Kilbarnet'. Kilvarnet is a townland near Ballinacarrow, Co. Sligo (*Irish*, Cill Bhearnais, the church in the gap).

4 *Mocharabuiee*: originally 'My cousin of Rosnaree' but altered in *WR* to 'Mocharabuiee'. A footnote supplied by Mrs W. B. Yeats reads 'pronounced as if

spelt ''Mockrabwee'''. (*CP* (1950) 82) (*Irish* Machra buidhe means Yellow Plain, the townland of Magheraboy, to the south-west of Sligo.)

8   *Sligo fair*: Sligo, a town in north-west Ireland where Yeats stayed frequently as a child with his maternal Pollexfen grandparents (see notes on 'Introductory Rhymes' (*PNE* 112) and notes on 'In Memory of Alfred Pollexfen' (*PNE* 173) and cf. 'Under Saturn' (*CP* 202)); later as a young man he stayed with his uncle George Pollexfen (see notes on 'In Memory of Major Robert Gregory' (*PNE* 144).

10   *Peter*: Saint Peter, who keeps the Gate of Heaven

20   *wave of the sea*: Henn (*LT* 305) compares Florizel's remark to Perdita, *A Winter's Tale*, IV, iv:

> When you do dance, I wish you
> A wave o' the sea.

Cf. *The Countess Cathleen*, sc. I, . . . 'singing like a wave of the sea'.

In the Seven Woods

Y EATS wrote that he had made some of these poems:

> walking about among the Seven Woods, before the big wind of nineteen
> hundred and three blew down so many trees, & troubled the wild creatures, &
> changed the look of things; and I thought out there a good part of the play
> which follows [*On Baile's Strand*]. The first shape of it came to me in a dream,
> but it changed much in the making, foreshadowing, it may be, a change that
> may bring a less dream-burdened will into my verses. I never re-wrote anything
> so many times; for at first I could not make these wills that stream into mere life
> poetical. But now I hope to do easily much more of the kind, and that our new
> Irish players will find the buskin and the sock.   (*ISW*)

In the Seven Woods was the first book published by Elizabeth Corbet Yeats's Dun
Emer Press, founded in 1903, later the Cuala Press. The book was printed in
Caslon Old Face type, a type used for all the seventy-eight books produced up to
1946. A brief note on the history of the press is given in the catalogue compiled
by R. O. Dougan, *WB Yeats. Manuscripts and Printed Books exhibited in the
Library of Trinity College, Dublin 1956*, 17–18. See also *The Irish Book* II,
(1963) 43–52 and 81–90, and Liam Miller, 'The Dun Emer and the Cuala
Press', *The World of W. B. Yeats* (ed. Skelton and Saddlemyer, 1965), 141–51.
A brief comment is given by Robin Skelton, 'Twentieth Century Irish Literature
and the Private Press Tradition', *Massachusetts Review* (Winter, 1964), 368–77.
The 1903 edition included the long poems 'The Old Age of Queen Maeve' and
'Baile and Aillinn' as well as the play *On Baile's Strand*. Three poems 'Old
Memory', 'Never Give All the Heart' and 'The Entrance of Deirdre' (later
removed and included in the play *Deirdre* (1907) were added in 1906 and two,
'The Hollow Wood' and 'O Do Not love too long' in 1908.

IN THE SEVEN WOODS   77

This poem first appeared in *ISW*, dated August 1902.   *85*

1   *the Seven Woods*: at Coole Park, the estate of Lady Gregory (1852–1932) in
Co. Galway. Yeats described the woods in his 'Introduction to a Dramatic Poem',
a poem which first appeared in the *Speaker* (1 Dec 1900) and was entitled 'I
walked among the Seven Woods of Coole' in *The Shadowy Waters* (1900). The
poem (*PNE* 378) opens:

> I walked among the seven woods of Coole;
> Shan-walla, where a willow-bordered pond

Gathers the wild duck from the winter dawn;
Shady Kyle-dortha; sunnier Kyle-na-no
Where many hundred squirrels are as happy
As though they had been hidden by green boughs
Where old age cannot find them; Pairc-na-lee,
Where hazel and ash and privet blind the paths;
Dim Pairc-na-carraig, where the wild bees fling
Their sudden fragrances on the green air;
Dim Pairc-na-tarav, where enchanted eyes
Have seen immortal, mild, proud shadows walk;
Dim Inchy wood, that hides badger and fox
And marten-cat, and borders that old wood
Wise Biddy Early called the wicked wood:
Seven odours, seven murmurs, seven woods.

3   *lime-tree*: cf. line 2 'The New Faces' (*PNE* 216) which describes Coole Park.

6   *Tara uprooted*: the Hill of Tara in Co. Meath, traditionally the seat of the ancient Irish kings. The reference is to a contemporary excavation of the site.
   Mr John Frayne has pointed out to me that Douglas Hyde, George Moore and Yeats wrote a letter to the *Times* (27 June 1902) which drew the attention of the public to the fact that labourers were destroying the site of the ancient Royal duns and houses 'apparently that the sect which believes the English to be descended from the ten tribes may find the Ark of the Covenant'. Tara (*Irish* Temair, Teamhair) means a place with a view.

7   *new commonness*: an allusion to the coronation of Edward VII and Alexandra

8   *paper flowers*: decorations in Dublin to celebrate the Coronation

12   *Great Archer*: Saul (*PYP* 77) glosses as Sagittarius. This hints at some revelation about to come. There is a possibility that the 'Quiet' of line 10 may refer to Maud Gonne, the archer being then some figure of love.

14   *Pairc-na-lee*: see note on line 1 above: (*Irish* Pairc na Laoi) the field of the calves, one of the seven woods of Coole. See notes on 'Introductory Lines' (*PNE* 378).

78   THE ARROW

85   This poem was written in 1901 and first appeared in *ISW*.

1   *your beauty*: Maud Gonne's beauty. Yeats had first met her in 1889.

this arrow: it is possible that Yeats had in mind a Blakean meaning for the arrow. When he and Edwin Ellis edited *The Works of William Blake* (3 vols., 1893) they supplied a commentry on these lines of Blake's 'Preface' to *Milton*:

Bring me my bow of burning gold:
Bring me my arrows of desire:
Bring me my spear: O clouds unfold!
Bring me my chariot of fire.

The commentary ran: 'He shall return again, aided by the Bow, sexual symbolism, the arrow, desire, the spear, male potency, the chariot, joy.'

6   *apple blossom*: Yeats associated apple blossom with his memories of his first meeting with Maud Gonne. See note on 'The Song of Wandering Aengus' (*PNE* 48), which quotes the accounts in his unpublished Autobiography and *Autobiographies* of this meeting.

THE FOLLY OF BEING COMFORTED   79

This poem first appeared in *The Speaker* (11 Jan. 1902). The poem refers to   86
Maud Gonne and marks a newly emerging note of realism in Yeats's poetry.

1   *One that is ever kind*: possibly Lady Gregory

6   *patience*: Ellmann, (*Y:M & M* 161) quotes two drafts for a lyric written about 1897 which indicates Yeats's hopes and despair:

> O my beloved you only are
>   not moved by my songs
> Which you only understand
> You only know that it is
>   of you I sing when I tell
>   of the swan on the water
>   or the eagle in the heavens
>   or the faun in the wood.
> Others weep but your eyes
>   are dry.
>
> II
> O my beloved. How happy
> I wish that day when you
> came here from the
> railway, and set your hair
> aright in my looking glass
> and then sat with me at
> my table, and lay resting
> in my big chair. I am
> like the children o my
> beloved and I play at
> marriage – I play
> with images of the life
> you will not give to me o
> my cruel one.

9   *nobleness*: 'Her beauty . . . was incredibly distinguished', see note on 'Old Memory' (*PNE* 80).

80   OLD MEMORY

86   This poem was written in November or December (probably the third week of December) 1903 and first appeared in *Wayfarer's Love* (ed. the Duchess of Sutherland, 1904). It was written when Yeats was 'shut up in a railway train coming from Canada'. He wrote to Lady Gregory, apropos of this poem, on 21 January 1904, that he thought a railroad train a good place to write in, if the journey was long enough, the scenery being exhausted in two or three hours, the newspaper – even an American one – in the second two or three hours and then towards the end of the day

> one can hardly help oneself but one has begun to write. Indeed I think that if some benevolent government would only . . . send one across the world one would really write two or three dozen lyrics in the year.   (*L* 427)

1   *her*: Maud Gonne, who married Major John MacBride in Paris in February 1903

5   *The queens*: Yeats wrote that there was an element in Maud Gonne's beauty that moved minds full of old Gaelic poems and stories, because she looked as if she lived in some ancient civilisation where superiority of mind or body were part of public ceremonial,

> were in some way the crowd's creation, as the entrance of the Pope into Saint Peter's is the crowd's creation. Her beauty, backed by her great stature, could instantly affect an assembly, and not, as often with our stage beauties, because obvious and florid, for it was incredibly distinguished, and if – as must be that it might seem that assembly's very self, fused, unified and solitary – her face, like the face of some Greek statue, showed little thought, her whole body seemed a master-work of long labouring thought, as though a Scopas [*fl*. 430 BC, an architect and sculptor of Ephesus who made the mausoleum which Artemisia raised to her husband, one of the seven wonders of the world] had measured and calculated, consorted with Egyptian sages, and mathematicians out of Babylon, that he might outface even Artemisia's sepulchral image with a living norm.   (*A* 364)

6   *he kneaded*: Yeats refers to his hopes of persuading Maud Gonne to give up politics and marry him, and his long work for the literary movement and his writing of poems for her – 'all was in her service'.

7   *the long years of youth*: he was twenty-three when he fell in love with Maud Gonne in 1889 at their first meeting.

8   *come to naught*: Maud Gonne's marriage to MacBride meant the end of his hopes.

NEVER GIVE ALL THE HEART   81

This poem first appeared in *McClure's Magazine* (December 1905).   87

1   *Never give*: this poem has affinities with Blake's 'Love's Secret':

> Never seek to tell thy love
> Love that never told can be;
> For the gentle wind doth move
> Silently, invisibly.
>
> I told my love, I told my love,
> I told her all my heart,
> Trembling, cold, in ghastly fears
> Ah! she did depart!

12   *deaf and dumb and blind*: Yeats refers to his own hopeless passion.

14   *and lost*: another reference to Maud Gonne's marriage

THE WITHERING OF THE BOUGHS   82

This poem first appeared in *The Speaker* (Aug. 1900) with the title 'Echtge of   87
Streams'.

6   *Echtge*: Sliabh Aughty (Echtge's mountain), mountain range in Co. Galway
and Co. Clare. Echtge was a goddess of the Tuatha de Danaan, who was given this
area of land as her marriage dowry.

7-8   *No boughs ... because of the wintry wind ... my dreams*: Yeats
commented elsewhere that Irish stories express the belief that as fruits and
vegetables, trees, or plants decay on earth, they ripen among the faeries, and that
dreams lose their wisdom 'when the sap rises in the trees, and that our dreams can
make the trees wither' (*M* 116).

12   *Danaan*: see note on line 3 'The Madness of King Goll' (*PNE* 9).   88

17, 18   *swans ... golden chains*: Baile and Aillinn were lovers but Aengus, the
Master of Love, wished them to be happy in his own land among the dead so he
told each the other was dead, their hearts were broken and they died. When they
died they took the shape of swans linked with a golden chain 'the shape that other
enchanted lovers took before them in the old stories'. See the 'Argument' and
footnote on Aillinn in *Baile and Aillinn* (1903) (*PNE* 377) and lines 135-8 of the
poem where the swans are 'Linked by a gold chain each to each.'

19   *A king and queen*: Baile and Aillinn

83 ADAM'S CURSE

88 This poem was written before 20 November 1902 and first appeared in the *Monthly Review* (Dec. 1902). It is written to Maud Gonne and is an autobiographical memory.

2 *That beautiful mild woman*: Maud Gonne's sister, Mrs Kathleen Pilcher

3 *And you and I*: Maud Gonne and Yeats

talked of poetry: The story of the poem's inspiration is contained in Madame MacBride's autobiography:

> While we were still at dinner Willie Yeats arrived to see me and we all went into the drawing-room for coffee. Kathleen [her sister, Mrs Pilcher] and I sat together on a big sofa amid piles of soft cushions. I was still in my dark clothes with the black veil I always wore when travelling instead of a hat, and we must have made a strange contrast. I saw Willie Yeats looking critically at me and he told Kathleen he liked her dress and that she was looking younger than ever. It was on that occasion Kathleen remarked that it was hard work being beautiful which Willie turned into his poem 'Adam's Curse'.
>
> Next day when he called to take me out to pay my customary visit to the Lia Fail, he said: 'You don't take care of yourself as Kathleen does, so she looks younger than you; your face is worn and thin; but you will always be beautiful, more beautiful than anyone I have known. You can't help that. Oh Maud, why don't you marry me and give up this tragic struggle and live a peaceful life? I could make such a beautiful life for you among artists and writers who would understand you.'
>
> 'Willie, are you not tired of asking that question? How often have I told you to thank the gods that I will not marry you. You would not be happy with me.'
>
> 'I am not happy without you.'
>
> 'Oh yes, you are, because you make beautiful poetry out of what you call your unhappiness and you are happy in that. Marriage would be such a dull affair. Poets should never marry. The world should thank me for not marrying you. I will tell you one thing, our friendship has meant a great deal to me; it has helped me often when I needed help, needed it perhaps more than you or anybody know, for I never talk or even think of these things.'
>
> 'Are you happy or unhappy?' he asked.
>
> 'I have been happier and unhappier than most, but I don't think about it. You and I are so different in this. It is a great thing to know one can never suffer again as much as one has suffered; it gives one great calm and great strength and makes one afraid of nothing. I am interested in the work I have undertaken; that is my life and I live, – while so many people only exist. Those are the people to be pitied; those who lead dull, uneventful lives; they might as well be dead in the ground. And now, Willie, let us talk of the Lia Fail. You know I hate talking of myself; I am not going to let you make me. (*SQ* 328–30)

4 . . . '*A line will take us hours maybe;/Yet if it does not seem a moment's thought/Our stitching and unstitching has been naught*: Corinna Salvadori comments that these lines are an exact definition of *sprezzatura*, and draws attention to Yeats's comment on a group of dancers whose toil must have been

long and difficult but whose movements were full of joy ('Certain Noble Plays of Japan' (*E & I* 223)), to his remark in *PASL* that it would be a hard toil to put what he had found into rhyme, and to his B.B.C. broadcast comment on 4 October 1932 'It gave me a devil of a lot of trouble to get into verse the poems that I am going to read'. (This is an echo of a remark by William Morris which he quoted elsewhere.) She defines the word as a spontaneous improvision, a careless rapture, but notes that Opdycke translated it as 'nonchalance' (*Yeats and Castiglione* 83–4).

19   *they do not talk of it at school*: cf. the final line of 'Michael Robartes and the   89
Dancer' (*PNE* 189), 'They say such different things at school.'

20   *labour to be beautiful*: Yeats wrote in *Discoveries* of 'the heroic discipline of the looking-glass', regarding beauty as one of the most difficult of the arts (*E & I* 270). Cf. lines 7–8 'To a Young Beauty' (*PNE* 152) 'You may, that mirror for a school'; and lines 14–15 'Michael Robartes and the Dancer' (*PNE* 189):

> . . . your lover's wage
> Is what your looking glass can show.

Adam's fall: Adam and Eve were expelled from the Garden of Eden for disobedience and afterwards had to live by their labour. See Genesis 3.

24   *compounded of high courtesy*: Yeats thought true love was a discipline that needed wisdom: 'Each divines the secret self of the other, and refusing to believe in the mere daily self, creates a mirror where the lover or the beloved sees an image to copy in daily life; for love also creates the Mask.' (*A* 464)

RED HANRAHAN'S SONG ABOUT IRELAND   84

This poem first appeared, untitled, in the story 'Kathleen-ny-Houlihan', in *NO*   90
(4 Aug. 1894). In *ISW* it was entitled 'The Song of Red Hanrahan' (having had the title 'Kathleen the Daughter of Hoolihan and Hanrahan the Red' in *TSR*). *VE* contains variant readings which show differences in the names of places in the poem. The poem may owe something to James Clarence Mangan's 'Kathleen-ny-Houlahan', *Irish Minstrelsy* (ed. H. Halliday Sparling), 141. Red Hanrahan is discussed in a note on 'The Tower' (*PNE* 205); see also note on [The poet, Owen Hanrahan, under a bush of may] (*PNE* A34). See also *B* 72 and *M* 243.

1   *Cummen Strand*: the southern shore of the estuary, to the northwest of Sligo on the road to Strandhill (*Irish* Caimin, the little common).

2   *left hand*: the left-hand side is unlucky in Irish, as in many other traditions.

5   *Cathleen, the daughter of Houlihan*: the poem is written to Maud Gonne (it was her favourite Yeats poem) who played the role of Cathleen, the old woman

who symbolises a freed Ireland, in Yeats's play *Cathleen ni Houlihan* (1902). ('My subject is Ireland and its struggle for independence', the *United Irishman*, 5 May 1902). The last lines of the play describe her thus:

Peter: Did you see an old woman going down the path?
Patrick: I did not, but I saw a young girl, and she had the walk of a queen.

Yeats described her playing the part 'very finely, and her great height made Cathleen seem a divine being fallen into our mortal infirmity' (appendix II, *Cathleen ni Houlihan*).

6 *Knocknarea*: Irish, mountain of the Kings; mountain overlooking Sligo. See note on 'The Hosting of the Sidhe' (*PNE* 40).

7 *stones . . . Maeve*: Queen Maeve's supposed burial cairn is on the top of Knocknarea. See note on 'The Hosting of the Sidhe' (*PNE* 40).

11 *Clooth-na-Bare*: Lough Ia, Sligo. Yeats wrote in 'The Untiring Ones':

Such a mortal too was Clooth-na-Bare [his footnote read 'Doubtless Clooth-na-Bare should be Cailleac Beare, which would mean the old Woman Beare. Beare or Bere or Verah or Dera or Dhera was a very famous person, perhaps the Mother of the Gods herself. Standish O'Grady found her, as he thinks, frequenting Lough Leath, or the Grey Lake on a mountain of the Fews. Perhaps Lough Ia is my mishearing or the story-teller's mispronunciation of Lough Leath, for there are many Lough Leaths] who went all over the world seeking a lake deep enough to drown her faery life, of which she had grown weary, leaping from hill to lake and lake to hill, and setting up a cairn of stones wherever her feet lighted, until at last she found the deepest water in the world in little Lough Ia, on the top of the Birds' Mountain at Sligo.
  The two little creatures may well dance on [they were faeries, one like a young man, the other like a young woman], and the woman of the log and Clooth-na-Bare sleep in peace, for they have known untrammelled hate and unmixed love, and have never wearied themselves with 'yes' and 'no', or entangled their feet with the sorry net of 'maybe' and 'perhaps'. The great winds came and took them up into themselves. (*M* 78)

See annotated notes on 'The Hosting of the Sidhe' (*PNE* 40).

14 *Rood*: cross. See note on 'The Song of the Happy Shepherd' (*PNE* 1).

85 THE OLD MEN ADMIRING THEMSELVES IN THE WATER

91 This poem was written before 20 November 1902 and first appeared in the *Pall Mall Magazine* (Jan. 1903).

86 UNDER THE MOON

91 This poem first appeared in *The Speaker* (15 June 1901).

1   *Brycelinde*: the forest of Broceliande in Brittany where Merlin was bewitched by Viviane

2   *Avalon*: King Arthur was brought here after his death. It was a mythical land like the Isles of the Blessed where the virtuous went after death. Cf. Sir Thomas Malory, *La Morte d'Arthur*, VIII, ch. 27; XII, chs. 7 and 9; and XXI, ch. 5. Yeats mocked at this poem in old age. See 'A Statesman's Holiday' (*PNE* A125).

2   *Joyous Isle*: Saul (*PYP* 80) comments that this place occurs in the Agravain portion of the prose vulgate *Lancelot.* Lancelot is an Arthurian knight, the lover of Queen Guinevere, who, finding Arthur dead, seeks the Queen and discovers she has taken the veil. He then becomes a priest and guards Arthur's grave. On his death he is carried to Joyous Gard.

3   *Where one*: John Rhys, *Studies in the Arthurian Legend* (1891) 147, is 'a probable source' (*PNE*) for Lancelot's living in the Joyous Isle with Elayne after her friend Dame Brysen cured him of madness, Elayne's father King Pelles having assigned them the Castle of Blyaunt to live in.

4   *Uladh*: Ulster, northern province of Ireland. See *McG* 87.

Naoise: a son of Usna, a young warrior who carried off Deirdre to Scotland and was eventually killed by Conchubar on his return to Ireland with her and his brothers. See note on 'The Rose of the World' (*PNE* 20).

6   *Land-under-Wave*: (*Irish* Tir-fa-Thonn) a name for the enchanted underworld beneath the sea

7   *Seven old sisters*: perhaps the planets, but more likely the Pleiades, the seven daughters of Atlas

8   *Land-of-the-Tower*: possibly the house of glass belonging to Aengus referred to in Yeats's footnote to *Baile and Aillinn* (1903) (*PNE* 377), and 'the tower of glass' mentioned in 'The Harp of Aengus', first published in the *North American Review*, May 1900 and afterwards in *The Shadowy Waters* (1900). See H. D'Arbois de Jubainville, *The Irish Mythological Cycle and Celtic Mythology*, tr. R. I. Best (1903) 67. In the latter poem Edain came, in a fit of jealousy, from the hill of Midhir [her husband, a king of the Sidhe] and lived 'Beside young Aengus in his tower of glass' weaving harp strings out of his hair. The Land of the Tower may be (*PNE*) Tory Island (*Irish* Toraigh, a place of Towers) in Co. Donegal. See *A* 50.

9   *Wood-of-Wonders . . . dawn*: this comes, as Sheila O'Sullivan has discovered (*YUIT* 267), from Douglas Hyde's edition of the tale of the 'Adventures of the Children of the King of Norway' contained in the first volume issued by the Irish Texts Society (1899) 128-9. The hero, Cod, meets in the Forest of Wonders a wondrous ox ('and two gold horns on him and a horn trumpet in his mouth') and kills him. Later (pp. 130-1) Cod sees 'a fair bevy of women' coming towards him

and 'a high-headed sensible queen at the head of that band' and a golden bier borne by four before her. 'Son of the King of Norway', said the lady, 'there is the ox for thee that thou woundedst a little while back, which we have in the bier'.

11 *Branwen*: daughter of Llyr in the *Mabinogion*; she was wife of the King of Ireland, Matholwch. Yeats read Lady Charlotte Guest's translation.

Guinevere: King Arthur's queen

92 12 *Niamh and Laban and Fand*: for Niamh see note on 'The Hosting of the Sidhi' (*PNE* 40); Laban was a sister of Fand, the wife of Manannan MacLir (Saul (*PYP* 81) remarks that she was changed to an otter by her magic well when she neglected it (see John Rhys (*LCH* 463). Her name (*Irish*, Li Ban) means woman's beauty); Fand was loved by Cuchulain (see note on 'The Secret Rose' (*PNE* 67)) though he returned to his mortal life in the end.

13 *Wood-woman*: In the 'Adventures of the Children of the King of Norway' (see note on 1.9 above) Cod meets her before he enters the Forest of Wonders and she tells him that her lover was turned to a blue-eyed hawk by the vindictive daughter of the King of Greece.

14 *dun: (Irish)* a fort

87 THE RAGGED WOOD

92 This poem first appeared, untitled, in the story 'The Twisting of the Rope', *Stories of Red Hanrahan* (1904). It was entitled 'The Hollow Wood' in *CW*.

6, 7 *silver-proud queen-woman . . . golden hood*: for the silver and gold symbols cf. 'The Song of Wandering Aengus' (*PNE* 48)

88 O DO NOT LOVE TOO LONG

93 This poem was written before 23 February 1905 and first appeared entitled 'Do Not Love Too Long', in *The Acorn* (Oct. 1905).

8 *so much at one*: cf. lines 13–16 'Among School Children' (*PNE* 222), 'it seemed that our two natures blent/Into a sphere from youthful sympathy'. Yeats is referring to his friendship with Maud Gonne.

9 *she changed*: probably a reference to Maud Gonne's marriage. Cf. the last line of 'Never give all the Heart' (*PNE* 81).

THE PLAYERS ASK FOR A BLESSING ON THE PSALTERIES AND ON THEMSELVES   **89**

This poem was probably written in June 1902 and first appeared in *ISW*.   *93*

Title   The Psalteries: an instrument made by Arnold Dometsch for Yeats and Florence Farr (Florence Farr Emery, d. 1917 in Ceylon, a member of the group of students of the occult who gathered round MacGregor Mathers (1854-1918). See note on her on 'All Souls' Night' (*PNE* 239)); it was 'half psaltery, half lyre' and contained all the chromatic intervals within the range of the speaking voice. Yeats wrote an essay on 'Speaking to the Psaltery' (*E & I* 13-27).

The psaltery, similar to a lyre, but with a trapezoidal sounding board, originated in the near East, was popular in Europe in the middle ages.

3   *O masters*: Yeats wrote to Arnold Dolmetsch on 3 June 1902 to say he was writing a 'Prayer to the Seven Archangels to bless the Seven Notes' (L 373). These 'masters' may therefore be the seven archangels. They are 'kinsmen of the Three in One' in line 14, a reference to the Christian Trinity.

THE HAPPY TOWNLAND   **90**

This poem first appeared in *The Weekly Critical Review* (4 June 1903). It was   *94* entitled 'The Rider from the North' in *ISW*, but the original title was resumed in *Poems, 1899-1905*. In a radio talk of 1932 Yeats said the poem symbolised striving after an impossible ideal.

3   *the townland*: Paradise. Saul (*PYP* 83) links it with 'that happy townland' [Paradise] in *The Unicorn from the Stars,* Act II. C. M. Bowra (*HS* 190) thinks there is a folklore source for the Irish notion that certain men are 'away', entirely absorbed in the search for an earthly Paradise which is hidden behind the appearance of the visible world. Sheila O'Sullivan links it (*YUIT* 275-6) with the Irish poet Raftery's poems of places, citing Lady Gregory's reference to them in *Poets and Dreamers* (1903) 30: ' ''Cnoicin Saibhir'', the Plentiful Little Hill, must have sounded like a dream to many a poor farmer'. 'The Happy Townland' was to be included in a play to be entitled *The Country of the Young*, in which a poor child, riding on a kitchen 'form' with a mysterious stranger was to be carried away by the magic of imagination to a townland like Raftery's Cill Aodain. Lady Gregory's 'poor farmer' becomes the 'strong farmer' of the poem, materialistic, full of worldly cares.

10   *golden and silver wood*: see note on 'The Man who dreamed of Faeryland' (*PNE* 33).

13   *the little fox*: Sheila O'Sullivan suggests that the little fox is an accomplice, also at war with the materialistic world, based on 'An Maidrin Rua' (the little red fox), a song often sung at Gaelic League Feiseanna, which she thinks Yeats might have heard at the Feis at Killeenan, which he attended in August 1902.

14   *the world's bane*: Grace Jackson, *Mysticism in AE and Yeats in relation to Oriental and American Thought,* 162, considers the 'world's bane' may echo Blake's 'Jerusalem':

> When God commanded this hand to write
> In the shadowy hours of deep midnight,
> He told me that all I wrote should prove
> The bane of all that on earth I love.
> (*The Works of William Blake* (1893) II, 224)

Yeats and Ellis in their note stress the meaning of 'bane', pointing out that Blake had his own career in mind in 'The Monk' as in 'Milton', that the lines 'He told me that all I wrote should prove/The bane of all that on earth I love' recalls lines written at Felpham at about the same time and sent in a letter to Mr Butts:

> Must my wife live in my sister's bane,
> And my sister survive on my love's pain?

95   24   *golden and silver boughs*: see note, line 10

41   *Michael*: the Archangel; elsewhere Yeats describes him with the trumpet (of the Last Judgement) 'that calls the body to resurrections' (*E & I* 316); this is usually the archangel Gabriel's role.

45   *Gabriel*: Saul points out that P. Gurd, *The Early Poetry of William Butler Yeats*, 83, links Gabriel with Bertrand, *La Religion des Gaulois*, with its figures 'with human heads and fish tails', and the 'old horn' (line 49) with one of hammered silver in the Dublin Museum. Yeats described Gabriel as the angel of the Moon in the Cabbala 'and might, I considered, command the waters at a pinch' (*A* 269).

The Green Helmet and Other Poems

THE poems of *The Green Helmet* (1910) are transitional; they are far from the languor and resignation, nostalgia and deliberate restriction of Yeats's earlier poetry. They echo a troubled period in the poet's life. The love poetry regrets the waste of spirit involved in loving Maud Gonne in vain (for she married John MacBride in Paris in 1903), yet excuses it because of her beauty in poems which are cold and simple in style, yet possess a dignity and symbolic rhetoric. The old ideal of romantic poetry had come to a stop, and there is an air of finality about the love poetry Yeats wrote after Maud's marriage: it is static, detached yet none the less poignant.

His other poems in this volume reveal an increasing poetic interest in public life: he had decided his Dionysiac phase was over and he must leave the modes of Mallarmé or Symons for an Apollonian activity: 'All things can tempt me from this craft of verse'. There are poems dealing with age, poems foreshadowing the political rhetoric which the Lane controversy would beget in his next volume; and there are poems which praise Coole and Lady Gregory.

This is varied work which reflects Yeats's own life increasingly; his work in the Abbey Theatre was demanding, and the poetry shows his occasional feeling of disappointment in the Irish audience, his frustration in love as well as the satiric and sensual side of his character. He was still forming a new style, stripping off the decoration of the old, but not yet managing to put all his interests together in his poetry, still feeling his way towards a fuller expression of himself.

The 1910 edition was published by the Cuala Press; the 1912 Macmillan edition added six poems; 'That the Night Come'*, 'Friends'*, 'The Cold Heaven'*, 'On hearing that the students of our New University have joined the Ancient Order of Hibernians and the Agitation against Immoral Literature', 'The Attack on the "Playboy" '*, and 'At the Abbey Theatre'. The four asterisked poems were moved to *RPP*.

HIS DREAM   **91**

This poem first appeared, entitled 'A Dream', in *N* (11 July 1908) dated July   99
[1908] in *GH*. Several poems in this volume, including this one, were grouped under the general title 'Raymond Lully and his wife Pernella' corrected in an erratum slip to 'Nicolas Flamel and his wife Pernella'. A note after the title reads:

A few days ago I dreamed that I was steering a very gay and elaborate ship upon some narrow water with many people upon its banks, and that there was a figure upon a bed in the middle of the ship. The people were pointing to the figure and questioning, and in my dream I sang verses which faded as I awoke, all but this fragmentary thought, 'We call it, it has such dignity of limb, by the sweet name of Death.' I have made my poem out of my dream and the sentiment of my dream, and can almost say, as Blake did, 'The Authors are in Eternity.' [For Blake quotation see notes on 'The Cap and Bells' (*PNE* 59).]

92   A WOMAN HOMER SUNG

100   This poem was written between 5 and 15 April 1910 (in Yeats's Diary). It first appeared with some alterations in *GH*.

3   *her*: Maud Gonne

9   *being grey*: Yeats was nearly forty-five when he wrote the poem.

13   *shadowed in a glass*: he was celebrating her beauty – a duty he thought beautiful women should not shirk, but Maud Gonne seemed to him to hate 'her own beauty, not its effect on others, but its image in the mirror'. This passage commented (in terms of *A V*) that beauty is from the antithetical self and a woman 'can scarce but hate it, for not only does it demand a painful daily service, but it calls for the denial or the dissolution of the self' (*A* 365). [There follow some lines from an untitled poem not in *CP*, now 11.7-14 of *PNE* A80]

How many centuries spent
The sedentary soul
In toils of measurement
Beyond eagle or mole,
Beyond hearing or seeing
Or Archimedes' guess,
To raise into being
That loveliness?

19   *A woman Homer sung*: for Helen of Troy, see note on 'The Rose of the World' (*PNE* 20). She appears in Homer's *Iliad* which tells of one episode in the Greco-Trojan war, 'The wrath of Achilles'; she also appears in his *Odyssey*, back in Sparta after the war. For Homer see note on 'Mad as the Mist and Snow' (*PNE* 281).

93   WORDS

100   This poem was first written in prose in Yeats's 1908 Diary, section 10, probably on 22 January, as revised verses written on 23 January are to be added to the poem 'written yesterday'. The entry reads:

To-day the thought came to me that P.I.A.L. [Maud Gonne] never really understands my plans, or nature or ideas. Then came the thought – what matter? How much of the best I have done and still do is but the attempt to explain myself to her? If she understood I should lack a reason for writing, and one can never have too many reasons for doing what is so laborious. (*WBY* 228)

The poem first appeared in *GH*.

2 *cannot understand*: Maud Gonne was always reproaching Yeats for not making his art into nationalist propaganda. She introduced him to Arthur Griffith of the Sinn Fein movement after she withdrew from the more extreme I.R.B. about the turn of the century, hoping to keep the literary movement in line with the policies of Sinn Fein. See *WBY* 173.

15 *poor words*: cf. 'The Choice' (*PNE* 258) with its choice of 'Perfection of the   *101* life, or of the work'

NO SECOND TROY   **94**

This poem heads Yeats's Diary with the date December 1908 beneath it: it first   *101* appeared in *GH*

1 *her*: Maud Gonne

2 *of late*: Maud Gonne withdrew from public life after the break-up of her marriage. See note on 'Against Unworthy Praise' (*PNE* 98).

3 *most violent ways*: before her marriage Maud Gonne was increasingly involved in anti-British activities; she linked the I.R.B. (an Irish secret revolutionary association) with French military intelligence; she offered a Boer agent in Brussels a plan to put bombs in British troopships bound for Africa. See *WBY* 169 and *Y:M & P* 133.

4 *little streets upon the great*: J. Hone, 'Yeats as political philosopher', *London Mercury* (April 1939) remarked that Yeats had come to distrust and quarrel with 'all the little semi-literary and semi-political clubs and societies out of which the Sinn Fein movement grew' (see notes on previous poem).

5 *courage equal to desire*: Conor Cruise O'Brien has also commented on this aspect of Yeats's attitude to politics in 'Passion and Cunning: an Essay on the Politics of W. B. Yeats', drawing attention to Yeats's picture of his political associates of the 'nineties: 'Men who had risen above the traditions of the countryman, without learning those of cultivated life, or even educating themselves and who because of their poverty, their ignorance, their superstitious piety, are much subject to all kinds of fear.' He comments that these views of Yeats are 'a classical statement of the Irish Protestant view of the rising Catholic middle-class' (*IER* 223).

8 *tightened bow*: sexual symbolism in Blake: see notes on 'The Arrow' (*PNE* 78).

9 *not natural in an age like this*: Yeats described her in 'The Trembling of the Veil' as looking as if 'she lived in an ancient civilisation', her face was 'like the face of some Greek statue' (*A* 364), and elsewhere he described her as a classical impersonation of the spring, 'the Virgilian commendation ''She walks like a goddess'' made for her alone' (*A* 123). See Jeffares, 'Pallas Athene Gonne', *Tributes in Prose and Verse to Shotaro Oshima* (1970) 4-7.

10 *high and solitary and most stern*: cf. the description in 'The Trembling of the Veil' which described her beauty as backed by her great stature, . . . solitary . . . her face, like the face of some Greek statue, showed little thought (*A* 364).

12 *Troy for her to burn*: Bowra (*HS* 199) remarks 'His only symbol for her is Helen of Troy: for like Helen she is beyond praise or comment.' See note on 'The Rose of the World' (*PNE* 20).

95 RECONCILIATION

102 This poem was included in section 7 of Yeats's Diary, which was dated 26 February 1909, but Ellmann (*IY* 288) dates it September 1908. The entry reads, 'I made the following poem about six months ago and write it here that it may not be lost.' It first appeared in *GH*.

1 *you*: Maud Gonne

3 *ears being deafened*: Yeats was lecturing in Dublin and received the news of Maud Gonne's marriage to John MacBride just before the lecture. He gave the lecture but never knew what he said in it.

5-6 *a song about . . . kings, Helmets and swords*: possibly a reference to the plays *The King's Threshold* and *On Baile's Strand*

10 *pit*: originally 'a' pit not 'the' pit. Here (despite the possible ambiguity of 'pit' referring to the Abbey Theatre's pit) it probably means grave, as one of the MS. versions had an erased line, 'Trample in the dull lime after them.'

12 *barren thoughts*: another version of the poem written in the Diary between August 1910 and November 1911 contained these lines:

> But every powerful life goes on its way
> Too blinded by the sight of the mind's eye
> Too deafened by the cries of the heart
> Not to have staggering feet and groping hands.

KING AND NO KING   96

This poem was written on 7 December 1909, and first appeared in *GH*.   *102*

1 *but merely voice*: Ellmann (*IY* 252) using information given him by Allan Wade, has pointed out that this poem is based on the Beaumont and Fletcher play *A King and No King* (staged 1611, published 1619) in which King Arbaces falls in love with his supposed sister Panthea: he tells her

> I have lived
> To conquer men, and now am overthrown
> Only by words, brother and sister. Where
> Have those words dwelling? I will find 'em out
> And utterly destroy 'em; but they are
> Not to be grasped: let 'em be men or beasts,
> And I will cut 'em from the earth; or towns,
> And I will raze 'em, and then blow 'em up:
> Let 'em be seas, and I will drink 'em off,
> And yet have unquenched fire left in my breast;
> Let 'em be anything but merely voice.

5 *Old Romance*: Arbaces is found to be an adopted child and 'No King', so he is finally able to marry Panthea and become King.

9 *that pledge you gave*: perhaps some vow Maud Gonne took not to marry, possibly in view of her relationship with Lucien Millevoye, a French Boulangist. There were reasons she could not marry, she told Yeats when he first proposed to her. But see Nancy Cardozo for their 'spiritual marriage' in 1898 and its renewal after a sexual relationship in 1907-8 (*MGLE* 157-8, 164-7 and 258-63).

11 *your faith*: Maud Gonne became a Roman Catholic in 1897; she was formally received into the Church in February 1903 before her marriage to John MacBride.

PEACE   97

This poem was written in May 1910 at Les Mouettes, Colville, Maud Gonne's   *103* house on the Normandy coast near Calvados. (It was destroyed in the Second World War.) It first appeared in *GH*.

2 *Homer's age*: the comparison between Maud Gonne and Homer's Helen of Troy is implicit. See note on 'A Woman Homer Sung' (*PNE* 92).

3 *a hero's wage*: Maud Gonne had married Major John MacBride, who had fought for the Boers in the South African War.

8, 9 *All that sternness amid charm, / All that sweetness amid strength*: these opposing qualities in Maud Gonne troubled Yeats. Cf. 'Against Unworthy Praise' (*PNE* 98) and 'The Tower' (*PNE* 205) where he alludes to her as 'a great labyrinth'.

98   AGAINST UNWORTHY PRAISE

103   This poem was written at Colville, Calvados, and is dated 11 May 1910 in Yeats's Diary. It first appeared in *GH*.

2   *knave or dolt*: this may refer to the behaviour of the Abbey audience when disturbances over Synge's *The Playboy of the Western World* occurred in 1907.

41   *for a woman's sake*: an undated entry in section 10 of Yeats's Diary epitomises the main thought of the poem: 'How much of the best that I have done and still do is but the attempt to explain myself to her.'

104   13   *labyrinth*: cf. 'The Tower' (*PNE* 205)

16, 17   . . . *slander, ingratitude, From self-same dolt and knave*: the Abbey audience hissed Maud Gonne when she appeared in the theatre on 20 October 1906, having received the official decree of separation from John MacBride. After this she virtually withdrew from Irish public life until 1918.

99   THE FASCINATION OF WHAT'S DIFFICULT

104   The subject matter of this poem was contained in prose in Yeats's Diary in September 1909. The poem was probably written between that date and March 1910; it first appeared in *GH*.

1   *The fascination*: the prose draft reads:

Subject: To complain at the fascination of what's difficult. It spoils spontaneity and pleasure, and wastes time. Repeat the line ending difficult three times and rhyme on bolt, exalt, coalt, jolt. One could use the thought that the winged and unbroken coalt must drag a cart of stones out of pride because it is difficult, and end by denouncing drama, accounts, public contests and all that's merely difficult.

4   *our colt*: Pegasus, the winged horse who sprang from the blood of Medusa and flew to Heaven. Ovid relates a legend in which Pegasus lived on Helicon where he raised the Fountain of Hippocrene, after which the Muses made him their favourite.

6   *Olympus*: the highest mountain in Greece, regarded as the home of the Gods in Greek mythology

8   *road-metal*: it is possible that Yeats got the image of Pegasus from T. Sturge Moore (1870–1944), who was a close friend of his at this period. Moore wrote

Swift, as a rule, used his Pegasus for a cart-horse, since it was strong, and he sorely importuned by the press of men and notions in need of condign punishment: but even when plodding in the ruts, its motion betrays the mettle in which it here revels.   (*Art and Life* (1910) 76)

Another possible source is Heine:

> In the land of fable prances
> My beloved Pegasus.
> He's no useful, safely virtuous
> Cart-horse of your citizen.
> (*Atta Troll*, III (1876) 9)

A DRINKING SONG   100

This poem is dated 17 February 1910 in Yeats's Diary: it first appeared in *GH*.   104

6   *I sigh*: the poem was written for *Mirandolina*, Lady Gregory's adaptation of   105
Goldoni's *La Locandiera*, and is a speech by Mirandolina, an innkeeper who is
flirting with the misogynist Captain. Clifford Bax's translation is perhaps nearer to
the original spirit of Goldoni, whose original version read:

> Viva Bacco e viva Amore
> L'uno e l'altro ci consola:
> Uno passa per la gola
> L'altro va dagli occhi al cuore
> Bevo il vin; cogli occhi poi . . .
> Faccio . . . quel che fate voi.
> (*Commedie scelte*, 1891)

Bax's version reads:

> Wine and love! With what sweet art
> Each can lay our sorrows flat!
> This goes down the throat, and that
> Down the eyes to take the heart.
> Look, I drink: and these eyes too
> Then do straightway what yours do.
> Goldoni, *Four Comedies* (ed. Bax, 1922)

This leads better into the Captain's reception of the toast, which has a sentimental
flavour in Yeats's version.

THE COMING OF WISDOM WITH TIME   101

This poem was written on 21 or 22 March 1909 in Yeats's Diary; it was   105
originally entitled 'Youth and Age' when it first appeared in *McClure's
Magazine* (Dec. 1910). The present title was used in *GH*.

102 ON HEARING THAT THE STUDENTS OF OUR NEW UNIVERSITY HAVE JOINED
THE AGITATION AGAINST IMMORAL LITERATURE

105 This poem was dated 3 April 1912 in Yeats's Diary, and entitled 'On hearing
that the students of our New University having joined the Ancient Order of
Hibernians are taking part in the Agitation against Immoral Literature'. The
poem first appeared in *The Green Helmet and Other Poems* (1912) with the title
'On hearing . . . University have joined the Ancient Order of Hibernians and the
Agitation against Immoral Literature'.

Title   New University: originally named the Royal University of Ireland. It was
founded in 1908 on a federal basis, and became the National University of
Ireland, composed of colleges in Dublin, Cork, Galway and Maynooth, that in
Dublin being originally begun by Newman as Rector in 1854, when it was named
the Catholic University of Ireland. It is 'new' as opposed to Trinity College,
Dublin, founded in 1591 by Queen Elizabeth I.

103 TO A POET, WHO WOULD HAVE ME PRAISE CERTAIN BAD POETS, IMITATORS
OF HIS AND MINE

105 This poem was written in Yeats's Diary between 23 and 26 April [1909], Section
166. It was headed 'To AE, who wants me [to] praise some of his poets imitators
of my own.' It first appeared in *GH*.

1   *You*: Yeats's friend George Russell (AE), who had a literary circle in Dublin.
'Seumas O'Sullivan', a member of it, replied, 'Where's the wild dog which ever
knew his father?'

104 THE MASK

106 The text of this poem was written in Yeats's Diary between August 1910 and
May 1911. It first appeared in *GH* entitled 'A Lyric from an Unpublished Play'.
It is a lyric from *The Player Queen* (1922). The parts are allocated to man and
woman more clearly in the play, e.g. the man speaks lines 1-2, 6-7, 11-12, and
the woman replies.

1   *that mask*: Yeats wrote 'What I have called "the Mask" is an emotional
antithesis to all that comes out of their [subjective men] internal nature' (*A* 189).

105 UPON A HOUSE SHAKEN BY THE LAND AGITATION

106 Yeats's Diary included a prose draft for this poem dated 7 August [1910], the text
of the poem and an explanation of it. The poem first appeared, entitled 'To a

Certain Country House in Time of Change' in *McClure's Magazine* (Dec. 1910). It was entitled 'Upon a Threatened House' in *GH*. The draft read:

> Subject for a Poem. A Shaken House. How should the world gain if this house failed, even though a hundred little houses were the better for it, for here power has gone forth, or lingered giving energy, precision; it gives to a far people beneficent rule; and still under its roof loving intellect is sweetened by old memories of its descents from far off; how should the world be better if the wren's nest flourish and the eagle's house is scattered.

The explanation read:

> I wrote this poem on hearing the result of reduction of rent made by the courts. One feels that when all must make their living they will live not for life's sake but the work's and all be the poorer. My work is very near to life itself and my father's very near to life itself but I am always feeling a lack of life's own values behind my thought. They should have been there before the stream began, before it became necessary to let the work create its values. This house has enriched my soul out of measure because here life moves within restraint through gracious forms. Here there has been no compelled labour, no poverty-thwarted impulse.

1 *this house*: Coole Park (*Irish* cuil, a corner), Lady Gregory's house near Gort in Co. Galway, demolished in 1942. See note on 'Man and the Echo' (*PNE* 372).

4 *the lidless eye*: this line refers to a belief that only an eagle can stare into the sun without blinking. Yeats uses the eagle as a symbol for an active objective person.

5 *eagle thoughts*: cf. Blake's lines, 'The Eagle, that doth gaze upon the sun' ('King Edward the Third', *The Poems of William Blake* (ed. Yeats) 29) and

> As the wing'd eagle scorns the towery fence . . .
> Then, bosomed in an amber cloud, around
> Plumes his wide wings, and seeks Sol's palace high
> ('An Imitation of Spenser', poetical sketches, *The Poems of William Blake* (ed. Yeats) 14)

and

> And the eagle returns . . .
> Shaking the dust from his immortal pinions to awake
> The sun that sleeps too long.
> (Visions of the Daughters of Albion, The Prophetical Books, *The Poems of William Blake* (ed. Yeats), 181)

There is also Blake's query '[Ask] the winged eagle why he loves the sun?' (*The Poems of William Blake* (ed. Yeats) 182).

8 *Mean roof-trees*: the cottages whose inhabitants would farm more of the estate. In September 1910 Yeats's Diary contains thoughts upon the contrasts of Irish life. Synge, exalted to the aristocracy of writers and persecuted by the mob, is like Coole Park threatened by the growing powers of the cottages (cf. 'Estrangement', *A* 482). Yeats wrote:

I thought of the house [Coole Park] slowly perfecting itself and the life within it in ever increasing intensity of labour and then of it probably sinking away, things courteous incomplete or rather sheer weakness of will, for ability has not failed in young Gregory, and I said to myself: Why is life a perpetual preparation for something that never happens? Even an Odyssey only seems a preparation, a thing of ruined reminiscence. It is not always the tragedy of the great that they see before the end the small and weak in friendship or in enmity pushing them from their place and ruining what they have built and doing one or the other in mere lightness of mind.

107   10   *The gifts that govern men*: Sir William Gregory (1817–92), Lady Gregory's husband, a politician, had served as Governor of Ceylon. (The first Gregory to own Coole (in 1768) was a Director of the East India Company.)

11   *a written speech*: Lady Gregory's plays and her two books of Irish legends, *Gods and Fighting Men* and *Cuchulain of Muirthemne*

106   AT THE ABBEY THEATRE

107   This poem was written in Paris in May 1911. A note to this effect, dated 17 August 1911, is in Yeats's Diary; the poem first appeared in *IR* (Dec. 1912) and *The Green Helmet and Other Poems* (1912).

Title: *Ronsard*: the poem is very close to the original sonnet:

> Tyard, on me blasmoit, à mon commencement,
> Dequoy j'estois obscur au simple populaire,
> Mais on dit aujourd'huy que je suis au contraire,
> Et que je me démens, parlant trop bassement.
> Toy de qui le labeur enfante doctement
> Des livres immortels, dy-moy, que doy-je faire?
> Dy-moi, car tu sçais tout, comme doy-je complaire
> A ce monstre testu, divers en jugement?
> Quand je tonne en mes vers, il a peur de me lire;
> Quand ma voix se desenfle, il ne fait qu'en mesdire.
> Dy-moy de quel lien, force, tenaille, ou clous
> Tiendray-je ce Proté qui se change à tous coups?
> Tyard, je t'enten bien, il le faut laisser dire,
> Et nous rire du luy, comme il se rit de nous.
> (*Œuvres complètes*, I, 116 (1950))

1   *Craobhin Aoibhin*: Irish for 'Little Pleasant Branch', the pen name of Dr Douglas Hyde (1860–1949), a poet, translator, politician, and first President of Eire. Yeats thought he had not fulfilled his early promise, and while praising his first book of verse thought he had not critical capacity but an uncritical folk genius: 'He had much frequented the company of old countrymen, and had so acquired the Irish language, and his taste for snuff, and for moderate quantities of a detestable species of illegal whiskey [potheen] distilled from the potato by certain of his neighbours' (*A* 217). He wrote out of an imitative sympathy; he was to

create a popular movement (the Gaelic League) but Yeats none the less mourned for ' ''the greatest folklorist who ever lived'' and for the great poet who died in his youth.' Yeats thought his incapacity for criticism made him 'the cajoler of crowds, and of individual men and women . . . and for certain years young Irish women were to display his pseudonym, ''Craoibhin Aoibhin'', in gilt letters upon their hat-bands' (*A* 219). Cf. 'Coole Park, 1929' (*PNE* 253):

> There Hyde before he had beaten into prose
> That noble blade the Muses buckled on . . .

2   *high and airy*: a reference to the heroic verse plays staged in the Abbey Theatre, Dublin, which did not attract large audiences. The theatre was established in 1904 by Yeats and others.

5   *Common things*: the realistic plays and 'cottage comedies' which were popular, though the treatment of peasant life in Synge's plays upset audiences.

11   *Proteus*: in Greek legend an old man of the sea who tended Poseidon's flocks. He had the gift of prophesy but he was difficult to consult because he could change his shape at will.

THESE ARE THE CLOUDS   107

This poem, which was written in May 1910, first appeared in *GH*.   *107*

3   *the weak lay hand on what the strong has done*: cf. notes on 'Upon a House shaken by the Land Agitation' (*PNE* 105). Yeats wrote in his Diary when he was at Stone Cottage in 1914: 'A long continuity of culture like that at Coole could not have arisen and has not arisen in a single Catholic family in Ireland since the Middle Ages.'

4   *lifted*: originally 'builded', probably a reference to the actual house at Coole Park

7   *friend*: the poem is written to Lady Gregory, to reassure her of the value of   *108*
her work and the intrinsic greatness she has created.

AT GALWAY RACES   108

This poem was written at Coole in the summer of 1908 according to Hone (*WBY*   *108*
225); on 21 October 1908 according to Ellmann (*IY* 288). It first appeared in *ER*
(Feb. 1909) entitled 'Galway Races'.

1   *the course*: horse races are held annually at Galway, in the west of Ireland

5   *We, too*: the poets. An entry of Yeats's Diary of this period compared poets to the aristocracy of birth, and horsemen (cf. line 7), as opposed to merchants and clerks (cf. line 8), are the descendants of the class that honoured bards.

7   *horsemen*: used as symbols of simple, violent and passionate men in 'The Gyres' (*PNE* 321)

10-16   *at some new moon . . . sleeping is not death . . . horses*: these lines reflect some of *AV*'s thought and resemble 'The Gyres' (*PNE* 321):

> What matter? Those that Rocky Face holds dear,
> Lovers of horses and of women, shall . . . [disinter]
> . . . The workman, noble and saint, and all things run
> On that unfashionable gyre again.

15-16   *hearteners among men/That ride upon horses*: Maud Gonne (MacBride) noticed the change in his acquaintances:

> He found himself among the comfortable and well-fed, who style themselves the 'upper classes', but whom Willie shuddering at the words and discriminating even among them, called 'Distinguished Persons'; and some undoubtedly deserved the title. (*Scattering Branches. Tributes to the Memory of W. B. Yeats*, ed. Stephen Gwynn (1940) 28)

109   A FRIEND'S ILLNESS

109   This poem was written out three times in Yeats's Diary, in section 52 in [February] 1909. It first appeared in *GH*.

1   *sickness*: the Diary entry for 4 February 1909 reads:

> This morning I got a letter telling me of Lady Gregory's illness. I did not recognise her son's writing at first and my mind wandered, I suppose because I am not well. I thought my mother was ill and that my sister was asking me to come at once: then I remembered my mother died years ago and that more than kin was at stake. She had been to me mother, friend, sister and brother. I cannot realise the world without her –she brought to my wavering thoughts steadfast nobility. All the day the thought of losing her is like a conflagration in the rafters. Friendship is all the house I have.

On 6 February [1909] the Diary continues:

> Lady Gregory better but writes in pencil that 'she very nearly slipped away'.

Section 50 of the Diary praised Lady Gregory's work (it is printed in *Estrangement*) and section 51 contained one sentence: 'Of Lady Gregory one can say what Shakespeare or another said, "She died every day she lived".' Section 52 contained the three versions of the poem, and section 53 continued:

> All Wednesday I heard Castiglione's phrase ringing in my memory, 'Never be it spoken without tears, the Duchess is dead,' that slight phrase coming

where it did among the numbering of his dead has often moved me till my eyes dimmed; and I feel his sorrow as though one saw the worth of life fade for ever.

See note on 'Coole Park, 1929' (*PNE* 253).

ALL THINGS CAN TEMPT ME   110

This poem was written at Coole Park in the summer of 1908, according to Hone   *109*
(*WBY* 226). It first appeared in *ER* (Feb. 1909), entitled 'Distraction', the
present title being used in *GH*.

1   *tempt me*: Yeats wrote little verse while he was Manager of the Abbey
Theatre (1904–10).

2   *woman's face*: Maud Gonne

BROWN PENNY   111

This poem first appeared in *GH* entitled 'The Young Man's Song'.   *109*

Responsibilities

SOME of the poems in this volume appeared in *The Green Helmet and Other Poems* (1912), others in periodicals, while public life stirred Yeats into the passionate speech of the poems written about the Lane Gallery which were published as *PWD* in 1913. These particular poems reflect his delight in the patronage given by the rulers of Italian Renaissance courts, with which he compared the attitude of Ireland's new rich. He weighed the new politicians against the old heroes and found them sadly lacking; in 'The Fisherman' he contrasted his hopes for Ireland with the reality. His experience of secret societies, committees, public meetings emerged in bitter political rhetoric: there was a bitterly disillusioned note in the love poetry too; the Celtic trappings were finally, decisively, renounced in 'A Coat' and his own ancestors were given mythological significance, while he continued to write love poems, still deeply moved by the beauty of Maud Gonne and, while angered by the way in which the Irish crowd had behaved to him and to her ('The People'), yet ready to accept her continuing regard for the people as selfless and impressive. These love poems have some gentleness and excitement; they are also compassionate in their evocation of old memories. There are also poems recording intense personal experiences, such as that superb and timeless poem 'The Cold Heaven'.

The volume published by the Cuala Press in 1914 included 'The Two Kings' and a play, *The Hour-Glass*. The 1916 edition omitted this play but added 'The Well and the Tree' (not included in *CP*).

FIRST EPIGRAPH

As yet unidentified

SECOND EPIGRAPH

PNE identifies this as from Confucius (*c*. 557–*c*. 479 BC), *Analects* vii, v, quoting Legge's translation: 'Extreme is my decay. For a long time I have not dreamed as I was wont to, that I saw the Duke of Châu' (Châu-Kung (d. 1105 BC), Chinese statesman and author) *PNE* points out that M. G. Pauthier's French translation *Confucius et Mencius* (1841), ii, gives 'Khoung-fout-seu', and suggests that Ezra Pound may have been assisting Yeats with these Chinese quotations.

This poem is dated 1912-14 in *Responsibilities and Other Poems* (1916).   *113*
Ellmann (*IY* 288) dates it December 1913. It first appeared in *RPP*.

1   *old fathers*: the poem was provoked by George Moore's attacks on Lady
Gregory and Yeats in portions of *Vale* printed in *ER* in January and February
1914:

> As soon as the applause died away, Yeats who had lately returned to us from
> the States with a paunch, a huge stride, and an immense fur overcoat, rose to
> speak. We were surprised at the change in his appearance, and could hardly
> believe our ears when, instead of talking to us as he used to do about the old
> stories come down from generation to generation he began to thunder like Ben
> Tillett against the middle classes, stamping his feet, working himself into a
> great temper, and all because the middle classes did not dip their hands into
> their pockets and give Lane the money he wanted for his exhibition. When he
> spoke the words, the middle classes, one would have thought that he was
> speaking against a personal foe, and we looked round asking each other with
> our eyes where on earth our Willie Yeats had picked up the strange belief that
> none but titled and carriage-folk could appreciate pictures. And we asked
> ourselves why our Willie Yeats should feel himself called upon to denounce his
> own class; millers and shipowners on one side, and on the other a portrait-
> painter of distinction; and we laughed, remembering AE's story, that one day
> whilst Yeats was crooning over his fire Yeats had said that if he had his rights
> he would be Duke of Ormonde. AE's answer was: I am afraid, Willie, you are
> overlooking your father – a detestable remark to make to a poet in search of an
> ancestry; and the addition: We both belong to the lower-middle classes, was in
> equally bad taste. AE knew that there were spoons in the Yeats family bearing
> the Butler crest, just as there are portraits in my family of Sir Thomas More,
> and he should have remembered that certain passages in *The Countess
> Cathleen* are clearly derivative from the spoons. He should have remembered
> that all the romantic poets have sought illustrious ancestry, and rightly, since
> romantic poetry is concerned only with nobles and castles, gonfalons and
> oriflammes. Villiers de l'Isle Adam believed firmly in his descent, and appeared
> on all public occasions with the Order of Malta pinned upon his coat; and
> Victor Hugo, too, had inquired out his ancestry in all the archives of Spain and
> France before sitting down to write *Hernani* . . . and with good reason, for with
> the disappearance of gonfalons and donjons it may be doubted if—My
> meditation was interrupted by Yeats's voice.
> We have sacrificed our lives for Art; but you, what have you done? What
> sacrifices have you made? he asked, and everybody began to search his memory
> for the sacrifices that Yeats had made, asking himself in what prison Yeats had
> languished, what rags he had worn, what broken victuals he had eaten. As far
> as anybody could remember, he had always lived very comfortably, sitting
> down invariably to regular meals, and the old green cloak that was in keeping
> with his profession of romantic poet he had exchanged for the magnificent fur
> coat which distracted our attention from what he was saying, so opulently did it
> cover the back of the chair out of which he had risen. But, quite forgetful of the
> coat behind him, he continued to denounce the middle classes, throwing his
> arms into the air, shouting at us, and we thinking not at all of what he was

saying, but of a story that had been floating about Dublin for some time.   (*Vale* (1947 ed.) 113-15)

The passage continues with a malicious discussion of Dublin criticism of Yeats ('a literary movement consists of five or six people who live in the same town and hate each other cordially'), the allegation that his work was finished, and a view that Yeats's love of Maud Gonne was 'the common mistake of a boy'. The rewritten passages which deal with Lady Gregory and her writing can be read in *Vale* (1947) 122-31, 145-7. Moore altered his suggestion in the *English Review* that she had gone amongst the cottages as a Bible reader when a young woman, with skill, and tongue in cheek:

> In her own words, 'early association had so much to do with that religion which is the secret of the heart with God'. In saying as much she wins our hearts, but our intelligence warns us against seduction, and we remember that we may not acquiesce in what we believe to be error.

Cf. notes on 'The Witch' (*PNE* 128) and on ['Closing Rhyme'] (*PNE* 142). Yeats regarded *Reveries* (part of *A*) which he finished on Christmas Day 1914, as 'some sort of apologia for the Yeats family' (Letter to Lily Yeats, 29 Dec. 1914), and had written earlier in his 1909 Diary that:

> Duncan has been looking up my coat of arms for a book plate. I gave him the crest . . . a goat's head on a coronet. He found that a Mary Yeats of Lifford who died in 1673 had the following [coat of arms]. Being a woman there was no crest but the English 'Yates' had the goat's head . . . Can my sister get back to 'Mary Yeates'? Mary is an old family name and we had relations not very far from Lifford in North Sligo.

The Prologue was also intended as a challenge to Moore to speak of his own ancestors. See *Y:M & P* 180, for an extract from Yeats's Diary discussing Moore's family. His revenge came in *DP*.

3   *Old Dublin merchant 'free of the ten and four'*: *Old* may refer to time rather than age. The merchant may be Jervis Yeats (d. 1712) a Dublin linen merchant, supposedly of Yorkshire stock, the first of the Yeats family to live in Ireland, or his son and inheritor Benjamin or Benjamin's son, also christened Benjamin (1750-95), the poet's great-great-grandfather, a linen merchant like his father and grandfather. The last was listed as 'free of the six and ten per cent tax at the Custom-house, Dublin', from 1783-94, a privilege seemingly lost on his death in 1795 (it may have been held by his father or grandfather. See Jeffares *Y:M & P*, 2-3, and *PNE* (citing Richard Eton in *A book of rates . . . merchandise* (1767) on wholesalers allowed a discount from the excise of ten per cent on wine and tobacco, six per cent on other goods). Yeats got most of his information about the Yeats family from his sister Lily. Yeats wrote that the term 'free of the ten and four' applied to merchants who were exempted from certain duties by the Irish Parliament (*RPP*) but a later note, dated 1914, corrected this statement:

> 'Free of the ten and four' is an error I cannot now correct, without more rewriting than I have a mind for. Some merchant in Villon, I forget the reference [*PNE* cites Francois Villon's (b. 1431) 'Epistre a ses amis', p. 22

'noble men, free of the quarter and tenth', two kinds of tax], was 'free of the ten and four'. Irish merchants exempted by the Irish Parliament were, unless memory deceives me again – I cannot remember my authority – 'free of the eight and six' [which should have been 'six and ten'].

4   *Galway into Spain*: a good deal of merchandise was carried in sailing vessels between Galway and Spain in the eighteenth and nineteenth centuries.

5   *Old country scholar, Robert Emmet's friend*: Yeats's great-grandfather John Yeats (1774-1846), Rector of Drumcliffe, Sligo, from 1805 till his death. He was a friend of Emmet (1778-1803), the patriot who led a Rebellion in 1803; it failed and Emmet was executed. Yeats's great-grandfather was suspected and imprisoned for a few hours (*A* 21).

6   *to the poor*: he was praised by Rev. T. P. O'Rorke, *History of Sligo: Town and Country*, II, 27, for his kindness and charity.

7   *Merchant and scholar*: Jervis Yeats and the Rev. John Yeats

8   *huckster's loin*: merchants had been derided in Yeats's poem 'At Galway Races' (*PNE* 108) where they were linked with 'clerks': now they are elevated by being linked with a scholar. A method of distinguishing between the old and the new middle classes of Ireland was to make a contrast between hucksters and the 'Merchant and scholar'. But line 7 originally read 'Traders or soldiers' and was no doubt emended to sharpen the contrast between his family and the 'hucksters'.

9   *Soldiers*: see line 10. This refers to Yeats's Butler and Armstrong ancestors. Cf. *A* 20, which deals with the military history of the family in vague terms.

10   *a Butler or an Armstrong*: Benjamin Yeats, grandson of Jervis, married Mary Butler (1751-1834), a member of the great Anglo-Irish Ormonde family, in 1773, and the poet set great store by this connection. The Rev. William Butler Yeats (1806-62), son of the Rev. John Yeats, was the poet's grandfather. He was Rector of Moira, Co. Down, and in 1835 married Jane Grace Corbet (1811-76), daughter of Grace Armstrong (1774-1864) and William Corbet (1757-1824), whose family had strong military traditions. Jane Corbet's brother owned Sandymount Castle, Dublin, where the poet's father, John Butler Yeats, spent much of his time when he was an undergraduate at Trinity College, Dublin. See Jeffares, 'John Butler Yeats' (*IER* 26-8).

11, 12   *Boyne . . . James . . . Dutchman*: the scene of the battle fought on 1 July 1690 in which James II was defeated by William of Orange (1650-1702). Yeats originally thought his ancestors fought on the Jacobite side and lines 9-12 first read as follows:

> Pardon, and you that did not weigh the cost,
> Old Butlers when you took to horse and stood
> Beside the brackish waters of the Boyne,
> Till your bad master blenched and all was lost.

101

The river Boyne enters the Irish Sea near Drogheda; its goddess Boann lived at Bruigh Na Boinne, now Newgrange, Co. Meath.

13   *Old merchant skipper*: William Middleton (1770-1832), the poet's maternal great-grandfather, of Sligo. He had a depot in the Channel Islands and brought goods to and from South America. His smuggling developed into a general cargo traffic between Sligo and the Iberian peninsula. He seems to have been a brave man. Cf. T. P. O'Rorke, *History of Sligo: Town and Country*, I, 384.

15   *silent and fierce old man*: Yeats's maternal grandfather, William Pollexfen (1811-92), a retired sea captain and merchant, a silent and proud man who had run away to sea as a boy. He was so silent his wife never knew until he was nearly eighty that he had been given the freedom of some Spanish city, a fact he never explained. Yeats was captivated by his personality and terrified by it as well: the old man kept a hatchet by his bedside in case of burglars and once the boy saw him hunt men with a horsewhip. Yeats's memories of him were clear: 'Even today when I read *King Lear* his image is always before me, and I often wonder if the delight in passionate men in my plays and in my poetry is more than his memory' (*A* 6 ff.).

18   *wasteful virtues*: probably an implicit comparison with the Middleton relatives in Sligo who were 'liked but had not the pride and reserve, the sense of decorum and order, the instinctive playing before themselves that belongs to those who strike the popular imagination' (*A* 17).

19   *barren passion's sake*: Yeats's unrequited love for Maud Gonne

20   *forty-nine*: Yeats was born on 13 June 1865; the poem was published on 25 May, 1914

113   THE GREY ROCK

115   This poem was written before 1913 but first appeared in *P(Ch)* and *BR* in April 1913.

Title: The Grey Rock is the grey stone (*Irish* Craig Liath), a 40 feet high rock near Killaloe, Co. Clare, the house of Aoibheal, a fairy goddess or banshee (*McG* 51). Yeats spells the name Aoibheal (*M* 152), Aoibhel (*E* 8), Eevell (*E* 283, 285), and here as Aoife. See also *FFT* 81. *McG* 95 corrects Saul, *PYP* 90.

1-2   *Poets ... Cheshire Cheese*: poets of the 'nineties, members of the Rhymers' Club which met in an upper room with a sanded floor in the Cheshire Cheese, a Fleet Street chop house. Yeats and Ernest Rhys ((1859-1946), an Anglo-Welsh editor and poet, who became a mining engineer but abandoned this career for writing in 1886; he edited the Camelot Series for Walter Scott's publishing house but was best known as the editor of the *Everyman* series) founded the Club (probably in 1891). It had as members Lionel Johnson, Ernest Dowson, Victor Plarr, Ernest Radford, John Davidson, Richard Le Gallienne, T. W. Rolleston, Selwyn Image, Edwin Ellis, and John Todhunter, all of whom 'came constantly for a time'. Arthur Symons and Herbert Horne came 'less constantly, while William Watson joined but never came and Francis Thompson came once but never joined; and sometimes if we met in a private house, which we did occasionally, Oscar Wilde came' (*A* 165). Many of the members were interested in Celtic literature. Allan Wade adds the names of G. A. Greene and A. C. Hillier (*L* 181). Elkin Matthews published a *Book of the Rhymers' Club* in 1892 and Elkin Matthews and John Lane a second volume in 1894. Ernest Rhys has described the gatherings:

> The first three members were T. W. Rolleston [1857–1920, Irish writer, German scholar and editor], W. B. Yeats and myself. Each of us asked other Rhymers to come to the club suppers, and we soon reached the allotted number of ten. Our custom was to sup downstairs in the old coffee-house boxes, something like high double-seated pews with a table between. After supper, at which we drank old ale and other time-honoured liquors, we adjourned to a smoking-room at the top of the house, which we came to look upon as our sanctum. There long clays or churchwarden pipes were smoked, and the Rhymers were expected to bring rhymes in their pockets, to be read aloud and left to the tender mercies of the club for criticism. (*Everyman Remembers* 105)

10   *Goban*: Goibrui or Goibniu, an ancient God, of the Tuatha de Danaan, described as 'the legendary mason' in *M* 66. He was bow-legged in the first published version; later known as an architect and builder, his ale gave immortality to those who drank it.

15   *Slievenamon*: the link between the Gods and the poets of the Cheshire Cheese is that they each consider man must keep faith with the eternal powers. Slievenamon (*Irish* Sliabh na mBan, the Mountain of the Women) is in Tipperary, and was the site of the god Bodb Derg's palace. (See *McG*, 95 and cf. *PYP* 91.)

23   *mountain top*: Sliabh Anierean, the iron mountain in Co. Leitrim

29   *like woman made*: Aoife, a woman of the Sidhe   116

32   *for a dead man*: the man who befriended Murrough, the King of Ireland's son. Cf. lines 71–106

41   *a woman*: Maud Gonne

47   *lout*: a word Yeats used elsewhere to describe John MacBride, 'a drunken, vainglorious lout'. Cf. 'Easter 1916' (*PNE* 193). Yeats may be comparing Maud Gonne's briefly successful marriage (1903–5) to Aoife's.

54   *wine or women*: the first may refer to Lionel Johnson, the second to Ernest

Dowson. Cf. line 62. Yeats wrote that they were 'dissipated men, the one a drunkard, the other a drunkard and mad about women, and yet they had the gravity of men who had found life out and were awakening from the dream' (*M* 331).

117 62 *Dowson and Johnson*: Ernest Dowson (1867-1900) and Lionel Johnson (1867-1902), both described in Yeats's 'The Tragic Generation'. Johnson drank heavily in his last years, as did Dowson. Johnson lectured Dowson on chastity, 'but the rest of us counted the glasses emptied in their talk'. Dowson 'drunk, desired whatever woman chance brought, clean or dirty' (*A* 308-15). Yeats wrote to his father on 16 February 1910, about these two poets in particular, apropos a lecture he was preparing:

> The doctrine of the group, or rather of the majority of it, was that lyric poetry should be personal. That a man should express his life and do this without shame or fear. Ernest Dowson did this and became a most extraordinary poet, one feels the pressure of his life behind every line as if he were a character in a play of Shakespeare's. Johnson had no theories of any sort but came to do much the same through the example of Dowson and others and because his life grew gradually so tragic that it filled his thoughts. (*L* 548)

Yeats's 'Modern Poetry: a broadcast' also described 'the lucklessness' of the Rhymers' Club, and, in particular, Johnson and Dowson, and estimated their effect on Yeats himself. Cf. *E & I* 491-5.

65-68 *The Danish troop . . . King of Ireland's dead*: the Scandinavians began to invade the British Isles from about 800 onwards. They virtually controlled Ireland about 977. Their rule was broken by Malachy, king of Meath, who freed Meath in 980, and Brian Boru, king of Munster, who became High King of Ireland, restored many of the ruined churches and replaced the lost books, and finally defeated the Norsemen at the Battle of Clontarf in 1014. He and his son Murchad fell in the battle. Clontarf (*Irish* Cluain Tarbh, the meadow of the bulls) is now a northern suburb of Dublin.

76-85 *an unseen man . . . a young man*: Dubhlaing O'Hartagan, the lover of Aoibhell, offered two hundred years of life by her if he did not fight along with Murchad; he refused and was killed. See Yeats's note on 'The Hosting of the Sidhe' (*PNE* 40), where she is Aebhin/Aebhen. A possible source is Nicholas O'Kearney 'The Festivities at the House of Conan', *Transactions of the Ossianic Society* II (1835), 98-102.

118 88 *Aoife*: Cuchulain conquered this Scottish warrior queen, forcing her to grant him three wishes. She was to become the vassal of Scathach (a warrior woman of Skye who taught Cuchulain the art of war), to sleep with him one night, and bear him a son. See note on 'Cuchulain's Fight with the Sea' (*PNE* 19), but in 'The Grey Rock' Aoife is the Irish goddess Aoibheal (see note on title).

119 125 *rock-born, rock-wandering foot*: there is an implicit comparison of Maud Gonne (the 'rock-wandering' perhaps a reference to her love of wandering on

Howth's rock paths) with Aoibheal of Craglee (the Grey Rock of the poem's title), the fairy goddess.

128   *loud host before the sea*: this may refer to Yeats being unpopular with the I.R.B. and the nationalists. He had accepted a British Civil List pension in 1910, and was sneered at as 'pensioner Yeats' by the nationalist press, but these papers had earlier attacked him over the 'Playboy' controversy of 1907, and his poems dealing with the Lane controversy had not made him popular. See 'September 1913' (*PNE* 115).

TO A WEALTHY MAN WHO PROMISED A SECOND SUBSCRIPTION TO THE   114
DUBLIN MUNICIPAL GALLERY IF IT WERE PROVED THE PEOPLE WANTED
PICTURES

This poem was dated 8 January 1913 by Yeats, but Ellmann (*IY* 288) dates it 24   *119*
December 1912. It first appeared in the *Irish Times* (11 Jan. 1913) entitled 'The
Gift/To a friend who promises a bigger subscription than his first to the Dublin
Municipal Gallery if the amount collected proves that there is a considerable
"popular demand" for the pictures'. The poem was included in *PWD* where the
'friend' of the title was altered to 'Man'. Sir Hugh Lane (1875-1915), Lady
Gregory's nephew, offered to give his collection of French paintings to Dublin if
they were properly housed. He favoured a bridge gallery over the river Liffey,
designed by Sir Edwin Lutyens. See Lady Gregory *Sir Hugh Lane: His Life and
Legacy* (1973) 90:

> this site . . . was near the centre of the city, would take the place of the ugly
> metal foot-bridge, and as the Corporation intended sooner or later to pull this
> down and build a more worthy one the cost would not be for the Gallery alone,
> it would still act as a foot-bridge. The Gallery would be detached, and especially
> safe from fire. But there is no doubt it was the beauty of the design that awoke
> and kindled enthusiasm.

This was the third public controversy which stirred Yeats's imagination, the
first being that over Parnell, the second the dispute over Synge's *The Playboy of
the Western World*.

In the thirty years or so during which I have been reading Irish newspapers,
three public controversies have stirred my imagination. The first was the
Parnell controversy [see note on 'To a Shade' (*PNE* 118)]. There were reasons
to justify a man's joining either party, but there were not to justify, on one side
or on the other, lying accusations forgetful of past service, a frenzy of
detraction. And another was the dispute over *The Playboy* [see note on 'On
Those that hated "The Playboy of the Western World"', 1907' (*PNE* 120)].
There may have been reasons for opposing as for supporting that violent,
laughing thing, though I can see the one side only, but there cannot have been
any for the lies, for the unscrupulous rhetoric spread against it in Ireland, and
from Ireland to America. The third prepared for the Corporation's refusal of a
building for Sir Hugh Lane's [Lane (1875-1915), founder of the Dublin
Municipal Gallery, offered a gift of mainly impressionist paintings but withdrew

the offer when the Dublin Corporation rejected a design for a gallery over the River Liffey. Lane had made it a condition of his offer that a permanent building should be erected to house the paintings. He bequeathed the paintings to the National Gallery, London; then added an unwitnessed codicil to his will leaving the pictures to Dublin. He was drowned when the *Lusitania* was sunk off Ireland by a German submarine in 1915. The English government did not regard the codicil as valid and retained the pictures. The controversy has only recently been settled between the English and Irish Governments with an agreement to share the pictures] famous collection of pictures.

One could respect the argument that Dublin, with much poverty and many slums, could not afford the £22,000 the building was to cost the city, but not the minds that used it. One frenzied man compared the pictures to Troy horse which 'destroyed a city,' and innumerable correspondents described Sir Hugh Lane and those who had subscribed many thousands to give Dublin paintings by Corot, Manet, Monet, Degas, and Renoir, as 'self-seekers,' 'self-advertisers,' 'picture-dealers,' 'log-rolling cranks and faddists,' and one clerical paper told 'picture-dealer Lane' to take himself and his pictures out of that. A member of the Corporation said there were Irish artists who could paint as good if they had a mind to, and another described a half-hour in the temporary gallery in Harcourt Street as the most dismal of his life. Someone else asked instead of these eccentric pictures to be given pictures 'like those beautiful productions displayed in the windows of our city picture shops.' Another thought that we would all be more patriotic if we devoted our energy to fighting the insurance act. Another would not hang them in his kitchen while yet another described the vogue of French impressionist painting as having gone to such a length among 'log-rolling enthusiasts' that they even admired 'works that were rejected from the Salon forty years ago by the finest critics in the world.'

The first serious opposition began in the *Irish Catholic*, the chief Dublin clerical paper, and Mr William Murphy the organiser of the recent lock-out and Mr Healy's financial supporter in his attack upon Parnell, a man of great influence, brought to its support a few days later his newspapers *The Evening Herald* and *The Irish Independent*, the most popular of Irish daily papers. He replied to my poem 'To a Wealthy Man' (I was thinking of a very different wealthy man) from what he described as 'Paudeen's point of view,' and 'Paudeen's point of view' it was. The enthusiasm for 'Sir Hugh Lane's Corots' – one paper spelled the name repeatedly 'Crot' – being but 'an exotic fashion,' waited 'some satirist like Gilbert' who 'killed the aesthetic craze,' and as for the rest 'there were no greater humbugs in the world than art critics and so-called experts'. As the first avowed reason for opposition, the necessities of the poor got but a few lines, not so many certainly as the objection of various persons to supply Sir Hugh Lane with 'a monument at the city's expense,' and as the gallery was supported by Mr James Larkin, the chief labour leader, and important slum workers, I assume that the purpose of the opposition was not exclusively charitable.

These controversies, political, literary, and artistic, have showed that neither religion nor politics can of itself create minds with enough receptivity to become wise, or just and generous enough to make a nation. Other cities have been as stupid – Samuel Butler [(1835–1902)] laughs at shocked Montreal for hiding the Discobolus [a plaster cast of a statue of a discus thrower by the Greek sculptor Myron (*fl. c.*480–445 BC) primarily a worker in bronze] in a lumber-room ['A Psalm of Montreal', *The Spectator*, 18 May 1878] – but Dublin is

106

the capital of a nation, and an ancient race has nowhere else to look for an education. Goethe [(1749-1832)] in *Wilhelm Meister* describes a saintly and naturally gracious woman, who, getting into a quarrel over some trumpery detail of religious observance, grows – she and all her little religious community – angry and vindictive. [In Book VI of *Wilhelm Meister's Lehrjehre* (1795-96) which Yeats may have read in Thomas Carlyle's (1795-1881) translation of 1824.] In Ireland I am constantly reminded of that fable of the futility of all discipline that is not of the whole being. Religious Ireland – and the pious Protestants of my childhood were signal examples – thinks of divine things as a round of duties separated from life and not as an element that may be discovered in all circumstance and emotion, while political Ireland sees the good citizen but as a man who holds to certain opinions and not as a man of good will. Against all this we have but a few educated men and the remnants of an old traditional culture among the poor. Both were stronger forty years ago, before the rise of our new middle class which made its first public display during the nine years of the Parnellite split, showing how base at moments of excitement are minds without culture.   (*RPP*)

(*Note*. – I leave out two long paragraphs ['One could respect . . . not exclusively charitable', *VE* 819-20] which have been published in earlier editions of these poems. There is no need now to defend Sir Hugh Lane's pictures against Dublin newspapers. The trustees of the London National Gallery, through his leaving a codicil to his will unwitnessed, have claimed the pictures for London, and propose to build a wing to the Tate Gallery to contain them. Some that were hostile are now contrite, and doing what they can, or letting others do unhindered what they can, to persuade Parliament to such action as may restore the collection to Ireland. – Jan. 1917.) (*Responsibilities and Other Poems*)

1 *You*: the 'wealthy man' is probably Lord Ardilaun, though William Martin Murphy has been suggested by Saul (*PYP* 91). Yeats mentioned Lord Ardilaun in a letter written to Lane on 1 January 1913: 'I have tried to meet the argument in Lady Ardilaun's letter to somebody, her objection to giving because of Home Rule and Lloyd George, and still more to meet the general argument of people like Ardilaun that they should not give unless there is a public demand' (*L* 573). Yeats also commented in his Notes, apropos William Martin Murphy's reply to 'To a Wealthy Man', 'I was thinking of a very different wealthy man'.

See also 'Some New Letters from W. B. Yeats to Lady Gregory' *A Review of English Literature*, 4, 3, July 1963, where Yeats says he has a poem about Lane's gallery and Lord Ardilaun which 'is not tactless and does not name Lord Ardilaun'.

2, 3 *Paudeen's . . . Biddy's*: the crowd, the people; sometimes used contemptuously as of beggars. Paudeen is a diminutive of Padraig.

4 *some . . . evidence*: a reference presumably to some argument of Lord or Lady Ardilaun about the need for public demand for a gallery.

7 *the blind and ignorant town*: Yeats particularly resented the attacks made on Lane in the *Irish Independent*, William Martin Murphy's paper. Cf. Conor Cruise

O'Brien, 'Passion and Cunning: An Essay on the Politics of W. B. Yeats' (*IER* 232 ff.).

9 *Duke Ercole*: Duke Ercole de l'Este (1431-1505), son of Duke Niccolo III and Rizzarda di Saluzzo, was bred at the Neapolitan Court and became Duke of Ferrara. Though his reign was not peaceful his court was renowned for luxury and the brilliancy of its art and letters which the Duke supported generously and with discrimination. Yeats had first read Castiglione's *The Book of the Courtier* in Hoby's translation in 1903 or 1904 (there are many references to it in his 1909-10 Diary). This described the Duke's court in Ferrara, and Yeats visited Ferrara and Urbino when he went to Italy for the first time with Lady Gregory and her son in 1907.

12 *his Plautus*: the Duke's patronage of the theatre is described by Castiglione and Opdycke's translation of *The Courtier* (1902) mentions this: 'no less than five plays of Plautus being performed during the wedding of his son Alphonso in 1502'. Though Yeats owned a copy of Hoby's translation he seems to have used Opdycke's also, from the notes of which he probably gathered the information about these plays of the Roman comic dramatist Plautus (*c.* 254-184 BC).

120 14 *Guidobaldo*: Guidobaldo di Montefeltro, Duke of Urbino (1472-1508), son of Duke Federico de Montefeltro and Battista Sforza, an accomplished niece of the first Sforza Duke of Milan.

15 *That grammar school*: he was highly praised in *The Courtier*. Talents, learning, grave deportment and fluency of speech were required of his courtiers, and the culture and refined manners of his court were renowned. Yeats sees it as a place where youth 'for certain brief years imposed upon drowsy learning the discipline of its joy' (*A* 545).

17 *Urbino's windy hill*: Urbino is superbly situated on the slopes of the Apennines. Castiglione described the palace as

> regarded by many as the most beautiful to be found in all Italy; and he so well furnished it with everything suitable that it seemed not a palace but a city in the form of a palace; and not merely with what is ordinarily used, – such as silver vases, hangings of richest cloth-of-gold and silk, and other similar things, – but for ornament he added countless antique statues in marble and bronze, pictures most choice, and musical instruments of every sort, nor would he admit anything there that was not very rare and excellent. Then at very great cost he collected a goodly number of most excellent and rare books in Greek, Latin and Hebrew, all of which he adorned with gold and silver, esteeming this to be the chiefest excellence of his great palace. (Castiglione, *The Courtier*, trans. L. E. Opdycke (1902))

Yeats walked to Urbino from San Sepolcro and described its situation vividly in 'A Tower on the Apennines' (*E & I* 290).

19 *the shepherds' will*: in *BS* Yeats remembered a friend (Lady Gregory)

108

reading out Castiglione's commendations of Urbino and remembered 'a cry of Bembo's made years after, ''Would that I were a shepherd that I might look down daily upon Urbino'' ' (*A* 545). The quotation is also made in *AV*, where men of Phase Three are described as images seen by lyric poets (particularly those of the seventeenth phase, to which Yeats belonged). See *AV* (B) 108-9.

20   *Cosimo*: Cosimo de Medici, exiled in 1433 to Venice, returned to Florence after a year.

23   *Michelozzo*: Michelozzo de Bartolomeo (1396-1472), an architect and pupil of Brunelleschi. He accompanied Cosimo to Venice and designed many public and private buildings there, returning in triumph with Cosimo in 1434. Yeats probably acquired knowledge of him and his work when in Venice in 1907. He designed, at Cosimo's order and expense, the Library of the Monastery of S. Giorgio Maggiore and the Library of St Mark's, Florence. Lines 21-4 originally ran:

> Unknowing their predestined man,
> So much more time and thought had he
> For Michelozzo's latest plan
> Of the San Marco library.

T. R. Henn, 'The Green Helmet' and 'Responsibilities' (*HG* 41), remarks Cosimo de Medici is Hugh Lane, Michelozzo is Lutyens, the San Marco Library is the projected gallery over the Liffey.

28   *dugs*: the word is a mark of Yeats's new style, and received a veiled reproof in a letter from 'Val d'Arno':

> Mr Yeats draws all his mental nourishment from the dry breasts of Greece, whose views of men and things please him for the simple reason that they equate with the prejudices of the class to which Mr Yeats presumably belongs. (*Irish Times*, 13 Jan. 1913)

32   *the sun's eye*: a reference to the eagle being able to stare unblinkingly at the sun. Cf. line 36 'eagle's nest', and note on 'Upon a House shaken by the Land Agitation' (*PNE* 105). The eagle symbolises nobility, activity, greatness, objectivity.

SEPTEMBER 1913   115

This poem was dated 7 September 1913 when it first appeared in the *Irish Times*   120
(8 Sept. 1913) entitled 'Romance in Ireland/(On reading much of the correspondence against the Art Gallery)'. In *Nine Poems* (1914) it was entitled 'Romantic Ireland (September 1913)' and the present title was adopted in *RPP*.

1   *you*: the people of Ireland, but particularly the new Catholic middle class which Yeats disliked

2 *greasy till*: the image came from a speech Yeats made in July 1913. He wrote to Lady Gregory that he had spoken with Lane as well as possible subscribers [to the Gallery] in his mind: 'I described Ireland, if the present intellectual movement failed, as a little greasy huxtering nation groping for halfpence in a greasy till but did not add except in thought, ''by the light of a holy candle'' ' (Lady Gregory, *Hugh Lane*, 137).

121 8 *O'Leary*: John O'Leary (1830–1907) when a medical student in Trinity College, Dublin, was influenced by the Young Ireland Movement, and became one of the Triumvirate in the Fenian movement which succeeded it. He was arrested in 1865, condemned to twenty years' penal servitude, but set free after serving nine years of his sentence, on condition that he did not return to Ireland for fifteen years. He spent his exile in Paris and returned to Dublin in 1885. He had a large collection of Irish books and greatly influenced Yeats. (He was also friendly with Yeats's father, John Butler Yeats.) It was through O'Leary's influence that Yeats moved from his father's Home Rule views to a more strongly nationalist point of view. O'Leary, 'the handsomest old man' Yeats had ever seen, was a romantic figure:

> Sometimes he would say things that would have sounded well in some heroic Elizabethan play. It became my delight to rouse him to these outbursts, for I was the poet in the presence of his theme. Once when I was defending an Irish politician who had made a great outcry because he was treated as a common felon, by showing that he did it for the cause's sake, he said, 'There are things that a man must not do to save a nation.' He would speak a sentence like that in ignorance of its passionate value, and would forget it the moment after. (*A* 95–6)

He despised inferior writing and told Yeats, 'Neither Ireland nor England knows the good from the bad in any art, but Ireland unlike England does not hate the good when it is pointed out to her' (*A* 101). From debates in a Young Ireland Society, from O'Leary's conversation and the Irish books he lent Yeats came 'all I have set my hand to since' (*A* 101). O'Leary belonged to Yeats's romantic conception of Irish nationality: he – like his disciple the barrister J. F. Taylor – seemed to Yeats to be the last 'to speak an understanding of life and Nationality, built up by the generation of Grattan, which read Homer and Virgil, and by the generation of Davis, which had been pierced through by the idealism of Mazzini, and of the European revolutionists of the mid-century' (*E & I* 246).

16 *in the grave*: Yeats could not bring himself to go to O'Leary's funeral, for he shrank from seeing about his grave 'so many whose Nationalism was different from anything he had taught or that I could share' (*E & I* 246).

17 *the wild geese*: Irishmen who served abroad in the armies of France, Spain, and Austria, largely as a result of the Penal Laws passed after 1691. Sarsfield and 11,000 men left for the French service, out of loyalty to James II, after the Treaty of Limerick was signed in 1691; the Irish Brigade fought with the French until the Revolution. In all, it is said that 120,000 'Wild Geese' left Ireland between 1690 and 1730. Cf. Curtis (*HI* 292).

20 *Edward Fitzgerald*: Lord Edward Fitzgerald (1763–98), a romantic figure who served in America, became M.P. for Athy and Kildare, and joined the United Irishmen in 1796. He was president of the military committee and died of wounds received while he was being arrested.

21 *Emmet*: Robert Emmet (1778–1803), who was educated at Trinity College Dublin, led an abortive revolt in 1803, was tried for high treason and hanged publicly in Dublin.

Wolfe Tone: Theobald Wolfe Tone (1763–98), educated at Trinity College Dublin, founded the United Irish Club, was appointed chef-de-brigade in France, and led a French force to Ireland. He was captured in Lough Swilly and condemned to death by a court martial. He committed suicide in prison.

22 *delirium*: this probably derives from Swinburne's contemptuous comment, in his *William Blake* (1906), vi, on Yeats's Introduction to Blake where he had tried to prove Blake a Celt:

> Some Hibernian commentator on Blake, if I rightly remember a fact so insignificant, has somewhere said something to some such effect that I, when writing about some fitfully audacious and fancifully delirious deliverance of the poet he claimed as a countryman, and trying to read into it some coherent and imaginative significance, was innocent of any knowledge of Blake's meaning. It is possible, if the spiritual fact of his Hibernian heredity has been or can be established, that I was: for the excellent reason that, being a Celt, he now and then too probably had none worth the labour of deciphering – or at least worth the serious attention of any student belonging to a race in which reason and imagination are the possible preferable substitutes for fever and fancy.

Yeats's father drew his attention to this passage (*LTHS* 92–3): 'It is a reference to you of a particularly insolent and contemptuous sort. . . . His criticism that the Celtic movement puts fever and fancy in the place of reason and imagination is I am afraid a true criticism – as true as to my mind it is obvious,' and Yeats probably remembered his own old love for 'fitfully audacious and fancifully delirious heroes' when he wrote in his notes to *Responsibilities*: 'Neither religion or politics can of itself create minds with enough receptivity to become wise, or just and generous enough to make a nation. Our new middle class . . . showed . . . how base at moments of excitement are minds without culture.'

He now contrasts the delirium of his heroes with the uncultured excitement of his own times, using Swinburne's word to exalt the old and belittle the new Ireland.

28 *You'd cry*: modern middle-class Ireland could not understand the love these men had for Ireland. Yeats himself is bound to the wild geese and the martyr heroes by his maddened love for Maud Gonne which was so linked with his love of Ireland. A passage in *BS* illustrates this:

> During our first long wait all kinds of pictures had passed before me in reverie and now my imagination renews its excitement. I had thought how we

Irish had served famous men and famous families, and had been, so long as our nation had intellect enough to shape anything of itself, good lovers of women, but had never served any abstract cause, except the one, and that we personified by a woman, and I wondered if the service of woman could be so different from that of a Court. I had thought how, before the emigration of our poor began, our gentlemen had gone all over Europe, offering their swords at every Court, and that many had stood, just as I, but with an anxiety I could but imagine, for their future hung upon a frown or a smile. I had run through old family fables and histories, to find if any man of my blood had so stood, and had thought that there were men living, meant by nature for that vicissitude, who had served a woman through folly, because they had found no Court to serve.   (*A* 544–5)

116 TO A FRIEND WHOSE WORK HAS COME TO NOTHING

122 This poem was dated 16 September [1913] in the Maud Gonne MS. book, and first appeared in *PWD*.

2 *Be secret*: Yeats's note, dated 1922 in *Later Poems* (1922), makes it clear that the poem was written to Lady Gregory, though she originally thought it written to Sir Hugh Lane. See her inclusion of the poem in *Hugh Lane's Life and Achievement* (1921) 138; and her subsequent description of the poem as 'to me, myself "A Friend . . . Nothing"' in her *Sir Hugh Lane. His Life and Legacy* (1973) 108.

5–6 *one Who*: William Martin Murphy. The poem probably relates to the final decision of the Dublin Corporation about the Lane pictures. Yeats wrote to Lady Gregory on the envelope of a letter posted in London on 1 July 1913: 'Can you send me I T [*Irish Times*] with final decision of Corporation? It may move me to another poem.'

117 PAUDEEN

122 The MS. of this poem, which was written at The Prelude, Coleman's Hatch, is dated 16 September 1913. It first appeared in *PWD*.

1 *the fumbling wits, the obscure spite*: this may refer to William Martin Murphy's attack on Yeats's first poem of the series on the Lane controversy, 'To a Wealthy Man . . .' (*PNE* 114). Murphy replied to Yeats's reference to 'Paudeen's pence' in that poem:

> I may here remark that, generally speaking, benefactors have to depend upon posterity for the erection of public monuments to their memory . . . . If 'Paudeen's Pennies', so contemptuously poetised a few days ago in the press by Mr W. B. Yeats, are to be abstracted from Paudeen's pockets, at least give him an opportunity of saying whether he approves of the process or not. . . . Speaking for myself I admire good pictures and I think I can appreciate them

but as a choice between the two, I would rather see in the city of Dublin one block of sanitary houses at low rents replacing a reeking slum than all the pictures Corot and Degas ever painted. (*Irish Independent*, 17 January 1913)

See note on 'To a Wealthy Man . . . Pictures' (*PNE* 114).

2 *our old Paudeen*: see Yeats's note, included in headnote to 'To a Wealthy Man . . .' (*PNE* 114) where he alludes to Murphy replying to his poem from 'Paudeen's point of view'.

6 *God's eye*: a passage in 'The Stirring of the Bones' may expand the thought. Yeats experienced an emotion which seemed to him what the devout Christian must feel when he surrenders his will to God. He woke next day to hear a voice saying, 'The love of God is infinite for every human soul because every human soul is unique; no other can satisfy the same need in God'. (*A* 378-9)

TO A SHADE   118

The MS. of this poem is dated 29 September [1913]; it was written at Coole and   *123*
first appeared in *PWD*. The subject is the blind bitterness with which true
benefactors of Ireland have been greeted.

1 *thin Shade*: the poem is addressed to Charles Stewart Parnell (1846–91), the Irish Parliamentary leader repudiated by Gladstone, the Irish Hierarchy, and the Irish Party, because of his affair with Mrs Kathleen O'Shea (1845-1921). Yeats's view of the deposition of Parnell is given in 'Modern Ireland', *Massachusetts Review* (Winter 1964), 257-9.

2 *monument*: the Parnell monument is situated at the northern end of O'Connell Street, Dublin.

7 *gaunt houses*: of Dublin

9 *A man*: Sir Hugh Lane, whose treatment by his fellow countrymen is compared to that of Parnell. See notes on 'To a Wealthy Man . . .' (*PNE* 114).

11 *what*: Lane's proffered gift of the French paintings

17 *Your enemy, an old foul mouth*: William Martin Murphy (1844-1919) [see notes on 'To a Wealthy Man . . .' (*PNE* 114), 'September 1913' (*PNE* 115), 'To a Friend whose Work has come to Nothing' and 'Paudeen' (*PNE* 117)], proprietor of the *Irish Independent* and the evening paper, the *Evening Herald.* Murphy had opposed the Lane benefaction; but he had also opposed Parnell, and supported Tim Healy (1855-1931), who led the attack on Parnell. He organised the recent lock-out which Yeats regarded as inhumane as well as an unprincipled attempt to stir up religious passion. (See Conor Cruise O'Brien,

'Politics and Cunning: An Essay on the Politics of W. B. Yeats' (*IER* 230), who quotes Yeats's letter published in *Irish Worker* (1 Nov. 1913.) Yeats's note links Murphy and Healy:

> The first serious opposition [to the Lane gallery] began in the *Irish Catholic*, the chief Dublin clerical paper, and Mr William Murphy the organiser of the recent lock-out and Mr Healy's financial supporter in his attack upon Parnell, a man of great influence, brought to its support a few days later his newspapers *The Evening Herald* and *The Irish Independent*, the most popular of Irish daily papers. He replied to my poem 'To a Wealthy Man' (I was thinking of a very different wealthy man) from what he described as 'Paudeen's point of view', and 'Paudeen's point of view' it was.   (*RPP*)

Yeats's poem appeared in *The Irish Times*, 11 January 1913, Murphy's reply on 18 January: in this he suggested that if Paudeen's pence were to be extracted from his pocket he might be given an opportunity of saying whether he approved of the process or not.

18   *The pack*: this refers to the influence Murphy's two newspapers possessed, and was probably inspired by a quotation from Goethe which 'ran through the papers [during the quarrel over Parnell's grave], describing our Irish jealousy: "The Irish seem to me like a pack of hounds, always dragging down some noble stag".' (Eckermann, *Conversations with Goethe*, 7 April 1829 (quoted by Yeats in *A* 316).) But Corinna Salvadori, *Yeats and Castiglione* 65, suggests that the image may come from Ugolino's dream in Dante, *La Divina Commedia*, Inferno, Canto XXXIII, 28–36.

19   *Glasnevin coverlet*: Parnell was buried in Glasnevin (*Irish* Glas-Naeidhen, Naeidhe's little stream) cemetery, situated in north Dublin, on 11 October 1891. Yeats did not attend the funeral but wrote a poem 'Mourn, and then Onward' on the occasion, which was published in *UI* (10 Oct. 1891).

119   WHEN HELEN LIVED

124   This poem was written between 20 and 29 September 1913 and first appeared in *P(Ch)* (May 1914).

8   *Those topless towers*: cf. Marlowe, *The Tragical History of Dr Faustus*, V, I, 94–95:

> Was this the face that launched a thousand ships,
> And burnt the topless towers of Ilium?

12   *A word and a jest*: in 'The Death of Synge' Yeats recorded that he had dreamed this thought on 6 July 1909: 'Why should we complain if men ill-treat our Muses, when all that they gave to Helen while she still lived was a song and a jest?' (*A* 521). Yeats's poetry and his work for the literary revival were theoretically for Maud Gonne's sake. The Helen–Maud Gonne symbolism is involved in the poem. See note on 'The Rose of the World' (*PNE* 20).

ON THOSE THAT HATED 'THE PLAYBOY OF THE WESTERN WORLD', 1907   **120**

This poem is written in Yeats's Diary with the date 5 April 1909. It was first   *124*
published in *IR* (Dec. 1911) entitled 'On those who Dislike The Playboy'.

Title '*The Playboy . . .*': Yeats had described the troubles in 'The Controversy
over The Playboy of the Western World':

> On the second performance of *The Playboy of the Western World*, about
> forty men who sat in the middle of the pit succeeded in making the play entirely
> inaudible. Some of them brought tin trumpets, and the noise began
> immediately upon the rise of the curtain. For days articles in the Press called for
> the withdrawal of the play, but we played for the seven nights we had
> announced; and before the week's end opinion had turned in our favour. There
> were, however, nightly disturbances and a good deal of rioting in the
> surrounding streets. On the last night of the play there were, I believe, five
> hundred police keeping order in the theatre and in its neighbourhood.   (*E*
> 226)

2   *Eunuchs*: Yeats wrote to Lady Gregory on 8 March 1909 telling her he had
written a number of notes, in one of which he had compared Griffith and his like
to the Eunuchs in Charles Ricketts's picture watching Don Juan riding through
Hell. This note was shortly made into the poem. Arthur Griffith (1872–1922)
founded the *United Irishman* after returning to Ireland from Africa in 1899; he
edited this paper and its successor (in 1906) *Sinn Fein*. He was arrested in 1916,
released in 1917, was Vice-President of Dail Eireann in 1918, and negotiated the
treaty of 1921. He became President of the Dail in 1922 and died that year.

Griffith had attacked Synge's plays. He held that literature should be
subordinate to politics (see *L* 422) but Yeats regarded the journalists and political
leaders as suffering from a cultivation of hatred which made them regard creative
power with the jealousy of the Eunuch (cf. *A* 486). The attack on Synge seemed
to him an attack on genius. In his Diary he wrote of the warping of repressed
desire, he regarded the sterility of Irish writing and thought as due to sexual
abstinence. An entry for 18 May 1910 reads:

> When any part of human life has been left unexperienced there is a hunger
> for the experience in large numbers of men and if the expression is prevented
> artificially the hunger becomes morbid and [then] if the educated do not beware
> is born the ignorant will.

See also the essay 'J. M. Synge and the Ireland of his Time' (*E & I*, 311), where
Yeats thought that the young men who had wished 'to silence what they
considered a slander upon Ireland's womanhood' had been slowly prepared to
adopt this attitude by patriotic but ignoble journalism ever since Synge's *The
Shadow of the Glen* had been performed. In a letter to Lady Gregory of 8 March
1908 he recorded writing 'culture is the sanctity of the intellect' and went on to
explain that he was 'thinking of men like Griffith and how they can renounce
external things without it but not envy, revenge, jealousy and so on' (*L* 525).

Charles Ricketts (1866–1931), whose painting was in Yeats's mind as he
wrote the poem, was a close friend, and was also a stage and book designer, a

115

sculptor and critic. He was co-editor of *The Dial* (1889–97). See Yeats's comment on his work in *A* 550. He met Ricketts and Charles Shannon (see *A* 169) frequently. See also *L* for several comments on both artists.

4   *Don Juan*: the legendary Spanish libertine, reputedly Don Juan Tenorio of Seville. The statue of the father of the girl he has attempted to ravish, murdered by Juan, comes to a banquet and delivers Juan to devils.

121   THE THREE BEGGARS

124   This poem first appeared in *Harper's Weekly* (15 Nov. 1913).

5   *lebeen-lone*: according to Henn (*LT* 92) using Dinneen's *Irish-English Dictionary*, probably *libín leamham*, a small fish, a minnow. *libín* is a minnow, *lón* food. Probably minnow's food is intended.

6   *crane*: heron. The symbolic significance of the bird is discussed by Henn (*HG* 45).

Gort: a market town in County Galway (*Irish* Innse Guaire, the island field of Guaire. See *McG* 50); the entrance to Coole Park is two miles to the north of it.

8   *King Guaire*: Guaire Aidne (*d.* 663) a king of Connacht, known for his hospitality and generosity; he appears in Yeats's play *The King's Threshold* (*CPl* 105)

122   THE THREE HERMITS

127   This poem was written at Stone Cottage, Sussex, on 5 March 1913 and first appeared in *The Smart Set* (Sept. 1913). Its tone may have resulted from Ezra Pound's influence. He was acting as secretary to Yeats at the time and was urging him to stiffen his style and become harsher in expression. F. F. Farag (*YCE* 43) points out that the poet is presenting different points of view on the question of rebirth. The theory that man cannot reincarnate as animal after reaching the human stage was, he points out, hotly debated in the Theosophical Society. He cites H. P. Blavatsky, *Isis Unveiled*, I, 179 and A. P. Sinnett, *Esoteric Buddhism*, 205–6. See lines 22–8 of the poem.

123   BEGGAR TO BEGGAR CRIED

128   The MS. of this poem is dated 5 March 1913, and it first appeared in *P(Ch)* (May 1914). Hone (*WBY* 301) has suggested its tone was probably caused by the breaking off of a love affair [with Mabel Dickinson] which ended in 1910. A

telegram was sent to Yeats when he was at Coole by the lady announcing she was pregnant. Yeats thought wrongly that an attempt was being made 'by an unmarried woman past her first youth' to force him into marriage, but this idea like the news in the telegram was wrong. There was a somewhat sardonic reaction on Yeats's part to Lady Gregory's treatment of the situation; she thought Yeats should marry lest some similar upset should disturb his peace in the future. See notes on 'The Dolls' (*PNE* 140) and 'Presences' (*PNE* 169).

4   *make my soul*: a common Irish expression meaning to prepare for death. Yeats used the phrase in 'The Tower', line 181 (*PNE* 205) 'Now shall I make my soul.'

RUNNING TO PARADISE   **124**

This poem was written at Coole on 20 September 1913 and first appeared in   *129*
P(Ch) (May 1914).

1-2   *As I came ... Gap ... cap*: Sheila O'Sullivan, who suggests the poem continues the theme of 'The Happy Townland' (*CP* 94), thinks (*YUIT* 276) the opening two lines were inspired by a popular riddle:

> As I was going through Slippery Gap
> I met a little man with a red cap.

Windy Gap: possibly the one in Co. Sligo opposite Carraroe Church (*McG* 90) or the valley (*Irish* Gleann-na-Gae; *English* Windy Gap) among the hills south of Galway Bay. (See Yeats, *The Speckled Bird: with Variant Versions*, ed. William H. O'Donnell (1977) p. 41.) There are very many Windy Gaps in Ireland. Cf. *M* 243.

3   *running to Paradise*: Sheila O'Sullivan suggests (*YUIT* 277) that the phrase may come from Lady Gregory's *A Book of Saints and Wonders* (1906) which gives a version of Whitley Stokes's translation of a tale about Saint Brigit in *The Book of Leinster*. In this the saint is with her sheep in the Curragh in Co. Kildare and sees Nindid the scholar running past her:

> 'What makes thee unsedate, O son of reading?' saith Brigit, 'and what seekst thou in that wise?'
> 'O Nun', saith the scholar, 'I am going to Heaven.'

(*Anecdota Oxoniensis, Lives of the Saints from the Book of Lismore*, ed. Whitley Stokes (1890) 194.)

7   *And there the king ... beggar*: Sheila O'Sullivan suggests (*YUIT* 277) that this refrain comes from Lady Gregory's translation (in *The Kiltartan Poetry Book* (1918) 57-8) of Douglas Hyde's poem 'He meditates on the Life of a Rich Man':

> A golden cradle under you ... cattle, means herds and flocks ... at the end

117

of your days death . . . What one better after to-night than Ned the beggar or Seaghan the fool?

9   *skelping*: beating

19   *a bare heel*: as a young man in London, Yeats inked his heels so the holes in his socks would not be noticeable.

20   *old sock full*: of money

125   THE HOUR BEFORE DAWN

130   The MS. of this poem is dated 19 October 1913. It was written at Coole, and first appeared in *RPP*. T. R. Henn (*HG* 47), thinks the poem may have arisen out of a Jack Yeats illustration of a Cuala Press Broadside, 2 July 1913, entitled 'Two Tinkers'. He also suggests two poems by Yen Hui (in the British Museum).

4   *Cruachan*: Yeats commented that this is pronounced as if spelt 'Crockan' in modern Gaelic. It was in Co. Roscommon and was the capital of Connacht.

8   *Maeve . . . Maines*: Queen of Connaught. The nine Maines were her sons by Ailill. See line 36. Traditionally there were seven or eight of them. See John Rhys, *LCH* 366-70.

25   *Hell Mouth*: the Cave of Cruachan, known as the Hell gate of Ireland. Cf. *PYP* 97. Line 120 read in the first version 'From the Hell Mouth at Cruachan'.

131   50   *Goban's mountain-top*: see note on 'The Grey Rock' (*PNE* 113). In one version line 54 read, ' ''That sacred Goban brewed'', he cried'.

58   *Midsummer Day*: 24 June, the feast of Saint John the Baptist

132   82-93   Louis MacNiece, *The Poetry of W. B. Yeats*, 113, thought these lines echoed Synge's tramp in *The Shadow of the Glen*:

> We'll be going now, I'm telling you, and the time you'll be feeling the cold, and the frost, and the great rain and the sun again, and the south wind blowing in the glens, you'll not be sitting up in a wet ditch, the way you're after sitting in this place making yourself old with looking on each day, and it passing you by. You'll be saying one time, 'It's a good evening, by the grace of God,' and another time 'It's a wild night, God help us; but it'll pass surely.'

86   *a good Easter wind*: The date of the celebration of Easter varies between 22 March and 25 April. March winds are notoriously cold in Ireland.

133   100   *Michael's trumpet*: on the day of Judgement. Cf. line 41, 'The Happy Townland' (*PNE* 90).

A SONG FROM 'THE PLAYER QUEEN' 126

Yeats spent many years working on this play. This song first appeared in *P* (Ch) 134
(May 1914). *The Player Queen*, first produced in 1919, was published in 1922.
In the play Decima introduces the song, which her husband Septimus has made,
as follows:

> It is the song of the mad singing daughter of a harlot. The only song she had.
> Her father was a drunken sailor waiting for the full tide, and yet she thought
> her mother had foretold that she would marry a prince and become a great
> queen.

8 *gold and silver*: see note on 'The Man who dreamed of Faeryland' (*PNE* 33).

THE REALISTS 127

This poem first appeared in *P(Ch)* (Dec. 1912). 135

3 The MS. had a half-scratched-out sentence which ran 'A poet known in
France used to sing to women to wive . . .' which suggests a possible French
source. Dragons may be derived from memories of paintings of the Perseus-
Andromeda or St George legends; but a possible source may be the legend
connected with Innisfree. Russell K. Alspach quotes William Gregory Wood-
Martin, *History of Sligo* (1882) for the account (which Yeats knew) of the dragon
which guarded the fruit of a tree on the island. The daughter of the chief of the
island asked her lover, named 'Free', to get her some. He defeated the dragon, ate
the fruit and died of its virtue. She ate it and died across his body. See also *A* 71-2,
quoted in notes on 'The Lake Isle of Innisfree' (*PNE* 24), and Alspach, *Yeats and
Innisfree* (1965), 71.

THE WITCH 128

The first version of this poem is dated 24 May 1912 in Yeats's Diary. The poem 135
first appeared in *P(Ch)* (May 1914).

1 *rich*: Yeats's financial position had begun to improve after 1910 because of
his pension (see note on line 128 'The Grey Rock' (*PNE* 113)) and funds from
his American lecturing tours. George Moore gave a malicious account of the
apparent signs of this in *Vale*:

> We have sacrificed our lives for Art; but you, what have you done? What
> sacrifices have you made? he asked, and everybody began to search his memory
> for the sacrifices that Yeats had made, asking himself in what prison Yeats had
> languished, what rags he had worn, what broken victuals he had eaten. As far
> as anybody could remember, he had always lived very comfortably, sitting
> down invariably to regular meals, and the old green cloak that was in keeping

with his profession of romantic poet he had exchanged for the magnificent fur
coat which distracted our attention from what he was saying, so opulently did it
cover the back of the chair out of which he had risen. . . . The poet advanced a
step or two nearer to the edge of the platform, and stamping his foot he asked
again what the middle classes had done for Art, and in a towering rage (the
phrase is no mere figure of speech for he raised himself up to tremendous
height) he called upon the ladies and gentlemen that had come to hear my
lecture to put their hands in their pockets and give sovereigns to the stewards
who were waiting at the doors to receive them, or, better still, to write large
cheques. We were led to understand that by virtue of our subscriptions we
should cease to belong to the middle classes, and having held out this hope to us
he retired to his chair and fell back overcome into the middle of the great fur
coat, and remained silent until the end of the debate. (George Moore, *Hail &
Farewell, Vale* 162–3. Text from 1914 ed.)

3   *witch*: originally read 'bitch' in MS.

7   *one long sought*: possibly a reference to Maud Gonne. (Yeats's early
courtship was inhibited by his lack of money: 'What sort of wife would she make,
I thought, for a poor student.' He did not propose to her for some years after they
first met in 1889.) But the poem is a general comment of disillusionment with
success.

129   THE PEACOCK

135   This poem first appeared in *P(Ch)* (May 1914).

1   *riches*: cf. the scorn of wealth in 'The Grey Rock' (*PNE* 113) '. . . never
made a song/That you might have a heavier purse.'

3   *Three Rock*: probably the Three Rock Mountain which overlooks Dublin

130   THE MOUNTAIN TOMB

136   This poem was written at Maud Gonne's house, Les Mouettes, Colville, Calvados
in August 1912. It first appeared in *P(Ch)* (Dec. 1912). Yeats's essay 'The Body
of the Father Christian Rosencrux' provides an explanation (he was a member of
the Order of the Golden Dawn, an occult society which used Rosicrucian material
and had written two pamphlets dealing with its future in 1901):

The followers of the Father Christian Rosencrux [who reputedly founded in
1484 the Rosicrucian order, which is first mentioned in 1614], says the old
tradition, wrapped his imperishable body in noble raiment and laid it under the
house of their Order, in a tomb containing the symbols of all things in heaven
and earth, and in the waters under the earth, and set about him
inextinguishable magical lamps, which burnt on generation after generation,
until other students of the Order came upon the tomb by chance. . . .

Yeats used the symbolism of the tomb to describe his own times; the following passage may shed light on the sense of the poem's 'in vain, in vain . . .', for it shows the futility of housing a body which does not reveal wisdom:

> It seems to me that the imagination has had no very different history during the last two hundred years, but has been laid in a great tomb of criticism, and had set over it inextinguishable magical lamps of wisdom and romance, and has been altogether so nobly housed and apparelled that we have forgotten that its wizard lips are closed, or but opened for the complaining of some melancholy and ghostly voice. . . .   (*E & I* 196 ff.)

See also Karl Kisewetter, 'The Rosicrucians', *Theosophical Siftings*, III.

TO A CHILD DANCING IN THE WIND   131

This poem was written at Les Mouettes, Colville, Calvados, in December 1912. It   *136*
first appeared in *P (Ch)* (Dec. 1912).

2   *you*: Iseult Gonne (1895–1954), Maud Gonne's daughter by Lucien Millevoye. She later married the novelist Francis Stuart. For a description of her (probably in 1916 or 1917, when Yeats and she were reading the French religious poets together, see *L* 628–9) in Normandy, see *AV*:

> I remember a beautiful young girl singing at the edge of the sea in Normandy words and music of her own composition. She thought herself alone, stood barefooted between sea and sand; sang with lifted head of the civilisations that there had come and gone, ending every verse with the cry: 'O Lord, let something remain.'   (*AV* (B) 220)

7   *The fool's triumph*: perhaps William Martin Murphy's campaign against   *137*
Lane's pictures

8   *Love lost as soon as won*: perhaps a reference to Maud Gonne's marriage which lasted two years. More likely is his relationship with her in 1907–8; See notes on 'King and No King' (*PNE* 96) and 'His Memories' (*PNE* 232).

9   *the best labourer*: J. Unterecker (*RG* 126) suggests this may refer to Synge's death in 1909.

TWO YEARS LATER   132

This poem was written on 3 December 1912 or 1913 and first appeared in *P*   *137*
(*Ch*), (May 1914).

3   *you*: Iseult Gonne

9   *your mother*: Maud Gonne

133   A MEMORY OF YOUTH

137   The MS. is undated but this poem was probably written on 13 August 1912 and first appeared in *P(Ch)* (Dec. 1912).

138   5   *her praise*: the poem is written about Maud Gonne.

15   *silent as a stone*: the stone image which was associated with Maud Gonne occurs in 'Easter 1916': 'Too long a sacrifice / Can make a stone of the heart' (*PNE* 193). It symbolises love ending in coldness or else a quality of coldness incapable of comprehending the love Yeats professed. It also conveyed a sense of political ruthlessness:

> Hearts with one purpose alone
> Through summer and winter seem
> Enchanted to a stone.

Cf. also *E & I* 312-14.

134   FALLEN MAJESTY

138   This poem was written at Maud Gonne's house, Les Mouettes, Colville, Calvados; the MS. is dated 1912 and the poem first appeared in *P (Ch)* (Dec. 1912).

1   *crowds gathered*: Yeats's comments on Maud Gonne as a speaker are contained in 'The Trembling of the Veil':

> Her power over crowds was at its height, and some portion of the power came because she could still, even where pushing an abstract principle to what seemed to me an absurdity, keep her own mind free, and so when men and women did her bidding they did it not only because she was beautiful, but because that beauty suggested joy and freedom.   (*A* 364)

2   *even old men's eyes*: the line echoes the admiration the elders of Troy felt for Helen, cf. 'When Helen lived' (*CP* 124). But the 'even' has its particular point here. Maud Gonne's attitude in the 'nineties was that of the more violent Fenian movement from which she later retired, and as an incipient stirrer-up of violence she had the disapproval of the older nationalists who deplored the use of force in any attempt to seek independence for Ireland.

5   *lineaments*: a word Yeats found in Blake and found poetically effective

6   *what's gone*: Maud Gonne virtually retired from public life after her marriage in 1903, which lasted until 1905. The crowds are probably those Yeats remembered from his experience while President of the '98 Commemoration Association when he went 'hither and thither speaking at meetings in England and Scotland and occasionally at tumultuous Dublin conventions, and endured

some of the worst months of my life' (*A* 355); he travelled by rail with Maud Gonne on many occasions and they had stirring conversations about the possibility of uniting the various Irish organisations (*A* 362).

The poem is concerned with how the memory of great beauty lingers on. There may be a hint in line 2 of the Homeric Helen, who lived on through Homer's praise. There is another parallel in the case of Mary Hynes, the peasant girl admired by crowds in much the same way:

> . . . I can see at no great distance a green field where stood once the thatched cottage of a famous country beauty, the mistress of a small local landed proprietor. I have spoken to old men and women who remembered her, though all are dead now, and they spoke of her as the old men upon the wall of Troy spoke of Helen, nor did man and woman differ in their praise.
> . . . And there were men that told of the crowds that gathered to look at her upon a fair day, and of a man 'who got his death swimming a river', that he might look at her. It was a song written by the Gaelic poet Raftery that brought her such great fame, and the cottagers still sing it, though there are not so many to sing it as when I was young. (*A* 561)

The comparisons are clear. Mary, Helen, and Maud moved crowds by their beauty; they were admired by older people; and their beauty lives on – Helen had Homer, Mary Raftery and Maud Yeats, through whose words this came about.

FRIENDS   135

The MS. date of this poem is January 1911; it first appeared in *The Green*   139
Helmet and Other Poems (1912)

4   *One*: Mrs Olivia Shakespear (1867-1938), a cousin of Lionel Johnson, whom Yeats first met in London in 1894. They corresponded until her death in 1938 when he wrote 'For more than forty years she has been the centre of my life in London, and during all that time we have never had a quarrel, sadness sometimes, but never a difference.' In 1895 Yeats and she exchanged many letters when he was in Sligo and she sent him the manuscript of her work *Beauty's Hour* while he wrote to her on his ideas of the coincidence of opposites. See note on 'The Lover mourns for the Loss of Love' (*PNE* 51).

10   *And one*: Lady Gregory, whom Yeats first met in 1896 and whose house Coole Park he visited during succeeding summers. She got him to help her in collecting folklore and became his ally in the movement to create an Irish theatre. She also helped him to put his 'house in order' and created conditions in which he could work regularly:

> She asked me to return there the next year, and for years to come I was to spend my summers at her house. When I was in good health again, I found myself indolent, partly perhaps because I was affrighted by that impossible novel, and asked her to send me to my work every day at eleven, and at some other hour to my letters, rating me with idleness if need be, and I doubt if I should have done much with my life but for her firmness and her care. (*A* 377)

See also 'Coole Park, 1929' (*PNE* 253) and 'Coole Park and Ballylee, 1931' (*PNE* 254).

16   *labouring in ecstasy*: Maud Gonne thought that this line referred to the Italian tour which Yeats made in 1907 with Lady Gregory and her son Robert. The summer gatherings at Coole Park afforded an Irish parallel to Urbino's court.

17   *her that took*: Maud Gonne, whom Yeats first met in 1889 when he was twenty-three. She married in 1903.

25   *eagle look*: the detachment and objectivity Yeats associated with active rather than contemplative persons. Yeats was always struck by Maud Gonne's refusal to discuss herself: 'You know I hate talking of myself; I am not going to let you make me' (*SQ* 330).

136   THE COLD HEAVEN

140   This poem first appeared in *The Green Helmet and Other Poems* (1912). Maud Gonne asked Yeats its meaning and was told that it was an attempt to describe the feelings aroused in him by the cold detached sky in winter. He felt he was alone, responsible in his loneliness for all the past mistakes that were torturing his peace of mind. This was a momentary intensity of perception, made more poignant for him by the memory of his lost love. It has the air of a dream clinging to it and Yeats wrote in 'The Trembling of the Veil' of his belief that after death men live their lives backwards (*A* 378). Henn (*LT* 93) sees in this poem the effect of Yeats's reading of Grierson's edition of Donne.

6   *love crossed long ago*: his love for Maud Gonne

7   *out of all sense and reason*: Henn (*LT* 94) comments that 'out of all sense' is an Irish (and ambiguous) expression meaning both 'to an extent far beyond what common-sense could justify' and 'beyond the reach of sensation'.

10–12 *Confusion of the death-bed over*: it has been suggested by Henn that these ideas are derived from Berkeley, but it is likely Yeats had not read him at this period.

137   THAT THE NIGHT COME

140   This poem first appeared in *The Green Helmet and Other Poems* (1912).

1   *She*: this poem is written about Maud Gonne.

This poem was written at Coole Park in 1907 or 1908: it first appeared in *ER*   *141*
(Feb. 1909) entitled 'On a Recent Government Appointment in Ireland'.

1   *government*: Yeats was enraged with Lord Aberdeen and Mr Birrell because
they had not given Sir Hugh Lane the position of Curator of the National
Museum in Dublin, but had appointed Count Plunkett.

3   *the proud, wayward squirrel*: a squirrel was described more conventionally in
The Island of Statues, I, iii.

8   *the tame will . . . timid brain*: Lady Gregory described the way Yeats received
the news of the appointment:

> It was, in his mind, one of the worst of crimes, that neglect to use the best man,
> the man of genius, in place of the timid obedient official. That use of the best
> had been practised in the great days of the Renaissance. He had grown calmer
> before my arrival, [she had telegraphed the news] because when walking in the
> woods, the sight of a squirrel had given him a thought for some verses, the first
> he had ever written on any public event: [Lady Gregory had probably not read
> 'Mourn – and then Onward' which had appeared in the *United Irishman* in
> 1891, but not been reprinted]. . . . Hugh, having a certain reverence for
> writers, was pleased, though a little puzzled, by the lines, which do but put in
> form of fantasy what another poet has called 'the difference between men of
> office and men of genius, between computed and uncomputed rank.'   (*Hugh
> Lane's Life and Achievement* (1921) 85)

She goes on to describe how Yeats wrote out the poem on a blank leaf of one of his
books and wrote above it, 'On the Appointment of Count Plunkett to the
Curatorship of the Dublin Museum, by Mr T. W. Russell and Mr Birrell, Hugh
Lane being a candidate'. Yeats wrote a poem on Birrell in his Diary for 16
September 1909 calling it an attempt to put in rhyme a joke Robert Gregory had
made at dinner – 'it is too savage to be much good – I had described my old
conversation with Birrell.' The title originally read 'On a certain middle-aged
office holder' which became 'On a prosperous mimic of others' thought' and the
poem ran

> He thinks to set his world aright
> As his [he's?] no longer parasite
> Now that he's master of the trick
> That turns a flea into a tick.

Yeats decided it was 'not worth giving by itself, would seem mere party politics,
but might come in part of old note of conversation at Baily – names left out.' . . .
'Cabinet Minister who had been a lively chatterbox in his youth' would, he
thought, be enough of a description.

139 THE MAGI

141 This poem was written on 20 September 1913 and first appeared in *P (Ch)*, (May 1914). The poem is complementary to 'The Dolls' (*PNE* 140). After he had made the latter Yeats

> looked up one day into the blue of the sky, and suddenly imagined, as if lost in the blue of the sky, stiff figures in procession. I remembered that they were the habitual image suggested by blue sky, and looking for a second fable called them 'The Magi', complementary forms of those enraged dolls. *(RPP)*

2 *unsatisfied*: the Magi are unsatisfied by the birth of Christ because they represent Yeats's belief that the Christian revelation was not final, that history occurs in alternate movements, or gyres (cf. 'The Gyres' (*PNE* 321)). Christ is uncontrollable because he is not final, he has ushered another cycle which will be succeeded by another. Cf. 'Two Songs from a Play' (*PNE* 218) and this is probably one of the first poems to be linked with the ideas later expressed in *AV* (A) and *AV* (B), in which Christ is a being of Phase one:

> When the old *primary* becomes the new *antithetical*, the old realisation of an objective moral law is changed into a subconscious turbulent instinct. The world of rigid custom and law is broken up by 'the uncontrollable mystery upon the bestial floor'. *(AV* (B) 105)

Cf. line 8 of 'The Magi', and 'The Second Coming' (*PNE* 200), which used the symbol of the rough beast, the antithesis of Christ, bringing in a new era.

7 *Calvary's turbulence*: Yeats wrote that at or near the central point of a lunar month of classical civilisation – the first degree of Aries in the Great Wheel – comes the Christian *primary* dispensation, the child born in the Cavern. 'At or near the central point of our civilisation must come *antithetical* revelation, the turbulent child of the Altar' (*AV* (B) 204). Here Yeats was thinking of symbols discovered by Frobenius in Africa, the cavern being a symbol of nations moving westwards, the Altar (at the centre of radiating roads) being a symbol of nations moving eastwards. For Yeats's use of Christianity see his play *Calvary (Four Plays for Dancers* (1921)) and the 'Galilean turbulence' of 'Two Songs from a Play' (*PNE* 218). Christ was crucified on Calvary, outside Jerusalem.

140 THE DOLLS

141 This poem was written on 20 September 1913, and first appeared in *RPP*. The fable for the poem came into Yeats's head, when giving lectures in Dublin (*CP* 531), 'I had noticed once again how all thought among us is frozen into "something other than human life" '. It is related to 'Beggar to Beggar Cried' (*PNE* 123) and 'Presences' (*PNE* 169). See Yeats's note quoted on 'The Magi' (*PNE* 139).

142 3 *That*: the baby the woman has brought into the house. There is a parallel passage in Synge, where a woman is blamed for bringing a doll into the house:

Today a grotesque twopenny doll was lying on the floor near the old woman. He picked it up and examined it as if comparing it with her. Then he held it up: 'Is it you is after bringing that thing into the world,' he said, 'woman of the house?'   (J. M. Synge, *The Aran Islands*, 37)

A COAT   **141**

This poem was written in 1912 and first appeared in *P* (*Ch*), May 1914). It   *142* marks Yeats's renunciation of his earlier style.

1   *my song a coat*: two extra lines in a MS. revision of the poem –

> And gave it to my song
> And my song wore it –

make clear the ambiguity of the first line, which means 'I made a coat for my song'.

3   *old mythologies*: the Gaelic legends Yeats had read in O'Grady's translations, and those of O'Donovan, O'Curry, O'Looney, Mangan, etc. The MS. version of the poem had for this line 'Dragons and Gods and moons'.

5   *the fools*: probably a reference to some of AE's protégés, among them 'Seumas O'Sullivan'. Cf. 'To a Poet who would have me Praise certain Bad Poets, Imitators of His and Mine' (*PNE* 103).

CLOSING RHYME [WHILE I, FROM THAT REED-THROATED WHISPERER] or   **142**
[EPILOGUE]

This poem was written in 1914 and was entitled 'Notoriety (suggested by a   *143* recent magazine article)' when it first appeared in The *New Statesman* (7 Feb. 1914).

Title   magazine article: the poem was provoked by an article by George Moore in *ER*. Yeats told Lady Gregory in a letter of 1 February 1914, written on board a Cunard liner (probably the *Lusitania*, though he refers to the *Mauretania* in *L* 586) that he had sent

> that second Moore poem to *The New Statesman* because they happened to ask for something, and asked Ezra [Pound] to see to the proofs. Sturge Moore wanted me to send it to *The English Review* itself but that would have been to condone Harrison's share in the thing. People have constantly spoken to me of the article with indignation.

5-6   *the dull ass's hoof . . . Jonson's phrase*: the phrase is used in 'An Ode to Himself', *Underwoods* (1640), and in the Epilogue to *The Poetaster* (staged 1601, published 1602) both by Ben Jonson (1572-1637):

Leave me. There's something come into my thought,
That must and shall be sung high and aloof,
Safe from the wolf's black jaw, and the dull ass's hoof.

7   *Kyle-na-no*: (*Irish* Coill na gCno) the Wood of Nuts, one of the seven woods of Coole. See 'To a Squirrel at Kyle-na-no' (*PNE* 171) and 'Introductory Lines' (*The Shadowy Waters, PNE* 378).

8   *that ancient roof*: Coole Park

14   *a post*: in his 1930 Diary Yeats wrote, 'I shall publish when ready – to adapt a metaphor from Erasmus – to make myself a post for dogs and journalists to defile.'

The Wild Swans at Coole, first published by the Cuala Press in 1917, contained a play *At the Hawk's Well*. This play was omitted from the Macmillan edition of 1919, in the Preface to which Yeats remarked that the play might be part of a book of new plays suggested by the dance plays of Japan (*Four Plays for Dancers*, 1921). The edition of 1919 included seventeen more poems, some of which first appeared in this edition: they were 'An Irish Airman forsees his Death', 'Shepherd and Goatherd', 'The Phases of the Moon', 'The Saint and the Hunchback', 'Two Songs of a Fool', 'Another Song of a Fool', and 'The Double Vision of Michael Robartes'.

Most of the poems in this volume were written between 1915 and 1918. During this period Yeats emerged from the slough of *Responsibilities*, yet was unhappy – until, after his marriage in 1917, he became preoccupied with writing *AV*. The poems in this volume reflect Yeats's development when placed in chronological order, but he deliberately arranged them differently (seven of the poems written to Maud Gonne, for instance, were written in 1915, but are placed at *CP* 168-174 (*PNE* 162-8)), not wanting people, as he told his wife, to know too much about his personal concerns. The main intellectual interest of the volume lies in the poetry it contains, which deals tentatively with the system of *AV*. In part, Yeats regained his poetic energy (whose loss he had lamented in *The Green Helmet*) by using poetry as a vehicle for his strange thoughts and for his own personal life. After the 1916 Rising he proposed to Maud Gonne (her husband having been shot as one of the leaders), then to her daughter Iseult. He married Georgie Hyde-Lees, whom he had known for some years, in October 1917. He was deeply disturbed after his marriage through a feeling of responsibility for Iseult (the hidden meaning of 'Two Songs of a Fool' (*PNE* 186), though some of these turbulent moods were not disclosed until later; 'Owen Aherne and his Dancers' (*PNE* 226) was not published until 1928). The automatic writing of Mrs Yeats and the creation of *AV* banished his emotional disturbance. There was also the excitement of making Thoor Ballylee habitable. Yeats had been impressed by this tower earlier; it became increasingly important in his poetry after he bought it in 1917 and began to live in it. The difference is shown in 'Ego Dominus Tuus' (*PNE* 181), written in 1915, and 'In Memory of Major Robert Gregory' (*PNE* 144) written in 1918.

'Ego Dominus Tuus' is an important poem because it deals with the material of *AV*. Into his poetry came a new kind of strength based upon 'getting it all in order'. The system of *AV* lurks behind many of the later poems even when these are not acting as direct mouthpieces for his thought. The results of his early reading of Theosophy, magic, occultism, Kabbalism, astrology, Blake, Swedenborg, and Boehme all combined steadily with his increasing knowledge of history and philosophy. 'The Double Vision of Michael Robartes' (*PNE* 188), for instance, can be clarified by reference to *AV*: it foreshadows the poems to follow such as 'The Second Coming' (*PNE* 200) or 'Sailing to Byzantium' (*PNE* 204) and 'Byzantium' (*PNE* 260), which through their cryptic yet concise confidence convey the excitement of, and impart authority to, Yeats's views.

Besides the innovations in subject matter, the poems in *WSC* reveal Yeats developing his use of ancestors and friends as subjects for poetry: he is now more prepared to delineate details of personality just as he is to use personal names. His regret that his own youth, even if it has been replaced by wisdom, is vanishing is the substance of his personal cry – 'O Heart we are old'. This awareness of approaching age, sharpened by contemplation of Iseult's beauty, echoes through the poems even if momentarily lulled by the symbolism of the Solomon and Sheba poems recording the early years of his marriage. These seemed to combine age and wisdom for a time until, indeed, the old complaint broke out once more in *The Tower* about

> Decrepit age that has been tied to me
> As to a dog's tail.

DEDICATION

Edmund Dulac (1882–1953). See note below on 'On a Picture of a Black Centaur by Edmund Dulac' (*PNE* 221)

143   THE WILD SWANS AT COOLE

147   This poem was written in 1916 and first appeared in the *Little Review* (June 1917) where it is dated October 1916. In the first printed version lines 25–30 were placed between lines 12 and 13. Yeats was fifty-one when he wrote the poem, and realised how he had changed since, at the age of thirty-two, he first visited Lady Gregory at Coole Park. When first staying there he was grieving over Maud Gonne's refusal to return his love: as he recorded in *DP*:

> I must have spent the summer of 1897 at Coole. I was involved in a miserable love affair, that had but for one brief interruption absorbed my thoughts for years past, and would for some years yet. My devotion might as well have been offered to an image in a milliner's window, or to a statue in a museum, but romantic doctrine had reached its extreme development. Dowson was in love with a girl in an Italian restaurant, courted her for two years; at first she was too young, then he too disreputable; she married the waiter and Dowson's life went to wreck.... My health was giving way, my nerves had been wrecked. Finding that I could not work, and thinking the open air salutary, Lady Gregory brought me from cottage to cottage collecting folk-lore. Every night she wrote out what we had heard in the dialect of the cottages.   (*A* 399 ff.)

In 1916 he was still grieving, but a new element had entered into his grief. Now he was troubled by his own lack of concern that Maud, after her husband John MacBride had been shot for his part in the 1916 Rebellion, had refused once more to marry him. Madame MacBride told the present editor in 1944 that she thought Yeats was relieved by this refusal, which was accompanied by her old comment of the 'nineties that neither she nor Yeats was the marrying kind. Romantic love could not be rekindled. Lady Gregory and Mrs Shakespear had each been urging him to marry, to have descendants, to be comfortable. Marriage with Maud, he now realised, could never have been comfortable.

1-4   *trees ... paths ... the water*: descriptions of the lake at Coole Park. Cf. Lady Gregory's description:

Our own river that we catch a glimpse of now and again through hazel and ash, or outshining the silver beech stems of Kyle Dortha, has ever been an idler. Its transit is as has been said of human life 'from a mystery through a mystery to a mystery'; suddenly appearing, as a French writer has put down in his book 'dans le beau parc privé de Coole, derrière le village de Kiltartan.' And dipping presently under great limestone flags that form a natural bridge 'la dernière réapparition se fait voir a 350 mètres de là toujours dans le parc de Coole.' Then, flowing free, it helps to form a lake, whose fulness, finding no channel above ground, is forced 'de chercher sa route par les passages souterains de lac vers la mer'; into which it flows under the very shadow of the Dun of the ancient legendary King of Guaire [or Gort]. (*Coole* 27-8)

Cf. 'Coole and Ballylee, 1931' (*PNE* 135).

6   *nine-and-fifty swans*: they were there, as Yeats told the late Professor H. O. White (describing the poem as written in a mood of intense depression). Lady Gregory quotes George Moore's description of them:

It was then I forgot Yeats and Edward [Martyn] and everything else in the delight caused by a great clamour of wings, and the snowy plumage of thirty-six great birds rushing down the lake, striving to rise from its surface. At last their wings caught the air, and after floating about the lake they settled in a distant corner where they thought they could rest undisturbed. Thirty-six swans rising out of a lake and floating round it, and settling down in it, is an unusual sight; it conveys a suggestion of fairyland, perhaps because thirty-six wild swans are so different from the silly China swan which sometimes floats and hisses in melancholy whiteness up and down a stone basin. That is all we know of swans – all I knew until the thirty-six rose out of the hushed lake at our feet, and prompted me to turn to Yeats, saying, You're writing your poem in its natural atmosphere.   (*Ave* (1947 ed), 190)

Lady Gregory adds the following sentence in her quotation from Moore in *Coole* 35: 'And Yeats himself in the volume to which he has given their name tells of an October evening when he made the count of a yet greater number. . . .'

7, 16   *nineteenth autumn ... first time*: Yeats's first brief visit to Coole took place in 1896 (he subsequently spent that summer in Paris in a very unhappy state, cf. *A* 343) but these lines refer to 1897, the year he regarded, in *DP*, as altering his life.

131

19   *lover by lover*: there may be a link between his poem and Shelley's *Alastor* (lines 277 ff.), where in each case the unhappiness of the *persona* is accentuated by the thought of mated swans:

> A swan was there,
> Beside a sluggish stream among the reeds,
> It rose as he approached, and with strong wings
> Scaling the upward sky, bent its bright course
> High over the immeasurable main.
> His eyes pursued its flight: – 'Thou hast a home,
> Beautiful bird! thou voyagest to thine home,
> Where thy sweet mate will twine her downy neck
> With thine, and welcome thy return with eyes
> Bright in the lustre of their own fond joy.
> And what am I that I should linger here,
> With voice far sweeter than thy dying notes,
> Spirit more vast than thine, frame more attuned
> To beauty, wasting these surpassing powers
> In the deaf air, to the blind earth, and heaven
> That echoes not my thoughts?' A gloomy smile
> Of desperate hope wrinkled his quivering lips.
> For Sleep, he knew, kept most relentlessly
> Its precious charge; and silent Death exposed,
> Faithless perhaps as Sleep, a shadowy lure,
> With doubtful smile mocking its own strange charms.

Cf. also Shelley's preface to *Alastor*, describing the poet imagining the Being whom he loves, attaching all of the wonderful, wise or beautiful which could be envisaged by poet, philosopher or lover, to a single image, and then searching in vain for a prototype of his conception.

22   *Their hearts. . . old*: the other love poems in *WSC* written to Maud Gonne ('His Phoenix', 'Broken Dreams', 'A Deep-Sworn Vow', 'Presences', etc.) were composed *before* 1916. But Yeats may have been troubled both by the death of his love for Maud Gonne and by the realisation that Iseult Gonne, to whom he proposed marriage in 1916 and 1917, would think of him as an old man. Cf. 'The Living Beauty' (*PNE* 150) and 'A Song' (*PNE* 151) or 'Men improve with the Years' (*PNE* 146). Throughout the poems of *WSC* runs this grief over the age of the heart. Cf. 'A Song' (*PNE* 151), '*O who could have foretold / That the heart grows old?*'

148   28   *By what lake's edge*: Lady Gregory (*Coole* 38) throws light on this query. In August 1928 Yeats saw two swans and three cygnets with them and said, 'I have known your lake for thirty years, and that is the first time a swan has built here. That is a good omen.'

144   IN MEMORY OF MAJOR ROBERT GREGORY

148   This poem was written by 14 June 1918, and first appeared in *ER* (Aug. 1918).

The word 'Major' was not included in the title then, but Yeats's note after the title read: 'Major Robert Gregory, R.F.C., M.C., Legion of Honour, was killed in action on the Italian Front, January 23, 1918'. Yeats wrote four poems in memory of Robert Gregory (1881-1918), Lady Gregory's only child; this one, 'Shepherd and Goatherd' (*PNE* 159), 'An Irish Airman foresees his Death' (*PNE* 145) and 'Reprisals' (unpublished during Yeats's lifetime, see *VE* 791).

1 *our house*: Thoor Ballylee, the Norman tower and cottages Yeats had purchased in 1917, in which he and his family were to spend their summers until 1929. For a detailed description see Mary Hanley, *Thoor Ballylee - Home of William Butler Yeats* (1965). The 'almost settled' describes the period when Yeats and his wife were supervising alterations to the tower to make it habitable and were living in Ballinamantane House which Lady Gregory had lent them.

5 *turf*: peat

tower: for subsequent treatment of the Tower see *PNE* 144, 181, 184, 201, 203, 207, 210, 212, 218, 243. For other descriptions in which the Tower is not specifically mentioned, see *PNE* 208, 213, 242.

5 *the narrow winding stair*: it gave a name to a subsequent volume of poems, and was associated in Yeats's mind with the spiral movement of the gyres. (For subsequent treatment of the stair see *PNE* 205, 208, 210, 213, 242, 243.)

6 *Discoverers of forgotten truth*: those interested in the occult tradition

8 *All, all*: cf. note on line 21 'Broken Dreams' (*PNE* 167):

17-24 *Lionel Johnson*: see note on 'The Grey Rock' (*PNE* 113). Yeats met him in 1888 or 1889 and described him in various prose passages. He was a member of the Rhymers' Club (according to Yeats (*E & I* 491) his thought dominated the scene and gave the club its character) and shared a house with Herbert Horne (1864-1916) an architect and writer on art, Selwyn Image (1849-1930) the artist, and others in Charlotte Street, Fitzroy Square, and impressed Yeats with his poise and learning (*A* 168); he had a considerable library, a knowledge of tongues and books which was very great (*A* 306).

19 *courteous to the worst*: Johnson's courtesy chiefly impressed Yeats, who was conscious of his own provincial clumsiness and lack of self-possession, and envied Johnson his acquaintance with 'everybody of importance'. It was only later he discovered many of Johnson's reported conversations with famous men were imaginary. The worst may refer to Ernest Dowson, Johnson's friend whose life was 'a sordid round of drink and cheap harlots' (*E & I* 492).

149

19-20 *much falling . . . sanctity*: Yeats described him in 'Ireland after Parnell':

He drank a great deal too much, and, though nothing could, it seemed, disturb his calm or unsteady his hand or foot, his doctrine, after a certain number of glasses, would become more ascetic, more contemptuous of all that we call human life. . . . Even without stimulant his theology conceded nothing to human weakness, and I can remember his saying with energy, 'I wish those people who deny the eternity of punishment could realise their unspeakable vulgarity. . . .' He sometimes spoke of drink as something which he could put aside at any moment. . . .   (*A* 222)

The 'much falling' may come from his poem 'Mystic and Cavalier' which Yeats quoted in *A* 224. The poem opens:

> Go from me: I am one of those who fall.
> What! hath no cold wind swept your heart at all,
> In my sad company? Before the end
> Go from me, dear my friend!

The historical setting of the poem, Yeats thought, was but masquerade, and Johnson rested 'in clouds of doom'. But 'much falling' may also refer to Johnson falling down in a drunken stupor. (See *A* 309.)

22-4   *A long blast . . . consummation*: cf. the last stanza of 'Mystic and Cavalier':

> O rich and sounding voices of the air!
> Interpreters and prophets of despair:
> Priests of a fearful sacrament! I come
> To make with you my home.

25   *John Synge*: Yeats's respect and admiration for his friend, the Irish author John Millington Synge (1871-1909) are well known. He wrote Prefaces to *The Well of the Saints* (1905) and *Poems and Translations* (1909) and an essay 'J. M. Synge and the Ireland of his Time'. Yeats first met Synge in Paris in 1896 and persuaded him to go to the Aran Islands (see line 30) and find there a life that had never been expressed in literature.

26   *dying*: Yeat's comment upon Synge's poems explains the line:

> . . . the greater number were written very recently, and many during his last illness. *An Epitaph* and *On an Anniversary* show how early the expectation of death came to him, for they were made long ago. But the book as a whole is a farewell, written when life began to slip from him. He was a reserved man, and wished no doubt by a vague date to hide, while still living, what he felt and thought, from those about him. I asked one of the nurses in the hospital where he died if he knew he was dying, and she said 'He may have known it for months, but he would not have spoken of it to anyone.' Even the translations of poems that he has made his own by putting them into that melancholy dialect of his, seem to express his emotion at the memory of poverty and the approach of death. . . .   (*E & I* 307)

27   *long travelling*: in 'The Tragic Generation' Yeats described Synge in terms of *AV*:

> According to my Lunar parable, he was a man of the twenty-third Phase; a man whose subjective lives – for a constant return to our life is a part of my

dream – were over; who must not pursue an image, but fly from it, all that subjective dreaming, that had once been power and joy, now corrupting within him. He had to take the first plunge into the world beyond himself, the first plunge away from himself that is always pure technique, the delight in doing, not because one would or should, but merely because one can do.   (*A* 344)

30   *a most desolate stony place*: the Aran Islands. Yeats's memories in *BS* illustrate his understanding of what Synge found there:

I had met John Synge in Paris in 1896. Somebody has said, 'There is an Irishman living on the top floor of your hotel; I will introduce you.' I was very poor, but he was much poorer. He belonged to a very old Irish family and, though a simple courteous man, remembered it and was haughty and lonely. With just enough to keep him from starvation and not always from half-starvation, he had wandered about Europe, travelling third-class or upon foot, playing his fiddle to poor men on the road or in their cottages. He was the man that we needed, because he was the only man I have ever known incapable of a political thought or of a humanitarian purpose. He could walk the roadside all day with some poor man without any desire to do him good or for any reason except that he liked him. He was to do for Ireland, though more by his influence on other dramatists than by his direct influence, what Robert Burns did for Scotland. When Scotland thought herself gloomy and religious, Providence restored her imaginative spontaneity by raising up Robert Burns to commend drink and the Devil. I did not, however, see what was to come when I advised John Synge to go to a wild island off the Galway coast and study its life because that life 'had never been expressed in literature'. He had learned Gaelic at College and I told him that, as I would have told it to any young man who had learned Gaelic and wanted to write. When he found that wild island he became happy for the first time, escaping, as he said, 'from the nullity of the rich and the squalor of the poor'. He had bad health, he could not stand the island hardship long, but he would go to and fro between there and Dublin.   (*A* 567–8)

32   *passionate and simple*: Yeats had visited Inishmaan and Inishmore in 1896, and when he met the oldest man on Inishmaan he was told by him that 'If any gentleman has done a crime, we'll hide him. There was a gentleman that killed his father, and I had him in my own house six months till he got away to America' (*A* 344). Synge himself was quiet –

timid, too shy for general conversation, an invalid and full of moral scruple, and he was to create now some ranting braggadocio, now some tipsy hag full of poetical speech, and now some young man or girl full of the most abounding health. He never spoke an unkind word, had admirable manners, and yet his art was to fill the streets with rioters, and to bring upon his dearest friends enemies that may last their lifetime.   (*A* 345)

33   *George Pollexfen*: Yeats's maternal uncle, with whom he spent holidays as a young man. They experimented with cabbalistic symbols and studied the visions and thoughts of the Sligo country people. See *A* 255–70. George Pollexfen (1839–1910) is fully described in *A* 69 as a pessimistic hypochrondriac:

A hypochondriac, he passed from winter to summer through a series of

135

woollens that had always to be weighed; for in April or May, or whatever the date was, he had to be sure he carried the exact number of ounces he had carried upon that date since boyhood. He lived in despondency, finding in the most cheerful news reasons of discouragement, and sighing every twenty-second of June over the shortening of the days. Once in later years, when I met him in Dublin sweating in a midsummer noon, I brought him into the hall of the Kildare Street Library, a cool and shady place, without lightening his spirits; for he but said in a melancholy voice, 'How very cold this place must be in winter-time'. Sometimes when I had pitted my cheerfulness against his gloom over the breakfast-table, maintaining that neither his talent nor his memory nor his health were running to the dregs, he would rout me with the sentence, 'How very old I shall be in twenty years'. See also *A* 70–1.

34   *muscular youth*: 'He had once ridden steeple-chases and had been, his horse-trainer said, the best rider in Connacht' (*A* 70).

Mayo: county north of Galway in the west of Ireland deriving its name from a village (*Irish* Muigheo), the plain of the yew tree.

37   *solid men*: 'He would take to club and dumb-bell if his waist thickened by a hair's breadth, and twenty years after, when a very old man, he had the erect shapely figure of his youth' (*A* 257).

39   *opposition, square and trine*: Pollexfen was interested in astrology and symbolism. He and Yeats used MacGregor Mathers's symbols to induce reveries. At Rosses Point, where George Pollexfen had a small house as a summer residence, Yeats walked by the seashore, his uncle on cliff or sandhill, and Yeats would imagine a symbol and George Pollexfen would notice what passed before his mind's eye, 'and in a short time he would practically never fail of the appropriate vision' (*A* 258 ff.). Yeats thought his uncle's long association with Mary Battle, a second-sighted servant, had led him to believe much in the supernatural world. Cf. 'In Memory of Alfred Pollexfen' (*PNE* 173). The astrological terms represent heavenly bodies separated, respectively, by 180°, 90° and 120°.

150   46   *dear friend's dear son*: the repetition is reminiscent of line 57 in John of Gaunt's dying speech in *Richard the Second*, II, i, 'This land of such dear souls, this dear dear land.'

47   *Our Sidney*: Robert Gregory had an Elizabethan versatility, and, like Sir Philip Sidney (1554–86) the English author, his love of action led him to an untimely death abroad. Gregory was educated at Harrow, New College, and the Slade. He also worked at Jacques Blanche's atelier in Paris; he had an exhibition of paintings in Chelsea in 1914. He was a good shot, a good bowler, a boxer, and a fearless horseman. He joined the 4th Connaught Rangers in 1915, then transferred to the Royal Flying Corps in 1916. He became Chevalier of the Légion d'Honneur in 1917, and was awarded a Military Cross that year also 'for conspicuous gallantry and devotion to duty'. He showed 'the highest courage and

skill' as a pilot. He was killed on 23 January 1918 on the north Italian front. Neither Yeats nor his family knew that he had been shot down in error by an Italian Pilot.

50   *Were loved by him*: Robert Gregory had encouraged Yeats to buy the tower. He made several drawings of it.

storm-broken trees: the trees are described elsewhere in *PNE* 182, 201, 205, 207, 212.

51-2   *road . . . bridge . . . stream*: are referred to in *PNE* 181, 183, 205, 207, 212, 254.

55   *water-hen*: the water-hens are referred to in *PNE* 144, 183, 207, 211, 254.

57-64   *he would ride*: these lines were added to the poem at the request of Gregory's widow.

58   *Castle Taylor . . . Roxborough*: Castle Taylor, formerly Caislean MacCraith of Ballymagrath near Craughwell, is in Co. Galway; Roxborough, near Coole, was Lady Gregory's home as a child; she was born a Persse. Originally Roche's Rock (*Irish* Craig a Roiste), the name was changed to Roxborough in 1707 (*McG* 78).

59   *Esserkelly*: in Co. Galway, near Ardrahan. (*Irish* Esirtkelly, Dysert/Disert Cheallagh) St Ceallagh's Hermitage

60   *Mooneen*: Mooneen (*Irish* Moinin, the little bog) near Esserkelly, Co. Galway

65   *a great painter*: Yeats had a painting by Gregory in Riversdale, Rathfarnham, and he recorded his opinion of Gregory's talent elsewhere:

> Robert Gregory painted the Burren Hills and thereby found what promised to grow into a great style, but he had hardly found it before he was killed. His two finished pictures, so full of austerity and sweetness, should find their way into Irish public galleries.   (*E & I* 209)

For a discussion of Gregory's work as a painter, see D. J. Gordon and Ian Fletcher, 'Persons and Places' (*IP* 30-4). Three of his paintings are reproduced in that volume on pp. 116, 117, and 118.

66   *Clare*: Irish county, south of Co. Galway

81   *consume . . . combustible*: the imagery was possibly suggested by a phrase in a letter of Henry James to Yeats, 25 August 1915:

> & happy you poets who can be present [in an anthology], & *so* present by a simple flicker of your genius, & not, like the clumsier race [of novelists], have to lay a train & pile up faggots that may not after all prove in the least combustible! . . .

151   83   *dried straw*: Yeats wrote on John Davidson in 'The Tragic Generation' in a way which explains something of his attitude to Gregory's life and work – the image of the 'fire of straw' being significantly common to the poem and this prose comment on Davidson:

> I think he might have grown to be a successful man . . . violent energy, which is like a fire of straw, consumes in a few minutes the nervous vitality, and is useless in the arts. Our fire must burn slowly, and we must constantly turn away to think, constantly analyse what we have done, be content even to have little life outside our work. . . . A few months after our meeting in the Museum, Davidson had spent his inspiration. 'The fires are out', he said, 'and I must hammer the cold iron.' When I heard a few years ago that he had drowned himself, I knew that I had always expected some such end. With enough passion to make a great poet, through meeting no man of culture in early life, he lacked intellectual receptivity, and, anarchic and indefinite, lacked pose and gesture, and now no verse of his clings to my memory.   (*A* 318)

There are several passages in Yeats's 1910 Diary which show that he envied Robert Gregory his lack of introspection. Gregory would not 'turn away to think' nor 'constantly analyse' what he had done nor 'have little life' outside his work. The stanza emerges from the thought of stanza VI which showed Yeats could not become accustomed to the idea of Gregory's death, a thought which closes the poem in stanza XII.

145   AN IRISH AIRMAN FORESEES HIS DEATH

152   This poem was written in 1918 and first appeared in *WSC* (1919).

1   *I know*: Robert Gregory

3   *Those that I fight*: the Germans

4   *Those that I guard*: the English

5   *Kiltartan Cross*: crossroads in Kiltartan, a barony near Coole Park, Co. Galway. Lady Gregory's style in her translations is sometimes known as Kiltartan. This reference to Kiltartan Cross suggests a comparison of this poem with 'Reprisals' (published posthumously in *Rann/An Ulster Quarterly of Poetry*, Autumn 1948; text is also in *VE* 791) where 'those that I fight' (line 3 above) become 'nineteen German planes'. 'Reprisals' was written for *The Nation* in 1921; see Jeffares *Y: M & P*, 328, *n*50 for its being withheld; its tone is bitter:

> *Reprisals*
> Some nineteen German planes, they say,
> You had brought down before you died.
> We called it a good death. Today
> Can ghost or man be satisfied?
> Although your last exciting year
> Outweighed all other years, you said,

Though battle joy may be so dear
A memory, even to the dead,
It chases other thought away,
Yet rise from your Italian tomb,
Flit to Kiltartan cross and stay
Till certain second thoughts have come
Upon the cause you served, that we
Imagined such a fine affair:
Half-drunk or whole-mad soldiery
Are murdering your tenants there.
Men that revere your father yet
Are shot at on the open plain.
Where may new-married women sit
And suckle children now? Armed men
May murder them in passing by
Nor law nor parliament take heed.
Then close your ears with dust and lie
Among the other cheated dead.

MEN IMPROVE WITH THE YEARS   146

This poem was written on 19 July 1916 and first appeared in the *Little Review*   152
(June 1917).

1 *worn out with dreams*: the poem is written about the effect of Iseult Gonne's
youth and beauty on Yeats. He endeavours to persuade himself that the wisdom
he has won out of the disappointments of life compensates him for the age that
prevents him from loving Iseult passionately, 'Delighted to be but wise'. But this
theory may be specious. Is it a dream or the truth? Love crowds in upon his
wisdom. The conclusion is very like that of a later poem, 'Politics' (*PNE* 374):

> But O that I were young again
> And held her in my arms!

Cf. also 'The Living Beauty' (*PNE* 150) and 'A Song' (*PNE* 151) which each
record the depressing realisation of age: 'The living beauty is for younger men'
and '. . . *who could have foretold/That the heart grows old?*'

2 *triton*: a statue of a Greek sea deity, usually represented with the upper parts
of a man and a fish tail, holding a trumpet made from a conch shell. Triton was a
sea god, son of Poseidon and Amphitrite.

THE COLLAR-BONE OF A HARE   147

This poem was written on 5 July 1916 and first appeared in the *Little Review*   153
(June 1917).

5   *. . . and the dancing*: Cf. a passage in *Visions and Beliefs*, II, 310: 'always in his [Blake's] boys and girls walking or dancing on smooth grass and in golden light, as on pastoral scenes cut upon wood or copper by his disciples Palmer and Calvert, one notices the peaceful Swedenborgian heaven' (*E* 44). Yeats valued the artists who could delineate a blissful state akin to that of Eden. Cf. lines 64–5 'Under Ben Bulben' (*PNE* 356). Cf. also the last stanza of 'John Kinsella's Lament for Mrs Mary Moore' (*PNE* 368) for a parallel picture of 'Eden's garden'.

10   *The collar-bone of a hare*: the image probably comes from a peasant story. In 'The Three O'Byrnes and the Evil Faeries'

> a peasant of the neighbourhood once saw the treasure [of the O'Byrnes]. He found the shin-bone of a hare lying on the grass. He took it up; there was a hole in it; he looked through the hole, and saw the gold heaped up under the ground. He hurried home to bring a spade, but when he got to the path again he could not find the spot where he had seen it.   (*M* 87)

13   *where they marry in churches*: the poem expresses a contrast between the ideal world and the real, perhaps sharpened by a situation where Lady Gregory was advising the poet to marry and Mrs Shakespear approved of the idea also. Marriage can seem a very enfettering prospect to a bachelor of fifty-one.

148   UNDER THE ROUND TOWER

154   This poem was written in March 1918 and first appeared in the *Little Review* (Oct. 1918).

4   *Billy Byrne*: William Byrne, a Catholic gentleman from Ballymanus, Co. Wicklow, was a member of the Leinster Directory of the United Irishmen, who was captured and hanged in 1798. He was a legendary figure in Glendalough at the time the Yeatses stayed there in the Royal Hotel in March 1918. For Byrne, see Thomas Pakenham, *The Year of Liberty* (1969) 83–4 and 285–8.

7–9   *tombstone*: the lines are a description of the Glendalough graveyard, in which the round tower is situated. These slender pencil-shaped stone round towers were built as a defence against the Scandinavian invaders. There are a remarkable number of O'Byrnes and Byrnes buried in the graveyard at Glendalough, near Laragh, Co. Wicklow. Glendalough (*Irish* Gleann Da Loch) means the Valley of the Two Lakes. A monastic centre was set up there by Saint Kevin (d. 618).

9   *O'Byrnes*: they were early rulers of southern Co. Wicklow, their stronghold situated in the virtually impenetrable defile of Glenmalure; see Edmund Curtis *HI*, 60, 107, 121, 128, 138, 195, 198 and 212.

11–13   *sun and moon . . . golden king and silver lady*: cf. 'The Man who dreamed of Faeryland' (*PNE* 33). The golden king and silver lady (the sun and moon) symbolise the continual oscillation which is representative of the horizontal movement of the historical cones described in Book V, 'Dove or Swan', cf. *AV* (B).

19 *wild lady*: the moon is 'wild' in 'Solomon and the Witch' (*PNE* 190). It becomes 'wilder'. There are sometimes sexual implications in the word in Irish usage.

In Yeats's *Stories of Red Hanrahan* the sun and the moon

> are the man and the girl, they are my life and your life, they are travelling and ever travelling through the skies as if under the one hood. It was God made them for one another. He made your life and my life before the beginning of the world, He made them that they might go through the world, up and down, like the two best dancers that go on with the dance up and down the long floor of the barn, fresh and laughing, when all the rest are tired out and leaning against the wall. (*M* 227-8)

SOLOMON TO SHEBA   149

This poem was written at Glendalough in [March?] 1918 and first appeared in   *155*
the *Little Review* (Oct. 1918).

1 *Solomon to Sheba*: Solomon symbolises Yeats, Sheba Mrs Yeats. Cf. 'Solomon and the Witch' (*PNE* 190). Solomon (*c.* 972-932 BC) was King of the Hebrews. See I Kings 10, 1-13, for Sheba's visit to him. She was a ruler in Arabia, in the Yemen. But there is also a lively account of their relationship in the *Kebra Negast*.

See *Magda, Queen of Sheba, from the ancient royal Abyssinian manuscript 'The Story of the Kings'* [Kebra Negast] *From the French of M. Le Roux by Mrs Van Horst with an Introduction by Hugues Le Roux* (1907). See also *The Queen of Sheba and her only son Menyelek. A complete translation of the Kebra Negast*, with Introduction by Sir E. A. Wallis Budge, (1922).

7 *theme of love*: in his 1910 Diary Yeats wrote:

> It seems to me that true love is a discipline, and it needs so much wisdom that the love of Solomon and Sheba must have lasted, for all the silence of the Scriptures. Each divines the secret self of the other, and refusing to believe in the mere daily self, creates a mirror where the lover or the beloved sees an image to copy in daily life; for love also creates the Mask. (*A* 464)

THE LIVING BEAUTY   150

The MS. of this poem is dated 1917 and it first appeared in the *Little Review* (Oct.   *156*
1918).

141

Title   The Living Beauty: Iseult Gonne (who could not recall when the poem was written). Yeats spent the summer of 1917 at Maud Gonne's house in Colville, Calvados, and renewed his offer of marriage to Iseult, which she finally refused when Maud Gonne and her family arrived in London in September. Yeats had accompanied them; they were not allowed to proceed to Ireland and Yeats then arranged that Iseult should be given the post of assistant librarian in the School of Oriental Languages. She cried 'because she was so ashamed "at being so selfish" in not wanting me to marry and so break her friendship with me'. See *WBY* 304-6.

1   *the wick and oil are spent*: cf. 'Men improve with the Years' (*PNE* 146), 'The Collar-bone of a Hare' (*PNE* 147), 'A Song' (*PNE* 151) and 'To a Young Beauty' (*PNE* 152).

151   A SONG

156   This poem was probably written in 1915 and first appeared in the *Little Review* (Oct. 1918).

3   *dumb-bell and foil*: Yeats did Sandow exercises and Ezra Pound taught him fencing in the winter of 1912-13. Yeats used the image in the essay 'Anima Hominis':

> I sometimes fence for half an hour at the day's end, and when I close my eyes upon the pillow I see a foil playing before me, the button to my face. We meet always in the deep of the mind, whatever our work, wherever our reverie carries us, that other Will.   (*M* 337)

5-6   *the heart grows old*: Saul (*PYP* 104) has compared this refrain with 'Ephemera' (*PNE* 8), 'how old my heart' and 'Passion has often worn our wandering hearts'.

152   TO A YOUNG BEAUTY

157   This poem was written in 1918 [probably in the autumn] and first appeared in *Nine Poems* [October] (1918).

1   *Dear fellow-artist*: the poem was written to Iseult Gonne.

3   *every Jack and Jill*: Yeats disapproved of the Bohemian company Iseult kept in London and in Dublin. Maud Gonne had acquired 73 St Stephen's Green, Dublin, which she lent to Yeats and his wife. She had been imprisoned on suspicion in England – having earlier defied the ban on her proceeding to Ireland (imposed in September 1917). Yeats had managed to get her removed to a sanatorium because of her health. By Christmas 1918 Yeats and his wife handed over the house to her.

7   *that mirror for a school*: cf. lines 14, 15, 50 of 'Michael Robartes and the Dancer' (*PNE* 189).

11   *Ezekiel's cherubim*: they are mentioned in Ezekiel ix. 3; x. 2, 6, 7, 14, 16, 19; xi. 22; xxviii. 16; xli. 18; and are presumably to be taken as more grandiose than the conceptions of Beauvarlet.

12   *Beauvarlet*: Jacques Firmin Beauvarlet (1731-97), a mediocre French painter and engraver. His name appears erroneously as Beaujolet until *Later Poems* (1926).

18   *With Landor and with Donne*: Yeats wrote to Professor Grierson on 14 November 1912 to thank him for his edition of Donne:

> I have been using it constantly and find that at last I can understand Donne. Your notes tell me exactly what I want to know. Poems that I could not understand or could but understand are now clear and I notice that the more precise and learned the thought the greater the beauty, the passion; the intricacy and subtleties of his imagination are the length and depth of the furrow made by his passion. His pedantry and his obscenity – the rock and the loam of his Eden – but make me the more certain that one who is but a man like us all has seen God.   (*L* 570)

In a passage in 'The Tragic Generation' Yeats linked capacity for the metaphysical with a vision of evil. The poet John Donne (1571/2-1631) could be as physical as he pleased; because he could say what he pleased: he was not tempted to linger, Yeats thought, between spirit and sense. And Yeats saw in some of his own early work a disagreeable sentimental sensuality. [This might have been in some of the 'nineties poems attacked by Paul Elmer More. Cf. the latter's *Shelburne Essays* (First Series) 181-2.]

> How often had I heard men of my time talk of the meeting of spirit and sense, yet there is no meeting but only change upon the instant, and it is by the perception of a change, like the sudden 'blacking out' of the lights of the stage, that passion creates its most violent sensation.   (*A* 326)

It is likely that Yeats read Walter Savage Landor (1775-1864) in the winters of 1914, 1915, and 1916. The 'dining' with Landor may be explained by the latter's appearance in *AV* in the same phase, the seventeenth, as Dante and Shelley (and Yeats himself, though this is not explicitly stated). Landor was

> The most violent of men, he uses his intellect to disengage a visionary image of perfect sanity (*Mask* at Phase 3) seen always in the most serene and classic art imaginable. He had perhaps as much Unity of Being as his age permitted, and possessed, though not in any full measure, the Vision of Evil.

(*AV* (B) 144-5)

Cf. the description in 'Anima Hominis': '. . . Savage Landor topped us all in calm nobility when the pen was in his hand, as in the daily violence of his passion when he had laid it down.' (*M* 328)

Landor was also described in 'Anima Hominis' in terms which gloss Yeats's personal situation – the facing of age – in 1917:

A poet, when he is growing old, will ask himself if he cannot keep his mask and his vision without new bitterness, new disappointment. Could he if he would, knowing how frail his vigour from youth up, copy Landor who lived loving and hating, ridiculous and unconquered, into extreme old age, all lost but the favour of his Muses?

> The Mother of the Muses, we are taught,
> Is Memory; she has left me; they remain,
> And shake my shoulder, urging me to sing.   (*M* 342)

153   TO A YOUNG GIRL

157   This poem is dated May 1915 in the Maud Gonne Manuscript Book. Ellmann (*IY* 289) dates it 1913 or 1915. It first appeared in the *Little Review* (Oct. 1918).

1   *My dear, my dear*: Iseult Gonne

158   4   *mother*: Maud Gonne. The 1915 date might suit this poem better than the earlier. Yeats did not take seriously the idea that he had fallen in love with Iseult Gonne until 1916. She proposed to him in 1915 (but presumably in lighthearted vein) and was refused because there was too much Mars in her horoscope. Cf. *Y:M & P* 190.

154   THE SCHOLARS

158   The manuscript of this poem which I have seen is dated April 1915. Ellmann (*IY* 289) gives 1914 and April 1915. It first appeared in *Catholic Anthology 1914–1915* (1915).

7   *all cough in ink*: a crossed-out version of this line in the MS. read 'They'll dip in the inkpots to world's end.' The stanza then ran:

> They'd cough in the ink till the world's end
> Wear out the carpet with their shoes
> Earn respect, have no strange friend;
> If they have sinned nobody knows;
> Lord what would they say
> Should their Catullus walk that way.

Yeats wrote on the back of this manuscript:

I am doubtful of the last verse. It began with a jerk – what do you think of this?

> There'll be their life to the world's end
> To wear the carpet with their shoes
> And earn respect; have no stranger friend;
> And only sin, when no one knows;
> Lord what would they say
> Should their Catullus walk that way.

If you choose this end, call it perhaps 'At the British Museum'. I don't like the new fourth line so well I think. Would the old men regret in the new context?

The softening down took place when Yeats was away from Ezra Pound's influence (information from Mrs W. B. Yeats). See *WBY* 272 for Yeats's friendship with Pound and the winters he spent with him at Stone Cottage, Coleman's Hatch, Sussex.

12   *Catullus*: the Roman love poet Caius Valerius Catullus (? 84–? 54 BC)

TOM O'ROUGHLEY   **155**

This poem was written on 16 February 1918 and first appeared in the *Little*   *158*
Review (Oct. 1918).

1 *logic-choppers*: Yeats was probably thinking of Newton, Hobbes, and Locke. Cf. a passage in his Introduction to *Fighting the Waves*:

> Science has driven out the legends, stories, superstitions that protected the immature and the ignorant with symbol, and now that the flower has crossed our rooms, science must take their place and demonstrate as philosophy has in all ages, that States are justified, not by multiplying or, as it would seem, comforting those that are inherently miserable, but because sustained by those for whom the hour seems 'awful' and by those born out of themselves, the best born of the best.
> Since my twentieth year, those thoughts have been in my mind, and now that I am old I sing them to the Garrets and the Cellars:
>
>> Move upon Newton's town,
>> The town of Hobbes and Locke,
>> Pine, spruce, come down
>> Cliff, ravine, rock:
>> What can disturb the corn?
>> What makes it shudder and bend?
>> The rose brings her thorn,
>> The Absolute walks behind.   (*W & B* 76–7)

4 *An aimless joy is a pure joy*: Yeats wrote in his essay 'Bishop Berkeley':

> In the *Commonplace Book* alone is Berkeley always sincere, and there I find in paragraph 639, 'Complacency seems rather to . . . constitute the essence of volition', which seems what an Irish poet meant who sang to some girl 'A joy within guides you', and what I meant when I wrote 'An aimless joy is a pure joy.' Berkeley must have been familiar with Archbishop King's *De Origine Mali* which makes all joy depend 'upon the act of the agent himself, and his election'; not upon an external object. The greater the purity the greater the joy. A Sligo countryman once said to me, 'God smiles even when He condemns the lost.' (*E & I*, fn. 408)

Cf. also note on line 22 'Demon and Beast' (*PNE* 199):

> For aimless joy had made me stop
> Beside the little lake.

159   5   *Tom O'Roughley*: he is probably invented as the kind of fool Yeats had in mind in Phase Twenty-eight of *A V*:

> He is but a straw blown by the wind, with no mind but the wind and no act but a nameless drifting and turning, and is sometimes called 'The Child of God'. At his worst his hands and feet and eyes, his will and his feelings, obey obscure subconscious fantasies, while at his best he would know all wisdom if he could know anything. The physical world suggests to his mind pictures and events that have no relation to his needs or even to his desires; his thoughts are an aimless reverie; his acts are aimless like his thoughts, and it is in this aimlessness that he finds his joy.   *(A V* (B) 182)

7–8   '*And wisdom is a butterfly/And not a gloomy bird of prey*': Yeats's note (dated 1928) on 'Meditations in Time of Civil War, VII' read:

> I suppose that I must have put hawks into the fourth stanza because I have a ring with a hawk and a butterfly upon it, to symbolise the straight road of logic, and so of mechanism, and the crooked road of intuition: 'For wisdom is a butterfly and not a gloomy bird of prey.'   *(CP)*

13   *trumpeter Michael*: see note on 'The Happy Townland' *(PNE* 90).

156   SHEPHERD AND GOATHERD

159   This poem was being written on 22 February 1918 and was finished on 19 March 1918; it first appeared in *WSC* (1919) entitled 'The Sad Shepherd' which was altered in *CP* to the present title.

Title   Shepherd and Goatherd: the poem was written in memory of Robert Gregory. See notes on 'In Memory of Major Robert Gregory' *(CP* 148). Yeats wrote to Lady Gregory on 22 February 1918, 'I am trying a poem in manner like one that Spenser wrote for Sir Philip Sidney', and, on 19 March 1918, 'I have to-day finished my poem about Robert, a pastoral, modelled on what Virgil wrote for some friend of his and on what Spenser wrote of Sidney' *(L* 646 and 647). The poem is nearer to *Astrophel* (Edmund Spenser (?1552–99)) in general spirit, possibly because Yeats knew Spenser better than he knew Virgil (he made a selection for a volume of Spenser's *Poems*, published in 1906), and possibly because the theme of *Astrophel* is nearer to Yeats's subject than is Virgil's Fifth Eclogue (a probable imitation of Theocritus' Elegy on Daphnis, and less personal than Spenser's or Yeats's lament). But the form of the poem is probably derived from Virgil's Eclogue, Virgil using a dialogue between two rustics as a setting for his lament for Daphnis; Menalcas and Mopsus each sing their own songs as do Yeats's Shepherd and Goatherd (whereas in *Astrophel* the singer repeats a song made by Clorinda, who is not present). There is a further similarity in structure in that the first singer sings of the death, Mopsus of Daphnis, the Shepherd of Gregory, while the second sings of the state after death, Menalcas of the deification of Daphnis, the Goatherd of the Yeatsian reincarnation of Gregory. Yeats brought to the poem his interest in the occult and in mystic thought.

17-20   *He that was best ... is dead*: Gregory was an excellent athlete,   *160*
horseman and shot. Cf. *Astrophel*:

> For both in deeds and words he noutred was.
> Both wise and hardie – too hardie alas!
> In wrestling, nimble; and in running, swift;
> In shooting, steddie; and in swimming, strong;
> Well made to strive, to throw, to leap, to lift,
> And all the sports that shepheards are among
> In every one, he vanquisht everyone
> He vanquisht all and vanquisht was of none.

21   *he had thrown the crook away*: see notes on 'In Memory of Major Robert
Gregory' (*PNE* 144), and cf. *Astrophel*:

> Such skill matcht with such courage as he had,
> Did prick him foorth with proud desire of praise;
> To seek abroad, of danger nought y'drad
> His mistress' name, and his owne fame to raise.

24   *their loneliness*: Yeats thought that Gregory had captured the nature of the
Galway scene in his paintings and Augustus John praised his work for
conveying its strange quality. See *IP* 31.

25   *his mother*: cf. *Astrophel*:

> For from the time that first the nymph his mother
> Him forth did bring; and taught her lambs to feed:
> A slender swaine, excelling far each other
> In comely shape, like her that did him breed.

30-2   *when I had neither goat nor grazing*: a reference to Lady Gregory's
friendship with Yeats, her lending him money so that he could give up journalism
(see Hone (*WBY* 195), who writes that it was not until 1914 that she would
accept repayment of a debt which then amounted to £500) and imposing a routine
on him during his visits to Coole. A letter to Florence Farr indicated something of
his regime there:

> After breakfast Chaucer – garden for twenty minutes – then work from 11 till
> 2, then lunch, then I fish from 3 till 5, then I read and work again at lighter
> tasks till dinner – after dinner walk. To this I have added Sandow exercises
> daily. (*L* 454)

32   *New welcome ... old wisdom*: refers to his summer visits to Coole Park
from 1897 onwards, and 'old wisdom', perhaps, to the folklore she persuaded
him to gather with her in the early summers he spent there when he was in ill
health and could not work. He wrote elsewhere of their visits to cottages
collecting stories:

> As that ancient system of belief unfolded before us, with unforeseen
> probabilities and plausibilities, it was as though we had begun to live in a

dream, and one day Lady Gregory said to me when we had passed an old man in the wood: 'That old man may know the secret of the ages.'   (*E* 30)

34   *his children and his wife*: for later mention of Robert Gregory's child Anne see 'For Anne Gregory' (*PNE* 255).

161   46   *Old goatherds and old goats*: Wilson (*Y & T* 200) draws attention to 'the Platonic use of sheep and goats as symbols for young and old souls respectively'.

62   *speckled bird*: *The Speckled Bird* was the title of an autobiographical novel Yeats never published.

162   78   *certain lost companies of my own*: possibly those friends lamented in 'In Memory of Major Robert Gregory' (*PNE* 144)

80   *the road that the soul treads*: this is autobiographical, and depicts Yeats's interest in the occult. It was published (Ed. William H. O'Donnell) in 1976.

89   *He grows younger*: this is the main theme of the poem, that Gregory will grow younger and live his life backwards, an idea dealt with in the Introduction to *WWP* in terms of Indian belief, where the unpurified dead

> examine their past if undisturbed by our importunity, tracing events to their source, and as they take the form their thought suggests, seem to live backward through time; or if incapable of such examination, creatures not of thought but of feeling, renew as shades certain detached events of their past lives, taking the greater excitements first.   (*E* 366)

This is a later version of the idea. In an essay on 'Swedenborg, Mediums and Desolate Places' of 1914 Yeats reported country people in the west of Ireland as saying that

> after death every man grows upward or downward to the likeness of thirty years, perhaps because at that age Christ began His ministry, and stays always in that likeness; and these angels move always towards the 'springtime of their life' and grow more and more beautiful, 'the more thousand years they live', . . . 'for to grow old in heaven is to grow young.'   (*E* 39)

Wilson (*Y & T* 201) traces the idea to Thomas Taylor's *A Dissertation* (1790) quoting a passage dealing with the Orphic theology which stated that souls under the government of Saturn, who is pure intellect, instead of progressing from youth to age advance from age to youth. In the Orphic mysteries the soul in heaven was represented as a child. Wilson goes on to quote Plato's myth of two cycles, of Jupiter and Saturn. The latter was the intellectual world, a prenatal condition from which the soul descended and to which it returned after death. In the Saturnian kingdom man was no longer seen advancing to old age but became younger and more delicate. But in the previous cycle Plato described the world as a paradise resembling the intellectual condition, and Wilson quotes this passage from Taylor's *Plato*, IV, 123: 'The white hairs of those more advanced in years became black, and the cheeks of those that had beards became smooth, and thus each was restored to the past flower of his age.' Wilson regards Yeats's commentary on a passage in Shelley's *Prometheus Unbound* as evidence that Yeats knew the Platonic myth because, he argues, Shelley drew on this myth of Plato for Asia's song in *Prometheus Unbound*, and Yeats saw in Asia's voyage a movement against the current from age to youth, from youth to infancy, and so to the prenatal condition, 'peopled by Shapes too bright to see'.

95 *Jaunting, journeying*: jaunting: to take a jaunt for pleasure (horse-drawn 163 jaunting cars were in common use in Ireland at this time).

96 *To his own dayspring*: the phrase 'dayspring' is reminiscent of Yeats's reading in Swedenborg. He quoted the phrase in a letter to T. Sturge Moore, in a comment on Dowson seeking from religion 'something of that which the angels find who move perpetually, as Swedenborg has said, "towards the dayspring of their youth" ' (*A* 311), and in *BS*:

now I am old and rheumatic, and nothing to look at, but my Muse is young. I am even persuaded she is like those Angels in Swedenborg's vision, and moves perpetually 'towards the dayspring of her youth'. (*A* 541)

97 *the loaded pern*: Yeats wrote the following note in 1919:

When I was a little child at Sligo I could see above my grandfather's trees a little column of smoke from the 'pern mill,' and was told that 'pern' was another name for the spool, as I was accustomed to call it, on which thread was wound. One could not see the chimney for the trees, and the smoke looked as if it came from the mountain, and one day a foreign sea-captain asked me if that was a burning mountain. (*WSC*)

Cf. line 5 of 'Demon and Beast' (*PNE* 199), 'The Fool by the Roadside' (*PNE* 225), and 'Hades' bobbin' of 'Byzantium' (*PNE* 260).

Cf. Scott's use of the word in *The Antiquary*: ' "I ken naething about that," said the Gaberlunzie, "but in my auld acquaintance be hersell, or onything like hersell, she may come to bind us a pirn." ' (Ch. 39).

103 *the close cropped grass*: this may be glossed by Yeats's essay on Swedenborg, who because he belonged

to an eighteenth century not yet touched by the romantic revival, feels horror amid rocky uninhabited places, and so believes that the evil are in such places while the good are amid smooth grass and garden walks and the clear sunlight of Claude Lorraine. (*E* 37)

Cf. Wilson (*Y & T* 204) who considers that Plato also may have provided the imagery. He quotes a passage which describes those distributed about Saturn:

The inhabitants also are naked and without beds, and for the most part are fed dwelling in the open air. The grass likewise springing abundantly from the earth supplies them with soft couches. (Taylor, *Plato*, IV, 120)

He also draws attention to a passage where Yeats describes how always in his [Blake's] boys and girls walking or dancing on smooth grass and in golden light, as on pastoral scenes cut upon wood or copper by his disciples Palmer and Calvert, one notices the peaceful Swedenborgian heaven.   (*E* 44)

107   *unwind*: cf. line 97

109-112   these lines are reminiscent of Blake's 'The Mental Traveller'.

115   *new-torn bark*: probably close to Virgil's lines:

> Immo haec in viridi nuper quae cortice fagi
> Carmina descripsi et modulans alterna notavi,
> Experiar.

157   LINES WRITTEN IN DEJECTION

163   This poem was written in 1915 (probably in October) and first appeared in *WSC*.

3   *the moon*: the sun and moon in this poem symbolise objectivity and subjectivity, cf. 'The Man who dreamed of Faeryland' (*PNE* 33). At this period of his life Yeats seemed at times to despair of writing poetry; this poem also carries the dejection of the heart grown old. Cf. 'Men improve with the Years' (*PNE* 146), 'The Living Beauty' (*PNE* 150) and 'A Song' (*PNE* 151).

7   *the holy centaurs*: Yeats wrote elsewhere 'I thought all art should be a Centaur finding in the popular lore its back and its strong legs' (*A* 191). Centaurs, in Greek mythology, usually have the head, torso and arms of a man, joined to a lower body with the four legs of a horse.

8   *embittered sun*: it is possible to consider the objective life as destroying the creative element in man. The tasks involved in 'theatre business, management of men' may have seemed objective in comparison to Yeats's earlier life. In *AV* he described a man of the seventeenth phase (to which he belonged) in terms which might suit his own position ('out of phase') at this period of his life:

> If it [the intellect] be out of phase it will avoid the subjective conflict, acquiesce, hope that the *Body of Fate* may die away; and then the *Mask* will cling to it and the *Image* lure it. It will feel itself betrayed, and persecuted till, entangled in *primary* conflict, it rages against all that destroys *Mask* and *Image*. It will be subject to nightmare, for its *Creative Mind* (deflected from the *Image* and *Mask* to the *Body of Fate*) gives an isolated mythological or abstract form to all that excites its hatred. It may even dream of escaping from ill-luck by possessing the impersonal *Body of Fate* of its opposite phase, and of exchanging passion for desk and ledger. Because of the habit of synthesis, and of the growing complexity of the energy, which gives many interests, and the still faint perception of things in their weight and mass, men of this phase are almost always partisans, propagandists and gregarious; yet because of the *Mask* of simplification, which holds up before them the solitary life of hunters and of

fishers [cf. Yeats's poem 'The Fisherman' (*PNE* 160)] and 'the groves pale passion loves,' they hate parties, crowds, propaganda.   (*AV* (A) 77)

Shelley when 'out of phase' dreamed of converting the world, and upsetting governments, yet returned 'again and again to these two images of solitude, a young man whose hair has grown white from the burden of his thoughts, an old man in some shell-strewn cave . . .' and the parallel between his life (as seen in these Yeatsian terms) and Yeats's own can be drawn. In *Estrangement* Yeats recorded his despair at the apparent dissipation of his poetic skill in varied work:

> I often wonder if my talent will ever recover from the heterogeneous labour of these last few years. The younger Hallam says that vice does not destroy genius but that the heterogeneous does. I cry out vainly for liberty and have ever less and less inner life. Evil comes to us men of imagination wearing as its mask all the virtues.   (*A* 484)

THE DAWN   **158**

This poem was written on 20 June 1914 and first appeared in *P* (*Ch*) (Feb. 1916).   *164*

3   *that old queen . . . a town*: the queen was Emain, the town Emain Macha (the Twins of Macha) or Armagh. In one tale Macha, the horse goddess, had twins and these, *PNE* suggests, may be the two hills in Armagh (*Irish* Ard Macha, Macha's Height). Emain, daughter of Hugh Roe, claimed to rule in her father's right after his death, and defeated his brother Dihorba in battle, married his brother Cimbaeth and captured Dihorba's five sons by a stratagem. She compelled the five princes to build her a palace. Armagh became the capital of Ulster in the Irish tales.

4   *With the pin of a brooch*: In Standish James O'Grady, *History of Ireland Critical and Philosophical* (1881), I, 181, she marked out the site of the palace with the bodkin or pin of her cloak – hence the name of her palace, in Latinised form Emania. See Edward Rogers, *Memoir of Armagh Cathedral* (1882) for further details of the legend.

5-6   *the withered men . . . pedantic Babylon*: a reference to what Yeats called 'the Babylonian mathematical starlight' in *AV* (B) 268. Babylon, famous for astronomy and astrology, was the chief city of ancient Mesopotamia, first settled 3000 BC. The Babylonian Empire flourished from *c.* 2200 to 538 BC.

11   *the glittering coach*: presumably the chariot of Phoebus, the sun, though the fact that one particular dawn is suggested might imply that that particular dawn had seen Phaëton, the son of Phoebus, on his disastrous attempt to drive the chariot, killed by a thunderbolt hurled by Zeus because Phaëton was likely to set the earth on fire.

159 ON WOMAN

164 This poem was dated 25 May 1914 in the Maud Gonne Manuscript Book; it first appeared in *P (Ch)* (Feb. 1916). The poem has some of the sardonic realism of 'Beggar to Beggar Cried' (*PNE* 123) and 'The Witch' (*PNE* 128). It was not written to Mrs Yeats.

165 11 *Solomon grew wise*: cf. Prov. iv. 5-7. See note on 'Solomon to Sheba' (*PNE* 149). Solomon's wisdom was proverbial.

19 *shuddered in the water*: sexual symbol. Cf. line 23 and 'Leda and the Swan' (*PNE* 220)

21 *yawn*: cf. 'Three Things' (*PNE* 282). 'And did after stretch and yawn'

30 *the Pestle of the moon*: Yeats's belief in rebirth is qualified – 'if the tale's true'. Cf. Hone (*WBY* 48), who quotes Mohini Chatterjee as saying: 'Everything that has been shall be again.' But the thought here probably relates to Swedenborg. There is an undated entry in the Maud Gonne Manuscript Book which reads:

. . . O God grant me for my gift not in this life for I begin to grow [old] but somewhere that I shall love some woman, so that every passion, pity, cruel desire, the affection that is full of tears to abasement as before an image . . .

160 THE FISHERMAN

166 This poem was dated 4 June 1914 in the Maud Gonne Manuscript Book, and first appeared in *P (Ch)* (Feb. 1916). The poem has as subject the contrast between an ideal man and the real men of Ireland.

1-8 *him*: the ideal man

4 *grey Connemara clothes*: homespun tweed. See *A* 361 for a comment on this subject. For Connemara see note on 'The Dedication . . . Irish Novelists' (*PNE* 34).

9-12 *All day . . . and the reality*: the lines refer to the ideal audience, the fisherman – 'What I had hoped 'twoud be / To write for my own race' and to the actual audience, 'the reality', which is so unlike the ideal. The reality is described in lines 13-24.

14 *the dead man*: probably J. M. Synge

167 23-4 *The beating down . . . Art beaten down*: probably a reference to the controversy over the Lane Gallery proposals

25 *a twelvemonth since*: there is an entry in the Maud Gonne Manuscript Book written between 18 and 25 May 1913, a year before 'The Fisherman' was written, which is headed 'Subject for a poem' and runs:

> Who is this by the edge of the stream
> That walks in a good homespun coat
> And carries a fishing [rod] in his hand
> We singers have nothing of our own.
> All our hopes, our loves, our dreams
> Are for the young, for those whom
> We stir into life. But [there is] one
> That I can see always though he is not yet born
> He walks by the edge of the stream
> In a good homespun coat
> And carries a fishing-rod in his hand.

These lines form the substance of the last sixteen lines of 'The Fisherman' and show that only an imagined person could fulfil the poet's dreams. The germ of the idea can be seen in 'At Galway Races' (*PNE* 108), where the horsemen are idealised 'natural' men.

33 *down-turn of his wrist*: Yeats was a good fisherman and this description of skilled casting was praised for its accuracy by Siegfried Sassoon.

THE HAWK   161

This poem first appeared in *P(Ch)* (Feb. 1916).   *167*

1 *the hawk*: cf. notes on 'Tom O'Roughley' (*PNE* 155). In 'Four Years: 1887–1891' Yeats described how he thought that in man and race there is something called Unity of Being. He thought the enemy of this Unity was abstraction, 'meaning by abstraction not the distinction but the isolation of occupation, or class or faculty'. He then added the first six lines of 'The Hawk'.

15 *Last evening?*: the conversation is not recorded. There is a certain amount of   *168* self-analysis in Yeats's Diaries where he recorded dissatisfaction with his methods of conversing, particularly in the Arts Club. There is an example of this rethinking of past conversations or debates in *Estrangement*, II. Out of this need to develop a poised personality came the doctrine of the mask: 'Style, personality – deliberately adopted and therefore a mask – is the only escape from the hot-faced bargainers and the money-changers' (*A* 461).

MEMORY   162

Ellmann (*IY* 290) dates this poem as 1915–16; it first appeared in *P(Ch)* (Feb.   *168* 1916).

1   *a lovely face*: Mrs Shakespear

5   *form*: the lair in which a hare crouches

6   *the mountain hare*: possibly Iseult Gonne. See notes on 'Two Songs of a Fool' (*PNE* 186).

163   HER PRAISE

168   The manuscript of this poem is dated 27 January 1915; it first appeared in *P(Ch)* (Feb. 1916), entitled 'The Thorn Tree'.

1   *She is foremost* . . . : the poem is about Maud Gonne, who withdrew from public life after her marriage. See *WBY* 210. Yeats sees society as forgetting her but the poor as remembering her. Maud Gonne was well known among the Dublin poor for her charity.

3   *turned the talk*: cf. line 14 'manage the talk'

169   11–18   *I will talk no more . . . But walk*: the original version of these lines ran:

> A man comes hither because of the harsh wind
> I am certain that where he finds the thorn he will stop
> To shelter a while, that puts it into my mind
> To turn the talk until her name has come up.
>
> And being but a ragged man he will know her name
> And be well pleased remembering it, for in old days
> Though she had young men's praise and old men's blame
> Among the poor both old and young gave her praise.

164   THE PEOPLE

169   The manuscript of this poem is dated 10 January 1915. It first appeared, entitled 'The Phoenix', in *P(Ch)* (Feb. 1916).

1   *'What have I earned . . .'*: this poem records a conversation with Maud Gonne, who is symbolised by the Phoenix in this poem and 'His Phoenix' (*PNE* 165).

2   *all that I have done*: probably a reference not only to Yeats's work for the Abbey Theatre but his earlier work for the literary and political movements.

3   *this unmannerly town*: Dublin, which had failed to appreciate the dramatic work of Synge (and Yeats) and the generosity of Hugh Lane.

4   *most defamed*: perhaps a mixture of dislike of Dublin's malicious gossip, its journalism, and George Moore's writings (see notes on the 'Introductory Rhymes' and 'Closing Rhyme' of *Responsibilities* (*PNE* 112 and 142)).

6-9   *I might have lived . . . Ferrara wall*: Wade included a fragment of a letter in his selection, which described a rehearsal at the Gaiety Theatre, Dublin, probably in October 1901, in which Yeats described his longing to get away from his work for an audience which he regarded as unsuitable:

> The kid Benson is to carry in his arms was wandering in and out among the artificial ivy. I was saying to myself 'Here are we a lot of intelligent people, who might have been doing some sort of work that leads to some fun. Yet here we are going through all sorts of trouble and annoyance for a mob that knows neither literature nor art. I might have been away in the country, in Italy, perhaps writing poems for my equals and betters. That kid is the only sensible creature on the stage. He knows his business and keeps to it.' At that very moment one of the actors called out 'Look at the goat eating the property ivy.'   (*L* 356)

9   *Ferrara*: Yeats visited the town in 1907. Duke Ercole was an excellent encourager of the arts. Cf. notes to 'To a Wealthy Man who promised a second Subscription to the Dublin Municipal Gallery if it were proved the People wanted Pictures' (*PNE* 114).

11-18   *the unperturbed and courtly images . . . dawn*: the source of these lines is probably Castiglione's *The Book of the Courtier*. Yeats possessed Hoby's Elizabethan translation (issued by David Nutt in 1900 with an Introduction by Sir Walter Raleigh), but he seems to have referred to Opdycke's translation also, published by Duckworth in 1902. The following extract is from Opdycke:

> . . . the custom of all the gentlemen of the house was to betake themselves straightway after supper to my lady Duchess; where, among the other pleasant pastimes and music and dancing that continually were practised, sometimes neat questions were proposed, sometimes ingenious games were devised at the choice of one or another, in which under various disguises the company disclosed their thoughts figuratively to whom they liked best. Sometimes other discussions arose about different matters, or biting retorts passed lightly back and forth. Often devices (*imprese*), as we now call them, were displayed, in discussing which there was wonderful diversion, the house being (as I have said) full of very noble talents.   (*The Courtier* (tr. 1902) 12)

The anecdote of the Duchess [of Urbino, Elisabetta Gonzaga (1471-1526)] and her people talking till dawn also derives from the description of a prolonged evening at Urbino:

> My lord Gaspar began making ready to reply, but my lady Duchess said:
> 'Of this let messer Pietro Bembo be the judge, and let us abide by his decision whether or not women are as capable of divine love as men are. But the controversy between you might be long, it will be well to postpone it until tomorrow.'
> 'Nay, until this evening,' said messer Cesare Gonzaga.

'How until this evening?' said my lady Duchess.

Messer Cesare replied:

'Because it is already day'; and he showed her the light that was beginning to come in through the cracks at the windows.

Then everyone rose to his feet in great surprise, for the discussion did not seem to have lasted longer than usual; but by reason of having been begun much later, and by its pleasantness, it had so beguiled the company that they had not perceived the flight of hours; nor was there anyone who felt the heaviness of sleep upon his eyes, which nearly always happens when the accustomed hour of sleep is passed in watching. The windows having then been opened on that side of the palace which looks towards the lofty crest of Mount Catria, they saw that a beautiful dawn of rosy hue was already born in the east, and that all the stars had vanished save Venus, sweet mistress of the sky, who holds the bonds of night and day: from which there seemed to breathe a gentle wind that filled the air with crisp coolness and began to waken sweet choruses of joyous birds in the murmuring forests of the hills hard by.

So, having reverently taken leave of my lady Duchess, they all started towards their chambers without light of torches, that of day being enough for them. . . . (*The Courtier* (tr. 1902) 308)

See also Yeats's comment on Urbino in 'Discoveries' (*ELI* 290 and 293)

170   22   *my phoenix*: Maud Gonne. Cf. Nancy Cardozo, *MGLE* 264

23   *when my luck changed*: a memory of the unpopularity which greeted Maud Gonne in Dublin. She was seeking a separation from her husband John MacBride in 1905.

27   *after nine years*: this would place the conversation in 1906.

165   HIS PHOENIX

170   This poem was written in January 1915 and first appeared, entitled 'There is a Queen in China' in *P(Ch)* (Feb. 1916).

1–7   *There is a queen . . . his mind*: the second stanza of the original manuscript version of the poem ran thus:

> And every morn and every night some newspaper applauds
> The unblemished character, whiteness that has no stain
> As though she'd warmed herself in Troy, and there are waggon loads
> Of Countesses and Duchesses surpassing womankind
> Or who have found a painter to make them so for pay
> And smooth out stain or blemish with the elegance of his mind.

4   *that sprightly girl*: Leda. Cf. 'Leda and the Swan' (*PNE* 220). Tread (of birds), to copulate.

8   *a phoenix*: Maud Gonne. See the essay on 'Poetry and Tradition':

This joy, because it must be always making and mastering, remains in the hands and in the tongue of the artist, but with his eyes he enters upon a submissive, sorrowful contemplation of the great irremediable things, and he is known from other men by making all he handles like himself, and yet by the unlikeness to himself of all that comes before him in a pure contemplation. It may have been his enemy or his love or his cause that set him dreaming, and certainly the phoenix can but open her young wings in a flaming nest; but all hate and hope vanishes in the dream, and if his mistress brag of the song or his enemy fear it, it is not that either has its praise or blame, but that the wings of the holy nest are not easily set afire. The verses may make his mistress famous as Helen or give a victory to his cause, not because he has been either's servant, but because men delight to honour and to remember all that have served contemplation. (*E & I* 254-5)

9-11 *their Gaby's laughing eye*: these lines were different in the original MS. and ran:

> Pavlova is beyond our praise, Gaby's a laughing eye
> Though Ruth St. Denis had no luck she had an Indian charm
> In 1908 or nine Miss Maud Allen had the cry.

9 *Gaby*: Gaby Deslys (1884-1920), a French actress

10 *Ruth St. Denis*: an American dancer (1887-1968)

11 *Pavlova*: Anna Matveyevna Pavlova (1885-1931), the famous Russian ballerina

12 *a player in the States*: Julia Marlowe (1866-1950), whom Yeats saw during his 1903-4 lecture tour in the United States, was known for her Shakespearean roles.

17 *Margaret ... Dorothy ... Mary*: Ellmann (*ED* 73) remarks that this was a list of Ezra Pound's girl friends. In April 1914 Pound married Dorothy Shakespear, daughter of Yeats's friend Mrs Olivia Shakespear. See *PYP* 66-7.

18 *in privacy*: a note in Yeats's handwriting on the final manuscript version of the poem reads: 'When I repeated this to Gogarty [Oliver St. John Gogarty (1878-1957)] he says I spoke of "chastity" not "privacy" and he prefers "chastity".'

28. *the simplicity of a child*: cf. 'Against Unworthy Praise' (*PNE* 98) where   *172* she is described as 'half lion, half child', and 'Long-legged Fly' (*PNE* 364) where she is 'part woman, three parts a child'.

29 *that proud look*: cf. 'Upon a House shaken by the Land Agitation' (*PNE* 105) with its 'lidless eye that loves the sun'. The eagle is supposed to be able to gaze into the sun unblinkingly.

166   A THOUGHT FROM PROPERTIUS

172   This poem was probably written before November 1915 and first appeared in *WSC*.

Title   Propertius: Sextus Propertius (*c*. 50–16 BC) a Roman love poet

1   *She might*: Maud Gonne

4   *walked to the altar*: the poem probably derives from the second poem in the second book of Propertius. Yeats seems to have selected images from it:

> Why abides such mortal beauty upon earth? Jupiter, I pardon thy gallantries of olden time. Yellow is her hair, and tapering her hands, tall and full her figure, and stately her walk, worthy the sister of Jove or like to Pallas, when she strides to Dulichian altars, her breast veiled by the Gorgons' snaky locks. Fair is she as Ischomache, heroic child of the Lapithae, the Centaurs' welcome spoil in the revel's midst, or as Brimo when by the sacred waters of Boebeis she laid her virgin body at Mercury's side. Yield now, ye goddesses, whom of old the shepherd saw lay aside your raiment on the heights of Ida! And oh! may old age never mar that face, though she reach the years of the Cumaean prophetess. (H. E. Butler's translation)

6   *Pallas Athene*: Yeats described Maud Gonne in terms of Pallas Athene in 'Beautiful Lofty Things' (*PNE* 334): 'Pallas Athena in that straight back and arrogant head.' When they first met in 1889 she seemed a classical impersonation of the spring, 'the Virgilian commendation ''She walks like a goddess'' made for her alone.' Cf. *A* 123. Pallas Athene in Greek mythology was a virgin goddess of wisdom, of practical skills, the arts of peace and of prudent warfare. See Jeffares, 'Pallas Athene Gonne', *Tributes in Prose and Verse to Shotaro Oshima* (1970) 4–7

7   *Centaur*: see note on 'Lines Written in Dejection' (*PNE* 157).

167   BROKEN DREAMS

172   This poem was dated 24 October 1915 in the Maud Gonne Manuscript Book: it first appeared, dated November 1915, in the *Little Review* (June 1917).

1   *your hair*: the poem is written to Maud Gonne.

173   18   *the poet stubborn with his passion*: Yeats

19   *chilled his blood*: Yeats was fifty when he wrote the poem

21   *all, all, shall be renewed*: cf. line 8 'In Memory of Major Robert Gregory (*PNE* 144); line 5 'The Results of Thought' (*PNE* 264); lines 118–37 'The

Shadowy Waters' (*PNE* 380); line 184 'The Gift of Harun Al-Rashid' (*PNE* 382).

28   *your body had a flaw*: in an essay on 'The Tragic Theatre' written five years earlier Yeats praised the attractiveness of the unusual in a beloved, the quality of uniqueness:

> Some little irrelevance of line, some promise of character to come, may indeed put us at our ease, 'give more interest' as the humour of the old man with the basket does to Cleopatra's dying; but should it come, as we had dreamed in love's frenzy, to our dying for that woman's sake, we would find that the discord had its value from the tune.   (*E & I* 244)

A DEEP-SWORN VOW   168

This poem is dated 17 October 1915 in the Maud Gonne Manuscript Book and   *174* first appeared in the *Little Review* (June 1917).

1   *you did not keep*: Maud Gonne

2   *That deep-sworn vow*: not to marry

3   *look death in the face*: the poem may possibly have been inspired by a poem by Arthur Symons because the entry in the Manuscript Book which precedes it reads:

> I have just found a scrap of paper in Nan Tobin's writing. It is a poem by Arthur Symons written in his first stages of madness – a state of delirium. Four lines thus:
>
> > I am undone. My course shall swiftly run
> > Yet lain enrapt in an enchanted swoon
> > I die of rapture yet I see that soon
> > The fated sisters shall my web have spun.

PRESENCES   169

This poem was dated November 1915 in the Maud Gonne Manuscript Book and   *174* first appeared in the *Little Review* (June 1917):

12   *One is a harlot*: probably the lady [Mabel Dickinson] referred to by Hone (*WBY* 301).

one a child: Iseult Gonne

14   *a queen*: Maud Gonne

170   THE BALLOON OF THE MIND

175   This poem was written before 1917 and first appeared in the *New Statesman* (29 Sept. 1917).

2   *the balloon of the mind*: in 'Reveries', written in 1914, Yeats traced a lack of organised thought back to his English schooldays, in the Godolphin School, Hammersmith. (The similarity of the idea and image in the poem and the prose might argue some closeness in the date of composition):

> I was unfitted for school work, and though I would often work well for weeks together, I have to give the whole evening to one lesson if I was to know it. My thoughts were a great excitement, but when I tried to do anything with them, it was like trying to pack a balloon into a shed in a high wind.   (*A* 41)

He blamed his father for not taking him away from school, this time the High School, Dublin:

> He would have taught me nothing but Greek and Latin, and I would now be a properly educated man, and would not have to look in useless longing at books that have been, through the poor mechanism of translation, the builders of my soul, nor face authority with the timidity born of excuse and evasion. Evasion and excuse were in the event as wise as the housebuilding instinct of the beaver.   (*A* 58)

171   TO A SQUIRREL AT KYLE-NA-NO

175   The manuscript of this poem is dated September 1912 and it first appeared in the *New Statesman* (29 Sept. 1917).

Title   Kyle-na-no: (*Irish* Coill na gCno), The Wood of Nuts, one of the seven woods at Coole, spelt 'Kyle-na-gno' in the first printing, later 'Kyle-Na-Gno' until it became Kyle-na-no in *CP*. Cf. 'An Appointment' (*PNE* 138). See note on 'Closing Rhyme' (*PNE* 142).

6   *all I would do*: Yeats's attitude to killing animals emerged early in life:

> I fished for pike at Castle Dargan and shot at birds with a muzzle-loading pistol until somebody shot a rabbit and I heard it squeal. From that on I would kill nothing but the dumb fish.   (*A* 55)

172   ON BEING ASKED FOR A WAR POEM

175   This poem was written on 6 February 1915 and first appeared in *The Book of the Homeless* (ed. Edith Wharton, 1916), entitled 'A Reason for Keeping Silent'. The original title was 'To a friend who has asked me to sign his manifesto to the neutral nations.'

1 *I think it better*: Yeats sent the poem to Henry James on 20 August [1915] in a letter from Coole Park and concluded the letter:

> It is the only thing I have written of the war or will write, so I hope it may not seem unfitting. I shall keep the neighbourhood of the seven sleepers of Ephesus, hoping to catch their comfortable snores till bloody frivolity is over.   (*L* 600)

IN MEMORY OF ALFRED POLLEXFEN   **173**

This poem was written in August 1916 according to Ellmann (*IY* 290); it first   *175*
appeared in the *Little Review* (June 1917), entitled 'In Memory'.

1 *Five-and-twenty years have gone*: William Pollexfen (b. 1811), Yeats's maternal grandfather, died in 1890. See 'Introductory Rhymes' (*PNE* 112) and 'Under Saturn' (*PNE* 192).

3 *his strong bones*: the use of 'bones' for 'body' in this line may be due to   *176*
Yeats's memory of his grandfather using the phrase 'I am not going to lie with those old bones' when deciding not to be buried with the Middletons:

> There was a Middleton tomb and a long list of Middletons on the wall, and an almost empty space for Pollexfen names . . . [obviously, as William Pollexfen was the first of the family to settle in Sligo] and already one saw his name in large gilt letters on the stone fence of a new tomb. He ended his walk at Saint John's churchyard [in Sligo] almost daily, for he liked everything neat and compendious as upon shipboard, and if he had not looked after the tomb himself the builder might have added some useless ornament.   (*A* 67-8)

4 *Elizabeth*: Elizabeth Pollexfen, *nee* Middleton (1819-92). For details of the Pollexfens see William M. Murphy, *The Yeats Family and the Pollexfens of Sligo* (1971).

> . . . his wife, a Middleton, was gentle and patient and did many charities in the little back parlour among frieze coats and shawled heads, and every night when she saw him asleep [he had a violent temper and kept a hatchet by his bed] went the round of the house alone with a candle to make certain there was no burglar in danger of the hatchet.'   (*A* 9)

6 *after twenty years*: George Pollexfen (b. 1839) died in September 1910.

9 *And Masons drove*: Yeats described the funeral in a letter of 29 September 1910 to Lady Gregory:

> The funeral was very touching – the church full of the working people, Catholics who had never been in a Protestant church before, and the man next me crying all the time. I thought of Synge's funeral – none at that, after some two or three, but enemies or conventional images of gloom. The Masons (there were 80 of them) had their own service and one by one threw acacia leaves into the grave with the traditional Masonic goodbye, 'Alas my brother so mote it

be.' Then there came two who threw each a white rose, and that was because they and he were 'Priori Masons', a high degree of Masonry.   (*L* 553)

11   *a melancholy man*: see notes on 'In Memory of Major Robert Gregory' (*PNE* 144). George Pollexfen was a hypochondriac, but Yeats wrote, 'it is a curious thing that George who complained so much when well, has always been brave and calm before real calamity' (*L* 551).

13   *Many a son and daughter*: Yeats's 'grandfather's many sons and daughters, came and went' (*A* 10).

15   *The Mall and . . . grammar school*: a street in Sligo and the grammar school which survives today

17   *the sailor John*: John Butler Yeats in a letter written in 1916 to the poet made the point that a sailor's self-control compelled him into personality, alluding to stories told by John Pollexfen (1845–1900; he died in Liverpool) about his life at sea (*LTHS* 224).

24   *the youngest son*: he 'was stout and humorous and had a tongue of leather over the keyhole of his door to keep the draught out' (*A* 10).

30   *journey home*: Alfred Pollexfen (1854–1916) – J. B. Yeats called him 'that mental simpleton Alfred' – came back from Liverpool where he had worked in the family firm (W. & G. T. Pollexfen & Co.) to take George's place in it in Sligo. His wife and children stayed in Sligo while he was away. The lines mean he returned to Sligo at fifty and died ten years later.

31   *fiftieth*: he actually returned in 1910.

177   37   *A visionary white sea-bird*: Yeats recorded that his sister had (six months before he wrote 'Reveries' in 1914) awoken dreaming that she held a wingless sea-bird in her arms and presently had heard that another uncle had died in his madhouse, 'for a sea-bird is the omen that announces the death or danger of a Pollexfen' (*A* 10). Yeats wrote to Lady Gregory that his sister Lily as well as the nurse heard the Banshee and George Pollexfen died the night after at the same hour the Banshee had cried the night before. He wrote to Lily to say it seemed a fitting thing, as George Pollexfen had an instinctive nature close to the supernatural (*L* 552 and 553).

38   *'Mr Alfred'*: Yeats's sister Lily (1866–1949) described his last six years in Sligo: 'He had money and was no longer one of a great army of nobodies in Liverpool but had become ''Mr Alfred'' in a place where he was know[n] and which had known and respected his people before him' (Letter to John Butler Yeats, 14 August 1916)

UPON A DYING LADY

These seven poems were written between January 1912 and July 1914. Section I *177* was written in January 1913, Section II in January 1912, and Section VII probably in July 1914. They first appeared in the *Little Review* (Aug. 1917) under the general title 'Seven Poems', the fourth, fifth and sixth being given numerical subtitles, the other being entitled as in *CP*.

HER COURTESY

Title   Her Courtesy: the subject of the poems is the painter Aubrey Beardsley's *177* sister Mabel who had married an actor, George Bealby Wright. She died of cancer in her early forties, and letters Yeats wrote to Lady Gregory on 8 January 1913 and on 11 February 1913 explain the circumstances in which the poems were written:

My dear Lady Gregory . . . I dined with Lane on Sunday. He is very pleased with the poem which Hone has now. Hone was excited with doing a leader elaborating the thought of the poem. I am not very hopeful. The Corporation has voted about £2000 a year and I told Lane I thought he should consider that as the country's support and not make the action of half a dozen people – who alone have money enough to subscribe £20,000 – the deciding thing. He replied that he hated Dublin. I said so do we. He then said that unless the gallery were built at once it would be a long time before he would have the pleasure of hanging the pictures. I urged him to buy the site himself, if need [be] by selling some of the pictures for the purpose. He said he could buy it without selling any of the pictures but thought it a mistake to do so unless £20,000 was subscribed, so we were back again at the half dozen people. He took all I said in good part and has asked me to invite myself to dinner when I liked. . . .

Strange that just after writing those lines on the Rhymers who 'unrepenting faced their ends' I should be at the bedside of the dying sister of Beardsley, who was practically one of us. She had had a week of great pain but on Sunday was I think free from it. She was propped up on pillows with her cheeks I think a little rouged and looking very beautiful. Beside her a Xmas tree with little toys containing sweets, which she gave us. Mr Davis – Ricketts' patron – had brought it – I daresay it was Ricketts' idea. I will keep the little toy she gave me and I daresay she knew this. On a table near were four dolls dressed like people out of her brother's drawings. Women with loose trousers and boys that looked like women. Ricketts had made them, modelling the faces and sewing the clothes. They must have taken him days. She had all her great lady airs and asked after my work and my health as if they were the most important things in the world to her. 'A palmist told me,' she said, 'that when I was forty-two my life would take a turn for the better and now I shall spend my forty-second year in heaven' and then emphatically 'O yes I shall go to heaven. Papists do.' When I told her where Mrs Emery was she said 'How fine of her, but a girls' school! why she used to make even me blush!' Then she began telling improper stories and inciting us (there were two men besides myself) to do the like. At moments she shook with laughter. Just before I was going her mother came and saw me to the door. As we were standing at 'it she said 'I do not think she wishes to live – how could she after such agony? She is all I have left now.' I lay awake most of the night with a poem in my head. I cannot over-state her strange charm – the pathetic gaiety. It was her brother but her brother was not I think loveable, only astounding and intrepid. She has been ill since June last. . . .

My dear Lady Gregory . . . Mabel Beardsley said to me on Sunday 'I wonder who will introduce me in heaven. It should be my brother but then they might not appreciate the introduction. They might not have good taste.' She said of her brother 'He hated the people who denied the existence of evil, and so being young he filled his pictures with evil. He had a passion for reality.' She has the same passion and puts aside any attempts to suggest recovery and yet I have never seen her in low spirits. She talked of a play she wanted to see. 'If I could only send my head and my legs,' she said, 'for they are quite well.' Till one questions her she tries to make one forget that she is ill. I always see her alone now. She keeps Sunday afternoon for me. I will send you the little series of poems when they are finished. One or two are I think very good.   (*L* 573-5)

8   *Petronius Arbiter*: Gaius Petronius (d. 66 AD) a Roman satirist, companion of Nero and author of the Satiricon. He was the director of the pleasures of the Emperor's Court, the *arbiter elegantiae*.

175   II CERTAIN ARTISTS BRING HER DOLLS AND DRAWINGS

177   2   *doll*: see letters to Lady Gregory quoted above.

176   III SHE TURNS THE DOLLS' FACES TO THE WALL

Title   the Dolls': made by Ricketts, see letters to Lady Gregory quoted above, and by Edmund Dulac.

178   7   *Longhi*: Pietro Longhi (1702-62), a Venetian genre painter

9   *our Beauty*: see letters to Lady Gregory quoted above.

10   *must have like every dog his day*: probably an echo of Paul Fort's phrase, quoted by Yeats in 'Modern Poetry: A Broadcast':

> And they came back so merrily: all at the dawn of day;
> A singing all so merrily: '*The dog must have his day!*'

Paul Fort, a French poet, was born in 1872; the translation was read by Yeats in one of his brother's *Broadsides* (a mixture of hand-coloured prints and poetry).

V HER RACE   178

11   *her dead brother's valour*: Aubrey Beardsley (1872–98) was art editor of   *179*
The Yellow Book (1894) and died of consumption at the age of twenty-six. An
unpublished section of the poem ran as follows:

> Although she has turned away
> The pretty waxen faces
> And hid their silk and laces
> For Mass was said to-day
> She has not begun denying
> Now that she is but dying
> The pleasures she loved well
> The strong milk of her mother
> The valour of her brother
> Are in her body still
> She will not die weeping
> May God be with her sleeping.

VI HER COURAGE   179

4–6   *Grania . . . Diarmuid*: see notes on 'A Faery Song' (*PNE* 23)

8   *Giorgione*: a famous Venetian painter (*c.* 1478–1510)

9   *Achilles*: Greek hero, son of Peleus and Thetis. He slew Hector in the siege of
Troy (see 'News for the Delphic Oracle' (*PNE* 363), was wounded in the heel
(the rest of his body being invulnerable) by Paris and died.

Timor: Tamburlaine (1336–1405), Mongol conqueror, ruler of Samarkand from
1369 to 1405

Babar: Zahir-ud-din Mohammed (?1480–1530), founder of the Moghul Empire
in India (1483–1530)

Barhaim: probably Bahram, the great hunter of Edward FitzGerald's (1809–83)
Rubáiyát of Omar Khayyam (1859); he was called Bahrám Gur, Bahram of the
Wild Ass, from his skill in hunting the animal

EGO DOMINUS TUUS   .   181

The poem was written by 5 October 1915, though a second manuscript bears the   *180*
date 5 December 1915. It first appeared in *P* (*Ch*) (Oct. 1917). In 1925 Yeats
wrote: 'I can now, if I have the energy, find the simplicity I have sought in vain. I
need no longer write poems like "The Phases of the Moon" [*PNE* 183] nor
"Ego Dominus Tuus" ' (*AV* (A) xii)

Title This comes from Dante Alighieri (1265-1321), *Vita Nuova*. The passage in *PASL* which gives this information indicates the main thought of the poem, that Yeats is open to the power that fills creative men, that the artist has a well of strength from which to draw, the source of which he does not know, there being an ununderstood unreality in life:

> How could I have mistaken for myself an heroic condition that from early boyhood has made me superstitious? That which comes as complete, as minutely organised, as are those elaborate, brightly lighted buildings and sceneries appearing in a moment, as I lie between sleeping and waking must come from above me and beyond me. At times I remember that place in Dante where he sees in his chamber the 'Lord of Terrible Aspect', and how, seeming 'to rejoice inwardly that it was a marvel to see, speaking, he said many things among the which I could understand but few, and of these this: ego dominus tuus' . . . (*M* 325-6)

Ego dominus tuus: (*Latin*) I am thy master. Yeats read various translations of Dante: Cary's, Shadwell's and Rosetti's.

1   *Hic*: the poem takes the form of a dialogue between *Hic* and *Ille*, the setting the neighbourhood of Thoor Ballylee (which Yeats bought in 1917). Yeats had written to his father that his thought was part of a religion more or less logically worked out:

> A system which will, I hope, interest you as a form of poetry. I find the setting of it all in order has helped my verse, has given me a new framework and new patterns. One goes on year after year getting the disorder of one's own mind in order, and this is the real impulse to create.   (Quoted by Hone (*WBY* 305))

He referred to *PASL* (first called 'An Alphabet') in which he developed the theories of the anti-self which are explored in 'Ego Dominus Tuus'. In the poem's dialogue *Hic* defends the objective, *Ille* the subjective; *hic* and *ille* are Latin demonstrative pronouns, 'this' and 'that', or 'the former' and 'the latter'; used here in the sense of 'the one' and 'the other'. (Contemporary comment in Dublin – Ellmann attributes the quip to Ezra Pound – had it that *Hic* and *Willie* would be more correct nomenclature.) *PASL* affords some explanation of parts of the poem.

2   *wind-beaten tower*: Yeats's Norman tower (*Irish*, tur, tor) at Ballylee, Co. Galway. See notes on 'In Memory of Major Robert Gregory' (*PNE* 144).

3   *A lamp*: cf. the symbolism of tower and lamp in 'The Tower' (*PNE* 205) and, particularly, notes (p. 268) on the section of 'Meditations in Time of Civil War' entitled 'My House' (*PNE* 207).

4   *Michael Robartes*: see notes on 'The Lover tells of the Rose in his Heart' (*PNE* 43). Robartes appeared in the story 'Rosa Alchemica' as a mysterious person who persuades the narrator to join a magical society which is attacked in a village riot. Robartes has travelled in the Near East. He and Aherne appear in the Introduction to *AV* where Aherne complains that 'Mr Yeats had given the name of Michael Robartes and that of Owen Aherne to fictitious characters, and made

those characters live through events that were a travesty of real events.' In *AV* (A) Robartes is described as finding the *Speculum Anglorum et Hominorum*, written by Giraldus and printed in Cracow in 1594. After this he found an Arab tribe of Judwalis who, though they have lost their sacred book, which was attributed to Kusta ben Luka, a Christian philosopher at the Court of Harun Al-Raschid, remember much of its doctrine, and this doctrine is akin to the material in the book by Giraldus. Yeats agreed to write an exposition of the Giraldus diagrams provided Aherne wrote the Introduction and any notes he pleased. The unreality of this myth-making was acknowledged openly in *A Packet for Ezra Pound* (1929) and in *AV* (B):

> The first version of this book, *A Vision*, except the section on the twenty-eight phases, and that called 'Dove or Swan' which I repeat without change, fills me with shame. I had misinterpreted the geometry, and in my ignorance of philosophy failed to understand distinctions upon which the coherence of the whole depended, and as my wife was unwilling that her share should be known, and I to seem sole author, I had invented an unnatural story of an Arabian traveller which I must amend and find a place for some day because I was fool enough to write half a dozen poems that are unintelligible without it. (*AV* (B) 19)

The notes on 'The Gift of Harun Al-Rashid' (*PNE* 382) should be consulted, and on 'The Phases of the Moon' (*PNE* 183).

5–7 *still trace . . . Magical shapes*: these are the shapes Robartes had previously traced on the Arabian sands:

> many diagrams where gyres and circles grew out of one another like strange vegetables; and there was a large diagram at the beginning where lunar phases and zodiacal signs were mixed with various unintelligible symbols. (*AV* (A) xviii)

8 *I call to my own opposite*: cf. this passage in Yeats's essay in 'The Death of Synge':

> I think that all happiness depends on the energy to assume the mask of some other self; that all joyous or creative life is a rebirth as something not oneself, something which has no memory and is created in a moment and perpetually renewed. We put on a grotesque or solemn painted face to hide us from the terrors of judgment, invent an imaginative Saturnalia where one forgets reality, a game like that of a child, where one loses the infinite pain of self-realization. Perhaps all the sins and energies of the world are but its flight from an infinite blinding beam. (*A* 503)

Yeats later referred to this passage; he had explained that once he had formed the idea of the mask he became over-allegorical and his imagination became sterile, for nearly five years, and he only escaped by mocking his own thought (in *The Player Queen*). He also quoted an earlier comment on the mask:

> If we cannot imagine ourselves as different from what we are, and try to assume that second self, we cannot impose a discipline upon ourselves though we may accept one from others. Active virtue, as distinguished from the passive

167

acceptance of a code, is therefore theatrical, consciously dramatic, the wearing of a mask. . . . (*M* 334)

In the poem we need to read to the end before the full significance of the phrase 'call to my own opposite' can be understood: it is expanded in the final speech of *Ille*: 'I call to the mysterious one . . .'. *Hic*, however, being objective, replies, in effect, 'Why pursue unreality?' He says that he would find himself, not an image.

12   *gentle sensitive mind*: cf. Yeats's comment in 'Anima Hominis' that he began to believe that

> our culture, with its doctrine of sincerity and self-realization, made us gentle and passive, and that the Middle Ages and the Renaissance were right to found theirs upon the imitation of Christ or of some classic hero. Saint Francis and Caesar Borgia made themselves overmastering, creative persons by turning from the mirror to meditation upon a mask.   (*M* 333)

This is *Ille*'s rejoinder: that there is a lack of inspiration or rapture in contemporary work.

18   *chief imagination*: Yeats is thinking of him here as the author of the *Divine Comedy* (?1309–?20), an allegorical account of his journey through Hell, Purgatory and Paradise guided by Virgil and his idealised love Beatrice (see note on lines 20 and 37 below).

181   19   *Dante . . . found himself*: in a somewhat rhetorical passage in 'Anima Hominis' Yeats wrote of himself when away from others inviting a Marmorean Muse, an art where no thought nor emotion has come to him because another man thought or felt something different:

> . . . for now there must be no reaction, action only, and the world must move my heart but to the heart's discovery of itself, and I begin to dream of eyelids that do not quiver before the bayonet: all my thoughts have ease and joy, I am all virtue and confidence. When I come to put in rhyme what I have found, it will be a hard toil, but for a moment I believe I have found myself and not my anti-self.   (*M* 325)

Hic's remarks on Dante finding himself reinforce his earlier comment, but provide an opportunity for *Ille* to develop the idea of the anti-self.

20   *that hollow face*: this line is probably owed to a memory of a sentence by Simeon Solomon (1840–1905), an English painter and draughtsman. Cf. 'Anima Hominis':

> Some thirty years ago I read a prose allegory by Simeon Solomon, long out of print and unprocurable, and remember or seem to remember a sentence, 'a hollow image of fulfilled desire.' All happy art seems to me that hollow image, but when its lineaments express also the poverty or the exasperation that set its maker to the work, we call it tragic art. Keats but gave us his dream of luxury; but while reading Dante we never long escape the conflict, partly because the verses are at moments a mirror of his history, and yet more because that history is so clear and simple that it has the quality of art. I am no Dante scholar, and I

but read him in Shadwell or in Dante Rossetti, but I am always persuaded that he celebrated the most pure lady poet ever sung and the Divine Justice, not merely because death took that lady and Florance banished her singer, but because he had to struggle in his own heart with his unjust anger and his lust; while, unlike those of the great poets who are at peace with the world and at war with themselves, he fought a double war.\'Always,' says Boccaccio, 'both in youth and maturity he found room among his virtues for lechery'; or as Matthew Arnold preferred to change the phrase, 'his conduct was exceeding irregular.' Guido Cavalcanti, as Rossetti translates him, finds 'too much baseness' in his friend:

> And still thy speech of me, heartfelt and kind,
> Hath made me treasure up thy poetry;
> But now I dare not, for thy abject life,
> Make manifest that I approve thy rhymes.

And when Dante meets Beatrice in Eden, does she not reproach him because, when she had taken her presence away, he followed, in spite of warning dreams, false images, and now, to save him in his own despite, she has 'visited . . . the Portals of the Dead,' and chosen Virgil for his courier? While Gino de Pistoia complains that in his *Commedia* his 'lovely heresies . . . beat the right down and let the wrong go free':

> Therefore his vain decrees, wherein he lied,
> Must be like empty nutshells flung aside;
> Yet through the rash false witness set to grow,
> French and Italian vengeance on such pride
> May fall like Antony on Cicero.

Dante himself sings to Giovanni Guirino 'at the approach of death':

> The King, by whose rich grave his servants be
> With plenty beyond measure set to dwell,
> Ordains that I may bitter wrath dispel,
> And lift mine eyes to the great Consistory.   (*M* 329-31)

23   *was the hunger*: in 'Hodos Chameliontos' Yeats wrote of personifying spirits which bring our souls to crisis:

We have dreamed a foolish dream these many centuries in thinking that they value a life of contemplation, for they scorn that more than any possible life, unless it be but a name for the worst crisis of all. They have but one purpose, to bring their chosen man to the greatest obstacle he may confront without despair. They contrived Dante's banishment, and snatched away his Beatrice, and thrust Villon into the arms of harlots, and sent him to gather cronies at the foot of the gallows, that Dante and Villon might through passion become conjoined to their buried selves, [he wrote earlier that genius is a crisis that joins that buried self (the age-long memorial self that shapes the shell of the mollusc and the child in the womb) for certain moments to our trivial daily mind], turn all to Mask and Image, and so be phantoms in their own eyes . . . but in a few in whom we recognise supreme masters of tragedy, the whole contest is brought into the circle of their beauty. Such masters – Villon and Dante, let us say – would not, when they speak through their art, change their luck; yet they are mirrored in all the sufferings of desire. The two halves of their

169

nature are so completely joined that they seem to labour for their objects, and yet to desire whatever happens, being at the same instant predestinate and free, creation's very self. We gaze at such men in awe, because we gaze not at a work of art, but at the re-creation of the man through that art, the birth of a new species of man, and it may even seem that the hairs of our heads stand up, because that birth, that re-creation, is from terror. Had not Dante and Villon understood that their fate wrecked what life could not rebuild, had they lacked their Vision of Evil, had they cherished any species of optimism, they could but have found a false beauty, or some momentary instinctive beauty, and suffered no change at all, or but changed as do the wild creatures, or from Devil well to Devil sick, and so round the clock.   (*A* 272-3)

26   *Lapo and Guido*: Lapo degli Uberti was said to have been the son of Farinata degli Uberti (the Ghibelline leader of Florence) and father of Fazio degli Uberti, the author of *Dittamondo*, which is thought, according to H. F. Cary, Dante's translator, to approach the *Divina Commedia* in the energy of its style. Guido Cavalcanti (*c.* 1230–1300) was an Italian poet. Yeats may have associated Lapo and Guido because of a note in Cary's translation of Dante which he was fond of reading, despite his remark that he was no Dante scholar and but read him in Shadwell or Dante Rossetti. This note ran:

> I perceive that some have known the excellence of the vernacular tongue, namely Guido Lapo. I [Cary] suspect Dante here means his two friends Cavalcanti and Uberti; though this has hitherto been taken for the name of one person.

But Lapo Gianni (*c.* 1270–1330) was, like Cavalcanti, also Dante's friend and contemporary, and he may have been the Lapo intended by Yeats. See Nicola Zingarelli, 'La Vita, tempe e le opere di Dante', *Storia Letteraria d'Italia* (Milan 1931) pp. 189, 197, 607 for discussion of Lapo degli Uberti, and pp. 92, 107, 197, 200, 205, 209, 225, 313, 586, for discussion of Lapo Gianni.

29   *a Bedouin's horse-hair roof*: cf. Shelley's *Queen Mab*:

> Behold yon sterile spot,
> Where now the wandering Arab's tent
> Flaps in the desert blast.

There is a childhood memory which may have recurred to Yeats which he recounts in 'Reveries over Childhood and Youth':

> . . . an old white-haired man, who had written volumes of easy, too-honeyed verse, and run through his money and gone clean out of his mind . . . was known to live in one room with a nail in the middle of the ceiling from which innumerable cords were stretched to other nails in the walls. In this way he kept up the illusion that he was living under canvas in some Arabian desert.
>
> (*A* 84)

The image of the Arab and his tent recurs in 'Coole Park and Ballylee, 1931' (*PNE* 254). The Bedouins are nomadic desert-dwelling Arabs.

30   *From doored and windowed cliff*: and the 'stony face' of line 29 may have been suggested by Petra.

33-7   *his lecherous life . . . the most exalted lady*: cf. the passage quoted above in note on line 20.

37   *lady*: Dante's beloved Beatrice (possibly Beatrice Portinari (1266-90) who married Simone dei Bardi) whom he said he first saw and fell in love with when he was nearly nine and she eight years and four months old.

45   *the fly in marmalade*: a phrase Yeats attributed to Landor, but in 'The Tragic Generation' he describes Verlaine as using it in a conversation in Paris in 1895 or 1896:

> He asked me, speaking in English, if I knew Paris well, and added, pointing to his leg, that it had scorched his leg, for he knew it 'well, too well', and 'lived in it like a fly in a pot of marmalade.'   (*A* 341)

46   *the rhetorician*: in 'Anima Hominis' Yeats wrote that 'Unlike the   *182* rhetoricians, who get a confident voice from remembering the crowd they have won or may win, we [the poets] sing amid our uncertainty'.   (*M* 331)

47   *the sentimentalist himself*: in 'Anima Hominis' he also put the view that the sentimentalists are

> practical men who believe in money, in position, in a marriage bell, and whose understanding of happiness is to be so busy whether at work or at play, that all is forgotten but the momentary aim. They find their pleasure in a cup that is filled from Lethe's wharf, and for the awakening, for the vision, for the revelation of reality, tradition offers us a different word – ecstasy.   (*M* 331)

48   *a vision of reality*: Yeats wrote that no artist he had read of or known had been a sentimentalist: 'The other self, the anti-self or the antithetical self, as one may choose to name it, comes but to those who are no longer deceived, whose passion is reality.'

51   *dissipation and despair*: Yeats wrote of Johnson and Dowson in 'Anima Hominis' in words which suggest he had them in mind as he wrote these lines:

> Johnson and Dowson, friends of my youth, were dissipated men, the one a drunkard, the other a drunkard and mad about women, and yet they had the gravity of men who had found life out and were awakening from the dream.   (*M* 331)

53   *Keats*: the English poet John Keats (1795-1821). *Hic*'s argument is opposed by *Ille*'s interpretation, in lines 25-33, of Keats's personality, which can be glossed by Yeats's comments in 'Anima Hominis':

> I imagine Keats to have been born with that thirst for luxury common to so many at the outsetting of the Romantic Movement, and not able, like wealthy Beckford, to slake it with beautiful and strange objects. It drove him to imaginary delights; ignorant, poor, and in poor health, and not perfectly well-bred, he knew himself driven from tangible luxury; meeting Shelley he was resentful and suspicious because he, as Leigh Hunt recalls, 'being a little too

171

sensitive on the score of his origin, felt inclined to see in every man of birth his natural enemy.' (*M* 329)

182 A PRAYER ON GOING INTO MY HOUSE

183 This poem was written in 1918, and first appeared in the *Little Review* (Oct. 1918).

1 *this tower and cottage*: Thoor Ballylee, the Norman tower which Yeats had bought on or before 17 June 1917: there were two cottages adjoining it which were converted. See M. Hanley, *Thoor Ballylee – Home of William Butler Yeats* (1965) and Sheelah Kirby, *The Yeats Country* (1962). See also note on 'In Memory of Major Robert Gregory' (*PNE* 144)

3 *No table or chair or stool*: local craftsmen made heavy beds, chairs and tables from a local elm tree.

4 *Galilee*: in Palestine, the scene of Christ's early ministry

5 *for portions of the year*: refers to the plan Yeats and his wife had formed of living at Ballylee in the summer months

10-11 *Sinbad the sailor's brought a painted chest,*
      Or image, from beyond the Loadstone Mountain: Henn (*TLT* 263) traces the image to the edition of *Sinbad the Sailor and other stories from the Arabian Nights* which was illustrated by Yeats's friend Edmund Dulac (1882–1953) and quotes a relevant passage:

> 'Tell me', I said, 'what is the history of the mountain?'
> 'It is black, steep and inaccessible', he replied. 'On its summit is a dome of brass, supported by ten pillars of brass; and on the dome is a brazen horseman, mounted on a brazen horse, bearing in his hand a spear of brass, and on his breast a plate of lead, engraved with mystic signs. Sirs, while that horseman sits upon his horse, the spell of the loadstone spares no ship in the surrounding seas, for without iron no ship is built.'

Sinbad's ship was wrecked on a loadstone mountain on his sixth voyage; the story 'Sinbad the Sailor' is included in the *Arabian Nights' Entertainment* (first unabridged translation made by Sir Richard Burton (1821–90) the explorer).

12 *limb of the Devil*: expression in common use in Ireland

16 *the Red Sea bottom*: cf. the letter to Michael Yeats's schoolmaster, quoted by Hone (*WBY* 420). The Red Sea separates Africa and Arabia.

This poem was written in 1918 and first appeared in *WSC*. Yeats's note in *CP*, *183*
dated 1922, reads:

> Years ago I wrote three stories in which occur the names of Michael Robartes
> and Owen Aherne. I now consider that I used the actual names of two friends,
> and that one of these friends, Michael Robartes, has but lately returned from
> Mesopotamia, where he has partly found and partly thought out much
> philosophy. I consider that Aherne and Robartes, men to whose namesakes I
> had attributed a turbulent life or death, have quarrelled with me. They take
> their place in a phantasmagoria in which I endeavour to explain my philosophy
> of life and death. To some extent I wrote these poems as a text for exposition.

In Preface to *WSC* (1919) Yeats had a fancy that he had read the name 'John
Aherne' among those prosecuted for making a disturbance at the first production
of ''the Playboy'' which may account for his animosity to myself'. This is
probably a joke.

This poem deals with one of the central ideas later used in *AV* and in a similar
manner to 'Ego Dominus Tuus' (*PNE* 181). See note on 'Michael Robartes and
the Dancer' (*PNE* 189).

2   *He and his friend*: the fanciful introduction to *AV* (A) xx–xxi, supposedly by
Aherne, refers to the poem:

> On a walking tour in Connaught we passed Thoor Ballylee where Mr Yeats
> had settled for the summer, and words were spoken between us slightly
> resembling those in 'The Phases of the Moon,' and I noticed that as his
> friendship with me grew closer his animosity against Mr Yeats revived.

4   *Connemara*: see note on 'The Fisherman' (*PNE* 160).

9   *an otter*: probably based on an early memory of the place, cf. 'an otter hurried *184*
away under a gray boulder' (*M* 23)

10   *bridge . . . that shadow is the tower*: a bridge crossed the river which flows
past the tower

12   *He*: Yeats

13   *Mere images*: refers to lines 14–18

15   *Milton's Platonist*: an allusion to an illustration by Samuel Palmer (1805–
81), water-colour landscape painter and etcher, in *The Shorter Poems of John
Milton* (1889) entitled 'The Lonely Tower' which illustrated Milton's *Il
Penseroso*, 186, 'Some high lonely tower'. This description accompanied the
illustration:

> Here poetic loneliness has been attempted: not the loneliness of a desert, but a
> secluded spot in a genial pastoral country, enriched also by antique relics such

as the so-called druidic stones upon the distant hill. The constellation of the
'Bear' may help to explain that the building is the tower of *Il Penseroso*. Two
shepherds watching their flocks speak together of the mysterious light above
them.

There is a waning crescent moon in the illustration which connects with the
poem's title – phases of the moon.

Il Penseroso is an abstraction, meaning Contemplation of a Platonic cast, the
title character in *Il Penseroso* ((1632) by John Milton (1608-74)).

16 *Shelley's visionary price*: it is possible that Percy Bysshe Shelley (1792–
1822) drew upon Milton's imagery in these lines of *Il Penseroso*:

> Or let my lamp, at midnight hour,
> Be seen in some high lonely tower,
> Where I may oft outwatch the *Bear*,
> With thrice great *Hermes*, or unsphere
> The spirit of *Plato*, to unfold
> What worlds, or what vast regions hold
> The immortal mind that hath forsook
> Her mansion in the fleshly nook; . . .

Milton's 'lamp at midnight hour' seen 'in some high tower' is echoed in
Shelley's lines in 'Prince Athanase':

> The Balearic fisher, driven from shore,
> Hanging upon the peaked wave afar,
> Then saw their lamp from Laian's turret gleam,
> Piercing the stormy darkness, like a star, . . .

Milton's reference to the Bear is paralleled by Shelley's 'Bright Arcturus through
your pines is glowing'. Both poets allude to Plato. Milton seeks to 'unsphere /
The spirit of Plato' to discover what world or regions hold the immortal mind,
and Shelley's old man comforts Prince Athanase with the recollection of 'Plato's
words of light' where Agathon and Diotima seemed 'From death and dark
forgetfulness released'.

Yeats wrote of his mind giving itself

> to gregarious Shelley's dream of a young man, his hair blanched with sorrow,
> studying philosophy in some lonely tower, or of his old man, master of all
> human knowledge, hidden from human sight in some shell-strewn cavern on
> the Mediterranean shore.   (*A* 171)

In the copy of Shelley's *Political Works*, which Katharine Tynan gave Yeats in
January 1888, p. 510 was turned down opposite the lines which introduce the
tower in 'Prince Athanase':

> His soul had wedded wisdom, and her dower
> Is love and justice, clothed in which she sate
> Apart from men, as in a lonely tower,
> Pitying the tumult of their dark estate –

The 'Visionary Prince', like Yeats himself in youth,

. . . as with toil and travel,
Had grown quite weak and gray before his time.

In 'Discoveries' Yeats remarked that 'there are many who are not moved as they would be by that solitary light burning in the tower of Prince Athanase, because it has not entered into men's prayers nor lighted any through the sacred dark of religious contemplation' (*E & I* 294)

17   *the lonely night*: see note on line 15 above.

26-27   *. . . that extravagant style*
      He had learnt from Pater:
a reference to the decorative and involved prose Yeats wrote in the 'nineties, perhaps particularly that of *TSR*.

27   *Pater*: Walter Pater (1839-94), English essayist and critic known for his polished involved style and aesthetic outlook.

28   *Said I was dead*: in the story 'Rosa Alchemica' (*M* 267 ff.). His end is also alluded to in 'The Tables of the Law' (*M* 293 ff.)

29   *the changes of the moon*: may be traced to Yeats's interest in Chaucer. In 1910 he was 'deep in Chaucer' and extremely interested in 'the eight and twenty mansiouns / That longen to the moon' of *The Frankelyn's Tayle* (lines 1115 ff.)

31   *Twenty-and-eight the phases of the moon*: these are discussed in *AV* (B) 105-84. See also the diagram from *AV* (B) 81, reproduced on p. 540.

32   *The full*: Phase fifteen, complete subjectivity, a phase of complete beauty

the moon's dark: Phase one, a supernatural incarnation, complete objectively, 'Body absorbed in its supernatural environment'. See *AV* (B) 105 and 183-4.

and all the crescents: Phases two to eight, Phases eight to fourteen, Phases sixteen to twenty-two, twenty-two to twenty-seven. See the diagram (p. 521).

33   *but six-and-twenty*: see lines 33, 34. Phase one and Phase fifteen are not   *185*
phases of human life.

36   *the first crescent to the half*: Phases two to eight. See *AV* (B) 105-16. The 'Bodies of Fate' given to these are 'None except monotony', 'Interest', 'Search', 'Natural Law', 'Humanity', 'Adventure that excites the individuality' and 'The Beginning of Strength'.

39   *the moon is rounding*: Phases nine to fourteen. See *AV* (B) 116-37. After Phase eight the 'Bodies of Fate' are 'enforced'.

45   *Athena takes Achilles*: cf. Homer, *Iliad*, XXII, 330; or I, 197. Yeats used

the image in *The Resurrection* when he wrote 'When the goddess came to Achilles in the battle she did not interfere with his soul, she took him by his yellow hair' (*C Pl* 587). See note on 'A Thought from Propertius' (*PNE* 166) and (p. 165) on 'Her Courage' (*PNE* 179).

46   *Hector is in the dust, Nietzsche is born*: the twelfth phase of *AV* (B) is that of the hero, the man who overcomes himself. 'Solitude has been born at last, though solitude invaded and hard to defend' (*AV* (B) 126-9). Hector, oldest son of Priam, was killed by Achilles in the Trojan War. Friederick Nietzsche (1844-1900), German philosopher, was known for his concept of the superman.

48   *twice born, twice buried*: the full moon is the fifteenth phase: therefore the thirteenth and fourteenth phases must occur first of all, and are subsequently described.

50   *the soul at war*: in *AV* the examples given of the thirteenth phase are Baudelaire, Beardsley and Ernest Dowson. It was the only phase 'where entire sensuality is possible, that is to say, sensuality without the intermixture of any other element' (*AV* (B) 129). The phase is one of emotional morbidity; there is a preoccupation with metaphors, symbols and images through which whatever is most morbid or strange is defined.

53   *the frenzy of the fourteenth moon*: the examples of the fourteenth phase given in *AV* are Keats, Giorgione and many beautiful women. In this phase responsibility is dropped. Helen is one of the beautiful women (and perhaps Maud Gonne also) of the phase; she is imagined as elaborating a delicate personal discipline, and, while seeming an image of softness and quiet she 'draws perpetually upon glass with a diamond' (*AV* (B) 132). Perhaps it is because she desires so little and gives so little that men die and murder in her service. In the poetry of Keats, Yeats wrote, there is, though little sexual passion, an exaggerated sensuousness that compels us to remember the pepper on the tongue as though that were his symbol.

> Thought is disappearing into image; and in Keats, in some ways a perfect type, intellectual curiosity is at its weakest; there is scarcely an image, where his poetry is at its best, whose subjectivity has not been heightened by its use in many great poets, painters, sculptors, artificers.   (*AV* (B) 134)

58   *becomes an image*: the description of this phase is given in *AV*:

> The being has selected, moulded and remoulded, narrowed its circle of living, been more and more the artist, grown more and more 'distinguished' in all preference. Now contemplation and desire, united into one, inhabit a world where every beloved image has bodily form, and every bodily form is loved. This love knows nothing of desire, for desire implies effort, and though there is still separation from the loved object, love accepts the separation as necessary to its own existence. *Fate* is known for the boundary that gives our *Destiny* its form, and – as we can desire nothing outside that form – as an expression of our freedom. Chance and Choice have become interchangeable without losing their

identity. As all effort has ceased, all thought has become image, because no thought could exist if it were not carried towards its own extinction, amid fear or in contemplation; and every image is separate from every other, for if image were linked to image, the soul would awake from its immovable trance. All that the being has experienced as thought is visible to its eyes as a whole, and in this way it perceives, not as they are to others, but according to its own perception, all orders of existence. Its own body possesses the greatest possible beauty, being indeed that body which the soul will permanently inhabit, when all its phases have been repeated according to the number allotted: that which we call the clarified or Celestial Body. Where the being has lived out of phase, seeking to live through *antithetical* phases as though they had been *primary*, there is now terror of solitude, its forced, painful and slow acceptance, and a life haunted by terrible dreams. Even for the most perfect, there is a time of pain, a passage through a vision, where evil reveals itself in its final meaning. In this passage Christ, it is said, mourned over the length of time and the unworthiness of man's lot to man, whereas his forerunner mourned and his successor will mourn over the shortness of time and the unworthiness of man to his lot; but this cannot yet be understood.   (*AV*(B) 135–7)

67   *Sinai's top*: Mount Sinai where Moses received the Ten Commandments, on the Sinai peninsula at the north end of the Red Sea; see Exodus 34 and 35.

85   *the man within*: Yeats   186

87   *the crumbling of the moon*: the next phase after the fifteenth is one which finds within itself an aimless excitement, and the examples given of it in *AV* are William Blake, Rabelais, Aretino, Paracelsus and some beautiful women. The description in *AV* is lively:

Capable of nothing but an incapable idealism (for it has no thought but in myth, or in defence of myth), it must, because it sees one side as all white, see the other side all black; what but a dragon could dream of thwarting a St George? In men of the phase there will commonly be both natures, for to be true to phase is a ceaseless struggle. At one moment they are full of hate – Blake writes of 'Flemish and Venetian demons' and of some picture of his own destroyed 'by some vile spell of Stoddart's' – and their hate is always close to madness; and at the next they produce the comedy of Aretino and of Rabelais or the mythology of Blake, and discover symbolism to express the overflowing and bursting of the mind. There is always an element of frenzy, and almost always a delight in certain glowing or shining images of concentrated force; in the smith's forge; in the heart; in the human form in its most vigorous development; in the solar disc; in some symbolical representation of the sexual organs; for the being must brag of its triumph over its own incoherence.

Since Phase 8 the man has more and more judged what is right in relation to time: a right action, or a right motive, has been one that he thought possible or desirable to think or do eternally; his soul would 'come into possession of itself for ever in one single moment'; but now he begins once more to judge an action or motive in relation to space. A right action or motive must soon be right for any other man in similar circumstance. Hitherto an action, or motive, has been right precisely because it is exactly right for one person only, though for that person always. After the change, the belief in the soul's immortality

177

declines, though the decline is slow, and it may only be recovered when Phase 1 is passed.

Among those who are of this phase may be great satirists, great caricaturists, but they pity the beautiful, for that is their *Mask*, and hate the ugly, for that is their *Body of Fate*, and so are unlike those of the *primary* phases, Rembrandt for instance, who pity the ugly, and sentimentalise the beautiful, or call it insipid, and turn away or secretly despise and hate it. Here too are beautiful women, whose bodies have taken upon themselves the image of the True *Mask*, and in these there is a radiant intensity, something of 'The Burning Babe' of the Elizabethan lyric. They walk like queens, and seem to carry upon their backs a quiver of arrows, but they are gentle only to those whom they have chosen or subdued, or to the dogs that follow at their heels. Boundless in generosity, and in illusion, they will give themselves to a beggar because he resembles a religious picture and be faithful all their lives, or if they take another turn and choose a dozen lovers, die convinced that none but the first or last has ever touched their lips, for they are of those whose 'virginity renews itself like the moon.' Out of phase they turn termagant, if their lover take a wrong step in a quadrille where all the figures are of their own composition and changed without notice when the fancy takes them. Indeed, perhaps if the body have great perfection, there is always something imperfect in the mind, some rejection of or inadequacy of *Mask*: Venus out of phase chose lame Vulcan. Here also are several very ugly persons, their bodies torn and twisted by the violence of the new *primary*, but where the body has this ugliness great beauty of mind is possible. This is indeed the only *antithetical* phase where ugliness is possible, it being complementary to Phase 2, the only *primary* phase where beauty is possible.

From this phase on we meet with those who do violence, instead of those who suffer it; and prepare for those who love some living person, and not an image of the mind, but as yet this love is hardly more than the 'fixed idea' of faithfulness. As the new love grows the sense of beauty will fade. (*A V* (B) 138–40)

184 THE CAT AND THE MOON

188   This poem was written in 1917 when Yeats was staying with the Gonnes in Normandy; it first appeared in *Nine Poems* (1918).

1   *The cat*: Minnaloushe, the Gonnes' black Persian cat. See line 5. Yeats wrote in his Introduction to *The Cat and the Moon*, a play first performed in the Abbey Theatre, Dublin, in 1926, that, as the populace might alter out of recognition or deprive some philosophical thought or verse of its meaning, he had written

a little poem where a cat is disturbed by the moon, and in the changing pupils of its eyes seems to repeat the movement of the moon's changes, and allowed myself as I wrote to think of the cat as the normal man and of the moon as the opposite he seeks perpetually, or as having any meaning I have conferred upon the moon elsewhere. Doubtless, too, when the lame man takes the saint upon his back, the normal man has become one with that opposite, but I had to bear in mind that I was among dreams and proverbs, that though I might discover what had been and might be again an abstract idea, no abstract idea must be present. The spectator should come away thinking the meaning as much his own manufacture as that of the blind man and the lame man [The play deals with an old Irish tradition that a blind man and a lame man dreamed that somewhere in Ireland a well would cure them and set out to find it, the lame man on the blind man's back, the lame man symbolising the body, the blind man the soul. In *DP* Yeats later suggested that the friendship of Edward Martyn and George Moore was symbolised in the play] had seemed mine. Perhaps some early Christian – Bardaisan had speculations about the sun and moon nobody seems to have investigated – thought as I do, saw in the changes of the moon all the cycles: the soul realising its separate being in the full moon, then, as the moon seems to approach the sun and dwindle away, all but realising its absorption in God, only to whirl away once more: the mind of a man, separating itself from the common matrix, through childish imaginations, through struggle – Vico's heroic age – to roundness, completeness, and then externalising, intellectualising, systematising, until at last it lies dead, a spider smothered in its own web: the choice offered by the sages, either with the soul from the myth to union with the source of all, the breaking of the circle, or from the myth to reflection and the circle renewed for better or worse. For better or worse according to one's life, but never progress as we understand it, never the straight line, always a necessity to break away and destroy, or to sink in and forget. (*E* 402–4)

THE SAINT AND THE HUNCHBACK 185

This poem was written in 1918, and first appeared in *WSC* (1919). The poem *189* epitomises two phases of *A V*, the Hunchback being of Phase twenty-six, the Saint of Phase twenty-seven.

2–5   . . . *great bitterness*
In thinking of his lost renown.
A Roman Caesar is held down
Under this hump: cf. Yeats's prose description in *A V*:

All the old abstraction, whether of morality or of belief, has now been exhausted; but in the seemingly natural man, in Phase 26 out of phase, there is an attempt to substitute a new abstraction, a simulacrum of self-expression. Desiring emotion the man becomes the most completely solitary of all possible men, for all normal communion with his kind, that of a common study, that of an interest in work done, that of a condition of life, a code, a belief shared, has passed; and without personality he is forced to create its artificial semblance. It is perhaps a slander of history that makes us see Nero so, for he lacked the physical deformity which is, we are told, first among this phase's inhibitions of personality. The deformity may be of any kind, great or little, for it is but symbolised in the hump that thwarts what seems the ambition of a Caesar or of an Achilles. He commits crimes, not because he wants to, or like Phase 23 out of phase because he can, but because he wants to feel certain that he can; and he is full of malice because, finding no impulse but in his own ambition, he is made jealous by the impulse of others. He is all emphasis, and the greater that emphasis the more does he show himself incapable of emotion, the more does he display his sterility. If he live amid a theologically minded people, his

179

greatest temptation may be to defy God, to become a Judas, who betrays, not for thirty pieces of silver, but that he may call himself creator.   (*AV* (B) 177–8)

4   *A Roman Caesar*: title (arising from Caius Julius Čaesar (? 102–44 BC) the Roman general, statesman and historian) given to Roman emperors from Augustus to Hadrian; it can mean any Roman emperor.

190   6   *a different plan*: perhaps a reference to the twenty-eight phases of the moon in *AV*.

8   *I lay about me with the taws*: taws, a form of birch; cf. the lines in 'Among School Children':

> Soldier Aristotle played the taws
> Upon the bottom of a king of kings (*PNE* 222)

The meaning of the speech of the Saint is clarified in *AV*:

> True to phase, he substitutes for emulation an emotion of renunciation, and for the old toil of judgment and discovery of sin, a beating upon his breast and an ecstatical crying out that he must do penance, that he is even the worst of men. He does not, like Phase 26, perceive separated lives and actions more clearly than the total life, for the total life has suddenly displayed its source. If he possess intellect he will use it but to serve perception and renunciation. His joy is to be nothing, to do nothing, to think nothing; but to permit the total life, expressed in its humanity, to flow in upon him and to express itself through his acts and thoughts. He is not identical with it, he is not absorbed in it, for if he were he would not know that he is nothing, that he no longer even possesses his own body, that he must renounce even his desire for his own salvation, and that this total life is in love with his nothingness.   (*AV*)(B) 180–1)

10   *Greek Alexander*: Alexander the Great (356–323 BC) King of Macedon, conqueror of Greece, Egypt, and the Persian Empire; founder of Alexandria

11   *Augustus Caesar*: Caius Julius Caesar Octavianus (63 BC–14 AD); first Emperor of Rome, he adopted the title Augustus (27 BC)

12   *Alcibiades*: Alcibiades (450–404 BC), Athenian statesman and general who was both brilliant and unstable

186   TWO SONGS OF A FOOL

190   These poems were written between July and September 1918 when Yeats and his wife were living at Ballinamantane House, near Gort, Co. Galway, which Lady Gregory had lent them. They first appeared in *WSC* (1919).

A letter written by Yeats to his father on 17 October 1918 discussed the poem as follows:

> Your last letter, however, shows the most curious of all this telepathic exchange. When it came, I said to George [Mrs W. B. Yeats] (without letting

her see the date of your letter), 'When did I write my poem of the Hare?' She said 'about September 20th.' Your letter is dated Sept. 22. My memory is that I was full of my subject for some days before Sept. 20th. I send you the two poems. One line, – 'The horn's sweet note and the tooth of the hound,' may have reached you, or the hare's cry – which is to you a symbol of exultation at death. 'The horn's sweet note' might well mean that. Your poem has a fine idea, but I cannot make out whether the symbolising the joy at death by the scream of the hare is, or is not, too strained an idea . . . (*LTHS* 251)

Hone's footnote connecting it with 'The Collar-bone of a Hare' is inaccurate.

I

1   *A specked cat*: Mrs W. B. Yates. Cf. a similar joke 'Who can keep company with the goddess Astraea if his eyes are on the brindled cat?' (*Essays 1931–1936*, 3).

a tame hare: Iseult Gonne. The poet's paternal feeling for Iseult appeared in a letter written to Lady Gregory in 1916:

I believe I was meant to be the father of an unruly family. I did not think that I liked little boys but I liked Shawn [Sean MacBride, Maud Gonne's son]. I am really managing Iseult very well . . . as father, but as father only, I have been a great success.   (*WBY* 303)

After his marriage in September 1917 Yeats had a feeling of responsibility for Iseult Gonne. The vague premonition of danger in the first section, more cogent in the second, is like that of 'To a Young Beauty' (*PNE* 152).

6   *Providence*: God, in his foreseeing care and protection of his creatures

II

2   *slept on my knee*: cf. the lines in 'Solomon to Sheba'   191

> To Solomon sang Sheba,
> Planted on his knees.   (*PNE* 149)

ANOTHER SONG OF A FOOL   187

This poem is not dated; it first appeared in *WSC* (1919).   191

1   *butterfly*: cf. 'Tom O'Roughley' (*PNE* 155) where the butterfly symbolises the wisdom of wide-ranging thought, and, for butterflies in the tower, cf. also 'Blood and the Moon', III (*PNE* 243).

THE DOUBLE VISION OF MICHAEL ROBARTES   188

This poem was written in 1919; it first appeared in *WSC* (1919).   192

Title   *Michael Robartes*: see headnote on 'The Lover tells of the Rose in his Heart' (*PNE* 43).

1   *Grey rock of Cashel*: the Rock of Cashel in Co. Tipperary, Ireland, has several ecclesiastical ruins, including the chapel built by Cormac MacCarthy (d. 1138) in the twelfth century. (See the last line of the poem.)

2   *the cold spirits*: these spirits come from the later phases of *AV*.

9   *Constrained*: the third stanza of the poem is quoted to illustrate the adoration of force which comes with the last gyre:

A decadence will descend, by perpetual moral improvement, upon a community which may seem like some woman of New York or Paris who has renounced her rouge pot to lose her figure and grow coarse of skin and dull of brain, feeding her calves and babies somewhere upon the edge of the wilderness. The decadence of the Greco-Roman world with its violent soldiers and its mahogany dark young athletes was as great, but that suggested the bubbles of life turned into marbles, whereas what awaits us, being democratic and *primary*, may suggest bubbles in a frozen pond – mathematical Babylonian starlight.
When the new era comes bringing its stream of irrational force it will, as did Christianity, find its philosophy already impressed upon the minority who have, true to phase, turned away in the last gyre from the *Physical Primary*. And it must awake into life, not Dürer's, nor Blade's nor Milton's human form divine – nor yet Nietzsche's superman, nor Patmore's catholic, boasting 'a tongue that's dead' – the brood of the Sistine Chapel – but organic groups, *covens* of physical or intellectual kin melted out of the frozen mass. I imagine new races, as it were, seeking domination, a world resembling but for its immensity that of the Greek tribes – each with its own Daimon or ancestral hero – the brood of Leda, War and Love; history grown symbolic, the biography changed into a myth. Above all I imagine everywhere the opposites, no mere alternation between nothing and something like the Christian brute and ascetic, but true opposites, each living the other's death, dying the other's life.   (*AV* (A) 213–14)

9–16   *Constrained ... that we obey*: Yeats quoted these eight lines in 'A People's Theatre' to conclude a passage in which he examined the 'two great energies of the world', and distinguished between the arts and 'visible history, the discoveries of science, the discussions of politics'. He saw change as coming from the anti-self of visible history:

Every new logical development of the objective energy intensifies in an exact correspondence a counter-energy. . . . Are we approaching a supreme moment of self-consciousness, the two halves of the soul separate and face to face? . . . Were it not for that other gyre turning inward in exact measure with the outward whirl of its fellow, we would fall in a generation or so under some tyranny that would cease at last to be a tyranny, so perfect our acquiescence.   (*E* 258–9)

18   *A Sphinx*: 'the introspective knowledge of the mind's self-begotten unity.'

The Sphinx, in Greek mythology, was a monster with a woman's head and bust, wings and a lion's body. The most famous figure of a sphinx is near the Great Pyramid at El-Ghizeh, Egypt.

19   *A Buddha*: 'the outward-looking mind.' Sphinx and Buddha are 'like   *193* heraldic supporters guarding the mystery of the 15th phase', and between them the dancer combines intellect and emotion for the moment. Gautama Siddhartha (*c.* 563–483 BC), an Indian nobleman and philosopher, founded Buddhism; the title of the Buddha was given to him.

21   *And right between these two a girl at play*: Ellmann (*IY* 255) comments:

> The Sphinx is the intellect, gazing on both known and unknown things; the Buddha is the heart, gazing on both loved and unloved things; and the dancing girl, most important of all, is primarily an image of art. She dances between them because art is neither intellectual nor emotional, but a balance of these qualities.

56   *Homer's paragon*: Helen of Troy. Cf. 'A woman Homer sung' (*PNE* 92),   *194* 'No Second Troy' (*PNE* 94) and 'When Helen lived' (*PNE* 119). The Helen symbol usually suggests Maud Gonne.

68   *Cormac's ruined house*: see note above on the first line of the poem and see *E* 266 for reference to the stout Church of Ireland bishop who took the lead roof from the gothic church to save his legs. (Archbishop Price used the roof for a new cathedral built on the plain in 1749.)

Michael Robartes and the Dancer

SOME of the poems in this volume were written in 1916 but not publicly circulated until 1920. His earlier mockery – 'Romantic Ireland's dead and gone' – has vanished, and he records in these poems his clear perception of what was achieved by the Rising, by the leaders who have joined the long procession of Ireland's martyrs. The magnificent poems based on *AV*'s thought blend imaginative experience and explanation in a manner which imparts a sense of revelation. 'A Prayer for my Daughter' (*PNE* 201) and 'Demon and Beast' (*PNE* 199) while not as completely linked with *AV* as 'The Second Coming' (*PNE* 200) are none the less illustrative of how much Yeats's life and thought interacted, how much he resembled at this period the poor man in his poem, who, having roved, loved and thought himself beloved, now 'from a glad kindness cannot take his eyes'.

MRD's Preface alludes to Michael Robartes's exposition of the *Speculum Angelorum et Hominum* of Giraldus and there are several notes on the poems of the volume dealing with this material (part of *AV*). Yeats quotes Goethe's saying that the poet needs philosophy but must keep it out of his work (probably deriving this from Goethe's *Conversations with Eckermann*, 23 July 1827 and 4 February 1829).

189   MICHAEL ROBARTES AND THE DANCER

197   This poem was written in 1919 and first appeared in *The Dial* (Nov. 1920). Yeats's note on the poem (*CP* 531) is quoted in note on 'The Phases of the Moon' (*PNE* 183). The characters Robartes and Aherne appear in 'Rose Alchemica' (1896), 'The Tables of the Law' (1896) and 'The Adoration of the Magi' (1897) as well as in *AV* (A).

1   *He*: *He* represents Yeats's views, *She* Iseult Gonne's.

2   *this altar piece*: probably 'Saint George and the Dragon' ascribed to Bordone (*c.* 1500–71) in the National Gallery, Dublin. Henn (*LT* 249) remarks that Cosimo Tura's 'St George and the Dragon', which Yeats saw in Ferrara Cathedral in 1907, may have suggested the idea of the 'altar-piece' which the Bordone is not. Cf. 'Her Triumph' (*PNE* 296).

19   *Athena*: see note on 'A Thought from Propertius' (*PNE* 166).

26   *Paul Veronese*: Paolo Veronese, cognomen of Paolo Cagliari (1525–88), the   198
last great Venetian painter, who settled in Venice in 1555.

29   *lagoon*: at Venice

32   *Michael Angelo's Sistine roof*: Yeats often visited the Sistine Chapel in
Rome in 1925, and while there bought reproductions of Michelangelo's
'fabulous' ceiling. See Hone (*WBY* 367–8) and cf. line 45 'Under Ben Bulben'
(*PNE* 356). Michelangelo Buonarroti (1475–1564) painted the ceiling from
1508 to 1512. See note on An Acre of Grass' (*PNE* 332).

33   *his 'Morning' and his 'Night'*: Yeats saw these statues in the Medici
Chapel, S. Lorenzo, Florence, on his visit there in 1907.

SOLOMON AND THE WITCH

This poem was written in 1918, and first appeared in *MRD*.   190

1   *that Arab lady*: the poem is written about Yeats and Mrs Yeats; it deals with   199
the possible annihilation of time through a perfect union of lovers. The cockerel
thinks that eternity has returned (cf. 'The miracle that gave them such a death' in
'Ribh at the Tomb of Baile and Aillinn' (*PNE* 309)). It has not, but the lovers try
again. The poem is one where meaning is cumulative; it becomes clearer as the
illustrations are developed.

4   *Solomon*: Yeats. See note on 'Solomon to Sheba' (*PNE* 149).

6   *Who*: Solomon

9   *'A cockerel...'*: Wilson (*YI* 280–1), identifies it as the Hermetic cock.

11   *the Fall*: the Fall of Man, when Adam and Eve ate the forbidden fruit of the
Tree of Knowledge (see Genesis 3)

14   *Chance being at one with Choice*: cf. line 23, and line 58 'All Souls' Night'
(*PNE* 239). An early use of the two words occurs in *The Island of Statues*, I, iii,
39: 'all choice, and give to chance, for guiding chance'. Yeats's note on his play
Calvary refers to Chance and Choice. He puts the words in the mouth of 'a certain
old Arab':

> I have used my bird-symbolism in these songs to increase the objective
> loneliness of Christ by contrasting it with a loneliness, opposite in kind, that
> unlike His can be, whether joyous or sorrowful, sufficient to itself. I have
> surrounded Him with the images of those He cannot save, not only with the
> birds, who have served neither God nor Caesar, and await for none or for a

185

different saviour, but with Lazarus and Judas and the Roman soldiers for whom He has died in vain. 'Christ,' writes Robartes, 'only pitied those whose suffering is rooted in death, in poverty, or in sickness, or in sin, in some shape of the common lot, and he came especially to the poor who are most subject to exterior vicissitude.' I have therefore represented in Lazarus and Judas types of that intellectual despair that lay beyond His sympathy, while in the Roman soldiers I suggest a form of objectivity that lay beyond His help. Robartes said in one of the conversations recorded by Aherne: 'I heard much of *Three Songs of Joy*, written by a certain old Arab, which owing to the circumstances of their origin were considered as proofs of great sanctity. He held the faith of Kusta ben Luki, but did not live with any of the two or three wandering companies of Judwalis. He lived in the town of Hâyel as servant to a rich Arab merchant. He himself had been a rich merchant of Aneyza and had been several times to India. On his return from one of these journeys he had found his house in possession of an enemy and was himself driven from Aneyza by the Wahâbies on some charge, I think of impiety, and it was then he made his first song of joy. A few years later his wife and child were murdered by robbers in the desert, and after certain weeks, during which it was thought that he must die of grief, his face cleared and his step grew firm and he made his second song. He gave away all his goods and became a servant in Hâyel, and a year or two later, believing that his death was near, he made his third song of joy. He lived, however, for several months, and when I met him had the use of all his faculties. I asked him about the 'Three Songs', for I knew that even on his deathbed, as became the votary of a small contentious sect, he would delight in exposition. I said (though I knew from his songs themselves, that this was not his thought, but I wanted his explanation in his own words): ''You have rejoiced that the Will of God should be done even though you and yours must suffer.'' He answered with some emotion: ''Oh, no, Kusta ben Luki has taught us to divide all things into Chance and Choice; one can think about the world and about man, or anything else until all has vanished but these two things, for they are indeed the first cause of the animate and inanimate world. They exist in God, for if they did not He would not have freedom, He would be bound by His own Choice. In God alone, indeed, can they be united, yet each be perfect and without limit or hindrance. If I should throw from the dice-box there would be but six possible sides on each of the dice, but when God throws He uses dice that have all numbers and sides. Some worship His Choice; that is easy; to know that He has willed for some unknown purpose all that happens is pleasant; but I have spent my life in worshipping His Chance, and that moment when I understand the immensity of His Chance is the moment when I am nearest Him. Because it is very difficult and because I have put my understanding into three songs I am famous among my people.'' ' (*Four Plays for Dancers*, 1921)

15   *the brigand apple*: that Eve ate, which brought Death into the world and all our woe. See Genesis 3.6.

17–18   *He that crowed out eternity*
    Thought to have crowed it in: cf. lines 28–9. The world ends or time comes to a stop when a perfect union takes place.

19   *spider's eye*: Henn (*LT* 57) remarks on the complicated nature of the image, alluding to the familiar aspect of the spider, the female destroying the mate after

copulation, to Donne's 'spider love that *transubstantiates* all' in 'Twicknam Garden', to the Jacobean use of dried spiders for poison, to the steeping of the spider of jealousy in a man's drink. He adds that Yeats would have known the Arachne in Doré's *Illustrations to Dante* and Blake's 'Black and White Spiders'. He suggests that the image also comes from natural history, the large eye of the spider containing refracting and magnifying lenses which 'gives superbly the capacity of lovers to discover, reflect, enlarge each other's shortcomings'.

AN IMAGE FROM A PAST LIFE   191

This poem was written in September 1919 and first appeared in *N* (6 Nov. 1920).   *200*
F. F. Farag (*YCE* 43) points out that Tagore's 'In the Dusky Path of a Dream' which Yeats included in the *Oxford Book of Modern Verse 1892-1935*, is a source for the poem's theme. Tagore begins his poem 'In the dusky path of a dream I went to seek the love who was mine in a former life.'

1   *He*: represents Yeats

5   *that scream*: associated with moments of insight or revelation or recollection. Cf. the last line with the scream of Juno's peacock. See note on line 32, 'Meditations in Time of Civil War' III (*PNE* 208) and the 'miraculous strange bird' of 'Her Triumph' (*PNE* 296).

7   *Image*: see the conclusion to Yeats's note on the poem, quoted below, line 42.

8   *She*: represents Mrs Yeats.

14   *its lesson*: that happiness is not unalloyed, that other women have been   *201*
loved by the poet

22   *A sweetheart*: this stanza reverts to the romantic languorous language of the early love poetry written to Maud Gonne and 'Diana Vernon', the exception being the adjective arrogant; 'distress', 'loveliness', 'tress', 'starry eddies' and 'paleness' echoing the early poems.

42   *the hovering thing*: the last paragraph of Yeats's note on the poem (here quoted in full) explains this as an 'Over Shadower or Ideal Form':

> Robartes writes to Aherne under the date May 12th, 1917. 'I found among the Judwalis ['diagrammatists', a name invented by Yeats] much biographical detail, probably legendary, about Kusta-ben-Luki. [Kusta ben Luka (820-92) an Arabian doctor and translator]. He saw occasionally during sleep a woman's face and later on found in a Persian painting a face resembling, though not identical with the dream-face, which he considered that of a woman loved in another life. Presently he met & loved a beautiful woman whose face also resembled, without being identical, that of his dream. Later on he

made a long journey to purchase the painting which was, he said, the better likeness, and found on his return that his mistress had left him in a fit of jealousy.' In a dialogue and in letters, Robartes gives a classification and analysis of dreams which explain the survival of this story among the followers of Kusta-ben-Luki. They distinguished between the memory of concrete images and the abstract memory, and affirm that no concrete dream-image is ever from our memory. This is not only true they say of dreams, but of those visions seen between sleeping and waking. This doctrine at first found me incredulous, for I thought it contradicted by my experience and by all I have read, not however a very great amount, in books of psychology and of psycho-analysis. Did I not frequently dream of some friend, or relation, or that I was at school? I found, however, when I studied my dreams, as I was directed in a dialogue, that the image seen was never really that of a friend, or relation, or my old school, though it might very closely resemble it. A substitution had taken place, often a very strange one, though I forgot this if I did not notice it at once on waking. The name of some friend, or the conceptions 'my father' and 'at school,' are a part of the abstract memory and therefore of the dream life, but the image of my father, or my friend, or my old school, being a part of the personal concrete memory appeared neither in sleep nor in visions between sleep and waking. I found sometimes that my father, or my friend, had been represented in sleep by a stool or a chair, and I concluded that it was the entire absence of my personal concrete memory that enabled me to accept such images without surprise. Was it not perhaps this very absence that constituted sleep? Would I perhaps awake if a single concrete image from my memory came before me? Even these images – stool, chair, etc. were never any particular stool, chair, etc. that I had known. Were these images, however, from the buried memory? had they floated up from the subsconscious? had I seen them perhaps a long time ago and forgotten having done so? Even if that were so, the exclusion of the conscious memory was a new, perhaps important truth; but Robartes denied their source even in the subconscious. It seems a corroboration that though I often see between sleep and waking elaborate landscape, I have never seen one that seemed a possible representation of any place I have ever lived near from childhood up. Robartes traces these substitute images to different sources. Those that come in sleep are (1) from the state immediately preceding our birth; (2) from the *Spiritus Mundi* – that is to say, from a general storehouse of images which have ceased to be a property of any personality or spirit. Those that come between sleeping and waking are, he says, re-shaped by what he calls the 'automatic faculty' which can create pattern, balance, etc. from the impressions made upon the senses, not of ourselves, but of others bound to us by certain emotional links though perhaps entire strangers, and preserved in a kind of impersonal mirror, often simply called the 'record,' which takes much the same place in his system [as] the lower strata of the astral light does among the disciples of Elephas Levi [pseudonym of Alphonse Louis Constant (? 1810-75) a French occultist]. This does not exhaust the contents of dreams for we have to account also for certain sentences, for certain ideas which are not concrete images and yet do not arise from our personal memory, but at the moment I have merely to account for certain images that affect passion or affection. Robartes writes to Aherne in a letter dated May 15th, 1917: 'No lover, no husband has ever met in dreams the true image of wife or mistress. She who has perhaps filled his whole life with joy or disquiet cannot enter there. Her image can fill every moment of his waking life but only its counterfeit comes to him in sleep; and he who classifies these counterfeits will find that just

188

in so far as they become concrete, sensuous, they are distinct individuals; never types but individuals. They are the forms of those whom he has loved in some past earthly life, chosen from *Spiritus Mundi* by the subconscious will, and through them, for they are not always hollow shades, the dead at whiles outface a living rival.' They are the forms of Over Shadowers as they are called. All violent passion has to be expiated or atoned, by one in life, by one in the state between life and life, because, as the Judwalis believe, there is always deceit or cruelty; but it is only in sleep that we can see these forms of those who as spirits may influence all our waking thought. Souls that are once linked by emotion never cease till the last drop of that emotion is exhausted – call it desire, hate or what you will – to affect one another, remaining always as it were in contact. Those whose passions are unatoned seldom love living man or woman but only those loved long ago, of whom the living man or woman is but a brief symbol forgotten when some phase of some atonement is finished; but because in general the form does not pass into the memory, it is the moral being of the dead that is symbolised. Under certain circumstances, which are precisely described, the form indirectly, and not necessarily from dreams, enters the living memory; the subconscious will, as in Kusta-ben-Luki in the story, selects among pictures, or other ideal representations, some form that resembles what was once the physical body of the Over Shadower, and this ideal form becomes to the living man an obsession, continually perplexing and frustrating natural instinct. It is therefore only after full atonement or expiation, perhaps after many lives, that a natural deep satisfying love becomes possible, and this love, in all subjective natures, must precede the Beatific Vision.

When I wrote An Image from a Past Life, I had merely begun my study of the various papers upon the subject, but I do not think I misstated Robartes' thought in permitting the woman and not the man to see the Over Shadower or Ideal Form, whichever it was. No mind's contents are necessarily shut off from another, and in moments of excitement images pass from one mind to another with extraordinary ease, perhaps most easily from that portion of the mind which for the time being is outside consciousness. I use the word 'pass' because it is familiar, not because I believe any movement in space to be necessary. The second mind sees what the first has already seen, that is all.   (*MRD*)

UNDER SATURN   192

This poem was written in November 1919 and first appeared in *The Dial* (Nov.   *202*
1920).

1   *Saturnine*: taciturn, gloomy, from the gloomy influence attributed to the influence of the planet Saturn

2   *lost love*: for Maud Gonne who consumed his youth

4   *the wisdom that you brought*: perhaps a reference to Mrs Yeats's share in *AV*

5   *the comfort*: in October 1919 Yeats and his wife leased a house in Broad Street, Oxford (since demolished), and he gave up the rooms in Woburn Buildings

which he had rented for twenty years. (They have been preserved by the hotel which now owns the buildings. John Masefield spoke at a ceremony to open them.) They did not buy their house in Dublin, 82 Merrion Square, until February 1922.

7   *an old cross Pollexfen*: William Pollexfen, Yeats's maternal grandfather. See note on '*Introductory Rhymes*' (*PNE* 112) and 'In Memory of Alfred Pollexfen' (*PNE* 173).

8   *a Middleton*: probably William Middleton (1806–62) a great-uncle of Yeats.

9   *a red-haired Yeats*: the Reverend William Butler Yeats (1806–62), Yeats's grandfather, the 'old country scholar' of 'Introductory Rhymes' (*PNE* 112).

193   EASTER 1916

202   The manuscript of this poem is dated 25 September 1916. Yeats wrote it when he was staying with Maud Gonne MacBride at Calvados; it first appeared in *Easter, 1916* (1916) an edition of twenty-five copies 'privately printed by Clement Shorter for distribution among his friends' and subsequently in the *New Statesman* (23 Oct. 1920).

This poem, which V. K. Menon, *The Development of William Butler Yeats*, 48, has called a palinode to 'September 1913' (*PNE* 115) gives Yeats's reaction to the Easter Rising in Dublin. The Irish Republic was proclaimed on Easter Monday, 24 April and the centre of Dublin occupied by the Republicans. They were the Irish Volunteers of the Irish Republican Brotherhood, probably about seven hundred in all. They held out until 29 April. From 3 to 12 May fifteen of the leaders were executed after a series of courts martial. A letter Yeats wrote to Lady Gregory on 11 May shows his sorrow:

> My dear Lady Gregory, The Dublin tragedy has been a great sorrow and anxiety. Cosgrave, who I saw a few months ago in connection with the Municipal Gallery project and found our best supporter, has got many years' imprisonment and to-day I see that an old friend Henry Dixon [according to Wade's note, this was Thomas Dickson, the Henry Dixon who took part in the Rising having been released from prison in June 1917, but Edward Malins, *Yeats and the Easter Rising*, 13, has not been able to discover his name among those of the prisoners released at that time] – unless there are two of the name – who began with me the whole work of the literary movement has been shot in a barrack yard without trial of any kind. I have little doubt there have been many miscarriages of justice. The wife of a Belgian Minister of War told me a few days ago that three British officers had told her that the command of the British army in France should be made over to the French generals, and that French generals have told her that they await with great anxiety the result of the coming German attack on the English lines because of the incompetence of the English Higher Command as a whole. Haig however they believed in – he was recommended by the French for the post. I see therefore no reason to believe that the delicate instrument of Justice is being worked with precision in Dublin.

I am trying to write a poem on the men executed – 'terrible beauty has been born again.' If the English Conservative party had made a declaration that they did not intend to rescind the Home Rule Bill there would have been no Rebellion. I had no idea that any public event could so deeply move me – and I am very despondent about the future. At the moment I feel that all the work of years has been overturned, all the bringing together of classes, all the freeing of Irish literature and criticism from politics. Maud Gonne reminds me that she saw the ruined houses about O'Connell Street and the wounded and dying lying about the streets, in the first few days of the war. I perfectly remember the vision and my making light of it and saying that if a true vision at all it could only have a symbolised meaning. This is the only letter I have had from her since she knew of the Rebellion. I have sent her the papers every day. I do not yet know what she feels about her husband's death. Her letter was written before she heard of it. Her main thought seems to be 'tragic dignity has returned to Ireland.' She had been told by two members of the Irish Party that 'Home Rule was betrayed.' She thinks now that the sacrifice has made it safe. She is coming to London if she can get a passport, but I doubt her getting one. Indeed I shall be glad if she does not come yet – it is better for her to go on nursing the French wounded till the trials are over. How strange that old Count Plunkett and his wife and his three sons should all be drawn into the net.

I sent on to you yesterday the proof sheets I had finished and fastened up at the start of the Rebellion. I sent a letter with them giving an explanation of what I want you to do. I have been able to do little work lately and that chiefly on *Player Queen* which always needs new touches in its one bad place – first half of second act. Yours W. B. Yeats.   (*L* 612–14)

1   *them*: the revolutionaries

4   *eighteenth-century houses*: many Dublin houses were built of granite from the hills, others of limestone from the plains.

12   *the club*: probably the Arts Club, Upper Merrion Street, Dublin (now   *203* situated in 3 Upper Fitzwilliam Street) of which Yeats was a member. A good description of it (and of Yeats eating two dinners there in one evening) is given in P. L. Dickinson, *The Dublin of Yesterday* (1929), 54.

17   *That woman's days*: Constance Gore-Booth (1868–1927), who married Count Casimir Markievicz (1847–1932). She is described in 'On a Political Prisoner' (*PNE* 196) and 'In Memory of Eva Gore-Booth and Con Markievicz' (*PNE* 240). She took part in the Rising; her sentence of death was commuted to penal servitude for life and she was later released.

Yeats first met the Gore-Booth sisters in 1894. He stayed at Lissadell, their late-Georgian grey granite house that looks out over Sligo Bay, and, as he wrote to his sister Lily, enjoyed himself greatly:

> They are delightful people. . . . All the while I was at Lissadell I was busy telling stories – old Irish stories – first to one then another and then telling them over again to the sick Miss Gore upstairs. Miss Eva Gore-Booth shows some promise as a writer of verse. Her work is very formless as yet but it is full of very telling little phrases. Lissadell is an exceedingly impressive house inside with a great sitting room as high as a church and all things in good taste. . . .

But outside it is grey, square and bare yet set amid delightful grounds. (*L* 239-40)

There is a biography by Sean O'Faolain. See also *IP* 40-3, but the best and fullest accounts of Constance's life are given in Anne Marreco, *The Rebel Countess* (1967) and Jacqueline Van Voris, *Constance de Markievicz in the Cause of Ireland* (1968).

23   *she rode to harriers*: cf. 'On a Political Prisoner' (*PNE* 196).

24   *This man*: Patrick Pearse (1879-1916), the founder of St Enda's School for Boys at Rathfarnham, Co. Dublin, was Commandant-General and President of the provisional government in Easter week, and surrendered in the Post Office. He was a member of the Irish Bar, an orator, and had published poetry and prose in Gaelic and English.

26   *This other*: Thomas MacDonagh (1878-1916), a poet, dramatist (his play *When the Dawn is Come* was staged in the Abbey in 1908) and critic whose *Literature in Ireland* (1916) was a discerning piece of criticism. He taught English Literature in University College, Dublin. Yeats wrote of him in *Estrangement*:

> Met MacDonagh[1] yesterday – a man with some literary faculty which will probably come to nothing through lack of culture and encouragement. He had just written an article for the *Leader*, and spoke much as I do myself of the destructiveness of journalism here in Ireland, and was apologetic about his article. He is managing a school on Irish and Gaelic League principles but says he is losing faith in the League. Its writers are infecting Irish not only with the English idiom but with the habits of thought of current Irish journalism, a most un-Celtic thing. 'The League', he said, 'is killing Celtic civilisation.' I told him that Synge about ten years ago foretold this in an article in the *Academy*. He thought the National Movement practically dead, that the language would be revived but without all that he loved it for. In England this man would have become remarkable in some way, here he is being crushed by the mechanical logic and commonplace eloquence which give power to the most empty mind, because, being 'something other than human life', they have no use for distinguished feeling or individual thought. I mean that within his own mind this mechanical thought is crushing as with an iron roller all that is organic. (*A* 488)

31   *This other man*: Major John MacBride (1865-1916), Maud Gonne's husband, who had fought against England in the Boer War

33   *most bitter wrong*: probably a reference to the break-up of MacBride's marriage in 1905

34   *some who are near my heart*: Maud Gonne, and perhaps Iseult and possibly even Sean MacBride

204   43   *a stone*: hearts enchanted to a stone were Yeats's symbol for those who had

[1] Executed in 1916.

devoted themselves to a cause without thought of life or love. The stone was a symbol of how politics had affected, in particular, Maud Gonne. To be choked with hate was the chief of all evil chances, Yeats wrote in 'A Prayer for my Daughter' (*PNE* 201), with Maud Gonne in mind. Constance Markievicz's mind had become 'a bitter, an abstract thing' in 'On a Political Prisoner' (*PNE* 196).

58   *a stone of the heart*: the sacrifice referred to is, in particular, Maud Gonne's long service given to revolutionary ideals. Cf. *E & I* 314.

67   *needless death*: the Rising was not generally welcome at first in Ireland. Edward Malins, *Yeats and the Easter Rising* (1965) 3, has remarked that there were 100,000 Irishmen serving with the forces of the Crown, and adds, p. 10, that 'within a month the British Government had lit a flame of martyrdom around the leaders, that turned the revolt into a triumphal success, providing an emotional stimulus for the birth of a nation no less than that of Paul Revere and the Minutemen of Lexington'.

68   *may keep faith*: the Bill for Home Rule for Ireland received the Royal assent in 1914 but was suspended at the beginning of the 1914–18 war, the English government promising to enact it after the war was over.

72   *excess of love*: possibly an echo of Pearse's invocation of Colmcille: 'If I die it shall be for the excess of love I bear the Gael'.

76   *Connolly*: James Connolly (1870–1916), a trade union organiser and *205* author of *Labour in Irish History*, founded the *Irish Worker* and Workers' Republic, organised the Citizen Army, was military commander of all Republican forces in Dublin and Commandant in the Post Office during the rising. He was wounded and was brought to his execution on 12 May 1916 in a wheel-chair. He is said to have remarked: 'You can shoot me if you like but I am dying for my country.'

78   *green is worn*: an echo of the songs inspired by the 1798 revolution 'Green on my Cape' and 'The wearing of the Green'. For variants see Georges-Denis Zimmermann, *Irish Political Street Ballads and Rebel Songs* (1966), 167–70.

SIXTEEN DEAD MEN   **194**

This poem was written on 17 December 1916 or 1917, and first appeared in *The* *205* *Dial* (Nov. 1920).

Title   Sixteen: Yeats has presumably added Sir Roger Casement (1864–1916) to the fifteen leaders shot in 1916. He was a member of the British Consular Service from 1875 to 1913; he joined the Sinn Fein movement in 1914, went to Germany, returned in a submarine to Ireland and was arrested in the south-west. He was tried for high treason in London and hanged on 3 August 1916. His remains were returned to Ireland on 23 February 1965, and subsequently reinterred at Glashevin Cemetery, Dublin.

6   *the boiling pot*: Yeats is emphasising the effect that the executions had had, of making those shot into martyrs.

10   *Pearse*: see note on 'Easter 1916' (*PNE* 193)

12   *MacDonagh's*: see note on line 26, 'Easter 1916' (*PNE* 193).

16   *Lord Edward and Wolfe Tone*: Lord Edward Fitzgerald and Wolfe Tone, unsuccessful leaders of the 1798 rebellion. See note on 'September 1913' (*PNE* 115).

195   THE ROSE TREE

206   This poem's manuscript is dated 7 April 1917 in the Maud Gonne Manuscript Book. It first appeared in *The Dial* (Nov. 1920).

2   *Pearse to Connolly*: see notes on 'Easter 1916' (*PNE* 193)

4   *our Rose Tree*: Ireland, but a different kind of Ireland from the Rose symbolism of the earlier poems. The Rising was a gesture by dedicated men prepared to die for their beliefs, which were based on the idea that the nation needed to be redeemed by blood. Pearse regarded the position of Ireland as one of enslavement, and thought this worse than 'Shedding blood'. See Yeats's 'Modern Ireland', *Massachusetts Review* (winter 1964), 264-5, for a description of Pearse and his belief in 'the blood sacrifice'. See note on 'To the Rose upon the Rood of Time' (*PNE* 17).

17   *our own red blood*: Pearse wrote that 'Bloodshed is a cleansing and sanctifying thing', *Political Writings*, 99. He thought that it would take 'the blood of the sons of Ireland to redeem Ireland'. The theme was an old one. See Georges-Denis Zimmermann, *Irish Political Street Ballads and Rebel Songs* (Geneva, 1966), 71-2. A ballad included in this study, 'Ireland's Liberty Tree', 255 [text in *Harding's Dublin Songster*, new series, 32, 757; sung to tune of 'Norah O'Neal', F. Roche, *Collection of Irish Airs*, I, 19] seems likely to have influenced Yeats in his composition of 'The Rose Tree':

> A tree has been planted in Ireland,
>   And watered with tears of the brave;
> By our Great-grandsires it was nourished,
>   Who scorned to be held like the slaves.
> The trust they transported to their children,
>   To keep it until they were free,
> And yearly the plant has grown stronger
>   'Tis called 'Ireland's Liberty-Tree!'

Chorus:
>   Protect then, the tree, sons of Erin,
>   Its branches from traitors keep free,
>   Though Martyrs before ye have perished
>   Neath Ireland's famed Liberty-Tree.

>   Its roots in the ground firmly woven,
>   Unshaken by threat'ning alarm,
>   Its branches will wave o'er the patriot
>   Who dies for his country in arms.
>   The eyes of the world are upon it,
>   And millions beyond the blue sea
>   Are eagerly waiting to gather
>   Beneath Ireland's Liberty-Tree.

>   Brave Emmet, Fitzgerald and Grattan
>   Have died in defence of the tree,
>   While Shiel and O'Connell predicted
>   That the plant would see Ireland free.
>   Then deem not those patriots dreamers,
>   Their prophetic visions could see
>   That properly nourished, no power
>   Could harm Ireland's Liberty-Tree.

>   Let each son of Erin contribute
>   Whate'er in his power doth lie;
>   The pure blood of Ireland's Martyrs
>   Gave it strength, and it shall never die.
>   Then gather beneath its broad branches,
>   All ye who dare strive to be free,
>   And Heaven will surely protect those
>   Who guard Ireland's Liberty-Tree!

Zimmermann, op. cit., 85, regards Aubrey De Vere's poem 'The Little Black Rose shall be red at last' as the model for 'The Rose Tree' (it is contained in *The Sisters, Inisfail and other poems*, 293). The Liberty-Tree was a patriotic symbol deriving from the 'arbres de la liberté' which appeared in France in 1790, planted to celebrate Revolution and Liberty. They were planted earlier in America, from 1765–75, as symbols of opposition to England. In Ireland the United Irishmen took up the idea in 1792. See Zimmermann, op. cit., 41.

ON A POLITICAL PRISONER   196

This poem was written between 10 and 29 January 1919, and first appeared in   *206*
The Dial (Nov. 1920).

1   *She*: The Countess Markievicz. See note on line 7 'Easter 1916' (*PNE* 193). Yeats wrote to Mrs Yeats from Lucan, Co. Dublin, in 1918: 'I'm writing one on Con to avoid writing one on Maud. All of them are in prison. . . .' At this time

she was in Holloway Gaol for the second time, having been arrested as a Sinn Fein leader making seditious speeches. At the time relations between Yeats and Maud Gonne were somewhat strained. In December she had escaped from the nursing home in England to which she had been transferred from prison on account of her health. Yeats and his wife had been renting her house, 73 St Stephen's Green, Dublin, and when she arrived in December Yeats refused to have her in the house, as his wife was seriously ill with the devastating influenza then prevalent. Yeats and his wife left the house shortly afterwards. Another cause of tension between Yeats and Maud Gonne was the treatment of women prisoners.

207   9   *a bitter, an abstract thing*: cf. 'Easter 1916' (*PNE* 193) with its 'stone of the heart' and the dispraise of 'an intellectual hatred' in 'A Prayer for my Daughter' (*PNE* 201).

11–12   *Blind and leader of the blind*
        Drinking the foul ditch: cf. the blind man and ditch imagery in 'A Dialogue of Self and Soul', II (*PNE* 242)

13   *I saw her ride*: cf. 'Easter 1916':

> . . . young and beautiful
> She rode to harriers.

Cf. *Y: M & P* 189 and note on line 16, below. Yeats retailed an anecdote of a hunt in his broadcast of 10 April 1932 which showed that he liked the arrogance which accompanied the beauty.

14   *Ben Bulben*: (*Irish* Beann Ghulban) Gulban's Peak, a mountain to the north of Sligo, where Conall Gulban, a son of Nial of the Nine Hostages, was fostered (*McG* 21). Cf. 'Under Ben Bulben' (*PNE* 356).

16   *youth's lonely wildness*: D. J. Gordon and Ian Fletcher (*IP* 41) have written that, for all its gracious leisure, the life of serenity and opulence at Lissadell could not contain Constance Gore-Booth and her sister Eva:

> The eagerness with which the two girls listened to Yeats in the bay-windowed room – great windows open to the South – full of the apparatus of their leisure, must have been an index of their restlessness. Constance, though a famous and reckless horsewoman – Eva too rode fearlessly, but Constance was said to be the finest horsewoman in Ireland – painted, and even those early photographs of her seem to show an element of wilfullness. She always, through gesture or expression, quite deliberately isolates herself from the carefully posed and smiling group.

See also Ian Fletcher, 'Yeats and Lissadell' (*YCE* 62–77).

This poem was written in 1918 and first appeared in *MRD*.   *207*

1   *They*: Saul (*PYP* 119), suggests they were the 'crowd' of Dublin Bohemians Constance Markievicz had joined.

6   *The abounding gutter had been Helicon*: perhaps a contrast between the popular press and poetry. Yeats particularly disliked the Sinn Fein press and Arthur Griffith. He wrote, too, of Maud Gonne's activities in 'Poetry and Tradition':

> . . . gradually the political movement she was associated with, finding it hard to build up any fine lasting thing, became content to attack little persons and little things. All movements are held together more by what they hate than by what they love, for love separates and individualises and quiets, but the nobler movements, the only movements on which literature can found itself, hate great and lasting things.   (*E & I* 249-50)

Helicon, a mountain in Boeotia, was sacred to the Muses: it had a fountain, Hippocrene, which rose from the ground when struck by the hoof of the horse Pegasus (cf. 'Our colt' in 'The Fascination of What's Difficult' (*PNE* 99)) and this fountain was also sacred to the Muses. The word 'gutter' may well have been used in contrast to Helicon (standing for Hippocrene) to emphasise how far Yeats had moved from his earlier revolutionary belief that 'we must be baptized of the gutter'. But the poem may refer solely to Dublin's would-be writers, artists, etc. See note on line 1.

Truth flourishes where the student's lamp has shone: this is the symbol of 'Ego Dominus Tuus' (*PNE* 181) where the lamp 'burns on beside the open book', of 'The Phases of the Moon' (*PNE* 183) where 'the light proves that he is reading still'. It is the image of 'mysterious wisdom won by toil'. See notes on these poems. The 'candle and written page' of 'Meditations in Time of Civil War', II (*PNE* 207) are also part of this idea.

9   *that have no solitude*: solitude is necessary for the pursuit of wisdom. Cf. the   *208*
phrase in *AV* (B) 143, which describes Shelley returning 'again and again to these two images of solitude', the young man whose hair has grown white, the old man in the cavern. This occurs when he is 'out of phase' and has been trying to be a man of action, and dreaming of converting the world.

12   *that lamp*: this may link the Miltonic, Shelleyan, Yeatsian image of study with the magical Rosicrucian lamps which also represented a search for hidden truth and were still alight when taken from the tomb of Father Christian Rosencrux. Cf. note on 'The Mountain Tomb' (*PNE* 130) and Yeats's essay 'The Body of the Father Christian Rosencrux' (*E & I* 196-7). Yeats asserted that 'wisdom is the property of the dead' in 'Blood and the Moon', IV (*PNE* 243).

208   This poem was probably written in January 1919 and first appeared in *The Dial* (Nov. 1920).

1   *the double of my dream*: the poem is a record of two dreams dreamed by the poet and his wife on the same night when they were staying at the Powerscourt Arms Hotel, Enniskerry, Co. Wicklow, in January 1919. A passage in *AV* (A) describes this kind of experience:

> When two people meditate upon the one theme, who have established a supersensual link, they will invariably in my experience no matter how many miles apart, see pass before the mind's eye complementary images, images that complete one another. One for instance may see a boat upon a still sea full of tumultuous people, and the other a boat full of motionless people upon a tumultuous sea. Even when the link is momentary and superficial this takes place, and sometimes includes within its range a considerable number of people. One, for instance, will receive from a dream figure a ripe apple, another an unripe; one a lighted and one an unlighted candle and so on.
>
> On the same night a mother will dream that her child is dead or dying, the child that her mother is dead, while the father will wake in the night with a sudden inexplicable anxiety for some material treasure. I put an experience of the kind into the poem that begins –
>
> Was it the double of my dream, . . .   (*AV* (A) 173)

5   *a waterfall*: possibly the waterfall (see note on 'The Stolen Child' (*PNE* 10)) called 'the stream against the height' (*Irish* Struth-in-aghaidh-an-Aird) flowing into Glencar Lake (see *McG* 49). Wilson (*YI* 259), regards it as an image of the *fons vitae*, the water of life, and argues that the dream indicates that the *su:nmum bonum* of woman's spirituality is outside the scope of sexual possession.

209   23   *The marvellous stag*: the reference is to the stag in Malory, *Le Morte d'Arthur*, III, 5, which appeared at the marriage feast of Arthur and Guinevere pursued by a white brachet and thirty couple of running hounds. Unterecker (*RG* 163) draws connections between the dreams: white waterfall, white stag; water, a female symbol, stag, masculine; his dream, naturalistic, his wife's, mythological; his possessive, his wife's detached; his full of 'over much' love, hers detached; his water falls, her stag leaps. Wilson (*YI* 258-9) regards the stag image as 'the elusive spiritual beauty which a woman may discern in a man'.

PNE suggests *The Mabinogion, tr.* Lady Charlotte Guest (1877) 141-84, but Mrs W. B. Yeats confirmed Malory as source (in conversation with present author).

Arthur: mythical King of Britain (possibly a chieftain of the fifth or sixth century) on whom the Arthurian legends centre

This poem was written on 23 November 1918 and first appeared in *The Dial*   209
(Nov. 1920).

The poem is a description of momentary blessedness. Peter Ure, 'Yeats's "Demon and Beast",' *Irish Writing*, 31 (1955), described the poem as a war between two passions, the demon of hatred and the beast of desire, which he regarded as images of 'a state of intense selfabsorption and subjectivity'.

5   *perned in the gyre*: see note on 'Shepherd and Goatherd' (*PNE* 156). To pern is to move with a circular, spinning motion. For gyres see notes on 'The Double Vision of Michael Robartes' (*PNE* 188); 'The Second Coming' (*PNE* 200); 'Two Songs from a Play' (*PNE* 218); and 'The Gyres' (*PNE* 321). See Jeffares, 'Gyres in Yeats's poetry', *The Circus Animals* (1970) 103-14 for a discussion of sources in among others Emmanuel Swedenborg (1688-1772) the Swedish mystical philosopher and Jacob Boehm (1575-1624) the German mystic.

10   *Luke Wadding*: a portrait of an Irish Franciscan, born in Waterford 1588, and educated at Lisbon, who became president of the Irish College at Salamanca. He founded the College of St Isodore at Rome, where he died in 1657. He presented this College, of which he was Rector for fourteen years, with 5000 books and 800 manuscripts. The portrait was painted by José Ribera (1588-1652), and is in the National Gallery, Dublin.

11   *the Ormondes*: portraits of titled members of the Butler family in the National Gallery, Dublin. Yeats was connected with this family, see notes on 'Introductory Rhymes' (*PNE* 112). The portraits are part of the Lane Bequest.

13   *Strafford*: Sir Thomas Wentworth, 1st Earl of Strafford (1593-1641). He was Lord Deputy of Ireland 1632-8, and Charles I's political adviser. His portrait is in the National Gallery, Dublin, and is of the school of Van Dyck.

17   *the Gallery*: the National Gallery, Dublin

22   *aimless joy*: cf. note on 'Tom O'Roughley' (*PNE* 155). In *OTB* Yeats wrote:

> The arts are all the bridal chambers of joy. No tragedy is legitimate unless it leads some great character to his final joy. Polonius may go out wretchedly, but I can hear the dance music in 'Absent thee from felicity awhile', or in Hamlet's speech over the dead Ophelia, and what of Cleopatra's last farewells, Lear's rage under the lightning, Oedipus sinking down at the story's end into an earth 'riven' by love? Some Frenchman has said that farce is the struggle against a ridiculous object, comedy against a movable object, tragedy against an immovable; and because the will, or energy, is greatest in tragedy, tragedy is the more noble; but I add that 'will or energy is eternal delight,' and when its limit is reached it may become a pure, aimless joy, though the man, the shade, still mourns his lost object. (*E* 448-9)

23   *the little lake*: in St Stephen's Green, Dublin. Yeats and his wife were living in Maud Gonne MacBride's house, 73 St Stephen's Green, when he wrote the poem.

210   27-8   *absurd . . . green-pated bird*: one of the many ducks on the lake

44   *barren Thebaid*: Yeats drew his knowledge of the early Christian monastic movement from two books by the Rev. J. O. Hannay (who wrote his novels under the pseudonym George A. Birmingham), *The Spirit and Origin of Christian Monasticism* (1903) and *The Wisdom of the Desert* (1904). Hannay's Introduction to the latter, pp. 7-10, stresses the barren nature of the Thebaid. Cf. Yeats's remark in 'Bishop Berkeley' that he remembered 'that monks in the Thebaid, or was it by the Mareotic Sea, claimed ''to keep the ramparts'', meaning perhaps that all men whose thoughts skimmed the ''unconscious'', God-abetting, affected others according to their state, that what some feel others think, what some think others do' (*E & I* 405). The Thebaid is in the area around Thebes in upper Egypt.

45   *Mareotic Sea*: one of the five regions listed by Hannay where Egyptian monasticism flourished. Cf. Shelley's *Witch of Atlas*. She glided down the Nile

> By Moeris and the Mareotid lakes
> Strewn with faint blooms like bridal-chamber floors

See note on lines 1-2 of 'Under Ben Bulben' (*PNE* 356). Lake Mareotis is south of Alexandria.

46   *Exultant Anthony*: St Anthony of Coma (240?-345), whose life was described in chapter iv of J. O. Hannay's *The Spirit and Origin of Christian Monasticism*. Hannay, p. 101, stressed his enthusiasm as an element of his greatness.

47   *twice a thousand more*: a reference to the spread of monasticism. For St Anthony's influence on the Egyptian monastic movement see also A. Cooper Marsdin, *The History of the Island of the Lerins* (1913) and *The School of the Lerins* (1905).

48   *starved*: this was probably suggested by Hannay's chapter on fasting in *The Wisdom of the Desert*, 143-54.

50   *the Caesars*: there is a possible link between St Anthony's connection with the scene of his namesake's disaster. From Mark Antony to Caesar is an easy transition of thought. With the idea of the Caesars comes the thought of the effect of Christianity clashing with the Empire. Christ was seen by Yeats in *PASL* as 'the antithetical self of the classic world'; he commented that the saint 'whose life is but a round of customary duty, needs nothing the whole world does not need, and day by day he scourges in his body the Roman and Christian conquerors: Alexander and Caesar are famished in his cell' (*M* 337). Cf. notes on 'The Saint

and the Hunchback' (*PNE* 185) which expresses the same thought and on 'Whence had they come?' (*PNE* 316) with its 'hand and lash that beat down frigid Rome'.

The Caesars had nothing but their thrones because they did not have the benefit of a check upon their power. The idea is included in 'The Tragic Generation' where 'The typical men of the classical age (I think of Commodus, with his half-animal beauty, his cruelty and his caprice) lived public lives, pursuing curiosities of appetite, and so found in Christianity, with its Thebaid and its Mareotic Sea, the needed curb' (*A* 313). This idea of the curb may have come from a memory of Hannay's assertion in *The Wisdom of the Desert*, 144, that 'the end which the hermits hoped to attain by fasting was the subjugation of the flesh'. The hermit who disdained the exercise of fasting was compared to a horse without a bridle.

The Caesars came between the ideals of Greek religion and Christianity in *AV*:

> God is now conceived of as something outside man and man's handiwork, and it follows that it must be idolatry to worship that which Phidias and Scopas made, and seeing that He is a Father in Heaven that Heaven will be found presently in the Thebaid where the world is changed into featureless clay and can be run through the fingers. (*AV*(A) 185–6)

but their thrones: another passage in *AV* contrasts Christ and Caesar, and deals with the question of Caesar becoming a king. He concludes the section:

> One thinks of Mommsen's conviction that though Caesar chose the lesser of two evils the Roman State was from his day to the end a dead thing, a mere mechanism. (*AV*(B) 244–5)

For Caesars, see note on 'The Saint and the Hunchback' (*PNE* 185).

THE SECOND COMING   200

This poem was written in January 1919; it first appeared in *The Dial* (Nov.   *210*
1920).

The poem which prophesies the arrival of a new god takes its title from Christian doctrine. (See Kathleen Raine, 'Yeats's Debt to Blake', *Dublin Magazine* (Summer 1966), 40–2, for links between 'The Mental Traveller' and Yeats's system.) It blends Christ's prediction of this second coming in Matthew xxiv and St John's description of the beast of the Apocalypse in Revelations. The location of the birthplace in Bethlehem, traditionally associated with the idea of the gentle innocence of infancy, and with maternal love, adds horror to the thought of the rough beast. Yeats annotated the poem in terms of the story of the mythical Judwalis and Robartes as follows:

> Robartes copied out and gave to Aherne several mathematical diagrams from the *Speculum*, squares and spheres, cones made up of revolving gyres intersecting each other at various angles, figures sometimes of great complexity. His explanation of these, obtained invariably from the followers of Kusta-ben-Luki, is founded upon a single fundamental thought. The mind,

whether expressed in history or in the individual life, has a precise movement, which can be quickened or slackened but cannot be fundamentally altered, and this movement can be expressed by a mathematical form. A plant or an animal has an order of development peculiar to it, a bamboo will not develop evenly like a willow, nor a willow from joint to joint, and both have branches, that lessen and grow more light as they rise, and no characteristic of the soil can alter these things. A poor soil may indeed check or stop the movement and a rich prolong and quicken it. Mendel [Gregor Johann Mendel (1822-84) Austrian monk and scientist, founder of genetics, whose findings, published in 1865, were unrecognised until 1900] has shown that his sweet-peas bred long and short, white and pink varieties in certain mathematical proportions suggesting a mathematical law governing the transmission of parental characteristics. To the Judwalis, as interpreted by Michael Robartes, all living mind has likewise a fundamental mathematical movement, however adapted in plant, or animal, or man to particular circumstance; and when you have found this movement and calculated its relations, you can foretell the entire future of that mind. A supreme religious act of their faith is to fix the attention on the mathematical form of this movement until the whole past and future of humanity, or of an individual man, shall be present to the intellect as if it were accomplished in a single moment. The intensity of the Beatific Vision when it comes depends upon the intensity of this realisation. It is possible in this way, seeing that death is itself marked upon the mathematical figure, which passes beyond it, to follow the soul into the highest heaven and the deepest hell. This doctrine is, they contend, not fatalistic because the mathematical figure is an expression of the mind's desire, and the more rapid the development of the figure the greater the freedom of the soul. The figure while the soul is in the body, or suffering from the consequences of that life, is frequently drawn as a double cone, the narrow end of each cone being in the centre of the broad end of the other.

It had its origin from a straight line which represents, now time, now emotion, now subjective life, and a plane at right angles to this line which represents, now space, now intellect, now objective life; while it is marked out by two gyres which represent the conflict, as it were, of plane and line, by two movements, which circle about a centre because a movement outward on the plane is checked by and in turn checks a movement onward upon the line; & the circling is always narrowing or spreading, because one movement or other is always the stronger. In other words, the human soul is always moving outward into the objective world or inward into itself; & this movement is double because the human soul would not be conscious were it not suspended between contraries, the greater the contrast the more intense the consciousness. The man, in whom the movement inward is stronger than the movement outward, the man who sees all reflected within himself, the subjective man, reaches the narrow end of a gyre at death, for death is always, they contend, even when it seems the result of accident, preceded by an intensification of the subjective life; and has a moment of revelation immediately after death, a revelation which they describe as his being carried into the presence of all his dead kindred, a moment whose objectivity is exactly equal to the subjectivity of death. The objective man on the other hand, whose gyre moves outward, receives at this moment the revelation, not of himself seen from within, for that is impossible to objective man, but of himself as if he were somebody else. This figure is true also of history, for the end of an age, which always receives the revelation of the character of the next age, is represented by the coming of one gyre to its place of greatest expansion and of the other to that of its greatest contraction. At the present moment the life gyre is sweeping outward, unlike that before the birth of Christ which was narrowing, and has almost reached its greatest expansion. The revelation which approaches will however take its character from the contrary movement of the interior gyre. All our scientific, democratic, fact-accumulating, heterogeneous civilisation belongs to the outward gyre and prepares not the continuance of itself but the revelation as in a lightning flash, though in a flash that will not strike only in one place, and will for a time be constantly repeated, of the civilisation that must slowly take its place. This is too simple a statement, for much detail is possible. There are certain points of stress on outer and inner gyre, a division of each, now into ten, now into twenty-eight, stages or phases. However in the exposition of this detail so far as it affects the future, Robartes had little help from the Judwalis either because they cannot grasp events outside their experience, or because certain studies seem to them unlucky. ' ''For a time the power'' they have said to me,' (writes Robartes) ' ''will be with us, who are as like one another as the grains of sand, but when the revelation comes it will not come to the poor but to the great and learned and establish again for two thousand years prince & vizier. Why should we resist? Have not our wise men marked it upon the sand, and it is because of these marks, made generation after generation by the old for the young, that we are named Judwalis.'' '

Their name means makers of measures, or as we would say, of diagrams. (*MRD*)

1-2   ... *widening gyre*
The falcon cannot hear the falconer: originally the falcon was a hawk (see Stallworthy (*BL* 17-18)) but these lines may derive from Dante's description of how he and Virgil reach the eighth circle of Hell seated on Geryon's back. In Cary's translation Geryon moves in wheeling gyres:

> Of ample circuit, easy thy descent ...
> As falcon that hath long been on the wing
> But lure nor bird hath seen, while in despair
> The falconer cries 'Ah me! thou stoop'st to earth'.

Yeats's falcon also travels in gyres. And the Doré illustration to this part of *The Vision of Hell* shows Geryon emerging from the Abyss with his body shaped like the path of a gyre on a cone. The falcon represents man, present civilisation, becoming out of touch with Christ, whose birth was the revelation which marked the beginning of the two thousand years of Christianity.

4   *mere anarchy*: in 'The Trembling of the Veil' Yeats wrote that he had not   *211*

foreseen (in the 1887-91 period) 'the growing murderousness of the world' (*A* 192) and he went on to quote 'The Second Coming'. He had 'the troubles' in Ireland in mind, no doubt, as well as the Russian Revolution.

A letter was written to George Russell (AE), probably in April 1919, in which Yeats refers to his having sent Russell (who told Iseult Gonne the Russians had only executed 400 people) certain Russian comments on the figure as well as on the figure of 13,000 which was published 'as coming from the Russian government itself'. He continued

> What I want is that Ireland be kept from giving itself (under the influence of its lunatic faculty of going against everything which it believes England to affirm) to Marxian revolution or Marxian definition of value in any form. I consider the Marxian criterion of values as in this age the spear-head of materialism and leading to inevitable murder. From that criterion follows the well-known phrase 'Can the bourgeois be innocent?' (*L* 655-6)

5 *blood-dimmed tide*: cf. 'The Gyres (*PNE* 321), 'Irrational streams of blood are staining earth'.

7 *the best*: Henn (*LT* 144) suggests these lines echo Shelley's *Prometheus Unbound*, 625-8.

> The good want power, but to weep barren tears,
> The powerful goodness want: . . .

10 *the Second Coming*: *AV* contains many passages discussing the succession of civilisations:

> Each age unwinds the threads another age had wound, and it amuses me to remember that before Phidias, and his westward moving art, Persia fell, and that when full moon came round again, amid eastward moving thought, and brought Byzantine glory, Rome fell; and that at the outset of our westward moving Renaissance Byzantium fell; all things dying each other's life, living each other's death. (*AV*(A) 183)

The new era looked likely to be one of irrational force, as another passage pointed out. It is quoted in the note on line 9 of 'The Double Vision of Michael Robartes' (*PNE* 188) and is particularly germane.

12 *Spiritus Mundi*: 'a general storehouse of images which have ceased to be a property of any personality or spirit'. See the note from *MRD* quoted, line 42 'An Image from a Past Life' (*PNE* 191).

14 *A shape with lion body*: lines 13-17 were quoted after the following passage of *AV*:

> The approaching *antithetical* influx and that particular *antithetical* dispensation for which the intellectual preparation has begun will reach its complete systematisation at that moment when, as I have already shown, the Great Year comes to its intellectual climax. Something of what I have said it must be, the myth declares, for it must reverse our era and resume past eras in itself; what

else it must be no man can say, for always at the critical moment the *Thirteenth Cone*, the sphere, the unique intervenes.   (*AV* (B) 263)

The image, as Peter Ure first pointed out in *TM*, may be related to the Introduction to *The Resurrection* where Yeats wrote: 'I began to imagine, as always at my left side just out of the range of the sight, a brazen winged beast that I associated with laughing, ecstatic destruction' (*E* 393).

Yeats remarked in a footnote that the beast was 'afterwards described in my poem ''The Second Coming''.' Ure has pointed out (*TM* 46) that this beast probably derived from Yeats's experiences with MacGregor Mathers's symbolism and quotes Yeats's account of how Mathers gave him a cardboard symbol and he closed his eyes:

> Sight came slowly, there was not that sudden miracle as if the darkness had been cut with a knife, for that miracle is mostly a woman's privilege, but there rose before me mental images that I could not control: a desert and a black Titan raising himself up by his hands from the middle of a heap of ancient ruins. Mathers explained that I had seen a being of the order of Salamanders because he had shown me their symbol. . . .   (*A* 185–6)

17   *desert birds*: these have the ominous aspect of birds of prey: they pick bones bare in *Calvary*.

19   *twenty centuries*: Yeats regarded the Christian era as being of two thousand years, like the era that went before it. Cf. *AV* (B) 267.

21   *rough beast*: Henn (*LT* 145) compares the line 'What from the forest came? What beast has licked its young?'' in 'Supernatural Songs', VII (*PNE* 315). He comments that the possibilities of the 'rough beast' are endless and suggests that it may be founded on the quotations given above, or on a Blake illustration, or on the man-headed sphinx Sturge Moore drew for a translation of Villiers de L'Isle Adam, or on the brazen winged beasts in Charles Ricketts's illustration for Wilde's *Salome*. Cf. the mystery 'on the bestial floor' of 'The Magi' (*PNE* 139). See also S. B. Bushrui, *Yeats's Verse Plays. The Revisions 1900–1910* (1965), 114, who points out that the death speech of the poet in *The King's Threshold* is linked to 'The Second Coming' with its lines:

> He needs no help that joy has lifted up
> Like some miraculous beast out of Ezekiel.

Professor A. M. Gibbs has suggested parallels between the 'rough beast' of this poem and the 'rough beast' in Shakespeare's *Lucrece*. The images of the falcon and the tide of blood were also used by Shakespeare in that poem.

22   *Bethlehem*: Christ's birthplace, therefore a most holy place in Christian tradition

201 A PRAYER FOR MY DAUGHTER

211 This poem was written between February and June 1919; it first appeared in *Poetry* (Nov. 1919).

Title my Daughter: Anne Butler Yeats was born on 26 February 1919. The poem was begun shortly after her birth and finished at Thoor Ballylee (see note on 'To be Carved on a Stone at Thoor Ballylee' (*PNE* 203)), Yeats's tower near Gort, Co. Galway, where its scene is set.

4 *Gregory's wood.* Thoor Ballylee was also near Lady Gregory's estate, Coole Park.

6 *the Atlantic*: some miles to the west of the tower

212 10 *the tower*: Yeats's tower

11 *the bridge*: it crossed the stream, which washed one wall of the tower.

14–16 *. . . future years had come,*
Dancing to a frenzied drum,
Out of the murderous innocence
Cf. the foreboding of 'The Second Coming' (*PNE* 200) and its lines:

The blood-dimmed tide is loosed, and everywhere
The ceremony of innocence is drowned.

25 *Helen*: the earlier association of Helen and Maud Gonne is a preparation for lines 57–64.

27 *that great Queen*: Aphrodite, Greek goddess of love, beauty and fertility. Hesiod told of her birth from the sea. Her name was supposed to be derived from Aphros, meaning foam. Hence she was 'fatherless'.

29 *bandy-leggèd smith*: her husband was Hephaestus, the lame god of fire.

32 *the Horn of Plenty*: Zeus received a cornucopia from Amalthea, the goat that suckled him: her horns flowed with nectar and ambrosia. This is a folk motif, where the possessor can get anything he wants out of the magical object.

33 *In courtesy*: Yeats regarded courtesy and self-possession and style in the arts as the result of 'a deliberate shaping of all things'. There is an interesting passage on the role of aristocrats, countrymen and artists in this connection in 'Poetry and Tradition' (*E & I* 251–6), which is echoed in 'The Municipal Gallery Revisited' (*PNE* 354).

37 *for beauty's very self*: probably Maud Gonne is implied.

38   *a poor man*: a reference to Yeats

40   *a glad kindness*: a reference to Yeats's marriage. Yeats wrote to Lady   *213*
Gregory shortly after his marriage (on 20 October 1917): 'My wife is a perfect
wife, kind, wise and unselfish. I think you were such another young girl once. She
has made my life serene and full of order' (*WBY* 307).

51   *prosper but little*: Maud Gonne returned to Ireland in December 1918.
Both she and Con Markievicz were in prison afterwards. See note on 'On a
Political Prisoner' (*PNE* 196).

57   *An intellectual hatred*: Yeats wrote in a Diary in 1910:

> Women because the main event of their lives has been a giving of themselves
> give themselves to an opinion as if it were a stone doll . . . women should have
> their play with dolls finished in childhood for, if they play with ideas again it is
> amid hatred and malice.

In 'The Death of Synge' this appears in a different guise:

> F—— is learning Gaelic. I would sooner see her in the Gaelic movement
> than in any Irish movement I can think of. I fear some new absorption in
> political opinion. Women, because the main event of their lives has been a
> giving themselves and giving birth, give all to an opinion as if it were some
> terrible stone doll . . . to women opinions become as their children or their
> sweethearts, and the greater their emotional capacity the more do they forget all
> other things. They grow cruel, as if in defence of lover or child, and all this is
> done for 'something other than human life'. At last the opinion is so much
> identified with their nature that it seems a part of their flesh becomes stone and
> passes out of life. . . . Women should have their play with dolls finished in
> childish happiness, for if they play with them again it is amid hatred and
> malice.   (*A* 504)

59   *the loveliest woman born*: Maud Gonne, who was hinted at in the Helen
symbol in the fourth stanza; the trouble that Helen had 'from a fool' being
paralleled by Aphrodite's choice of Hephaestus and Maud's choice of MacBride
as husband.

60   *Plenty's horn*: see note on line 32.

66   *radical innocence*: contrasting with the 'murderous innocence' of line 16?

A MEDITATION IN TIME OF WAR   **202**

This was written on 9 November 1914 in the Maud Gonne Manuscript Book; it   *214*
first appeared in *The Dial* (Nov. 1920), with the title 'A Mediation in Time of
War' (probably a misprint), and in *N* (13 Nov. 1920).

1   *one throb of the artery*: William Blake's 'Time' is probably a source for the

poem; it is included in Blake, *Works* (1893) I, 278, and in Yeats's selection of Blake's *Poems* of 1893:

> Everytime less than a pulsation of the artery
> Is equal in its period and value to six thousand years.
> For in this period the poet's work is done, and all the great
> Events of time start forth and are conceived in such a period,
> Within a moment; a pulsation of the artery.

An essay in *CT*, dated 1902, possibly gives an account of an experience which has contributed to this poem:

> One day I was walking over a bit of marshy ground close to Inchy Wood when I felt, all of a sudden, and only for a second, an emotion which I said to myself was the root of Christian mysticism. There had swept over me a sense of weakness, of dependence on a great personal Being somewhere far off yet near at hand. No thought of mine had prepared me for this emotion, for I had been preoccupied with Aengus and Edain, and with Manannan, Son of the Sea. That night I awoke lying upon my back and hearing a voice speaking above me and saying, 'No human soul is like any other human soul, and therefore the love of God for any human soul is infinite, for no other soul can satisfy the same need in God.' A few nights after this I awoke to see the loveliest people I have ever seen. A young man and a young girl dressed in olive-green raiment, cut like old Greek raiment, were standing at my bedside. I looked at the girl and noticed that her dress was gathered about her neck into a kind of chain, or perhaps into some kind of stiff embroidery which represented ivy-leaves. But what filled me with wonder was the miraculous mildness of her face. There are no such faces now. It was beautiful as few faces are beautiful, but it had not, one would think, the light that is in desire or in hope or in fear or in speculation. It was peaceful like the faces of animals, or like mountain pools at evening, so peaceful that it was a little sad. I thought for a moment that she might be the beloved of Aengus, but how could that hunted, alluring, happy, immortal wretch have a face like this? (*M* 68-9)

An essay in *PASL* deals with the same subject:

> There are two realities, the terrestrial and the condition of fire.[1] All power is from the terrestrial condition, for there all opposites meet and there only is the extreme of choice possible, full freedom. And there the heterogeneous is, and evil, for evil is the strain one upon another of opposites; but in the condition of fire is all music and all rest. Between is the condition of air where images have but a borrowed life, that of memory or that reflected upon them when they symbolise colours and intensities of fire: the place of shades who are 'in the whirl of those who are fading' and who cry like those amorous shades in the Japanese play:

> > That we may acquire power
> > Even in our faint substance,

---

[1] When writing this essay I did not see how complete must be the antithesis between man and Daimon. The repose of man is the choice of the Daimon, and the repose of the Daimon the choice of man; and what I have called man's terrestrial state the Daimon's condition of fire. I might have seen this, as it all follows from the words written by the beggar in *The Hour Glass* upon the walls of Babylon.

We will show forth even now,
And though it be but in a dream,
Our form of repentance.

After so many rhythmic beats the soul must cease to desire its images, and can, as it were, close its eyes.

When all sequence comes to an end, time comes to an end, and the soul puts on the rhythmic or spiritual body or luminous body and contemplates all the events of its memory and every possible impulse in an eternal possession of itself in one single moment. That condition is alone animate, all the rest is fantasy, and from thence come all the passions and, some have held, the very heat of the body.

Time drops in decay,
Like a candle burnt out,
And the mountains and woods
Have their day, have their day.
What one, in the rout
Of the fire-born moods,
Has fallen away? ['The Moods' (*PNE* 42)] (*M* 356-7)

In the same essay Yeats wrote 'we perceive in a pulsation of the artery, and after slowly decline' (*M* 361). See also his reference to Villiers de l'Isle-Adam quoting Aquinas: 'Eternity is the possession of one's self, as in a single moment' (*E* 37).

TO BE CARVED ON A STONE AT THOOR BALLYLEE   **203**

This poem was written in 1918, probably between May and July, and first   *214*
appeared in *MRD*.

Title   *Thoor* from the Irish *tor, tur*, a tower. Ballylee is the townland in which Yeats's tower was situated, its name derived from the Leech (O'Liagh) family, hereditary leeches to the O'Flaherties of Connemara (*McG* 19-20). Yeats bought the tower for £35 in 1917. See A. Norman Jeffares, 'Poet's Tower', *The Circus Animals* (1970), 29-46.

2   *old mill boards*: Yeats wrote to John Quinn on 23 July 1918, from Ballylee Castle:

We are surrounded with plans. This morning designs arrived from the drunken man of genius, Scott, for two beds. The war is improving the work for, being unable to import anything, we have bought the whole contents of an old mill – great beams and three-inch planks, and old paving stones; and the local carpenter and mason and blacksmith are at work for us. On a great stone beside the front door will be inscribed these lines:

I, the poet, William Yeats,
With common sedge and broken slates,
And smithy work from the Gort forge,
Restored this tower for my wife George;

> And on my heirs I lay a curse
> If they should alter for the worse,
> From fashion or an empty mind,
> What Raftery built and Scott designed.

Raftery is the local builder . . . (*L* 651)

3   *the Gort forge*: the tower was about four miles from the village of Gort.

4   *George*: Mrs Yeats, *née* Bertha Georgina Hyde-Lees (1894–1968). Yeats wrote to his father a week or two after his marriage (20 October 1917):

> I am dictating this to my wife. I call her George to avoid Georgie which she has been called hitherto in spite of her protests. I enclose her photograph. She permits me to say that it flatters her good looks at the expense of her character. She is not so black and white, but has red-brown hair and a high colour which she sets off by wearing dark green in her clothes and earrings, etc.   (*WBY* 307)

6   *ruin once again*: the tower fell into disrepair after Yeats's death. The last summer the family spent there was in 1929: its somewhat isolated situation made it a difficult household to manage, and the damp climate was bad for Yeats's rheumatism. The tower and the cottages have, however, recently been renovated, and the story of this is told in Mary Hanley, *Thoor Ballylee – Home of William Butler Yeats* (1965), which includes photographs of the rooms which now contain replicas of the furniture made for Yeats. See also A. Norman Jeffares, 'Poet's Tower', *Envoy*, V, 20 (July 1951).

YEATS'S change of style and his maturity were probably not generally recognised until the publication of *The Tower* in 1928. This volume was a collection of poems which reflect the richness of his life: marriage, a family, senatorship of the Irish Free State, the Nobel Prize for poetry, *AV* published, the discovery of his Anglo-Irish ancestry in politics and literature. There was also the sharpened apprehension, brought by Ireland's civil war, of approaching conflagration in the world and, by approaching age, of ruin and decay. Yeats had become 'a smiling sixty-year-old public man', but with ironic memories of lost youth and love, with the tower to remind him that the glory of a family or a house can vanish, and an idealised Byzantium to set against the realities of living in a country of the young. His verse took on new eloquence, it dealt freely with many of his moods and interests: politics, philosophy, friendship, and love. He wrote of them as they affected his own imaginative life: and his imagination grew stronger as his body decayed: an idea he had seized upon in Blake when he himself was only thirty-four. He looked back on the poetry of *The Tower* in surprise at its bitterness and power, yet it also carried an antithetical view:

> When such as I cast out remorse
> So great a sweetness flows into the breast
> We must laugh and we must sing,
> We are blest by everything,
> Everything we look upon is blest.

The poems in *The Tower* (1928) had previously been included in *Seven Poems and A Fragment* (1922), *The Cat and the Moon* (1924) and *October Blast* (1927). Poems included in these volumes were brought together in *The Tower* (1928); 'Fragments' was added to *The Tower CP* (1933); in this the order of the poems was altered and 'The Hero, the Girl and the Fool' replaced by 'The Fool by the Roadside'.

SAILING TO BYZANTIUM   **204**

This poem was written in the autumn of 1926; the two typescripts (there are *217* seventeen other MS. sheets) are dated 26 Sept. 1926. The poem first appeared in *OB*.

Title Byzantium: Yeats's knowledge of the city was largely derived from reading W. G. Holmes, *The Age of Justinian and Theodora* (1905), Mrs A. Strong, *Apotheosis and After Life: Three Lectures on Certain Phases of Art and Religion in the Roman Empire* (1915), and O. M. Dalton, *Byzantine Art and Archaeology* (1911). He also read Gibbon's *Decline and Fall of the Roman*

Empire, The Cambridge Mediaeval History, the *Encyclopaedia Britannica* and other general reference works. R. Ellmann has suggested that J. B. Bury the historian, who was Latin master for a time at the High School, Dublin, may first have interested Yeats in Byzantium.

The symbolic meaning of Byzantium can be discovered in Yeats's prose ('Sailing to Byzantium' and 'Byzantium' (*PNE* 260) are complementary poems in many respects). In *AV* it was described at about the end of the first Christian millennium. Byzantium is a holy city, as the capital of eastern Christianity, and as the place where God exists because of the life after death Yeats imagines existing there. His description of Byzantium (the ancient city rebuilt by the Roman Emperor Constantine I (? 287–337) and renamed Constantinople) in *AV* shows that he valued the position of the artist in the city:

> I think if I could be given a month of Antiquity and leave to spend it where I chose, I would spend it in Byzantium, a little before Justinian opened St Sophia and closed the Academy of Plato. I think I could find in some little wine-shop some philosophical worker in mosaic who could answer all my questions, the supernatural descending nearer to him than to Plotinus even, for the pride of his delicate skill would make what was an instrument of power to princes and clerics, a murderous madness in the mob, show as a lovely flexible presence like that of a perfect human body.
>
> I think that in early Byzantium, maybe never before or since in recorded history, religious, aesthetic and practical life were one, that architect and artificers – though not, it may be, poets, for language had been the instrument of controversy and must have grown abstract – spoke to the multitude and the few alike. The painter, the mosaic worker, the worker in gold and silver, the illuminator of sacred books, were almost impersonal, almost perhaps without the consciousness of individual design, absorbed in their subject-matter and that the vision of a whole people. They could copy out of old gospel books those pictures that seemed as sacred as the text, and yet weave all into a vast design, the work of many that seemed the work of one, that made building, picture, pattern, metal-work of rail and lamp, seem but a single image; and this vision, this proclamation of their invisible master, had the Greek nobility, Satan always the still half-divine Serpent, never the horned scarecrow of the didactic Middle Ages.
>
> The ascetic, called in Alexandria 'God's Athlete', has taken the place of those Greek athletes whose statues have been melted or broken up or stand deserted in the midst of cornfields, but all about him is an incredible splendour like that which we see pass under our closed eyelids as we lie between sleep and waking, no representation of a living world but the dream of a somnambulist. Even the drilled pupil of the eye, when the drill is in the hand of some Byzantine worker in ivory, undergoes a somnambulistic change, for its deep shadow among the faint lines of the tablet, its mechanical circle, where all else is rhythmical and flowing, give to Saint or Angel a look of some great bird staring at miracle. Could any visionary of those days, passing through the Church named with so un-theological a grace 'The Holy Wisdom', can even a visionary of today wandering among the mosaics at Ravenne or in Sicily, fail to recognise some one image seen under his closed eyelids? To me it seems that He, who among the first Christian communities was little but a ghostly exorcist, had in His assent to a full Divinity made possible this sinking-in upon a supernatural splendour, these walls with their little glimmering cubes of blue

and green and gold.   (*AV* (B) 279–80) [Ravenne is presumably a misprint for Ravenna.]

In November 1924 Yeats had been ill, out of breath, with high blood pressure, and Mrs Yeats brought him to Sicily where he saw the Byzantine mosaics of Monreale and the Capella Palatina at Palermo. This visit may have revived his memories of the mosaics at Ravenna. He had visited the church of S. Apollinare Nuovo in 1907 and seen its frieze of holy virgins and martyrs. See Gwendolen Murphy, *The Modern Poet*, 153. On 5 September 1926 Yeats wrote to Mrs Shakespear: 'There have been constant interruptions – the last time I wrote a poem about Byzantium to recover my spirits.'

The best comment on the poem, however, is contained in a paragraph Yeats wrote for a broadcast of his poems (BBC Belfast, 8 Sept. 1931) which was not included in the final version of the script:

Now I am trying to write about the state of my soul, for it is right for an old man to make his soul, and some of my thoughts upon that subject I have put into a poem called 'Sailing to Byzantium'. When Irishmen were illuminating the Books of Kells [in the eighth century] and making the jewelled croziers in the National Museum, Byzantium was the centre of European civilisation and the source of its spiritual philosophy, so I symbolise the search for the spiritual life by a journey to that city.

1   *That country*: Ireland. A version in MS. has 'This is no country for old men'.

old men: Yeats was thinking of the disadvantages of age in relation to love. Early versions of the poem in MSS. show him balancing the young Christ with the ageless pagan gods of Ireland. Then the contrast between the sensual and the soul is developed. There are three discussions of the MSS. versions of the poem: Jeffares, 'The Byzantine Poems of W. B. Yeats', *RES* XXII, 44–52; Curtis Bradford, 'Yeats's Byzantine Poems', *PMLA* LXXV, 1, 110–25 and J. Stallworthy, *BL*, 87–136. The last gives the fullest account of the development of the poems.

2   *In one another's arms*: Stallworthy quotes a first and illegible draft in which the poet writes that the time has come to speak of his loves 'in my first youth' and contains these lines 'For many loves have I taken off my clothes' . . . 'but now I will take off my body/That they might be enfolded in that for which they (had longed)'. In 'that', as Stallworthy points out, is probably the poet's soul.

4   *The salmon-falls*: probably a memory of the salmon at Galway (one of the first things Yeats wanted his wife to see when she came to Ireland after their marriage) waiting to leap their way upstream to spawn. George Moore has described Yeats's delight in the Galway salmon weir:

There were other idlers besides ourselves enjoying the fair weather, and their arms resting on the stone bridge they looked into the brown rippling water, remarking from time to time that the river was very low (no one had ever seen it lower), and that the fish would have to wait a long time before there was sufficient water for them to get up the weir. But my eyes could not distinguish a fish until Yeats told me to look straight down through the brown water, and I saw one, and immediately afterwards a second and a third and a fourth. And then the great show, hundreds, thousands of salmon, each fish keeping its place in the current, a slight movement of the tail being sufficient.

But if they should get tired of waiting and return to the sea?

Yeats is a bit of a naturalist, and in an indolent mood it was pleasant to listen to him telling of the habits of the salmon which only feeds in the sea. If the fishermen were to get a rise it would be because the fish were tired of waiting and snapped at anything to relieve the tedium of existence. . . . (*Salve* (1947 Edition) 102)

There was also a famous salmon-leap at Leixlip, Co. Dublin, and Cuchulain was famous for his 'salmon-leap', his vigour being compared to that of a bird. In an old Irish song the sensual music of summer is stressed through images of birds and fish:

> The blackbird sings a loud strain
> To him the live world is a heritage
> The sad angry sea is fallen asleep
> The speckled salmon leaps.
> (*Old Irish Songs of Summer and Winter*, trans. and
> ed. Kuno Meyer, 1903)

mackerel-crowded seas: probably founded on memories of the mackerel 'coming in' to harbours and shores in the west of Ireland

5   *Fish, flesh, or fowl, commend*: Henn (*LT* 225) compares 'The Dancer at Cruachan and Cro-Patrick' (*PNE* 288).

10   *a tattered coat*: cf. 'A Coat' (*PNE* 141) and the fourth stanza of 'Among School Children' (*PNE* 222) with its 'old scarecrow'

11   *Soul clap its hands and sing*: L. A. G. Strong, *Personal Record*, 32, suggested this image derived from Blake's vision of his brother's soul clapping its hands as it flew up to heaven.

14   *Monuments of its own magnificence*: D. J. Greene suggests that this may derive from Samuel Johnson, *Journey to the Western Islands of Scotland*.

17   *sages standing in God's holy fire*: they are the martyrs in the frieze at S. Apollinare Nuovo at Ravenna. See introductory note to poem above. In a letter to Mrs Shakespear written on 27 October 1927 Yeats told her that

When I went to London I had just finished a poem in which I appeal to the saints in 'the holy fire' to send death on their ecstasy. In London I went to a medium called Cooper and on the way called to my people for their especial wisdom. The medium gave me 'a book test' – Third book from R bottom shelf – study – Page 48 or 84. I have only this morning looked it up. The book was the complete Dante designs of Blake. It was not numbered by pages but by plates. Plate 84 is Dante entering the Holy Fire (Purgatorio–Canto 27). Plate 48 is 'The serpent attacking Vanni Fucci.' When I looked this up in Dante I found that at the serpent's sting Vanni Fucci is burnt to ashes and then recreated from the ashes and that this symbolises 'the temporal Fire.' The medium is the most stupid I know and certainly the knowledge was not in my head. After this and all that has gone before I must capitulate if the dark mind lets me. Certainly we suck always at the eternal dugs. How well too it puts my own mood between spiritual excitement, and the sexual torture and the knowledge that they are somehow inseparable! It is the eyes of the Earthly Beatrice – she has not yet put on her divinity – that makes Dante risk the fire 'like a child that is offered an apple.' Immediately after comes the Earthly Paradise and the Heavenly Beatrice. (*L* 730-1)

19   *perne in a gyre*: see notes on 'Shepherd and Goatherd' (*PNE* 156) and 'Demon and Beast' (*PNE* 199).

23-4   *gather me*   *218*
           Into the artifice of eternity
Cf. a passage in *The Tables of the Law* where Yeats wrote:

Just as poets and painters and musicians labour at their works, building them with lawless and lawful things alike, so long as they embody the beauty that is beyond the grave, these children of the Holy Spirit labour at their moments with eyes upon the shining substance on which Time has heaped the refuse of creation; for the world only exists to be a tale in the ears of coming generations; and terror and content, birth and death, love and hatred, and the fruit of the Tree, are but instruments for that supreme art which is to win us from life and gather us into eternity like doves into their dove-cots. (*M* 300-1)

Yeats regarded Justinian's reign in Byzantium as a great age of building in which Byzantine art was perfected. A building like St Sophia preceded the climax of that civilisation. Cf. *AV* (B) 281-2.

27   *such a form as Grecian goldsmiths make*: Yeats's note read: 'I have read somewhere that in the Emperor's palace at Byzantium was a tree made of gold and silver, and artificial birds that sang' (*OB*).
   Much speculation has occurred on the subject of the bird's origin. (See Jeffares, 'Yeats's Byzantine Poems and the Critics', *English Studies in Africa*, 1962.) T. L. Dume, for instance, in 'Yeats's Golden Tree and Birds in the Byzantine Poems', *Modern Language Notes*, LXVII, 404-7, suggests passages in *The Cambridge Mediaeval History* and Edward Gibbon (1737-94)'s *The History of the Decline and Fall of the Roman Empire* (1776-88) which Yeats read in J. B. Bury's edition (1909-14) (see VI, 81 of this edition) as likely sources. Other sources, including the Byzantine, are discussed by Jeffares, 'The Byzantine Poems of W. B. Yeats', *RES*, XXII, 85 (Jan. 1946) 48-9. But the best suggestion put forward is that of E. Schanzer, ' "Sailing to Byzantium", Keats and Anderson', *English Studies*, XLI (Dec. 1960), who thinks Yeats remembered being read, as a child, Hans Andersen's tale 'The Emperor's Nightingale' (probably from the edition which had for cover an illustration of the Emperor and his court listening to the artificial bird). In about 1910 Yeats was told by Eric Maclagan of the well-known passage in Liutprand of

215

Cremona describing the singing bird in the Imperial Palace (referred to in *RES* article cited above).

29-31   ... *Emperor awake;*
              Or set upon a golden bough to sing
              To lords and ladies:

see note above.

32   *past, or passing, or to come*: this line echoes the first stanza's 'Whatever is begotten, born, and dies'. Stallworthy (*BL* 99) sees an echo here of Blake's lines:

> Hear the voice of the Bard,
> Who present, past and future, sees;

205   THE TOWER

218   The manuscript of the last section is dated 7 Oct. 1925; the poem first appeared in *The New Republic* (29 June 1927).

3-6   *Decrepit age ... imagination ... the impossible*: Yeats was sixty: he had been ill the previous autumn. The seeming contradiction of having more energy as he grew older is possibly an echo of Blake whom he had quoted in a letter to the *Boston Pilot* in 1889:

> I have been very near the gates of Death, and have returned very weak, and an old man feeble and tottering, but not in spirits and life, not in the real man, the imagination which liveth for ever. In that I am stronger as this foolish body decays. (*Letters to the New Island*, 42)

8   *rod and fly*: cf. note on 'The Fisherman' (*PNE* 160).

9   *Ben Bulben*: mountain to the north of Sligo. See note on 'On a Political Prisoner' (*PNE* 196) and cf. 'Under Ben Bulben' (*PNE* 356).

11   *bid the Muse go pack*: cf. the final lines of 'Vacillation', VIII (*PNE* 262). The Nine Muses in Greek mythology are the patronesses of art and science; here the Muse of Poetry is intended.

12   *Plato and Plotinus*: Yeats wrote in 1928:

> When I wrote the lines about Plato and Plotinus I forgot that it is something in our own eyes that makes us see them as all transcendence. Has not Plotinus written: 'Let every soul recall, then, at the outset the truth that soul is the author of all living things, that it has breathed the life into them all, whatever is nourished by earth and sea, all the creatures of the air, the divine stars in the sky; it is the maker of the sun; itself formed and ordered this vast heaven and conducts all that rhythmic motion - and it is a principle distinct from all these to which it gives law and movement and life, and it must of necessity be more

216

honourable than they, for they gather or dissolve as soul brings them life or abandons them, but soul, since it never can abandon itself, is of eternal being?' (*CP* 533)

Yeats read Plotinus (?203–62), the Greek Neo-Platonic philosopher, in Stephen MacKenna's translation. (The quotation is from *Plotinus: the Divine Mind Being the Treatises of the Fifth Ennead* (1926) 2.) A letter from MacKenna to E. R. Debenham, written in October 1926, records MacKenna's pleasure at this:

> Another little encouragement: Yeats, a friend tells me, came to London, glided into a bookshop and dreamily asked for the new Plotinus, began to read there and then, and read on and on till he'd finished (he has really a colossal brain, you know), and now is preaching Plotinus to all his train of attendant duchesses: he told my friend he intended to give the winter in Dublin to Plotinus. (*Journal and Letters of Stephen MacKenna*, ed. E. R. Dodds, 235)

MacKenna's five-volume translation of Plotinus appeared from 1917 to 1930. Mrs Yeats knew Taylor's translations of *Plotinus* (*AV* (B) 19). An edition of his *Select Works of Plotinus* was published in 1895; his *Five Books of Plotinus* had been published in 1794. Yeats began to read the Greek philosopher Plato (?427– 348 BC) (see notes on 'Among School Children' (*PNE* 222) and on 'Mad as the Mist and Snow' (*PNE* 285)) at Lionel Johnson's instigation in the 'nineties; he may have used Thomas Taylor's *Plato* (5 vols., 1804).

17   *the battlements*: on Yeats's tower. He compared winding stairs of towers 'to the philosophical gyres' (*CP* 535).   *219*

25–9   *Mrs. French*: Yeats wrote that

> The persons mentioned are associated by legend, story and tradition with the neighbourhood of Thoor Ballylee or Ballylee Castle, where the poem was written. Mrs. French lived at Peterswell in the eighteenth century and was related to Sir Jonah Barrington who described the incident of the ears and the trouble that came of it. The peasant beauty and the blind poet are Mary Hynes and Raftery, and the incident of the man drowned in Cloone Bog is recorded in my *Celtic Twilight*. Hanrahan's pursuit of the phantom hare and hounds is from my *Stories of Red Hanrahan* [1904]. The ghosts have been seen at their game of dice in what is now my bedroom, and the old bankrupt man lived about a hundred years ago. According to one legend he could only leave the Castle upon a Sunday because of his creditors, and according to another he hid in the secret passage.   (*CP* 532)

Sir Jonah Barrington (whom Mrs Yeats was reading aloud to her husband at this time) gave a racy description of the incident, which took place in 1778:

> Some relics of feudal arrogance set the neighbours and their adherents together by the ears. My grandfather (Mr French of County Galway) had conceived a contempt for, and antipathy to, a sturdy *half* mounted gentleman, one Mr Dennis Bodkin, who entertained an equal aversion to the arrogance of my grandfather, and took every possible opportunity of irritating and opposing him. My grandmother, an O'Brien, was high and proud, steady and sensible, but disposed to be rather violent at times, in her contempt and animosities, and entirely agreed with her husband on his detestation of Mr Dennis Bodkin.

On some occasion or other Mr Dennis had chagrined the squire and his lady most outrageously. A large company dined at my grandfather's and my grandmother concluded her abuse of Dennis with an energetic expression that could not have been literally meant, in these words – 'I wish the fellow's ears were cut off! That might quiet him.'

This passed over as usual, the subject was changed, and all went on comfortably till supper; at which time when everybody was in full glee, the old butler, Ned Regan, who had drunk enough, came in – joy was in his eye – and whispering something to his mistress which she did not comprehend, he put a large snuff box into her hand. Fancying it was some whim of her old domestic, she opened the box and shook out its contents; when, lo! a considerable portion of a pair of bloody ears dropped on the table! Nothing could surpass the horror and surprise of the company. Old Ned exclaimed, – 'Sure, my lady, you wished that Dennis Bodkin's ears were cut off; so I told old Gahagan (the gamekeeper) and he took a few boys with him, and brought back Dennis Bodkin's ears – and there they are: and I hope you are plazed, my lady!'

The scene may be imagined; but its results had like to have been of a more serious nature. The sportsman and the boys were ordered to get off as fast as they could; but my grandfather and grandmother were held to heavy bail, and were tried at the ensuing assizes at Galway. The evidence of the entire company, however, united in proving that my grandmother never had an idea of any such order, and that it was a mistake on the part of the servants. They were, of course, acquitted. The sportsman never reappeared in the county till after the death of Dennis Bodkin, which took place three years subsequently.

The quotation is from Sir Jonah Barrington (1760–1834), *Personal Sketches of his own Time*, 26–7. Torchiana (*Y & GI* 301) points out that Mrs Yeats read to the poet from *Recollections of Jonah Barrington*, with an introduction by George A. Birmingham [1918]. There are slight differences in the text of the latter, pp. 30–1.

33–4 *Some few remembered still when I was young*

   A peasant girl commended by a song: Yeats wrote in the essay 'Dust hath closed Helen's eye' of Mary Hynes and how her memory was 'still a wonder by turf fires'. She died at Ballylee sixty years before he wrote the essay (in 1900). He heard of her from an old man, an old woman, an old weaver, another old man, two other old women and an old man who lived at Duras.

35 *that rocky place*: the area is one of limestone.

36 *the colour of her face*: Yeats's essay quotes the old man's description 'her skin was like dribbled snow . . . and she had blushes in her cheeks', and the old woman's: 'The sun and the moon never shone on anybody so handsome, and her skin was so white that it looked blue, and she had two little blushes on her cheeks.'

37 *the greater joy*: Yeats commented in his essay:

These poor countrymen and countrywomen in their beliefs, and in their emotions, are many years nearer to that old Greek world, that set beauty beside the fountain of things, than are our men of learning. She 'had seen too much of the world'; but these old men and women, when they tell of her, blame another and not her, and though they can be hard, they grow gentle as the old men of Troy grew gentle when Helen passed by on the walls. (*M* 28)

39 *Farmers jostled at the fair*: fair in the sense of market. 'And if she went to any kind of meeting, they would all be killing one another for a sight of her, and there was a great many in love with her, but she died young' (*M* 27).

40 *the song*: Raftery's (see note on line 49) capacity for praise and blame was famous.

41–8 *And certain men, being maddened by those rhymes,*   220
   Or else by toasting her a score of times,
   Rose from the table and declared it right
   To test their fancy by their sight
   But they mistook the brightness of the moon
   For the prosaic light of day –
   Music had driven their wits astray –
   And one was drowned in the great bog of Cloone

Yeats was told by the old weaver that Mary Hynes was the most beautiful thing ever made:

 My mother used to tell me about her, for she'd be at every hurling, and wherever she was she was dressed in white. As many as eleven men asked her in marriage in one day, but she wouldn't have any of them. There was a lot of men up beyond Kilbecanty one night sitting together drinking, and talking of her, and one of them got up and set out to go to Ballylee and see her; but Cloone Bog [near Gort, Co. Galway] was open then, and when he came to it he fell into the water, and they found him dead there in the morning. (*M* 25–6)

49 *the man who made the song*: Anthony Raftery (1784–1834), the blind Gaelic poet. The Irish poem he wrote (see 'Mary Hynes, or the Posy Bright', *Songs ascribed to Raftery*, ed. Douglas Hyde (1903) 331–3) on Mary Hynes runs thus in Lady Gregory's translation, quoted in *CT* (1902 edn):

   Going to Mass by the will of God,
   The day came wet and the wind rose;
   I met Mary Hynes at the cross of Kiltartan,
   And I fell in love with her then and there.

   I spoke to her kind and mannerly,
   As by report was her own way;
   And she said, 'Raftery, my mind is easy,
   You may come to-day to Ballylee.'

   When I heard her offer I did not linger,
   When her talk went to my heart my heart rose.
   We had only to go across the three fields,
   We had daylight with us to Ballylee.

The table was laid with glasses and a quart measure,
She had fair hair, and she sitting beside me;
And she said, 'Drink, Raftery, and a hundred welcomes,
There is a strong cellar in Ballylee.'

O star of light and O sun in harvest,
O amber hair, O my share of the world,
Will you come with me upon Sunday
Till we agree together before all the people?

I would not grudge you a song every Sunday evening,
Punch on the table, or wine if you would drink it,
But, O King of Glory, dry the roads before me,
Till I find the way to Ballylee.

There is sweet air on the side of the hill
Where you are looking down upon Ballylee;
When you are walking in the valley picking nuts and blackberries,
There is music of the birds in it and music of the Sidhe.

What is the worth of greatness till you have the light
Of the flower of the branch that is by your side?
There is no god to deny it or to try and hide it,
She is the sun in the heavens who wounded my heart.

There was no part of Ireland I did not travel,
From the rivers to the tops of the mountains,
To the edge of Lough Greine whose mouth is hidden,
And I saw no beauty but was behind hers.

Her face was shining, and her brows were shining too;
Her face was like herself, her mouth pleasant and sweet.
She is the pride, and I give her the branch,
She is the shining flower of Ballylee.

It is Mary Hynes, the calm and easy woman,
Has beauty in her mind and in her face,
If a hundred clerks were gathered together,
They could not write down a half of her ways.   (*M* 24–5)

52   *Homer*: the connection is a double one. Raftery was blind and so was Homer. Each sang of a woman who was spoken of in the same way by the old: Yeats wrote in *BS* of his speaking to old men and women who remembered Mary Hynes and 'they spoke of her as the old men upon the wall of Troy spoke of Helen, nor did man and woman differ in their praise' (*A* 561).

53   *Helen*: Mary Hynes resembled her, see note on line 37. And Helen is a symbol for Maud Gonne, see note on 'The Rose of the World' (*PNR* 20). This leads to the poet himself in lines 56 ff.

54   *moon and sunlight*: the same imagery is used in 'The Man who dreamed of Faeryland' (*PNE* 33).

57   *Hanrahan*: a character invented by Yeats, who appeared in *Stories of Red*

Hanrahan (1904) and *TSR* (1907). Lines 57–73 retell the story entitled 'Red Hanrahan' (*M* 212 ff.) in an abbreviated form, leaving out mention of the fact that Hanrahan was journeying to his sweetheart Mary Lavelle when he met the old man in the old bawn. Giles W. L. Telfer, *Yeats's Idea of the Gael* (1965), 92, points out that Hanrahan has a striking resemblance to Eoghan Ruadh O Suileabhan (1748–84).

65   *an old bawn*: this may be a misprint for 'barn' which is used in the prose story 'Red Hanrahan' (*M* 213). Bawn (*Irish* ban) means a fortified enclosure and is used in Spenser's *State of Ireland,* 502b, which Yeats read. It can also mean a cattle ford, a term in use in the south of Ireland. (See *Notes and Queries*, I, ii, 60.)

69   *a pack of hounds*: a similar trick is described in Lady Gregory, *Gods and Fighting Men*, 109, where several animals and men are created consecutively, who follow each other up into the sky.

76   *he was harried*: this is the old bankrupt man who lived about a hundred years before: see Yeats's note, line 25.   221

79   *his dog's day*: the phrase may derive from *Hamlet*:

> Let Hercules himself do what he may
> The cat will mew and dog will have his day

or, more likely, from York Powell's translation of Paul Fort:

> And they came back so merrily: all at the dawn of day;
> A-singing all so merrily: '*The dog must have his day!*'   (*E & I* 498)

95   *whose images*: the ghosts are referred to in Yeats's comments. See note on line 25.

the Great Memory: a stock of archetypal images. See 'Anima Mundi', *M* 343–61

90   *half-mounted man*: the bankrupt owner. The phrase probably derives from Sir Jonah Barrington, op. cit.

91   *rambling celebrant*: Antony Raftery (*c.* 1784–1835), who was an itinerant poet; his poems were edited by Douglas Hyde in *Songs Ascribed to Raftery* (1903).

92   *the red man*: Red Hanrahan

94   *so fine an ear*: Dennis Bodkin who lost both his ears in Barrington's anecdote

105   *Old lecher*: Hanrahan, who turns into Yeats in the next stanza   222

112   *labyrinth*: cf. 'the labyrinth that he has made / In art and politics' of

'Nineteen Hundred and Nineteen', III (*PNE* 213), and the same poem's 'the labyrinth of the wind'.

114   *woman lost*: Maud Gonne

121   *It is time*: This section of the poem anticipates 'Sailing to Byzantium' (*PNE* 204).

123   *that climb the streams*: cf. 'The Fisherman' (*PNE* 160).

223   130-1   *. . . were spat on,*
           Nor to the tyrants that spat: a private joke referring to friends of Yeats whom he called Spit, Spat and Spat on. Lines 132-3 replaced a line in the MS. 'with nothing on but spats on' referring to a bathing party given by these friends.

132   *The people of Burke and of Grattan*: at this period Yeats was discovering his Anglo-Irish inheritance. In the debate on divorce in the Irish Senate on 11 June 1925, he wound up his speech (the text can be read in *SSY* 90-102) – which argued that to forbid divorce was a measure which the Protestant minority considered grossly oppressive – with a magnificent peroration:

> I am proud to consider myself a typical man of that minority. We against whom you have done this thing are no petty people. We are one of the great stocks of Europe. We are the people of Burke; we are the people of Grattan; we are the people of Swift, the people of Emmet, the people of Parnell. We have created the most of the modern literature of this country. We have created the best of its political intelligence.

Edmund Burke (1729-97), the political philosopher, orator and politician, was Irish. Henry Grattan (1746-1820) a protestant Irish leader of vision who opposed the Union of 1800 and afterwards supported Catholic emancipation. See note on 'The Seven Sages' (*PNE* 251).

136   *fabulous horn*: see note on line 32 of 'A Prayer for my Daughter' (*PNE* 201)

137   *sudden shower*: this image resembles the first stanza of 'Meditations in Time of Civil War' (*PNE* 206).

140   *the swan*: Yeats's note read:

> In the passage about the Swan in Part III I have unconsciously echoed one of the loveliest lyrics of our time – Mr Sturge Moore's 'Dying Swan.' I often recited it during an American lecturing tour, which explains the theft.

THE DYING SWAN
O silver-throated Swan
Struck, struck! A golden dart
Clean through thy breast has gone
Home to thy heart.

> Thrill, thrill, O silver throat!
> O silver trumpet, pour
> Love for defiance back
> On him who smote!
> And brim, brim o'er
> With love; and ruby-dye thy track
> Down thy last living reach
> Of river, sail the golden light –
> Enter the sun's heart – even teach,
> O wondrous-gifted Pain, teach thou
> The god to love, let him learn how.   (*CP* 533)

Thomas Sturge Moore (1870–1944) the English poet, critic and wood engraver who was a friend of Yeats for many years. See his *The Poems* (1932) II, 7 for the poem in slightly different form.

146–7   *Plotinus' thought*
         And cry in Plato's teeth: cf. note on line 12.

156   *Translunar Paradise*: beyond the moon, out of time

158   *learned Italian things*: his visits to Italy, his interest in Dante, in Castiglione, the Italian painters and sculptors

159   *stones of Greece*: he visited the British Museum, and *AV* has several passages on the significance of Greek sculpture. See 'The Statues' (*PNE* 362).

166   *loophole there*: in the tower   224

181   *make my soul*: an expression in common use in Ireland, meaning to prepare for death

                                                                        206–
MEDITATIONS IN TIME OF CIVIL WAR   212

These seven poems were mainly written at Thoor Ballylee during the Irish Civil   225
War of 1922–3. The Republicans led by Eamonn de Valera (see note on 'Parnell's Funeral' (*PNE* 304)) refused to accept the terms of the Anglo-Irish Treaty (signed in London in December 1921, ratified by the Irish parliament, 7 January 1922); the Civil War was between the new Irish Free State Government and the de Valera-led Republicans. The first of these poems was written in England in 1921; they first appeared in *The Dial*, January 1923.

General Title: Yeats's note reads:

> These poems were written at Thoor Ballylee in 1922, during the civil war. Before they were finished the Republicans blew up our 'ancient bridge' one midnight. They forbade us to leave the house, but were otherwise polite, even saying at last 'Good-night, thank you,' as though we had given them the bridge.

The sixth poem is called 'The Stare's Nest by My Window.' In the west of Ireland we call a starling a stare, and during the civil war one built in a hole in the masonry by my bedroom window.

In the second stanza of the seventh poem occur the words 'Vengeance on the murderers of Jacques Molay.' A cry for vengeance because of the murder of the Grand Master of the Templars seems to me fit symbol for those who labour from hatred, and so for sterility in various kinds. It is said to have been incorporated in the ritual of certain Masonic societies of the eighteenth century, and to have fed class-hatred.

I suppose that I must have put hawks into the fourth stanza because I have a ring with a hawk and a butterfly upon it, to symbolise the straight road of logic, and so of mechanism, and the crooked road of intuition: 'For wisdom is a butterfly and not a gloomy bird of prey.' (*CP* 534)

The letters Yeats wrote between April 1921 and November 1922 give some details of his life in the tower during this period. See *L* 680–692. The Knights Templar were members of a military monastic order founded in 1118, dissolved in 1312; their role was to defend christendom and protect pilgrims visiting the Holy Land. The ring was designed by Edmund Dulac, see note on 'On a picture . . . Dulac' (*PNE* 221).

206   I ANCESTRAL HOUSES

225   *Title   Ancestral Houses*: the poem perhaps echoes the thought of *A V*, that the new kind of violence which was coming into the world would be unlike the kind of violence which had brought the houses of the rich (in particular the country houses of Ireland) into being. And the present state of the inherited glory of the rich casts doubt upon the value of ancestral houses. Greatness may need violence.

12   *The abounding glittering jet*: Russell K. Alspach, *Yeats and Innisfree* (1965), 78–9, comments on the frequency of the image. He lists the occurrences; in *The Shadowy Waters* (1906 version), *Poems* 1899–1905, 63; the prose essay 'At Stratford-on-Avon', *Ideas of Good and Evil* (1903), 163; in this poem; two occurrences in 'The Gift of Harun Al-Raschid' (*PNE* 382); another in 'The Tower' (*PNE* 205) and one in 'Blood and the Moon' (*PNE* 243). He regards the fountain and the fountain jet as a symbol for an almost fierce joy in mere living. And Yeats's essay 'The Thinking of the Body' summed up its meaning: 'Art bids us touch and taste and hear and see the world and shrinks from what Blake calls mathematical form, from every abstract thing, from all that is of the brain only, from all that is not a fountain jetting from the entire hopes, memories, and sensations of the body' (*E & I* 292–3).

13   *sea-shell*: the image may derive from Shelley's *The Revolt of Islam* (Canto Fourth, I):

> Upon whose floor the spangling sands were strown
> And rarest sea-shells, which the eternal flood,
> Slave to the mother of the months, had thrown
> Within the walls of that grey tower.

but see also Canto Seventh, XIII, for the images of shells, a fountain, and 'the state: Of kingless thrones, which Earth did in her heart create.'

Cf. also *The Only Jealousy of Emer* (*CPl* 281-2).

25-9   *gardens where the peacock strays*: these are memories of Lady Ottoline   *226*
Morrell's house and gardens at Garsington, near Oxford.

27   *Juno*: queen of the gods in Roman mythology

II MY HOUSE   207

Title   My House: this poem describes Yeats's tower, built by the de Burgo   *226*
family, mentioned as Islandmore Castle in 1585, and the property of Edward
Ulick de Burgo who died in it in 1597. The property is now in trust, and open to
the public. See Mary Hanley, *Thoor Ballylee – Home of William Butler Yeats*
(1965).

1   *an ancient bridge*: cf. various other references to the bridge in *A Concordance
to the Poems of W. B. Yeats* (ed. Parrish and Painter).

4   *the symbolic rose*: see notes on 'To the Rose upon the Rood of Time' (*PNE*
17). Althea Gyles designed the cover for Yeats's *TSR* and this design has been
described well by Joan Coldwell, ' ''Images That Yet Fresh Images Beget'': A
Note on Book Covers', *The World of W. B. Yeats* (1965), 154:

> In the centre of the gold-stamped design is the four-petalled rose attached to a
> cross which had been the focal point of the *Poems* cover. Now the rose and
> cross are embedded in the heart of a serpent-like tree at whose tip appears a
> trinity of smaller roses, and beneath these are the kissing faces of a man and
> woman.

8   *stilted water-hen*: cf. line 8, 'The Phases of the Moon' (*PNE* 183).

9   *Homer*: see note on 'A Woman Homer Sung' (*PNE* 92).

11   *A winding stair*: see notes (p. 267) on *The Winding Stair and Other Poems*.   227

a chamber arched with stone: this was Yeats's bedroom on the first floor of the
tower which he also used as a study. It had an open fire for turf and an elm-wood
bed and wooden ceiling. (See *L* 687.)

14   *Il Penseroso's Platonist*: see note on line 15 'The Phases of the Moon'
(*PNE* 183).

18   *Benighted travellers*: cf. Palmer's illustration to Milton's poem, and the
opening lines of 'Ego Dominus Tuus' (*PNE* 181) and the opening and closing

lines of 'The Phases of the Moon' (*PNE* 183). Shelley's lines in 'Prince Athanase' may also have been in Yeats's mind:

> The Balearic fisher, driven from shore,
> Hanging upon the peaked wave afar,
> Then saw their lamp from Laian's turret gleam, . . .

22   *a score of horse*: cf. the 'Rough men-at-arms, cross-gartered to the knees' of 'The Tower' II (*PNE* 205).

28   *My bodily heirs*: Anne Butler Yeats, born 26 February 1919, and Michael Butler Yeats, born 22 August 1921

208   III MY TABLE

227   2   *Sato's gift*: Yeats wrote a letter to Edmund Dulac on 22 March 1920 which explains how the sword came into his possession:

> A rather wonderful thing happened the day before yesterday. A very distinguished looking Japanese came to see us. He had read my poetry when in Japan and had now just heard me lecture. He had something in his hand wrapped up in embroidered silk. He said it was a present for me. He untied the silk cord that bound it and brought out a sword which had been for 500 years in his family. It had been made 550 years ago and he showed me the maker's name upon the hilt. I was greatly embarrassed at the thought of such a gift and went to fetch George, thinking that we might find some way of refusing it. When she came I said 'But surely this ought always to remain in your family?' He answered 'My family have many swords.' But later he brought back my embarrassment by speaking of having given me 'his sword.' I had to accept it but I have written him a letter saying that I 'put him under a vow' to write and tell me when his first child is born – he is not yet married – that I may leave the sword back to his family in my will.   (*L* 662)

Cf. also the lines describing the sword in 'A Dialogue of Self and Soul' (*PNE* 242) and in 'Symbols' (*PNE* 246).

8   *Chaucer had not*: he had, if the sword was made 550 years before 1920; but the figure is a round one. Geoffrey Chaucer was born *c*. 1340.

228   9   *Sato's house*: Junzo Sato, then Japanese consul at Portland, Oregon, gave Yeats an ancestral ceremonial sword, which he said he would have returned to Junzo Sato after his own death.

32   *Juno's peacock*: cf. a passage in *AV*:

> A civilisation is a struggle to keep self-control, and in this it is like some great tragic person, some Niobe who must display an almost superhuman will or the cry will not touch our sympathy. The loss of control over thought comes towards the end; first a sinking in upon the moral being, then the last

surrender, the irrational cry, revelation – the scream of Juno's peacock.   (*A V* (B) 268)

The peacock was sacred to Juno as a symbol of immortality; no source has been found for its scream symbolising the end of civilisation.

IV MY DESCENDANTS   209

2   *my old fathers*: Yeats's father, grandfather and great-grandfather were   *228* educated at Trinity College, Dublin.

3   *a woman and a man*: Anne and Michael Yeats. See note on 'II My House' (*PNE* 207).

9–12   *And what if my descendants lose the flower*   *229*
       Through natural declension of the soul,
       Through too much business with the passing hour,
       Through too much play, or marriage with a fool?: Yeats was worried about the future of his children, as were many Anglo-Irish parents at the time of the Treaty and the subsequent civil war. A letter he wrote to Olivia Shakespear on 22 December 1921 put the problem frankly, out of a deep gloom about Ireland and its bitterness:

> In the last week I have been planning to live in Dublin – George very urgent for this – but I feel now that all may be blood and misery. If that comes we may abandon Ballylee to the owls and the rats, and England too (where passions will rise and I shall find myself with no answer), and live in some far land. Should England and Ireland be divided beyond all hope of remedy, what else could one do for the children's sake, or one's own work? I could not bring them to Ireland, where they would inherit bitterness, nor leave them in England where, being Irish by tradition, and by family and fame, they would be in an unnatural condition of mind and grow, as so many Irishmen who live here [he was writing from Oxford] do, sour and argumentative.   (*L* 675)

14–18   *Becomes a roofless ruin that the owl*
        May build in the cracked masonry and cry
        Her desolation to the desolate sky.

        The Primum Mobile that fashioned us
        Has made the very owls in circles move: Yeats may have been remembering Swedenborg's dicta in *Arcana Coelestia*, 5149, that 'gross and dense falsities are signified by owls and ravens; by owls because they live in the darkness of night, and by ravens because they are black'. The owls 'in circles' almost conform to the cyclic ideas of *A V* and thus prepare us for the 'flourish or decline' of its history.

17   *Primum Mobile*: the Primum Mobile was part of the Ptolemaic system, 'the wheel or rhomb called the Primum Mobile, the motion of which is supposed to cause the revolution of the nine inner spheres round the earth in twenty-four hours'. There is a passage in *Paradise Lost*, VII, 449–501, which is explicit:

> Now Heaven in all her glory shone, and rolled
> Her motions, as the great First Mover's hand
> First wheeled their course.

21   *for an old neighbour's friendship*: Lady Gregory's estate, Coole Park, was within walking distance of Ballylee.

22   *a girl's love*: a reference to Mrs Yeats

210   V THE ROAD AT MY DOOR

229   1   *Irregular*: a member of the Irish Republican Army, which opposed the signing of the Ango-Irish treaty and thus caused the Civil War in 1922. The Republicans later blew up the bridge beside the tower in the autumn of 1922. See *L* 692.

2   *Falstaffian*: after Sir John Falstaff, Shakespeare's fat comic character in *Henry IV* and *The Merry Wives of Windsor*

6   *A brown Lieutenant and his men*: 'Free Staters' or members of the National Army loyal to the Irish Free State provisional government

211   VI THE STARE'S NEST BY MY WINDOW

230   *Title   The Stare's Nest*: Yeats wrote a long explanation of this poem in *BS*:

> I was in my Galway house during the first months of civil war, the railway bridges blown up and the roads blocked with stones and trees. For the first week there were no newspapers, no reliable news, we did not know who had won nor who had lost, and even after newspapers came, one never knew what was happening on the other side of the hill or of the line of trees. Ford cars passed the house from time to time with coffins standing upon end between the seats, and sometimes at night we heard an explosion, and once by day saw the smoke made by the burning of a great neighbouring house. Men must have lived so through many tumultuous centuries. One felt an overmastering desire not to grow unhappy or embittered, not to lose all sense of the beauty of nature. A stare (our West of Ireland name for a starling) had built in a hole beside my window and I made these verses out of the feeling of the moment:

> > The bees build in the crevices
> > Of loosening masonry, and there
> > The mother birds bring grubs and flies.
> > My wall is loosening; honey bees,
> > Come build in the empty house of the stare.

> > We are closed in, and the key is turned
> > On our uncertainty, somewhere
> > A man is killed, or a house is burned,
> > Yet no clear fact to be discerned:
> > Come build in the empty house of the stare.

228

That is only the beginning but it runs on in the same mood. Presently a strange thing happened. I began to smell honey in places where honey could not be, at the end of a stone passage or at some windy turn of the road, and it came always with certain thoughts. When I got back to Dublin I was with angry people who argued over everything or were eager to know the exact facts: in the midst of the mood that makes realistic drama.   (*A* 579-80)

VII I SEE PHANTOMS OF HATRED AND OF THE HEART'S FULLNESS AND   **212**
OF THE COMING EMPTINESS

10   *Jacques Molay*: Jacques de Molay (b. 1244) was arrested in 1307 and   *231*
burned in March 1314. See M. Summers, *The Geography of Witchcraft*, 367-76, and Thomas Wright, *Narratives of Sorcery and Magic*. See Yeats's own note quoted in note on general title 'Meditations in Time of Civil War' (*PNE* 206).

17-19   *Their legs long, delicate and slender, aquamarine their eyes,*
        Magical unicorns bear ladies on their backs: Henn (*LT* 255) pointed out that these lines describe Gustave Moreau's painting *Ladies and Unicorns* (described in a letter of 8 November 1936, as on a wall of Yeats's house (*DWL* 100)). It is included in the illustrations in Giorgio Melchiori (*WMA* 74-5). These phantoms are 'of the Heart's fullness' in contrast to the brazen hearts which follow, symbols of logic as opposed to intuition.

29   *brazen hawks*: see Yeats's note, quoted in note on general title 'Meditations   *232*
in Time of Civil War' (*PNE* 206).

32   *clanging wings*: these may be, as Unterecker (*RC* 181) has suggested, a symbol of the emptiness of the coming cycle, which eliminates the subjectivity symbolised by the moon. He draws attention to the last stanza's parody of Wordsworth which, he suggests, Yeats uses 'to celebrate occult investigations of "Demonic images" ' . . . and 'to insist that such investigations have brought him intimations of immortality quite as accurate in old age as in youth'.

NINETEEN HUNDRED AND NINETEEN   **213**

This poem was written in 1919 and first appeared in *The Dial* (Sept. 1921). In   *232*
LM (Nov. 1921) the title was 'Thoughts upon the Present State of the World'.
    The poem arose out of 'some horrors at Gort', Co. Galway during the period when fighting between the Irish Republican Army (the IRA) and the English army and Royal Irish Constabulary (the RIC) increased. See notes on line 25 and lines 26-8.

6   *An ancient image*: probably derives from Sophocles, *Oedipus at Colonus*, but   *233*
the original story is in Herodotus, VIII, 65, where the sacred olive is recounted to have grown a cubit (Pausanias, I, 27, 2, improved on Herodotus' version of the

story by making the plant grow a shoot two cubits long on the same day) by the second day after the Persians had sacked and burnt Athens, including the old Erechtheum, which contained the spring of salt water and the sacred olive which were created by Erechtheus and Athene in their rivalry to become deity of the city. Yeats translated the Sophoclean chorus (*PNE* 223) from Paul Masqueray's French translation of *Oedipus at Colonus*. There was an olive-wood statue of Athena Polias in the Erechtheum at Athens.

7   *Phidias*: the famous Athenian sculptor (*c*. 490-417 BC); primarily a bronze-worker, he also acquired his fame from chryselephantine statutes, of gold and ivory, of which his Athena Parthenos survives in copies, though his Zeus of Olympia is only a memory. Pericles commissioned him to design the marble sculptures of the Parthenon and he made the models for the sculptors who worked under him.

8   *golden grasshoppers and bees*: from Thucydides I, vi, which describes the use by the Athenians of golden brooches in the form of grasshoppers to hold up their hair. *PNE* suggests Walter Pater, *Greek Studies: A Series of Essays* (1875) as a source for the bees.

9-32   *We too had many pretty toys when young:*
A law indifferent to blame or praise,
To bribe or threat; habits that made old wrong
Melt down, as it were wax in the sun's rays;
Public opinion ripening for so long
We thought it would outlive all future days.
O what fine thought we had because we thought
That the worst rogues and rascals had died out.

All teeth were drawn, all ancient tricks unlearned,
And a great army but a showy thing;
What matter that no cannon had been turned
Into a ploughshare? Parliament and king
Thought that unless a little powder burned
The trumpeters might burst with trumpeting
And yet it lack all glory; and perchance
The guardsmen's drowsy chargers would not prance.

These stanzas describe events before 1914 or perhaps before the Boer War.

16   *rogues and rascals had died out*: Torchiana (*Y & GI* 317) quotes Yeats's speech at the Tailteann Banquet, 2 August 1924, which refers to the 'eighties at this point:

Everyone, certainly everyone who counted, everyone who influenced events believed that the world was growing better and better, and could not even help doing so owing to physical science and democratic politics, and that dream lasted for many years.

19-20   *no cannon had been turned Into a ploughshare*: these lines relate to Isaiah ii. 4: 'And they shall beat their swords into plowshares and their spears into pruning hooks: nation shall not lift up sword against nation neither shall they learn war any more.' Cf. Micah iv. 3 and Joel iii. 10 (where the plowshares are beaten into swords).

21-3   *unless a little powder burned ... chargers would not prance*: cf. the speech Yeats made at the Tailteann Banquet, 2 August 1924, quoted in *Y & GI* 317-18:

> A fortnight before the great war a friend of mine was standing beside an English Member of Parliament watching a Review in one of the London Parks. My friend said as the troops marched past 'It is a fine sight.' And the Member of Parliament answered 'It is a fine sight, but it is nothing else, there will never be another war.'
> 'There will never be another war', that was our opium dream.

25   *Now days are dragon-ridden*: this stanza refers to atrocities committed by members of the Auxiliaries and the Black and Tans in the pre-Treaty fighting in Ireland. For details see Brian Graney, 'Days of Terror in South Galway', *Vexilla Regis* (1954-5) 85-98. See note on lines 26-8.

26-8   *a drunken soldiery*
           Can leave the mother, murdered at her door,
           To crawl in her own blood, and go scot-free: these lines also refer to particularly unpleasant atrocities at Gort. See *WBY* 329 and *Lady Gregory's Journals* (ed. Lennox Robinson) 129-46. Mrs Ellen Quinn was killed by the Black and Tans, and the Loughnane brothers were murdered and mutilated. See also 'Reprisals' (*VE* 791) quoted in notes on 'An Irish Airman Foresees his Death' (*PNE* 145).

32   *weasels fighting in a hole*: cf. line 92. Yeats had seen weasels fighting at Coole. Lady Gregory recorded their bad name with gamekeepers, the need other country people expressed 'to behave well to them' and the advice of an old acquaintance not to insult one – 'For they are enchanted and understand all things' (*Coole* 26). Lady Wilde, *Ancient Legends of Ireland*, 179, recorded that they are 'spiteful and malignant, and old withered witches sometimes take this form'. Yeats may have been influenced by his reading of Landor who placed in Sheridan's mouth an argument that there should be no church establishment for less than one hundred adults:

> But seriously, in turning this acid on such putridity there would be a violent fermentation; there would be animosities and conflicts. However, what harm if there should be? Turn out the weasel against the rat, and, at least while they are fighting, neither of them can corrode the rafters or infect the larder.   (W. S. Landor, *Collected Works*, 'Conversations with Windham and Sheridan', III, 127)

43   *That country round*: the burning of the great houses would have been   *234* unthinkable in Ireland before the fighting between the IRA and the British forces.

46   *that stump*: see note above on line 6, 'an ancient image'.

49–50   *Loie Fuller's Chinese dancers enwound*
       A shining web, a floating ribbon of cloth: Loie Fuller (1862–1928), an American dancer who danced 'in a whirl of shining draperies manipulated on sticks' at the *Folies Bergère* in the 'nineties. Mallarmé wrote about her and Toulouse-Lautrec painted her. Cf. Kermode, 'Poet and Dancer before Diaghilev', *Partisan Review* (Jan./Feb. 1961) 48–76; *RI* 71 and *IP* 122. She had a troupe of Japanese dancers.

54   *Platonic Year*: this is derived from Plato. Yeats discussed the Great Year in *AV* (B) 245–54, basing his ideas on Pierre Duhem, *Le Système du Monde*. He also used Cicero's definition:

> But when the whole of the constellations shall return to the positions from which they once set forth, thus after a long interval re-making the first map of the heavens, that may indeed be called the Great Year wherein I scarce dare say how many are the generations of men.

He added his own comment that the Great Year was

> sometimes divided into lesser periods by the return of the sun and moon to some original position, by the return of a planet or of all the planets to some original position, or by their making an astrological aspect with that position; and sometimes it was dissociated from the actual position of the stars and divided into twelve months, each month a brightening and a darkening fortnight, and at the same time perhaps a year with its four seasons.   (*AV* (B) 246)

There are some interesting divergences between the two versions of *AV* in the discussion of Plato's great year. The earlier version speaks of 'the elaborate geometry of *The Timaeus* and certain numerical calculations in *The Republic* of which modern scholars have seventeen incompatible explanations', and continues:

> that no one, not even Plato with all his mathematical calculations, calculated the periods back through the World Year implies an acceptance or half acceptance of that Year, not for its astronomical but for its moral value. Our interest in Plato's comment is precisely that he does use it as we use the lunar phases, as if it were the moving hands upon a vast clock, or a picturesque symbolism that helped him to make more vivid, and perhaps date, developments of the human mind that can be proved dialectically. In the Republic he identifies the passage of his typical community through Timocracy, Oligarchy, Democracy, Tyranny, and so back to Aristocracy again, as a passage through Ages of Gold, Silver, etc., that may have seemed to the eyes of the Sibyl and perhaps to the eyes of Virgil identical with some classification of the Ten Ages: he saw what had seemed *Fate* as *Destiny*. In another passage he makes his typical community bring its different periods to an end by carrying some character to excess, and attributes the changes of the year to a like cause.   (*AV* (A) 154–5)

Later he returned to the contrast of the Platonic year:

The alternation of *antithetical* and *primary* months is certainly Platonic, for his Golden Age men are born old and grow young, whereas in that which follows they are born young and grow old. He, however, made Gold *antithetical*; upon the other hand the Babylonians had the same alternation but began we are told with Silver and the Moon.   (*AV*(A) 157-8)

In *AV* (B) Yeats writes:

Yet Plato's statements are there that scholars may solve the Golden Number, and they have found fourteen different solutions. To Taylor they suggest 36,000 years, 360 incarnations of Plato's Man of Ur. Proclus thought the duration of the world is found 'when we bring into contemplation the numerical unity, the one self-unfolding power, the sole creation that completes its work, that which fills all things with universal life. One must see all things wind up their careers and come round again to the beginning; one must see everything return to itself and so complete by itself the circle allotted to that number; or that unity which encloses an infinity of numbers, contains within itself the instability of the Duad and yet determines the whole movement, its end and its beginning, and is for that reason called the Number and the Perfect Number.' It is as though innumerable dials, some that recorded minutes alone, some seconds alone, some hours alone, some months alone, some years alone, were all to complete their circles when Big Ben struck twelve upon the last night of the century.   (*AV* (B) 248)

See also part II of the Introduction to *The Resurrection* (*E* 392-8) quoted on p. 240.

59   *Some moralist or mythological poet*: possibly Shelley in *Prometheus Unbound*, II, v, 72-4:

> My soul is like an enchanted boat,
> Which, like a sleeping swan, doth float
> Upon the silver waves of thy sweet singing; . . .

72   *Some Platonist*: possibly Thomas Taylor, *De Antro Nympharum*, where after the dead pass the Styx they are ignorant of their former lives on earth, but recognise material forms 'and recollect their pristine condition on the earth' (*PNE*).

89   *We, who seven years ago*: Yeats is possibly contrasting the speeches of   *235* British politicians at the time of the 1912 Ulster crisis with those which later favoured the activities of the Auxiliaries and Black and Tans. In this case 'We' may be ironic. Or 'We' may measure the change in Irish nationalists' attitudes. Or, most likely, 'We' may represent generally civilised people in the British Isles, and deplore a loss of control, a lapse from idealism into faction by both Irish and English.

90   *talked*: Cf. 'Sixteen Dead Men' (*PNE* 194): 'O But we talked at large before/The sixteen men were shot'.

92   *the weasel's twist; the weasel's tooth*: see note on line 32   *236*

93   *mock at the great*: this section of the poem seems to be founded on Yeats's memory of Blake's poem 'Scoffers' with its lines:

> Mock on, mock on, Voltaire, Rousseau,
> Mock on, mock on; 'tis all in vain;
> You throw the dust against the wind,
> And the wind blows it back again.

Yeats included this poem in his selection of Blake (Blake, *Poems* (1893), 108).

97   *the levelling wind*: the wind in this section of the poem and the next are reminiscent of James Clarence Mangan's 'Gone in the Wind' with its refrain taken from Rückert:

> Solomon! Where is thy throne? It is gone in the wind.
> Babylon! Where is thy might? It is gone in the wind
> Like the swift shadows of Noon, like the dreams of the Blind,
> Vanish the glories and pomps of the world in the wind.

237   118   *Herodias' daughters have returned again,*
        A sudden blast of dusty wind: in a note (pp. 42 ff.) quoted in headnote to 'The Hosting of the Sidhe' (*PNE* 40) Yeats wrote that Sidhe is the Gaelic for wind and that the Sidhe had much to do with the wind: 'They journey in whirling winds, the winds that were called the dance of the daughters of Herodias in the Middle Ages, Herodias doubtless taking the place of some old goddess.' Yeats may have been thinking of the traditional procession of witches on St John the Baptist's Eve. See M. Summers, *The Geography of Witchcraft* (1927) 76, who quotes St Ivo of Chartres on this:

> Certain abandoned women turning aside to follow Satan, being seduced by the illusions and phantasms of demons, believe and openly profess that in the dead of night they ride upon certain beasts with the pagan goddess Diana and a countless horde of women, and that in these silent hours they fly over vast tracts of country and obey her as their mistress while on other nights they are summoned to pay her homage.

Summers, op. cit., 79, also cites John of Salisbury for Herodias as a witchqueen who called the sorcerers together to meetings (sabbaths) by night, when they feasted, sacrificed babes to ghouls and ghosts, and gave themselves up to blasphemies and debauchery. See also M. H. Murray, *The witch cult in Western Europe*, 102. The legend of the pageant of witches is also to be found in Heine's *Atta Troll*, XVIII-XX, 67-86. It is possible that Yeats was remembering Arthur Symons's poem 'The Dance of the Daughters of Herodias' where the daughters dance

> With their eternal, white, unfaltering feet,
> And always, when they dance, for their delight,
> Always a man's head falls because of them.
> Yet they desire not death, they would not slay
> Body or soul, no, not to do them pleasure:
> They desire love, and the desire of men;
> And they are the eternal enemy.

They are unreal:

> Shapes on a mirror, perishable shapes
> Fleeting, and without substance, or abode,
> In a fixed place.

Symons's lines describe their effect on what men hold dear:

> The wisdom which is wiser than Kings know,
> The beauty which is fairer than things seen,
> Dreams which are nearer to eternity
> Than that most mortal tumult of the blood
> Which wars on itself in loving, droop and die.

128   *That insolent fiend Robert Artisson*: Yeats's note read:

The country people see at times certain apparitions whom they name now 'fallen angels', now 'ancient inhabitants of the country' and describe as riding at whiles 'with flowers upon the heads of the horses'. I have assumed in the sixth poem that these horsemen, now that the times worsen, give way to worse. My last symbol, Robert Artisson, was an evil spirit much run after in Kilkenny at the start of the fourteenth century. Are not those who travel in the whirling dust also in the Platonic Year? – May 1921 (This version follows the text in *The Dial* (Sept. 1921).)

Robert Artisson was the fourteenth-century incubus of Dame Alice Kyteler. Yeats read the MS. accounts in the British Museum of the proceedings against her and her confederates. He also read Dr Carrigan's *History of the Diocese of Ossory* which deals with the events. Thomas Wright edited the MS. for the Camden Society, and his 'Narratives of Witchcraft and Sorcery' in *The Transactions of the Ossory Archaeological Society* (vol. I), also contain an account of the trial. St John D. Seymour, *Irish Witchcraft and Demonology* (1913) devotes a chapter to Dame Alice Kyteler, whom he describes as the '*facile princeps*' of Irish witches. Condemned as a witch on 2 July 1324, she was:

a member of a good Anglo-Norman family that had been settled in the city of Kilkenny for many years. The coffin-shaped tombstone of one of her ancestors, Jose de Keteller, who died in 128-, is preserved at St Mary's Church; the inscription is in Norman French and the lettering in Lombardic. The lady in question must have been far removed from the popular concepts of a witch as an old woman of striking ugliness, or else her powers of attraction were very remarkable, for she had succeeded in leading four husbands to the altar. She had been married first, to William Outlawe of Kilkenny, banker; secondly, to Adam le Blund of Callan; thirdly, to Richard de Valle – all of whom she was supposed to have got rid of by poison: and fourthly, to Sir John le Poer, whom it was said she deprived of his sense by philtres and incantations. The Bishop of Ossory at this period was Richard de Ledrede, a Franciscan friar, and an Englishman by birth. He soon learnt that things were not as they should be, for when making a visitation of his diocese early in 1324 he found by an Inquisition, in which were five Knights and numerous nobles, that there was in the city a band of heretical sorcerers, at the head of whom was Dame Alice.

Among the charges laid against this band were two of special significance:

235

2. They offered in sacrifice to demons living animals, which they dismembered, and then distributed at cross-roads to a certain evil spirit of low rank, named the son of Art.

7. The said dame had a certain demon, an incubus, named Son of Art, or Robin son of Art, who had carnal knowledge of her, and from whom she admitted that she had received her wealth. This incubus made its appearance under various forms, sometimes as a cat, or as a hairy black dog, or in the likeness of a negro (Ethiops), accompanied by two others who were larger and taller than he, and of whom one carried an iron rod.

According to Holinshed's *The Historie of Ireland* (1577) the sacrifice to the evil spirit is said to have consisted of nine red cocks, and nine peacocks' eyes.

214 THE WHEEL

237 This poem was written on 13 September 1921 and first appeared in *SPF*.

Yeats wrote the poem in the Euston Hotel; see Jeffares 'Yeats and his methods of writing verse', *The Permanence of Yeats* (ed. Hall and Steinmann, 1950; 1961). The poem is compared by Saul (*PYP* 127), to a passage in *Mythologies*:

Joachim of Flora acknowledged openly the authority of the Church, and even asked that all his published writings, and those to be published by his desire after his death, should be submitted to the censorship of the Pope. He considered that those whose work was to live and not to reveal were children and that the Pope was their father; but he taught in secret that certain others, and in always increasing numbers, were elected, not to live, but to reveal that hidden substance of God which is colour and music and softness and a sweet odour; and that these have no father but the Holy Spirit. Just as poets and painters and musicians labour at their works, building them with lawless and lawful things alike, so long as they embody the beauty that is beyond the grave, these children of the Holy Spirit labour at their moments with eyes upon the shining substance on which Time has heaped the refuse of creation; for the world only exists to be a tale in the ears of coming generations; and terror and content, birth and death, love and hatred, and the fruit of the Tree, are but instruments for that supreme art which is to win us from life and gather us into eternity like doves into their dove-cots. (*M* 300-1)

215 YOUTH AND AGE

237 This poem was written in 1924 and first appeared in *The Cat and the Moon and Certain Poems* (1924)

216 THE NEW FACES

238 This poem was written in December 1912 and first appeared in *SPF*.

1 *you*: Lady Gregory. Yeats first met her in 1896 when he was thirty-one: she was then 'a plainly dressed woman of forty-five'. See Jeffares, ' "The New Faces" a new explanation', *RES*, XXIII (Oct. 1947) 92.

2 *catalpa tree*: Lady Gregory described it with delight:

> We are looking . . . from the bench that is under the shadow of the catalpa tree – 'A weeping ash,' George Moore has called it telling of his quarrels as he sat there with Yeats 'in the warmth and fragrance of the garden', over that play *Diarmuid and Grania* they were writing, not without differences of opinion. But my own quarrel with him must be for the libel of calling this catalpa by the name of among all trees the one for which I have least affection, even a slight feeling of dislike. I did not find, or ever plant one here at Coole. . . .
> But the catalpa coming as I believe from the gentle Pacific zone has no fault to keep it outside the garden walls. The clean limbs spreading over garden bench and wall give no noxious shade, for the leaves larger than the palm of a man's hand . . . are but few beside those of our native trees. The trusses of white blossom add beauty to their pale green. They cast a pleasant shadow on the long bench and a part of the flower border, yet not such darkness as to check the blossoming of tulip or larkspur, or anemone, or the growth of that delicately leaved laurel painters lay on a poet's brow; or of rosemary and the sweet tufted herbs. *(Coole* (1931) 42-4)

4 *Where we wrought*: Coole Park in general; but this line may anticipate line 7's 'garden gravel'. This is described by Lady Gregory:

> The long grey wall that encloses the garden protects a flower border from the ocean salt, for all the miles between flung in great storms on the very windows of the house, and is itself in part protected by an outer line of great beeches. The seeds of these, flung on to the border, often take root, and appear, two or three inches of foreign tree, among the hyacinth and phlox. The ground dips eastward to the orchard, the tennis ground. . . .
> Yeats planned many a play or poem pacing up and down this gravelled walk before facing the blank paper on the writing table in his room; I stealing a pleasant half hour with him between the ordering of the day's meals and the endless answering of letters that falls to a woman's share; turning just once again towards the great ilex, its silver grey calling to mind that of the olive against the Italian blue. *(Coole* (1931) 44-5)

A PRAYER FOR MY SON   217

This poem was written in December 1921 and first appeared in *SPF*.   *238*

2 *my Michael*: Michael Butler Yeats was born in August 1921 at Castlebrook House, Thame, Oxfordshire.

10 *Some there are*: Yeats discussed the strange phenomena which accompanied the automatic writing in *AV*:

> Sometimes if I had been ill some astringent smell like that of resinous wood

filled the room, and sometimes, though rare, a bad smell. These were often warnings; a smell of cat's excrement announced some being that had to be expelled, the smell of an extinguished candle that the communicators were 'starved'. A little after my son's birth I came home to confront my wife with the statement 'Michael is ill'. A smell of burnt feathers had announced what she and the doctor had hidden. When regular communication was near its end and my work of study and arrangement begun, I was told that henceforth the Frustrators would attack my health and that of my children, and one afternoon, knowing from the smell of burnt feathers that one of my children would be ill within three hours, I felt before I could recover self-control the mediaeval helpless horror at witchcraft.   (*A V* (B) 16)

He continued:

Sometimes my wife saw apparitions: before the birth of our son a great black bird, persons in clothes of the late sixteenth century and of the late seventeeth. There were still stranger phenomena that I prefer to remain silent about for the present because they seemed so incredible that they need a long story and much discussion.   (*A V* (B) 17)

239   17   *You*: Christ

26   *Your enemy*: King Herod, who feared the prophecy that a ruler would come out of Bethlehem (where Christ was born, and where Herod had all male children under two slain. See Matthew 2.16)

27   *a woman and a man*: Joseph and Mary took Jesus to Egypt to escape Herod, and stayed there until Herod's death. (See Matthew 2. 19–23.)

28   *Holy Writings*: the Bible, see Matthew 2.

218   TWO SONGS FROM A PLAY

239   The poems were written in 1926 with the exception of the latter stanza in II which was probably written in 1930-1. Poem I and the first stanza of II first appeared in *The Adelphi* (June 1927) then in *OB*. The full text first appeared in *Stories of Michael Robartes and His Friends* (1931). There are marked differences between the text of the play in *The Adelphi* and those in other printings, see *VPl*. 900-36.

Yeats's ~~note~~ explained that these two songs are sung by the Chorus of Musicians in *Resurrection*, a play that has for its theme Christ's first appearance to the Apostles after the Crucifixion. The play was meant to be performed in a drawing-room or studio (*OB*) and was first performed in the Abbey Theatre, Dublin, on 20 July 1934. The play deals with Yeats's view expressed in *A V* that Christianity terminated a 2000-year period of history and ushered in the beginnings of another era with radical violence. His Introduction to the play in *W & B* makes clear his aim:

This play, or the first sketch of it, more dialogue than play, was intended for my drawing-room, where my *Hawk's Well* had just been played.

For years I have been preoccupied with a certain myth that was itself a reply to a myth. I do not mean a fiction, but one of those statements our nature is compelled to make and employ as a truth though there cannot be sufficient evidence. When I was a boy everybody talked about progress, and rebellion against my elders took the form of aversion to that myth. I took satisfaction in certain public disasters, felt a sort of ecstasy at the contemplation of ruin, and then I came upon the story of Oisin in Tir nà nOg [spelt Tir-nan-Oge in *W & B*] and reshaped it into my *Wanderings of Oisin*. He rides across the sea with a spirit, he passes phantoms, a boy following a girl, a hound chasing a hare, emblematical of eternal pursuit, he comes to an island of choral dancing, leaves that after many years, passes the phantoms once again, comes to an island of endless battle for an object never achieved, leaves that after many years, passes the phantoms once again, comes to an island of sleep, leaves that and comes to Ireland, to Saint Patrick and old age. I did not pick these images because of any theory, but because I found them impressive, yet all the while abstractions haunted me. I remember rejecting, because it spoilt the simplicity, an elaborate metaphor of a breaking wave intended to prove that all life rose and fell as in my poem. How hard it was to refrain from pointing out that Oisin after old age, its illumination half accepted, half rejected, would pass in death over another sea to another island. Presently Oisin and his islands faded and the sort of images that come into *Rosa Alchemica* and *The Adoration of the Magi* took their place. Our civilisation was about to reverse itself, or some new civilisation about to be born from all that our age had rejected, from all that my stories symbolised as a harlot, and take after its mother [this refers to the gyres, described in the notes to *CP* (535) as occurring in Swedenborg, Thomas Aquinas and certain classical authors. See note on 'Demon and Beast' (*PNE* 199)]; because we had worshipped a single god it would worship many or receive from Joachim de Flora's Holy Spirit a multitudinous influx. A passage in *La Peau de chagrin* may have started me, but because I knew no ally but Balzac, I kept silent about all I could not get into fantastic romance. So did the abstract ideas persecute me that *On Baile's Strand*, founded upon a dream, was only finished when, after a struggle of two years, I had made the Fool and Blind Man, Cuchulain and Conchubar whose shadows they are, all image, and now I can no longer remember what they meant except that they meant in some sense those combatants who turn the wheel of life. Had I begun *On Baile's Strand* or not when I began to imagine, as always at my left side just out of the range of the sight, a brazen winged beast [the beast in 'The Second Coming'] that I associated with laughing, ecstatic destruction? Then I wrote, spurred by an external necessity, *Where There is Nothing,* a crude play with some dramatic force, since changed with Lady Gregory's help into *The Unicorn from the Stars*. A neighbourhood inflamed with drink, a country house burnt down, a spiritual anarchy preached! Then, after some years came the thought that a man always tried to become his opposite, to become what he would abhor if he did not desire it, and I wasted some three summers and some part of each winter before I had banished the ghost and turned what I had meant for tragedy into a farce: *The Player Queen*. Then unexpectedly and under circumstances described in *A Packet to Ezra Pound* came a symbolical system displaying the conflict in all its forms:

> Where got I that truth?
> Out of a medium's mouth,
> Out of nothing it came,

Out of the forest loam,
Out of dark night where lay
The crowns of Nineveh.

II

And then did all the Muses sing
Of Magnus Annus at the spring.

In 1894 Gorky and Lunacharsky tried to correct the philosophy of Marxian socialism by the best German philosophy of their time, founding schools at Capri and Bologna for the purpose, but Lenin founded a rival school at Paris and brought Marxian socialism back to orthodoxy: 'we remain materialist, anything else would lead to religion.' Four or five years later Pius X saw a Commission of Catholic scholars considering the text of the Bible and its attribution to certain authors and dissolved the Commission: 'Moses and the Four Evangelists wrote the Books that are called by their names; any other conclusion would lead to scepticism.' In this way did two great men prepare two great movements, purified of modernism, for a crisis when, in the words of Archbishop Downey, they must dispute the mastery of the world.

So far I have the sympathy of the Garrets and Cellars, for they are, I am told, without exception Catholic, Communist, or both! Yet there is a third myth or philosophy that has made an equal stir in the world. Ptolemy thought the precession of the equinoxes moved at the rate of a degree every hundred years, and that somewhere about the time of Christ and Caesar the equinoctial sun had returned to its original place in the constellations, completing and recommencing the thirty-six thousand years, or three hundred and sixty incarnations of a hundred years apiece, of Plato's man of Ur. Hitherto almost every philosopher had some different measure for the Greatest Year, but this Platonic Year, as it was called, soon displaced all others; it was a Christian heresy in the twelfth century, and in the East, multiplied by twelve as if it were but a month of a still greater year, it became the Manvantra of 432,000 years, until animated by the Indian jungle it generated new noughts and multiplied itself into Kalpas.

It was perhaps obvious, when Plotinus substituted the archetypes of individual men in all their possible incarnations for a limited number of Platonic Ideas, that a Greatest Year for whale and gudgeon alike must exhaust the multiplication table. Whatever its length, it divided, and so did every unit whose multiple it was, into waxing and waning, day and night, or summer and winter. There was everywhere a conflict like that of my play between two principles or 'elemental forms of the mind,' each 'living the other's life, dying the other's death.' I have a Chinese painting of three old sages sitting together, one with a deer at his side, one with a scroll open at the symbol of *yen* and *yin*, those two forms that whirl perpetually, creating and re-creating all things. But because of our modern discovery that the equinox shifts its ground more rapidly than Ptolemy believed, one must, somebody says, invent a new symbolic scheme. No, a thousand times no; I insist that the equinox does shift a degree in a hundred years; anything else would lead to confusion.

All ancient nations believed in the re-birth of the soul and had probably empirical evidence like that Lafcadio Hearn found among the Japanese. In our time Schopenhauer believed it, and McTaggart thinks Hegel did, though lack of interest in the individual soul had kept him silent. It is the foundation of McTaggart's own philosophical system. Cardinal Mercier saw no evidence for it, but did not think it heretical; and its rejection compelled the sincere and noble Von Hügel to say that children dead too young to have earned Heaven suffered no wrong, never having heard of a better place than Limbo. Even though we think temporal existence illusionary it cannot be capricious; it is what Plotinus called the characteristic act of the soul and must reflect the soul's coherence. All our thought seems to lead by antithesis to some new affirmation of the supernatural. In a few years, perhaps, we may have much empirical evidence, the only evidence that moves the mass of men to-day, that man has lived many times; there is some not yet perfectly examined – I think of that Professor's daughter in Palermo. This belief held by Plato and Plotinus, and supported by weighty argument, resembles the mathematical doctrines of Einstein before the experimental proof of the curvature of light.

We may come to think that nothing exists but a stream of souls, that all knowledge is biography, and with Plotinus that every soul is unique; that these souls, these eternal archetypes, combine into greater units as days and nights into months, months into years, and at last into the final unit that differs in nothing from that which they were at the beginning: everywhere that antinomy of the One and the Many that Plato thought in his *Parmenides* insoluble, though Blake thought it soluble 'at the bottom of the graves.' Such belief may arise from Communism by antithesis, declaring at last even to the common ear that all things have value according to the clarity of their expression of themselves, and not as functions of changing economic conditions or as a preparation for some Utopia. There is perhaps no final happy state except in so far as men may gradually grow better; escape may be for individuals alone who know how to exhaust their possible lives, to set, as it were, the hands of the clock racing. Perhaps we shall learn to accept even innumerable lives with happy humility ('I have been always an insect in the roots of the grass') and putting aside calculating scruples, be ever ready to wager all upon the dice.

Even our best histories treat men as function. Why must I think the victorious cause the better? Why should Mommsen think the less of Cicero because Caesar beat him? I am satisfied, the Platonic Year in my head, to find but drama. I prefer that the defeated cause should be more vividly described than that which has the advertisement of victory. No battle has been finally won or lost; 'to Garret or Cellar a wheel I send.'   (*E* 392–8)

I

1   *a staring virgin*: this stanza draws a parallel between the myth of Dionysus, the Greek God of wine and fertility, and the death and resurrection of Christ. Ellmann (*IY* 260) draws on Sir James Frazer's *The Golden Bough* (which Yeats read) for this explanation:

Dionysus, child of a mortal Persephone, and an immortal, Zeus, was torn to pieces by the Titans. Athene (the 'staring virgin' of the poems, staring indicating that she acts as if in a trance because the events are pre-ordained) snatched the heart from his body, brought it on her hand to Zeus, who killed the Titans, swallowed the heart, and begat Dionysus again, upon another mortal, Semele. Yeats's introduction (see general note on the poem, above) gives Sir William Crookes, *Studies in Psychical Research* as a source. Sir William Crookes (1832–1919) was an English chemist and physicist.

6–7   *the Muses sing Of Magnus Annus*: they sing of this as a play because they

241

regard the ritual death and rebirth of the god as a recurring event, part of the cycles of history. Ellmann points out that 'both Gods had died and been reborn in March when the sun was between the Ram and the Fish, and when the moon was beside the constellation Virgo, who carries the star Spica in her hand'. In these stanzas Yeats is thinking of Virgil, *Eclogue*, IV, 6, '*Iam redit et Virgo . . .*' where Virgo, daughter of Jupiter and Themis, is the last to leave Earth at the end of the golden age; but will return, bringing back the golden age. This Virgilian prophecy was later read as a foretelling of the coming of Mary (as Virgo) and Christ, the star of Bethlehem (as Spica):

> 'The latest age of Cumean Song is at hand; the cycles in their vast array begin anew; Virgin Astrea comes, the reign of Saturn comes, and from the heights of Heaven a new generation of mankind descends. . . . Apollo now is King and in your consulship, in yours, Pollio, the age of glory shall commence and the mighty months begin to run their course.' . . . Three hundred years, two degrees of the Great Year, would but correspond to two days of the Sun's annual journey, and his transition from Pisces to Aries had for generations been associated with the ceremonial death and resurrection of Dionysus. Near that transition the women wailed him, and night showed the full moon separating from the constellation Virgo, with the star in the wheatsheaf, or in the child, for in the old maps she is represented carrying now one now the other. It may be that instead of a vague line, the Sibyl knew some star that fixed the exact moment of transition. I find but four explanations compatible with man's agency, and all four incredible, for Christ being born at or near the moment of transition. (*AV* (A) 152, 156-7)

See Yeats's Introduction to *W & B*, cited above, p. 240.

9-12   *Another Troy . . .*
       Another Argo's painted prow
       Drive to a flashier bauble yet
These lines develop the *Eclogue* (40 BC) IV, 31-6 of Virgil (70-19 BC):

> Yet shall some few traces of olden sin lurk behind, to call men to essay the sea in ships, to gird towns with walls, and to cleave the earth with furrows. A second Tiphys shall then arise, and a second Argo to carry chosen heroes; a second warfare, too, shall there be, and again shall a great Achilles be sent to Troy.

Cf. a passage in a rewritten version of 'The Adoration of the Magi' where while one of these old men is reading out 'the Fifth *Eclogue* of Virgil' and falls asleep and 'a strange voice spoke through him, and bid them set out for Paris, where a dying woman would give them secret names and thereby so transform the world that another Leda would open her knees to the swan, another Achilles beleaguer Troy' (*M* 310).

There is another reference to this in *Samhain* (1904): 'for has not Virgil, a knowledgeable man and a wizard, foretold that other Argonauts shall row between cliff and cliff and other fair-haired Achaeans sack another Troy?' (*E* 150).

Yeats is also echoing the imagery of Shelley's *Hellas*, 1060-79, though not its optimistic tone.

11   *Another Argo's painted prow*: cf. William Morris, *Life and Death of Jason*   240
Bk. IV, where the prow itself is prophetic:

> For just as a part of the ship Argo, keel or prow, was made of the Dodonaean
> oak, and Argo's crew heard with astonishment the ship herself prophesy to
> them on the sea. But Jason and the builder Argus knew whereby the prow
> foretold things strange and new.

13   *The Roman Empire stood appalled*: because though there were but six
million Christians in the Roman Empire's sixty million, the world was to become
Christian, and the Empire to be destroyed by Christianity (a view Yeats shared
with Gibbon).

13-16   *The Roman Empire . . .*
      Out of the fabulous darkness called: Ellmann (*IY* 261) remarks that
these lines daringly assert a parallelism and even identity between the three pairs,
Astraea and Spica, Athene and Dionysus, and Mary and Christ. Cf. Lady Gregory
(*Journals*, ed. Lennox Robinson (1946) 263) for an early version reading 'Virgo
[the constellation] and the mystic star'.

16   *The fabulous darkness*: from a description of Christianity by Proclus, a
fourth-century Neo-platonic philosopher (whom Yeats read in Thomas Taylor's
translation of 1816). Cf. Wilson (*Y & T* 59). Cf. *AV* (B) 277 and 278 and *AV*
(A) 185 ff.

> . . . the irrational force that would create confusion and uproar as with the cry
> "The Babe, the Babe, is born" – the women speaking unknown tongues, the
> barbers and weavers expounding Divine revelation with all the vulgarity of
> their servitude, the tables that move or resound with raps – but creates a
> negligible sect.
>   All about it is an *antithetical* aristocratic civilisation in its completed form,
> every detail of life hierarchical, every great man's door crowded at dawn by
> petitioners, great wealth everywhere in few men's hands, all dependent upon a
> few, up to the Emperor himself who is a God dependent upon a greater God,
> and everywhere in court, in the family, an inequality made law, and floating
> over all the Romanised Gods of Greece in their physical superiority . . . the
> world became Christian and 'that fabulous formless darkness' as it seemed to a
> philosopher of the fourth century, blotted out 'every beautiful thing', not
> through the conversion of crowds or general change of opinion or through any
> pressure from below, for civilisation was *antithetical* still, but by an act of
> power.

PNE draws on E. R. Dodds, *Select Passages Illustrating Neo-Platonism* (1923) for
the Greek sophist Eunapius (?347–420) who recounts (see Philostratus and
Eunapius, *The Lives of the Sophists*, tr. Walmer Cave Wright, 1922, p. 417) how
Antonius (?d. 290) foretold that as a result of Christianity the temple would cease
to be and even the great and holy temples of Serapis would pass into 'formless
darkness' and be transformed and that 'a fabulous and unseemly gloom would
hold sway over the fairest things on earth'.

II

2   *that room*: where the last supper took place. See Matthew 26, 30; Mark 14, 26; Luke 22, 39; John 18.1.

3   *Galilean turbulence*: foretold by astronomers in Babylon who reduce man's status by their science; Man is being taught that he is nothing in comparison to the universe; he is becoming featureless:

> God is now conceived of as something outside man and man's handiwork, and it follows that it must be idolatry to worship that which Phidias and Scopas made, and seeing that He is a Father in Heaven, that Heaven will be found presently in the Thebaid, where the world is changed into a featureless dust and can be run through the fingers; and these things are testified to from books that are outside human genius, being miraculous, and by a miraculous Church, and this Church, as the gyre sweeps wider, will make man also featureless as clay or dust. Night will fall upon man's wisdom now that man has been taught that he is nothing. . . .
> The mind that brought the change, if considered as man only, is a climax of whatever Greek and Roman thought was most a contradiction to its age; but considered as more than man He controlled what Neo-Pythagorean and Stoic could not – irrational force. He could announce the new age, all that had not been thought of, or touched, or seen, because He could substitute for reason, miracle.   (*AV* (B) 273 ff.)

For *Galilean,* see note on 'A Prayer on Going into my House' (*PNE* 182)

4   *Babylonian*: see note on 'The Dawn' (*PNE* 158)

7-8   *Platonic tolerance . . . Doric discipline*: the philosophy and architecture of the classical world of Greece, succeeded by Christianity. (There may possibly be a contrast here between the culture of Athens (Plato's city) and the military discipline of the Spartans (Dorians), the extremes of Greek civilisation.)

9-16   *Everything that man esteems . . .*
Man's own resinous heart has fed: these lines praise man who goes on creating heroically despite the fact that all things pass away (cf. *A* 315).

12   *painter's brush*: cf. a passage in 'The Tragic Generation': 'no school of painting outlasts its founders, every stroke of the brush exhausts the impulse, Pre-Raphaelitism had some twenty years; Impressionism thirty perhaps' (*A* 315).

219   FRAGMENTS

240   The date of composition of these poems is probably 1931. The first stanza first appeared in *DM* (Oct.-Dec. 1931) as part of the poet's commentary on *WWP,* the second in *CP.*

1   *Locke*: Yeats hated the ideas of John Locke (1632–1784), the English empirical philosopher. In this he probably followed Blake's example. In his Diary he wrote 'Descartes, Locke and Newton took away the world and gave us its excrement instead' (*E* 325). Cf. [Move upon Newton's Town] (*PNE* A 99).

2–4   *The Garden died*;
       God took the spinning-jenny
       Out of his side: the poem is a parody of Eve's coming into the world in Genesis 2, 18–23. In the Introduction to *WWP* Yeats wrote that he could see

> in a sort of nightmare vision the 'primary qualities' torn from the side of Locke, Johnson's ponderous body bent above the letter to Lord Chesterfield, some obscure person somewhere inventing the spinning-jenny [invented by James Hargreaves (d. 1778)]; upon his face that look of benevolence kept by painters and engravers, from the middle of the eighteenth century to the time of the Prince Consort [(1819–61)], for such as he, or, to simplify the tale –
> [then follow lines 1–4]   (*E* 358–9)

The spinning-jenny symbolises the Industrial Revolution which followed on Locke's mechanical philosophy, as Yeats argued in his essay on Berkeley:

> It is customary to praise English empirical genius, English sense of reality, and yet throughout the eighteenth century when her Indian Empire was founded England lived for certain great constructions that were true only in relation to the will. I spoke in the Irish Senate on the Catholic refusal of divorce and assumed that all lovers who ignored priest or registrar were immoral; upon education, and assumed that everybody who could not read the newspaper was a poor degraded creature; and had I been sent there by some religious organisation must have assumed that a child captured by a rival faith lost its soul; and had my country been at war – but who does not serve these abstractions? Without them corporate life would be impossible. They are as serviceable as those leaf-like shapes of tin that mould the ornament for the apple-pie, and we give them belief, service, devotion. How can we believe in truth that is always moth-like and fluttering and yet can terrify? – A friend and myself, both grown men, talked ourselves once into a terror of a little white moth in Burnham Beeches. And of all these the most comprehensive, the most useful, was invented by Locke when he separated the primary and secondary qualities; and from that day to this the conception of a physical world without colour, sound, taste, tangibility, though indicted by Berkeley as Burke was to indict Warren Hastings fifty years later, and proved mere abstract extension, a mere category of the mind, has remained the assumption of science, the groundwork of every text-book. It worked, and the mechanical inventions of the next age, its symbols that seemed its confirmation, worked even better, and it worked best of all in England where Edmund Spenser's inscription over the gates of his magic city seemed to end 'Do not believe too much': elsewhere it is the grosser half of that dialectical materialism the Socialist Prince Mirsky calls 'the firm foundation-rock of European Socialism', and works all the mischief Berkeley foretold.   (*E & I* 400–1)

II   *241*

This poem deals with the nature of poetic inspiration and insight. It returns to the belief Yeats held in his youth, that whatever the great poets had affirmed in their finest moments of inspiration was the nearest one could get to an authoritative religion. (Cf. *WBY* 47.) An essay on 'The Symbolism of Poetry' refers to Nineveh:

> It is indeed only those things which seem useless or very feeble that have any power, and all those things that seem useful or strong, armies, moving wheels, modes of architecture, modes of government, speculations of the reason, would have been a little different if some mind long ago had not given itself to some emotion, as a woman gives herself to her lover, and shaped sounds or colours or forms, or all of these, into a musical relation, that their emotion might live in other minds. A little lyric evokes an emotion, and this emotion gathers others about it and melts into their being in the making of some great epic; and at last, needing an always less delicate body, or symbol, as it grows more powerful, it flows out, with all it has gathered, among the blind instincts of daily life, where it moves a power within powers, as one sees ring within ring in the stem of an old tree. This is maybe what Arthur O'Shaughnessy meant when he made his poets say they had built Nineveh with their sighing; and I am certainly never sure, when I hear of some war, or of some religious excitement, or of some new manufacture, or of anything else that fills the ear of the world, that it has not all happened because of something that a boy piped in Thessaly. I remember once telling a seeress to ask one among the gods who, as she believed, were standing about her in their symbolic bodies, what would come of a charming but seeming trivial labour of a friend, and the form answering, 'the devastation of people and the overwhelming of cities.' I doubt indeed if the crude circumstance of the world, which seems to create all our emotions, does more than reflect, as in multiplying mirrors, the emotions that have come to solitary men in moments of poetical contemplation; or that love itself would be more than an animal hunger but for the poet and his shadow the priest, for unless we believe that outer things are the reality, we must believe that the gross is the shadow of the subtle, that things are wise before they become foolish, and secret before they cry out in the market-place. Solitary men in moments of contemplation receive, as I think, the creative impulse from the lowest of the Nine Hierarchies, and so make and unmake mankind, and even the world itself, for does not 'the eye altering alter all'?

> > Our towns are copied fragments from our breast;
> > And all man's Babylons strive but to impart
> > The grandeurs of his Babylonian heart.   (*E & I* 157-9)

The only mention of Nineveh made by O'Shaughnessy is his *Ode*, which describes the poets of the ages:

> We, in the ages lying
> In the buried part of the earth
> Built Nineveh with our sighing
> And Babel itself with our mirth;
> And o'erthrew them with prophesying
> To the old of the new world's worth;
> For each age is a dream that is dying,
> Or one that is coming to birth.
> > (Arthur O'Shaughnessy, *Music and Moonlight*, 2)

The lines on Nineveh and Babel were misquoted in Yeats's *Pages from a Diary*

Written in Nineteen Hundred and Thirty (E 337). He wrote another version on this theme in *W & B*:

> Decline of day,
> A leaf drifts down;
> O dark leaf clay
> On Nineveh's crown!   (*E* 401)

Cf. line 63 'Vacillation' V (*PNE* 262).

6   *Nineveh*: the capital of the Assyrian Empire, at its height in the eighth and seven centuries BC. It was destroyed by the Medes and Babylonians in 612 BC.

LEDA AND THE SWAN   **220**

This poem was written on 18 September 1923 and first appeared in *The Dial*   *241*
(June 1924).

Yeats wrote a note to explain that he

> wrote Leda and the Swan because the editor [George Russell, AE, see note on Dedication to *Crossways*] of a political review [*The Irishman Statesman*] asked me for a poem. I thought 'After the individualist, demagogic movement, founded by Hobbes [Thomas Hobbes (1588-1679) English utilitarian philosopher] and popularised by the Encyclopaedists [the authors of *L'Encyclopedie* (1751-72) who included Voltaire, Rousseau, Buffon and Turgot; they were edited by Diderot and D'Alembert, and influenced the course of the French revolution (1789-99)] and the French Revolution, we have a soil so exhausted that it cannot grow that crop again for centuries.' Then I thought 'Nothing is now possible but some movement, or birth from above, preceded by some violent annunciation'. My fancy began to play with Leda and the Swan for metaphor [the 'metaphor' is founded upon the Greek myth of Zeus, father of the gods, taking the form of a swan and impregnating the mortal Leda, daughter of Tyndareus, King of Sparta. She bore the twins Castor and Pollux and Helen (see note on 'A Woman Homer Sung' (*PNE* 92))] and I began this poem; but as I wrote, bird and lady took such possession of the scene that all politics went out of it, and my friend tells me that 'his conservative readers would misunderstand the poem.'
>
> (*The Cat and the Moon and Certain Poems*, 1924)

Melchiori (*WMA* 73-114) discusses the genesis and symbolism of the poem very fully. He sees the short poem 'The Mother of God' (*PNE* 261) as a Christian counterpart to the Leda annunciation, and he traces the effect of Gogarty's poems on the composition of 'Leda and the Swan' and its imagery, in particular that of 'To the Liffey with the Swans':

> . . . As fair as was that doubled Bird
> By love of Leda so besotten,
> That she was all with wonder stirred:
> And the Twin Sportsmen were begotten.

The poem appears in *AV* (A) heading the section *Dove or Swan* in which

Yeats wrote 'I imagine the annunciation that founded Greece as made to Leda, remembering that they showed in a Spartan temple, strung up to the roof as a holy relic, an unhatched egg of hers; and that from one of her eggs came Love and from the other War.' Cf. also *AV* (B) 268.

Yeats had a coloured photographic copy of Michelangelo's famous picture at Venice, but Charles Madge, the *Times Literary Supplement* (20 July 1962) has argued that an Etruscan bas-relief in the British Museum is closer to the poem's imagery and a more likely source for it than the Michelangelo painting. Yeats had probably also seen the statue of Leda and the Swan which was at Markree Castle, Colloney, Co. Sligo, the Coopers' seat. (It is now in the garden of a house north of Sligo.) See *McG* 69. For Michelangelo, see note on 'An Acre of Grass' (*PNE* 332) and see also 'Long-legged Fly' (*PNE* 364) and 'Under Ben Bulben', IV (*PNE* 356).

7   *that white rush*: Melchiori, *WMA*, draws attention to Spenser, *Prothalamion*, 3, 39–45:

> Two fairer birds I yet did never see:
> The snow which doth the top of *Pindus* strew,
> Did never whiter shew,
> Nor *Jove* himself when he a Swan would be
> For love of *Leda*, whiter did appeare:
> Yet *Leda* was, they say, as white as he,
> Yet not so white as those, nor nothing neare.

10   *wall . . . tower*: the walled city of Troy was destroyed after a ten-year siege by the Greeks. See note on 'The Rose of the World' (*PNE* 20). Henn (*LT* 255) quotes Todhunter's *Helena in Troas* which Yeats admired for the link between Leda and Helen of Troy:

> O pitiless mischief! Thee no woman bore
> Wooed by the billing of the amorous swan.
> Yea, Leda bore thee not but Nemesis
> To be the doom of Troy and Priam's house.

Henn has also discussed the meaning of the poem:

> Two Annunciations form a pattern in history: Leda and the Virgin. The Virgin is linked, mistakenly, to St Anne, *via* Pater's Essay. Both events concern the union of godhead and woman. Both produce momentous births. The eggs of Leda give rise to the fall of Troy; from them emerge the legend of two destined women Helen and Clytemnestra. Helen has long been a personal symbol for Maud Gonne. The swans are archetypal, everywhere; in Spenser, emblems, paintings, Celtic myth, and concretely on the Lakes at Coole. The swan stands for power, phallic strength, purity, spirit and spirits (as all white birds), fidelity; fire and air (as the dove); the ineffable Godhead. In the act of congress the *loosening thighs* and the *white rush* are antithetical aspects. Into the softness and whiteness is concentrated all the sensuality of touch. The outcome of the union is further history or myth, pagan or Christian, Love and War. But what of the woman? Yeats speculates continually on the emotions of woman in such a crisis. Did Leda or Mary by that act become half or wholly

divine? Did a god share with beast the lassitude that overcomes all animals, save only the lion and the cock? *Shudder* is of the sexual act, the moment of orgasm, as all husband-men know; but it is also anticipation in fear.

(LT 256-7)

11   *Agamemnon dead*: Agamemnon, brother of Menelaus, was murdered on his return from Troy by his wife Clytaemnestra and her lover Aegisthus. She was a daughter of Leda by Tyndareus.

ON A PICTURE OF A BLACK CENTAUR BY EDMUND DULAC   **221**

This poem was written in September 1920 and first appeared in *SPF* with the title *242*
'Suggested by a Picture of a Black Centaur'.

Title   for *centaur* see note on 'Lines Written in Dejection' (*PNE* 157). Edmund Dulac (1882-1953) English artist, designer of masks and costumes for *At the Hawk's Well* (1916), illustrated several of Yeats's books, and set several of his poems to music. *WS* is dedicated to him. The poem, according to Mrs Yeats, was begun in relation to a picture by Dulac but altered in relation to one by Cecil Salkeld, whose account of the poem's composition appears in *WBY* 326-8:

Madame Gonne MacBride smiled at me and said: 'Willie is booming and buzzing like a bumble bee . . . that means he is writing something. . . .' To my great surprise, Yeats, who appeared shortly, obviously preoccupied and absent-minded, asked me if I would walk up the glen with him. We walked, treading our way among boulders and small stones along the river bank for nearly half an hour in silence. By that I mean no word was spoken; but, all the while, Yeats kept up a persistent murmur – under his breath, as it were. Suddenly, he pulled up short at a big stone and said: 'Do you realise that eternity is not a long time but a *short* time . . . ?' I just said, I didn't quite understand. 'Eternity,' Yeats said, 'Eternity is in the glitter on the beetle's wing . . . it is something infinitely short . . .' I said that I could well conceive 'Infinity' being excessively small as well as being excessively large. 'Yes,' he said, apparently irrelevantly, 'I was thinking of those Ephesian topers. . . .'
    He pulled out of his pocket a very small piece of paper on which he had written 8 lines which had been perhaps ten times corrected. It was almost impossible for me to read a line of it. I only saw one phrase which I knew was obsessing him at that time – for Yeats was at all times a man dominated – sometimes for weeks on end – by a single phrase: this one was 'Mummy wheat' – a phrase destined to appear in a much later poem – a phrase he never forgot.
    That night I sat up late, long after the others had gone to bed, and finished a water-colour picture of a weird centaur at the edge of a dark wood: in the foreground, in the shade of the wood, lay the seven Ephesian 'topers' in a drunken stupor, while far behind on a sunny distant desert plain elephants and the glory of a great army passed away into the distance. Next day I showed the picture to Yeats. He looked at it so critically that I suddenly remembered that he had been an Art Student. He peered at me over the top of his glasses. 'Who is your teacher?' he asked. 'Has he told you about values?' 'What are values?' I asked. Yeats laughed his deep ferocious chuckle: 'Do you really tell me you

don't know what "values" are?' I said 'No', and waited for instruction. 'Well, I'm certainly not going to tell you! . . . "Values" were the bane of my youth.' When I walked out with him that day he made no reference to the poem, but talked continuously of the conception of the 'Daimon' which was particularly interesting him at the time: he also told me the history of his play *The Player Queen*, saying (perhaps with a faint reminiscence of Goethe's *Faust* in his head) that he had spent 20 years on the play.

Later that night, W. B. came down to supper with a perfectly clear countenance; it was plain the poem was finished. He did not speak throughout the meal, yet I felt he would say something before the night was through. When the ladies had withdrawn, he produced a pigskin-covered brandy flask and a small beautifully written manuscript: 'Your picture made the thing clear', he said. 'I am going to dedicate the poem to you. I shall call it The Black Centaur'. . . . It was then for the first time I heard those miraculous lines, one of which is:

Stretch out your limbs and sleep a long Saturnian sleep.

I was impressed and gratified. But when printed in 1928, in *The Tower*, the poem was altered; it was corrected and it was entitled: 'On a Picture of a Black Centaur by Edmund Dulac'.

7   *mummy wheat*: Yeats implies hidden wisdom which can be ripened centuries after its sowing. When he wrote this poem and 'All Souls' Night' (*PNE* 239) where the phrase is used in the second stanza, he was full of the ideas of *AV* and felt that they were revelations of hidden truth which he was bringing into the light out of the darkness where it had been concealed. The image came from his reading of the discoveries of Egyptian tombs (cf. 'The Gyres', *PNE* 321).

PNE cites J. Gardner Wilkinson, *A Popular Account of the Ancient Egyptians* (1854) II, 39, for wheat grown in England from seed found in the tombs of Thebes.

11   *seven Ephesian topers*: the seven sleepers of Ephesus, who slept for two centuries in a cave near Ephesus, from the persecution of the Christians by the Emperor Decius (*c.* 200–251) to the time of the Emperor Theodosius II (401–450) whose faith was confirmed when they were brought to him after their awakening.

12   *Alexander's Empire*: Alexander the Great (356–323 BC) pacified Ephesus, and lived there in 334 BC. His Empire collapsed shortly after his death.

13   *Saturnian sleep*: the reign of Saturn, an ancient Italian god of agriculture (later identified with the Greek God Cronos) was so beneficent that it was regarded as the Golden Age.

222   AMONG SCHOOL CHILDREN

242   This poem was written on 14 June 1926 and first appeared in *The Dial* (Aug. 1927) and *LM* (Aug. 1927).

A draft in Yeats's white vellum notebook written about 14 March 1926 reads 'Topic for poem – School children and the thought that live [life] will waste them perhaps that no possible life can fulfill our dreams or even their teacher's hope. Bring in the old thought that life prepares for what never happens'. The 'old thought' is probably a memory of ideas written in the Diary begun in 1908. In an unpublished entry, 6 Sept. 1909, Yeats asked himself why life is 'a perpetual preparation for something that never happens'. See also *A* 473 and note on line 39 below.

1 *the long schoolroom*: Yeats visited St Otteran's School, Waterford, in February 1926. This school was run on Montessori principles and Yeats praised its work in the Senate (see *SSY* 111).

2 *a kind old nun*: Rev. Mother Philomena, the Mistress of Schools. See Donald T. Torchiana, ' ''Among School Children'' and the Education of the Irish Spirit', *IER* 123-50.

5-6 *be neat in everything In the best modern way*: Dr Maria Montessori (1870–1952) aimed at creating neatness and spontaneity in children:

9-16 *Ledaean body*: Maud Gonne. Leda suggests the story of the eggs and this the Platonic image from the Symposium, 190 ('Plato's parable' of line 15). See note on line 22. *243*

15 *Plato's parable*: Plato (*c.* 427–348 BC) pupil and admirer of Socrates, taught in the Academy at Athens, composed dialogues, among them the *Symposium*, where Aristophanes (l. 450–385 BC) the Athenian comic dramatist argues that man was originally double, in a spherical shape. Love is a search for the unity lost when Zeus divided man in two, like a cooked egg. See note on line 22 and note on 'Leda and the Swan' (*PNE* 220).

22 *that colour*: Torchiana (*IER* 138-9) makes some interesting remarks on the childlike relationship between Yeats and Maud Gonne. He takes a description of Fionnuala and Aodh from Ella Young's *Celtic Wonder-Tales* (1910) which Maud Gonne illustrated with a recurring motif of a sphere containing two swans intertwined, ultimately blent as one, an obvious symbol of kindred souls (see note on 'Baile and Aillinn' (*PNE* 377).

25 *Her present image*: Maud Gonne's appearance at the time he was writing the poem.

26 *Quattrocento finger*: this was 'quinto-cento' finger in the early version. It was altered to 'Da Vinci' [Leonardo da Vinci (1452–1519)] finger in the version of the poem printed in *LM* (Aug. 1927).

30 *pretty plumage*: Yeats's former raven-coloured hair

32 *scarecrow*: cf. 'Sailing to Byzantium' (*PNE* 204)

244   33-40   *What youthful mother, a shape upon her lap*
Honey of generation had betrayed,
And that must sleep, shriek, struggle to escape
As recollection or the drug decide,
Would think her son, did she but see that shape
With sixty or more winters on its head,
A compensation for the pang of his birth,
Or the uncertainty of his setting forth?: Torchiana quotes a passage
from Gentile (*The Reform of Education* 194) which Yeats read in Dino
Bigongiari's translation of 1923 for which Croce wrote a foreword. (In this book
Gentile argues that only our thought gives unity to material reality, that culture is
an activity, a constant becoming):

> The mother who tenderly nurses her sick child is indeed anxious for the
> health of the body over which she worries, and she would like to see it vigorous
> and strong. But that body is so endeared to her, because by means of it the child
> is enabled to live happily with her; through it his fond soul can requite maternal
> love by filial devotion; or in it he may develop a powerful and beautiful
> personality worthy to be adored as the ideal creature of maternal affection. If in
> the bloom of physical health he were to reveal himself stupid and insensate,
> endowed with mere instinctive sensuality and bestial appetites, this son would
> cease to be the object of his mother's fondness, nay, he would arouse in her a
> feeling of loathing and revulsion. It is this sense of loathing . . . that we . . . feel
> for the human corpse from which life has departed; for life is the basis of every
> psychological relation, and therefore of every possible sympathy.　(*IER* 134)

34   *Honey of generation*: this image comes from the Neoplatonic philosopher
Porphyry (*c.* 233-304), *On the Cave of the Nymphs* (1917) 22. Yeats wrote that
he found no warrant in Porphyry for considering it the 'drug' that destroys the
'recollection' of prenatal freedom. He blamed a cup of oblivion given in the
zodiacal sign of Cancer (*CP* 535). Porphyry's work is a comment, dedicated to the
Nymphs, on the symbolism of Homer's *Odyssey*. In the cave which Homer
described in the thirteenth book of the *Odyssey* were bowls and works of divine
workmanship in which the busy bees placed delicious honey. Porphyry gives a
long explanation; he describes the cathartic and preservative functions of honey
and its ebriating effect on Saturn ('the sweetness of honey signifies, with
theologians, the same thing as the pleasure arising from generation, by which
Saturn, being ensnared, was castrated') and finally links the 'honey of generation'
with the aquatic Nymphs. Wilson (*Y & T* 212) explains that in Platonic tradition
the soul journeys from the Isles of the Blessed in life; in death it lives backwards in
time and returns to its starting point. The wanderings of Odysseus symbolise life:
he returns to Ithaca (which symbolises the Isles of the Blessed) after he has been
converted to intellectual life at the Holy City of Phaeacia, but he must return via
the cave, where the honey is the pleasure arising from generation and the
Nymphs and honey-bees are symbols for two kinds of souls born into the world:

> Since, therefore, honey is assumed in purgations, and as an antidote to
> putrefaction, and is indicative of the pleasure which draws souls downward to
> generation; it is a symbol well adapted to aquatic Nymphs, on account of the
> unputrescent nature of the waters over which they preside, their purifying

power, and their co-operation with generation. For water cooperates in the work of generation. On this account the bees are said, by the poet, to deposit their honey in bowls and amphorae; the bowls being a symbol of fountains, and therefore a bowl is placed near to Mithra, instead of a fountain; but the amphorae are symbols of the vessels with which we draw water from fountains. And fountains and streams are adapted to aquatic Nymphs, and still more so in the Nymphs that are souls, which the ancients peculiarly called bees, as the efficient causes of sweetness. . . . All souls, however, proceeding into generation, are not simply called bees, but those who will live in it justly and who, after having performed such things as are acceptable to the Gods, will again return (to their kindred stars). . . . We must therefore admit, that honeycombs and bees are appropriate and common symbols of the aquatic nymphs, and of souls that are married (as it were) to (the humid and fluctuating nature of) generation. (Porphyry, *On the Cave of the Nymphs* 23–5)

In his essay on 'The Philosophy of Shelley's poetry' Yeats traced Porphyry's influence on Shelley's cave symbolism, particularly in the Witch of Atlas. Cf. (*E & I* 80–6). Yeats may have used Thomas Taylor's (1758–1835) translation, included in his *Select Works* (1823).

38 *sixty or more winters*: probably derives from John Donne's 'A Song': 'Till age snow white hairs on thee' according to (*PYP* 131) and possibly to an old beggar telling Lady Gregory she was 'in the winter of her age'.

39 *A compensation*: cf. *At the Hawk's Well*:

> What were his life soon done!
> Would he lose by that or win?
> A mother that saw her son
> Doubled over a speckled shin,
> Cross-grained with ninety years,
> Would cry, 'How little worth
> Were all my hopes and fears
> And the hard pain of his birth.'   (*CPl* 208)

41–8 *Plato thought nature but a spume that plays*
Upon a ghostly paradigm of things;
Solider Aristotle played the taws
Upon the bottom of a king of kings;
World-famous golden-thighed Pythagoras
Fingered upon a fiddle-stick or strings
What a star sang and careless Muses heard:
Old clothes upon old sticks to scare a bird: Yeats wrote to Mrs Shakespear on 24 September 1926 that he was reading Croce, writing verse and hence had nothing to say:

Here is a fragment of my last curse on old age. It means that even the greatest men are owls, scarecrows, by the time their fame has come. Aristotle, remember, was Alexander's tutor, hence the taws (form of birch)

> Plato imagined all existence plays
> Among the ghostly images of things;
> Solider Aristotle played the taws
> Upon the bottom of the King of Kings;
> World famous, golden-thighed Pythagoras
> Fingered upon a fiddle stick, or strings,
> What the stars sang and careless Muses heard. –
> Old coats upon old sticks to scare a bird.

Pythagoras made some measurement of the intervals between notes on a stretched string. (*L* 719).

There is an interesting MS. version of this stanza:

> Caesar Augustus that made all the laws
> And the ordering of everything
> Plato that learned geometry and was
> The foremost man at the soul's meaning
> That golden thighed far famed Pythagoras
> World famous, golden thighed Pythagoras
> Who taught the stars of heaven what to sing
> And the musicians how to measure cords
> Old clothes upon old sticks to scare the birds.

Thomas Parkinson (*YTLP* 101) comments on 'the reasoned rhetorical order' of this draft, from 'the individual soul as seen by Plato to the state as organised by Augustus, to the universe as directed by Pythagoras'. He discusses the unpublished MSS. of the poem in detail, pp. 92–113.

42   *paradigm*: Parkinson (*YTLP* 103) points out that 'paradigm' was Thomas Taylor's favourite term for Archetype or Platonic idea of essence. Yeats used Taylor's translations of Plato and read his other work.

44–5   *Aristotle . . . King of Kings*: the Greek philosopher (384–322 BC) who tutored Alexander in Macedonia. On returning to Athens in 335 he composed most of his works.

45   *golden-thighed*: the phrase comes from Thomas Taylor's translation of Iamblichus, *Life of Pythagoras*, p. 49:

> Pythagoras, however, receiving the dart, and neither being astonished at the novelty of the thing, nor asking the reason why it was given to him, but as if he was in reality a god himself, taking Abacis aside, he showed him his golden thigh, as an indication he was not [wholly] deceived [in the opinion he had formed of him].

Pythagoras, the sixth-century Greek philosopher, developed the doctrine of the transmigration of souls, and assigned a mathematical basis to the universe and to musical intervals.

47   *Muses*: see note on 'The Tower' (*PNE* 205)

53   *O Presences*: Parkinson (*YTLP* 105) comments that these can only be taken to mean the statues and children that are knowable by passion, piety, or affection.

64   *the dancer from the dance*: Torchiana quotes a passage from Gentile (*The Reform of Education* 228-9), the thought of which he thinks is used by Yeats in the last stanza of the poem: 245

> The spirit's being is its alteration. The more it *is*, - that is, the more it becomes, the more it lives, - the more difficult it is for it to recognise itself in the object. It might therefore be said that he who increases his knowledge also increases his ignorance, if he is unable to trace this knowledge back to its origin, and if the spirit's rally does not induce him to rediscover himself at the bottom of the object, which has been allowed to alter and alienate itself more and more from the secret source of its own becoming. Thus it happens, as was said of old, that 'He that increaseth knowledge increaseth sorrow.' All human sorrow proceeds from our incapacity to recognise ourselves in the object, and consequently to feel our own infinite liberty.   (*IER* 135)

Parkinson (*YTLP* 108) comments on the final stanza that the problems posed by the poem 'were transported into a world of transcendent possibilities, successes beyond the reach of the divided life embodied in the first four stanzas of the poem and in the aspirations of the great intellects'.

COLONUS' PRAISE   223

This translation of a chorus by the Athenian dramatist Sophocles (*c*. 495-406 BC) in his *Oedipus at Colonus* was written on (approximately) 24 March 1927, and first appeared in *The Tower* (1928).   245

Yeats used a French translation by Paul Masqueray as he did not read Greek. (He made a translation of *Oedipus Rex* in 1911-12, but never used it. For references to plans for 'Edipus' (by Gogarty and John Eglinton as well as Yeats), see *Theatre Business*, selected and ed. Ann Saddlemyer (1982), 127, 147, 151-2, 159, 178, 216 and 295.) His translation of Oedipus Rex was first produced at the Abbey Theatre on 6 December 1926. His translation of *Oedipus at Colonus* was produced at the Abbey Theatre on 12 September 1927, and first appeared in *CPl*.

1   *Colonus*: Κολωνὸϛ ἵππιοϛ,Colonus of the horses, an Attic deme or district, the birthplace of Sophocles (495-406 BC), a hill a mile north of Athens, so called because the god Poseidon, who gave the gift of horses to men, was worshipped there

8   *Semele's lad*: Dionysus, son of Zeus and of Semele, a daughter of Cadmus. Hera, who was jealous of her association with Zeus, disguised herself and advised Semele to test the divinity of her lover by asking him to come to her in his true shape. Semele tricked Zeus into granting her whatever she would ask, and she was killed by the fire of his thunderbolts. Zeus put the unborn child in his thigh.

He was born at full time, went into Hades and brought Semele up and she became an Olympian goddess. See note on 'Two Songs from a Play' (*PNE* 218).

9   *the gymnasts' garden*: the Lyceum at Athens on the banks of the river Cephisus, a sacred grove at Athens on the banks of the river Cephisus, a grove sacred to the hero Academus and the site of the Academy founded by Plato about 386 BC

12   *olive-tree*: cf. line 46 'Nineteen Hundred and Nineteen' (*PNE* 213). Athene gave the olive as a gift to man; the original olive was on the Acropolis at Athens; the olive at the Academy was reputed to have been the next to grow.

16   *grey-eyed Athene*: was the patron goddess of Athens; she produced the olive tree in a struggle with Poseidon for ownership of the land in Attica and won the contest. 'Grey-eyed' was one of the standard descriptions of the goddess.

19   *Great Mother*: Demeter (or Ceres) a corn goddess mourning for her daughter Persephone who was carried into the underworld by Pluto (or Hades), the brother of Zeus and Poseidon. Jupiter granted Persephone (Proserpine) permission to spend half the year with her mother, half with Pluto. This is a vegetation myth.

246   23   *abounding Cephisus*: river in Attica

28   *Poseidon . . . bit and oar*: Poseidon, god of horses and the sea. See note on line 16. He taught men to manage boats as well as horses.

224   WISDOM

246   It is not possible to date the composition of this poem accurately; it probably belongs to the period of 'Two Songs from a Play' (*PNE* 218) and first appeared in *OB*.

6–7   *the sawdust from the floor of that working carpenter*: Yeats may have been thinking of pre-Raphaelite paintings, Millais's 'Christ in the house of his parents', for example. The first printed version read for lines 6 and 7

> Dream of shavings on a floor
> And dirty nails of carpenters.

Joseph, husband of the Virgin Mary, was a carpenter.

9–13   *In damask clothed and on a seat*
Chryselephantine, cedar-boarded,
His majestic Mother: Henn (*LT* 257) states this is based 'almost beyond doubt on a poorish seventeenth-century painting by an unknown painter formerly hung in the National Gallery, Dublin, then stored in its cellars and now hung

again. It was originally labelled 'The Annunciation' but a more possible title, according to Henn, is 'The Seamless Garment'.

13   *He*: Jesus Christ

14   *starry towers of Babylon*: Mrs Yeats thought these came from Yeats's visit to the Ravenna mosaics (1907), cf. 'the Babylonian starlight' of 'Two Songs from a Play' (*PNE* 218).

15   *Noah's freshet*: the flood that covered the whole world (see Genesis 6, 5–19); only Noah and those on the Ark with him survived

16–17   *King Abundance . . . Innocence*: God's creation of Christ through the Virgin Mary.

THE FOOL BY THE ROADSIDE   225

This poem's date of composition cannot be determined with accuracy; it first   *247*
appeared in *SPF* as 'Cuchulain The Girl and the Fool'. Only lines 18–29 were printed in *CP*. The lines 1–17 appear to deal with an imaginary conversation between Yeats and Iseult Gonne, and are akin to some of the imagery in 'Michael Robartes and the Dancer' (*PNE* 189).

5   *upon a spool*: the poem is reminiscent of Plato's spindle in *The Republic* and the pern mill in Sligo (see note on line 97 'Shepherd and Goatherd' (*PNE* 156)). Cf. notes on 'His Bargain' (*PNE* 281).

OWEN AHERNE AND HIS DANCERS   226

The first part of this poem was written shortly after Yeats's marriage when he and   *247*
his wife were staying at Ashdown Forest Hotel, Forest Row, on 24 October, and the second on 27 October 1917. It first appeared in *The Dial* (June 1924) with the first section entitled 'The Lover Speaks', the second 'The Heart Replies'.

Title   Owen Aherne: a name for an invented persona: he is described in *The Tables of the Law* (see *M* 293–4). See note on 'The Phases of the Moon' (*PNE* 183). But here he is a disguise for Yeats himself. Henn (*LT* 47) regards the 'Dancers' as 'the delighted senses, the principle of desire'.

1–2   *. . . love had come unsought*
      Upon the Norman upland: a reference to Yeats's love for Iseult Gonne. While the poem describes Yeats's feelings in the summer of 1917 the 'unsought' may refer to Iseult proposing to Yeats in Normandy at the age of fifteen and being rejected 'because there was too much Mars in her horoscope'. Lady Gregory

favoured his marrying Iseult. Iseult's mother, Maud Gonne (Madame MacBride), had a house in Normandy, France. See notes on 'The Mountain Tomb' (*PNE* 130) and 'To a Child dancing in the Wind' (*PNE* 131).

248   14   *that young child*: Iseult Gonne (1895–1954). Yeats continually asked her to marry him in 1917. He delivered an ultimatum to her on the boat when he accompanied Madame MacBride and Iseult to England from France in September 1917. She must make up her mind one way or the other: he found the situation a great strain and, if she would not marry him, he had a friend who would, a girl strikingly beautiful in a barbaric manner. He must receive her answer within a week. She refused and on 20 October 1917 he married Georgie Hyde-Lees.

      19   *the woman at my side*: Mrs Yeats

249   21   *Speak all your mind*: this may refer to the effect of the automatic writing which began *AV* and released much of the poet's tension and unhappiness. Cf. a letter Yeats wrote to Lady Gregory on 29 October 1917:

> . . . There has been something very like a miraculous intervention. Two days ago I was in great gloom (of which I hope, and believe, George knew nothing). I was saying to myself 'I have betrayed three people'; then I thought 'I have lived all through this before.' Then George spoke of the sensation of having lived through something before (she knew nothing of my thought). Then she said she felt that something was to be written through her. She got a piece of paper, and talking to me all the while so that her thoughts would not affect what she wrote, wrote these words (which she did not understand) 'with the bird' (Iseult) 'all is well at heart. Your action was right for both but in London you mistook its meaning.' I had begun to believe just before my marriage that I had acted, not as I thought more for Iseult's sake than for my own, but because my mind was unhinged by strain. The strange thing was that within half an hour after writing of this message my rheumatic pains and my neuralgia and my fatigue had gone and I was very happy. From being more miserable than I ever remember being since Maud Gonne's marriage I became extremely happy. That sense of happiness has lasted ever since. The misery produced two poems which I will send you presently to hide away for me – they are among the best I have done.
>
> I enclose a letter of congratulation from Helen Bayly (now Mrs Lawless) you will remember her at Florence. I send it as it shows you how well George is liked – I have had other like testimonies. I think George has your own moral genius. She says by the by that you are the only friend of mine she has never feared. Should have said that after George had written that sentence I asked mentally 'when shall I have peace of mind' and her hand wrote 'you will neither regret nor repine' and I think certainly that I never shall again. . . .   (*L* 633–4)

A MAN YOUNG AND OLD

These poems were written in 1926 and 1927 and first appeared in *LM* (May 1927) with the title 'Four Songs from the Young Countryman'. Numbers VI, VII, VIII, and X first appeared under the title 'More Songs from an Old Countryman' *LM* (April 1926). They were reprinted under the title 'A Man Young and Old' in *The Tower* (1928). 'From ''Oedipus at Colonus'' ' was first included as XI in *CP* (1933).

I FIRST LOVE 227

Title First Love: this poem describes Yeats's youthful love for Maud Gonne. He 249 wrote a letter to Olivia Shakespear on 7 December 1926 in which he enclosed an early version of the second stanza of this poem with the comment 'I told you and showed you part of two series of poems in which a man and a woman in old or later life remember love. I am writing for each series contrasting poems of youth' (*L* 720).

8 *heart of stone*: cf. note on line 43 of 'Easter 1916' (*PNE* 193).

II HUMAN DIGNITY 228

1 *her kindness*: this poem also describes Yeats's love for Maud Gonne. 250

3 *no comprehension*: in his Diary for 22 January 1909 Yeats wrote that Maud Gonne

> never really understands my plans or nature or ideas. Then came the thought – what matter? – How much of the best I have done and still do is but the attempt to explain myself to her? If she understood I should lack a reason for writing, and one can never have too many reasons for doing what is so laborious. (*WBY* 228)

Cf. the poem 'Words' (*PNE* 93).

9 *if I shrieked*: cf. a passage in an unpublished MS. in which Yeats described his state of mind in 1897: 'I was tortured with sexual desire and disappointed love. Often as I walked in the woods at Coole it would have been a relief to have screamed aloud.'

III THE MERMAID 229

1 *A mermaid*: this refers to Yeats's brief relationship with 'Diana Vernon' in 250 1896. A literary source may be Lady Gregory, *Visions and Beliefs*, II; 'And there

was a boy saw a mermaid down by Spiddal [Galway] not long ago, but he saw her before she saw him, so she did him no harm. But if she'd seen him first, she'd have brought him away and drowned him.'

230 IV THE DEATH OF THE HARE

250 This poem was written on 3 January 1926.

2 *The hare*: the hare is Iseult Gonne. Yeats wrote to Maurice Wollman who edited *Modern Poetry 1922-1934* (1935) on 23 September 1935 to say that he didn't want to interpret the poem.

> I can help you to write a note, if that note is to be over your own name, but you must not give me as your authority. If an author interprets a poem of his own he limits its suggestibility. You can say that the poem means that the lover may, while loving, feel sympathy with his beloved's dread of captivity. I don't know how else to put it.   (*L* 840-1)

251 12 *the death*: may allude to her marriage to Francis Stuart. See notes on 'Stream and Sun at Glendalough' (*PNE* 267) and on 'Why should not Old Men be Mad?' (*PNE* A122). See Francis Stuart's autobiographical novel, *Black List, Section H* (1971) for his view of their marriage.

231 V THE EMPTY CUP

251 This poem was probably written in December 1926.

1 *A crazy man*: Yeats

cup: the poem is about Yeats's relationship with 'Diana Vernon', cf. a letter to Olivia Shakespear written on 6 December 1926:

> I came upon two early photographs of you yesterday, while going through my file - one that from *Literary Year Book*. Who ever had a like profile? - a profile from a Sicilian coin. One looks back to one's youth as to [a] cup that a mad man dying of thirst left half tasted. I wonder if you feel like that.

The version of the poem included in the letter ran as follows:

> A madman found a cup of wine
> And half dead of thirst
> Hardly dared to wet his mouth,
> Imagining, moon accurst,
> That another mouthful
> And his beating heart would burst

> But my discovery of the change
> For it cannot be denied
> That all is ancient metal now
> The four winds have dried –
> Has kept me waking half the night
> And made me hollow-eyed.   (*L* 721–2)

4   *moon-accursed*: cf. 'First Love' (*PNE* 227) and 'Human Dignity' (*PNE* 228). The liaison between Yeats and 'Diana Vernon' lasted only a year. Maud Gonne had written to him that she was in London and would come and dine with him, and he had not let her. He was upset by this letter, and when Diana Vernon next came to see him, found he could not answer her and knew there was someone else in his heart. Cf. note on 'The Lover mourns for the Loss of Love' (*PNE* 51).

7   *October last*: Yeats had a meeting with 'Diana Vernon' (Mrs Shakespear) in October 1926.

VI HIS MEMORIES   232

15   *She*: Helen of Troy. See note on 'The Rose of the World' (*PNE* 20).   251
Virginia Moore, *The Unicorn* (1954) 202, and Richard Ellmann, *Golden Codgers* (1973), 108 fn, think the poem refers to Yeats sleeping with Maud Gonne about 1907. See notes on 'King and No King' (*PNE* 96).

Hector: see note on 'The Phases of the Moon' (*PNE* 183).

VII THE FRIENDS OF HIS YOUTH   233

This poem was written on 2 July 1926.   252

VIII SUMMER AND SPRING   234

6–8   *. . . halved a soul*   253
      And fell the one in t'other's arms
      That we might make it whole: this imagery is related to that of lines 13–17 of 'Among School Children' (*PNE* 222), and the imagery of the tree in lines 13–15 is akin to the last stanza of that poem.

IX THE SECRETS OF THE OLD   235

17–18   *bed of straw / Or the bed of down*: possibly a cottage or great house   253
antithesis

236   X HIS WILDNESS

254   3-4   *Paris' love That had so straight a back*: a description of Helen or Maud Gonne whose 'straight back' is praised in 'Beautiful Lofty Things' (*PNE* 334). For Paris see note (p. 27) on 'The Rose of the World' (*PNE* 20).

237   XI FROM 'OEDIPUS AT COLONUS'

255   This poem was written on or before 13 March 1927. See note on 'Colonus' Praise' (*PNE* 223).

255   12   *The second best's a gay goodnight*: Yeats wrote to Olivia Shakespear on 13 March 1927 that the last line was 'very bad Grecian, but very good Elizabethan and so it must stay' (*L* 723).

238   THE THREE MONUMENTS

255   This poem was written, according to Mrs Yeats, *before* the Irish Senate debate on divorce on 11 June 1925 (not after, as in *WBY* 370 nor, as in *SSY* 98, 'a couple of years later'), and first appeared in *OB*.

2   *Our most renownèd patriots stand*: a reference to the statues of the Irish politicians Daniel O'Connell (1745-1833) and Charles Stewart Parnell (1846-91), and the English naval commander Horatio, Lord Nelson (1758-1805).

4   *stumpier*: Nelson's Pillar (this was recently blown up, and the remains of the elegant column have been removed) which was higher than the Parnell monument, at the northern end of O'Connel Street (formerly Sackville Street) and the monument to O'Connell at the southern end.

255   12   *The three old rascals*: Yeats's speech in the Senate was challenging:

> I have said that this is a tolerant country, yet, remembering that we have in our principal streets certain monuments, I feel it necessary to say that it would be wiser if I had said this country is hesitating.
> I have no doubt whatever that, when the iceberg melts it will become an exceedingly tolerant country. The monuments are on the whole encouraging. I am thinking of O'Connell, Parnell, and Nelson. We never had any trouble about O'Connell. It was said about O'Connell, in his own day, that you could not throw a stick over a workhouse wall without hitting one of his children, but he believed in the indissolubility of marriage, and when he died his heart was very properly preserved in Rome. I am not quite sure whether it was in a bronze or marble urn, but it is there, and I have no doubt the art of that urn was as bad as the other art of the period. We had a good deal of trouble about Parnell when he married a woman who became thereby Mrs Parnell.

An Cathaoirleach: Do you not think we might leave the dead alone?

Dr Yeats: I am passing on. I would hate to leave the dead alone. When that happened, I can remember the Irish Catholic Bishops coming out with a declaration that he had thereby doubled his offence. That is, fundamentally, the difference between us. In the opinion of every Irish Protestant gentleman in this country he did what was essential as a man of honour. Now you are going to make the essential act impossible and thereby affront an important minority of your countrymen. I am anxious to draw the attention of the Bishop of Meath to Nelson. There is a proposal to remove Nelson because he interferes with the traffic. Now, I would suggest to the Protestant Bishop of Meath that he should advocate the removal of Nelson on strictly moral grounds. We will then have the whole thing out, and discover whether the English people who teach the history of Nelson to their children, and hold it before the country as a patriotic ideal, or the Bishop of Meath represent, on the whole, public opinion. The Bishop of Meath would not, like his predecessors in Ireland eighty years ago, have given Nelson a pillar. He would have preferred to give him a gallows, because Nelson should have been either hanged or transported. I think I have not greatly wronged the dead in suggesting that we have in our midst three very salutary objects of meditation which may, perhaps, make us a little more tolerant.   (*SSY* 97-8)

ALL SOULS' NIGHT   239

Epilogue to 'A Vision'   256

This poem was written in November 1920 at Oxford (Yeats wrote 'I have moments of exaltation like that in which I wrote ''All Souls' Night'' ' (*AV* (A) xii)) and it first appeared in *The New Republic* (9 March 1921) and *LM* (March 1921). The poem concludes both *AV* (A) and *AV* (B).

1   *Christ Church Bell*: Christ Church, Oxford, a college founded by Cardinal Wolsey (*c*. 1475-1530). Yeats was living in a house (now destroyed) in Broad Street, Oxford, when he wrote the poem.

3   *All Souls' Night*: when members of the Roman Catholic Church pray for the souls of the faithful still in Purgatory (usually 2 November)

21   *Horton's the first*: William Thomas Horton (1864-1919), an Irvingite who   257
produced mystical drawings for *S* in 1896, and for whose *A Book of Images* (1898) Years wrote a Preface. Horton also wrote *The Way of the Soul* (1910) with symbolic illustrations; he was influenced by Blake and Beardsley; many of his drawings are preserved in the University of Reading and in Bodley. He is listed among the members of the Order of the Golden Dawn in 1898. See two letters about the Order written to him by Yeats in 1896 (*L* 260-1). See Yeats's reference to him in his notes, *CP* 524; quoted p. 20

23   *platonic love*: Yeats wrote of him in *AV*:

[He] lived through that strange adventure, perhaps the strangest of all adventures – Platonic love. When he was a child his nurse said to him 'An Angel bent over your bed last night', and in his seventeenth year he awoke to see the phantom of a beautiful woman at his bedside. Presently he gave himself up to all kinds of amorous adventures, until at last, in I think his fiftieth year but when he had still all his physical vigour, he thought 'I do not need women but God.' Then he and a very good, charming, young fellow-student fell in love with one another, and though he could only keep his passion down with the most bitter struggle, they lived together platonically, and this they did, not from prejudice, for I think they had none, but from a clear sense of something to be attained by what seemed a most needless trampling of the grapes of life. She died and he survived her but a little time during which he saw her in apparition and attained through her certain of the traditional experiences of the saint.   (*AV*(A) p. x)

25   *when his lady died*: Audrey Locke (1881–1916)

35   *a slight companionable ghost*: D. J. Gordon and Ian Fletcher have quoted from a letter that Yeats wrote to Horton after Miss Locke's death: 'She had talent, and great charm and must have been much interwoven in your thought . . . the dead are not far from us . . . they cling in some strange way to what is most deep and still within us.'

They comment that when Horton tried to record this in a self-portrait showing the spiritual presence of the lady, the year after her death, the inadequacy of feeling and will to produce the image is almost desperately apparent (*IP* 103).

40   *a gold-fish swimming in a bowl*: a bowl of goldfish was kept on one of the windows of Yeats's house in Broad Street, Oxford, to amuse Anne Yeats.

41   *Florence Emery*: Florence Farr Emery (1869–1917) first met Yeats in 1890 when she was acting in *A Sicilian Idyll* by John Todhunter (1839–1916); she produced Yeats's *The Land of Heart's Desire* as a curtain raiser at the Avenue Theatre on 29 March 1894, acted the part of Aleel in *The Countess Cathleen* in Dublin 1899, and gave a performance of his *The Shadowy Waters* for a Theosophical Convention at the Court Theatre, London on 8 July 1905. She was a member of the group of students of the occult which centred on MacGregor Mathers, her initials in the Order of the Golden Dawn being SSDD (Sapientia Sapienti Dono Data). She recited Yeats's poems to the Psaltery and wrote *The Music of Speech* (1909). Ellmann (*Y:M & M* 182) says Yeats had an affair with her after 1903. Shaw described her as

a young independent professional woman, who enjoyed, as such, an exceptional freedom of social intercourse in artistic circles in London. As she was clever, good natured, and very good-looking, all her men friends fell in love with her. This had occurred so often that she had lost all patience with the hesitating preliminaries of her less practised adorers. Accordingly, when they clearly longed to kiss her, and she did not dislike them sufficiently to make their gratification too great a strain on her excessive good nature, she would seize the stammering suitor firmly by the wrists, bring him into her arms by a smart pull and saying 'Let's get it over' allow the startled gentleman to have his kiss, and then proceed to converse with him at her ease on subjects of more general interest. (Hesketh Pearson, *Bernard Shaw: His Life and Personality* (1942) 120-1)

Cf. *Florence Farr, Bernard Shaw and W. B. Yeats*, a volume of letters published by the Cuala Press in 1941.

Yeats described her in 'Four Years: 1887-1891' as possessing

three great gifts, a tranquil beauty like that of Demeter's image near the British Museum Reading-Room door, and an incomparable sense of rhythm and a beautiful voice, the seeming natural expression of the image. . . . Her sitting-room at the Brook Green lodging-house was soon a reflection of her mind, the walls covered with musical instruments, pieces of Oriental drapery, and Egyptian gods and goddesses painted by herself in the British Museum (*A* 121-3)

46   *teach a school*: In 1912 Mrs Emery went to teach in a Buddhist Institution, Ramanathan College, in Ceylon, where she died on 29 April 1917. This was founded by Sri Ponnambalam Ramanathan. For details of her life in Ceylon see Jayanta Padmanabha's articles in the *Ceylon Daily News*, 2 & 3 February 1947 and 29 & 30 April 1947.

49   *foul years*: cancer was diagnosed in December 1916; she had a mastectomy then, and died from heart failure the following April.

52-3   *. . . discourse in figurative speech*
   By some learned Indian . . .: F. F. Farag (*YCE* 41) suggests that the Indian was Mohini Chatterjee. 'free and yet fast' (line 57) may relate to his view that people do not 'possess even their bodies.' But Yeats probably meant Sir Ponnambalam Ramanathan (1851-1930) whom Florence Farr met in England in 1902. He exercised considerable influence on her; see Josephine Johnson, *Florence Farr Bernard Shaw's 'New Woman'* (1975) 93, 181, 192.

58   *Chance and Choice*: see note on 'Solomon and the Witch' (*PNE* 190).   *258*

61   *MacGregor*: MacGregor Mathers (1854-1918), originally Samuel Liddle Mathers, studied occultism in London from 1885. He was appointed Curator of the Horniman Museum at Forest Hill in 1890, lost this post through a quarrel and lived in Paris from (probably) 1894. Interested in Rosicrucianism and Freemasonry, he translated the *Kabalah Denudata*. Yeats probably met him in 1887, and wrote of him in 'Four Years: 1887-1891':

At the British Museum Reading-Room I often saw a man of thirty-six, or thirty-seven, in a brown velveteen coat, with a gaunt resolute face, and an athletic body, who seemed, before I heard his name, or knew the nature of his studies, a figure of romance. Presently I was introduced, where or by what man or woman I do not remember. He was called Liddell Mathers, but would soon, under the touch of 'The Celtic Movement', become MacGregor Mathers, and then plain MacGregor. He was the author of *The Kabbala Unveiled*, and his studies were two only – magic and the theory of war, for he believed himself a born commander and all but equal in wisdom and in power to that old Jew. He had copied many manuscripts on magic ceremonial and doctrine in the British Museum, and was to copy many more in Continental libraries, and it was through him mainly that I began certain studies and experiences, that were to convince me that images well up before the mind's eye from a deeper source than conscious or subconscious memory. I believe that his mind in those early days did not belie his face and body – though in later years it became unhinged, as Don Quixote's was unhinged – for he kept a proud head amid great poverty. One that boxed with him nightly has told me that for many weeks he could knock him down, though Mathers was the stronger man, and only knew long after that during those weeks Mathers starved. He had spoken to me, I think at our first introduction, of a society which sometimes called itself – it had a different name among its members – 'The Hermetic Students', and in May or June 1887 I was initiated into that society in a Charlotte Street studio, and being at a most receptive age, shaped and isolated. Mathers was its governing mind, a born teacher and organiser. (*A* 182-3)

61   *from the grave*: he had 'fallen on hard times' and died in 1918.

63   *of late estranged*: Yeats was involved in the split in the Order of the Golden Dawn. Mathers accused Dr Wynn Wescott of forging documents and Yeats was on the committee of the second order (RR & AC) – The order of Rosae Rubeae and Aureae Crucis – which investigated this charge. Mathers sent Aleister Crowley to act as his envoy. Mathers and others were suspended from membership of the Second Order by the Committee on 19 April 1900.

He had earlier written several letters to Lady Gregory about the trouble in the Order, about Crowley, 'a person of unspeakable life', and in May 1900 was able to write that

> MacGregor apart from certain definite ill doings and absurdities, on which we had to act, has behaved with dignity and even courtesy. A fine nature gone to wrack. At last we have got a perfectly honest order, with no false mystery and no mystagogues of any kind. Everybody is working, as I have never seen them work, and we have fought out our fight without one discourteous phrase or irrelevant issue. (*L* 344)

Yeats's own view of how the Order of RR and AC should develop is contained in two pamphlets he wrote, the first, 'Is the order of RR and AC to remain a magical order?', written in March 1901, and the second, 'A Postscript to Essay called Is the Order of RR and AC to remain a magical Order?', written on 4 May 1907.

Ellic Howe's book *The Magicians of the Golden Dawn* (1972) lists diary entries of the Second Order which mention Yeats (as DEDI), pp. 290-1. See also George Harper, *Yeats's Golden Dawn* (1974) for a full history of the difficulties within the Order from 1896 onwards.

259   86   *mummy truths*: cf. 'old mummy wheat' in and note on 'On a Picture of a Black Centaur by Edmund Dulac' (*PNE* 221).

The Winding Stair and Other Poems

The Winding Stair was first published in 1929 by the Fountain Press, New York. It contained five poems and those of *A Woman Young and Old.* The poems of *Words for Music Perhaps* were included in the 1933 Macmillan edition *WS* which also contained 'Crazy Jane talks with the Bishop'. *The Winding Stair*, Yeats wrote to Sturge Moore on 26 September 1930 when discussing the design for the cover of the volume, is 'the winding stair of Ballylee enlarged in a symbol but you may not think the stair, even when a mere symbol, pictorial. It might be a mere gyre – Blake's design of Jacob's ladder – with figures, little figures'. Memories became distilled as Yeats grew older, yet the range of his poetry was wide. Longer lyrics and shorter in *The Winding Stair* celebrate his friendships and their results. He remembered the Gore-Booth sisters and weighed up the achievement of Lady Gregory at Coole in noble poems; and even more condensed personal memories appeared in such poems as 'Quarrel in Old Age' (*PNE* 263); 'The Results of Thought' (*PNE* 264); and 'Stream and Sun at Glendalough' (*PNE* 267). The dialogue of self and soul developed; the claims of the supernatural were weighed in 'Byzantium' and 'Vacillation'; and new characters, Crazy Jane and Old Tom the lunatic, emerged in short poems which dealt with desecration and the lover's night. Deeper reading in philosophy and fresh reading in literature was recorded in such poems as 'The Delphic Oracle upon Plotinus' (*PNE* 292) or 'I am of Ireland' (*PNE* 287). Indeed Plotinus may have sanctioned the belief that immortality exists, outside the lovers' immediate existence. When Crazy Jane cried to the Bishop in 'Crazy Jane talks with the Bishop' (*PNE* 273):

> 'Fair and foul are near of kin
> And fair needs foul'

the poem is based on the thought the lover affirms in 'Young Man's Song' (*PNE* 276):

> She would as bravely show
> Did all the fabric fade;
> No withered crone I saw
> Before the world was made.

DEDICATION

For Dulac, see note on 'On a picture . . . Dulac' (*PNE* 221). In his notes (*CP* 536) Yeats includes the letter he wrote as dedication for the Macmillan edition of the volume:

DEAR DULAC,

I saw my *Hawk's Well* played by students of our Schools of Dancing and of Acting a couple of years ago in a beautiful little theatre called 'The Peacock,' which shares a roof with the Abbey Theatre. Watching Cuchulain in his lovely mask and costume, that ragged old masked man who seems hundreds of years old, that Guardian of the Well, with your great golden wings and dancing to your music, I had one of those moments of excitement that are the dramatist's reward and decided there and then to dedicate to you my next book of verse.

240 IN MEMORY OF EVA GORE-BOOTH AND CON MARKIEVICZ

263 The manuscript of this poem is dated 21 September 1927. The date given in *CP* is October 1927. Mrs Yeats considers that this date was incorrectly supplied; she remembers Yeats working on the poem in November 1927 in Seville. Constance Markievicz died in August 1927, and Eva the year before. The poem first appeared in *WS*. In a letter of 23 July 1916 Yeats wrote to Eva Gore-Booth 'Your sister & yourself, two beautiful figures among the great trees of Lisadell, are among the dear memories of my youth' (quoted by I. Fletcher (*YCE* 69)).

1 *Lissadell*: the Gore-Booth house (*Irish* Lis-a-Doill, the Courtyard of the Blind Man) in Sligo, which Yeats visited in the winter of 1894-5. See notes on line 17 'Easter 1916' (*PNE* 193) and 'On a Political Prisoner' (*PNE* 196). The house was built in 1832-4 to the design of Francis Goodwin. Cf 'The Man who dreamed of Faeryland' (*PNE* 33)

4 *one a gazelle*: Eva (1870-1926), who wrote poetry and later worked for the women's suffrage movement; she read deeply in Indian mysticism and Neoplatonism, and was strongly committed to social work.

7 *The older*: Constance (1868-1927) was two years older than her sister. She left Lissadell in 1898 to study painting in Paris. She married Count Casimir Markievicz and they settled in Dublin. See Anne Marreco, *The Rebel Countess* (1967) *passim*.

9 *conspiring*: she gave military training to the Fianna Scouts, worked with Fianna Fail Clubs, and joined the Citizen Army in 1914. She fell deeply under the spell of James Connolly, the Dublin Labour leader. She was deputy leader of the group who held St Stephen's Green in the 1916 Rising. Her subsequent death sentence was commuted to life imprisonment; she was released in the amnesty of 1917. After she was released from prison she busied herself with the affairs of *Cumann na mBan*, was elected an M.P., became the Minister for Labour in *Dail Eireann*, but did not take her seat at Westminster, was gaoled on several occasions. She was reappointed Minister in the second *Dail Eireann* (1921), but supported de Valera and the Republicans at the time of the 1922 Treaty which brought the Irish Free State into being. She fought in the Civil War and won her seat back in 1923. She became ill and died in 1927, her husband and step-son having arrived a few days before from Warsaw.

the ignorant: cf. P. L. Dickinson, *The Dublin of Yesterday* (1929), 92 ff.

11   *Utopia*: an ideal state, the title of a speculative political essay about the best form of government written in Latin (1516) by Sir Thomas More (1478-1535) and translated into English (1551).

16   *Georgian mansion*: Lissadell was built in 1832; technically the Georgian period of architecture runs from 1714 to 1820. The adjective applies to the style of the house.

27   *till time catch*: cf. 'The Untiring Ones' which has a reference to God   *264*
burning up the world with a kiss (*M* 78); there is a reference to God burning Nature with a kiss in the penultimate line of 'The Man who dreamed of Faeryland' (*PNE* 33), and to 'God burning time' in the penultimate line of 'He tells of the Perfect Beauty' (*PNE* 63). 'The Moods' (*PNE* 42) has an image of time dropping in decay 'Like a candle burnt out' and 'Vacillation' (*PNE* 262) has a brand or flaming breath coming to destroy

> All those antinomies
> Of day and night.

Stanza xi of 'In Memory of Major Robert Gregory' (*PNE* 143) has a similar idea.

30   *the great gazebo*: Ian Fletcher, 'Yeats and Lissadell' (*YCE* 68-9) suggests three meanings for the word: a summer house in the grounds of Lissadell; the Anglo-Irish meaning of the word, e.g. to make a gazebo of yourself or look ridiculous; and a place to look from (suggested by Stallworthy (*BL*)). The word appeared first in 1752.

DEATH   **241**

This poem was written on 13 or 17 September 1927 and first appeared in *WS*.   *264*
Yeats's note (*CP* 536) recounts that he was roused to write this poem by the assassination of Kevin O'Higgins (1892-1927), Vice-President and Minister of Justice in the Irish Free State, whom Yeats saw as following in the Anglo-Irish tradition: he added his name to those of Berkeley, Swift, Burke, Grattan, Parnell, and Augusta Gregory and Synge in a list which followed a statement in *OTB* that he wrote with two certainties in mind:

> first that a hundred men, their creative power wrought to the highest pitch, their will trained but not broken, can do more for the welfare of a people, whether in war or peace, than a million of any lesser sort no matter how expensive their education, and that although the Irish masses are vague and excitable because they have not yet been moulded and cast, we have as good blood as there is in Europe.   (*E* 441-2)

O'Higgins was shot on 10 July 1927 at Booterstown, Co. Dublin, on his way to Mass. In the Civil War period the Free State government had executed anyone captured carrying arms and a total of 77 irregulars was executed. O'Higgins had been convinced that this tough policy was correct; and it was thought that he was shot as an act of revenge. Yeats regarded him as 'the finest intellect in Irish life and, I think I may add, to some extent my friend' (*CP* 536). He wrote to Olivia Shakespear about the assassination in July or August 1927:

> You were right about our peace not lasting. The murder of O'Higgins was no mere public event to us. He was our personal friend, as well as the one strong intellect in Irish public life and then too his pretty young wife was our friend. We got the news just when we reached the Gresham Hotel where we were to dine and we left without dining and walked about the streets till bed-time. The night before George had suddenly called the dog out of the way of what she thought was a motor car – there was no car – and a moment after when inside our own door we both heard two bursts of music, voices singing together. At the funeral at the Mass for the dead I recognised the music as that of the choir which – just before the elevation of the host – sang in just such short burst of song. You will remember the part the motor car had in the murder. Had we seen more he might have been saved, for recent evidence seems to show that those things are fate unless foreseen by clairvoyance and so brought within the range of free-will. A French man of science thinks that we all – including murderers and victims – will and so create the future. I would bring in the dead. Are we, that foreknow, the actual or potential traitors of the race-process? Do we, as it were, forbid the banns when the event is struggling to be born? Is this why – even if what we foresee is not some trivial thing – we foresee too little to understand?
>
> I have finished those love poems – 19 in all – and am now at a new Tower series, partly driven to it by this murder. Next week I must go to Dublin to help vote the more stringent police laws the government think necessary. I hear with anxiety that they will increase the number of crimes punishable by death, and with satisfaction that they will take certain crimes out of the hands of jurors. But I know nothing except what I find in the papers.
>
> I am expecting a visit from my Italian translator – perhaps if we have lived good lives we may be reborn in some peaceful eastern village and have sweethearts with beautiful golden brown skins.   (*L* 726-7)

Cf. 'Blood and the Moon' (*PNE* 243) which was also written under the stimulus of O'Higgins's assassination.

5-6   *Many times he died*
   Many times rose again: cf. F. F. Farag (*YCE* 41) for the suggestion that this is the same idea of reincarnation expressed in 'Mohini Chatterjee' (*PNE* 259), cf. also 'Quarrel in Old Age' (*PNE* 263) and 'Under Ben Bulben' (*PNE* 356) with its 'two eternities'

11   *He knows death to the bone*: cf. Yeats's letter to Olivia Shakespear written in April 1933:

> This country is exciting. I am told that De Valera has said in private that within three years he will be torn in pieces. It reminds me of a saying by O'Higgins to his wife 'Nobody can expect to live who has done what I have.' No sooner does a politician get into power than he begins to seek unpopularity. It is the cult of sacrifice planted in the nation by the executions of 1916. Read [Liam] O'Flaherty's novel *The Martyr*, a book forbidden by our censor, and very mad

270

in the end, but powerful and curious as an attack upon the cult. I asked a high government officer once if he could describe the head of the I.R.A. He began 'That is so and so who has (the) cult of suffering and is always putting himself in positions where he will be persecuted.'   (*L* 809)

A DIALOGUE OF SELF AND SOUL   242

According to Mrs Yeats, this poem was written between July and December   265
1927, and first appeared in *WS*. It was written (Yeats, notes *CP* 537) 'in the
spring of 1928 during a long illness, indeed finished the day before a Cannes
doctor told me to stop writing'.

1   *the winding ancient stair*: of Thoor Ballylee

3   *broken, crumbling battlement*: cf. 'I climb to the tower-top and lean upon
broken stone', 'Meditations in Time of Civil War', VII (*PNE* 212)

9   *The consecrated blade*: see note on 'Meditations in Time of Civil War', III
(*PNE* 208)

10   *Sato's ancient blade*: Junzo Sato attended a lecture given by Yeats at
Portland, Oregon. See note on 'Meditations in Time of Civil War' (*PNE* 208).
He told the present author in Tokyo in 1981 that he still had vivid memories of
the lecture.

13   *That flowering, silken, old embroidery*: Yeats wrote on 2 or 4 October
1927 to Olivia Shakespear to say he had been writing verse: 'a new tower poem
"Sword and Tower", which is a choice of rebirth rather than deliverance from
birth. I make my Japanese sword and its silk covering my symbol of life' (*L* 729).
    The form of the poem may have been suggested by Marvell's 'A Dialogue
between the Soul and the Body' (included in Grierson's *Metaphysical Lyrics and
Poems* (1921), 163, which Yeats read).

25   *Montashigi*: Bishu Osafumé Motoshigé, the maker of the sword, who lived
in Osafume in the era of Oei (1394-1428)

32   *the crime*: cf. 'Consolation' (*PNE* 297):   266

                    But where the crime's committed
                    The crime can be forgot.

33-4   *Such fullness in that quarter overflows*
        And falls into the basin of the mind: cf.

                'Life overflows without ambitious pains;
                And rains down life until the basin spills,'

lines 3-4, 'Meditations in Time of Civil War' (*PNE* 206)

271

267   64   *a proud woman*: Maud Gonne

67-72   *Measure the lot; forgive myself the lot!*
When such as I cast out remorse
So great a sweetness flows into the breast
We must laugh and we must sing,
We are blest by everything,
Everything we look upon is blest: there is a passage in Yeats's essay 'J.
M. Synge and the Ireland of his Time' which describes the artists's joy which is of
one substance with that of sanctity:

> There is in the creative joy an acceptance of what life brings, because we have
> understood the beauty of what it brings, or a hatred of death for what it takes
> away, which arouses within us, through some sympathy perhaps with all other
> men, an energy so noble, so powerful, that we laugh aloud and mock, in the
> terror or the sweetness of our exaltation, at death and oblivion.   (*E & I* 322)

Cf. 'Vacillation' IV (*PNE* 262) for a description of happiness:

> It seemed, so great my happiness,
> That I was blessèd and could bless.

243   BLOOD AND THE MOON

267   This poem was written in August 1927 and first appeared in *The Exile* (Spring
1928).

1   *this place*: Thoor Ballylee

7   *cottages*: the cottages adjoined the tower, and were rethatched by 1919.

12   *Half dead at the top*: the tower was never completely restored; one room was
empty at the top. Concrete was used for the roof rather than an ornate structure
designed by Lutyens. Henn (*LT* 13), connects the empty room with the
traditional symbol of the Seventh Room in alchemy (referring to *The Chymical
Marriage of Christian Rosencrux*) and the ultimate room in St Teresa's *The
Interior Castle* (which Yeats had read). He regards the empty room at the top as
that in which spiritual revelation is given, and he suggests that 'half dead at the
top' refers not to the flat cement roof (as suggested by Hone (*WBY* 331)) but to
the impossibility of spiritual enlightenment in this era. See Jeffares, *The Circus
Animals* (1970) 43 and cf. Edward Young's anecdote about Swift ('Conjectures
on original composition', *Works* (1798) III, 196) gazing at 'a noble tree, which in
its uppermost branches was much withered and decayed. Pointing at it, he said "I
shall be like that tree, I shall die at top" '.

13   *beacon tower*: the Pharos, a lighthouse (one of the seven wonders of the
World) built (*c.* 280 BC) on an island off Alexandria in Egypt, destroyed by an
earthquake in the fourteenth century

15 *Shelley had his towers*: Yeats wrote an essay on 'The Philosophy of   *268*
Shelley's Poetry' in which he discussed this symbol:

> As Shelley sailed along those great rivers and saw or imagined the cave that
> associated itself with rivers in his mind, he saw half-ruined towers upon the hill-
> tops, and once at any rate a tower is used to symbolise a meaning that is the
> contrary to the meaning symbolised by caves. Cythna's lover is brought
> through the cave where there is a polluted fountain to a high tower, for being
> man's far-seeing mind, when the world has cast him out he must to the 'towers
> of thought's crowned powers' [the reference is to Shelley's *Prometheus
> Unbound* (1820) IV, 103]; nor is it possible for Shelley to have forgotten this
> first imprisonment when he made men imprison Lionel in a tower for a like
> offence; and because I know how hard it is to forget a symbolical meaning, once
> one has found it, I believe Shelley had more than a romantic scene in his mind
> when he made Prince Athanase follow his mysterious studies in a lighted tower
> above the sea, and when he made the old hermit watch over Laon in his
> sickness in a half-ruined tower, wherein the sea, here doubtless, as to Cythna
> 'the one mind,' threw 'spangled sands' and 'rarest sea shells.' The tower,
> important in Maeterlinck, as in Shelley, is, like the sea, and rivers, and caves
> with fountains, a very ancient symbol, and would perhaps, as years went by,
> have grown more important in his poetry.   (*E & I* 86–7)

Cf. also notes on 'Ego Dominus Tuus' (*PNE* 181) and on line 16 'The Phases of
the Moon' (*PNE* 183).

17 *my ancestral stair*: this poem, like 'The Seven Sages' (*PNE* 251), expresses
Yeats's pride in his intellectual ancestry, the Anglo-Irish Protestant predecessors
whom he enumerates in the next line.

He had these men in his mind frequently during his period as a Senator. (In the
winter of 1922–3 he met 'the revolutionary soldier' [Capt. D. A. MacManus]
who introduced him to Berkeley's works: shortly afterwards Lennox Robinson
gave him a two-volume edition of Berkeley.) He regarded them as the founders of
Irish thought. In his Introduction to J. M. Hone and M. M. Rossi, *Bishop
Berkeley* (1931) he wrote:

> Born in such a community, Berkeley with his belief in perception, that
> abstract ideas are mere words, Swift with his love of perfect nature, of the
> Houyhnhnms, his disbelief in Newton's system and every sort of machine,
> Goldsmith and his delight in the particulars of common life that shocked his
> contemporaries, Burke with his conviction that all States not grown slowly like
> a forest tree are tyrannies, found in England the opposite that stung their
> thought into expression and made it lucid.   (*E & I* 402)

Yeats had turned from Goldsmith and Burke in his youth because they seemed a
part of the English system, while Swift had not been a romantic; but he changed
his attitude to them and wrote in *WB* that now he 'read Swift for months
together, Burke and Berkeley less often but always with excitement, and
Goldsmith lures and waits' (*E* 344).

He recorded in his 1930 Diary that 'the thought of Swift, enlarged and
enriched by Burke, saddled and bitted reality, and that materialism was
hamstrung by Berkeley, and ancient wisdom brought back; that modern Europe
had known no men more powerful' (*E* 297–8).

18   *Goldsmith*: Oliver Goldsmith (1728–74), the Irish author

the Dean: Jonathan Swift (1667–1745). Dean of St Patrick's Cathedral, Dublin

Berkeley: George Berkeley (1685–1753) the Irish philosopher, Bishop of Cloyne in Co. Cork

Burke: see note on 'The Tower' (*PNE* 205) and on 'The Seven Sages' (*PNE* 251).

21   *honey-pot*: probably a reference to Goldsmith's periodical *The Bee*. See Torchiara *Y & GI*, 275–9, who also quotes John Butler Yeats's referring frequently to Goldsmith's gentleness and sympathy with the Irish poor.

22   *proved the state a tree*: cf. Yeats's comment on 'our tradition' 'that Berkeley was the first to say the world is a vision; Burke was the first to say a nation is a tree. And those two sayings are a foundation of modern thought' (Lady Gregory, *Journals*, 265).
   Burke's passage on the oak, *Reflections, Works*, II, 357, inspired several of Yeats's comments on the State: for instance, 'Burke [proved] that the State was a tree, no mechanism to be pulled in pieces and put up again, but an oak tree that had grown through centuries' (*SSY* 172). See also *Pages from a Diary* (*E* 318). Torchiana (*Y & GI* 192–3) has shown that the symbol was used by Yeats in a speech given in 1893, and in another given in 1903–4 (in the latter he said 'A nation is like a great tree . . .'), both before he had read Burke in detail.

25   *God-appointed Berkeley*: Yeats met the true Berkeley, according to Professor A. A. Luce, 'in the pages of the *Commonplace Book* with its snorts of defiance . . . the poet revelled in these notebooks, and from them he learned the simple truth which he expressed in the words "Descartes, Locke and Newton took away the world . . . Berkeley restored the world" '. Cf. A. A. Luce, *Berkeley's Immaterialism: a commentary on his Principles of Human Knowledge* (1945).
   A speech Yeats delivered on 'The Child and the State' at the Irish Literary Society on 30 November 1925 shows how he thought the main lines of the old Anglo-Irish culture could be extended into a new Catholic nationalist Ireland of his own time:

> There are two great classics of the eighteenth century which have deeply influenced modern thought, great Irish classics too difficult to be taught to children of any age, but some day those among us who think that all things should begin with the nation and with the genius of the nation, may press them upon the attention of the State. It is impossible to consider any modern philosophical or political question without being influenced knowingly or unknowingly by movements of thought that originated with Berkeley, who founded the Trinity College Philosophical Society, or with Burke, who founded the Historical. [The College Historical Society, the oldest debating club in the British Isles, which still flourishes in Trinity College, Dublin.] It would be but natural if they and those movements were studied in Irish colleges, perhaps

especially in those colleges where our teachers themselves are trained . . .

In Gaelic literature we have something that the English-speaking countries have never possessed – a great folk literature. We have in Berkeley and in Burke a philosophy on which it is possible to base the whole life of a nation. That, too, is something which England, great as she is in modern scientific thought and every kind of literature, has not, I think. The modern Irish intellect was born more than two hundred years ago when Berkeley defined in three or four sentences the mechanical philosophy of Newton, Locke and Hobbes, the philosophy of England in his day, and I think of England up to our day, and wrote after each 'We Irish do not hold with this,' or some like sentence.

Feed the immature imagination upon that old folk life, and the mature intellect upon Berkeley and the great modern idealist philosophy created by his influence, upon Burke who restored to political thought its sense of history, and Ireland is reborn, potent, armed and wise. Berkeley proved that the world was a vision, and Burke that the State was a tree, no mechanism to be pulled in pieces and put up again, but an oak tree that had grown through centuries. (*SSY* 171–2)

Swift and Berkeley, 'these two images, standing and sounding together' were combined by Yeats in the Introduction to *Bishop Berkeley*: they concerned all those 'who feel a responsibility for the thought of modern Ireland that can take away their sleep'.

26   *pragmatical . . . pig*: this may derive (see Hugh Kenner *ACE* 44) from Yeats's experience as Chairman of the Senate Committee on Ireland's coinage; the image of the pig had to be altered: 'better merchandise but less living' (*SSY* 166)

28   *Saeva Indignatio*: the phrase is from Swift's epitaph which Yeats translated.   *269*
See 'Swift's Epitaph' (*PNE* 256).

45   *Tortoiseshell butterflies, peacock butterflies*: see Yeats's notes (*CP* 535–6). Butterflies entered the top room of the tower by the loopholes and died against the window panes.

48   *half dead at the top*: see note on line 12

OIL AND BLOOD   **244**

This poem was probably written in December 1927 and worked over in 1928 and   *270*
1929. It first appeared in *WS*.

Yeats read several books on St Teresa (1515–82), the Spanish Carmelite nun. They were the *Life of St Teresa* (notes by Walter Elliott, 1899); *The Book of Foundations* (1913); *Life of St Teresa* (1924); *The Interior Castle* (1921).

3   *odour of violet*: Lady Lovat writes that

the wood of the coffin was found to be split and decayed, and the coffin was filled with earth and water but the body of the Saint was intact, her flesh white and soft, as flexible as when she was buried, and still emitted the same delicious and penetrating smell. Moreover the limbs exuded a miraculous oil which bore a similar perfume and embalmed the air and everything with which it came in contact. (Lady Lovat, *The Life of St Teresa* (1911), 606)

Yeats wrote to T. Sturge Moore from Cannes on 2 February 1928 about 'that very British brother of yours' [G. E. Moore, the philosopher]:

By the bye, please don't quote him again till you have asked him this question: 'How do you account for the fact that when the Tomb of St Teresa was opened her body exuded miraculous oil and smelt of violets?' If he cannot account for such primary facts he knows nothing. (*Y & TSM* 121-2)

5 *the vampires*: Yeats had read Bram Stoker's *Dracula* (1897) and Sheridan Le Fanu's vampire story (dramatised by Lord Longford under the title *Carmilla* and first produced 3 May 1932, at the Gate Theatre Dublin).

245 VERONICA'S NAPKIN

270 This poem was written at Portofina in 1929 and first appeared in *WMP*.

Title Veronica's Napkin: Yeats's source for the story of Veronica is not known. The legend is that

the Holy Face of Veronica is one of the three great, remarkable and very holy relics which the patriarchal Basilica of St Peter of the Vatican preserves with a jealous care, and which have been in every age of the Church, the object of the veneration of the faithful. The Veronica is a veil, or handkerchief, on which is impressed the true likeness of the adorable face of Our Lord and Saviour Jesus Christ, miraculously imprinted, not produced by artificial colours but by the divine power of God the Son made man. . . . From a constant tradition which is founded on the most authentic documents, we are informed that whilst our Saviour was on the way to Calvary loaded with the heavy wood of the cross, the altar on which he was to sacrifice His life for the redemption of mankind, a holy woman, moved by compassion. presented Him a handkerchief, or towel to wipe His face, all covered with sweat, spittle, dust and blood; and that Jesus, having used it, gave it back to her, having impressed on it His majestic and venerable image, so full of the deep sorrow into which He was plunged by the weight of the sin of the world. (*Veronica or The Holy Face* (translated from the French, 1870), 5)

1 *The Heavenly Circuit*: the title of an essay by Plotinus. Plotinus regarded God as the centre of a perfect circle, and the heavenly bodies rotate about God. The planets are fixed at a particular distance from God. So is the human soul, which circles about him since it cannot coincide with him, though it keeps as near to him as it can since he is the being on which all depends. Cf. *Y & T* 207-9 and Plotinus, *Psychic and Physical Treatises; comprising the Second and Third Enneads*, tr. Stephen MacKenna (1921) pp. 154-9. See note on 'The Delphic Oracle upon Plotinus' (*PNE* 292).

Berenice's Hair: Yeats used this as a symbol of romantic love in 'Her Dream' (*PNE* 280). Berenice II (*c*. 273-221 BC) was the daughter of King Magas of Cyrene and Apama the daughter of Antiochus I. Berenice was betrothed to Ptolemy III but when her father died her mother tried to marry her to Demetrius, a Macedonian prince. She led a rebellion against both of them and ordered the death of Demetrius. She married Ptolemy III in 247, and he named a constellation 'Berenice's Curls' after her, her hair having been offered for his safe return from war. Her son Ptolemy IV murdered her after her husband's death. Yeats probably read of her in Catullus LXVI.

2   *Tent-pole of Eden*: possibly the Pole Star, or the pole of the heavens (*PNE*); see note on 'He Hears the Cry of the Sedge' (*PNE* 64).

6   *the circuit of a needle's eye*: cf. 'Supernatural Songs' (*PNE* 319) with its lines:

> All the stream that's roaring by
> Came out of a needle's eye;
> Things unborn, things that are gone,
> From needle's eye still goad it on.

7   *a different pole*: the cross on which Jesus Christ was crucified

8   *napkin*: the handkerchief Veronica offered to Jesus. Henn (*LT* 260) remarks that there is a picture of the Styrian School in the National Gallery, Dublin, which shows the Apostles setting forth. It bears on the reverse side a large crude painting of St Veronica's napkin.

SYMBOLS   246

This poem was written in October 1927 and first appeared in *WMP*.   *270*

1-2   *watch-tower, / A blind hermit*: The source for these lines is probably an experience recorded in 'Discoveries':

The other day I was walking towards Urbino, where I was to spend the night, having crossed the Apennines from San Sepolcro, and had come to a level place on the mountain-top near the journey's end. My friends were in a carriage somewhere behind, on a road which was still ascending in great loops, and I was alone amid a visionary, fantastic, impossible scenery. It was sunset and the stormy clouds hung upon mountain after mountain, and far off on one great summit a cloud darker than the rest glimmered with lightning. Away south upon another mountain a mediaeval tower, with no building near nor any sign of life, rose into the clouds. I saw suddenly in the mind's eye an old man, erect and a little gaunt, standing in the door of the tower, while about him broke a windy light. He was the poet who had at last, because he had done so much for the world's sake, come to share in the dignity of the saint. He had hidden nothing of himself, but he had taken care of 'that dignity . . . the

277

perfection of form . . . this lofty and severe quality . . . this virtue.' And though he had but sought it for the word's sake, or for a woman's praise, it had come at last into his body and his mind. Certainly as he stood there he knew how from behind that laborious mood, that pose, that genius, no flower of himself but all himself, looked out as from behind a mask that other Who alone of all men, the countrypeople say, is not a hair's breadth more nor less than six feet high. He has in his ears well-instructed voices, and seeming-solid sights are before his eyes, and not, as we say of many a one, speaking in metaphor, but as this were Delphi or Eleusis, and the substance and the voice come to him among his memories which are of women's faces; for was it Columbanus or another that wrote, 'There is one among the birds that is perfect, and one perfect among the fish'?   (*E & I* 290–1)

3–5   *All destroying sword-blade still*
        Carried by the wandering fool.

        Gold-sewn silk on the sword-blade: probably a thought prompted by Junzo Sato's sword. Cf. 'Meditations in Time of Civil War', III (*PNE* 208) and 'A Dialogue of Self and Soul' (*PNE* 242).

5   *gold-sewn silk*: the Japanese sword was wrapped in a piece of silk from a Japanese lady's Court dress (*E* 320). Yeats wrote to Olivia Shakespear of the sword and its silk covering being a symbol of life and in a letter to Dorothy Wellesley dated October 1935 commented that the only swashbuckler in his immediate circle

delighted in those lines about love. He has only two interests, war and women, and that keeps him vital. Do you know my couplet

        The sword, a cross; thereon He died:
        On breast of Mars the goddess sighed.
                        ['Conjunctions' (*PNE* 318)]

That other better couplet

        Gold-sewn silk on the sword-blade
        Beauty and fool together laid.

                        (*DWL* 33)

It is possible that Yeats was influenced in the cross-sword equation by a passage in G. R. S. Mead, *The Gnostic Crucifixion*, 64: 'The outer story was centred round a dramatic crisis of death on a stationary cross – a dead symbol and a symbol of death. But the inner rite was one of movement and ''dancing'', a living symbol and a symbol of life.'

Henn (*LT* 134) regards these couplets as a microcosm of 'A Dialogue of Self and Soul'.

The tower is the emblem of the night of war, of violence, of man's aspirations to philosophy, of the decay of civilisation, of ancient ceremony, disintegrating in the face of the world – 'the broken crumbling battlements'. The tower is night; but its stability is only apparent. Behind it is the cosmic universe, permanent only in 'the star that marks the hidden pole'. The tower becomes astronomical, the departure-point for man's thought facing the universe. Set against it is the objective man, clinging, in old age, to the emblem of love and war, the sword and the embroidery.

SPILT MILK   247

This poem was written on 8 November 1930 and first appeared in *WMP*. Yeats   271
wrote to his wife that it was 'the upshot of my talk upon a metaphor of Lady Ottoline's'. Yeats and Walter de la Mare had visited Lady Ottoline Morrell on 7 November 1930.

THE NINETEENTH CENTURY AND AFTER   248

This poem was written between January and 2 March 1929 and first appeared in   271
WMP.

On 2 March 1929 Yeats wrote to Mrs Shakespear from Rapallo that he had turned from Browning

> to Morris and read through his *Defence of Guinevere* and some unfinished prose fragments with great wonder. I have come to fear the world's last great poetical period is over.

> Though the great song return no more
> There's keen delight in what we have –
> A rattle of pebbles on the shore
> Under the receding wave.

The young do not feel like that – George does not, nor Ezra – but men far off feel it – in Japan for instance.   (*L* 759)

STATISTICS   249

This poem was written in 1931 and first appeared in *WMP*.   271

1   *Platonists*: followers of the Greek philosopher Plato; see note on 'Among School Children' (*PNE* 222).

THREE MOVEMENTS   250

Yeats wrote a prose version of this poem in his White Manuscript book and dated   271
it 20 January 1932; the poem is dated 26 January 1932 by Ellmann (*IY* 267). It first appeared in *WMP*.

1   *Shakespearean fish*: the prose draft reads: 'Passion in Shakespeare was a great fish in the sea, but from Goethe to the end of the Romantic movement the fish was

in the net. It will soon be dead upon the shore.' There is a kindred sentiment in the essay on Bishop Berkeley which begins, 'Imagination, whether in literature, painting, or sculpture, sank after the death of Shakespeare' (*E & I* 396).

2   *Romantic fish*: Shakespeare lived from 1564 to 1616; the romantic movement began in the late eighteenth century and continued in the nineteenth. Yeats described Lady Gregory and himself as 'the last romantics' (*PNE* 254).

251   THE SEVEN SAGES

271   This poem was written on 30 January 1931 and first appeared in *WMP*.

1   *Edmund Burke*: Edmund Burke (1729-97) was educated at Trinity College Dublin, where he founded the College Historical Society, the oldest debating society – it is still flourishing – in the British Isles. He started the Annual Register, became a powerful and persuasive orator, attacking the Tory government, advocating the cause of the Americans, Catholics and Irish trade. He impeached Warren Hastings, supported Wilberforce in advocating the abolition of the slave trade, and, disturbed by the excesses of French Revolution, sided with the Tories. His published works include *A Philosophical Inquiry into the Sublime and the Beautiful* (1796), *Thoughts on the Present Discontents* (1770) and *Reflections on the French Revolution* (1770).

2   *Grattan's house*: Henry Grattan (1746-1820) was educated at Trinity College Dublin. He carried an address demanding legislative independence for Ireland (1782), and the parliament known as Grattan's Parliament sat during one of Ireland's brief periods of prosperity, but this ended with the passing of the Act of Union in 1800, which Grattan opposed in vain. He was MP for Dublin 1806-20. Yeats wrote that:

> Protestant Ireland should ask permission to bring back the body of Grattan from Westminster Abbey to Saint Patrick's. He was buried in Westminster against the protests of his friends and followers – according to Sir Jonah Barrington, that there might be no place of pilgrimage – abandoned there without bust or monument. I would have him brought back through streets lined with soldiers that we might affirm that Saint Patrick's is more to us than Westminster; but, though Protestant Ireland should first move in this matter, I would have all descendants of Grattan's party, or those who voted against the Union, lead the procession.   (*E* 296-7)

3   *Goldsmith*: see note on 'Blood and the Moon' (*PNE* 243).

272   4   *my great-grandfather's father*: in this poem Yeats is searching for his originals (see note on 'Blood and the Moon' (*PNE* 243)):

> How much of my reading is to discover the English and Irish originals of my thought, its first language, and, where no such originals exist, its relation to what original did. I seek more than idioms, for thoughts become more vivid

when I find they were thought out in historical circumstances which affect those in which I live, or, which is perhaps the same thing, were thought first by men my ancestors may have known. Some of my ancestors may have seen Swift, and probably my Huguenot grandmother who asked burial near Bishop King spoke both to Swift and Berkeley. I have before me an ideal expression in which all that I have, clay and spirit alike, assists; it is as though I most approximate towards that expression when I carry with me the greatest possible amount of hereditary thought and feeling, even national and family hatred and pride. (*E* 293)

5   *tar-water with the Bishop of Cloyne*: the tar-water in which Bishop Berkeley believed has been described by J. H. Barnard:

His attention was directed to medical matters, and in his attempts to alleviate the sufferings of the sick he discovered, as he thought, a remedy which would cure every ailment under heaven. When among the Indians in America he had heard much of the medicinal properties of tar-water, and trying this, among other drugs, he was led to believe in its efficacy. He was completely led away by this idea, and for years devoted himself to perfecting both the theory and practice of the administration of tar-water. As to theory, he held that tar contained a large amount of the vital element of the universe, and so must be efficacious in prolonging life. In practice he was enthusiastic; he set up a tar-water manufactory in his own house and dosed his friends and neighbours indiscriminately. The virtues of the drug were extolled in his famous work 'Siris; a chain of Philosophical Reflections'; and in this medical tract, where we would least expect it, we have the culmination of his philosophic teaching – It was the most popular of his publications in his own day; but this was as a medical not as a philosophical treatise. Tar-water became a fashionable drug. We read in one of the good Bishop's letters to America: 'My correspondence with patients that drink tar-water obliges me to be less punctual in corresponding with my friends'. Curious stories are told of its efficacy. The famous Irish giant, Magrath, is said to have been brought up in Berkeley's house on tar-water; hence his height 7 feet 10 inches. ('Berkeley', *DUR* March 1885). This article was probably read by Yeats.)

In his essay 'Bishop Berkeley' Yeats asked rhetorically

Did tar-water, a cure-all learnt from American Indians, suggest that though he could not quiet men's minds he might give their bodies quiet, and so bring to life that incredible benign image, the dream of a time that after the anarchy of the religious wars, the spiritual torture of Donne, of El Greco and Spinoza, longed to be protected and flattered?   (*E & I* 399. See also *E* 322-4)

6   *Stella*: Swift's name for Esther Johnson (d. 1728) whom he first met at Moor Park, Sir William Temple's house. His *Journal to Stella* consists of letters to her and her friend Rebecca Dingley during the period 1710-13. Their friendship lasted throughout Stella's life; their relationship was platonic and has caused much speculation. The best account of Stella is that written by Swift at the time of her death.

7   *Whiggery*: The English Whig party believed in a limited monarchy and represented the aristocracy and monied middle-class interest in the eighteenth

century; in the nineteenth the desire of Dissenters and some industrialists for reform.

8   *Burke was a Whig*: so, initially, was Swift. What Yeats intended is, perhaps, to be discovered in a passage from *OTB*:

> A time has come when man must have certainty, and man knows what he has made. Man has made mathematics, but God reality. Instead of hierarchical society, where all men are different, came democracy; instead of a science which had re-discovered *Anima Mundi*, its experiments and observations confirming the speculations of Henry More, came materialism: all that Whiggish world Swift stared on till he became a raging man. The ancient foundations had scarcely dispersed when Swift's young acquaintance Berkeley destroyed the new for all that would listen, created modern philosophy and established for ever the subjectivity of space. No educated man to-day accepts the objective matter and space of popular science, and yet deductions made by those who believed in both dominate the world, make possible the stimulation and condonation of revolutionary massacre and the multiplication of murderous weapons by substituting for the old humanity with its unique irreplaceable individuals something that can be chopped and measured like a piece of cheese; compel denial of the immortality of the soul by hiding from the mass of the people that the grave-diggers have no place to bury us but in the human mind.   (*E* 435–6)

The same basic idea appeared in the Introduction to *WWP*.

> 'He foresaw the ruin to come, Democracy, Rousseau, the French Revolution; that is why he hated the common run of men –, "I hate lawyers, I hate doctors", he said, "though I love Dr So-and-so and Judge So-and-so", – that is why he wrote *Gulliver*, that is why he wore out his brain, that is why he felt *saeva indignatio*, that is why he sleeps under the greatest epitaph in history.' The *Discourse of the Contests and Dissensions between the Nobles and the Commons in Athens and Rome*, published in 1703 to warn the Tory Opposition of the day against the impeachment of Ministers, is Swift's one philosophical work. All States depend for their health upon a right balance between the One, the Few, and the Many. The One is the executive, which may in fact be more than one – the Roman republic had two Consuls – but must for the sake of rapid decision be as few as possible; the Few are those who through the possession of hereditary wealth, or great personal gifts, have come to identify their lives with the life of the State, whereas the lives and ambitions of the Many are private. The Many do their day's work well, and so far from copying even the wisest of their neighbours, affect 'a singularity' in action and in thought; but set them to the work of the State and every man Jack is 'listed in a party', becomes the fanatical follower of men of whose characters he knows next to nothing, and from that day on puts nothing into his mouth that some other man has not already chewed and digested. And furthermore, from the moment of enlistment thinks himself above other men and struggles for power until all is in confusion. I divine an Irish hatred of abstraction likewise expressed by that fable of Gulliver among the inventors and men of science, by Berkeley in his *Commonplace Book*, by Goldsmith in the satire of *The Good-Natured Man*, in the picturesque, minute observation of *The Deserted Village*, and by Burke in his attack upon mathematical democracy. Swift enforced his moral by

proving that Rome and Greece were destroyed by the war of the Many upon the Few; in Rome, where the Few had kept their class organisation, it was a war of classes, in Greece, where they had not, war upon character and genius. Miltiades, Aristides, Themistocles, Pericles, Alcibiades, Phocion, 'impeached for high crimes and misdemeanours . . . were honoured and lamented by their country as the preservers of it, and have had the veneration of all ages since paid justly to their memories'. In Rome parties so developed that men born and bred among the Few were compelled to join one party or the other and to flatter and bribe. All civilisations must end in some such way, for the Many obsessed by emotion create a multitude of religious sects but give themselves at last to some one master of bribes and flatteries and sink into the ignoble tranquillity of servitude. He defines a tyranny as the predominance of the One, the Few, or the Many, but thinks that of the Many the immediate threat. All States at their outset possess a ruling power seated in the whole body as that of the soul in the human body, a perfect balance of the three estates, the king some sort of chief magistrate, and then comes 'a tyranny: first either of the Few or the Many; but at last infallibly of a single person.' He thinks the English balance most perfect in the time of Queen Elizabeth, but that in the next age a tyranny of the Many produced that of Cromwell, and that, though recovery followed, 'all forms of government must be mortal like their authors', and he quotes from Polybius, 'those abuses and corruptions, which in time destroy a government, are sown along with the very seeds of it' and destroy it 'as rust eats away iron, and worms devour wood'. Whether the final tyranny is created by the Many – in his eyes all Caesars were tyrants – or imposed by foreign power, the result is the same. At the fall of liberty came 'a dark insipid period through all Greece' – had he Ireland in his mind also? – and the people became, in the words of Polybius, 'great reverencers of crowned heads'. (*E* 350–3)

16 *Burke's great melody*: Burke devoted his political life to the emancipation of the House of Commons from the control of George III, the emancipation of the American Colonies, the emancipation of Irish trade, parliament and Catholics, the emancipation of India from the rule of the East India Company, and he opposed the Jacobinism of the French Revolution.

18 *Roads full of beggars, cattle in the fields*: Goldsmith depicted rural depopulation in his poem 'The Deserted Village'.

22 *Cloyne*: see note on Berkeley on 'Blood and the Moon' (*PNE* 243). Cloyne (*Irish* Cluain-Uamha) means the meadow of the cave.

THE CRAZED MOON   252

This poem was written in April 1923 and first appeared in *WMP*.   *273*

1 *much child-bearing*: Henn (*LT*) has suggested that a passage from Cornelius Agrippa (*Occult Philosophy* II, ch. xxxii), where the moon is described as the life of all the stars, may be the source of this:

The sun is the lord of all elementary virtues, and the moon by virtue of the sun is the mistress of generation, increase or decrease . . . but the moon, the nighest to the earth, the receptacle of all the heavenly influences, by the sweetness of her course is joined to the sun and the other planets and stars, every month, and being as it were the wife of all the stars and receiving the beams and influences of all the other planets and stars as a conception and imaging them forth to the inferior world as being next to itself, is the parent of all conceptions.   (*LT* 174)

Henn also suggests (*LT* 186) that the moon is womanhood. Mankind seeks for 'the children born of her pain' the events that come from her predestined round. But in the next there is virginal womanhood, and he regards the second stanza as a picture of an earlier richer life and a memory of Constance Gore-Booth, cf. 'On a Political Prisoner' (*PNE* 196). And in the third verse woman and circumstance unite.

253   COOLE PARK, 1929

273   This poem was completed at Lady Gregory's house, Coole Park, Co. Galway, on 7 September 1928 and first appeared in Lady Gregory, *Coole* (1931). A prose draft of the poem reads:

Describe house in first stanza. Here Synge came, Hugh Lane, Shaw Taylor, many names. I too in my timid youth. Coming and going like migratory birds. Then address the swallows fluttering in their dream like circles. Speak of the rarity of the circumstances that bring together such concords of men. Each man more than himself through whom an unknown life speaks. A circle ever returning into itself.

This is discussed by Parkinson (*YTLP* 80-1), who examines the change from the initial idea to final form.

1   *a swallow's flight*: see note on line 17

2   *an aged woman and her house*: Yeats wrote of Lady Isabella Augusta Gregory (1852-1932), translator and dramatist and co-founder of the Abbey Theatre, in *DP*, that when her husband died she had devoted herself to her estate and her son. She was born a Persse, a family that settled in the Irish midlands in the seventeenth century, but had moved to Galway, where Lady Gregory grew up in Roxborough House beside the road from Gort to Loughrea:

The house contained neither pictures nor furniture of historic interest. The Persses had been soldiers, farmers, riders to hounds and, in the time of the Irish Parliament, politicians; a bridge within the wall commemorated the victory of the Irish Volunteers in 1782, but all had lacked intellectual curiosity until the downfall of their class had all but come. In the latter half of the nineteenth century Lady Gregory was born, an older and a younger sister gave birth to Sir Hugh Lane, and to that John Shawe-Taylor who, by an act of daring I must presently describe, made the settlement of the Land Question possible.   (*A* 392-3)

9   *Hyde*: Dr Douglas Hyde (1860-1949) Irish poet, translator and scholar, was   274
educated at Trinity College Dublin. He succeeded John O'Leary as President of
the Irish National Literary Society. Yeats remarked in *DP* that his presidential
lecture on 'The De-Anglicisation of Ireland' led to the foundation in 1893 of the
Gaelic League, which was, in Yeats's words, 'for many years to substitute for
political argument a Gaelic grammar, and for political meetings village gatherings,
where songs were sung and stories told in the Gaelic language' (*A* 559). Hyde
was the first president of Eire (1938-45) and author of *Love Songs of Connacht*.
He wrote under the Gaelic name 'An Craoibhin Aoibhin', the pleasant little
branch, and lived at French Park, Co. Roscommon. Yeats described him in 1888
as the best of the Irish folklorists: 'His style is perfect – so sincere and simple – so
little literary' (*L* 88). His review of Douglas Hyde's *Beside the Fire* was reprinted
in the first edition of *CT* under the title 'The Four Winds of Desire'.

10   *That noble blade*: see notes on 'At the Abbey Theatre' (*PNE* 106). Yeats
described his style in *DP* in connection with a visit Hyde made to Coole Park in
1899 (Lady Gregory had founded a branch of the Gaelic League in her area):

> His ordinary English style is without charm; he explores facts without
> explaining them, and in the language of the newspapers – Moore compared one
> of his speeches to frothing porter. His Gaelic, like the dialect of his *Love Songs
> of Connacht*, written a couple of years earlier, had charm, seemed all
> spontaneous, all joyous, every speech born out of itself. Had he shared our
> modern preoccupation with the mystery of life, learnt our modern
> construction, he might have grown into another and happier Synge. But
> emotion and imagery came as they would, not as he would; somebody else had
> to put them together. He had the folk mind as no modern man has had it, its
> qualities and its defects, and for a few days in the year Lady Gregory and I
> shared his absorption in that mind. When I wrote verse, five or six lines in two
> or three laborious hours were a day's work, and I longed for somebody to
> interrupt me; but he wrote all day, whether in verse or prose, and without
> apparent effort. Effort was there, but in the unconscious. He had given up verse
> writing because it affected his lungs or his heart. Lady Gregory kept watch, to
> draw him from his table after so many hours; the gamekeeper had the boat and
> the guns ready; there were ducks upon the lake. He wrote in joy and at great
> speed because emotion brought the appropriate word. Nothing in that language
> of his was abstract, nothing worn-out; he need not, as must the writer of some
> language exhausted by modern civilisation, reject word after word, cadence
> after cadence; he had escaped our perpetual, painful, purification. I read him,
> translated by Lady Gregory or by himself into that dialect which gets from
> Gaelic its syntax and keeps its still partly Tudor vocabulary; little was, I think,
> lost.   (*A* 439-40)

10   *The Muses*: see note on 'The Tower' (*PNE* 205).

11   *There one that ruffled in a manly pose*: Yeats himself. Cf. *A* 457. The
'pose' included the quality Castiglione described as *sprezzatura*. Cf. a passage on
courtesy in 'The Cutting of an Agate' where Yeats remarked: 'Even knowledge
is not enough, for the "recklessness" Castiglione thought necessary in good
manners is necessary in this likewise, and if a man has it not he will be gloomy and

had better to his marketing again' (*E & I* 256). See Corinna Salvadori, *Yeats and Castiglione: poet and courtier*, 3 and 12–13.

12   *that slow man*: J. M. Synge, see note on 'In Memory of Major Robert Gregory' (*PNE* 144); cf. the extracts from Yeats's 1909 Diary entitled in published form 'The Death of Synge', and the particular remarks 'For him nothing existed but his thought. . . . He was too confident for self-assertion' (*A* 512)

14   *Impetuous men*: Yeats described John Shawe-Taylor, Lady Gregory's nephew (1866–1911) in an essay:

There is a portrait of John Shawe-Taylor by a celebrated painter in the Dublin Municipal Gallery, but, painted in the midst of a movement of the arts that exalts characteristics above the more typical qualities, it does not show us that beautiful and gracious nature. There is an exaggeration of the hollows of the cheeks and of the form of the bones which empties the face of the balance and delicacy of its lines. He was a very handsome man, as women who have imagination and tradition understand those words, and had he not been so, mind and character had been different. There are certain men, certain famous commanders of antiquity, for instance, of whose good looks the historian always speaks, and whose good looks are the image of their faculty; and these men, copying hawk or leopard, have an energy of swift decision, a power of sudden action, as if their whole body were their brain.

A few years ago he was returning from America, and the liner reached Queenstown in a storm so great that the tender that came out to it for passengers returned with only one man. It was John Shawe-Taylor, who had leaped as it was swept away from the ship.

The achievement that has made his name historic and changed the history of Ireland came from the same faculty of calculation and daring, from that instant decision of the hawk, between the movement of whose wings and the perception of whose eye no time passes capable of division. A proposal for a Land Conference had been made, and cleverer men than he were but talking the life out of it. Every argument for and against had been debated over and over, and it was plain that nothing but argument would come of it. One day we found a letter in the daily papers, signed with his name, saying that a conference would be held on a certain date, and that certain leaders of the landlords and of the tenants were invited. He had made his swift calculation, probably he could not have told the reason for it: a decision had arisen out of his instinct. He was then almost an unknown man. Had the letter failed, he would have seemed a crack-brained fool to his life's end; but the calculation of his genius was justified. He had, as men of his type have often, given an expression to the hidden popular desires; and the expression of the hidden is the daring of the mind. When he had spoken, so many others spoke that the thing was taken out of the mouths of the leaders; it was as though some power deeper than our daily thought had spoken, and men recognised that common instinct, that common sense which is genius. Men like him live near this power because of something simple and impersonal within them which is, as I believe, imaged in the fire of their minds, as in the shape of their bodies and their faces.

I do not think I have known another man whose motives were so entirely pure, so entirely unmixed with any personal calculation, whether of ambition, of prudence or of vanity. He caught up into his imagination the public gain as other men their private gain. For much of his life he had seemed, though a good soldier and a good shot, and a good rider to hounds, to care deeply for nothing but religion, and this religion, so curiously lacking in denominational limits, concerned itself alone with the communion of the soul with God. Such men, before some great decision, will sometimes give to the analysis of their own motive the energy that other men give to the examination of the circumstances wherein they act, and it is often those who attain in this way to purity of motive who act most wisely at moments of great crisis. It is as though they sank a well through the soil where our habits have been built, and where our hopes take root or lie uprooted, to the lasting rock and to the living stream. They are those for whom Tennyson claimed the strength of ten, and the common and clever wonder at their simplicity and at a triumph that has always an air of miracle. (*E & I* 343-5)

There is a good brief account of his life in Torchiana (*Y & GI* 44-57).

Sir Hugh Lane (1875-1915), another nephew of Lady Gregory. See notes on 'To a Wealthy Man who promised a second Subscription to the Dublin Municipal Gallery if it were proved the People wanted Pictures' (*PNE* 114).

17 *like swallows*: this stanza has some points in common with a passage in Pythagoras who wrote:

> Receive not a swallow into your house. Explanation – This symbol admonishes as follows: Do not admit to your dogmas a man who is indolent, who does not labour incessantly, and who is not a firm adherent to the Pythagorean sect and endued with intelligence; for these dogmas require continued and most strenuous attention, and an endurance of labour through the mutation and circumvolition of the various disciplines which they contain. But it uses the swallow as an image of indolence and an interruption of time, because this bird visits us for a certain part of the year, and for a short time, becomes as it were our guest; but leaves us for the greater part of the year and is not seen by us. (G. R. S. Mead, *The Golden Verses of Pythagoras and Other Pythagorean fragments*, 72)

18 *a woman's powerful character*: Yeats wrote that:

> She knew Ireland always in its permanent relationships, associations – violence but a brief interruption –, never lost her sense of feudal responsibility, not of duty as the word is generally understood, but of burdens laid upon her by her station and her character, a choice constantly renewed in solitude. 'She has been', said an old man to me, 'like a serving-maid among us. She is plain and simple, like the Mother of God, and that was the greatest lady that ever lived.' When in later years her literary style became in my ears the best written by woman, she had made the people a part of her soul; a phrase of Aristotle's had become her motto: 'To think like a wise man, but to express oneself like the common people'. (*A* 395)

26 *those rooms and passages are gone*: the Forestry Department took over the house, garden, fields and woods during Lady Gregory's lifetime: she then rented the house from the Department which sold the house after her death. The purchaser pulled it down.

275   This poem was written in February 1931 and first appeared in *WMP*.

1   *my window ledge*: at Thoor Ballylee. See Yeats's notes to *The Tower* (*CP* 532, 534).

4   *'dark' Raftery's 'cellar'*: Raftery (1784–1835) blind (hence 'dark') Irish poet. See notes on 'The Tower' II (*PNE* 205). The limestone is porous and there are several underground rivers in the area. Cf. Lady Gregory's description in *Coole*, quoted in notes on 'The Wild Swans at Coole' (*PNE* 143). The river forms the 'cellar' (*Irish* an soilear), a swallow-hole, not far from the tower.

8   *the generated soul?*: In 'Earth, Fire and Water' Yeats wrote: 'Did not the wise Porphyry think that all souls come to be born because of water, and that "even the generation of images in the mind is from water"?' (*M* 80). Elsewhere he wrote: 'I think it was Porphyry who wrote that the generation of images in the mind is from water.' The Neoplatonics used water as a symbol of generation, and the passage Yeats had in mind was probably the following:

> For in consequence of containing perpetually-flowing streams of water, it will not be a symbol of an intelligible hypostasis, but of a material essence. On this account also it is sacred to Nymphs, not the mountain *or rural Nymphs*, or others of the like kind, but to the Naiades, who are thus denominated from streams of water. For we peculiarly call the Naiades, and the powers that preside over waters, Nymphs; and this term also is commonly applied to all souls descending into generation. For the ancients thought that these souls are incumbent on water which is inspired by divinity, as Numenius says, who adds, that on this account, a prophet asserts, that the Spirit of God moved on the waters. The Egyptians likewise, on this account, represent all dæmons and also the sun, and, in short, all the planets . . . not standing on anything solid, but on a sailing vessel; for souls descending into generation fly to moisture. Hence also, Heraclitus says, 'that moisture appears delightful and not deadly to souls'; but the lapse into generation is delightful to them. And in another place (speaking of unembodied souls), he says, 'We live their death, and we die their life.' Hence the poet calls those that are in generation *humid*, because they have souls which are *profoundly* steeped in moisture. . . . But pure souls are averse from generation; so that, as Heraclitus says, '*a dry soul is the wisest.*' Hence, here also the spirit becomes moist and more aqueous through the desire of generation, the soul thus attracting a humid vapour from verging to generation. Souls, therefore, proceeding into generation are the nymphs called naiades. Hence it is usual to call those that are married nymphs, as being conjoined to generation, and to pour water into baths from fountains, or rivers, or perpetual rills.   (Porphyry, *On the Cave of the Nymphs* 15–18)

14   *mounting swan*: in a letter to Mrs Yeats written on 3 February 1932 Yeats told her 'I am turning the introductory verses to Lady Gregory's 'Coole' (Cuala) into a poem of some length – various sections with more or less symbolic matter. Yesterday I wrote an account of the sudden ascent of a swan – a symbol of inspiration I think' (*WBY* 425).

24　*murdered with a spot of ink*: in 'The Irish Dramatic Movement' Yeats　*276*
wrote 'Did not M. Tribulat Bonhomet discover that one spot of ink would kill a
swan?' (*E* 90). Henn (*LT* 138) comments that the allusion must be to Villiers de
l'Isle-Adam's satiric novel *M. Triboulat Bonhomet* (1887), in which Dr
Bonhomet is a hunter of swans.

16　*somebody that toils from chair to chair*: Lady Gregory

27-28　*Beloved books that famous hands have bound,*
　　　Old marble heads, old pictures everywhere: the house was described by
Lady Gregory in *Coole* and Yeats himself described it in *DP*:

A glimpse of a long vista of trees, over an undergrowth of clipped laurels, seen
for a moment as the outside car approached her house on my first visit, is a
vivid memory. Coole House, though it has lost the great park full of ancient
trees, is still set in the midst of a thick wood, which spreads out behind the
house in two directions, in one along the edges of a lake which, as there is no
escape for its water except a narrow subterranean passage, doubles or trebles its
size in winter. In later years I was to know the edges of that lake better than any
spot on earth, to know it in all the changes of the seasons, to find there always
some new beauty. Wondering at myself, I remember that when I first saw that
house I was so full of the mediaevalism of William Morris that I did not like the
gold frames, some deep and full of ornament, round the pictures in the drawing-
room; years were to pass before I came to understand the earlier nineteenth and
later eighteenth century, and to love that house more than all other houses.
Every generation had left its memorial; every generation had been highly
educated; eldest sons had gone the grand tour, returning with statues or
pictures; Mogul or Persian paintings had been brought from the Far East by a
Gregory chairman of the East India Company, great earthenware ewers and
basins, great silver bowls, by Lady Gregory's husband, a famous Governor of
Ceylon, who had married in old age, and was now some seven years dead; but of
all those Gregorys, the least distinguished, judged by accepted standards, most
roused my interest – a Richard who at the close of the eighteenth century was a
popular brilliant officer in the Guards. He was accused of pleading ill-health to
escape active service, and though exonerated by some official inquiry, resigned
his commission, gave up London and his friends. He made the acquaintance of
a school-girl, carried her off, put her into a little house in Coole demesne,
afterwards the steward's house, where she lived disguised as a boy until his
father died. They married, and at the end of last century the people still kept the
memory of her kindness and her charity. One of the latest planted of the woods
bore her name, and is, I hope, still called, now that the Government Foresters
are in possession, 'The Isabella Wood'. While compelled to live in boy's clothes
she had called herself 'Jack the Sailor' from a song of Dibdin's. Richard had
brought in bullock-carts through Italy the marble copy of the Venus de' Medici
in the drawing-room, added to the library the Greek and Roman Classics bound
by famous French and English binders, substituted for the old straight avenue
two great sweeping avenues each a mile or a little more in length. Was it he or
his father who had possessed the Arab horses, painted by Stubbs? It was
perhaps Lady Gregory's husband, a Trustee of the English National Gallery,
who had bought the greater number of the pictures. Those that I keep most in
memory are a Canaletto, a Guardi, a Zurbarán. Two or three that once hung

there had, before I saw those great rooms, gone to the National Gallery, and the fine portraits by Augustus John and Charles Shannon were still to come. The mezzotints and engravings of the masters and friends of the old Gregorys that hung round the small downstairs breakfast-room, Pitt, Fox, Lord Wellesley, Palmerston, Gladstone, many that I have forgotten, had increased generation by generation, and amongst them Lady Gregory had hung a letter from Burke to the Gregory that was chairman of the East India Company saying that he committed to his care, now that he himself had grown old, the people of India. In the hall, or at one's right hand as one ascended the stairs, hung Persian helmets, Indian shields, Indian swords in elaborate sheaths, stuffed birds from various parts of the world, shot by whom nobody could remember, portraits of the members of Grillion's Club, illuminated addresses presented in Ceylon or Galway, signed photographs or engravings of Tennyson, Mark Twain, Browning, Thackeray, at a later date paintings of Galway scenery by Sir Richard Burton, bequeathed at his death, and etchings by Augustus John. I can remember somebody saying: 'Balzac would have given twenty pages to the stairs'. The house itself was plain and box-like, except on the side towards the lake, where somebody, probably Richard Gregory, had enlarged the drawing-room and dining-room with great bow windows. Edward Martyn's burnt house had been like it doubtless, for it was into such houses men moved, when it was safe to leave their castles, or the thatched cottages under castle walls; architecture did not return until the cut stone Georgian houses of a later date. (*A* 388-91)

30   *a last inheritor*: her only child Robert was killed in Italy. See notes on 'In Memory of Major Robert Gregory' (*PNE* 144). When Lady Gregory sold Coole to the Irish Land Commission and Department of Forestry in 1927 she wrote in her Diary that it

no longer belongs to anyone of our family or name, I am thankful to have been able to keep back a sale for these years past, for giving it into the hands of the Forestry people makes the maintenance of the woods secure and will give employment and be for the good and dignity of the country. As to the house I will stay and keep it as the children's home as long as I keep strength enough and can earn money enough. It had a good name before I came here, its owners were of good, even of high repute; and that has been continued, has increased, in Robert's time and mine. Perhaps some day one of the children may care enough for it to come back; they have been happy here. (*Lady Gregory's Journals*, ed. Lennox Robinson (1946) 39)

31   *none has reigned*: cf. Yeats's lines in the play *Purgatory*:

Great people lived and died in this house;
Magistrates, colonels, members of Parliament,
Captains and Governors, and long ago
Men that fought at Aughrim and the Boyne.   (*CPl* 683)

40   *some poor Arab tribesman*: Yeats had read Doughty's *Arabia Deserta*, but the image may derive from Shelley, cf. note on 'Ego Dominus Tuus' (*PNE* 181) and its 'Bedouin's horse-hair roof'.

41   *the last romantics*: cf. stanza VI of 'The Municipal Gallery Revisited' (*PNE* 354)

43-4   *poets name/The book of the people*: Ian Fletcher 'Coole Park and Lady Gregory', *W. B. Yeats. Images of a Poet* (1961) 28, points out that Raftery (see note on 'The Tower' (*PNE* 205)) used the phrase. Lady Gregory, *Poets and Dreamers* (1903; 5th edn, 1974) 27, alludes to 'the truths of God that he [Raftery] strove in his last years, as he says, to have written in the book of the people'.

46   *that high horse*: Pegasus. Cf. note on 'The Fascination of What's Difficult' (*PNE* 99).

FOR ANNE GREGORY   255

This poem was written in September 1930 and first appeared in *WMP*.   277

Title   *Anne Gregory*: Anne Gregory (*b.* 1911) was Lady Gregory's grandchild.

SWIFT'S EPITAPH   256

This poem was first drafted at Coole in 1929 and completed in September 1930.   277
It first appeared in *DM* (Oct.–Dec. 1931).

   The Latin epitaph in St Patrick's Cathedral, Dublin, where Swift is buried, reads:

> *Hic* depositum est Corpus
> IONATHAN SWIFT S.T.D.
> Hujus Ecclesiæ Cathedralis
> Decani,
> *Ubi* saeva Indignatio
> Ulterius
> Cor lacerare nequit.
> Abi Viator
> Et imitare, si poteris,
> Strenuum pro virili
> Libertatis Vindicatorem
> Obiit 19° Die Mensis Octobris
> A.D. 1745 Anno Aetatis 78.

See J. V. Luce, 'A note on the composition of Swift's epitaph', *Hermathena*, CIV (Spring 1967) 78-81. 'World-besotted' is Yeats's importation.
   Cf. lines 19-20 'Blood and the Moon', II (*PNE* 243).

257   AT ALGECIRAS - A MEDITATION UPON DEATH

278   This poem was written at Algeciras when Yeats was staying at the Hotel Reina Cristina during November 1928; it first appeared in *A Packet for Ezra Pound* (1929) dated 4 February 1929 (Ellmann dated it 23 January 1929 (*IY* 291)) and it is dated November 1928 in *CP*. The title given it in *WMP* was 'A Meditation written during Summers at Algeciras'. Algeciras is in southern Spain.

1   *the heron-billed pale cattle-birds*: Yeats watched the birds flying in to roost near the hotel.

3   *Moroccan*: Morocco in North Africa, on the southern side of the straits of Gibraltar

11   *Newton's metaphor*: Sir Isaac Newton's (1642-1717) words were:

I do not know how I may appear to the world; but to myself I seem to have been only like a boy, playing on the seashore, and diverting myself, in now and then finding another pebble or prettier shell than ordinary, while the great ocean of truth lay all undiscovered before me. (David Brewster, *Memories . . . of Sir Isaac Newton* (1855), II, 407)

12   *Rosses' level shore*: district near Sligo. Cf. lines 14-15 of 'The Stolen Child' (*PNE* 10).

16   *Great Questioner*: God. Yeats had been very seriously ill in October 1928. A cold developed into congestion of the lungs and he had been sent to Spain in search of sunshine.

258   THE CHOICE

278   This poem was probably written in February 1931 (it was originally the penultimate stanza of 'Coole Park and Ballylee 1931' (*PNE* 254)).

259   MOHINI CHATTERJEE

279   This poem is incorrectly dated 1928 in *CP*. Yeats wrote it between 23 January and 9 February 1929, and it first appeared in *A Packet for Ezra Pound* (1929).

Title   Mohini Chatterjee: he was a Bengali Brahmin whom Yeats and his friends in the Hermetic Society invited to come to Dublin to lecture to them in 1885 or 1886: 'It was my first meeting with a philosophy that confirmed my vague speculations and seemed at once logical and boundless' (*A* 91-2). Cf. *CW*, VIII, 279.

1   *if I should pray*: Yeats wrote a note in which he recounted how someone had asked Mohini Chatterjee, a Bengali Brahmin (1858–1936), if we should pray:

> but even prayer was too full of hope, of desire, of life, to have any part in that acquiescence that was his beginning of wisdom, and he answered that one should say, before sleeping: 'I have lived many lives, I have been a slave and a prince. Many a beloved has sat upon my knees, and I have sat upon the knees of many a beloved. Everything that has been shall be again.' Beautiful words that I spoilt once by turning them into clumsy verse.

The lines were in 'Kanva on Himself'

> Hast thou not sat of yore upon the knees
> Of myriads of beloveds, and on thine
> Have not a myriad swayed below strange trees
> In other lives? Hast thou not quaffed old wine
> By tables that were fallen into dust
> Ere yonder palm commenced his thousand years.   (*WO*)

Hone commented that the Brahmin had been one of the earliest members of the Theosophical Society in India and taught that everything we perceive exists in the external world; this is a stream which is out of human control, and we are but a mirror, and our deliverance consists in turning the mirror away so that it reflects nothing. He quoted Yeats's lines written out of satisfaction with this philosophy:

> Long thou for nothing, neither sad nor gay.
> Long thou for nothing, neither night nor day,
> Not even, 'I long to see thy longing over,'
> To the ever longing and mournful spirit say.   (*WBY* 48)

17   *Old lovers yet may have*: this is similar to the idea in 'Broken Dreams' (*PNE* 167):

> Vague memories, nothing but memories,
> But in the grave all, all, shall be renewed.

24   *cannonade*: this echoes the imagery of 'King and no King' (*PNE* 96).   *280*

BYZANTIUM   **260**

This poem was written in September 1930 and first appeared in *WMP*.   *280*

'Then ill again', Yeats wrote in the Notes to *CP*, 'I warmed myself back into life with "Byzantium" and "Veronica's Napkin", looking for a theme that might befit my years.' He had had Malta fever in the autumn of 1929 at Rapallo.

The prose draft of 'Byzantium' contained in Yeats's 1930 *Diary* ran:

> Subject for a poem. Death of a friend. . . . Describe Byzantium as it is in the system towards the end of the first Christian millennium. A walking mummy. Flames at the street corners where the soul is purified, birds of hammered gold singing in the golden trees, in the harbour [dolphins] offering their backs to the wailing dead that they may carry them to Paradise.

These subjects have been in my head for some time, especially the last. (*E* 290)

Yeats's view of Byzantium is also given in *A V*:

> I think that if I could be given a month of Antiquity and leave to spend it where I chose, I would spend it in Byzantium, a little before Justinian opened St Sophia and closed the Academy of Plato. I think I could find in some little wine-shop some philosophical worker in mosaic who could answer all my questions, the supernatural descending nearer to him than to Plotinus even, for the pride of his delicate skill would make what was an instrument of power to princes and clerics, a murderous madness in the mob, show as a lovely flexible presence like that of a perfect human body.
>
> I think that in early Byzantium, and maybe never before or since in recorded history, religious, aesthetic and practical life were one, that architect and artificers – though not, it may be, poets, for language had been the instrument of controversy and must have grown abstract – spoke to the multitude and the few alike. The painter, the mosaic worker, the worker in gold and silver, the illuminator of sacred books, were almost impersonal, almost perhaps without the consciousness of individual design, absorbed in their subject-matter and that the vision of a whole people. They could copy out of old Gospel books those pictures that seemed as sacred as the text, and yet weave all into a vast design, the work of many that seemed the work of one, that made building, picture, pattern, metal-work of rail and lamp, seem but a single image; and this vision, this proclamation of their invisible master, had the Greek nobility, Satan always the still half-divine Serpent, never the horned scarecrow of the didactic Middle Ages. (*A V*(B) 279)

See note on 'Sailing to Byzantium' (*PNE* 204) for continuation of this quotation.

In 'Modern Ireland' *Massachusetts Review* (Winter 1964), Yeats cancelled this passage, formerly in the MS.:

> In my later poems I have called it Byzantium ['it' was 'an example of magnificence: and style, whether in literature or life, comes, I think, from excess, from that something over and above utility, which wrings the heart'], that city where the Saints showed their wasted forms upon a background of gold mosaic, and an artificial bird sang upon a tree of gold in the presence of the Emperor; and in one poem I have pictured the ghosts swimming, mounted upon dolphins, through the sensual seas, that they may dance upon its pavements.

On 16 April 1930 T. Sturge Moore wrote to Yeats that 'Sailing to Byzantium' had let him down in the fourth stanza 'as such a goldsmith's bird is as much nature as a man's body, especially if it only sings like Homer and Shakespeare of what is past or passing or to come to Lords and Ladies' (*Y & TSM* 162). On 4 October Yeats wrote to Sturge Moore to tell him that 'Byzantium' originated from his criticism of 'Sailing to Byzantium' which had showed Yeats 'that the idea needed exposition'. (*Y & TSM* 164)

1–8   *The unpurged images of day recede;*
       The Emperor's drunken soldiery are abed;
       Night resonance recedes, night-walkers' song
       After great cathedral gong;

> *A starlit or a moonlit dome disdains*
> *All that man is,*
> *All mere complexities,*
> *The fury and the mire of human veins*: the first stanza describes what
Stallworthy has called 'the whole, complicated, physical world'; he has suggested
that Blake's poem 'London' was in Yeats's mind:

> the hapless soldier's sigh
> Runs in blood down palace walls.
>
> But most through midnight streets I hear
> How the youthful harlot's curse
> Blasts the new born infant's tear.

Edward Engelberg, *The Vast Design* (1964), 147-8, considers the first two
sections of 'Byzantium' echo Dante, *Purgatorio*, VIII, 1-12. For other similarities
between 'Byzantium' and Dante's *Purgatorio* see F. N. Lees, 'Yeats's
"Byzantium", Dante and Shelley', *Notes & Queries* (July 1957), 312-13.

4   *cathedral gong*: Yeats pencilled the word 'gong' in the margin of p. 110 of
W. G. Holmes, *The Age of Justinian and Theodora*, opposite this description:
'At the boom of the great *semantron*, a sonorous board suspended in the porch of
each church, and beaten with mallets by a deacon.' Wilson regards the gong as
being a warning sign, an intimation of the nearness of death (*Y & T* 232-3).

5   *A starlit or a moonlit dome*: the dome of Santa Sophia or Haga Sophia, the
church that the Emperor Justinian I (483-565; ruled 527-565) had constructed
(532-7) in Byzantium

9   *an image, man or shade*: in Yeats's note on his play *The Dreaming of the
Bones* he wrote of

> the world wide belief that the dead dream back for a certain time, through the
> more personal thoughts and deeds of life. The wicked, according to Cornelius
> Agrippa, dream themselves to be consumed by flames and persecuted by
> demons. . . . The Shade is said to fade out at last, but the Spiritual Being does
> not fade, passing on to other states of existence after it has attained a spiritual
> state, of which the surroundings and aptitudes of early life are a
> correspondence.   (*Four Plays for Dancers* (1921), 77-8)

There is a passage in 'Anima Mundi' which deals with the soul's capacity to
mould the body to any shape:

> All souls have a vehicle or body, and when one has said that with More and
> the Platonists one has escaped from the abstract schools who seek always the
> power of some Church or institution, and found oneself with great poetry, and
> superstition which is but popular poetry, in a pleasant, dangerous world.
> Beauty is indeed but bodily life in some ideal condition. The vehicle of the
> human soul is what used to be called the animal spirits, and Henry More quotes
> from Hippocrates this sentence: 'The mind of man is . . . not nourished from
> meats and drinks from the belly, but by a clear luminous substance that
> redounds by separation from the blood.' These animal spirits fill up all parts of

295

the body and make up the body of air, as certain writers of the seventeenth century have called it. The soul has a plastic power, and can after death, or during life, should the vehicle leave the body for a while, mould it to any shape it will by an act of imagination, though the more unlike to the habitual that shape is, the greater the effort. To living and dead alike, the purity and abundance of the animal spirits are a chief power. The soul can mould from these an apparition clothed as if in life, and make it visible by showing it to our mind's eye, or by building into its substance certain particles drawn from the body of a medium till it is as visible and tangible as any other object. To help that building the ancients offered sheaves of corn, fragrant gum, and the odour of fruit and flowers, and the blood of victims. The half-materialised vehicle slowly exudes from the skin in dull luminous drops or condenses from a luminous cloud, the light fading as weight and density increase. The witch, going beyond the medium, offered to the slowly animating phantom certain drops of her blood. The vehicle once separate from the living man or woman may be moulded by the souls of others as readily as by its own soul, and even, it seems, by the souls of the living. It becomes a part for a while of that stream of images which I have compared to reflections upon water. But how does it follow that souls who never have handled the modelling tool or the brush make perfect images? Those materialisations who imprint their powerful faces upon paraffin wax, leave there sculpture that would have taken a good artist, making and imagining, many hours. How did it follow that an ignorant woman could, as Henry More believed, project her vehicle in so good a likeness of a hare that horse and hound and huntsman followed with the bugle blowing? Is not the problem the same as of those finely articulated scenes and patterns that come out of the dark, seemingly completed in the winking of an eye, as we are lying half asleep, and of all those elaborate images that drift in moments of inspiration or evocation before the mind's eye? Our animal spirits or vehicles are but, as it were, a condensation of the vehicle of *Anima Mundi*, and give substance to its images in the faint materialisation of our common thought, or more grossly when a ghost is our visitor.   (*M* 348–50)

11   *Hades' bobbin*: probably taken from Plato's mythology in the myth of Er (see *The Republic* (trans. Davies and Vaughan) § 620). Cf. 'His Bargain' (*PNE* 281) where the 'spindle' probably has the same source. G. R. S. Mead compares the soul to a spindle (*Echoes from the Gnosis*, 18). Yeats's draft suggests 'Hades' bobbin' is a spirit. Hades (or Pluto) was lord of the underworld, the realm of the dead.

13   *A mouth that has no moisture and no breath*: cf. Yeats's comment in *WWP*:

The Indian ascetic passing into his death-like trance knows that if his mind is not pure, if there is anything there but the symbol of his God, some passion, ambition, desire, or phantasy will confer upon him its shape or purpose, for he is entering upon a state where thought and existence are the same. One remembers those witches described by Glanvil who course the field in the likeness of hares while their bodies lie at home, and certain mediumistic phenomena. The ascetic would say, did we question him, that the unpurified dead are subject to transformation that would be similar were it not that in their case no physical body remains in cave or bed or chair, all is transformed. They examine their past if undisturbed by our importunity, tracing events to their source, and as they take the form their thought suggests, seems to live backward through time; or if incapable of such examination, creatures not of thought but of feeling, renew as shades certain detached events of their past lives, taking the greater excitements first. When Achilles came to the edge of the blood-pool (an ancient substitute for the medium) he was such a shade. Tradition affirms that, deprived of the living present by death, they can create nothing, or, in the Indian phrase, can originate no new Karma. Their aim, like that of the ascetic in meditation, is to enter at last into their own archetype, or into all being: into that which is there always. They are not, however, the personalities which haunt the séance-room: these when they speak from, or imply, supernormal knowledge, when they are more than transformations of the medium, are, as it were, new beings begotten by spirit upon medium to live short but veritable lives, whereas the secondary personalities resemble those eggs brought forth without the assistance of the male bird. They, within their narrow limits, create; they speak truth when they repeat some message suggested by the past lives of the spirit, remembered like some prenatal memory, or when, though such instances must be few, begotten by some spirit obedient to its source, or, as we might say, blessed; but when they neither repeat such message nor were so begotten they may justify passages in Swedenborg that denounce them as the newspapers denounce cheating mediums, seeing that they find but little check in their fragmentary knowledge or vague conscience.

> Let images of basalt, black, immovable,
> Chiselled in Egypt, or ovoids of bright steel
> Hammered and polished by Brancusi's hand,
> Represent spirits. If spirits seem to stand
> Before the bodily eyes, speak into the bodily ears,
> They are not present but their messengers.
> Of double nature these, one nature is
> Compounded of accidental phantasies.
> We question; it but answers what we would
> Or as phantasy directs – because they have drunk the blood.   (*E* 366-7)

Wilson (*Y & T* 237) remarks that these lines refer indirectly to Tiresias, Homer's summoner of the shades.

16   *death-in-life*: Stallworthy (*BL* 121) regards this stanza as growing round the nucleus of a Coleridgean image:

> The Nightmare Life-in-Death was she,
> Who thicks man's blood with cold.

And see Denis Donoghue, 'An honoured guest on "The Winding Stair" ' (*HG* 116), who quotes the sentence in *The Resurrection* spoken by the Greek student of Heracleitus: 'God and man die each other's life, live each other's death.' He argues that Heracleitus vouched for the superhuman element of the image.

17   *Miracle, bird or golden handiwork*: see notes on lines 27-32 'Sailing to Byzantium' (*PNE* 204). The bird may have more symbolical meanings; it might be related to the 'one white fowl wearing a crown' on the highest bough of the

Tree of Life which was seen by a young Irishwoman in trance. See 'Magic' (*E & I*
44-5). Kermode distinguishes between the birds in 'Sailing to Byzantium' and
that in this poem.   (*RI* 87)

281   20   *like the cocks of Hades*: cf. a passage in 'The Adoration of the Magi' where
the second of the three old men crowed like a cock and the youngest of them
assumed a devil had gone into him. But the voice is that of Hermes, the Shepherd
of the Dead (*M* 311-312). Cf. the cockerel in 'Solomon and the Witch' (*PNE*
190). Ellmann (*IY* 220) remarks that Yeats is here distinguishing between birds
that sing the common strain of the continuing cycle of human lives and those that
scorn the cycle and sing only of escape from it.

25   *the Emperor's pavement*: this is probably derived from W. G. Holmes, *The
Age of Justinian and Theodora*, 69. Yeats marked this passage in his copy: 'We
. . . arrive at the Forum of Constantine, which presents itself as an expansion of
the Mese. This open space, the most signal ornament of Constantinople, is called
prescriptively the Forum; and sometimes from its finished marble floor ''The
Pavement''.'

25-6   *flit Flames*: cf. 'Anima Mundi' where Yeats describes ghosts held by
memories (*M* 354-7) as well as their being refashioned, and the description of the
dead 'dreaming back' through their lives in the notes to *The Dreaming of the
Bones* (*Four Plays for Dancers*, 1921).

28   *blood-begotten spirits*: Gwendolen Murphy described them as human ghosts
(*The Modern Poet*, 153) and Ellmann (*IY* 221-2) remarked that they have to be
immortalised by fire, quoting notes Yeats made for *AV* two years before writing
'Byzantium':

> At first we are subject to Destiny . . . but the point in the Zodiac where the
> whirl becomes a sphere once reached, we may escape from the constraint of our
> nature and from that of external things, entering upon a state where all fuel has
> become flame, where there is nothing but the state itself, nothing to constrain it
> or end it. We attain it always in the creation or enjoyment of a work of art, but
> that moment though eternal in the Daimon passes from us because it is not an
> attainment of our whole being . . .

29   *complexities of fury leave*: after purgation. Cf. prose passages referred to in
notes on lines 25-6.

33   *the dolphin's mire and blood*: cf. Mrs Strong, *Apotheosis and the After Life*,
153, 195, 266. She comments that the dolphin is an 'emblem of the soul or its
transit', and states 'The dead man – or his soul – might be conveyed thither by
boat, or on the back of a sea monster, a dolphin, sea-horse or triton.' The dolphins
form 'a mystic escort of the dead' to the Islands of the Blest (p. 219). See notes on
'News for the Delphic Oracle' (*PNE* 363).

34   *The smithies*: these are derived from W. G. Holmes, *The Age of Justinian
and Theodora*, 69.

36 *Marbles of the dancing floor*: see note on line 25

38 *images*: cf. a section of 'Hodos Chameliontos' (*A* 272-4)

THE MOTHER OF GOD   **261**

This poem was written on 3 September 1931 and finally revised on 12 September   *281*
1931, and first appeared in *WMP*.

1 *a fallen flare*: Yeats's note reads:

> In 'The Mother of God' the words 'A fallen flare through the hollow of an ear'
> are, I am told, obscure. I had in my memory Byzantine mosaic pictures of the
> Annunciation, which show a line drawn from a star to the ear of the Virgin.
> She received the word through the ear, a star fell, and a star was born.

Henn (*LT* 258) suggests as sources Blake's tempera drawing 'Annunciation',
in which Gabriel stands with massive eagle wings on the left of the picture, and
Charles Ricketts's drawing 'Eros leaving Psyche', in which the departing winged
God stands beside the bed and the naked Psyche clutches at his feet.

5 *The Heavens in my womb*: Raymond Lister, 'Beulah to Byzantium. . .' II,
Dolmen Press Yeats Centenary Papers (1965), suggests that a likely source for
this image could have been the Krishna legend that tells of Krishna, when a small
boy, eating some dirt and being scolded by his foster mother Yasoda. She ordered
him to open his mouth and looked inside to see the whole universe. He refers to
W. G. Archer, *The Loves of Krishna* (1957) 32.

15 *my hair stand up*: cf. the lines in *The Herne's Egg*:   *282*

> When beak and claw their work begin
> Shall horror stir in the roots of my hair?
> *Sang the bride of the Herne, and the great Herne's bride*   (*CPl* 664-5)

VACILLATION   **262**

This poem was written in 1931 and 1932. Section I was written in December   *282*
1931. In a letter to Olivia Shakespear of 15 December 1931 Yeats alludes to his
having begun 'a longish poem called "Wisdom" in the attempt to shake off
"Crazy Jane", and I begin to think I shall take to religion unless you save me
from it' (*L* 788). It first appeared in *WMP*. The titles of the sections in the first
printing were: I What is Joy; II The Burning Tree (this included the stanzas
numbered II and III in subsequent printings); III (IV subsequently) Happiness; IV (V
subsequently) Conscience; V (VI subsequently) Conquerors; VI (VII subsequently)
A Dialogue; VII (VIII subsequently) Von Hügel. The subsequent arrangement first
appeared in *WS*. The writing of the poem is discussed by Curtis Bradford (*Yeats at*

Work, 128-34); Ellmann (*IY* 268-74); Jeffares (*Y:M & P* 272-3); and Parkinson (*YTLP*, 220-8).

Section IV was written in November 1931 and Section VI between January and 5 March 1932, see Ellmann (*IY* 292); Section VII was written on 3 and 4 January 1932 and Section VII on 3 January 1932 (*L* 789-90).

I

282   This stanza was enclosed in a letter to Olivia Shakespear written in November 1931 (postmark, 23 November; letter dated 'Last Sunday', but there was another that month) a paragraph of which described the subject of the poem:

> The night before letters came I went for a walk after dark and there among some great trees became absorbed in the most lofty philosophical conception I have found while writing *A Vision*. I suddenly seemed to understand at last and then I smelt roses. I now realised the nature of the timeless spirit. Then I began to walk and with my excitement came – how shall I say? – that old glow so beautiful with its autumnal tint. The longing to touch it was almost unendurable. The next night I was walking in the same path and now the two excitements came together. The autumnal image, remote, incredibly spiritual, erect, delicate featured, and mixed with it the violent physical image, the black mass of Eden. Yesterday I put my thoughts into a poem which I enclose, but it seems to me a poor shadow of the intensity of the experience. (*L* 785. Wade's footnote is, I think, incorrect)

1   *extremities*: this opening section owes much to Blake's theory of contraries (with which Yeats dealt in the 1893 edition of Blake) and probably to Boehme also. The following passage in Yeats's copy of Denis Saurat, *Blake and Modern Thought* received a pencilled comment:

> Without contraries there is no progression. Attraction and Repulsion, Love and Hate, are necessary to Human existence. From these contraries spring what the religious call Good and Evil. Good is the passive that obeys Reason. Evil is the active springing from Energy. Good is Heaven – Evil is Hell.

Yeats's comment was: 'I think there was no such thought known in England in Blake's day. It is fundamental in Blake.' For the occurrence of the idea in Boehme see H. L. Martensen, *Jacob Boehme: His Life and Teaching*, 77.

II

11   *A tree there is*: this is a tree described in *The Mabinogion*, which Yeats mentioned in an essay 'The Celtic Element in Literature':

> . . . our 'natural magic' is but the ancient religion of the world, the ancient worship of Nature and that troubled ecstasy before her, that certainty of all beautiful places being haunted, which it brought into men's minds. The ancient religion is in that passage of the *Mabinogion* about the making of 'Flower Aspect' . . . and one finds it in the not less beautiful passage about the burning tree, that has half its beauty from calling up a fancy of leaves so living and beautiful, they can be of no less living and beautiful a thing than flame:

'They saw a tall tree by the side of the river, one half of which was in flames from the root to the top, and the other half was green and in full leaf'. (*E & I* 176)

(The quotation is from Lady Charlotte Guest, *The Mabinogion, translated from the Red Book of Hergest* (1877), 86. The passage is marked in Yeats's copy.)

16 *he that Attis' image hangs*: in the procession at the festival of Attis the priest used to hang the god's image on the sacred pine tree. Ellmann (*IY* 172) suggests that Yeats identifies the poet with the priest, himself castrated like the god (Attis was a vegetation god who castrated himself when Cybele, the earth mother, drove him to frenzy, and his devotees castrated themselves at his March festival) because he conceived of the artist as forced to sacrifice his life for the sake of his art: 'For its sake he becomes one with Attis and in this union, which is also the union of body and soul, he experiences the ecstasy of seeing beyond the cross or gyres into the rose or sphere of things.' The devotee hanging the image of Attis between the body and soul of the tree rejects normal experiences but knows, according to Ellmann, 'the ecstatic state of non-grief which may be called joy'. Yeats obtained his main knowledge of the Attis ritual from Sir James Frazer's *Attis, Adonis and Osiris*, 219–49. Henn (*LT* 259) suggests Julian's 'Hymn to the Mother of God' as a source and Wilson (*YI* 276), mentions Arthur Symons's version of Catullus' 'Attis' (LXVI), and Parkinson (*YTLP* 221) mentions *Hastings' Encyclopaedia of Religion and Ethics* as another source. See also Sir James Frazer, *The Golden Bough: A Study in Comparative Religion* (1890) I, 297–9. *283*

17 *That staring fury*: Parkinson (*YTLP* 226) remarks that this is Yeats's way of identifying flame, death and knowledge, each a destructive peril. 'And the blind lush leaf is seen as equally menacing to those who seek revelation beyond grief.'

III *283*
This section also answers the query of Section I 'What is joy?' It was included with II in the first printed version.

21 *trivial days*: there may be some thought here of the years Yeats spent working for the Abbey Theatre. From 1902 to 1912 he wrote 'little verse and no prose that did not arise out of some need of the Irish players, or from some thought suggested by their work, or in the defence of some friend connected with that work, or with the movement of events that made it possible' (*E & I* 219).

ram them: the image comes from Ben Jonson – Yeats misquoted his *Poetaster* in 'Anima Mundi': 'Surely of the passionate dead we can but cry in words Ben Jonson meant for none but Shakespeare: "So rammed" are they "with life they can but grow in life with being" ' (*M* 360).

27 *Lethean foliage*: in classical mythology Lethe meant oblivion. In Latin poetry

the waters of Lethe, a river in Hades, were drunk by souls about to be reincarnated so they forgot their past lives.

29   *fortieth year*: Yeats had settled on his new bare style by 1905, when he was forty. It is possible that this year, when Maud Gonne and John MacBride separated (when she, despite having become a Roman Catholic, had sought to divorce him. See *MGLE* 252-4) was indeed a time for testing works of 'intellect or faith'.

IV

35   *fiftieth year*: Yeats was fifty in 1915-16; a passage in his 'Anima Mundi' describes this experience:

> At certain moments, always unforeseen, I become happy, most commonly when at hazard I have opened some book of verse. Sometimes it is my own verse when, instead of discovering new technical flaws, I read with all the excitement of the first writing. Perhaps I am sitting in some crowded restaurant, the open book beside me, or closed, my excitement having over-brimmed the page. I look at the strangers near as if I had known them all my life, and it seems strange that I cannot speak to them: everything fills me with affection, I have no longer any fears or any needs; I do not even remember that this happy mood must come to an end. It seems as if the vehicle had suddenly grown pure and far extended and so luminous that the images from *Anima Mundi*, embodied there and drunk with that sweetness, would, like a country drunkard who has thrown a wisp into his own thatch, burn up time.
>
> It may be an hour before the mood passes, but latterly I seem to understand that I enter upon it the moment I cease to hate. I think the common condition of our life is hatred – I know that this is so with me – irritation with public or private events or persons.   (*M* 364-5)

284   V

50   *Responsibility*: cf. a phrase in the Introduction to Hone and Rossi, *Berkeley* (*E & I* 397) dealing with those who feel a responsibility for the thought of modern Ireland that can 'take away their sleep' and the memory of the '98 riots in *A* 368: 'I count the links in the chain of responsibility, run them across my fingers, and wonder if any link there is from my workshop.'

51   *Things said or done*: cf. 'Man and the Echo' (*PNE* 372).

VI

59   *Chou*: probably, according to Saul (*PYP* 144) Chóu-Kung, a twelfth-century member of the Chou dynasty. Yeats had possibly been reading Richard Wilhelm's translation of *The Secret of the Golden Flower* (*L* 786). See also note (p. 98) on the second epigraph to *Responsibilities*, suggesting Confucius as Yeats's source for the Duke.

63   *Babylon or Nineveh*: for Babylon see note on 'The Dawn' (*PNE* 158); for

Nineveh see note on 'Fragments' (*PNE* 219); this image may derive from Arthur O'Shaughnessy's poem.

67   *man's blood-sodden heart*: cf. 'Man's own resinous heart' of 'Two Songs   *285* from a Play' (*PNE* 218).

VII

72   *The Soul*: Yeats wrote from Coole Park to Mrs Shakespear on 3 January 1932:

> I meant to write to you this morning (it is now 3.15) but thought of that sentence of yours [probably she wrote, 'You will be too great a bore if you get religion'] and then wrote a poem, which puts clearly an argument that has gone on in my head for years. When I have finished the poem I began yesterday I will take up the theme in greater fullness. Here is the poem. Heart and Soul are speaking:
>
> *Soul.* Search out reality, leave things that seem.
> *Heart.* What be a singer born and lack a theme?
> *Soul.* Ezekiel's coal and speed [speech?] leaps out anew.
> *Heart.* Can there be living speech in heaven's blue?
> *Soul.* Knock on that door, salvation waits within.
> *Heart.* And what sang Homer but original sin.
>
> I feel that this is the choice of the saint (St Theresa's ecstasy, Gandhi's smiling face): comedy; and the heroic choice; Tragedy (Dante, Don Quixote). Live Tragically but be not deceived (not the fool's Tragedy). Yet I accept all the miracles. Why should not the old embalmers come back as ghosts and bestow upon the saint all the care once bestowed upon Rameses? why should I doubt the tale that when St Theresa's tomb was opened in the middle of the nineteenth century the still undecayed body dripped with fragrant oil? I shall be a sinful man to the end, and think upon my death-bed of all the nights I wasted in my youth.   (*L* 789-90)

74   *Isaiah's coal*: cf. Isaiah vi;

> Then flew one of the seraphims unto me, having a live coal in his hand which he had taken with the tongs from off the altar; and he laid it upon my mouth and said, Lo, this hath touched thy lips, and thine iniquity is taken away and thy sin purged. Also I heard the voice of the Lord saying, 'Whom shall I send, and who will go for us? Then said I, Here am I; send me. And he said, Go and tell this people, Hear ye indeed, but understand not; and see ye indeed, but perceive not.

The change from the Ezekiel of the draft of the poem to Isaiah in the published text may have been because Yeats found von Hügel dealing with Ezekiel in some detail as a representative of the higher elements of religion.

75-6 . . . *Simplicity of fire! . . . salvation walks within*: Henn (*LT* 140) cites a passage from *PASL* which is based on Plotinus:

There are two realities, the terrestrial and the condition of fire. All power is from the terrestrial condition, for there all opposites meet and there only is the extreme of choice possible, full freedom. And there the heterogeneous is, and evil, for evil is the strain one upon another of opposites; but in the condition of fire is all music and all rest.   (*M* 356–7)

77   *Homer but original sin?*: the theme of the poem was epitomised by a remark of Lady Gregory to Yeats a few weeks before she died, that she preferred the poems (in a book Yeats had shown her) which were translated from the Irish, because they came out of original sin. Cf. Frank O'Connor, 'Synge', *The Irish Theatre*, 38.

VIII
The composition of this section is discussed in Bradford, *Yeats at Work*, 128–34.
   Yeats was reading Baron Friedrich von Hügel's (1852–1925) *The Mystical Element of Religion, as Studied in St. Catherine of Genoa and Her Friends* (1908); this poem's contrast between Homeric and Christian ideas probably came from a passage in von Hügel (186 ff.):

For the survival after the body's death indubitably attributed to the Psyche in the Homeric poems, is conceived there, throughout, as a miserably shrunken consciousness, and one which is dependent for its continuance upon the good offices bestowed by the survivors upon the corpse and grave. And the translation of the still living Menelaus to Elysium (*Odyssey* IV, 560–8) is probably a later insertion; it belongs to a small class of exceptional cases; implies the writer's inability to conceive a heightened consciousness for the soul, after the soul's separation from the body; and is based not upon any virtue or reward, but upon Menelaus' family-relationship to Zeus. Ganymede gets similarly translated because of his physical beauty.   (*Ilias*, XX, 232 ff.)

79   *Accept the miracles*: Yeats wrote in his preface to *The Ten Principal Upanishads* (1937), 10, that '*The Golden Bough* has made Christianity look modern and fragmentary'.

80   *Saint Teresa*: see notes on 'Oil and Blood' (*PNE* 244).

82   *self-same hands ... Pharoah's mummy*: embalmers. The bodies of the Egyptian pharaohs were mummified. Cf. Wilson (*YI* 165), who thinks Yeats 'suggests that the ghosts of ancient Egyptian embalmers may have been sent in the astral body to preserve it' [the body of St Theresa].

286   88   *the lion and the honeycomb*: cf. Judges xiv, 5–18. Samson, a judge of Israel, performed feats of strength against the Philistines. He extracted honey from the carcase of a lion he killed and made a riddle out of this. (Lyle's Golden Syrup illustrates the dead lion and bees on its tins with part of the riddle from Judges: 'out of the strong came forth sweetness'; the tins were known to Yeats!)

QUARREL IN OLD AGE   **263**

This poem was written in November 1931 and first appeared in *WMP*.   *286*

1   *her sweetness*: Maud Gonne's. The poem records a quarrel with her, probably over the treatment of women prisoners on a hunger strike organised by Mary McSwiney.

3   *blind bitter town*: Dublin. Cf. 'this blind bitter land' of 'Words' (*PNE* 93), the 'blind and ignorant town' of 'To a Wealthy Man who promised a second Subscription to the Dublin Municipal Gallery if it were Proved the People wanted Pictures' (*PNE* 114), and 'this unmannerly town' of 'The People' (*PNE* 164).

9   *All lives that has lived*: F. F. Farag (*YCE* 41) points out that the idea of reincarnation gave Yeats hope whenever he felt death approaching. Cf. 'Mohini Chatterjee' (*PNE* 259).

14   *that lonely thing*: cf. 'Broken Dreams' (*PNE* 167).

16   *Targeted*: protected as with a round shield or targe. Cf. Hone (*WBY* 441) who confirms Yeats's approval of the note on this in *Modern Poetry 1922-1934* (ed. M. Wollman).

like spring: cf. *A* 123, where Yeats described his memory of his first meeting with Maud Gonne, who seemed 'a classical impersonation of the spring'

THE RESULTS OF THOUGHT   **264**

This poem was written between 18 and 28 August 1931 and first appeared in   *286*
WMP.

1   *Acquaintance*: not identified

companion: Mrs Shakespear

2   *One dear brilliant woman*: Lady Gregory

5   *All, all*: cf. note on line 21 'Broken Dreams' (*PNE* 167).   *287*

GRATITUDE TO THE UNKNOWN INSTRUCTORS   **265**

The date of composition is unknown; the poem first appeared in *WMP*.   *287*

1   *they*: those who inspired *AV*. Passages in the Introduction to that work

describe how Mrs Yeats surprised the poet on 24 October 1917 by attempting automatic writing:

> What came in disjointed sentences, in almost illegible writing, was so exciting, sometimes so profound, that I persuaded her to give an hour or two day after day to the unknown writer, and after some half-dozen such hours offered to spend what remained of life explaining and piecing together those scattered sentences. 'No' was the answer, 'we have come to give you metaphors for poetry'. (*AV* (B) 8)

> Early in 1919 the communicator of the moment – they were constantly changed – said they would soon change the method from the written to the spoken word as that would fatigue her less, but the change did not come for some months'. (*AV* (B) 9)

> Much that has happened, much that has been said, suggests that the communicators are the personalities of a dream shared by my wife, by myself, occasionally by others. . . . (*AV* (B) 22-3)

266   REMORSE FOR INTEMPERATE SPEECH

287   This poem was written on 28 August 1931 and first appeared in *WMP*.

1   *the knave and fool*: probably a reference to Yeats's youthful work as a nationalist

288   4   *Fit audience*: probably the friends Yeats made after he was thirty, Lady Gregory in Ireland, and many others in England

8   *hatred*: Yeats wrote on 7 September 1927 to Mrs Shakespear, referring to the 'hatred that is a commonplace here – It lays hold on our class I think more easily than upon the mass of the people. It finds a more complicated and determined conscience to prey upon.'

10   *fanatic*: Yeats's note reads 'I pronounce ''fanatic'' in what is, I suppose, the older and more Irish way, so that the last line of each stanza contains but two beats' (*PNE* 266).

267   STREAM AND SUN AT GLENDALOUGH

288   This poem was written on 23 June 1932, and first appeared in *WMP*.

Title   Glendalough: in Co. Wicklow. Cf. 'Under the Round Tower' (*PNE* 148). Iseult Gonne and her husband Francis Stuart lived at Laragh, a few miles from Glendalough. See notes on 'The Death of the Hare' (*PNE* 230) and on 'Why should not Old Men be Mad?' (*PNE* A122).

YEATS wrote in his Introduction to *WS* that in the spring of 1929:

> life returned to me as an impression of the uncontrollable energy and daring of
> the great creators; it seemed to me that but for journalism and criticism, all that
> evasion and explanation, the world would be torn in pieces. I wrote *Mad as the
> Mist and Snow*, a mechanical little song, and after that almost all that group of
> poems, called in memory of those exultant weeks *Words for Music Perhaps*.

In a letter of 2 March 1929, Yeats wrote to Mrs Shakespear from Rapallo that
he was 'writing *Twelve poems for music* – have done three of them (and two other
poems) – no [t] so much that they may be sung as that I may define their kind of
emotion to myself. I want them to be all emotion and all impersonal' (*L* 758). On
13 September 1929 he wrote to her from Dublin that he would finish at Rapallo
'the book of thirty poems for music I am more than half through. ''For Music'' is
only a name, nobody will sing them' (*L* 769). On 17 August he wrote to her from
Riversdale, Rathfarnham, that the 'Crazy Jane' poems 'and the little group of love
poems that follow are, I think, exciting and strange. Sexual abstinence fed their
fire – I was ill and yet full of desire. They sometimes came out of the greatest
mental excitement I am capable of' (*L* 814).

These poems were written between 1929 and 1932. See *WBY* 401 for some
dates, and ibid., 425, where Yeats's letter (of the winter of 1931-2) to his wife is
quoted: 'I want to exorcise that slut, Crazy Jane, whose language has become
unendurable.' 'Crazy Jane' was substituted for 'Cracked Mary', the title given in
the first printing.

'Cracked Mary' was an old woman who lived near Lady Gregory and was 'the
local satirist and a really terrible one', as Yeats wrote in a letter to Mrs Shakespear
of November 1931. In this he described Crazy Jane as more or less founded on
this old woman:

> who lives in a cottage near Gort. She loves her flower garden – She has just sent
> Lady Gregory some flowers in spite of the season and [has] an amazing power of
> audacious speech. One of her great performances is a description of how the
> meanness of a Gort shopkeeper's wife over the price of a glass of porter made
> her so despair of the human race that she got drunk. The incidents of the
> drunkenness are of an epic magnificence.

There is a Jane in 'The Limerick Rake' who may have been a possible source.
See Colm O'Loghlain, *Irish Street Ballads*. D. E. S. Maxwell, 'Swift's Dark
Grove: Yeats and the Anglo-Irish tradition' (*YCE*, 28-9) suggests the parallels
between Yeats's Crazy Jane poems and some of Swift's.

And Yeats may have known 'Crazy Jane' by Matthew Gregory ('Monk')
Lewis (1775-1818), a ballad included in his *Poems* (1812) pp. 24-5.

268 CRAZY JANE AND THE BISHOP

290 This poem was written on 2 March 1929, and first appeared in the *New Republic* (12 Nov. 1930) and *LM* (Nov. 1930). The title was initially 'Cracked Mary and the Bishop'.

1 *the blasted oak*: this was 'the chapel wall' in an early MS. version.

9 *Jack the Journeyman*: Ellmann (*IY* 275), points out that Jack the Journeyman appeared as a character in Yeats's play *The Pot of Broth* (1902), and in a note to that play Yeats remarked that the words and air of the tramp's song in that play, 'There's Broth in the Pot' came from an old woman known as Cracked Mary 'who wanders about the plain of Aidhne, and who sometimes sees unearthly riders on white horses coming through stony fields to her hovel door in the night time.' Lady Gregory used the name 'Jack the Journeyman' in her play *The Losing Game* (1902) – see note on [There's broth in the pot for you, Old Man] (*PNE* A48).

269 CRAZY JANE REPROVED

291 This poem was written on 27 March 1929 and first appeared in the *New Republic* (12 Nov. 1930) and *LM* (Nov. 1930) entitled 'Cracked Mary Reproved'.

2-4 *All those dreadful thunder-stones,*
All that storm that blots the day
Can but show that Heaven yawns: cf. a passage on 'Ireland after Parnell':

. . . politics, for a vision-seeking man, can be but half achievement, a choice of an almost easy kind of skill instead of that kind which is, of all those not impossible, the most difficult. Is it not certain that the Creator yawns in earthquake and thunder and other popular displays, but toils in rounding the delicate spiral of a shell.' (*A* 249)

This suggests that Crazy Jane is being reproved for her choice of lovers.

5 *Europa*: the daughter of Agenor, King of Tyre. Zeus fell in love with her, assumed the shape of a bull, and carried her off to Crete: there she became the mother of Minos, Sarpedon, and Rhadamanthus. Zeus' appearance to her as a bull was part of his less serious activity, and ranks, with his production of storms, as inferior to his creation of a shell.

270 CRAZY JANE ON THE DAY OF JUDGMENT

291 This poem was written in October 1930 and first appeared in *WMP*.

Title: The Day of Judgment, when humans will be judged and sent to heaven or hell.

3-4 . . . *the whole/Body and soul*: Saul (*PYP* 147) draws attention to Sir W. Rothenstein, *Since Fifty*, 242, who quoted Yeats's remark that 'the tragedy of sexual intercourse is the perpetual virginity of the souls'.

CRAZY JANE AND JACK THE JOURNEYMAN   271

This poem was written in November 1931 and first appeared in *WMP*.   *292*

5   *a skin unwound*: cf. 'His Bargain' (*PNE* 281).

7   *A lonely ghost*: some of Yeats's ideas about ghosts and their relationships are   *293*
put in 'Anima Mundi':

> The dead, as the passionate necessity wears out, come into a measure of freedom and may turn the impulse of events, started while living, in some new direction, but they cannot originate except through the living. Then gradually they perceive, although they are still but living in their memories, harmonies, symbols, and patterns, as though all were being refashioned by an artist, and they are moved by emotions, sweet for no imagined good but in themselves, like those of children dancing in a ring; and I do not doubt that they make love in that union which Swedenborg has said is of the whole body and seems from far off an incandescence. Hitherto shade has communicated with shade in moments of common memory that recur like the figures of a dance in terror or in joy, but now they run together like to like, and their covens and fleets have rhythm and pattern. This running together and running of all to a centre, and yet without loss of identity, has been prepared for by their exploration of their moral life, of its beneficiaries and its victims, and even of all its untrodden paths, and all their thoughts have moulded the vehicle and become event and circumstance.   (*M* 355-6)

CRAZY JANE ON GOD   272

This poem was written on 18 July 1931 and first appeared in *WMP*.   *293*

5   *Men come, men go*: the first stanza describes Crazy Jane's realisation that love is transitory, but is yet aware of permanence. Ellmann (*IY* 277) suggests that Yeats originally got the idea from Madame Blavatsky, quoting from Yeats's words in Lady Gregory, *Visions and Beliefs* I, 277: '. . . she tried to explain predestination, our freedom and God's full knowledge of the use that we should make of it. All things past and to come were present in the mind of God and yet all things were free.'

7   *Banners choke the sky*: a passage in the introduction to *WWP* provides a gloss:

It is fitting that Plotinus should have been the first philosopher to meet his daimon face to face, though the boy attendant out of jealousy or in convulsive terror strangled the doves, for he was the first to establish as sole source the timeless individuality or daimon instead of the Platonic Idea, to prefer Socrates to his thought. This timeless individuality contains archetypes of all possible existences whether of man or brute, and as it traverses its circle of allotted lives, now one, now another, prevails. We may fail to express an archetype or alter it by reason, but all done from nature is its unfolding into time. Some other existence may take the place of Socrates, yet Socrates can never cease to exist. Once a friend of mine was digging in a long-neglected garden and suddenly out of the air came a voice thanking her, an old owner of the garden, she was told later, long since reborn, yet still in the garden. Plotinus said that we should not 'baulk at this limitlessness of the intellectual; it is an infinitude having nothing to do with number or part' (*Ennead* V. 7. I); yet it seems that it can at will re-enter number and part and thereby make itself apparent to our minds. If we accept this idea many strange or beautiful things become credible. The Indian pilgrim has not deceived us; he did hear the bed where the sage of his devotion slept a thousand years ago creak as though someone turned over in it, and he did see – he himself and the old shrine-keeper – the blankets all tossed about at dawn as if someone had just risen; the Irish countrywoman did see the ruined castle lit up, the bridge across the river dropping; these two Oxford ladies [Charlotte Anne Elizabeth Moberly (1846-1937), Principal of St Hugh's College, Oxford (1886-1915) and Eleanor Frances Jourdain (d. 1924), Principal of St Hugh's College (1915-24)] did find themselves in the garden of the Petit Trianon with Marie Antoinette and her courtiers, see that garden as those saw it; the gamekeeper did hear those footsteps the other night that sounded like the footsteps of a stag where stag has not passed these hundred years. All about us there seems to start up a precise inexplicable teeming life, and the earth becomes once more, not in rhetorical metaphor, but in reality, sacred. (*E* 368-9)

An earlier passage in 'Anima Mundi' dealt with the same idea:

Spiritism, whether of folk-lore or of the séance-room, the visions of Swedenborg, and the speculation of the Platonists and Japanese plays, will have it that we may see at certain roads and in certain houses old murders acted over again, and in certain fields dead hunstmen riding with horse and hound, or ancient armies fighting above bones or ashes. We carry to *Anima Mundi* our memory, and that memory is for a time our external world; and all passionate moments recur again and again, for passion desires its own recurrence more than any event, and whatever there is of corresponding complacency or remorse is our beginning of judgement. . . . (*M* 354)

Ellmann (*IY* 277), remarks that the image of the army may derive from the fact that the original Cracked Mary sometimes saw 'unearthly riders on white horses'.

294   13-16   *Before their eyes a house*
            That from childhood stood
            Uninhabited, ruinous,
            Suddenly lit up: This is probably the ruined castle referred to in the Introduction to *WWP* quoted above, and it was probably Castle Dargan, near Sligo, also described in Yeats's play *The King of the Great Clock Tower*:

Castle Dargan's ruin all lit,
Lovely ladies dancing in it . . .
. . . Yet all the lovely things that were
Live, for I saw them dancing there.   (*CPl* 640)

This castle is also alluded to, *A* 53. Cf. also *A* 77 and the description of the ruined house 'that was burnt down' in Yeats's play *Purgatory*, a window of which is lit up with a young girl in it (*CPl* 685–7). And cf. the ruined house in 'The Curse of Cromwell' (*PNE* 337). There is also a possibility that Yeats had Leap Castle in mind, which 'though burnt down during our Civil War and still a ruin, is haunted by what is called an evil spirit which appears as a sheep with short legs and decaying human head' (*AV* (B) 224). Cf. p. 513. Leap Castle (*Irish* Leirn-Ui-Bhanain, O'Bannon's Leap) in Co. Offaly was on the site of a castle of the O'Carrols of Ely.

CRAZY JANE TALKS WITH THE BISHOP   273

This poem was written in November 1931 and first appeared in *WS*.   294

3   *Those breasts*: cf. a passage in Synge's translation of Villon's 'An Old Woman's Lamentation':

'The man I had a love for – a great rascal would kick me in the gutter – is dead thirty years and over it, and it is I am left behind, grey and aged. When I do be minding the good days I had, minding what I was one time, and that it is I'm come to, and when I do look on my own self, poor and dry, and pinched together, it wouldn't be much would set me raging in the streets.

Where is the round forehead I had, and the fine hair, and the two eyebrows, and the eyes with a big gay look out of them would bring folly from a great scholar? Where is my straight shapely nose, and two ears, and my chin with a valley in it, and my lips were red and open?

Where are the pointed shoulders that were on me, and the long arms and nice hands to them? Where is my bosom was as white as any, or my straight rounded sides?

It's the way I am this day – my forehead is gone into furrows, the hair of my head is grey and whitish, my eyebrows are tumbled from me, and my two eyes have died out within my head – those eyes that would be laughing to the men – my nose has a hook on it, my ears are hanging down and my lips are sharp and skinny.

That's what's left over from the beauty of a right woman – a bag of bones, and legs the like of two shrivelled sausages going beneath it.

It's the like of what we old hags do be thinking, of the good times that are gone away from us, and we crouched on our hunkers by a little fire of twigs, soon kindled and soon spent, we that were the pick of many.   (Synge, *Poems and Translations*, 44)

16   *The place of excrement*: cf. Blake's line in *Jerusalem*: 'For I will make their   295
places of love and joy excrementitious'.

274 CRAZY JANE GROWN OLD LOOKS AT THE DANCERS

295 This poem was written on 6 March 1929 and first appeared in *The New Republic* (12 Nov. 1930).

1   *that ivory image*: the source of the poem is revealed in a letter Yeats wrote to Mrs Shakespear from Rapallo on 2 March 1929:

> Last night I saw in a dream strange ragged excited people singing in a crowd. The most visible were a man and woman who were I think dancing. The man was swinging around his head a weight at the end of a rope or leather thong and I knew that he did not know whether he would strike her dead or not, and both had their eyes fixed on each other, and both sang their love for one another. I suppose it was Blake's old thought 'sexual love is founded on spiritual hate' – I will probably find I have written it in a poem in a few days – though my remembering my dream may prevent that – by making my criticism work upon it. (At least there is evidence to that effect.)   (*L* 758)

The passage on sexual love and spiritual hate in 'Anima Hominis' is concerned with similar matters, where Yeats sees the warfare of man and Daimon as imaged in love. See *M* 336-7.

296 18   *thraneen*: probably from Synge's *The Playboy of the Western World*, II, and the phrase means not to care. Thraneen (*Irish*), a dry stalk of grass, a straw.

275 GIRL'S SONG

296 This poem was written on 29 March 1929 and first appeared in the *New Republic* (22 Oct. 1930).

11   *an old man young*: this is reminiscent of Blake

276 YOUNG MAN'S SONG

296 This poem was written after 29 March 1929, according to Ellmann (*IY* 292). It first appeared in the *New Republic* (22 Oct. 1930).

297 12   *Before the world was made*: cf. 'Before the World was Made' (*PNE* 294).

16   *shall bend the knee*: this phrase frequently occurred in Irish political oratory in the nineteenth century.

277 HER ANXIETY

297 This was written after 17 April 1929, and first appeared in the *New Republic* (22 Oct. 1930).

HIS CONFIDENCE   **278**

This poem was written after 29 March 1929 and first appeared in the *New*   *298*
Republic (22 Oct. 1930).

LOVE'S LONELINESS   **279**

This poem was written on 17 April 1929 and first appeared in the *New Republic*   *298*
(22 Oct. 1930).

HER DREAM   **280**

This poem was written after 29 March 1929 and first appeared in the *New*   *299*
Republic (22 Oct. 1930).

    A possible source for the poem is Catullus LXVI.

1-8   *I dreamed as in my bed I lay,*
        All night's fathomless wisdom come,
        That I had shorn my locks away
        And laid them on Love's lettered tomb:
        But something bore them out of sight
        In a great tumult of the air,
        And after nailed upon the night
        Berenice's burning hair: cf. a passage in 'Anima Mundi':

    The soul cannot have much knowledge till it has shaken off the habit of time and of place, but till that hour it must fix its attention upon what is near, thinking of objects one after another as we run the eye or the finger over them. Its intellectual power cannot but increase and alter as its perceptions grow simultaneous. Yet even now we seem at moments to escape from time in what we call prevision, and from place when we see distant things in a dream and in concurrent dreams. A couple of years ago, while in meditation, my head seemed surrounded by a conventional sun's rays, and when I went to bed I had a long dream of a woman with her hair on fire. I awoke and lit a candle, and discovered presently from the odour that in doing so I had set my own hair on fire. I dreamed very lately that I was writing a story, and at the same time I dreamed that I was one of the characters in that story and seeking to touch the heart of some girl in defiance of the author's intention; and concurrently with all that, I was as another self trying to strike with the button of a foil a great china jar. The obscurity of the 'Prophetic Books' of William Blake, which were composed in a state of vision, comes almost wholly from these concurrent dreams. Everybody has some story or some experience of the sudden knowledge in sleep or waking of some event, a misfortune for the most part, happening to some friend far off.   (*M* 358)

8   *Berenice's burning hair*: see note on 'Veronica's Napkin' (*PNE* 245).

281 HIS BARGAIN

299   This poem was written after 29 March 1929 and first appeared in the *New Republic* (22 Oct. 1930). The first version contained six extra lines probably through a printer's error as they are lines 13–18 of 'Young Man's Song' (*PNE* 276).

1   *Plato's spindle*: this probably derives from Plato's myth of Er in Book X of *The Republic* (which Yeats's conception of the gyres resembles):

> For this light binds the sky together, like the hawser that strengthens a trireme, and thus holds together the whole revolving universe. To the extremities is fastened the distaff of Necessity, by means of which all the revolutions of the universe are kept up. The shaft and hook of this distaff are made of steel; the whorl is a compound of steel and other materials. The nature of the whorl may be thus described. In shape it is like an ordinary whorl; but from Er's account we must picture it to ourselves under the form of a large hollow whorl, scooped out right through, into which a similar, but smaller whorl is nicely inserted, like those boxes which fit into one another. In the same way a third whorl is inserted within the second, a fourth within the third, and so on to four more. . . . Now the distaff as a whole spins round with uniform velocity; but while the whole revolves, the seven inner circles travel slowly round in the opposite direction. . . . The distaff spins round upon the knees of Necessity. . . . At equal distances around sit three other personages, each on a throne. These are the daughters of Necessity, the Fates, Lachesis, Clotho, and Atropos . . . (*Republic* 616–17, translated by J. L. Davies and D. J. Vaughan).

The lover protests that he has chosen to love only her with whose hair he made the bargain. This choice of faithful love 'before the thread began' may be due to this passage:

> Now the souls, immediately on their arrival, were required to go to Lachesis. An interpreter first of all marshalled them in order, and then having taken from the lap of Lachesis a number of lots and plans of life, mounted a high pulpit and spoke as follows: 'Thus saith the maiden Lachesis, the daughter of Necessity. Ye short-lived souls, a generation of men shall here begin the cycle of its mortal existence. Your destiny shall not be allotted to you, but you shall choose it for yourselves.' (*Republic* 617)

The myth continues to describe the different lives of living things laid before the soul. No settled character of soul was included because the soul inevitably becomes changed with the change of life. The choice 'is apparently the moment when everything is at stake with a man' and

> With iron resolution must he hold fast this opinion when he enters the future world, in order that, there as well as here, he may escape being dazzled by wealth and similar evils; and may not plunge into usurpations or other corresponding courses of action, to the inevitable detriment of others, and to his own still heavier affliction; but may know how to select that life which always steers a middle course between such extremes, and to shun excess on either side to the best of his power, not only in this life, but in that which is to come. For, by acting thus, he is sure to become a most happy man.

314

Yeats did not like the platonic μηδὲν ἄγαν - his lover made his choice 'before the thread began' - but he had made a choice which overrides fate, a choice superior to the common one in which the imagined characters

> Dan and Jerry Lout
> Change their loves about

Plato's story allots the souls a due span of time:

> Now, when all the souls had chosen their lives in the order of the lots, they advanced in their turn to Lachesis, who dispatched with each of them the Destiny he had selected, to guard his life and satisfy his choice. This Destiny first led the soul to Clotho in such a way as to pass beneath her hand and the whirling motion of the distaff, and thus ratified the fate which each had chosen in the order of precedence. After touching her, the same Destiny led the soul next to the spinning of Atropos, and thus rendered the doom of Clotho irreversible. From thence the souls passed straightforward under the throne of Necessity. (*Republic* 620)

This idea was also used in Yeats's play *Diarmuid and Grania* where Diarmuid says to Grania: 'Life of my life, I [k]new you before I was born, I made a bargain with this brown hair before the beginning of time and it shall not be broken through unending time' (*VPl* 1195).

8 *Before the thread began*: Yeats quoted in a letter to Katharine Tynan of June 1891 Mrs Radford's lines:

> The love within my heart for thee
> Before the world was had its birth . . .

And cf. also 'Before the World was Made' (*PNE* 294).

11 *A bargain with that hair*: this un-Greek extravagance, typical of the manner in which Yeats could turn from philosophy to love poetry, may be an adaptation of his philosophical sources to another model taken from the love poetry of Hafiz for its image of great and lasting love. (The cynical view of the possibility of this great love is to be found in 'The Fool by the Roadside' (*PNE* 225) which uses the same imagery to different ends.) Cf. 'The Tresses of the Hair':

> Hafiz cried to his beloved, 'I made a bargain with that brown hair before the beginning of time, and it shall not be broken through unending time,' and it may be that Mistress Nature knows that we have lived many times, and that whatsoever changes and winds into itself belongs to us. She covers her eyes away from us, but she lets us play with the tresses of her hair. (*E & I* 290)

THREE THINGS 282

This poem was written in March 1929 and first appeared in the *New Republic* 300 (2 Oct. 1929).

17 *stretch and yawn*: David R. Clark (*YASAC* 44-50) considers that the phrase

stands for sexual arousal rather than consummation; he suggests further (p. 52) that Ezra Pound's translation of Arnault Daniel's 'Doutz brais e critz' may have been a literary source. Daniel describes his lady 'of whom I have great hunger . . . A thousand times a day I yawn and stretch because of that fair who surpasseth all others even as true joy surpasseth ire and fury'. The translation is included in Pound's *The Spirit of Romance* (1910).

283 LULLABY

300 This poem was written on either 20 or 27 March 1929 and first appeared in the *New Keepsake* (London, 1931). Frank O'Connor stated that this poem is based on his translation *Grania* (*Kings, Lords, and Commons,* 49).

Yeats wrote to Olivia Shakespear on 29 March 1929 that this was

> a *Lullaby* that I like. A mother sings to her child [Then followed a version of the poem]. I have done two or three others that seem to me lucky and that does not often happen. Yet I am full of doubt. I am writing more easily than I ever wrote and I am happy, whereas I have always been unhappy when I wrote and worked with great difficulty. I feel like one of those Japanese who in the middle ages retired from the world at 50 or so – not like an Indian of that age to live in jungle but to devote himself 'to art and letters' which was considered sacred. If this new work do not seem as good as the old to my friends then I can take to some lesser task and live very contentedly. The happiness of finding idleness a duty. No more opinions, no more politics, no more practical tasks.   (*L* 760–1)

4 *Paris*: son of Priam, King of Troy, and his wife Hecuba, who was exposed on Mount Ida as it was prophesied he would bring ruin on his country. He was brought up by shepherds, and lived with Oenone, a nymph, until he was appointed to award the prize for beauty to one of the three goddesses, Hera, Athene and Aphrodite. Aphrodite offered him the fairest woman in the world if she gained the prize. Afterwards Paris visited Sparta and persuaded Helen, the wife of King Menelaus, to elope with him. This caused the Greek siege of Troy in which Paris was mortally wounded by an arrow. He was brought to Oenone, but it was too late for her to cure him and in her grief she committed suicide.

301 8 *Tristram*: in Malory's *Le Morte d'Arthur* Tristram, the son of the King of Lyonesse, is sent to Ireland to be cured of a wound. He falls in love there with La Beale Isoud the King's daughter, but he leaves the court, as he has killed the brother of the Queen of Ireland. He returns to Cornwall and King Mark sends him to Ireland to ask La Beale Isoud to marry King Mark. She marries Mark, but continues relations with Tristram (they fell irresistibly in love having drunk a love potion unwittingly) till they are betrayed to Mark. He then leaves Mark's court and falls in love with Isoud la Blanche Mains when fighting for King Howel of Brittany. But he returns to Cornwall, is banished, and is killed by Mark as he sits harping before La Beale Isoud.

Another version of the legend tells how Tristram, wounded by a poisoned arrow in Brittany, sends for La Beale Isoud – she is to come in a ship with a white sail. But when the ship returns Isoud of Brittany tells him the sail is black and he dies. La Beale Isoud discovers his body, lies beside it and dies herself.

9   *potion's work*: see note on line 8.

14   *Eurotas*: the main river in Sparta

15   *holy bird*: Zeus who took the shape of a swan. Cf. 'Leda and the Swan' (*PNE* 220).

17   *Leda*: Leda, the wife of Tyndareus the King of Sparta, was bathing in the Eurotas when Zeus saw her. She bore Castor and Pollux and Helen to Zeus.

Maud Gonne is described as having a 'Ledaean body' in 'Among School Children' (*PNE* 220).

AFTER LONG SILENCE   **284**

This poem was written in November 1929 and first appeared in *WMP*.   *301*

Yeats wrote on 16 December 1929 to Mrs Shakespear from Rapallo to say 'When I first got here I was fairly vigorous though shaky, and wrote this little poem of which I showed you the prose draft' (*L* 772).

The prose draft is quoted by Ellmann (*IY* 280)

> Subject
> Your hair is white
> My hair is white
> Come let us talk of love
> What other theme do we know
> When we were young
> We were in love with one another
> And therefore ignorant

8   *We loved each other*: the poem was written about Yeats and Mrs Shakespear, according to Mrs Yeats. Donald R. Clark, however, has argued (*YASAC* 65-89) that Yeats's visit to Mrs Mathers (whom he had not seen for thirty years) which occurred before January 1924, brought about a reconciliation. She had been irritated by Yeats's treatment of her late husband MacGregor Mathers (see comment on him in notes on 'All Souls' Night', *PNE* 239) in *Autobiographies*. Clark suggests that Yeats may have been reminded of the Dedication of *A Vision* (1925) to Mrs Mathers (as 'Vestigia') when he was writing this poem, as he was also revising *A Vision* and substituting *A Packet for Ezra Pound* for the earlier edition's Dedication and Introduction. He may have been prompted by that recollection to write the poem about his friendship with Mrs Shakespear in a manner reminiscent of the earlier Dedication. The 'Bodily decrepitude' ('decrepitude', Clark thinks, may have come from James Clarence Mangan's 'Lament for the Princes of Tyrone and Tyrconnell' which Yeats included in his *A Book of Irish Verse* (1895):

317

> Theirs were not souls wherein dull Time
> Could domicile Decay or house
> Decrepitude!)

was something Yeats knew well at the time, as Clark points out, citing the note Yeats added in November 1930 to the November 1929 version of the poem:

> When I wrote this poem, I had already been ill for three weeks or so – I had just arrived at Rapallo and struggled with constant sleepiness – the first stages of suffer[ing] of Malta fever. Now it is the end of March & for the last five days I have begun to write again revising 'The Vision'. I am at Portofina Vetta and can look from my windows out over a vast tranquil sea & a coast dotted with sunlight houses as far as Genoa. I know seven or eight people at Rapallo & had stage-fright in my walks of a few hundred yards. Here I can slip in or out without a word & improve hourly. It is now five months since my haemorrhage from the lung in London & I have written nothing but one poem & the doctor says I will not be well again for another three months, which means I suppose not able to write verse.

285   MAD AS THE MIST AND SNOW

301   This poem was written on 12 February 1929 and first appeared in *WMP*.
      Yeats wrote in *OTB*:

> When I began to grow old I could no longer spend all my time amid masterpieces and in trying to make the like. I gave part of every day to mere entertainment, and it seemed when I was ill that great genius was 'mad as the mist and snow'. Already in mid-Renaissance the world was weary of wisdom, science began to appear in the elaborate perspectives of its painters, in their sense of weight and tangibility; man was looking for some block where he could lay his head. But better than that, with Jacob's dream threatening, get rid of man himself. Civilisation slept in the masses, wisdom in science. Is it criminal to sleep? I do not know; I do not say it.   (*E* 436)

302   7   *Horace*: Quintus Horatius Flaccus (65–8 BC), Roman poet, pardoned after fighting on the losing side at Philippi, and became a friend of Maecenas who gave him a Sabine farm. He wrote satires, odes, epodes, epistles, and the *Ars Poetica*. His lyric poetry had an epicurean bias.

Homer: the Greek epic poet, regarded by the ancients as the author of the *Iliad* and the *Odyssey* (? born between 1050 and 850 BC). Seven cities claimed to be his birthplace. Tradition represents him as blind and poor in his old age.

8   *Plato*: the Greek philosopher (427–348 BC) was born at Athens or Aegina. He was a pupil and admirer of Socrates and retired to Megara and Sicily after his death, returning to Athens in 386 BC to teach in the Academy there. He spent the rest of his life teaching and composing Dialogues in some of which Socrates figures.

9   *Tully's open page*: Marcus Tullius Cicero (106–43 BC) became consul in 63

BC. He was pardoned by Caesar after Pharsalia, having fought on Pompey's side. He attacked Mark Anthony in his Philippic orations, was proscribed by the triumvirate and put to death in 43 BC. He wrote on rhetoric, political philosophy and moral philosophy. His orations are masterpieces of Latin prose style and his letters give an excellent picture of his life.

THOSE DANCING DAYS ARE GONE   286

This poem was written on 8 March 1929 and first appeared in the *New Republic*   302
(12 Nov. 1930), and *LM* (Nov. 1930).

7-8   *I carry the sun in a golden cup,*
       The moon in a silver bag: cf. 'The Man who dreamed of Faeryland' (*PNE*
33). The first line of the refrain is taken from Ezra Pound's (1885-1972) *Canto*
XXIII (Notes *CP*). Yeats read it in *A Draft of the Cantos 17-27* (1928) 33.

'I AM OF IRELAND'   287

This poem was written in August 1929 and first appeared in *WMP*. There is a   303
note on the MS. in R. O. Dougan, *W. B. Yeats. Manuscripts and Printed Books
exhibited in the Library of Trinity College, Dublin* 1956, 37.

1   *I am of Ireland*: Ellmann (*IY* 280) gives an account of Frank O'Connor
reading aloud an early fourteenth-century English lyric:

> Icham of Irlande
> Aut of the holy lande of Irlande
> Gode sir pray ich ye
> For of saynte charite
> Come and daunce wyt me,
> in Irlaunde

This version is from J. E. Wells, *Manual of Middle English Writing*, 492. Yeats's note (in *CP*) is that 'the poem is developed from three or four lines of an Irish fourteenth-century dance song somebody [Frank O'Connor (1903-66)] repeated to me a few years ago' but the source may be, according to Mrs Yeats, St John D. Seymour's *Anglo-Irish Literature 1200-1582*. In this book there is a passage which may have suggested elements of the poem to Yeats:

> Wells describes a fragment of an English manuscript (1300-1350) containing popular songs, of some of which only a line remains: these, he says, were rude pieces for singing by the roadside or at the ale house as may have been the case with our Kilkenny fragments. One of these is of interest to him, as he considers it to be perhaps the earliest English dance song extant. It is of more interest to us, as it is placed in the mouth of an Irish girl, and so presumably was composed by an Anglo-Irish minstrel.

Here are the elements of the poem: a singing, dancing, Irish girl; the English crowd by the roadside or in the alehouse; only one man pays any attention to the girl. Ellmann (*IY* 280-1) comments:

> But only one man listens, and he finds many pretexts for preferring comfortable expedience to the discomforts of idealism. When she repeats her appeal he gives a further reason: there can be no dancing in a country where all things are awry, and he gives her back her own words by pointing out that there is no time to remedy these things. Yet her cry continues, as if indifferent to his prudential explanations, like the cry of all idealism and heroism.

288   THE DANCER AT CRUACHAN AND CRO-PATRICK

304   This poem was written in August 1931 and first appeared in *WMP*, with 'Cro-Patrick' spelt as 'Croagh Patrick' in the title. Yeats's note read that 'Cruachan' was pronounced 'Crockhan in modern Gaelic'.

Title   *Cruachan*: see note on 'The Hour before Dawn' (*PNE* 125)

Cro-Patrick: Croagh Patrick (*Irish* Cruach Phadraig, Patrick's Heap), a mountain in Connemara. It is near Westport, Co. Mayo, and is a centre for Christian pilgrimage.

1   *I, proclaiming*: St Cellach. Cf. 'An Indian Monk' where Yeats remarks 'Some Irish saint, whose name I have forgotten, sang "There is one among the birds that is so perfect, one among the fish, one perfect among men" ' (*E & I* 431).
    Another essay in 'Discoveries' puts the question: 'was it Columbanus or another that wrote, "There is one among the birds that is perfect, and one perfect among the fish"?' (*E & I* 291).

There were two Irish Cellachs who should not be confused, one pagan and one Christian. Halt Cellach was the protector of the pagan bards who were overcome by the Christians at the battle of Moyra. Cellach tried to capture Congal, the pagan leader, alive during this battle, but before he could lay hands on him, to quote Sir Samuel Ferguson's *Congal* p. 132:

> Sudden and black, the storm came down; with scourge of
>   hissing hail
> It lashed the blinded, stumbling hosts: a shrill loud
>   whistling wail
> And thundrous clamours filled the sky . . .

The Christian Saint Cellach was Cellach MacAodh, Archbishop of Armagh from 1105-29. See Standish Hayes O'Grady, *Silver Gadelica*, II, 50-69, for the 'Life of Cellach of Killala'.

289   TOM THE LUNATIC

305   This poem was written on 27 July 1931 and first appeared in *WMP*. Tom O'Bedlam was a name applied to inmates of Bedlam (the hospital of St Mary of

Bethlehem, a London lunatic asylum); Tom Fool is a traditional name for fool or buffoon. See also Shakespeare's 'Poor Tom', *King Lear*, III, 4, 123–34, and the intensification of 'fool' as 'Tom-fool'

7 *Huddon and Duddon and Daniel O'Leary*: cf. *AV* (B) 32, where these three characters appear in a poem:

> Huddon, Duddon and Daniel O'Leary
> Delighted me as a child;
> But where that roaring, ranting crew
> Danced, laughed, loved, fought through
> Their brief lives I never knew.
>
> Huddon, Duddon and Daniel O'Leary
> Delighted me as a child.
> I put three persons in their place
> That despair and keep the pace
> And love wench Wisdom's cruel face.
>
> Huddon, Duddon and Daniel O'Leary
> Delighted me as a child.
> Hard-living men and men of thought
> Burn their bodies up for nought,
> I mock at all so burning out.

Daniel O'Leary (Yeats's footnote to the poem in *AV* reads 'As a child I pronounced the word as though it rhymed to "dairy" ') explains himself in the prose of *Stories of Michael Robartes and his friends: an extract from a record made by his pupils* (*AV* (B) 33–55).

See 'Hudden and Dudden and Donald O'Neary', *Celtic Fairy Tales*, ed. Joseph Jacobs (1892) 47–55).

8 *Holy Joe*: presumably invented. The term is used (often in contempt) for excessively religious persons in Ireland.

The use Yeats made of invented characters may perhaps relate to his experiments in thought transference and interest in complementary dreams. A passage in 'Hodos Chameliontos' shows that his interest in these characters may have come from the experiences of his uncle's second-sighted servant Mary Battle:

> Considering that Mary Battle received our thoughts in sleep, though coarsened or turned to caricature, do not the thoughts of the scholar or the hermit, though they speak no word, or something of their shape and impulse, pass into the general mind? Does not the emotion of some woman of fashion, caught in the subtle torture of self-analysing passion, pass down, although she speak no word, to Joan with her Pot, Jill with her Pail, and it may be, with one knows not what nightmare melancholy, to Tom the Fool? (*A* 262)

290   TOM AT CRUACHAN

306   This poem was written on 29 July 1931 and first appeared in *WMP*

Title: For Tom see note above on 'Tom the Lunatic' (*PNE* 289). For Cruachan see note on 'The Hour Before Dawn' (*PNE* 125) and headnote on 'The Dancer at Cruachan and Cro-Patrick' (*PNE* 288).

291   OLD TOM AGAIN

306   This poem was written in October 1931 and first appeared in *WMP*.
   See note on 'Tom the Lunatic' (*PNE* 289). Yeats described the poem in a letter to his wife as 'a reply to the Dancer's Song', probably 'The Dancer at Cruachan and Cro-Patrick' (*PNE* 288).

292   THE DELPHIC ORACLE UPON PLOTINUS

306   This poem was written on 19 August 1931 and first appeared in *WMP*.
   This poem is based on the verse oracle, in Porphyry's *Life of Plotinus*, given to Amelius who consulted Delphi (the most famous Greek oracle, most influential from the eighth to the fifth centuries BC, in Phocis on the slopes of Mount Parnassus) to discover where Plotinus' soul had gone after his death. Yeats knew Thomas Taylor's translation of Plotinus and read Dempsey's *The Delphic Oracle* carefully, but the source for this poem, describing the Greek idea of Heaven, is Stephen MacKenna's translation:

> . . . the bonds of human necessity are loosed for you and, strong of heart, you beat your eager way from out the roaring tumult of the fleshly life to the shores of that wave-washed coast free from the thronging of the guilty, thence to take the grateful path of the sinless soul:/where glows the splendour of God, where Right is throned in the stainless place, far from the wrong that mocks at law./Oft-times as you strove to rise above the bitter waves of this blood-drenched life, above the sickening whirl, toiling in the mid-most of the rushing flood and the unimaginable turmoil, oft-times, from the Ever-Blessed, there was shown to you the Term still close at hand:/Oft-times, when your mind thrust out awry and was like to be rapt down unsanctioned paths, the Immortals themselves prevented, guiding you on the straightgoing way to the celestial spheres, pouring down before you a dense shaft of light that your eyes might see from amid the mournful gloom./ Sleep never closed those eyes: high above the heavy murk of the mist you held them; tossed in the welter, you still had vision; still you saw sights many and fair not granted to all that labour in wisdom's quest./But now that you have cast the screen aside, quitted the tomb that held your lofty soul, you enter at once the heavenly consort:/where fragrant breezes play, where all is unison and winning tenderness and guileless joy and the place is lavish of the nectar streams the unfailing Gods bestow, with the blandishments of the Loves, and delicious airs, and tranquil sky:/where Minos and Rhadamanthus dwell,

322

great brethren of the golden race of mighty Zeus; where dwells the just Aeacus, and Plato, consecrated power, and stately Pythagoras and all else that form the choir of Immortal Love, there where the heart is ever lifted in joyous festival.

O Blessed One, you have fought your many fights; now crowned with unfailing life, your days are with the Ever-Holy./

Rejoicing Muses, let us stay our song and the subtle windings of our dance; thus much I could but tell, to my golden lyre, of Plotinus, the hallowed soul.

Good and kindly, singularly gentle and engaging: thus the oracle presents him, and so in fact we found him. Sleeplessly alert – Apollo tells – pure of soul, ever striving towards the divine which he loved with all his being, he laboured strenuously to free himself and rise above the bitter waves of this blood-drenched life: and this is why to Plotinus – God-like and lifting himself often, by the ways of meditation and by the methods Plato teaches in the Banquet, to the first and all-transcendent God – that God appeared, the God throned above the Intellectual-Principle and all the Intellectual-Sphere. . . .

We are told that often when he was leaving the way, the Gods set him on the true path again, pouring down before him a dense shaft of light; here we are to understand that in his writing he was overlooked and guided by the divine powers.

'In this sleepless vision within and without,' – the oracle says, 'your eyes have beheld sights many and fair not vouchsafed to all that take the philosophic path': contemplation in man may sometimes be more than human, but compare it with the True-Knowing of the Gods and, wonderful though it be, it can never plunge into the depths their divine vision fathoms.

Thus far the Oracle recounts what Plotinus accomplished and to what heights he attained while still in the body: emancipated from the body, we are told how he entered the celestial circle where all is friendship, tender delight, happiness and loving union with God, where Minos and Rhadamanthus and Aeacus, the sons of God, are enthroned as judges of souls – not however to hold him to judgment but as welcoming him to their consort to which are bidden spirits pleasing to the Gods – Plato, Pythagoras and all the people of the Choir of Immortal Love, there where the blessed spirits have their birth-home and live in days made happy by the Gods. (S. MacKenna, *Plotinus*, 'Porphyry's Life of Plotinus', 22–4; revd. edn (1946) 16.)

1   *that great Plotinus*: Plotinus (AD 205–270) was born in Egypt and studied at Alexandria. He then opened a School at Rome and founded Neoplatonic philosophy; he was a mystic and had knowledge of oriental philosophy.

2   *such seas*: Yeats kept closely to the original, the seas being strengthened by 'buffeted' in the poem. The 'roaring tumult', the 'bitter waves', the 'sickening whirl', the 'rushing flood' and 'unimaginable turmoil' are echoed in this line, for Plotinus was 'tossed in the welter'.

3   *Bland Rhadamanthus*: the adjective may have come from the 'blandishments' of the sentence in MacKenna's translation which precedes the introduction of Rhadamanthus. He, along with Aeacus and Minos, was a judge of souls in the underworld and is bland because he is welcoming Plotinus, not judging him. He

was a son of Zeus and Europa, renowned for his impartial justice when he reigned in the Cyclades.

4   *the Golden Race*: Porphyry describes Minos, Rhadamanthus and Aeacus, the sons of God, as enthroned as judges of souls: Minos and Rhadamanthus are 'great brethren of the golden race of Zeus'. Minos was also a son of Zeus and Europa. They looked dim to Plotinus, but they had guided him by pouring down a dense shaft of light that his eyes 'might see from amid the mournful gloom'. While 'tossed in the welter' he still had vision.

5   *Salt blood*: Plotinus was labouring strenuously to free himself and 'rise above the bitter waves of this blood-drenched life'.

307   6-7   *Scattered on the level grass*
            Or winding through the grove: Plotinus having cast the screen aside, enters 'the heavenly consort: where fragrant breezes play'.

8-10   *Plato there and Minos pass,*
            There stately Pythagoras
            And all the choir: cf. MacKenna's translation:

> Where Minos and Rhadamanthus dwell, great brethren of the golden race of mighty Zeus; where dwells the just Aeacus, and Plato, consecrated power, and stately Pythagoras and all else that form the choir of Immortal Love, there where the heart is ever lifted in joyous festival.

This is echoed in Yeats's essay 'Bishop Berkeley' as one of his favourite quotations: 'That wave-washed shore . . . the golden race of mighty Zeus . . . the just Aeacus, Plato, stately Pythagoras, and all the choir of immortal love' (*E & I* 409). For Plato see note on 'Mad as the Mist and Snow' (*PNE* 285) and for Pythagoras see note on 'Among School Children' (*PNE* 222). Cf. 'The Statues' (*PNE* 362) and 'News for the Delphic Oracle' (*PNE* 363).

A Woman Young and Old

THIS series of poems was written between 1926 and 1929; the 'woman speaks first in youth, then in age' (*WBY* 374). They are, to a certain extent, companion poems to those of *A Man Young and Old*, in *The Tower*, which were written in 1926 or 1927. Yeats's note (*CP* 536) says that the series was written before the publication of *The Tower* but left out for some reason I cannot recall'.

FATHER AND CHILD   293

This poem was probably written in 1926 or 1927; it first appeared in *WS*.   *308*

1   *She hears me*: Anne Butler Yeats, Yeats's daughter

strike the board: an echo of George Herbert's 'The Collar':

>   'I struck the board, and cry'd, No more.'

4   *a man*: the poem records an incident in the Yeats household when Anne, then a child, praised the appearance of a friend, Fergus Fitzgerald.

BEFORE THE WORLD WAS MADE   294

Ellmann (*IY* 292), dates this poem's composition as February 1928. The poem   *308*
first appeared in *WS*.

7   *I'm looking for the face*: cf. line 12 'Young Man's Song' (*PNE* 276) and 'His Bargain' (*PNE* 281). Here the woman is searching for her archetypal face. This is parallel to Plato's ideas, though they were abstract. Cf. Grace Jackson, *Mysticism in Yeats and AE in relation to Oriental and American Thought*, 152. There are three possible places in Plato where Yeats might have found a source for his image: *Republic* 597, where Plato applied his theory of ideas to constructing a bed and pointed out that God was the creator of the models of all things; *Timaeus* 28, where Timaeus ventures the idea that in making the world God looked to his created pattern; and *Phaedrus* 250, where Socrates speaks of earthly copies of higher ideas.

295   A FIRST CONFESSION

309   Ellmann (*IY* 292) gives June 1927 as the date of composition for this poem; it first appeared in *WS*.

This poem was included in a letter Yeats wrote to Olivia Shakespear from Thoor Ballylee on 23 June 1927 with the introduction 'Here is an innocent little song – one of the first [of] my woman series to balance that of ''The Young and Old Countryman'' ' . . . (*L* 725). In a note on this poem in *TWS* (New York Edition, 1929) Yeats said he had symbolised 'a woman's love as the struggle of the darkness to keep the sun from rising from its earthly bed' (but had changed the symbol in 'The Choice' (later 'Chosen' (*PNE* 298)).

14   *Zodiac*: cf. note on 'Chosen' (*PNE* 298)

296   HER TRIUMPH

310   This poem was written on 29 November 1926 and first appeared in *WS*.

The MS. version of the poem ran as follows:

> I am not evil now; until you came
> I thought the shamefulest things imaginable
> And they but seemed the sweeter for the shame:
> Thought love the better was it casual:
> I had an opium eating friend, a friend
> Who had drunk to drown a melancholy fit.
> The coils of the dragon had no end
> Its breath had touched me but you mastered it
> And broke the chain and set my ankle free
> Panoplied saint, wing-heeled Persius
> And now we stare at the sea
> And a miraculous strange bird shrieks at us.
>
> I laughed at poet's calls until you came
> And thought a common life more natural
> And Nature but a comedy and a game
> And love the better if but casual.

1   *the dragon's will*: Yeats may have had the picture 'Saint George and the Dragon' (ascribed to Bordone) in mind when he wrote this poem (it is described in 'Michael Robartes and the Dancer' (*CP* 197). It is in the National Gallery, Dublin. Another possible source is Cosimo Tura's 'St George and the Dragon', which Yeats saw in Ferrara Cathedral in 1907. Kathleen Raine, 'Yeats's Debt to Blake' *DM* (Summer 1966) 39, suggests that the dragon reason may be Blake's Urizen.

10   *Saint George or else a pagan Perseus*: see previous note. Yeats had a

reproduction (Ed^ne Alinari, p^e 2ª, No. 11884) of Perino del Vaga's *Andromeda and Perseus* from the Papal apartments at Castel S. Angelo, which may have been in his mind when he wrote this poem. Perseus was a son of Zeus and Danae (visited by Zeus in a shower of gold), the daughter of Acrisius, King of Argos, later killed by Perseus by mistake. Perseus, who killed Medusa the Gorgon also, rescued Andromeda (daughter of Cepheus, King of Ethiopia and Cassiopea) from a dragon.

12 *strange bird*: cf. 'Juno's peacock' of 'My Table' (*PNE* 208). David R. Clark (*YASAC* 98-9) argues that Plate 38 of Blake's *Milton* may have supplied the strange bird, but that William Morris's 'The Doom of King Acrisius' in *The Earthly Paridise* is a more likely source.

CONSOLATION   297

This poem was probably written in June 1927, and it first appeared in *WS*.   *310*
   Yeats described the poem as 'one not so innocent' in a letter of 23 June 1927 to Olivia Shakespear (*L* 725).

9 *crime of being born*: cf. 'A Dialogue of Self and Soul' (*PNE* 242) with 'the crime of death and birth'

CHOSEN   298

This poem was probably written early in 1926. Yeats wrote to Professor Grierson *311*
on 21 February 1926 that he had used the arrangement of the rhymes in Donne's *Nocturnall upon St Lucie's Day* for a poem of his own (*L* 710). 'Chosen' first appeared in *The Winding Stair* (1929) with the title 'The Choice'.
   The writing of the poem is discussed in *BL* 137-63 and Wilson (*Y & T* 205-11) discusses it at length.

1 *chosen*: this may come from Plato's myth of Er, in which the souls of men and women in heaven choose the lots (cf. *LT* 105 and *Y & T* 207) which represent their future destinies.

3 *the whirling Zodiac*: the sun progresses through the whirling zodiac. Yeats's first note on the poem read:

> I have symbolised a woman's love as the struggle of the darkness to keep the sun from rising from its earthly bed. In the last stanza of the Choice [the original title of 'Chosen'] I change the symbol to that of the souls of man and woman ascending through the Zodiac. In some Neoplatonist or Hermatist – whose name I forget – the whorl changes into a sphere at one of the points where the Milky Way crosses the Zodiac.   (*The Winding Stair* (1929))

The note was expanded in *WS*:

The 'learned astrologer' in *Chosen* was Macrobius [Ambrosius Theodosius Macrobius, a fifth-century Neoplatonist], and the particular passage was found for me by Dr. Sturm [Dr F. P. Sturm (d. 1942), a doctor who practised in Lancashire; he published three books of poems and was interested in the occult] that too little known poet and mystic. It is from Macrobius's comment upon 'Scipio's Dream' (Lib. I, Cap. XII, Sec. 5): '. . . when the sun is in Aquarius, we sacrifice to the Shades, for it is in the sign inimical to human life; and from thence, the meeting-place of Zodiac and/Milky Way, the descending soul by its defluction is drawn out of the spherical, the sole divine form, into the cone'. Cf. note on line 28, 'Byzantium' (*PNE* 260) and see *Frank Pearce Sturm: His Life, Letters and Collected Work*, ed. Richard Taylor (1969) 92, for Sturm's letter of 22 January 1926 to Yeats.

16 *both adrift on the miraculous stream*: the Milky Way, a symbol used for the abode of the soul before birth

17 *wrote a learned astrologer*: Wilson (*Y & T* 210) quotes the passage from Macrobius: 'Since those who are about to descend are yet in Cancer, and have not left the Milky Way, they rank in the order of the gods. . . . From the confine, therefore, in which the zodiac and galaxy touch one another, the soul, descending from a round figure which is the only divine form, is produced into a cone' (T. Taylor, *Porphyry*, 187). Wilson points out that Cancer is 'the confine in which the zodiac and galaxy touch one another', where Milky Way and zodiac meet, and Cancer is therefore 'the gate'. The soul passes through it, loses its spherical shape. It descends through the signs; after death it returns through the gate of Capricorn, eventually returning to its source. Wilson remarks (*Y & T* 210), that the harmonious soul is a sphere and the lovers' souls seem to be united, on their starting point on the Milky Way, 'both adrift' where spiritual and material worlds intersect and the imperfect is turned into the perfect.

18 *The Zodiac is changed into a sphere*: cf. Yeats's explanation of the Thirteenth Cycle or Thirteenth Cone in *AV*:

It is that cycle which may deliver us from the twelve cycles of time and space. The cone which intersects ours is a cone in so far as we think of it as the antithesis to our thesis, but if the time has come for our deliverance it is the phaseless sphere, sometimes called the Thirteenth Sphere, for every lesser cycle contains within itself a sphere that is, as it were, the reflection or messenger of the final deliverance. Within it live all souls that have been set free and every *Daimon* and *Ghostly Self*; our expanding cone seems to cut through its gyre; spiritual influx is from its circumference, animate life from its centre. 'Eternity also', says Hermes in the Aeslepius dialogue, 'though motionless itself, appears to be in motion.' When Shelley's Demogorgon – eternity – comes from the centre of the earth it may so come because Shelley substituted the earth for such a sphere.[1]   (*AV* (B) 210–11)

[1] Shelley, who had more philosophy than men thought when I was young, probably knew that Parmenides represented reality as a motionless sphere. Mrs Shelley speaks of the 'mystic meanings' of *Prometheus Unbound* as only intelligible to a 'mind as subtle as his own'.

He also commented on it as follows:

> The *Thirteenth Cone* is a sphere because sufficient to itself; but as seen by Man it is a cone. It becomes even conscious of itself as so seen, like some great dancer, the perfect flower of modern culture, dancing some primitive dance and conscious of his or her own life and of the dance. There is a mediaeval story of a man persecuted by his Guardian Angel because it was jealous of his sweetheart, and such stories seem closer to reality than our abstract theology. All imaginable relations may arise between a man and his God. I only speak of the *Thirteenth Cone* as a sphere and yet I might say that the gyre or cone of the *Principles* is in reality a sphere, though to Man, bound to birth and death, it can never seem so, and that it is the antinomies that force us to find it a cone. Only one symbol exists, though the reflecting mirrors make many appear and all different. (*AV* (B) 240)

PARTING   299

This poem was written in August 1926 and first appeared in *The Winding Stair*   *311* (1929).

The composition of the poem, which is linked with 'A First Confession' (*PNE* 295) and 'The Choice' ['Chosen'] (*PNE* 298) in Yeats's notes, is discussed in *BL* 138-63.

7   *his loud song*: Hone (*WBY* 433) suggested that there is an echo here of   *312* *Romeo and Juliet* III, v:

> No, night's bird and love's
> Bids all true lovers rest,
> While his loud song reproves
> The murderous stealth of day.

HER VISION IN THE WOOD   300

This poem was written in August 1926, and first appeared in *The Winding Stair*   *312* (1929).

14   *a litter with a wounded man*: Ellmann (*IY* 172-3) regards this as a portrayal of the Adonis legend. Henn (*LT* 260) suggests Adonis, or Diarmuid, who was killed by a boar on a Sligo mountain. He refers also to the Attis ritual in *The Golden Bough* in section II of 'Vacillation' (*PNE* 262).

16   *the beast*: a wild boar killed Adonis, a beautiful youth beloved by Aphrodite. The flower anemone was said to have sprung from his blood. He was restored to life by Persephone on condition that he spent six months of the year with her, six with Aphrodite. (This implied a summer-winter symbol.) His death and revival were celebrated in various festivals.

19 *Quattrocento*: *(Italian)* the fifteenth century. See note on 'Among School Children' (*CP* 222)

313 20 *Mantegna's thought*: Andrea Mantegna (1431–1506), born near Vicenza, left Padua *c.* 1459 where he painted the *Eremitani* frescoes and the *Agony in the Garden*, lived chiefly at Mantua where he painted the *Madonna della Vittoria* and the *Triumph of Caesar*.

25 *all blood and mire*: cf. 'the fury and the mire of human veins' and the dolphin's 'mire and blood' of 'Byzantium' (*PNE* 260) and the 'blood and mire' of 'The Gyres' (*PNE* 321).

31 *no fabulous symbol*: the body is not that of a god or hero, but of her lover.

301 A LAST CONFESSION

313 The MSS. dates of this poem are June, July 23 and 24 and August 1926. It first appeared in *The Winding Stair* (1929).

314 12 *Beast gave beast as much*: Henn (*LT* 66) draws attention to Yeats's remark to John Sparrow that the tragedy of sexual intercourse is in the perpetual virginity of the soul, quoted in *Y:M & P* 267.

23 *bird of day*: cf. the 'most ridiculous little bird' of 'A Memory of Youth' (*PNE* 133), the 'miraculous strange bird' of 'Her Triumph' (*PNE* 296), and the bird in 'Parting' (*PNE* 299). Henn (*LT* 59) remarks that it seems to have among its values a kind of eternalising function: it is not only a link with daytime and the dissipation of the ecstasies of the lovers but it is also

> a half-malicious, half-mystical symbol that suggests a supernatural and eternal commentary on the act. It is 'ridiculous', 'miraculous', 'betraying'. Perhaps it is linked to the golden bird of 'Byzantium'; something permanent and spiritual, and mocking, beside love's ecstasy.

302 MEETING

314 The date of composition of this poem is uncertain (probably 1926). It first appeared in *The Winding Stair* (1929).

303 FROM THE 'ANTIGONE'

315 This translation was probably largely finished by December 1927. Ezra Pound altered the order of the lines in a TS of 1928. The poem first appeared in *The Winding Stair* (1929). Yeats knew the translations by Richard Jebb, Lewis

Campbell and Paul Masqueray; according to Mrs W. B. Yeats he used the Masqueray version when writing this poem, as he did when writing *Oedipus the King* and *Oedipus at Colonus*.

6   *Parnassus*: This mountain, a few miles from Delphi, was sacred to the Muses in Greek mythology, one peak was sacred to Apollo, the other to Dionysus.

7   *Empyrean*: the highest part of the supposedly spherical heavens thought to contain the element of fire in classical cosmology. Early Christians thought it the abode of god and the angels.

10   *Brother and brother*: Antigone's brothers, Eteocles and Polynices, kill each other.

15   *Oedipus' child*: Antigone the daughter of Oedipus, commits suicide in the *Antigone*, having been buried alive by Creon, king of Thebes. His son Haemon, who loved her, killed himself on her grave.

Parnell's Funeral and Other Poems

AFTER Yeats had written the last poems of *WS* he thought his inspiration was drying up: for a time he wondered if Lady Gregory's death and the closing of Coole had ended the subconscious drama of his imaginative life. Then he returned to verse with 'Parnell's Funeral', in which he 'rhymed passages from a lecture' given in America, where he was on a lecture tour from October 1932 to January 1933. See his 'Modern Ireland: an Address to American Audiences 1932-33', *Irish Renaissance: a Gathering of Essays, Memoirs and Letters from the Massachusetts Review*, ed. Robin Skelton and David R. Clark (1965) pp. 13-25. In Dublin there followed an intense interlude of politics, and a reawakened interest in *AV* expressed in the *Supernatural Songs* – metaphysical, passionate and a brilliant answer to his earlier worry that perhaps he was too old for poetry.

304   PARNELL'S FUNERAL

319   This poem was completed in April 1933. Lines 16-23 first appeared, untitled, in *DM* (April–June 1932), as part of the 'Introduction to Fighting the Waves', which was included in *W & B*.

The poem first appeared in entirety in the *Spectator* (19 Oct. 1934); and the title given to the first section was 'A Parnellite at Parnell's Funeral'. The second section was entitled 'Forty Years Later'. It also appeared in the *Spectator* (19 Oct. 1934). The second section was untitled in *KGCT*. The first appearance of the whole poem with the present title was in *FMM*. Yeats wrote a commentary (annotated at the end of the extract below) on the poem in *KGCT* which reads:

I

When lecturing in America I spoke of Four Bells, four deep tragic notes, equally divided in time, so symbolising the war that ended in the Flight of the Earls; the Battle of the Boyne; the coming of French influence among our peasants; the beginning of our own age; events that closed the sixteenth, seventeenth, eighteenth and nineteenth centuries. My historical knowledge, such as it is, begins with the Second Bell.

II

When Huguenot artists designed the tapestries for the Irish House of Lords, depicting the Battle of the Boyne and the siege of Derry, they celebrated the defeat of their old enemy Louis XIV, and the establishment of a Protestant Ascendency which was to impose upon Catholic Ireland, an oppression copied in all details from that imposed upon the French Protestants. Did my own great-great-grandmother, the Huguenot Marie Voisin feel a vindictive triumph, or did she remember that her friend Archbishop King had been a loyal servant of James II and had, unless greatly slandered, accepted his present master after much vacillation, and that despite episcopal vehemence, his clergy were suspected of a desire to restore a Catholic family to the English throne. The Irish House of Lords, however, when it ordered the Huguenot tapestries, probably accepted the weavers' argument that the Battle of the Boyne was to Ireland what the defeat of the Armada had been to England. Armed with this new power, they were to modernise the social structure, with great cruelty but effectively, and to establish our political nationality by quarrelling with England over the wool trade, a protestant monopoly [monopoly]. At the base of the social structure, but hardly within it, the peasantry dreamed on in their medieval sleep; the Gaelic poets sang of the banished Catholic aristocracy; 'My fathers served their fathers before Christ was crucified' sang one of the most famous. Ireland had found new masters, and was to discover for the first time in its history that it possessed a cold, logical intellect. That intellect announced its independence when Berkeley, then an undergraduate of Trinity College, wrote in his *Commonplace Book*, after a description of the philosophy of Hobbes, Newton and Locke, the fashionable English philosophy of his day, 'We Irish do not think so.' An emotion of pride and confidence at that time ran through what there was of an intellectual minority. The friends who gave Berkeley his first audience, were to found 'The Dublin' now 'The Royal Dublin Society,' perhaps to establish that scientific agriculture described and praised by Arthur Young. The historical dialectic trampled upon their minds in that brutal Ireland, product of two generations of civil war, described by Swift in a well-known sermon; they were the trodden grapes and became wine. When Berkeley landed in America, he found himself in a nation running the same course, though Ireland was too close to England to keep its independence through the Napoleonic Wars. America, however, as his letters show, had neither the wealth nor the education of contemporary Ireland; no such violence of contraries, as of black upon white, had stung it into life.

III

The influence of the French Revolution woke the peasantry from the medieval sleep, gave them ideas of social justice and equality, but prepared for a century disastrous to the national intellect. Instead of the Protestant Ascendancy with its sense of responsibility, we had the Garrison, a political party of Protestant and Catholic landowners, merchants and officials. They loved the soil of Ireland; the returned Colonial Governor crossed the Channel to see the May flowers in his park; the merchant loved with an ardour I have not met elsewhere, some sea-board town where he had made his money, or spent his youth, but they could give to a people they thought unfit for self-government, nothing but a condescending affection. They preferred frieze-coated humanists, dare-devils upon horseback, to ordinary men and women; created in Ireland and elsewhere an audience that welcomed the vivid imaginations of Lever, Lover, Somerville and Ross. These writers, especially the first have historical importance, so completely have they expressed a social phase. Instead of the old half medieval peasantry came an agrarian political

333

party, that degraded literature with rhetoric and insincerity. Its novels, poems, essays, histories showed Irish virtue struggling against English and landlord crime; historical characters that we must admire or abhor according to the side they took in politics. Certain songs by Davis, Carleton's *Valentine McClutchy*, Kickham's *Knocknagow*, Mitchel's *History of Ireland*, numberless forgotten books in prose and verse founded or fostered a distortion we have not yet escaped. In the eighties of the last century came a third school: three men too conscious of intellectual power to belong to party, George Bernard Shaw, Oscar Wilde, George Moore, the most complete individualists in the history of literature, abstract, isolated minds, without a memory or a landscape. It is this very isolation, this defect, as it seems to me, which has given Bernard Shaw an equal welcome in all countries, the greatest fame in his own lifetime any writer has known. Without it, his wit would have waited for acceptance upon studious exposition and commendation.

IV

I heard the first note of the Fourth Bell forty years ago on a stormy October morning. I had gone to Kingsto[w]n Pier to meet the Mail Boat that arrived about 6 a.m. I was expecting a friend, but met what I thought much less of at the time, the body of Parnell. I did not go to the funeral, because, being in my sensitive and timid youth, I hated crowds, and what crowds implied, but my friend went. She told me that evening of the star that fell in broad daylight as Parnell's body was lowered into the grave – was it a collective hallucination or an actual event? Years after Standish O'Grady was to write:

'I state a fact – it was witnessed by thousands. While his followers were committing Charles Parnell's remains to the earth, the sky was bright with strange lights and flames. Only a coincidence possibly, and yet persons not superstitious have maintained that there is some mysterious sympathy between the human soul and the elements, and that storm, and other elemental disturbances have too often succeeded or accompanied great battles to be regarded as only fortuitous. . . . Those flames recall to my memory what is told of similar phenomena, said to have been witnessed when tidings of the death of Saint Columba overran the north-west of Europe.'

I think of the symbolism of the star shot with an arrow, described in the appendix to my book *Autobiographies*. I ask if the fall of a star may not upon occasion, symbolise an accepted sacrifice.

Dublin had once been a well-mannered, smooth-spoken city. I knew an old woman who had met Davis constantly and never knew that he was in politics until she read his obituary in the newspaper. Then came agrarian passion; Unionists and Nationalists ceased to meet, but each lived behind his party wall an amiable life. This new dispute broke through all walls; there were old men and women I avoid because they have kept that day's bitter tongue. Upon the other hand, we began to value truth. According to my memory and the memory of others, free discussion appeared among us for the first time, bringing the passion for reality, the satiric genius that informs *Ulysses, The Playboy of the Western World, The Informer, The Puritan* and other books, and plays; the accumulated hatred of years was suddenly transferred from England to Ireland. James Joyce has no doubt described something remembered from his youth in that dinner table scene in *The Portrait of the Artist as a Young Man*, when after a violent quarrel about Parnell and the priests, the host sobs, his head upon the table; 'My dead King.'

We had passed through an initiation like that of the Tibetan ascetic, who staggers half dead from a trance, where he has seen himself eaten alive and has not yet learned that the eater was himself.

V

As we discussed and argued, the national character changed, O'Connell, the great comedian, left the scene the tragedian Parnell took his place. When we talked of his pride; of his apparent impassivity when his hands were full of blood because he had torn them with his nails, the proceeding epoch with its democratic bonhomie, seemed to grin through a horse collar. He was the symbol that made apparent, or made possible (are there not historical limbos where nothing is possible?) that epoch's contrary: contrary, not negation, not refutation; the spring vegetables may be over, they have not been refuted. I am Blake's disciple, not Hegel's: 'contraries are positive. A negation is not a contrary.' (*KGCT*)

3 *Flight of the Earls*: Hugh O'Neill (1550-1616), second Earl of Tyrone, and Rory O'Donnell (1575-1608), first earl of Tyrconnel, left Ireland secretly with a hundred others on 14 September 1607; they went to France, then to Rome. They had submitted to James I (1566-1628), King of England, in 1603; in Tyrone and Tirconnel English law was established in 1603 and 1604; but the earls despaired of being left in peace on their estates by the officials and adventurers who had hoped to confiscate these lands as part of the English colonisation policy. After the flight nearly all the fertile land of six counties (over half a million acres) was confiscated in 1608 and 'planted' mainly with Scottish presbyterians and English protestants.

Battle of the Boyne: in this battle in 1690 William of Orange (1650-1702), King William III of England, defeated James II (1633-1701), the former King.

4 *French influence*: a French naval force sailed for Ireland in 1796 but returned as a result of bad weather. A small French force under General Humbert landed in Killala in Co. Mayo in August 1798 (after the Irish rebellion had been crushed) and subsequently surrendered. Next a French naval force with 3,000 troops under Admiral Bompart, was defeated off Lough Swilly, Co. Donegal.

9 *Huguenot artists . . . tapestries*: Ireland had many Huguenot refugees (who left France after Louis XIV (1638-1715) revoked the edict of Nantes (1595) which had guaranteed their religious freedom (they were Calvinists); many of them were weavers and were involved in the linen trade). *PNE* comments that the tapestries that Yeats mentions were installed in 1733; the chief artist was Melcior Van der Hagen, the chief weaver Jan Van Beaver, and the manufacturer Robert Baillie of Dublin. Only two of the six contracted tapestries were produced.

11 *Siege of Derry*: the tapestry entitled The Defence of Londonderry commemorates the city's resistance to James II's unsuccessful fifteen-week siege in 1689.

16   *Mary Voisin*: her father Claude Voisin came to Ireland in 1634; by marrying Edmond Butler she introduced the Butler strain (of which Yeats was so proud) into the family. She was Yeats's paternal great-great-great-grandmother.

17   *Archbishop King*: William King (1650–1729), Dean of St. Patrick's Cathedral in 1688, a Williamite, was imprisoned and released after the Battle of the Boyne. He wrote the *State of the Protestants of Ireland under the late King James' Government* (1691), a vindication of the revolution, and became Archbishop of Dublin in 1703.

25   *the Armada*: the Spanish fleet, defeated by the English in 1588

28   *the wool trade*: Lord Wentworth, later the earl of Strafford, when Deputy in Ireland, took measures to curtail the Irish woollen trade (though encouraging the linen trade, particularly in Ulster) in the seventeenth century. From 1699 to 1739 the Westminster Parliament prohibited the export of woollen goods from Ireland except to restricted ports in England (which imposed high import duties on them); the ban on Irish trading with other countries remained in force up to 1779, when the export duties on wool were also removed. In 1699 the Dublin parliament had imposed severe export duties on wool, frieze and flannel; the subsequent decline in the wool trade caused a large puritan emigration from Ireland to New England.

32–33   *my fathers . . . crucified*: the quotation is from Frank O'Connor's translation (with 'served' substituted by Yeats for 'followed') of the 'Last Lines' of Egan O'Rahilly (1670–1726), the Irish poet. See Yeats's note on 'Three Songs to the Same Tune' (*PNE* A101)

36   *Berkeley*: see note on 'Blood and the Moon' (*PNE* 243).

38   *Hobbes*: see note below on [Move Upon Newton's Town] (*PNE* A99).

39   *Newton*: see note on 'At Algeciras – A Meditation upon Death' (*PNE* 257).

Locke: see note on 'Fragments' (*PNE* 219).

43–44   *Royal Dublin Society*: fourteen men met in Trinity College in 1731 to found the Dublin society 'for improving Husbandry Manufactures and other useful arts'. See A. Norman Jeffares, *Anglo-Irish Literature* (1982) p. 41.

45   *Arthur Young*: Young (1741–1820) the English agriculturalist, wrote *A Tour in Ireland with General Observation on the Present State of that Kingdom* [1780]

47–48   *Swift . . . well-known sermon*: 'A Sermon on the Wretched condition of Ireland', *The Works of Rev. Dr. Jonathan Swift* (1784) XII, 122–37

49   *America*: Berkeley went there in 1728 to found a College at the Bermudas 'for the Christian civilization of America'; he stayed at Rhode Island for three years, but returned in 1731 whem the promised government grant was withdrawn.

52   *Napoleonic Wars*: The period when France under Napoleon (1769-1821) was at war, from 1803 to 1815.

56   *French Revolution*: the period from 1789 to 1799

59   *Protestant Ascendancy*: the period after the Williamite wars up to the Act of Union (1800) after which the Irish parliament in Dublin ceased to exist.

60   *the Garrison*: a general term for those in Ireland who supported British rule

63   *colonial governor*: a generalising statement, but Yeats probably had Sir William Gregory, Lady Gregory's husband, in mind here.

71   *Lever*: Charles Lever (1806-72), Irish novelist. See A. Norman Jeffares, 'Yeats and the wrong Lever', *Yeats, Sligo and Ireland* (ed. Jeffares, 1980) 98-111.

Lover: Samuel Lover (1797-1868), artist, novelist and song writer

Somerville and Ross: Edith Somerville (1858-1949) and Violet Martin (1862-1915) who wrote their novels and stories under the names Somerville and Ross.

79   *Davis*: Thomas Davis (1814-45); see note on 'To Ireland in the Coming Times' (*PNE* 39).

Carleton: William Carleton (1794-1869), Irish novelist and short story writer.

80   *Kickham's Knocknagow*: see note on 'The Ballad of the Fox Hunter' (*PNE* 16).

80-81   *Mitchel's History of Ireland*: published in 1868, by John Mitchel (1815-75); see note on 'Under Ben Bulben' (*PNE* 356).

85   *George Bernard Shaw*: Shaw (1856-1950) left Dublin for London in 1876. He wrote in the 1921 preface to his novel *Immaturity* that 'every Irishman who felt that his business in life was on the higher planes of the cultural professions felt that he must have a metropolitan domicile and an international culture: that is, he felt that his first business was to get out of Ireland. I had the same feeling'. See Bernard Shaw, *The Matter with Ireland*, ed. David H. Greene and Dan H. Lawrence (1962) 10.

Oscar Wilde: Oscar Wilde (1854-1900), dramatist and wit; see note on 'A Statesman's Holiday' (*PNE* A125).

George Moore: George Moore (1853-1933), novelist; see notes on 'Introductory Rhymes' (*PNE* 112) and 'Closing Rhyme' (*PNE* 142)

94   *Kingsto[w]n Pier*: now Dun Laoghaire, where the Mail Boat from Holyhead docks. Yeats had gone there to meet Maud Gonne off the boat.

97-100   *Parnell ... the star*: see notes below on ll. 4-7 of the poem. Parnell (1846-91) died in October 1891 in Brighton, was buried in Glasnevin Cemetery, Dublin, on 11 October 1891.

102   *O'Grady ... write*: in *The Story of Ireland* (1894) 210-12, by Standish James O'Grady

113   *Saint Columba*: Columba (521-97), excommunicated and exiled from Ireland, founded the famous monastery at Iona in 563.

116   *appendix ... Autobiographies*: Part IV in *A* (1926), previously published in *The Criterion* 1923, and *The Dial*, July 1923. See Yeats's note on 'Parnell's Funeral' (*PNE* 304). The appendix describes Yeats's vision of the centaur and the naked woman.

130   *Ulysses*: novel by James Joyce (1882-1941)

130-131   *The Playboy of the Western World*: play published in 1907 by John Millington Synge (1871-1909). See note on 'On those that hated "The Playboy of the Western World"' (*PNE* 120).

131   *The Informer, The Puritan*: novels by Liam O'Flaherty (b. 1896) published, respectively, in 1925 and 1931.

135   *The Portrait ... Artist*: in this novel by Joyce, published in 1916, the quarrel is in chapter one; a remark is made by a guest, Mr Casey, not by the host.

144   *Parnell ... took his place*: Parnell was a supremely powerful figure in Irish political life from 1879 to 1890, when he lost his leadership of the party because of his relationship with Mrs O'Shea.

143   *O'Connell*: see note below, on line 1, 'the Great Comedian'.

152   *Blake's ... not Hegel's*: Yeats is quoting from Blake's *Milton*, Book II; George Wilhelm Friedrich Hegel (1770-1831) was a German philosopher.

I

1   *the Great Comedian's tomb*: Daniel O'Connell (1775-1847), was educated at St Omer, driven out at the Revolution, read law in London and practised successfully. He killed D'Esterne in a duel, 1815; was returned as MP for Clare,

1828; pushed through Catholic Emancipation, 1829; MP for Dublin, 1832; held balance of power in House of Commons, 1835. He founded the Repeal Association, 1840, and was aided by the *Nation* (founded 1942). He was prosecuted in 1844, his sentence of a year's imprisonment quashed by House of Lords. He quarrelled with the Young Irelanders because of their belief in force. He died on a pilgrimage to Rome, but his body is buried at Glasnevin Cemetery, Co. Dublin. Yeats particularly disliked him, and said of him in a Senate speech:

> We never had any trouble about O'Connell. It was said about O'Connell, in his own day, that you could not throw a stick over a workhouse wall without hitting one of his children, but he believed in the dissolubility of marriage, and when he died his heart was very properly preserved in Rome. I am not quite sure whether it was in a bronze or marble urn, but it is there, and I have no doubt the art of that urn was as bad as the other art of the period.   (*SSY* 97–8)

He described him as 'the too compromised and compromising Daniel O'Connell' (*A* 353), and disliked 'the bragging rhetoric and gregarious humour of O'Connell's generation and school' (*A* 195).

4   *a brighter star shoots down*: this is the star, of which Maud Gonne told Yeats, which fell as Parnell's body was lowered into the grave. For Parnell, see note on 'To a Shade' (*PNE* 118)

7   *the Cretan barb that pierced a star*: this can be explained by a passage in *A* which Yeats annotated very fully. The passage is in 'The Stirring of the Bones':

> As Arthur Symons and I were about to stay with Mr Edward Martyn at Tulira Castle, in Galway, I decided that it was there I must make my invocation of the moon. I made it night after night just before I went to bed, and after many nights – eight or nine perhaps – I saw between sleeping and waking, as in a kinematograph, a galloping centaur, and a moment later a naked woman of incredible beauty, standing upon a pedestal and shooting an arrow at a star. I still remember the tint of that marvellous flesh which makes all human flesh seem unhealthy, and remember that others who have seen such forms have remembered the same characteristic. Next morning before breakfast Arthur Symons took me out on to the lawn to recite a scrap of verse, the only verse he had ever written to a dream. He had dreamt the night before of a woman of great beauty, but she was clothed and had not a bow and arrow. When he got back to London, he found awaiting him a story sent to the *Savoy* by Fiona Macleod and called, I think, *The Archer*. Some one in the story had a vision of a woman shooting an arrow into the sky and later of an arrow shot at a faun that pierced the faun's body and remained, the faun's heart torn out and clinging to it, embedded in a tree. Some weeks later I, too, was in London, and found among Mathers' pupils a woman whose little child – perhaps at the time of my vision, perhaps a little later – had come running in from the garden calling out, 'O, mother, I have seen a woman shooting an arrow into the sky and I am afraid that she has killed God'. I have somewhere among my papers a letter from a very old friend describing how her little cousin – perhaps a few months later – dreamed of a man who shot at a star with a gun and that the star fell down, but, 'I do not think', the child said, 'it minded dying because it was so very old', and how presently the child saw the star lying in a cradle. Had

some great event taken place in some world where myth is reality and had we seen some portion of it? One of my fellow-students quoted a Greek saying, 'Myths are the activities of the Daimons', or had we but seen in the memory of the race something believed thousands of years ago, or had somebody – I myself perhaps – but dreamed a fantastic dream which had come to those others by transference of thought? I came to no conclusion, but I was sure there was some symbolic meaning could I but find it. I went to my friend who had spoken to Megarithma, and she went once more into her trance-like meditation and heard but a single unexplained sentence: 'There were three that saw: three will attain a wisdom older than the serpent, but the child will die.' Did this refer to myself, to Arthur Symons, to Fiona Macleod, to the child who feared that the archer had killed God? I thought not, for Symons had no deep interest in the subject, and there was the second child to account for. It was probably some new detail of the myth or an interpretation of its meaning. There was a London coroner in those days, learned in the Cabbala, whom I had once known though we had not met for some years. I called upon him and told all that I have set down here. He opened a drawer and took out of it two water-colour paintings, made by a clumsy painter who had no object but a symbolical record: one was of a centaur, the other of a woman standing upon a stone pedestal and shooting her arrow at what seemed a star. He asked me to look carefully at the star, and I saw that it was a little golden heart. He said: 'You have hit upon things that you can never have read of in any book; these symbols belong to a part of the Christian Cabbala' – perhaps this was not his exact term – 'that you know nothing of. The centaur is the elemental spirit and the woman the divine spirit of the path Samekh, and the golden heart is the central point upon the cabbalistic Tree of Life and corresponds to the Sephiroth Tiphareth.' I was full of excitement, for now at last I began to understand. The Tree of Life is a geometrical figure made up of ten circles or spheres called Sephiroth joined by straight lines. Once men must have thought of it as like some great tree covered with its fruit and its foliage, but at some period, in the thirteenth century perhaps, touched by the mathematical genius of Arabia in all likelihood, it had lost its natural form. The Sephiroth Tiphareth, attributed to the sun, is joined to the Sephiroth Yesod, attributed to the moon, by a straight line called the path Samekh, and this line is attributed to the constellation Sagittarius. He would not or could not tell me more, but when I repeated what I had heard to one of my fellow-students, a yachtsman and yacht-designer and cabbalist, he said, 'Now you know what was meant by a wisdom older than the serpent'. He reminded me that the cabbalistic tree has a green serpent winding through it which represents the winding path of nature or of instinct, and that the path Samekh is part of the long straight line that goes up through the centre of the tree, and that it was interpreted as the path of 'deliberate effort'. The three who saw must, he said, be those who could attain to wisdom by the study of magic, for that was 'deliberate effort'. I remember that I quoted Balzac's description of the straight line as the line of man, but he could not throw light on the other symbols except that the short arrow must symbolise effort, nor did I get any further light. (*A* 372–5)

Yeats's notes refer to this vision of an archer:

The description of the vision was not in the first edition of this book, and I add it now on the advice of a man learned in East Mediterranean antiquities, met on a lecturing tour in England, who thought it important, and promised annotation. I would like to give his name, or at any rate to write and ask if I might, but though I have spent several hours in the search I cannot find his letter, nor can I trace him at the house where I thought we met [he was Vacher Burch, author and lecturer at Liverpool Cathedral (*PNE*)]. He was no phantom, though a correspondent seems to think so, and I can only offer an apology for my seeming discourtesy. He sent me several pages of notes which I will comment upon and summarise.

(a) *The Child and the Tree*

On a certain night in Devonshire, farmers and farm-labourers and their wives and children perform a ceremony at the finest apple-tree in the orchard. Punch is poured out at the roots and bread put among the branches, and a boy set among the branches 'who is either the tree in boy-form or the tree in bird-form', and the men fire blank charges at him. All dance round the tree, singing some such rhyme as this:

> 'Here's to thee, good apple-tree,
> To bear and blow apples enow', etc.

(*Transactions of the Devonshire Association*, 1867. Whitcombe, *Bygone Days in Devonshire and Cornwall*.)

'This rhyme calls to mind its ancient prototype, the Hymn of the Kouretes, found at Palaikastro in Crete. The Kouretes ''leap'' the ''full jars and rich fruit crops''. Moreover, in a previous stanza is celebrated the baby made immortal for Rhea.'

'This boy finds his analogue in Balder, ''who is shot to death that is life by means of a sprig or arrow of mistletoe''.'

In my vision, the star is shot by an arrow from a bow, and in one of the children's dreams which I have described, God is shot with an arrow, while in another child's dream, a star is shot with a gun. 'Balder is the tree embodied. His name tells us that. Recent philology has said that the name means, or is related to, apple-tree, Abble, Apfel, etc. But that is not true enough. When the first decipherment of Cretan pictographs is published, it will be seen that his name goes back to the Cretan Apollo who in old Cretan belief was a tree-god.' It is plain too that he is the 'Child hidden in the scented Dikton near Mount Ida' (*Phaen*. 32 ff.) of Aratus' lines, and that part of his significance is solar. 'He was believed to be born and grow up in a year (Aratus; Callimachus, *Zeus*, 552 ff., etc.) and to die once more. Orpheus made much use of these facts (Lobeck, *Aglaophamus*, i. 552 ff.).'

I had used Hebrew names connected with the symbolic tree, and the star at which the arrow was shot seems to have symbolised Kether, a Sephiroth attributed to the sun, and my invocation had for its object the killing or overcoming in some way of a 'solar influence'.

(b) *The Woman who shot the Arrow*

She was, it seems, the Mother-Goddess, whose representative priestess shot the arrow at the child, whose sacrificial death symbolised the death and resurrection of the Tree-spirit, or Apollo. 'She is pictured upon certain Cretan coins of the fifth century BC as a slightly draped, beautiful woman, sitting in the heart of a branching tree (G. F. Hill, *A Handbook of Greek and Roman Coins*, 163). She goes back to the very earliest form of the religion of Crete, and is, it seems probable, the Tree as Mother, killing the Tree as Son. But she is also Artemis, and there is a beautiful vase at Naples (Reinach, *Répertoire des vases*

341

peints grecs, i. 379. 1) which shows her archaic image upon a tall pillar with a strung bow in her left hand and a *patera* in her right.'

(c) *The Heart torn out*

A Father of the Church, Firmicus Maternus, in his book, *On the Errors of the Profane Religions*, turns the Myth of the Child Slain and Reborn into a story of murder and adultery. The Cretan Jupiter 'made an image of his son in gypsum and placed the boy's heart . . . in that part of the figure where the curve of the chest was to be seen.' It had been kept by his sister, Minerva, and a temple was made to contain the image. There were festivals and noisy processions that followed 'a basket in which the sister had hidden the heart'. 'It may be conjectured, perhaps', writes my learned man, 'that images were made with a chest cavity to contain the heart of the sacrificed.'

(d) *The Star*

The Star goes right back to the Cretan Mother-Goddess. The later Greek form of it was Asterios or Asterion. The latter, for example, is said to be Jupiter's son by Idaia (Pausanias, ii. 31. 1). 'This Star name did not mean in its primary use any particular star. It appears to have meant the Starry Heavens. . . . Zeus-Asterios is a late Gortynian (Cretan) collocation (Johannes Malala, *Chronicum*, 5). In the earlier thought of Crete, her deified kings bore the same name, Asterion or Asterios (e.g. Bacchylides, frag. 47, and Diodorus, iv. 60).'

(e) *The Centaur*

'There is a fragment of a very early Greek pot showing two roughly drawn centaurs with long thin legs, one of the centaurs touching with his hand a tree which has long leaves and what seems to be a round fruit. Above the centaurs, but apparently separate from the tree, a bird perches on a twig (Salzmann, *Nécropole de Camires*, plate XXXIX).'

(f) *Sagitta*

'About the third century BC we find Apollo is closely linked with the constellation Sagitta.' I find in a book upon astrology published this year: 'Sagittarius. The symbol is an arrow shot into the unknown. It is a sign of Initiation and Rebirth.' *A Student's Textbook of Astrology*, by Vivian E. Robson, p. 178.

Yeats wrote in August 1896 from Tillyra Castle to William Strang about the beautiful woman. See *L* 266; there is another mention of the woman in 'Anima Hominis':

Many years ago I saw, between sleeping and waking, a woman of incredible beauty shooting an arrow into the sky, and from the moment when I made my first guess at her meaning I have thought much of the difference between the winding movement of Nature and the straight line, which is called in Balzac's *Séraphita* the 'Mark of Man', but is better described as the mark of saint or sage. I think that we who are poets and artists, not being permitted to shoot beyond the tangible, must go from desire to weariness and so to desire again, and live but for the moment when vision comes to our weariness like terrible lightning, in the humility of the brutes. I do not doubt those heaving circles, those winding arcs, whether in one man's life or in that of an age, are mathematical, and that some in the world, or beyond the world, have foreknown the event and pricked upon the calendar the life-span of a Christ, a

Buddha, a Napoleon: that every movement, in feeling or in thought, prepares in the dark by its own increasing clarity and confidence its own executioner. We seek reality with the slow toil of our weakness and are smitten from the boundless and the unforeseen. Only when we are saint or sage, and renounce experience itself, can we, in imagery of the Christian Cabbala, leave the sudden lightning and the path of the serpent and become the bowman who aims his arrow at the centre of the sun. *(M 340)*

10   *A beautiful seated boy*: cf. Yeats's note, above, on *The Child and the Tree*.

13   *the Great Mother*: cf. Yeats's note, above, on *The Woman who shot the Arrow*. A priestess, imaging the Great Mother, shot the arrow.

14   *his heart*: see Yeats's note, above, on *The Heart torn out*.

15   *Sicilian coin*: see Yeats's note, above, on *The Woman who shot the Arrow*.

17   *strangers*: non-Irish. The three leaders rebelled against English rule: Robert Emmet (1778-1803) was hanged; Lord Edward Fitzgerald (1763-98) died of wounds; Wolfe Tone (1763-1798) committed suicide in prison. But Parnell was destroyed by the Irish people whose champion he was.

21   *Hysterica passio*: from Lear II, iv, 57: 'Hysterica passio, down, thou climbing sorrow'. Shakespeare's source was probably Harsnet, *Declaration of Popish Impostures*. Yeats used the phrase in 'Rosa Alchemia': '. . . I also have felt fixed habits and principles dissolving before a power, which was *hysterica passio* or sheer madness, if you will, but was so powerful in its melancholy exultation that I tremble lest it wake again and drive me from my new-found peace' *(M 278)*, and in 'A Bronze Head' *(PNE 365)*. The *hysterica passio* of Ireland is alluded to in *Estrangement (A 489)* and Yeats used the words in a letter to Dorothy Wellesley:

> I have never 'produced' a play in verse without showing the actors that the passion of the verse comes from the fact that the speakers are holding down violence or madness –'down Hysterica passio'. All depends on the completeness of the holding down, on the stirring of the beast underneath. *(DWL 86)*

dragged this quarry down: see notes on 'To a Shade' *(PNE 118)* which quote Goethe's description of the Irish being like a pack of hounds always 'dragging down some noble stag' *(A 483)*

22   *None shared our guilt*: Yeats wrote to John O'Leary on 22 January 1891 that it would seem plain that a combination of priests with the 'Sullivan gang' [A. M. Sullivan and his brother T. D. Sullivan and their friends and connections by marriage, Tim and Maurice Healey (who were MPs) were embittered against Parnell, and A. M. Sullivan controlled the *Nation*, an influential Nationalist weekly paper which voiced their views] is not likely to have on its side in political matters divine justice.' *(L 163-4)*

23   *we devoured his heart*: Parnell is envisaged as being like a god devoured in a ritual. Cf. Yeats's note quoted above on *The Heart torn out*.

320   25   *I thirst*: Yeats is challenging the Nationalists because they spurned Parnell.

27   *contagion of the throng*: cf. the 'great hatred, little room' of 'Remorse for Intemperate Speech' (*PNE* 266).

28   *the rhyme rats hear*: Henn (*LT* 46) suggests as a source for the rats *As You Like It*, III, ii, 170: 'I was never so berhymed since Pythagoras' time that I was an Irish rat, which I can hardly remember', an allusion to the idea of Pythagoras that souls could transmigrate into the bodies of animals. It was popularly believed that Irish witches could use rhymes to kill men and beasts. See *PNE* for James H. Todd's paper referring to the power believed to be possessed by Irish bards of rhyming rats to death or causing them to migrate by powers of rhyme. This paper is alluded to in *Transactions of the Ossianic Society*, 5 (1860) by Professor Connellan, where the poet Senchan through his satire causes ten mice to die. There is also an account of the poet Michael Chormaic O'Suillebhan reading the cursing psalm and pronouncing the poet's curse on rats that were eating corpses in the Mainistir cemetry in the nineteenth-century famine; the rats rushed out of the graveyard, led by an old grey rat, supported by four younger rats. Hugh Kenner, *ACE* 81, cites the 1856 Halliday edition of *As You Like It* for the bard Senchan Torpest killing 10 rats at Gort.

II

320   2   *de Valéra*: Eamonn de Valera (1882-1975), President of Ireland. He was sentenced to death for his part in the 1916 Rising; this sentence was commuted to life imprisonment, and he was released in 1917. President of Sinn Fein party, 1917-26; President of the Irish Volunteers, 1917-22; imprisoned Lincoln Gaol 1918 and escaped 1919. President of the Fianna Fail party 1926-59. de Valera was in power as President of the Executive Council of the Irish Free State 1932-48, 1951-54 and 1957-59. Yeats disliked him for being leader of the anti-treaty party in the Civil War; he thought Olivia Shakespear right (in a letter of February 1933) to compare him to Mussolini or Hitler (*L* 805), but in a letter written in the following month, on 9 March 1933, he told her after an hour's interview with de Valera that he had never met him before and was impressed 'by his simplicity and honesty though we differed throughout. It was a curious experience, each recognised the other's point of view so completely. I had gone there full of suspicion but my suspicion vanished at once' (*L* 806). Later he wrote to Mrs Shakespear in April 1933 that:

'This country is exciting. I am told that De Valera has said in private that within three years he will be torn in pieces. . . . No sooner does a politician get into power than he begins to seek unpopularity. It is the cult of sacrifice planted in the nation by the executions of 1916' (*L* 809).

Then on 13 July 1933 he wrote to her again

Politics are growing heroic. De Valera has forced political thought to face the

344

most fundamental issues. A Fascist opposition is forming behind the scenes to be ready should some tragic situation develop. I find myself constantly urging the despotic rule of the educated classes as the only end to our troubles. .... (*L* 811-12)

Parnell's heart: Charles Stewart Parnell (1846-91), Irish landowner and leader of the Irish Parliamentary Party, who was repudiated by Gladstone, the Irish Hierarchy and the Irish Party when his relationship with Mrs O'Shea became public. See note on 'To a Shade' (*PNE* 118), and the poem (written on the day Parnell died) which Yeats published on 10 October 1891 in *UI* but did not reprint. It is included in *VE* 737. See also the later poems on Parnell, 'Come Gather round Me, Parnellites' (*PNE* 341) and 'Parnell' (*PNE* 344).

5 *Cosgrave*: William T. Cosgrave (1880-1966), who was first President of Dail Eireann (1922-32) and previously Sinn Fein MP: member of Dail Eireann (1922-44).

8 *O'Higgins*: Kevin O'Higgins. See note on 'Death' (*PNE* 241).

9 *O'Duffy*: Eoin O'Duffy (1892-1944), member of IRA 1917, head of civic guards (Irish police) until dismissed by de Valera in 1933, Director of the Blue Shirt organisation, later leader of the Opposition United party 1933, and subsequently Brigadier-General in the Spanish Nationalist Army in the Spanish Civil War. A letter Yeats wrote to Olivia Shakespear on 23 July 1933 reveals his attitude to O'Duffy:

> The great secret is out – a convention of blue-shirts – 'National Guards' – have received their new leader with the Fascist salute and the new leader announces reform of Parliament as his business.
> When I wrote to you, the Fascist organiser of the blue shirts had told me that he was about to bring to see me the man he had selected for leader that I might talk my anti-democratic philosophy. I was ready, for I had just re-written for the seventh time the part of *A Vision* that deals with the future. The leader turned out to be Gen[eral] O'Duffy, head of the Irish police for twelve years, and a famous organiser. The man who brought him was one of the two men who came to me when we were threatened with a mutiny in the army. He is an old friend of mine, served in India, is crippled with wounds ... and therefore dreams an heroic dream. 'We shall be assassinated,' he said, 'but others have been chosen to take our place' – his dream perhaps but possibly not. Italy, Poland, Germany, then perhaps Ireland. Doubtless I shall hate it (though not so much as I hate Irish democracy) but it is September and we must not behave like the gay young sparks of May or June. Swinburne called September 'the month of the long decline of roses.' The *Observer*, the *Sunday Times*, the only English papers I see, have noticed nothing though Cosgrave's ablest ministers are with O'Duffy. O'Duffy himself is autocratic, directing the movement from above down as if it were an army. I did not think him a great man though a pleasant one, but one never knows, his face and mind may harden or clarify. (*L* 812-13)

Yeats wrote to her about the situation in Ireland on 20 September 1933; this letter reveals what Conor Cruise O'Brien ('Passion and Cunning: an Essay on the Politics of Yeats' (*IER* 256)) has called 'the climax' of Yeats's interest in O'Duffy:

> I wonder if the English newspapers have given you any idea of our political comedy. Act I. Capt Macmanus, the ex-British officer I spoke of, his head full of vague Fascism, got probably from me, decided that Gen[eral] O'Duffy should be made leader of a body of young men formed to keep meetings from being broken up. He put into O'Duffy's head – he describes him as 'a simple peasant' – Fascist ideas and started him off to organise that body of young men. Act II. Some journalist announced that 30,000 of these young men were going to march through Dublin on a certain day (the correct number was 3,000). Government panic. Would not O'Duffy, who had once been head of the army, and more recently head of the police, march on the Government with 30,000, plus army and police? Result, martial law – in its Irish form – armoured cars in the streets, and new police force drawn from the IRA to guard the government, and O'Duffy's organisation proclaimed. Act III. O'Duffy is made thereby so important that Cosgrave surrenders the leadership of his party to O'Duffy and all the opposition united under him. Two months ago he was unknown, politically . . . (*L* 815).

Cf. his letter to Ethel Mannin, 11 Feb. 1937 (*L* 881) for anti-O'Duffy sentiment and horror of modern politics. See also the refutation of Cruise O'Brien in 'Yeats, Fascism and Conor O'Brien', *London Magazine* 7, 4, July 1967, pp. 22–41 and Elizabeth Cullingford, *Yeats, Ireland and Fascism* (1981).

12   *bitter wisdom*: Yeats may be referring to Swift's *Discourse of the Contests and Dissensions between the Nobles and the Commons in Athens and Rome*, which was, he wrote in the Introduction to *WMP*, 'published in 1763 to warn the Tory Opposition of the impeachment of Ministers'. He regarded it as Swift's 'one philosophical work', and sees it as Swift's indictment of the War of the Many against the Few that destroyed Greece and Rome. In Rome there was a class war, in Greece a war upon character and genius. The thoughts he selected from Swift would apply to the situation in Ireland both in Parnell's time and 1933–4; he described Swift's view that the health of all states depends upon a right balance between the One, the Few, and the Many:

> The One is the executive, which may in fact be more than one – the Roman republic had two Consuls – but must for the sake of rapid decision be as few as possible; the Few are those who through the possession of hereditary wealth, or great personal gifts, have come to identify their lives with the life of the State, whereas the lives and ambitions of the Many are private. The Many do their day's work well, and so far from copying even the wisest of their neighbours, affect 'a singularity' in action and thought; but set them to the work of the State and every man Jack is 'listed in a party', becomes the fanatical follower of men of whose characters he knows next to nothing, and from that day on puts nothing into his mouth that some other man has not already chewed and digested. And furthermore, from the moment of enlistment thinks himself above other men and struggles for power until all is in confusion. (*E* 351)

This poem was probably written in 1934; it first appeared in *Life and Letters*   *324*
(Nov. 1934).

2   *Ben Bulben and Knocknarea*: mountains overlooking Sligo. Cf. 'Under Ben
Bulben' (*PNE* 356), 'The Hosting of the Sidhe' (*PNE* 40) and 'Red Hanrahan's
Song about Ireland' (*PNE* 84).

5   *Rosses' crawling tide*: sea coast and village near Sligo. Cf. note on line 15 'The
Stolen Child' (*PNE* 10).

9   *Cuchulain that fought night long with the foam*: cf. 'Cuchulain's Fight with
the Sea' (*PNE* 19).

11   *Niamh that rode on it*: cf. 'The Wanderings of Oisin' (*PNE* 375) for the

> . . . pearl-pale, high-born lady, who rose
> On a horse with bridle of findrinny;

and the opening lines of Book III:

> Fled foam underneath us, and round us, a wandering
> and milky smoke,
> High as the saddle-girth, covering away from our
> glances the tide;

Cf. notes on Niamh in 'The Hosting of the Sidhe' (*PNE* 40) and 'Under the
Moon' (*PNE* 86).

11   *lad and lass*: Naoise and Deirdre when captured by Conchubar (and kept in a
guest house in a wood in Yeats's play). Cf. *Deirdreu* 432-56. Naoise's speech sees
Deirdre and himself re-enacting the situation of Lugaidh Redstripe (a warrior of
the Red Branch cycle of tales). Deirdre was formerly Conchubar's ward whom he
kept in the hills in the care of an old nurse Lavarcam, intending to marry her.
Naoise, one of his warriors, saw her, fell in love with her and ran away with her to
Scotland, accompanied by his brothers, the other sons of Usna. When they
returned to Ireland, and Fergus, their safe-conduct, has had to leave them Naoise
says to Deirdre:

> What do they say?
> That Lugaidh Redstripe and that wife of his
> Sat at this chess-board, waiting for their end.
> They knew there was nothing that could save them,
> And so played chess as they had any night
> For years, and waited for the stroke of sword.
> I never heard a death so out of reach
> Of common hearts, a high and comely end . . .

15   *Aleel, his Countess*: the poet and the heroine in Yeats's play *The Countess Cathleen (CPl)*. See note on 'The Countess Cathleen in Paradise' *(PNE 31)*.

Hanrahan: cf. note on 'The Tower' II *(PNE 205)*.

325   19-20   *The King that could make his people stare,*
Because he had feathers instead of hair: cf. 'The Wisdom of the King' in *TSR (M* 165-70). The child of the High Queen of Ireland was visited by the crones of the grey hawk (the Sidhe), one of whom let a drop of her blood fall on the infant's lips. Two years later the King died, and the child grew very wise, but the feathers of the grey hawk grew in his hair. The child was deceived by the poets and men of law about these feathers: they told him everyone else had had feathers too, and ordered that everyone should wear them, but that anyone who told the child the truth should be put to death. The reason for this was a law that no one who had a bodily blemish could sit on the throne. The King eventually discovered the truth, ordered that Eochaid should rule in his stead and vanished.

306   TWO SONGS REWRITTEN FOR THE TUNE'S SAKE

325   These two songs appeared in *Plays in Prose and Verse* (1922), the first song (i.e. lines 1-4, 7-10, 13-16) in *The Pot of Broth* and the second song (i.e. lines 1 and 6-12) in *The Player Queen*. The second song first appeared in *The Dial* (Nov. 1922), then in *Plays in Prose and Verse*. The first song is altered more and the variations are to be found in *VE* 550-1. The revised versions of the first song appeared in *FMM*.

I
1   *Paistin Finn*: a Munster folk tune, sung to a lively air. It may be a popularised version of a song from the Ossianic cycle as the title means 'Little child of Fionn'. Fionn was Oisin's father. Since the Ossianic cycle was more popular than the Ulster cycle, Dr Brendan Kennelly suggests that Paistin Finn, purely folk, was originally heroic in the Fenian manner. Another translation is 'Fair-haired little child.' Yeats probably had in mind Sir Samuel Ferguson's version, in *Lays of the Western Gael* (1874).

II
5   *dreepy*: dreary, doleful, droopy (a dialect word in Ireland). From Scots *dree*, to endure or suffer, an archaic word revived by Sir Walter Scott.

307   A PRAYER FOR OLD AGE

326   This poem was written in 1934 and first appeared in the *Spectator* (2 Nov. 1934).
This poem was provoked by Ezra Pound's condemnation of *KGCT*, and expressed Yeats's dislike of 'intellectual' poetry. 'We only believe,' he wrote in

'The Cutting of an Agate', 'in those thoughts which have been conceived not in the brain but in the whole body' (*E & I* 235). After Lady Gregory's death Yeats had written no verse for two years:

. . . I had never been so long barren; I had nothing in my head, and there used to be more than I could write. Perhaps Coole Park where I had escaped from politics, from all that Dublin talked of, when it was shut, shut me out from my theme; or did the subconscious drama that was my imaginative life end with its owner? but it was more likely that I had grown too old for poetry. I decided to force myself to write, then take advice. In 'At Parnell's Funeral' I rhymed passages from a lecture I had given in America; a poem upon mount Meru came spontaneously, but philosophy is a dangerous theme; then I was barren again. I wrote the prose dialogue of *The King of the Great Clock Tower* that I might be forced to make lyrics for its imaginary people. When I had written all but the last lyric I went a considerable journey partly to get the advice of a poet not of my school [Ezra Pound] who would, as he did some years ago, say what he thought. I asked him to dine, tried to get his attention. 'I am in my sixty ninth year' I said, 'probably I should stop writing verse, I want your opinion upon some verse I have written lately.' I had hoped he would ask me to read it but he would not speak of art, or of literature, or of anything related to them. I had however been talking to his latest disciple and knew that his opinions had not changed: Phidias had corrupted sculpture, we had nothing of true Greece but certain *Nike* dug up out of the foundations of the Parthenon, and that corruption ran through all our art; Shakespeare and Dante had corrupted literature, Shakespeare by his too abounding sentiment, Dante by his compromise with the Church.

He said, apropos of nothing, 'Arthur Balfour was a scoundrel,' and from that on would talk of nothing but politics. All the other modern statesmen were more or less scoundrels except 'Mussolini and that hysterical imitator of his Hitler.' When I objected to his violence he declared that Dante considered all sins intellectual, even sins of the flesh, he himself refused to make the modern distinction between error and sin. He urged me to read the works of Captain Douglas who alone knew what caused our suffering. He took my manuscript and went away denouncing Dublin as 'a reactionary hole' because I had said that I was re-reading Shakespeare, would go on to Chaucer, and found all that I wanted of modern life in 'detection and the wild west.' Next day his judgment came and that in a single word 'Putrid'.

Then I took my verses to a friend of my own school, and this friend said 'go on just like that. Plays like *The Great Clock Tower* would always seem unfinished but that is no matter. Begin plays without knowing how to end them for the sake of the lyrics. I once wrote a play and after I had filled it with lyrics abolished the play.' Then I brought my work to two painters and a poet until I was like Panurge consulting oracles as to whether he should get married and rejecting all that did not confirm his own desire. (Preface to *KGCT*)

CHURCH AND STATE 308

This poem was written in August 1934 and first appeared in the *Spectator* (23 327 Nov. 1934) entitled 'A Vain Hope'.

This poem (untitled) followed Yeats's *Commentary on the Three Songs* in *P(Ch)* (Dec. 1934). See notes on *Three Songs to the Same Tune* (PNE A101).

309-
320 SUPERNATURAL SONGS

327-
334 Yeats wrote a general comment (annotated at the end of the quotation) on these poems which was included in *KGCT* (*KGCT* was published in 1934, the play produced at the Abbey Theatre, Dublin, on 30 July 1934):

> An Irish poet during a country walk talked of the Church of Ireland, he had preferences for this or that preacher, Archbishop Gregg had pleased him by accepting certain recent Lambeth decrees; one could be a devout communicant and accept all the counsels before the Great Schism that separated Western from Eastern Christianity in the ninth century. In course of time the Church of Ireland would feel itself more in sympathy with early Christian Ireland than could a Church that admitted later developments of doctrine. I said that for the moment I associated early Christian Ireland with India; Shri Purohit Swami, protected during his pilgrimage to a remote Himalayan shrine by a strange great dog that disappeared when danger was past, might have been that blessed Cellach who sang upon his deathbed of bird and beast; Bagwan Shri Hamsa's pilgrimage to Mount Kaílás, the legendary Meru, and to lake Manas Sarowa, suggested pilgrimages to Croagh Patrick and to Lough Derg. A famous philosopher believed that every civilisation began, no matter what its geographical origin, with Asia, certain men of science that all of us when still in the nursery were, if not African, exceedingly Asiatic. Saint Patrick must have found in Ireland, for he was not its first missionary, men whose Christianity had come from Egypt, and retained characteristics of those older faiths that have become so important to our invention. Perhaps some man young enough for so great a task might discover there men and women he could honour – to adapt the words of Goethe – by conferring their names upon his own thoughts; perhaps I myself had made a beginning.
>
> While this book was passing through the press I wrote the poems for that old hermit Ribh. I did not explain the poems in *The King of the Great Clock Tower*, nor will I explain these. I would consider Ribh, were it not for his ideas about the Trinity, an orthodox man.   (*KGCT*)

1   *Irish poet*: probably F. R. Higgins (1896-1941), joint editor with Yeats of a series of Cuala Press Broadsides, 1935; appointed a director of the Abbey Theatre in 1936.

2-3   *Archbishop Gregg*: John Allen Fitzgerald Gregg (1873-1961), Archbishop of Dublin (1920-28)

4   *Lambeth decrees*: so called because Anglican bishops hold decennial conferences at Lambeth Palace, London, official residence of the Archbishop of Canterbury, head of the Anglican church. Those decrees intended are probably of 1952, 1930 and 1932, of a cautious ecumenical kind. In 1924 the validity of ordinations by Eastern Orthodox churches was recognised; in 1930 Anglicans were allowed to take Holy Communion in other churches when unable to attend an Anglican service; and in 1932 the Anglican Church established inter-communion with some Old Catholic churches in Europe.

5   *Great Schism*: the Schism between the Eastern Orthodox church and the

Roman Catholic church was caused by the objection of Photius (*c.* 820–892), Patriarch of Constantinople, to a phrase in the Nicene Creed: he was excommunicated by the Fourth Council of Constantinople (869–70).

11   *Shri Purohit Swami . . . dog*: Shri Purohit Swami (b. 1882) included the story of the dog in *An Indian Monk: His Life and Adventures* (1932) to which Yeats wrote an Introduction.

14   *Cellach*: Cellach MacAodh, Archbishop of Armagh from 1105–29. See Standish Hayes O'Grady, *Silva Gadelica* (1892) II, 50–69, and see note on 'The Dancer at Cruachan and Cro-Patrick' (*PNE* 288).

14–15   *Bhagwan Shri Hamsa's . . . Kailás*: Bhagwan Shri Hamsa wrote *The Holy Mountain: Being the Story of a Pilgrimage to Lake Manas and of Initiation on Mount Kailas in Tibet* (1934); this was a translation by Shri Purohit Swami, to which Yeats contributed an Introduction. See note on 'Meru' (*PNE* 320).

17   *Croagh Patrick*: see note on 'The Dancer at Cruachan and Cro-Patrick' (*PNE* 288).

Lough Derg: see note on 'The Pilgrim' (*PNE* 348).

a famous philosopher: *PNE* suggests Friederick Hegel; see Introduction to his *Philosophy of History*, tr. P. F. Collier, 1902, p. 158: 'In Asia arose the light of the spirit and therefore the history of the world' and '. . . Europe is absolutely the end of history, Asia the beginning' (p. 163).

16   *certain men of science*: *PNE* suggests William King Gregory (1876–1976), *Our Face from Fish to Man* (1929).

24   *words of Goethe*: This remark was quoted by Yeats in connection with historical drama in *Samhain* 1904 as 'we do the people of history the honour of naming after them the creations of our own minds' (*E* 144). Yeats did not read German himself so presumably used a translation or heard the phrase in conversation. *PNE*, however, suggests as source for the quotation from *Il conte de Carmagnola. Tragedia de Alessandro Mazoni. Milano*, in *Über Kunst und Alterhum*, 2, 3 (1820), a 1902 volume in the Weimar edition of *Goethes Werke*.

27   *old hermit Ribh*: In the Preface to *FMM* Yeats remarked that the hermit Ribh in 'Supernatural Songs' is 'an imaginary critic of St Patrick. His Christianity, come perhaps from Egypt like much early Irish Christianity, echoes pre-Christian thought'.

327   This poem was written by 24 July 1934 and first appeared in *P(Ch)* and *LM* in Dec. 1934.

Yeats wrote to Mrs Shakespear on 24 July 1934:

> I have another poem in my head where a monk reads his breviary at midnight upon the tomb of long-dead lovers on the anniversary of their death, for on that night they are united above the tomb, their embrace being not partial but a conflagration of the entire body and so shedding the light he reads by.   (*L* 824)

1   *me*: Ribh, an imaginary character, see Yeats's notes quoted above.

6   *Baile and Aillinn*: legendary Irish lovers. See Yeats's *Baile and Aillinn* (*PNE* 377) and notes on 'The Withering of the Boughs' (*PNE* 82).

8   *the apple and the yew*: to each of the lovers Aengus, God of Love, gave false news of the other's death; they died of broken hearts, and were changed into swans linked by a golden chain. A yew tree grew where Baile's body lay, a wild apple over Aillinn's; their love stories were written on boards made of yew and apple. There is an interesting discussion of the poem in *LT* 311-17.

328   15   *the intercourse of angels is a light*: it is probable that Yeats got this idea from Swedenborg. In 'Anima Mundi' Yeats wrote of the dead 'I do not doubt that they make love in that union which Swedenborg has said is of the whole body and seems from far off an incandescence.' In a letter of 21 February 1933 he wrote to Mrs Shakespear:

> . . . *Louis Lambert* [by Balzac] might have been [an echo] of that saying of Swedenborg's that the sexual intercourse of the angels is a conflagration of the whole being

and on 9 March:

> Yet why not take Swedenborg literally and think we attain, in a partial contact, what the spirits know throughout their being. He somewhere describes two spirits meeting and as they touch they become a single conflagration. His vision may be true, Newton's cannot be. . . .

26-7   . . . *in a circle on the grass; therein*
I turn the pages of my holy book: the light is circular to indicate the perfect harmony achieved by the lovers. It is possible that the idea of putting priest and lovers into one poem came from Yeats's reading in Japanese plays. In 'Certain Noble Plays of Japan' he wrote:

> The love-sorrows - the love of father and daughter, of mother and son, of boy and girl - may owe their nobility to a courtly life, but he to whom the adventures happen, a traveller commonly from some distant place, is most often a Buddhist priest; and the occasional intellectual subtlety is perhaps Buddhist.

The adventure itself is often the meeting with ghost, god, or goddess at some holy place or much-legended tomb; and god, goddess, or ghost reminds me at times of our own Irish legends and beliefs, which once, if may be, differed little from those of the Shinto worshipper. (*E & I* 232)

The *Nishikigi*, in particular, may have influenced him. The tale of the lovers would lose its pathos 'if we did not see that forgotten tomb' (*E & I* 233), and again this passage suggests that the grass may have been suggested by the *Nishikigi*:

The lovers, now that in an aëry body they must sorrow for unconsummated love, are 'tangled up as the grass patterns are tangled.' Again they are like an unfinished cloth: 'these bodies, having no weft, even now are not come together; truly a shameful story, a tale to bring shame on the gods.' Before they can bring the priest to the tomb they spend the day 'pushing aside the grass from the overgrown ways in Kefu', and the countryman who directs them is 'cutting grass on the hill'; and when at last the prayer of the priest unites them in marriage the bride says that he has made 'a dream-bridge over wild grass, over the grass I dwell in'; and in the end bride and bridegroom show themselves for a moment 'from under the shadow of the love-grass'. (*E & I* 234)

RIBH DENOUNCES PATRICK   310

This poem was written in late July 1934 and first appeared in *LM* and *P(Ch)* in   *328*
December 1934.

See Yeats's *Commentary on Supernatural Songs* included above. In a letter of 24 July 1934 to Mrs Shakespear he included the second and third verses with the comment that the point of the poem was that 'we beget and bear because of the incompleteness of our love' (*L* 824).

6   *the Great Smaragdine Tablet*: a medieval Latin work on alchemy published in 1541, attributed to the Egyptian Hermes Trismegistus. Yeats's source was probably G. R. S. Mead's *Thrice Greatest Hermes*, Saul (*PYP* 158) suggests that Madame Blavatsky, *Isis Unveiled*, also makes the point that what is below is like what is above.

9   *in their embraces twined*: cf. a sentence in an essay 'What is Popular Poetry?': 'I always knew that the line of Nature is crooked, that, though we dig the canal-beds as straight as we can, the rivers run hither and thither in their wildness' (*E & I* 5).
   A similar image exists in *A* 480.

10   *serpent is multiplicity*: cf. a passage in *Discoveries*, 'On the Serpent's Mouth':

If it be true that God is a circle whose centre is everywhere, the saint goes to the centre, the poet and artist to the ring where everything comes round again. The poet must not seek for what is still and fixed, for that has no life for him; and if he did, his style would become cold and monotonous, and his sense of beauty faint and sickly, as are both style and beauty to my imagination in the prose and poetry of Newman, but be content to find his pleasure in all that is for ever passing away that it may come again, in the beauty of woman, in the fragile flowers of spring, in momentary heroic passion, in whatever is most fleeting, most impassioned, as it were, for its own perfection, most eager to return in its glory. Yet perhaps he must endure the impermanent a little, for these things return, but not wholly, for no two faces are alike, and, it may be, had we more learned eyes, no two flowers. It is that all things are made by the struggle of the individual and the world, of the unchanging and the returning, and that the saint and the poet are over all, and that the poet has made his home in the serpent's mouth?   (*E & I* 287-8)

---

311   RIBH IN ECSTASY

329   This poem was probably written in late 1934, and first appeared in *FMM*.

1   *you understood*: possibly Maud Gonne, cf. '*Words*' (*PNE* 93) – or else Frank O'Connor, who, when Yeats read 'Ribh denounces Patrick' to some friends at his home and asked them if they understood it, replied, 'No, I didn't understand a word of it' (*IY* 282).

7   *Those amorous cries*: the poem describes Yeats's own feeling of unity or happiness – cf. 'Vacillation' IV (*PNE* 262) – when he had written a philosophical poem (Ellmann suggests the previous one) which is interrupted again by 'the common round of day'.
In 1934 Yeats underwent the Steinach operation for rejuvenation.

---

312   THERE

329   This poem's date is not established but it was probably late in 1934 or early in 1935. It first appeared in *FMM*.

1   *There*: this is perfection, the 'sphere' of *AV*'s thirteenth cone:

> The *Thirteenth Cone* is a sphere because sufficient to itself; but as seen by Man it is a cone. It becomes even conscious of itself, as so seen, like some great dancer, the perfect flower of modern culture, dancing some primitive dance and conscious of his or her own life and of the dance. There is a mediaeval story of a man persecuted by his Guardian Angel because it was jealous of his sweetheart, and such stories seem closer to reality than our abstract theology. All imaginable relations may arise between a man and his God. I only speak of the *Thirteenth Cone* as a sphere and yet I might say that the gyre or cone of the *Principles* is in reality a sphere, though to Man, bound to birth and death, it can never seem so, and that it is the antinomies that force us to find it a cone. Only one symbol exists, though the reflecting mirrors make many appear and all different.   (*AV* (B) 240).

Thomas R. Whitaker, *Swan and Shadow*, 118, remarks that solar apocalypse, which Yeats terms the 'Sphere' in *AV*, Ribh calls 'There' – the term by which (in the MacKenna translation) Plotinus refers to the Divine Sphere: 'the Sun, There, is all the stars; and every star, again, is all the stars and sun.' There, as Boehme said, 'life windeth itself *Inwards* to the Sun.'

barrel-hoops: possibly a memory of the drowning of the dogs caused this imagery and that of 'Meru' (*PNE* 320) where civilisation 'is hooped together'.

2   *the serpent-tails*: possibly derived from Theosophical reading. Cf. 'Alchemy', *Theosophical Siftings* II (1889-90).

RIBH CONSIDERS CHRISTIAN LOVE INSUFFICIENT   313

This poem was probably written in 1934 and first appeared in *LM* and *P (Ch)* in   *330*
December 1934.

3   *I study hatred*: cf. 'Remorse for Intemperate Speech' (*PNE* 266). Ellmann (*IY* 283) suggests that the poem developed out of some automatic writing of Mrs Yeats. Yeats wrote in a journal of the ideas of a 'communicator' which she was writing down:

> He insisted on being questioned. I asked about further multiple influx. He said 'hate God,' we must hate all ideas concerning God that we possess, that if we did not absorption in God would be impossible . . . always he repeated 'hatred, hatred' or 'hatred of God' . . . said, 'I think about hatred.' That seems to me the growing hatred among men [which] has long been a problem with me.
> The soul has to enter some significant relationship with God even if this be one of hatred.

19   *stroke of midnight*: this phrase was used by Yeats in 'The Four Ages of Man' (*PNE* 317); it implies the end of life.

HE AND SHE   314

This was written before 25 August 1934, and first appeared in *LM* and *P (Ch)*   *331*
(Dec. 1934).
    Yeats wrote to Mrs Shakespear on 25 August 1934 that this poem was on the soul: 'It is of course, my central myth'. The poem relates to *AV*, 'She' being the soul or humanity, following the notes on phases of the moon. Cf. 'The Phases of the Moon' (*PNE* 183) for the relationship between these phases and the soul.

WHAT MAGIC DRUM?   315

This poem was probably written in 1934, and first appeared in *FMM*.   *331*
    This poem deals with the union of some god or hero with (perhaps) a human

355

mother, as in 'Leda and the Swan' (*PNE* 220). The poem is also reminiscent of 'The Second Coming' (*PNE* 200), the final emphasis on the 'beast' in each case coming as a jolt of horror to the reader.

4   *magic drum*: cf. the 'frenzied drum' of line 15 of 'A Prayer for my Daughter' (*PNE* 201).

316   WHENCE HAD THEY COME?

332   This poem was probably written in 1934; it first appeared in *FMM*.

This poem asks what imponderables lie behind the happenings of personal love or general history, behind the system of *AV*'s interpretation of both. The lovers are but a symbol of love (cf. 'His Bargain' (*PNE* 281)); the thought resembles that of the Platonic Idea, and there are parallels between the sexual symbolism of 'Leda and the Swan' (*PNE* 220), this poem and 'What Magic Drum?' (*PNE* 315).

4   *Dramatis Personae*: the characters in the play

12   *Charlemagne*: Charlemagne (742-814), King of the Franks, in 800 was crowned Emperor of the Holy Roman Empire, which extended from the Ebro to the Elbe. His court was the centre of a revival of learning.

317   THE FOUR AGES OF MAN

332   This poem was written on 6 August 1934, and first appeared in *LM* and *P(Ch)* (Dec. 1934).

Yeats wrote about the poem to Mrs Shakespear in a letter from Riversdale, Rathfarnham, on 24 July 1934:

. . . Yes that book is important. Notice this symbolism

Waters under the earth $\}$		
The Earth $\}$	The bowels etc.	*Instinct*
The Water	= The blood and the sex organ	*Passion*
The Air	= The lungs, logical thought	*Thought*
The Fire	=	*Soul*

They are my four quarters. The Earth before 8, the waters before 15, the Air before 22, the Fire before 1 (see *AV*, page 86). Note that on page 85 of *A Vision* [this was a wrong reference, corrected later in a letter of 24 July 1934, to p. 35 of *AV* (A) where 'it is there written that in the last quarter of a civilisation (the quarter we have just entered;) the fight is against body and body should win. You can define soul as "that which has value in itself" or you can say of it "it [is] that which we only know through analogies".'] the conflict on which we now enter is 'against the Soul' as in the quarter we have just left it was 'against the intellect'. The conflict is to restore the body . . .

Later in this letter Yeats wrote:

The Earth   = Every early nature-dominated civilisation
The Water = An armed sexual age, chivalry, Froissart's chronicles
The Air   = From the Renaissance to the end of the 19th Century
The Fire   = The purging away of our civilisation by our hatred
                (on these two I have a poem)   (*L* 823–5)

In a later letter of 7 August 1934 to Olivia Shakespear, Yeats remarked that he had put into rhyme what he had written in his last letter, and included the poem (with a variant second line 'Body won and values upright') with the comment

> They are the four ages of individual man, but they are also the four ages of civilisation. You will find them in that book you have been reading. First age, *earth*, negative functions. Second age, *water*, blood, sex. Third age, *air*, breath, intellect. Fourth age, *fire*, soul etc. In the first two the moon comes to the full – resurrection of Christ and Dionysus. Man becomes rational, no longer driven from below or above. My two plays, of which I send you the *Sunday Times* notices, both deal with that moment – the slain god, the risen god.   (*L* 826)

8   *stroke of midnight*: cf. 'Ribh considers Christian Love insufficient' (*PNE* 313).

CONJUNCTIONS   318

This poem was written before 25 August 1934 and first appeared in *LM* and   *333* *P(Ch)* (Dec. 1934).

Yeats wrote about the poem in a letter to Mrs Shakespear of 25 August 1934:

> ... I was told, you may remember, that my two children would be Mars conjunctive Venus, Saturn conjunctive Jupiter respectively; and so they were – Ann the Mars-Venus personality. Then I was told that they would develop so that I could study in them the alternating dispensations, the Christian or objective, then the Antithetical or subjective. The Christian is the Mars-Venus – it is democratic. The Jupiter-Saturn civilisation is born free among the most cultivated, out of tradition, out of rule.

> > Should Jupiter and Saturn meet,
> > What a crop of mummy wheat!

> > The sword's a cross; thereon He died:
> > On breast of Mars the goddess sighed.

> I wrote those lines some days ago. George said it is very strange but whereas Michael is always thinking about life Anne always thinks of death. Then I remembered that the children were the two dispensations. Anne collects skeletons. She buries little birds and beasts and then digs them up when worms and insects have eaten their flesh. She has a shelf of very white little skeletons. She has asked leave to go to the geological museum to draw skeletons. Then she loves tragedies, has read all Shakespeare's, and a couple of weeks ago was searching reference books to learn all about the poison that killed Hamlet's father. When she grows up she will either have some passionate love affair or

357

have some close friend that has – the old association of love and death. (*L* 827-8)

2 *mummy-wheat*: Cf. note on the 'old mummy wheat' of 'On a Picture of a Black Centaur by Edmund Dulac' (*PNE* 221)

3 *He*: Jesus Christ

4 *Mars*: Roman god of war

the Goddess: Venus, goddess of beauty and love, who was unfaithful to her husband Vulcan with Mars

319 A NEEDLE'S EYE

333 This poem's date is uncertain; it first appeared in *LM* and *P(Ch)*, (Dec. 1934).

2 *needle's eye*: cf. 'the needle's eye' of 'Veronica's Napkin' (*PNE* 245).

320 MERU

333 This poem was probably written about August 1933 and June 1934; it first appeared in *LM* and *P*(Ch) (Dec. 1934).
    Yeats had finished his study of various authorities and was about to start his Introduction to Shri Purohit Swami's *The Holy Mountain* (1934) in August 1933 (*L* 813). He sent back the final proofs, having read it all through in June 1934 and described it in a letter of June to Olivia Shakespear as 'one of those rare books that are fundamental' (*L* 823). There is an account of the Swami's experiences in Yeats's Introduction (*E & I* 448-73). The poem envisages man as a destroyer of what he creates, and the hermits learn this truth, of the succession of civilisations.

334 9 *Meru or Everest*: Shri Purohit Swami did not accompany his friend who had been ordered in a meditation known as *Savikalpa-Samadhi* 'to seek *Turiya*, the greater or conscious Samadhi at Mount Kailas, the legendary Meru' as he thought himself unworthy (*E & I* 453). Mount Kailasa in Tibet is the twin of Mount Meru, placed at the Centre of Paradise in Hindu mythology. Everest, highest mountain in the World, is in the Himalayas, on the borders of Tibet and Nepal.

10 *caverned*: see note on 'The Gyres' (*PNE* 321). The hermits are a new version of Shelley's Ahasuerus, Indian because of Yeats's intensified interest in Indian mysticism and religious thought at the time of writing the poem.

New Poems

CURTIS BRADFORD in 'Yeats's *Last Poems* Again', VIII, *Dolmen Press Yeats Centenary Papers* (1965) wrote that those poems in *CP* starting with 'The Gyres' and ending with 'Are You Content?' are Yeats's *New Poems*, as published by the Cuala Press in 1938. He points out that *CP*'s heading *Last Poems* can be properly applied only to those poems Yeats wrote or finished in the last year of his life. They were published in *Last Poems and Two Plays* in the order he intended by the Cuala Press in 1939. Curtis Bradford reproduces the order of Yeats's manuscript list as follows: 1. 'Under Ben Bulben'; 2. 'Three Songs to One Burden'; 3. 'The Black Tower'; 4. 'Cuchulain Comforted'; 5. 'Three Marching Songs'; 6. 'In Tara's Halls'; 7. 'The Statues'; 8. 'News for the Delphic Oracle'; 9. 'The Long-Legged Fly'; 10. 'A Bronze Head'; 11. 'A Stick of Incense'; 12. 'Hound Voice'; 13. 'John Kinsella's Lament etc'; 14. 'High Talk'; 15. 'The Apparitions'; 16. 'A Nativity'; 17. 'Man and Echo'; 18. 'The Circus Animal's Desertion'; 19. 'Politics'; 20. 'Cuchulain's Death'; 21. 'Purgatory'. The list does not include three poems Yeats included in *OTB*: 'Why should not old Men be Mad?', 'Crazy Jane on the Mountain' and 'Statesman's Holiday'.

THE GYRES   321

This poem was probably written between July 1936 and January 1937. It first   *337*
appeared in *NP*.

1   *The gyres*: see note on the gyres, 'Demon and Beast' (*PNE* 199) and cf. line 469, 'The Gift of Harun Al-Rashid' (*PNE* 382), Line 1, 'The Second Coming' (*PNE* 200), line 19, 'Sailing to Byzantium' (*PNE* 204), and line 62, 'Under Ben Bulben' (*PNE* 356).

Old Rocky Face: there have been several different identifications of this figure. The MS. version refers to the 'old cavern man' [and Yeats referred to 'the old ascetic of the cavern' (*E & I* 464)] and this suggests that Yeats was remembering Shelley's Ahasuerus, the cavern-dwelling Jew in Hellas:

> I have described what image – always opposite to the natural self or the natural world – Wilde, Henley, Morris copied or tried to copy, but I have not said if I found an image for myself. I know very little about myself and much less of the anti-self: probably the woman who cooks my dinner or the woman who sweeps out my study knows more than I do. It is perhaps because Nature made me a gregarious man, going hither and thither looking for conversation, and ready to deny from fear or favour his dearest conviction, that I love proud

and lonely things. When I was a child and went daily to the sexton's daughter for writing lessons, I found one poem in her School Reader that delighted me beyond all others: a fragment of some metrical translation from Aristophanes wherein the birds sing scorn upon mankind. In later years my mind gave itself to gregarious Shelley's dream of a young man, his hair blanched with sorrow, studying philosophy in some lonely tower, or of his old man, master of all human knowledge, hidden from human sight in some shell-strewn cavern on the Mediterranean shore. One passage above all ran perpetually in my ears:

> Some feign that he is Enoch: others dream
> He was pre-Adamite, and has survived
> Cycles of generation and of ruin.
> The sage, in truth, by dreadful abstinence,
> And conquering penance of the mutinous flesh,
> Deep contemplation and unwearied study,
> In years outstretched beyond the date of man,
> May have attained to sovereignty and science
> Over those strong and secret things and thoughts
> Which others fear and know not.

> MAHMUD
>   I would talk

With this old Jew.

> HASSAN
>   Thy will is even now
> Made known to him where he dwells in a sea-cavern
> 'Mid the Demonesi, less accessible
> Than thou or God! He who would question him
> Must sail alone at sunset, where the stream
> Of Ocean sleeps around those foamless isles,
> When the young moon is westering as now,
> And evening airs wander upon the wave;
> And, when the pines of that bee-pasturing isle,
> Green Erebinthus, quench the fiery shadow
> Of his gilt prow within the sapphire water,
> Then must the lonely helmsman cry aloud
> 'Ahasuerus!' and the caverns round
> Will answer 'Ahasuerus!' If his prayer
> Be granted, a faint meteor will arise,
> Lighting him over Marmora; and a wind
> Will rush out of the sighing pine-forest,
> And with the wind a storm of harmony
> Unutterably sweet, and pilot him
> Through the soft twilight to the Bosphorus:
> Thence, at the hour and place and circumstance
> Fit for the matter of their conference,
> The Jew appears. Few dare, and few who dare
> Win the desired communion.   (*A* 171–3)

In *AV*, Phase seventeen contains him: 'This *Mask* may represent intellectual or sexual passion; seem some Ahasuerus or Athanase' (*AV* (B) 141). This phase contained Dante and Shelley, and it was Yeats's phase also:

Because of the habit of synthesis, and of the growing complexity of the energy, which gives many interests, and the still faint perception of things in their weight and mass, men of this phase are almost always partisans, propagandists and gregarious; yet because of the *Mask* of simplification, which holds up before them the solitary life of hunters and of fishers and 'the groves pale passion loves', they hate parties, crowds, propaganda. Shelley out of phase writes pamphlets, and dreams of converting the world, [a parallel to Yeats's political activity in the 'nineties] or of turning man of affairs and upsetting governments, and yet returns again and again to these two images of solitude, a young man whose hair has grown white from the burden of his thoughts, an old man in some shell-strewn cave whom it is possible to call, when speaking to the Sultan, 'as inaccessible as God or thou'.   (*AV* (B) 143)

Cf. also the passage cited by Henn (*LT* 321) from Yeats's *Letters to AE*:

> Had some young Greek found Shelley's 'Ahasuerus' in that shell-strewn cavern, the sage would not have talked mathematics or even 'those strong and secret thoughts . . . which others fear and know not', but given, I think, very simple advice, not indeed fitted to any momentary crisis but fitted perhaps for the next fifty years.   (*DM*, July/Sept. 1939)

Henn also quoted a passage from Spengler which blended the symbolism with world events

> The second wave swelled up steeply in the Apocalyptic Currents after 300. Here it was the Magian waking consciousness that arose and built itself a metaphysic of Last Things, based already 'upon the prime symbol of the coming Culture, the Cavern'.   (*Decline of the West*, II, 249)

Yeats alluded to the symbol of the cavern in connection with Spengler's speculations in *AV* (B) 258-60: 'The Cavern is Time. . . .'.

It is likely, (see notes on 'Meru' (*PNE* 320)), that the idea of the cavern and the wise man came back into Yeats's mind as he read of the Indian sages and their pursuit of detached wisdom. Cf. the 'old ascetic of the cavern' (*E & I* 464).

5   *streams of blood*: cf. 'the blood-dimmed tide' of 'The Second Coming' (*PNE* 200), 'all that blood was shed' of 'September 1913' (*PNE* 115), the various mentions of blood in 'Blood and the Moon' (*PNE* 243), how 'base drove out the better blood' in 'A Statesman's Holiday' (*PNE* A124). In 'Two Songs from a Play' (*PNE* 218)

> Odour of blood when Christ was slain
> Made all Platonic tolerance vain
> And vain all Doric discipline.

6   *Empedocles*: a Greek philosopher (*c.* 490-430 BC) who regarded all things as composed of earth, air, fire, and water, mingled by love or separated by strife. Yeats quoted him in the opening of the section of the *Great Wheel*:

I

'When Discord', writes Empedocles, 'has fallen into the lowest depths of the vortex' - the extreme bound, not the centre, Burnet points out - 'Concord has reached the centre, into it do all things come together so as to be only one, not all at once but gradually from different quarters, and as they come Discord retires to the extreme boundary . . . in proportion as it runs out Concord in a soft immortal boundless stream runs in.' And again: 'Never will boundless time be emptied of that pair; and they prevail in turn as that circle comes round, and pass away before one another and increase in their appointed turn'. It was this Discord or War that Heraclitus called 'God of all and Father of all, some it has made gods and some men, some bond and some free', and I recall that Love and War came from the eggs of Leda.

II

According to Simplicius, a late commentator upon Aristotle, the Concord of Empedocles fabricates all things into 'an homogeneous sphere', and then Discord separates the elements and so makes the world we inhabit, but even the sphere formed by Concord is not the changeless eternity, for Concord or Love but offers us the image of that which is changeless.   *(AV* (B) 67–8)

7   *Hector is dead*: cf. 'The Phases of the Moon' *(PNE* 183):

> Athene takes Achilles by the hair,
> Hector is in the dust, Nietzsche is born,
> Because the hero's crescent is the twelfth.

8   *tragic joy*: this brave opposition to decay and death was part of Yeats's mental make-up. Cf. a passage in 'J. M. Synge and the Ireland of his Time':

> There is in the creative joy of acceptance of what life brings, because we have understood the beauty of what it brings, or a hatred of death for what it takes away, which arouses within us, through some sympathy perhaps with all other men, an energy so noble, so powerful, that we laugh aloud and mock, in the terror or the sweetness of our exaltation, at death and oblivion.   *(E & I* 322)

This idea was repeated in *OTB*, where after a side-swipe at 'the vulgar jocularity of certain ignorant Irish dramatists', no doubt contrasted in his mind with Synge, Yeats remarked 'No tragedy is legitimate unless it leads some great character to his final joy' *(E* 448). See the passage quoted from this essay in note on line 22 'Demon and Beast' *(PNE* 199) and note on 'Tom O'Roughley' *(PNE* 155).
   And he wrote to Dorothy Wellesley on 26 July 1935 that to him 'the supreme aim is an act of faith and reason to make one rejoice in the midst of tragedy' *(DWL* 12).

9   *numb nightmare*: no doubt these lines owed much to Yeats's knowledge of the troubles and the Irish Civil War. Cf. the 'dragon-ridden' days of 'Nineteen Hundred and Nineteen' *(PNE* 213) and 'Meditations in Time of Civil War' *(PNE* 206–212).

10   *blood and mire*: cf. note on line 25 'Her Vision in the Wood' *(PNE* 300).

11   *What matter?*: cf. 'Parnell's Funeral' *(PNE* 304).

> 'What matter for the scene, the scene once gone.'

338

Yeats wrote this poem in July 1936 (finishing it on the 25th): it first appeared in *LM* (March 1938) and the *New Republic* (13 April 1938). For a discussion of its meaning see *IY* 185-7 and Jeffares, 'Notes on Yeats's ''Lapis Lazuli'' ', *Modern Language Notes* (Nov. 1950) and 'The general and particular meanings of ''Lapis Lazuli'' ' in *Yeats: Last Poems* (ed. J. Stallworthy, 1968), 160 ff. See also Edward Engelberg, *The Vast Design*, 170-5. The carving (dating from Chien Lung period 1739-93 (*PNE*)) was given to Yeats in July 1935 as a seventieth birthday present by Henry (Harvey) Clifton (b. 1908).

3   *poets that are always gay*: in 'Modern Poetry: A Broadcast' Yeats quoted the lines:

> Unto us they belong,
> Us the bitter and gay,
> Wine and women and song.

He referred to Dowson, and remarked that it had never occurred to him to wonder why the Dowson he knew seemed neither gay nor bitter (*E & I* 492). But here the theme of gaiety is linked to the need to face tragedy heroically. Engelberg (*The Vast Design*, 170) remarks that Arnold's essay 'On the Study of Celtic Literature' (which Yeats read as a young man and commented on in his own essay 'The Celtic Element in Literature of 1897') stresses the Celtic origin of the word 'gay'.

5   *if nothing drastic is done*: the Germans reoccupied the Rhineland in 1936; the Italians were invading Abyssinia in 1935; and the Spanish Civil War was a testing ground for new armaments.

6   *Aeroplane and Zeppelin*: the Zeppelin was anachronistic for bombing purposes in 1936 but Yeats had memories of the Zeppelin bombing raids on London in the 1914-18 war. Frank O'Connor, *The Backward Look* (1967), 174, gives an account of how, at the time Yeats was writing a poem to the donor of the piece of lapis lazuli, Edmund Dulac had written to him to express his terror of what was going to happen if London was bombed from the air. Zeppelins, rigid-framed airships, were named after their designer Graf von Zeppelin (1838-1917).

7   *Pitch like King Billy bomb-balls in*: the 'bomb-balls' probably derive from 'The Battle of the Boyne', a ballad included in *Irish Minstrelsy* (1888), an anthology edited by H. Halliday Sparling whom Yeats probably met at the home of William Morris. The anthology contained a poem by Yeats, and an inscribed copy is in the poet's library. Cf. a passage from Elizabeth Yeats's diary for 1888-9 quoted by Joseph Hone, 'A scattered Fair', *The Wind and the Rain* (Autumn 1946), 113. The ballad lines ran:

> King James has pitched his tent between
> The lines for to retire
> But King William threw his bomb-balls in
> And set them all on fire.

The echo is stronger than the original. Yeats calls King William 'King Billy', a name more likely to rouse memories and political association in Ireland. He also took over the word 'pitch' and used it for the bomb-balls instead of for the tent. It has the touch of violence he required. And William may also suggest 'Kaiser Bill', Kaiser Wilhelm II (1859-1941), German emperor from 1888 to 1918.

11   *That's Ophelia, that Cordelia*: Shakespeare's characters Hamlet and Ophelia are in *Hamlet*, Lear and Cordelia in *King Lear*. Ophelia and Cordelia are implicitly contrasted with the 'hysterical women' (line 1) of 1936.

12-15   *Yet they, should the last scene be there,*
         The great stage curtain about to drop,
         If worthy their prominent part in the play,
         Do not break up their lines to weep: these lines are probably an answer to Frank O'Connor, who told Yeats how troubled he was over an unsatisfactory production of Lady Gregory's *Devorgilla* in which the heroine wept at the curtain. He asked Yeats (who had been talking of the lapis lazuli) 'Is it ever permissible for an actor to sob at the curtain of a play?' and he replied 'Never!' O'Connor remarked, not quite accurately, that this poem renders the lapis lazuli and the Chinese scenes, the bombardment and his own advice to the players, in strict chronological order as though copied from a diary (*The Backward Look* 174-5).

16   *They know that Hamlet and Lear are gay*: in 'A General Introduction for my Work' Yeats wrote that:

The heroes of Shakespeare convey to us through their looks, or through the metaphorical patterns of their speech, the sudden enlargement of their vision, their ecstasy at the approach of death: 'She should have died hereafter,' 'Of many thousand kisses, the poor last,' 'Absent thee from felicity awhile.' They have become God or Mother Goddess, the pelican, 'My baby at my breast,' but all must be cold; no actress has ever sobbed when she played Cleopatra, even the shallow brain of a producer has never thought of such a thing. The supernatural is present, cold winds blow across our hands, upon our faces, the thermometer falls, and because of that cold we are hated by journalists and groundlings. There may be in this or that detail painful tragedy, but in the whole work none. I have heard Lady Gregory say, rejecting some play in the modern manner sent to the Abbey Theatre, 'Tragedy must be a joy to the man who dies.' Nor is it any different with lyrics, songs, narrative poems; neither scholars nor the populace have sung or read anything generation after generation because of its pain. The maid of honour whose tragedy they sing must be lifted out of history and timeless pattern, she is one of the four Maries, the rhythm is old and familiar, imagination must dance, must be carried beyond feeling into the aboriginal ice. Is ice the correct word? I once boasted, copying the phrase from a letter of my father's, that I would write a poem 'cold and passionate as the dawn.'   (*E & I* 522-3)

Cf. also note on 'tragic joy' line 8 'The Gyres' (*PNE* 321). J. Kleinstück, 'Yeats and Shakespeare' (*YCE* 12-14) discusses this poem at length and suggests the 'tragic joy' was owed, in part, to Nietzsche.

24   *It cannot grow*: Engelberg (*The Vast Design*, 171) remarks that 'It' must clearly refer to the 'tragedy wrought to its utmost'.

29   *No handiwork of Callimachus*: cf. a passage in *AV* describing the period   *339*
2000 BC to AD 1:

> With Callimachus pure Ionic revives again, as Furtwängler has proved, and upon the only example of his work known to us, a marble chair, a Persian is represented, and may one not discover a Persian symbol in that bronze lamp, shaped like a palm, known to us by a description in Pausanias? But he was an archaistic workman, and those who set him to work brought back public life to an older form. One may see in masters and man a momentary dip into ebbing Asia.   (*AV* (B) 270)

Callimachus (late fifth century BC) Greek sculptor, reputed inventor of the Corinthian capital, first user of the running drill, made a golden lamp for the Erectheum at Athens. See Pausanias (fl. 150), *Description of Greece*, I, 261, 6-7. See also 'Certain Noble Plays of Japan':

> It may be well if we go to school in Asia, for the distance from life in European art has come from little but difficulty with material. In half-Asiatic Greece Callimachus could still return to a stylistic management of the falling folds of display, after the naturalistic drapery of Phidias. . . .   (*E & I* 225)

Callimachus was, in fact, known as Κατατηξιτεχνος, the man who spoiled his art by excessive elaboration.

37   *Two Chinamen*: this is a description of the piece of lapis lazuli. Cf. a letter of 6 July 1935 in which Yeats describes it:

> . . . someone [Harry Clifton] has sent me a present of a great piece carved by some Chinese sculptor into the semblance of a mountain with temple, trees, paths and an ascetic and pupil about to climb the mountain. Ascetic, pupil, hard stone, eternal theme of the sensual east. The heroic cry in the midst of despair. But no, I am wrong, the east has its solutions always and therefore knows nothing of tragedy. It is we, not the east, that must raise the heroic cry.   (*DWL* 8)

See David Parker, 'Yeats's Lapis Lazuli' *N & Q* (*n.s.*) 24, 5, Oct. 1977, pp. 452-4, for Yeats's more knowledgeable use of the carving in the poem, written a year later than this letter.

IMITATED FROM THE JAPANESE   323

This poem was written towards the end of December 1936 (see *DWL*, 116); the   *340*
final version was dated 30 October 1937. It first appeared in *NP*.

A letter Yeats wrote to Dorothy Wellesley in December 1936 records the writing of the poem and includes a version slightly differing from that printed in *New Poems*: 'I have been in bed unable to do anything but sleep, yesterday I got up for the first time. I made this poem out of a prose translation of a Japanese Hokku in praise of Spring' (*DWL* 116).

A hokku is a poem of seventeen syllables, in three lines of 5, 7 and 5 syllables. *PNE* suggests as source Gekkyo (1745-1824), 'My longing after the departed Spring/Is not the same every year' in *An Anthology of Haiku Ancient and Modern,* tr. Asatoro Miyamori (1932).

324 SWEET DANCER

340 This poem was written in January 1937 and first appeared in *LM* (April 1938).

1 *The girl*: Margot Collis, who wrote under the name Margot Ruddock. Yeats wrote an Introduction to a small volume of her verse, *The Lemon Tree* (1937). She took part in some broadcasts of poetry arranged by Yeats in 1937. She is the subject of 'A Crazed Girl' (*CP* 348). Yeats wrote an account of this happening to Mrs Shakespear in a letter of 22 May 1936:

> The girl who is quite a beautiful person came here seven or eight days ago. She walked in at 6.30, her luggage in her hand and, when she had been given breakfast, said she had come to find out if her verse was any good. I had known her for some years and had told her to stop writing as her technique was getting worse. I was amazed by the tragic magnificence of some fragments and said so. She went out in pouring rain, thought, as she said afterwards, that if she killed herself her verse would live instead of her. Went to the shore to jump in, then thought that she loved life and began to dance. She went to the lodging house where Shri Purohit Swami was, to sleep. She was wet through, so Swami gave her some of his clothes; she had no money, he gave her some. Next day she went to Barcelona and there went mad, climbing out of a window, falling through a baker's roof, breaking a kneecap, hiding in a ship's hold, singing her own poems most of the time. The British consul in Barcelona appealed to me, so George and I went there, found her with recovered sanity sitting up in bed at a clinic writing an account of her madness. It was impossible to get adequate money out of her family, so I accepted financial responsibility and she was despatched to England and now I won't be able to afford new clothes for a year. When her husband wrote it had not been to send money, but to congratulate her on the magnificent publicity. The paragraph you saw is certainly his work. Will she stay sane? it is impossible to know.
> When I am in London I shall probably hide because the husband may send me journalists and because I want to keep at a distance from a tragedy where I can be no further help. (*L* 856)

For their friendship see *Ah, Sweet Dancer. W. B. Yeats, Margot Ruddock. A Correspondence Edited by Roger McHugh* (1970). This includes Yeats's poem 'Margot', not included in *VE* or *PNE*:

I

All famine struck sat I, and then
Those generous eyes on mine were cast,
Sat like other agèd men
Dumfoundered, gazing on a past
That appeared constructed of
Lost opportunities to love.

II

O how can I that interest hold?
What offer to attentive eyes?
Mind grows young and body old;
When half closed her eye-lid lies
A sort of hidden glory shall
About these stooping shoulders fall.

III

The Age of Miracles renew,
Let me be loved as though still young
Or let me fancy that it's true,
When my brief final years are gone
You shall have time to turn away
And cram those open eyes with day.

THE THREE BUSHES   325

341

This poem was written in July 1936 and first appeared in *LM* (Jan. 1937). The
source is invented, though there was a Pierre de Bourdeille (*c*. 1540–1614)
abbot and lord of Brantôme, France. It derived from a ballad of Dorothy
Wellesley's which Yeats, in Kathleen Raine's words, 'appropriated, worked upon
and published as "The Three Bushes" and its accompanying songs'. The story
of the poem's elaboration can be read in the poet's correspondence with his friend
the English minor poet Dorothy Wellesley (1889–1956):

Riversdale, July 2nd, 1936
. . . I am longing to read your ballad. I will not send you mine until yours is
finished.

Yours with love and affection,
P.S. Just come.   W. B. Yeats

My dear,
   Here you have a masterpiece. (I have just put in the rhymes, made it a
ballad.)

I

She sent her maid unto the man
That would her leman be
'O Psyche mimic me at love
With him I will not lie
'Tis sweetly done, 'tis easy done
So child make love for me'.

367

II

'Why will you never meet the dawn,
    Nor light the torch my child?'
Said lover to the serving maid
    'Lie down, lie down you are wild,
O you are wild for love of me
    And I with love am wild'.

III

The black death came or another death
    And took the lady and lord,
The serving maid, the sewing maid
    Sat down to hem the shroud.
'O all goes well, O all goes well
    And I can sing it aloud'.

IV

She that did what she was bid
    Sang to the feather stitch,
'What of the man and the lady
    No matter which is which,
All goes well with a man in the dark,
    And well with the feather stitch'.

This is far better than my laboured livelier verses. This is complete, lovely, lucky, born out of itself, or born out of nothing. My blessing upon you and it.

Riversdale,
[July 10, 1936]
Friday.

My dear Dorothy,
    Here is another version of second & third stanzas. I start changing things because the rhyme 'lord' & 'loud' etc. is not admissible in any prosody, then went on to the rest.

Yrs,

W. B. Yeats.

'I go if that candle is lit'
'Lie down, lie down you are wild'
'O you are wild for love of me
And I with love am wild'
'I came to lie with a man in the dark'
'Lie down again dear child'
        or
But the black death took the lady & lord
'I sew but what I am bid
And all goes well O all goes well'
But why does she sing so loud
The serving maid, the sewing maid
She that hems the shroud.

368

Penns in the Rocks,
July 14.

My dear W. B.,
    I send the revised version of the Ballad, and except for a minor change here
or there I regard it as written. Have added lines to fit an air.
    May I have yours now? I long to see it.

Loving

D.

P.S. I like my ballad; anyway for the moment.

Riversdale,
[A] Tuesday [in July, 1936]

I have added 'The Three Bushes', etc.
My dear Dorothy,
    I send to you what seems to me a better version of the little poem. There is
no reason why you should not write a separate poem on the Rose Bushes or
rather put what you have written into ballad rhyme. Forgive me for my work
on the present poem. I thought from what you wrote that you meant to leave it
un-rhymed & I wanted to prove you wrong. Perhaps it will go well with the
'Street Corner Songs' – it has their mood. I have recovered from the shock of
your archaic modernity, which for a moment made me lose faith in myself. I
now like my long ballad of the Three Bushes again. I have written two other
poems on the same theme. I will send all as soon as I can. I think them among
my best things. . . .

Poem by Dorothy Wellesley [the footnote reads 'A second version, by W. B.
Y.']

I

She sent her sewing girl to the man
That would her leman be
'O Psyche mimic me at love
With him I will not lie
'Tis sweetly done, 'tis easy done
So child make love for me.'

II

'I go, should you light a candle'
'Lie down, lie down you are wild,
O you are wild for love of me
And I with love am wild'
'I came to lie with a man in the dark'
'Lie down again, dear child.'

III

But the black death took the lord & the lady
'Who is singing so loud'
'A sewing girl, a sewing girl
That sings hemming a shroud
'All goes well, O all goes well
And all that I did she bid.'

369

IV

High up lady, or sewing girl
What does it matter which!
Has found it sweet to lie in the dark
Nor cared who made the match;
O all goes well in the dark with a man
And well with the feather stitch!

THE THREE BUSHES
(By W. B. Y.)

1

'Man's love that lacks its proper food
None can rely upon
And could you sing no more of love
Your genius would be gone
And could that happen what were you
But a starving man'
  O my dear, O my dear.

2

'Light no candles in your room'
That lovely lady said
'When twelve o'clock is sounding
I shall creep into your bed
But if I saw myself creep in
I think I should drop dead'
  O my dear, O my dear.

3

'I love a man in secret
Dear chambermaid,' said she.
'I know that I must drop down dead
If he stop loving me,
Yet what could I but drop down dead
If I lost my chastity?'
  O my dear, O my dear.

4

'So you must lie beside him
And let him think me there
Maybe we are all the same
Where no candles are,
Maybe we are all the same
When the body's bare.'
  O my dear, O my dear.

370

5

'No, not another song' said he
'Because my lady came
'A year ago for the first time
At midnight to my room
And I must lie between the sheets
        the clock[1]
When bells[1] begin to boom'
    O my dear, O my dear.

6

'A laughing, crying, sacred song
A leching song' said they.
Did ever man hear such a song?
No not before that day.
Did ever man ride such a race?
Not till he rode away.
    O my dear, O my dear.

7

But when his horse had put its hoof
Into a rabbit hole,
He dropped upon his head and died
His lady that saw it all
Dropped and died thereon for she
Loved him with her soul.
    O my dear, O my dear.

8

The chambermaid lived on and took
Their graves into her charge
And there two bushes planted,
That when they had grown large
Seemed sprung from but a single root
So did their roses merge.
    O my dear, O my dear.

9

When she was old and dying
The priest came where she was
She made a full confession
Long looked he in her face,
And O he was a good man
And understood her case.
    O my dear, O my dear.

10

He bade them take and bury her
Beside her lady's man
And set a rose tree on her grave
And now none living can
When they have plucked a rose there
Know where its roots began.
    O my dear, O my dear.

[1] These are alternative readings. – D.W.

371

THE LADY TO HER CHAMBERMAID
(By W. B. Y.)

I

What manner of man is coming
To lie between your feet?

What matter we are but women;
Wash, make your body sweet,

I shall find a perfume
To scatter on the sheet.

    The Lord have mercy on us.

He shall love my soul as though
Body were not all

He shall love your body
Untroubled by the soul

Love crams his two divisions
Yet keeps his substance whole

    The Lord have mercy on us.

Soul must learn a love that is
Proper to my breast.

Limbs a love in common
With every noble beast

If soul may look and body touch
Which is the more blest?

    The Lord have mercy on us.

II

When you and my true lover meet
And he plays tunes between your feet,

If you dare abuse the soul,
Or think the body is the whole

I must, that am his daylight lady,
Outrageously abuse the body;

Swear that he shall never stray
From either neither night and day,

That I may hear, if we should kiss,
That contrapuntal serpent hiss,

You, should hand explore a thigh,
All the labouring heaven sigh.

Riversdale,
[postmark
July 18, 1936]
Thursday.

My dear Dorothy,

You have got me down to fundamental rock. I cannot say the good is bad or the bad good, even though the good is by my bitterest enemy, the bad by my dearest friend. When I got your first sketch I went down stairs humming over the opening stanzas, getting the rhymes regular & said to somebody 'I have something here that will not die'. Yet what you send me is bad. What has the beginning to do with the end? 'With him I will not lie' can only mean (I thought it a masterly simplification) left unqualified that she is not in love with the man, that she does not want him at all. Why then should she in her talk wih the briar lament that he was never hers. Why should this be 'truth after death'. Then why should the fact that she never gave herself cause the squire to lose not the lady but Psyche. Then in the last stanza I do not understand why Psyche has a living heart & why she can rise & deck their graves. Of course you know why, but it is not in the poem.

Then look through any old book of ballads & you will find that they have all perfectly regular rhyme schemes.

'O my dear, O my dear'

W. B. Y.

Perhaps your mind is meditative not narrative. I am putting your little poem with its music in one number with my ballad.

Penns in the Rocks,
July.

My dear W. B.

I have this minute received your letter, slanging my 'ballad'. I take your points as they come.

1. It is not obvious that the lady was a minx, a demi-vierge, an 'allumeuse', leading the young man on, letting him down? A mental baggage, a jade, a hussy, slut, demirep, and so on?

2. *Argument*. So she left it to her maid, when it came to grips.

3. You say why then when the rose tells her the truth does she mind? Because she, like all the women described above, regrets what she never knew she wanted.

4. The squire of course minded. He had been cheated. (Psyche is merely a symbol.) And he lamented after death. It disturbed his sleep.

5. Why has Psyche a 'living heart'? Because she loved the man and got what she wanted, and even the bitter truth after death could not destroy her memories. So she rose to deck all their graves.

6. Now as to technical errors about riming ballads. I hadn't attempted a true ballad. Had tried to graft a modern form upon the skeleton of the old. That is all. I don't believe in 'going back' in any sense, but this was an experiment. The modern mind cannot perhaps avoid short cuts, the assumption being that the reader has jumped to it.

I thought your verses very beautiful. Some I thought as fine as anything you have done. All yesterday I was in despair about the Muse.

Will you send back that false ballad? Just stick it into an envelope. I might rewrite it or not. There is something false in any case about archaic modernity.

Yrs, with affection,

D.

P.S. Have you kept the first version of my 'ballad'? I destroyed mine. You called it a 'masterpiece' in your letter of that date, a fortnight or so ago. I was certainly astonished at your praise. Could I have that version back too?

Riversdale,
July 21st, 1936.

Dear Lady Dorothy,

I enclose your first draft, which does not differ much from the second. When I read it I think I only glanced at the end about the thorntree. I thought that you had put it in because it was part of the story, and would as a matter of course leave it out. The first part surprised me, the new point of view and the absence of rhyme. Just as I thought you would leave out the end, so I was certain you either intended or could be persuaded to add rhyme. I ended the poem at 'Sang sewing maid to shroud'. In those first four verses I found something that had never been sung. The maid who had seemed 'wild with love' was able to 'sing aloud' as she hemmed the shroud. 'All goes well, Oh all goes well, No matter who she be, All in the dark unto a man' (I read this to mean 'in the dark with a man'). She was gay. She was without grief. —— said once to George Moore 'I wish I had a slave to do this for me. I would not have to think of him afterwards.' Your sewing maid gets the same result by being a slave – she had not to think of him afterwards. He was merely a man in the dark. In my excitement I began using my acquired skill to make your meaning plainer than you had made it. I sent you a first version with rhymes – I thought you would use it as a quarry for rhyme. Then against my first intention I sent you what I thought a finished version.

Regular rhyme is needed in this kind of work. The swing of the sentence makes the reader expect it. 'Said lover to the serving maid', ''Tis sweetly done, 'tis easy done' and so on are ballad cadences, and then the six line stanzas suggest ballad stanzas. There is another reason. In narrative verse we want to concentrate the attention on the fact or the story, not on the form. The form must be present as something we all accept – 'the fundamental sing-song'. I do not know a single example of good narrative where the rhyme scheme is varied . . . Ah my dear how it added to my excitement when I re-made the poem of yours to know it was your poem. I re-made you and myself into a single being. We triumphed over each other and I thought of *The Turtle and the Phoenix.* (*DWL* 69–82)

7   *O my dear, O my dear*: cf. the refrain 'O my dear, my dear' in [I was going the Road one day] (*PNE* A64) about which Yeats wrote 'one sometimes has need of more lines of the little song, and I have put into English rhyme three of the many verses of a Gaelic ballad' (*CW* iv)

342   55   *Loved him with her soul*: cf. the lines in 'The Lady's First Song' (*PNE* 326).

What hurts the soul
My soul adores

This was written by 20 November 1936 and first appeared in *NP*.   *343*
 Yeats wrote of it as 'not in itself very good but it will heighten the drama' [of
'The Three Bushes'] (*DWL* 105).

11   *No better than a beast*: cf. 'A Last Confession' (*PNE* 301):   *344*

> And laughed upon his breast to think
> Beast gave beast as much.

This poem was written in July 1936 and first appeared in *NP*. This poem is   *344*
quoted in early form in the letters between Yeats and Dorothy Wellesley. See
notes on 'The Three Bushes' (*PNE* 325).

7   *The Lord have mercy on us*: Henn (*LT* 332) points out that this liturgial
refrain 'not only throws forward to the Chambermaid's final confession to the
priest, but is a counterpointed gesture, as by some bystander, on the ''heresy''
that the Lady propounds'.

This poem was written in July 1936 and first appeared in *NP*.   *345*

10   *A contrapuntal serpent*: a symbol of the Fall of man caused by Satan who,
when tempting Eve, took the form of a serpent (see Genesis 3. 1-6) and hence,
presumably, sex: contrapuntal because of the opposition of the soul-body conflict.

This poem was written on 9 November 1936 and first appeared in *NP*.   *345*
 Yeats wrote on 9 November 1936 to Dorothy Wellesley

> After I had written to you I tried to find better words to explain what I meant
> by the touch from behind the curtain. This morning, this came. [The poem is
> then quoted.] It is *Matrix* again but air not earth. In Fragonard's 'Cup of Life'
> the young man is not in his first youth, his face is lined with thought & that
> makes that picture too mysterious – a double thirst.   (*DWL* 102)

He had written to her on 8 November 1936

> On the other wall are drawings, paintings or photographs of paintings of friends
> & relatives, & three reproductions of pictures, Botticelli's 'Spring', Gustave
> Moreau's 'Women and Unicorns', Fragonard's 'Cup of Life', a beautiful

young man and girl running with eager lips towards a cup held towards them by a winged form. The first & last sense, & the second mystery – the mystery that touches the genitals, a blurred touch through a curtain. . . .   (*DWL* 100)

330   THE CHAMBERMAID'S FIRST SONG

345   This poem was written in November 1936 and first appeared in *NP.*

346   10   *Weak as a worm*: Yeats's letters of 15, 20 and 28 November 1936 to Dorothy Wellesley enclosing this poem and 'The Chambermaid's Second Song' (*PNE* 331). In reply to Dorothy Wellesley's letter of 25 November 1936 (cf. *DWL* 103–8) protesting against the worm imagery Yeats changed the adjectives in the poems and wrote:

> The 'worm' is right, its repulsiveness is right – so are the adjectives – 'dull', 'limp', 'thin', 'bare', all suggested by the naked body of the man & taken with the worm by that body abject and helpless. All suggest her detachment, her 'cold breast', her motherlike prayer.   (*DWL* 108)

He had used the image earlier in 'The Phases of the Moon ' (*PNE* 183), 'helpless as a worm'.

331   THE CHAMBERMAID'S SECOND SONG

346   This poem was written in November 1936 and first appeared in *NP*. See notes on 'The Chambermaid's first Song' (*PNE* 330).

332   AN ACRE OF GRASS

346   This poem was written in November 1936 and first appeared in *Atlantic Monthly* and *LM* (April 1938).

2   *An acre of green grass*: Yeats described his new residence, Riversdale, Rathfarnham, Co. Dublin, in letters to Olivia Shakespear in the summer of 1932: 'There apple trees, cherry trees, roses, smooth lawns and no long climb upstairs (*L* 798) . . . 'I shall have a big old fruit garden all to myself – the study opens into it and it is shut off from the flower garden and the croquet and tennis lawns and from the bowling-green' (*L* 799).

5   *an old house*: Riversdale, which Yeats described in a letter of 8 July 1932 to Mrs Shakespear as leased 'for but thirteen years but that will see me out of life. . . . At any rate the home will be there while the children are being educated and making friends' (*L* 799)

7 *My temptation is quiet*: cf. a passage in a letter to Mrs Shakespear of 25 July 1932:

> I am writing in my new study – sometimes I go out of the glass-door into the fruit garden to share the gooseberries with the bullfinches. I can hear the workmen putting in the electric bells; through the window to my left I can see pergolas covered with roses. At first I was unhappy, for everything made me remember the great rooms and the great trees of Coole, my home for nearly forty years, but now that the pictures are up I feel more content. This little creeper-covered farm-house might be in a Calvert woodcut, and what could be more suitable for one's last decade? George's fine taste has made the inside almost as beautiful as the garden which has some fame among gardeners.   (*L* 799)

8 *at life's end*: Yeats had anticipated this stanza – and this situation – in an essay written in February 1917:

> A poet, when he is growing old, will ask himself if he cannot keep his mask and his vision without new bitterness, new disappointment. Could he if he would, knowing how frail his vigour from youth up, copy Landor who lived loving and hating, ridiculous and unconquered, into extreme old age, all lost but the favour of his Muses?

> > The Mother of the Muses, we are taught
> > Is Memory; she has left me; they remain,
> > And shake my shoulder, urging me to sing.

> Surely, he may think, now that I have found vision and mask I need not suffer any longer. He will buy perhaps some small old house, where, like Ariosto, he can dig his garden, and think that in the return of birds and leaves, or moon and sun, and in the evening flight of the roofs he may discover rhythm and pattern like those in sleep and so never awake out of vision. Then he will remember Wordsworth withering into eighty years, honoured and empty-witted, and climb to some waste room and find, forgotten there by youth, some bitter crust.   (*M* 342)

11 *its rag and bone*: cf. 'The Circus Animals' Desertion' (*PNE* 373)

> > Old kettles, old bottles, and a broken can,
> > Old iron, old bones, old rags, . . .

and

> > the foul rag-and-bone shop of the heart.

13 *an old man's frenzy*: this may draw on Nietzsche's quotation, *The Dawn of Day*, 21, of Plato's remark that 'All the greatest benefits of Greece have sprung from madness'. Yeats was rereading Nietzsche in 1936–7.

15 *Timon . . . Lear*: characters in Shakespeare's *Timon of Athens* and *King Lear*

16 *William Blake*: Blake (1757–1827), English poet and engraver. Cf.

'Michael Robartes and the Dancer' (*PNE* 189) and 'Under Ben Bulben' IV (*PNE* 356).

19 *Michael Angelo*: Michelangelo Buonarroti (1475-1564), Italian sculptor, painter and poet. His patron was Lorenzo de Medici; his main works include the statue of David (begun 1501), the ceiling of the Sistine Chapel at Rome (1508-12) and the fresco of the Last Judgement on the east wall of the Sistine Chapel (1535-41). Cf. 'Under Ben Bulben' IV (*PNE* 356).

20-2   *. . . pierce the clouds,*
        Or inspired by frenzy
        Shake the dead. . . .: a contented easy old age would lead to the forgetfulness of later generations. A passage in Nietzsche (*The Dawn of Day*, 369) casts light on this ambition of Yeats to avoid easy content:

> At this time, too, as the result of the love which all weary and old people feel for enjoyment, such men as those I am speaking of wish to enjoy the results of their thinking instead of again testing them and scattering the seeds abroad once more. This leads them to make their thoughts palatable and enjoyable, and to take away dryness, coldness, and want of flavour; and thus it comes about that the old thinker apparently raises himself above his life's work, while in reality he spoils it by infusing into it a certain amount of fantasy, sweetness, flavour, poetic mists, and mystic lights. This is how Plato ended, as did also that great and honest Frenchman August Comte. . . .

24   *An old man's eagle mind*: this may owe something to Nietzsche's view of genius, *The Dawn of Day*, 347:

> We have the best reason for speaking of 'genius' in men – for example, Plato, Spinoza, and Goethe – whose minds appear to be but loosely linked to their character and temperament, like winged beings which easily separate themselves from them, and then rise far above them.

333   WHAT THEN?

347   This poem was probably written in 1936; it first appeared in *The Erasmian* (April 1937).
    Yeats described the poem in a letter to Edith Shackleton Heald as 'a melancholy biographical poem' (*L* 895) and to the present author (then editor of *The Erasmian*) as one of the few poems he had written lately that might be fit for a school magazine. This poem, like 'An Acre of Grass' (*PNE* 332) was inspired by Yeats's re-reading of Nietzsche, the refrain of 'What then?' is similar to Nietzsche's conclusion of *The Dawn of Day*, which is headed 'We Aeronauts of the Intellect':

> All those daring birds that soar far and ever farther into space, will somewhere or other be certain to find themselves unable to continue their flight and they will perch on a mast or some narrow ledge – and they will be grateful even for this miserable accommodation! But who could conclude from this that

there was not an endless free space stretching far in front of them, and that they had flown as far as they possibly could? In the end, however, all our great teachers and predecessors have come to a standstill, and it is by no means in the noblest or most graceful attitude that their weariness has brought them to a pause: the same thing will happen to you and me! but what does this matter to either of us? *Other birds will fly farther!* Our minds and hopes vie with them far out and on high; they rise far above our heads and our failures, and from this height they look far into the distant horizon and see hundreds of birds much more powerful than we are, striving whither we ourselves have also striven, and where all is sea, sea, and nothing but sea!

And where then are we aiming at? Do we wish to cross the sea? Whither does this overpowering passion urge us, this passion which we value more highly than any other delight? Why do we fly precisely in this direction, where all the suns of humanity have hitherto set? Is it possible that people may one day say of us that we also steered westward, hoping to reach India – but that it was our fate to be wrecked on the infinite? Or, my brethren? or – ?

1   *chosen comrades thought at school*: Yeats went to a dame school in Sligo, next to the Godolphin School, Hammersmith, and then to the High School, Dublin, an Erasmus Smith foundation. *The Erasmian*, in which this poem first appeared, is its school magazine. An article in it by 'John Eglinton' [W. K. Magee], who was there with Yeats, describes the nature of the school in the eighteen-seventies and eighties. See 'Yeats at the High School', *Erasmian*, XXX (June 1939). Charles Johnston would have been one of his closest friends. See notes on 'The Indian upon God' (*PNE* 5)

5   *Plato's ghost*: Plato may have been suggested by the passage in Nietzsche quoted in note on line 24, 'An Acre of Grass' (*PNE* 332). For Plato, see note on 'Mad as the Mist and Snow' (*PNE* 285).

12   *A small old house*: Riversdale, Rathfarnham, Co. Dublin. See notes on 'An Acre of Grass' (*PNE* 332).

BEAUTIFUL LOFTY THINGS   334

This poem's date of composition is not known, though it was probably written in   *348*
1937 (in 'A General Introduction for my Work', written in 1937, Yeats mentions O'Leary, O'Grady, and Lady Gregory in 'II Subject Matter' in ways which are complementary to the poem. See *E & I* 510–16). It first appeared in *NP*.

1   *O'Leary's noble head*: Yeats called O'Leary 'the handsomest old man' he had ever seen (*A* 94). See notes on 'September 1913' (*PNE* 115) for information on O'Leary.

2–4   *My father*: John Butler Yeats (1839–1922). For a brief account of his life see Jeffares, *TCA* 117–46 and p. 403 below. He spoke at the debate in the

379

Abbey Theatre on the issues arising out of the riots about Synge's *The Playboy of the Western World* in 1907: 'No man of all literary Dublin dared show his face but my own father . . .' (*A* 483). The account of the incident given by J. B. Yeats is no less vivid than that given by his son in the poem. He wrote to a friend:

> Of course I did not make a speech in favour of patricide. How could I? Here is what I said. I began with some information about Synge which interested my listeners and then: 'Of course I know Ireland is an island of Saints, but thank God it is also an island of sinners – only unfortunately in this Country people cannot live or die except behind a curtain of deceit.' At this point the chairman and my son both called out, 'Time's up, Time's up.' I saw the lifted sign and like the devil in *Paradise Lost* I fled. The papers next morning said I was howled down. It was worse, I was pulled down. . . . The sentence about the curtain of deceit flashed on my mind at the moment, and was a good sentence, but manifestly a blunder, although I did enjoy it. . . . (*LTHS* 214).

5   *Standish O'Grady*: (1846–1928) an Irish historian and novelist, author of *The History of Ireland – The Heroic Period* (1878), which had an important influence on the Irish Renaissance. This event occurred at a dinner given by T. P. Gill, leader writer of the *Daily Express*, in Dublin, on 11 May 1899, in honour of the Irish Literary Theatre, in effect Edward Martyn and Yeats.

The dinner was described by George Moore in *Ave* (1947 edn) 102 ff., and Yeats also dealt with it in *DP*:

> Towards the end of the evening, when everybody was more or less drunk, O'Grady spoke. He was very drunk, but neither his voice nor his manner showed it. I had never heard him speak, and at first he reminded me of Cardinal Manning. There was the same simplicity, the same gentleness. He stood between two tables, touching one or the other for support, and said in a low penetrating voice: 'We have now a literary movement, it is not very important; it will be followed by a political movement, that will not be very important; then must come a military movement, that will be important indeed'. Tyrrell, Professor of Greek in Trinity College, known to scholars for his share in the Tyrrell–Purser edition of Cicero's Letters, a Unionist, but very drunk, led the applause. Then O'Grady described the Boy Scout Act, which had just passed, urged the landlords of Ireland to avail themselves of that Act and drill the sons of their tenants – 'paying but little attention to the age limit' – then, pointing to where he supposed England to be, they must bid them 'march to the conquest of that decadent nation'. I knew what was in his mind. England was decadent because, democratic and so without fixed principles, it had used Irish landlords, his own ancestors or living relatives, as its garrison, and later left them deserted among their enemies. Tyrrell, understanding nothing but the sweetness of that voice, the nobility of that gesture, continued to lead the applause. (*A* 423–4)

O'Grady's influence predominated, Yeats recorded, when modern Irish literature began:

> He could delight us with an extravagance we were too critical to share; a day will come, he said, when Slieve-na-mon will be more famous than Olympus; yet he was no Nationalist as we understood the word, but in rebellion, as he was fond of explaining, against the House of Commons, not against the King. (*E &I* 512)

This was an Irish attitude of mind which began with Molyneux's *Case of Ireland Stated* (1691), which argued for the independence of the Irish parliament, and asserted its loyalty to the King, not to the House of Commons in England.

7   *Augusta Gregory*: Lady Gregory told Yeats of this particular threat to her life which occurred in 'the troubles' when she was about seventy. Yeats chose 'eightieth' arbitrarily. See *Lady Gregory's Journals: Volume One: Books One to Twenty Nine, 10 October 1916–24 February 1925*, ed. Daniel J. Murphy (1978) 337, where she showed a tenant who wanted to take over some Coole Park land, 'how easy it would be' to shoot her 'through the unshuttered window' if he wanted to use violence. She used to sit regularly from six to seven o'clock at the window writing letters before dinner.

The movement from Standish O'Grady to Lady Gregory is paralleled in 'A General Introduction to my Work' where after describing Standish O'Grady and his cousin as representing the old Irish landowning aristocracy, Yeats went on to describe Lady Gregory as another member of that order, though he distinguished between O'Grady's style, founded on Carlyle, and Lady Gregory's, on the Anglo-Irish dialect of her neighbourhood. See note on 'Coole Park, 1929' (*PNE* 253).

10   *Maud Gonne*: this memory goes back to their walks at Howth, the promontory forming the northern arm of Dublin Bay (pronounced Hō-th) where Yeats first proposed to her in August 1891. There are some lyric descriptions of its scenery in *SQ*. The name is Danish, Hovud; the Irish name Ben Eadair.

11   *Pallas Athena*: cf. the passage in *A* 123 where 'the Virgilian commendation "She walks like a goddess" [was] made for her alone'. Cf. also 'Her beauty, backed by her great stature . . . her face, like the face of some Greek statue' (*A* 264) and cf. 'The Arrow' (*PNE* 78). See also note on 'Among School Children' (*PNE* 222) and on 'Mad as the Mist and Snow' (*PNE* 285) and A. Norman Jeffares, 'Pallas Athene Gonne' *Tributes in Prose and Verse to Shotaro Oshima* (1970) 4–7.

A CRAZED GIRL   335

This poem was written at Barcelona in May 1936 and first appeared in *The*   348
Lemon Tree (1937), a book of Margot Ruddock's poems for which Yeats wrote
an Introduction. The poem was entitled 'At Barcelona' in that volume.

1   *That crazed girl*: Margot Collis [Ruddock]. See notes on 'Sweet Dancer' (*PNE* 324).

14   '*O sea-starved . . . sea*': from a song in the essay 'Almost I tasted ecstasy', *The Lemon Tree* (1937) 9.

349   This poem was written in August 1936 and first appeared with the title 'To a Friend' in *LM* (March 1938) and *N* (12 March 1938). See note on 'The Three Bushes' (*PNE* 325).

7   (*For since the horizon's bought strange dogs are still*): a comma between 'bought' and 'strange' would clarify the sense. The original version, included in a letter from Yeats written to Dorothy Wellesley on 1 August 1936, read 'For since you bought the horizon all is still'. A letter from Dorothy Wellesley dated 4 March 1936 explains the line: 'I have saved by twenty-four hours this little corner of Sussex from a town of scarlet bungalows. So I now own the lovely ridge opposite and feel I have done something for "Deserted House" ' (*DWL* 53).

In a footnote Dorothy Wellesley remarked: 'I have never understood, however, what he meant by the last half of the line, unless he had a fantastic idea that after buying the few acres I evicted the people who lived on it, together with their dogs!' But Yeats was probably using the present tense as a future. No newcomers' 'strange' dogs would make a noise.

10   *a Great Dane*: Brutus, Dorothy Wellesley's dog, which she described:

Brutus himself had a great majesty, both of form and conduct, and Yeats had observed it. When he seemed too tired to reach a garden seat, the three of us would walk abreast, Yeats's hand and part of his great weight supported on my right shoulder, while my left hand and shoulder was supported by the great dog. I was always afraid of a landslide, but the great hound pacing slowly beside me never let me down. The seat was reached, the end achieved, and the tremendous Dane would settle down and turn into a piece of black and white marble until, our conversation ended, he would help us back again to the house.   (*DWL* 145-6)

350   16   *The Proud Furies*: Yeats's letter to Dorothy Wellesley explains what he meant the poem to achieve:

We have all something within ourselves to batter down and get our power from this fighting. I have never 'produced' a play in verse without showing the actors that the passion of the verse comes from the fact that the speakers are holding down violence or madness – 'down Hysterica passio'. All depends on the completeness of the holding down, on the stirring of the beast underneath. Even my poem 'To D. W.' should give this impression. The moon, the moonless night, the dark velvet, the sensual silence, the silent room and the violent bright Furies. Without this conflict we have no passion only sentiment and thought. . . .
. . . About the conflict in 'To D. W.', I did not plan it deliberately. That conflict is deep in my subconsciousness, perhaps in everybody's. I dream of clear water, perhaps two or three times (the moon of the poem), then come erotic dreams. Then for weeks perhaps I write poetry with sex for theme. Then comes the reversal – it came when I was young with some dream or some vision between waking and sleep with a flame in it. Then for weeks I get a symbolism like that in my Byzantium poem or in 'To D. W.' with flame for theme. All

this may come from the chance that when I was a young man I was accustomed to a Kabalistic ceremony where there were two pillars, one symbolic of water and one of fire. The fire mark is $\triangle$, the water mark is $\triangledown$, these are combined to make Solomon's seal $\Large\Leftrightarrow$. The water is sensation, peace, night, silence, indolence; the fire is passion, tension, day, music, energy.

(*DWL* 86-7)

14-16 *that great family ... authors misrepresent/The Proud Furies*: PNE suggests Yeats drew on Jane Ellen Harrison, *Prolegomena to the Study of Greek Religion* (3rd edn 1922) for descriptions of the Furies, the Erinyes or Eumenides (a euphemism, the kindly ones) of Greek mythology who are avenging spirits, executing curses pronounced on criminals or inflicting famines or pestilences. Aeschylus may have misrepresented them according to Lewis Richard Farnell, *The Cults of the Greek States* (1909) v 440.

THE CURSE OF CROMWELL   337

This poem was written between November 1936 and 8 January 1937 and first *350* appeared in *A Broadside*, No. 8 (New Series) (Aug. 1937).

Yeats wrote on 8 January 1937 to Dorothy Wellesley 'At this moment I am expressing my rage against the intelligentsia by writing about Oliver Cromwell who was the Lennin of his day – I speak through the mouth of some wandering peasant poet in Ireland' (*DWL* 119).

2 *Cromwell's house*: Oliver Cromwell (1599-1658) arrived in Ireland as Lord Lieutenant and general for the Parliament of England. He sacked Drogheda and Wexford, and left Ireland in 1650: his military rule lasted till 1658. By the Settlement Act of 1652 and an Act of Sequestration of 1653 only Clare and Connaught were left to Irish landowners while the rest, about eleven million out of the remaining twenty million acres of Irish land, was confiscated.

3 *beaten into the clay*: cf. section V of 'Under Ben Bulben' (*PNE* 356):

> . . . the lords and ladies gay
> That were beaten into the clay

The phrase comes, according to G. B. Saul (*PYP* 176), from Frank O'Connor's translation, *Kilcash*: 'The earls, the lady, the people beaten into the clay.'

11 *He that's mounting up*: cf. 'The Gyres' (*PNE* 321). This is a reference to the ebb and flow of civilisations.

12 *Muses*: see note on 'The Tower' (*PNE* 205).

18 *the Spartan boy's*: a Spartan boy stole a fox and when apprehended let it gnaw him to death under his clothes rather than be detected in crime. The story comes from a Life of Lycurgus (*c.* 390-*c.* 225 BC) the Athenian statesman, in the

Lives of Ten Orators attributed to the Greek philosopher and biographer Plutarch (*c.* 46-*c.* 120).

351 19 *things both can and cannot be*: this line may derive from Shelley, *The Sensitive Plant*, 3rd stanza of 'Conclusion':

Where nothing is but all things seem . . .

25 *great house*: cf. Yeats's play *Purgatory*, and notes on 'Crazy Jane on God' (*PNE* 272) with its 'uninhabited, ruinous' house.

32 *What is there left to say*: cf. 'Nineteen Hundred and Nineteen' (*PNE* 213), 'What more is there to say?'

338 ROGER CASEMENT

351 This poem was written in November 1936 (the MS. is dated 'October/November 1936') and first appeared in the *Irish Press* (2 Feb. 1937). A revised version appeared in the *Irish Press* (12 Feb. 1937); see notes on line 17. The ballad was meant to be sung to the tune of 'The Glen of Aherlow'.

Yeats wrote to Ethel Mannin on 15 November 1936 that he was in a rage:

I have just got a book published by the Talbot Press called *The Forged Casement Diaries* [(1936)]. It is by a Dr Maloney [(1881-1952)] I knew in New York and he has spent years collecting evidence. He has proved that the diaries, supposed to prove Casement 'a Degenerate' and successfully used to prevent an agitation for his reprieve, were forged. Casement was not a very able man but he was gallant and unselfish, and had surely his right to leave what he would have considered an unsullied name. I long to break my rule against politics and call these men criminals but I must not. Perhaps a verse may come to me, now or a year hence. I have lately written a song in defence of Parnell (about love and marriage less foul lies were circulated), a drinking song to a popular tune and will have it sung from the Abbey stage at Xmas. All my life it has been hard to keep from action, as I wrote when a boy, - 'to be not of the things I dream.' (*L* 867-8)

Yeats's letters to Dorothy Wellesley provide a background to this poem and 'The Ghost of Roger Casement' (*CP* 352). He wrote on 28 November 1936

. . . I sent off a ferocious ballad written to a popular tune, to a newspaper. It is on 'The Forged Diaries of Roger Casement' a book published here, & denounces by name —— and —— for their share in abetting the forgeries. I shall not be happy until I hear that it is sung by Irish undergraduates at Oxford. I wrote to the editor saying I had not hitherto sent him a poem because almost [all] my poems were unsuitable because they came out of rage or lust. (*DWL* 107)

The postscript read:

You will not find the four line stanza 'too easy' if you struggle to make your spirit at once natural & imaginative. My 'Casement' is better written than my 'Parnell' because I passed things when I had to find three rhymes & did not pass when I had to find two.

On 4 December he wrote:

> I could not stop that ballad if I would, people have copies, & I don't want to. —— belongs to a type of man for whom I have no respect. Such men have no moral sense. They are painted cardboard manipulated by intreaguers. If he had been a man he would before circulating those charges against Casement have asked 'was the evidence shown to Casement?' & have learned that Casement denied the charges & asked in vain to be shown the evidence. I was present when the Editor of *The Times* spoke of making the same charges in *The Times*. He did not do so, probably because of the infuriated comment of Roger Fry & myself. It was impossible to talk for five minutes to Roger Fry without finding out that he was honest. However I hate 'Leagues of Nations' & Leagues of all kinds & am not likely to be just.
> [A discussion of the well-known Casement charge follows.]
> But the Casement evidence was not true as we know – it was one of a number of acts of forgery committed at that time. I can only repeat words spoken to me by the old head of the Fenians [John O'Leary], years ago. 'There are things a man must not do even to save a nation.'
> By the by my ballad should begin
>
> > 'I say that Roger Casement
> > Did what he had to do
> > But died upon the scaffold,
> > But that is nothing new.'
>
> I feel that one's verse must be as direct & natural as spoken words. The opening I sent you was not quite natural.
> No I shall not get the ballad sung in Oxford: that was but a 'passing' thought because I happen to know a certain wild student who would have been made quite happy by the task – the idea amused me.
> We will have no great popular literature until we get rid of the moral sycophants. Montaigne says that a prince must sometimes commit a crime to save his people, but if he does so he must mourn all his life. I only hate the men who do not mourn.
> Forgive all this my dear, but I have told you that my poetry all comes from rage or lust.   (*DWL* 108-9)

On 7 December he wrote

> I am upset & full of remorse. You were quite right. I have wronged ——, though not ——. I got in a blind rage & only half read the passage that excited it. . . . All my life I have been subject to these fits of rage though thank God seldom if ever about any matter that effects myself. In this case I lost the book & trusted to memory. I am full of shame.   (*DWL* 110)

On 10 December 1936 he wrote:

> This post brings me a letter from an Irishwoman in England to whom I had sent the corrected Casement poem, she writes approving of what she supposes to be my hatred of England. It has shocked me for it has made me fear that you think the same. I have written to my correspondent. 'How can I hate England,

385

owing what I do to Shakespeare, Blake & Morris. England is the only country I cannot hate.' She is an extreme revolutionist but writes 'I drank the toast of the king for the first time in my life the other day.' (*DWL* 111)

1 *Roger Casement*: Sir Roger Casement, KCMG (1864-1916), a British consular official 1895-1913, who joined the Sinn Fein movement in 1914, went to Germany to ask for armed aid, returned in a submarine in 1916 and was arrested in south-west Ireland. He was tried in London on a charge of high treason, found guilty and hanged. See note on 'Sixteen Dead Men' (*PNE* 194).
   Yeats wrote to Dorothy Wellesley on 8 February 1937

On Feb. 2 my wife went to Dublin shopping & was surprised at the defference everybody showed her in buses & shop. Then she found what it was – the Casement poem was in the morning paper. Next day I was publicly thanked by the vice-president of the Executive Council, by De Valera's political secretary, by our chief antiquarian & an old revolutionist, Count Plunket, who calls my poem 'a ballad the people much needed'. De Valera's newspaper gave me a long leader saying that for generations to come my poem will pour scorn on the forgers & their backers. The only English comment is in the *Evening Standard* which points out my bad rhymes & says that after so many years it is impossible to discuss the authenticity of the diaries. (The British Government has hidden them for years.) (*DWL* 126)

7 *a trick by forgery*: cf. note on line 17. Yeats meant that 'a slander based on forged diaries was spread through the world'. The diaries are now not thought to be false; see Brian Inglis, *Roger Casement* (1973) 377-81 for an excellent account of the controversy after the period of Yeats's poems.

352 *Spring Rice*: Sir Cecil Arthur Spring-Rice (1859-1918), British Ambassador to the US from 1912.

17 *Come Tom and Dick, come all the troop*: in the MS. of the poem an extra stanza was inserted after line 16.

> No, no matter what the names they wear
> A dog must have his day
> And whether a man be rich or poor
> He takes the Devil's pay.

Line 17 originally ran 'Come Alfred Noyes and all the troop' which he altered to 'Come Gilbert Murray, Alfred Noyes'. Maloney had quoted from an article by the English poet Alfred Noyes (1880-1958), then Professor of English at Princeton University, in the *Philadelphia Public Ledger*, 31 August 1916, describing Casement's confessions as 'filthy beyond all descriptions'. The first version of the *Irish Press* (2 Feb. 1937) ran 'Come Alfred Noyes and all the troop' but was altered to 'No matter what the names they wear!' in a revised version of the ballad which accompanied Yeats's letter written after Alfred Noyes had written a disclaimer to the *Irish Press* (12 February 1937), suggesting a tribunal should examine the diaries. Yeats's letter was published in the paper on 13 February 1937:

Dear Sir, I accept Mr Alfred Noyes' explanation and I thank him for his noble letter. I, too, think that the British Government should lay the diaries before some tribunal acceptable to Ireland and to England. He suggests that Dr G. P. Gooch [(1873-1968), editor of the *Contemporary Review*], a great expert in such matters, and I should be 'associated with such an enquiry.' I have neither legal training nor training in the examination of documents, nor have I the trust of the people. But I thank him for his courtesy in suggesting my name.

I add a new version of my song. Mr Noyes' name is left out: but I repeat my accusation that a slander based on forged diaries was spread through the world and that, whatever the compulsion, 'Spring-Rice had to whisper it.' He was an honourable, able man in the ordinary affairs of life; why then did he not ask whether the evidence had been submitted to the accused? The British Government would have been compelled to answer.

I was dining with the wife of a Belgian Cabinet Minister after Casement's condemnation, perhaps after his execution, somebody connected with *The Times* was there; he said they had been asked to draw attention to the diaries. I said it was infamous to blacken Casement's name with evidence that had neither been submitted to him nor examined at his trial. Presently Roger Fry, the famous art critic, came in, and the journalist repeated his statement, and Roger Fry commented with unmeasured fury. I do not remember whether *The Times* spoke of the diaries or not. [It did, in an editorial, 4 August 1916 (the day after Casement's execution), attacking the 'inspired innuendoes' as 'irrelevant, improper and un-English'.]

Had Spring-Rice been a free man he would have shared my indignation and that of Roger Fry. [Roger Fry (1886-1934), an English art critic, associated with the Bloomsbury group, champion of the French impressionist painters in Britain] (*L* 882-3)

24 *That is in quicklime laid*: bodies of those hanged were buried in quicklime within British prisons. Casement's remains were recently returned to Ireland; he was reburied with military honours in Arbour Hill Barracks, Dublin.

THE GHOST OF ROGER CASEMENT   339

The MS. of this poem is dated October 1936; it went through much rewriting   *352* and first appeared in *NP*.

This poem is complementary to 'Roger Casement'. It was meant to be sung to the tune of 'The Church's One Foundation'. Yeats wrote to Dorothy Wellesley on 21 December 1936 of the nervous strain caused by writing it (*DWL* 113). He wrote to her on 23 December 1936:

I will send that ballad but will not be able to do so for a few days. My last typed copies went off to America on Monday & it is always difficult to get a typist who can read my writing or take my dictation. Then you may as well have the two Casement ballads together, they are meant to support each other. I am fighting in those ballads for what I have been fighting all my life, it is our Irish fight though it has nothing to do with this or that country. Bernard Shaw fights with the same object. When somebody talks of justice, who knows that justice is accompanied by secret forgery, when an archbishop wants a man to go to the communion table, when that man says he is not spiritually fit, when we remember our age old quarrel against gold-brayed and ermine & that our ancestor Swift has gone where 'fierce indignation can lacerate his heart no more', & we go stark, staring mad.

I said when I started my movement in my 25th or 26th year 'I am going to stiffen the back-bone'. Bernard Shaw may have said the same in his youth; it has been stiffened in Ireland with results. I am an old man now & month by month my capacity & energy must slip away, so what is the use of saying that both in England & Ireland I want to stiffen the back bone of the high hearted and high-minded & the sweet hearted & sweet-minded, so that they may no longer shrink & hedge, when they face rag merchants like ——. Indeed before all I want to strengthen myself. It is not our business to reply to this & that, but to set up our love and indignation against their pity & hate – but how I run on – Forgive me. (*DWL* 115)

4 *John Bull*: personification of the English nation and character; a typical Englishman, after John Arbuthnot's (1667–1735) *The History of John Bull* (1712)

353 12 *A dog must have his day*: cf. note on line 10, 'Upon a Dying Lady' III (*PNE* 176). This phrase was originally included in the MS. of 'Roger Casement' (*PNE* 338). See note on line 17 of that poem.

21 *India*: India came under British supremacy in 1763, passed to the British crown in 1858; the subcontinent was divided into India and Pakistan in 1947, and India became a republic within the commonwealth in 1950.

31 *I poked about a village church*: this stanza echoes Gray's 'Elegy written in a country churchyard.'

> Some village Hampden that with dauntless breast
> The little tyrant of his fields withstood,
> Some mute inglorious Milton, here may rest,
> Some Cromwell guiltless of his country's blood.

See Jeffares, 'Yeats and his methods of writing verse', *The Permanence of Yeats* (ed. Hall and Steinmann, 1950; 1961). Yeats was reading Gray at this period (*OTB* 17).

Yeats's MS. contained the following versions which he eventually discarded:

> For all that Hampden thought
> All that later Milton wrote

> It told of all his virtues there
> His words had been his bond
> Of such a man had Milton dreamed
> For such had Hampden planned

> For all that Hampden thought
> All that Milton knew
> Had blazed in heart and head
> Although John Hampden's dead.

Another variant of the last stanza described the family tomb:

> It told of all their virtues
> Their glory and estate
> And told it all in Latin
> To give it greater weight.

A contributory source for the introduction of the Casement tomb (apart from the contrast between the quicklime in which Casement was buried and the family tomb in which he might have expected to rest) was probably Thomas Davis's poem on Wolfe Tone, 'Tone's Grave', *National and Other Poems*, 78.

32 *his family tomb*: when waiting to be hanged Casement asked his cousin Gertrude Bannister on her last visit to him in Pentonville Gaol to have his body buried 'in the old churchyard at Murlough Bay'. See Brian Inglis, *Roger Casement* (1973), p. 369. Casement was, in fact, buried in Pentonville, but his remains were returned to Ireland in 1965. See note on 'Roger Casement' (*CP* 351).

THE O'RAHILLY   340

This poem was written in January 1937 and first appeared in *NP*. The original   *354*
refrain was 'Praise the Proud'. The O'Rahilly was killed in the fighting in 1916.

1 *the O'Rahilly*: The O'Rahilly (1875–1916) was shot in the 1916 Rising, in Henry Street, beside the General Post Office. He was 'a strikingly handsome young man always dressed in a saffron kilt'. See Arnold Bax, *Farewell my Youth*, 100.

3 *a 'the'*: 'the' is a hereditary title in Ireland.

12 *Pearse and Connolly*: see notes on 'Easter 1916' (*PNE* 193).

14 *the Kerry men*: the O'Rahilly was from Co. Kerry in south-west Ireland and head of his clan.

31 *Henry Street*: a street running at right angles to O'Connell Street, Dublin,   *355*
beside the GPO, linking O'Connell Street and Mary Street.

COME GATHER ROUND ME, PARNELLITES   341

This poem was written on 8 September 1936 and first appeared in *A Broadside*,   *355*
No. 1 (New Series) (Jan. 1937).

1 *Parnellites*: those who supported Parnell after the O'Shea divorce case and the consequent split in the Irish party. See *A* 356–7.

11   *fought the might of England*: Parnell was leader of the Irish parliamentary party, 1880, was imprisoned 1881, threw out the Liberal government, 1885, and supported the Conservatives. He held the balance of power at Westminster in 1886, and converted Gladstone to Home Rule.

14   *He brought it all to pass*: Yeats is stressing the strength of Parnell's leadership.

16   *a lass*: Mrs Kitty O'Shea. Parnell was co-respondent in the divorce case, brought by Captain William Henry O'Shea (1840-1905) in 1890. For Yeats's brief account of this see 'Modern Ireland', *Massachusetts Review* (Winter 1964), 257-9.

356   21   *Parnell was a proud man*: cf. Yeats's account in *A V* of Parnell's passionate pride:

> . . . a follower has recorded that, after a speech that seemed brutal and callous, his hands were full of blood because he had torn them with his nails. . . . Mrs Parnell tells how upon a night of storm on Brighton Pier, and at the height of his power, he held her out over the waters and she lay still, stretched upon his two hands, knowing that if she moved, he would drown himself and her.   (*A V* (B) 124)

See Yeats's commentary on 'Parnell's Funeral' (*PNE* 304).

25   *The Bishops and the Party*: Parnell was repudiated by Gladstone and the Irish hierarchy; he fought a bitter, but losing fight in 1891. He died in Brighton in 1891.

27-8   *A husband that had sold his wife*
   And after that betrayed: cf. notes on line 16, and Yeats's letter of 8 September 1936 to Dorothy Wellesley in which he commented on Henry Harrison, *Parnell Vindicated* (1931) and added:

> Mrs O'Shea was a free woman when she met Parnell, O'Shea had been paid to leave her free, and if Parnell had been able to raise £20,000 would have let himself be divorced instead of Parnell. The Irish Catholic press had ignored his book. It preferred to think that the Protestant had deceived the Catholic husband.   (*L* 862-3)

Yeats published his own views in 'Parnell' in *Essays 1931 to 1936* (*E & I* 486-90).

342   THE WILD OLD WICKED MAN

356   This poem was written when Yeats wanted to go to India with Lady Elizabeth Pelham. It first appeared in the *Atlantic Monthly* and *LM* (April 1938). Cf. letters of 21 March, 1 June and 7 July 1937 in Shankar Mokashi-Punekar, *The Later Phase in the Development of W. B. Yeats* (1966), pp. 264-5.

30   *Girls down on the seashore*: this stanza probably is a youthful memory. Cf.   *357*
this passage in *Reveries*:

> Once when I was sailing with my cousin, the boy who was our crew talked of
> a music-hall at a neighbouring seaport, and how the girls there gave themselves
> to men, and his language was as extravagant as though he praised that
> courtesan after whom they named a city or the Queen of Sheba herself.
> Another day he wanted my cousin to sail some fifty miles along the coast and
> put in near some cottages where he had heard there were girls 'and we could
> have a great welcome before us'. He pleaded with excitement (I imagine that
> his eyes shone) but hardly hoped to persuade us, and perhaps but played with
> fabulous images of life and of sex.   (*A* 75)

43   *all those warty lads*: Yeats wrote on 22 May 1936 to Dorothy Wellesley: *358*

> ... I wrote to-day to Laura Riding, with whom I carry on a slight
> correspondence, that her school was too thoughtful, reasonable & truthful, that
> poets were good liars who never forgot that the Muses were women who liked
> the embrace of gay warty lads. I wonder if she knows that warts are considered
> by the Irish peasantry a sign of sexual power? Those little poems of yours are
> nonchalant, & nonchalance is declared by Castiglione essential to all true
> courtiers – so it is to warty lads & poets.   (*DWL* 63)

THE GREAT DAY   343

This poem was written in January 1937 and first appeared in *LM* (March 1938),   *358*
under the title 'Fragments' which included 'Parnell' (*PNE* 344), 'What was
Lost' (*PNE* 345) and 'The Spur' (*PNE* 346). A line which ran 'Many violent
leading articles; the cannons shoot' was originally included in the MS.

PARNELL   344

This poem was written in January 1937 and first appeared in *LM* (March 1938).   *359*
See note on 'The Great Day' (*PNE* 343), and Yeats's commentary *KGCT* on
'Parnell's Funeral' (*PNE* 304).

WHAT WAS LOST   345

This poem was written in January 1937 and first appeared in *LM* (March 1938).   *359*
See note on 'The Great Day' (*PNE* 343).
    The poem relates to the thoughts of *AV* and, in particular, to a passage in
Yeats's Introduction to *The Resurrection*:

> Even our best histories treat men as function. Why must I think the
> victorious cause the better? Why should Mommsen think the less of Cicero
> because Caesar beat him? I am satisfied, the Platonic Year in my head, to find

but drama. I prefer that the defeated cause should be more vividly described than that which has the advertisement of victory. No battle has been finally won or lost; 'to Garret or Cellar a wheel I send'.   (*E* 398)

346   THE SPUR

359   This poem was written on 7 October 1936, and first appeared in *LM* (March 1938). See note on 'The Great Day' (*PNE* 343).

Yeats included this poem in a letter of 9 December 1936 to Dorothy Wellesley, calling it his 'final apology' (*DWL* 110). He had ended a letter of 4 December to her (*DWL* 109) with the remark 'Forgive all this my dear but I have told you that my poetry all comes from rage or lust.' The poem was also included in a letter to Ethel Mannin written on 11 December 1936, prefaced by the sentence 'Certain things drive me mad and I lose control of my tongue' (*L* 872).

347   A DRUNKEN MAN'S PRAISE OF SOBRIETY

359   The date of composition of this poem is uncertain; it first appeared in *NP*.

10   *dancing like a wave*: cf. 'The Fiddler of Dooney' lines 2 and 20, 'dance like a wave of the sea' (*PNE* 76).

348   THE PILGRIM

360   The date of composition of this poem is uncertain; it first appeared in *A Broadside*, No. 10 (N.S.) (Oct. 1937).

The most likely source is Archdeacon St John Seymour, *St Patrick's Purgatory. A medieval Pilgrimage in Ireland* (1919). See A. Norman Jeffares, 'A great black ragged bird', *Hermathena*, CXVIII, winter 1974, 69–81 for sources. A play on the Purgatory by the Spanish playwright Calderon (1600–81) considered by the Abbey (*c.* 1910) would also have been read by Yeats. St. Patrick is supposed to have fasted in the cave and had a vision of the next world there; the place, however, also has pagan legends attached to it and reminds the reader of Yeats's blending of Fenian and Christian tradition in *WO*.

6   *Lough Derg*: This small lake is on the borders of Co. Donegal and Co. Fermanagh. Cf. a passage in *If I were Four-and-Twenty*:

But if I were four-and-twenty, and without rheumatism, I should not, I think, be content with getting up performances of French plays and with reading papers. I think I would go – though certainly I am no Catholic and never shall be one – upon both of our great pilgrimages, to Croagh Patrick and to Lough Derg. Our churches have been unroofed or stripped; the stained glass of Saint Canice, once famous throughout Europe, was destroyed three centuries ago, and Christ Church looks as clean and unhistorical as a Methodist chapel, its sculptured tombs and tablets broken up or heaped one on t'other in the crypt; no congregation has climbed to the Rock of Cashel since the stout Church of Ireland bishop took the lead roof from the Gothic church to save his legs: but Europe has nothing older than our pilgrimages.   (*E* 266-7)

7   *the Stations*: the Stations of the cross, usually fourteen, depicting Christ's passion and crucifixion

13   *Purgatory*: state after death where, in Roman Catholic belief, the soul is purified before going to heaven

16   *A great black ragged bird*: probably the bird in Manini's description of 1411   *361*
quoted by Seymour, op. cit., 55-7. Cf. a passage in *If I were Four-and Twenty*:

... and I would, being but four-and-twenty and a lover of lost causes, memorialise bishops to open once again that Lough Derg cave of vision once beset by an evil spirit in the form of a long-legged bird with no feathers on its wings.   (*E* 267)

See also the apparition of 'a great black bird' recorded in *AV* (B) 17.

COLONEL MARTIN   349

This poem was written on 10 August 1937 and first appeared in *A Broadside*,   *361*
No. 12 (N.S.) (Dec. 1937). F. R. Higgins had suggested to Yeats that the refrain should be 'Lullabulloo, buloo, buloo, lullabulloo, buloo' as more suited to singing, and this was printed in the *Broadside* version. A letter to Edith Shackleton Heald written on 10 August 1937 deals with the poem:

I have just finished a long ballad – seven eight-line stanzas – on a Galway story. [There are eight in the printed version.] It has a curious pathos which I cannot define. I have known from the start what I wanted to do, and yet the idea seemed to lie below the threshold of consciousness – and still does. There is a chorus almost without meaning, followed by concertina and whistle.

                                                                            (*L* 896-7)

and a letter of 13 August 1937 to Dorothy Wellesley described the poem as 'among the best things, almost the strangest thing I have written' (*DWL* 144).

Ellmann provides another version of the story, which Yeats gave in a lecture in 1910 reported by the Dublin *Evening Telegraph*:

Mr Yeats said the thing that was destroying the theatre in Ireland was the substitution of humanitarianism for artistic feeling. The business of art was the exposition of human nature in itself, making us delight in personality, in character, in emotion, in human life, when it is not troubled or persecuted by anything artificial. These things were being crushed away by all kinds of special interests. One man would spend his life in making money; another man would spend his life on a mathematical problem. Human nature should not be merely endured; it should keep its delight, its energy, and its simplicity. He believed that the countryman in Ireland, as the countryman who has kept his simplicity everywhere in the world, had kept his delight in human nature. In proof of this assertion the lecturer related a story which, he said, had been told him by a Galway shepherd, about a certain Colonel Martin, whose wife was unfaithful to him. Colonel Martin discovered his wife in the company of a wealthy neighbour. There were two revolvers on a table, but Colonel Martin did not like to take advantage of an unarmed man. He took other proceedings, and obtained two kegs of gold from the wealthy neighbour. He ordered his man, Tom, to put the kegs on the ass's back, and he went through the streets of Galway distributing the money amongst the poor. The wealthy man had men at every corner ready to attack Colonel Martin, but he could not attack a man who had been so good to the poor. At the end there was no money left, and the man, Tom, said his master would be in want before he died. And he was. That showed how the people delighted in a striking personality. It showed the mysterious love of that mysterious thing, human nature. When they could get free from the daily newspapers, from the rubbish, and get down to this rich soil, there could be a great artistic movement.   (*IY* 205-6)

Torchiana (*Y & GI* 335) remarks that the poem is closer to the version in Lady Gregory's *Kiltartan History Book* (1926), and he considers the factual source is contained in the report of a case that came before Lord Kenyon at the Guildhall; this was reported in the *Connaught Telegraph* (22 Dec. 1791) and cited by S. J. Maguire, 'Notes. Martin v. Petrie', *The Galway Reader*, IV (Winter 1954), 122-3. The action was taken by Richard Martin of Dargan against John Petrie of Soho. The jury returned a verdict against Petrie and gave damages of ten thousand pounds. Torchiana mentions two accounts in the possession of the Irish Folklore Commission: James Berry, *Tales of the West. Recollections of Early Boyhood*, 72-4 and 'Tim O'Harte and Colonel Martin' in Sean Mac Giollarnáth, *Annála Beaga o Iorrus Aithneach* (1941), 197-9.

361   1   *The Colonel*: Richard Martin (1754-1834) was MP for Galway, JP and High Sheriff of County Galway and Colonel of the Galway Volunteers. He married in 1777 and again in 1796; he was a well-known duellist. See A. E. S. Martin, *Genealogy of the Family of Martin of Ballinahinch Castle* (1890).

43   *the rich man*: John Petrie, of Soho, London.

46   *Assize Court*: in Galway (possibly a preliminary hearing). The case was tried in London in 1797, before Lord Kenyon in the Guildhall.

49   *damages*: the colonel was awarded £10,000 damages.

364   71   *from the seaweed*: by gathering it for selling. It is used in the production of edible materials and is still spread on fields in the west of Ireland as a form of manure.

350   A MODEL FOR THE LAUREATE

364   This poem was written in late July 1937 and first appeared in *NP*.

New Poems

Title   Laureate: the lifetime office of Poet Laureate, court poet of Britain. The
first holder was Ben Jonson in 1616; when Yeats wrote the poem, his friend
John Masefield (1878-1967) was Poet Laureate. The Laureate is expected to
write poems on official occasions. Yeats wrote to Dorothy Wellesley on 26 July
1937: 'Three times I have opened the envelope to add a new version of the
enclosed poem. It is the kind of thing I would have written had I been made
Laureate, which is perhaps why I was not made Laureate' (*DWL* 141)

The poem was entitled 'A Marriage Ode' in this letter. It was written on King
Edward VIII's abdication. Yeats had written earlier, on 21 December 1936, that
he thought 'the ex-king's broadcast moving, restrained & dignified & of what I
hear the Archbishop's was the reverse' (*DWL* 113). The text of the poem in the
letter of 26 July 1937 differs slightly from the unpublished versions.

1   *from China to Peru*: an echo of the opening of Johnson's *The Vanity of
Human Wishes*:

> Let observation with extensive view,
> Survey mankind, from China to Peru.

17   *The Muse*: see note on 'The Tower' (*PNE* 205).

THE OLD STONE CROSS   351

This poem was written between April and June 1937. Yeats began it when   *365*
staying with the Misses Heald at the Chantry House, Steyning, Sussex. It first
appeared in *N* (12 March 1938) and *LM* (March 1938).

3   *A journalist makes up his lies*: cf. *OTB*, where Yeats denounced the English
mind, which, 'excited by its newspaper proprietors and its schoolmasters, has
turned into a bed-hot harlot' (*E* 443).

7-8   *man . . . stone Cross*: *PNE* suggests Denadhach (d. 871), buried at
Drumcliffe, Co. Sligo. See Yeats's story 'Drumcliff and Rosses' *TCT* (*M* 92-3)
where he is described as a pious soldier of the race of Conn lying under hazel
crosses, and watching over the graveyard in his armour.

20   *To shuffle, grunt and groan*: Yeats's own method of chanting verse is well   *366*
known. He was probably influenced by the acting of Heron Allen ('a solicitor,
fiddler and popular writer on palmistry') and Florence Farr who both

> read poetry for their pleasure. While they were upon the stage [of the Bedford
> Park Clubhouse] no one else could hold an eye or an ear. Their speech was
> music, the poetry acquired a nobility, a passionate austerity that made it akin
> for certain moments to the great poetry of the world. Heron Allen, who had
> never spoken in public before except to lecture upon the violin, had the wisdom
> to reduce his acting to a series of poses, to be the stately shepherd with not more
> gesture than was needed to 'twitch his mantle blue' and to let his grace be foil

to Florence Farr's more impassioned delivery. When they closed their mouths, and some other player opened his, breaking up the verse to make it conversational, jerking his body or his arms that he might seem no austere poetical image but very man, I listened in raging hatred. I kept my seat with difficulty, I searched my memory for insulting phrases, I even muttered them to myself that the people about might hear. I had discovered for the first time that in the performance of all drama that depends for its effect upon beauty of language, poetical culture may be more important than professional experience.   (*A* 120–1)

In the notes on *KGCT* Yeats wrote that the singer cannot sing poetry and explained how before he 'gave up the fight' he had tried to establish a style of verse speaking with the aid of Florence Farr [see notes on 'The Players ask for a Blessing on the Psalteries and on Themselves' (*PNE* 89)]:

I am not musical; I have the poet's exact time sense, only the vaguest sense of pitch; yet I get the greatest pleasure from certain combinations of singing, acting, speaking, drum, gong, flute, string, provided that some or all the words keep their natural passionate rhythm. Thirty years ago I persuaded Florence Farr, beautiful woman, incomparable elocutionist, to rediscover with the help of Arnold Dolmetsch [(1858–1940), a British musician], what seemed the ancient art of singing or speaking poetry to notes: Greek music if Greek music was, as some authorities think, 'regulated declamation.' Many people came to learn but she had only one successful pupil – I think her name was Taylor, I have not heard of her for many years – all others had the sense of pitch without the understanding of words or the understanding of words without the sense of pitch. I gave a number of lectures; Miss Farr spoke or sang to her psaltery passages from Homer, Shelley, Keats or from my own writings. When one spoke to members of the audience they seemed divided like her pupils into musicians who said that she was out of tune and well satisfied readers of poetry. I remember a famous war-correspondent saying, in an aggressive voice as he left the hall 'singing is a decadent art.' It seemed that in the twelfth century everybody had but one set of ears and that it is now possible to have two sets that cannot be pleased at the same time. I was puzzled, sometimes doubtful, but encouraged now and again when some acknowledged authority – I remember a long notice by the musical critic of the *Manchester Guardian* – said that we had discovered a great lost beauty. I, at any rate, keep among my most vivid memories a moment when, during the performance of a Greek play translated by Gilbert Murray, Florence Farr and her one pupil sang or spoke about 'the daughters of the sunset' with alternating voices; so I thought, so I still think, did the ancient world where the poets' 'I sing' seemed but literal truth, hear poetry.

When I had enough knowledge to discover some dramatic form to give her the opportunity she lacked Florence Farr had accepted a post in a Cingalese girls school that she might hide her ageing beauty.   (*KGCT*)

In letters to Dorothy Wellesley he returned to his dislike of actors reading poetry:

I have no news except that I went to Richard II last night, as fine a performance [as] possible considering that the rhythm of all the great passages is abolished. The modern actor can speak to another actor, but he is incapable of revery. On the advice of Bloomsbury he has packed his soul in a bag and left it with the bar-attendant. Did Shakespeare in Richard II discover poetic revery?   (*DWL* 145)

THE SPIRIT MEDIUM   352

This poem was written in Penns in the Rocks, Dorothy Wellesley's house in   *366*
Sussex, and first appeared in *NP*.

4   *Confusion of the bed*: cf. 'The Cold Heaven' (*PNE* 136)

6   *Perning*: cf. notes on 'Shepherd and Goatherd' (*PNE* 156), 'Demon and
Beast' (*PNE* 199) and 'Sailing to Byzantium' (*PNE* 204).

7   *my body to the spade*: the refrain is a composite picture of Mrs Yeats and
Dorothy Wellesley, both gardeners.

11   *Some that being unbegotten*: possibly an echo of Phase one in *AV*:

This is a supernatural incarnation, like Phase 15, because there is complete
objectivity, and human life cannot be completely objective. At Phase 15 mind
was completely absorbed by being, but now body is completely absorbed in its
supernatural environment. The images of mind are no longer irrelevant even,
for there is no longer anything to which they can be relevant, and acts can no
longer be immoral or stupid, for there is no one there that can be judged.
Thought and inclination, fact and object of desire, are indistinguishable (*Mask*
is submerged in *Body of Fate, Will* in *Creative Mind*), that is to say, there is
complete passivity, complete plasticity. Mind has become indifferent to good
and evil, to truth and falsehood; body has become undifferentiated, dough-like;
the more perfect be the soul, the more indifferent the mind, the more dough-
like the body; and mind and body take whatever shape, accept whatever image
is imprinted upon them, transact whatever purpose is imposed upon them, are
indeed the instruments of supernatural manifestation, the final link between the
living and more powerful beings. There may be great joy; but it is the joy of a
conscious plasticity; and it is this plasticity, this liquefaction, or pounding up,
whereby all that has been knowledge becomes instinct and faculty. All
plasticities do not obey all masters, and when we have considered cycle and
horoscope it will be seen how those that are the instruments of subtle
supernatural will differ from the instruments of cruder energy; but all, highest
and lowest, are alike in being automatic.   (*AV* (B) 183-4)

THOSE IMAGES   353

This poem was written on or before 10 August 1937. It first appeared in *LM*   *367*
(March 1938).
    This poem was inspired by a dislike of C. E. M. Joad's talk on politics. Yeats
met him during one of his visits to Penns in the Rocks, Sussex, in April 1937. A
letter of 13 August 1937 to Dorothy Wellesley indicates the frame of mind
behind the poem:

I am well enough to face the public banquet [This was the Banquet of the Irish
Academy of Letters held in Dublin on 17 August 1937] and make the
necessary senatorial speech. [The speech was included in *A Speech and Two*

Poems (1937)]. 'Our movement is essential to the nation – only by songs, plays, stories, can we hold our thirty millions together, [Yeats was thinking of the Irish abroad. See *VE* 839] keep them one people from New Zealand to California. I have always worked with this purpose in my mind.' Yet my dear I am as anarchic as a sparrow. 'For things like these what decent man would keep his lover waiting?' 'Kings and Parliaments,' said Blake, 'seem to me something other than human life,' or as Hugo said, 'they are not worth one blade of grass that God gives for the nest of the linnet.' (*DWL* 142-3)

The poem follows: it 'says what I have just said'.

2   *The cavern of the mind*: a phrase symbolising pure intellect

6   *To Moscow or to Rome*: Mussolini rather than Hitler – after Abyssinia and the Spanish War – would have seemed the obvious symbol to use for fascism.

8   *the Muses*: see note on 'The Tower' (*PNE* 205).

11-12   *The lion and the virgin*
          The harlot and the child

Cf. the final passage of *An Introduction for my Plays*:

As I altered my syntax I altered my intellect. Browning said that he could not write a successful play because interested not in character in action but in action in character. I had begun to get rid of everything that is not, whether in lyric or dramatic poetry, in some sense character in action; a pause in the midst of action perhaps, but action always its end and theme. 'Write for the ear', I thought, so that you may be instantly understood as when actor or folk singer stands before an audience. I delight in active men, taking the same delight in soldier and craftsman; I would have poetry turn its back upon all that modish curiosity, psychology – the poetic theme has always been present. I recall an Indian tale: certain men said to the greatest of sages, 'Who are your Masters?' And he replied, 'The wind and the harlot, the virgin and the child, the lion and the eagle.' (*E & I* 530)

354   THE MUNICIPAL GALLERY REVISITED

368   This poem was begun in August and completed in early September 1937; it first appeared in *A Speech and Two Poems* (1937).

Yeats referred to this poem about the Municipal Gallery of Modern Art, Parnell Square, Dublin – formerly Charlemont House, the residence of the Earl of Charlemont (1728–99) – in his speech at the Banquet of the Irish Academy of Letters on 17 August 1937:

For a long time I had not visited the Municipal Gallery. I went there a week ago and was restored to many friends. I sat down, after a few minutes, overwhelmed with emotion. There were pictures painted by men, now dead, who were once my intimate friends. There were the portraits of my fellow-workers; there was that portrait of Lady Gregory, by Mancini, which John

Synge thought the greatest portrait since Rembrandt; there was John Synge himself; there, too, were portraits of our Statesmen; the events of the last thirty years in fine pictures: a peasant ambush, the trial of Roger Casement, a pilgrimage to Lough Derg, event after event: Ireland not as she is displayed in guide book or history, but, Ireland seen because of the magnificent vitality of her painters, in the glory of her passions.

For the moment I could think of nothing but that Ireland: that great pictured song. The next time I go, I shall stand once more in veneration before the work of the great Frenchmen. It is said that an Indian ascetic, when he has taken a certain initiation on a mountain [Mount Kailasa, see Yeats's commentary *KGCT* (quoted, p. 350 on 'Supernatural Songs' (*PNE* 309)] in Tibet, is visited by all the Gods. In those rooms of the Municipal Gallery I saw Ireland in spiritual freedom, and the Corots, the Rodins, the Rousseaus were the visiting gods. [Works by Jean Corot (1796-1875), Auguste Rodin (1840-1917) and Theodore Rousseau (1812-67) were in the Gallery.] (*A Speech and Two Poems* (1937))

The best introduction to the poem is Arland Ussher (b. 1883), *Yeats and the Municipal Gallery* (1959). Yeats wrote to Edith Shackleton Heald on 5 September 1937 that he had 'first to make the prose notes and then write the verses at a little over a verse a day' (*L* 898). He described it to her as 'one of his best poems' and in a letter to Dorothy Wellesley on 5 September 1937 called it 'perhaps the best poem I have written for some years, unless the ''Curse of Cromwell'' is' (*DWL* 144).

2   *An ambush*: possibly Sean Keating's 'The Men of the West'

pilgrims: in 'St Patrick's Purgatory' by Sir John Lavery (1856-1941)

3   *Casement upon trial*: Lavery's 'The Court of Criminal Appeal'. See notes on 'Roger Casement' (*PNE* 338) and on 'The Ghost of Roger Casement' (*PNE* 339).

4   *Griffith*: see note on line 2, 'On Those that hated ''The Playboy of the Western World'' ' (*PNE* 120). The painting referred to is probably the portrait by Lavery but the gallery does include one by Lily Williams. Arthur Griffith (1871-1922), a political leader, edited *The United Irishman* and *Sinn Fein*. He led the Irish plenipotentiaries in the negotiations leading to the Anglo-Irish Treaty of 1921.

5   *Kevin O'Higgins*: painted by Lavery. See notes on 'Death' (*PNE* 241), and 'Blood and the Moon' (*PNE* 243).

8-10   *A revolutionary soldier kneeling to be blessed;*
        An Abbot or Archbishop with an upraised hand
        Blessing the Tricolour: This is Lavery's painting, 'Blessing of the Colours', the tricolour being the orange, white and green flag adopted by the Irish Free State after 1922.

12   *terrible and gay*: cf. the 'terrible' beauty of 'Easter 1916' (*PNE* 193)

13   *a woman's portrait*: Arland Ussher suggests that this may be a portrait of Lady Charles Beresford by the English painter John Singer Sargent (1856–1925). She was the wife of William de la Poer, Baron Beresford of Metemmeh and Curraghmore, Co. Waterford.

17   *Heart-smitten*: in a letter of 7 September 1937 Yeats wrote to James A. Healey: 'I spoke of my renewed visits to the Municipal Gallery where my friends' portraits were – visits made possible, or at any rate easy, now that I could go by taxi. I spoke of my emotion in the Gallery where Modern Ireland is pictured . . .' (*L* 899).

18   *My heart recovering*: Yeats was suffering from heart trouble at the time of his visit.

21   *Augusta Gregory's son*: Robert Gregory, see notes on 'In Memory of Major Robert Gregory' (*PNE* 144). The portrait of Gregory is by Charles Shannon (1863–1937), an English painter and lithographer, a friend of Charles Ricketts and Yeats. Both Shannon and Ricketts (1866–1931), painter, sculptor, art critic, stage designer and co-editor of *The Dial*, were described by Yeats in section XVII of *Four Years* (see *A* 169).

22   *her sister's son, Hugh Lane*: Probably the painting of Sir Hugh Lane by John Singer Sargent, see notes on 'To a Wealthy Man who promised a second Subscription to the Dublin Municipal Gallery, if it were proved the People wanted Pictures' (*PNE* 114).

'onlie begetter': the 'permanent images' above may have been suggested by the eternity promised by the 'the ever-living poet' to Mr W. H. (presumably regarded by Yeats as a patron or encourager of art) in the Dedication to Shakespeare's *Sonnets*:

> TO THE ONLY BEGETTER OF
> THESE ENSUING SONNETS
> MR. W. H. ALL HAPPINESS
> AND THAT ETERNITY
> PROMISED
> BY
> OUR EVER-LIVING POET
> WISHETH
> THE WELL-WISHING
> ADVENTURER IN
> SETTING
> FORTH   T. T.

23   *Hazel Lavery living and dying*: she was Sir John Lavery's second wife, born in Chicago, who died in 1935. The 'living' painting is entitled 'Hazel Lavery at her Easel', the 'dying' 'The Unfinished Harmony' ('It is finished').

25   *Mancini's portrait*: the Italian artist Antonio Mancini (1852–1930) painted
a portrait of Lady Gregory which is hung in the Municipal Gallery.

26   *Rembrandt*: Rembrandt van Rijn (1606–69), the famous Dutch painter and
etcher

33   *My medieval knees*: this may refer to Yeats's courtier-like manners. A letter
of 25 August 1934 to Mrs Shakespear mentions the Swedish compliment that
'has pleased me better than [any] I have ever had.' A Swede had said to Mrs
Yeats: ' "Our Royal family liked your husband better than any other Nobel prize
winner. They said he has the manners of a Courtier." ' I would like to think this
true but I doubt – my kind of critical mind creates harshness and roughness' (*L*
827).

34   *that woman, in that household*: Lady Gregory and Coole Park. See notes on
'Coole Park, 1929' (*PNE* 253) and on 'Beautiful Lofty Things' (*PNE* 334).

35   *all lacking found*: this stanza is of 7 lines. In the original version of the poem
lines 35–9 had an extra line included and ran differently:

> Honour had lived so long, their health I found.
> Childless, I thought, 'My children may learn here
> What deep roots are,' and never foresaw the end
> Of all that scholarly generations had held dear;
> But now the end has come I have not wept
> No fox can foul the lair the badger swept:

37   *never foresaw its end*: this stanza is referring to the settled Ireland of Yeats's
youth. He was childless when he first visited Coole Park in 1896, and his first
child was born in 1919. He did prophesy the end of the house in the last stanza of
'Coole Park, 1929' (*PNE* 253).

> When all those rooms and passages are gone,
> When nettles wave upon a shapeless mound
> And saplings root among the broken stone . . .

Lady Gregory was described (because of the death of her only son Robert in Italy
in 1917) as 'a last inheritor' in 'Coole Park and Ballylee, 1931' (*PNE* 254).

39   *No fox can foul*: an image from Spenser (? 1552–99), referred to in Yeats's
essay *Edmund Spenser* (1902), in which he remarks that Spenser's 'The Death of
the Earl of Leicester' (Spenser's title was 'The Ruins of Time') is 'more than a
conventional Ode to a dead patron . . . he laments that unworthy men should be
in the dead Earl's place, and compares them to the fox – an unclean feeder –
hiding in the lair "the badger swept".' Cf. Unterecker (*RG* 275–6) who
comments, 'Echoing both his own note on Spenser and Spenser himself, Yeats
points up the implicit parallel between his own patroness Lady Gregory and
Spenser's "great Earl".' The poem in question was included in Yeats's *Poems of*

Spenser (1906) 72: 'He is now gone, the whiles the Foxe is crept/Into the hole, the which the badger swept'. See also note on this selection in *B* 233-4.

41   *John Synge, I and Augusta Gregory*: Yeats's view of the people and popular lore is put in *A* 191, and in several essays. See, for instance, 'A People's Theatre' (*E* 244-59) and 'The Galway Plains' in which he wrote of the Galway people as a community 'bound together by imaginative possessions' (*E & I* 213). In *BS* Yeats paid tribute to Lady Gregory and Synge: 'their work and mine has delighted in history and tradition' (*A* 554). Cf. also *A* 395 for her making the people 'a part of her soul'.

44   *Antaeus-like*: Antaeus, son of Poseidon and Earth, when attacked by Hercules drew new strength from his mother whenever he touched the ground.

47   *Dream of the noble and the beggar-man*: in the Introduction to *Fighting the Waves* Yeats mentions Lady Gregory's habit of quoting from Aristotle: 'To think like a wise man, but express oneself like the common people' (*E* 371). He also discussed in this Introduction his own attempt to bring his blank verse as close to common speech as possible (*E* 371).

48   *Synge himself*: cf. line 25 'In Memory of Major Robert Gregory' (*PNE* 144). The portrait is by Yeats's father, John Butler Yeats (1839-1922).

that rooted man: Yeats may be referring here to Synge's finding 'his genius and his peace' on Inishmaan and the Blaskets (*E & I* 325).

355   ARE YOU CONTENT?

370   This poem's date of composition cannot be determined accurately: it first appeared in *Atlantic Monthly* and *LM* (April 1938).

9-10   *He that in Sligo at Drumcliff*
       Set up the old stone Cross: The Rev. John Yeats (1774-1846), who won the Bishop Berkeley Medal in Greek while at Trinity College, Dublin, was appointed to the living at Drumcliff, Co. Sligo, in 1805, and remained as Rector there until his death. The three-storied rectory is now demolished. Drumcliff (*Irish* Druim-Chliah), the ridge of the hazels' is at the foot of Ben Bulben. See *McG* 43 for details of the Churchyard.

11   *That red-headed rector*: the Rev. John Yeats's son, the Rev. William Butler Yeats (1806-62), who was a curate in the parish of Moira, Co. Down, before becoming Rector of Tullylish, near Portadown. In 1835 he married Jane Corbet, whose brother Robert (d. 1872) owned Sandymount Castle, Dublin.

13   *Sandymount Corbets*: cf. John Butler Yeats, *Early Memories* (1923), 54-5,

where he describes how Robert Corbet (his uncle), once he bought or leased Sandymount Castle, 'began creating all around him beautiful gardens'. Corbet lived there with his mother Grace Armstrong Corbet (1774–1861) and his aunt Jane Armstrong Clendenin.

John Butler Yeats spent most of his time there when he was an undergraduate, and regarded it as his Capua. When he married he rented 1 George's Ville, a house nearby in Sandymount Avenue, where W. B. Yeats was born in 1865. William M. Murphy's *Prodigal Father. The Life of John Butler Yeats (1839–1922)* (1978) is an excellent full-length biography of the poet's father.

14 *Old William Pollexfen*: Yeats's grandfather. See notes on 'Introductory Rhymes' (*PNE* 112).

15 *The smuggler Middleton*: William Middleton (d. 1832), who had a depot in the Channel Islands. See notes on 'Introductory Rhymes' (*PNE* 112).

Butlers far back: see notes on 'Introductory Rhymes' (*PNE* 112).

22 *What Robert Browning meant*: the reference is to *Pauline* (1833) by Robert Browning (1812–89):

> . . . an old hunter
> Talking with gods, or a high-crested chief
> Sailing with troops of friends to Tenedos.

It was one of Yeats's favourite quotations (see his *Introduction* to Hone and Rossi, *Berkeley* (1931), (*E & I* 409)). He also used it in his Introduction to Lady Gregory's *Gods and Fighting Men*, and in *AV*, where the old hunter is seen as an image of peace by men of the opposite phase 'worn out by a wisdom held with labour and uncertainty' (*AV* (B) 110).

[*Last Poems (1938-39)*]

397   This poem was completed by 4 September 1938 and first appeared in the *Irish Times*, the *Irish Independent* and the *Irish Press*, 3 February 1939.

I
1-2   *. . . what the sages spoke*
   Round the Mareotic Lake: see notes (*p.* 200) on line 44 ff. 'Demon and Beast' (*PNE* 199). Yeats wrote of Lionel Johnson in 'The Tragic Generation' that when he said 'wilderness' he thought of 'some historical, some bookish desert, the Thebaid, or the lands about the Mareotic sea' (*A* 307), areas known for Christian monasticism in the fourth century.

3   *the witch of Atlas*: she symbolised the beauty of wisdom in Shelley's poem of the same name (1824). She was 'a Naiad, and was born from one of the Atlantides, who lay in a "chamber of grey rock" until she was changed by the sun's embrace into a cloud' (*E & I* 84). Yeats wrote of her:

> When the Witch has passed in her boat from the caverned river, that is doubtless her own destiny, she passes along the Nile 'by Moeris and the Mareotid lakes,' and sees all human life shadowed upon its waters in shadows that 'never are erased but tremble ever'; and in 'many a dark and subterranean street under the Nile' – new caverns – and along the bank of the Nile; and as she bends over the unhappy, she compares unhappiness to the strife that 'stirs the liquid surface of man's life'; and because she can see the reality of things she is described as journeying 'in the calm depths' of 'the wide lake' we journey over unpiloted.   (*E & I* 85)

5   *those horsemen, by those women*: probably the visionary beings George Pollexfen's servant Mary Battle described to Yeats:

> 'Some of them have their hair down, but they look quite different, more like the sleepy-looking ladies one sees in the papers. . . . They are fine and dashing-looking, like the men one sees riding their horses in twos and threes on the slopes of the mountains with their swords swinging. There is no such race living now, none so finely proportioned.'   (*A* 266)

398   11   *Ben Bulben*: this mountain north of the town of Sligo was associated with the Fianna, the horsemen who served Finn.

II

14-15   *two eternities,*
        That of race and that of soul: perhaps this related to Yeats's idea of the
conflict of two states of consciousness, 'beings or persons which die each others
life, live each other's death' (*L* 918). A letter of 22 June 1938 to Dorothy
Wellesley puts the same idea: 'This is the proposition on which I write: "There is
now overwhelming evidence that man stands between two eternities, that of his
family and that of his soul"' (*L* 910).

III

25   *Mitchel*: John Mitchel (1815-1875) replaced Thomas Davis on *N*, founded
the *United Irishman* 1843, was transported, escaped to America, and on his
return to Ireland was made an MP. 'Give us war in our time, O Lord', comes
from his famous *Jail Journal* (1854), entry for 19 November 1853. It parodies a
sentence from the daily order of service: 'Give us peace in our time, O Lord'.

30   *his partial mind*: the idea may come from Rilke. Yeats wrote to Ethel
Mannin on 9 October 1938 to say he had been rereading an essay on the idea of
death in the poetry of Rilke: 'According to Rilke a man's death is born with him
and if his life is successful and he escapes mere "mass death" his nature is
completed by his final union with it' (*L* 917).

IV

41   *fill the cradles*: cf. this imagery in 'The Phases of the Moon' (*PNE* 183).   *399*

42   *Measurement began our might*: cf. notes on 'The Statues' (*PNE* 362).

42   *a stark Egyptian*: Plotinus (205-?270) born in Lycopolis, Egypt. *PNE* refers
to Stephen MacKenna's translation *Plotinus: the Divine Mind, Being the
Treatises of the Fifth Ennead* (1926) 74: the arts create by imitating natural
objects which are themselves imitations; they do not merely reproduce things;
they 'go back to the Ideas from which Nature itself derives'. Much of their work
is their own: 'they are holders of beauty and add where nature is lacking. Thus
Pheidias wrought the Zeus upon no model among things of sense but by
apprehending what form Zeus must take if he chose to become manifest to sight'.

44   *Gentler Phidias*: Phidias (*c.* 490-*c.* 432) the famous Greek sculptor best
known to us by the marble sculptures on the Parthenon at Athens. His bronze
statue of Athena Promachos on the Acropolis at Athens, his Athena Parthenos
and his Zeus at Olympia were among his best known work.

45   *Michael Angelo*: Yeats kept reproductions of Michelangelo's work in his
house and when Shaw's *The Black Girl in Search of God* was banned he brought
a reproduction of the Sistine Chapel Adam to the Censorship authorities for
purposes of comparison and to show them the error of their ways. In this painting
in the Sistine Chapel in the Vatican in Rome Adam is about to be wakened into

life by God. See note on 'Long-Legged Fly' (*PNE* 364) and note on 'An Acre of Grass' (*PNE* 332).

400   62   *Gyres*: see notes on 'The Gyres' (*PNE* 321)

64   *Calvert*: Denis Calvert (Calvaert) 1540–1619 was a Flemish painter who founded the School of Bologna and was the master of Guido Reni; but Yeats is here probably thinking of Edward Calvert (1799–1883) an English visionary artist on whom he once thought of writing a book. Raymond Lister, 'Beulah to Byzantium . . .' *Dolmen Press Yeats Centenary Papers*, II, 36, thinks Yeats read *A Memoir of Edward Calvert by his Third Son* (1893), and points out that Charles Ricketts had an impression of Calvert's line-engraving 'The Bride' and published two of his word-engravings in *The Pageant* in 1897. Calvert and Samuel Palmer were among the group of young men who were disciples of Blake and called themselves 'Ancients'. See a reference to him as a disciple of Blake in *E* 44. Raymond Lister suggests a link between Calvert's 'A Primitive City', Blake's Golgonooza and Yeats's Byzantium. He sees Calvert as looking towards a golden age, like Wilson, Blake, Claude and Palmer. See also Raymond Lister, *Edward Calvert* (1962).

Wilson: probably Richard Wilson (1714–82), British landscape painter. (Yeats refers to George Wilson, a pre-Raphaelite painter, in *A* 156.)

Claude: Claude Lorrain (1600–82) French landscape artist, master of the picturesque

66   *Palmer's phrase*: cf. Yeats's essay on 'Blake's Illustrations to Dante'. He regarded Samuel Palmer (1805–81), English painter of visionary landscapes, as Blake's disciple:

> The member of the group [which gathered around Blake in his old age] whom I have already so often quoted has alone praised worthily these illustrations to the first Eclogue [in Thornton's *Virgil*]: 'There is in all such a misty and dreamy glimmer as penetrates and kindles the inmost soul and gives complete and unreserved delight, unlike the gaudy daylight of this world. They are like all this wonderful artist's work, the drawing aside of the fleshly curtain, and the glimpse which all the most holy, studious saints and sages have enjoyed, of the rest which remains to the people of God. (*E & I* 125)

(The quotation is from A. H. Palmer, *The Life and Letters of Samuel Palmer* (1892) 15–16.)

V

78–9   *the lords and ladies gay*
     That were beaten into the clay: Saul (*PYP* 177) has pointed out that the source for these lines is Frank O'Connor's translation *Kilcash*. 'The earls, the lady, the people beaten into the clay.'

VI

84   *Under bare Ben Bulben's head*: in a letter to Ethel Mannin of 22 August 1938 Yeats wrote:

> I am arranging my burial place. It will be in a little remote country churchyard in Sligo where my great grandfather was the clergyman a hundred years ago. Just my name and dates and these lines:
>
> > Cast a cold eye
> > On life, on death;
> > Horsemen pass by.   (*L* 914)

In a letter of 15 August 1938 he had written to Dorothy Wellesley:

> I have found a book of essays about Rilke [R. M. Rilke, *Some Aspects and his Mind and Poetry*] waiting me; one on Rilke's ideas about death [by William Rose] annoyed me. I wrote on the margin [There follows the epitaph with this line prefixed
> > 'Draw rein; draw breath']   (*L* 913)

Hone remarks accurately (*WBY* 473 n) that there is no note on the margin of Yeats's copy of this book. Yeats may have derived the idea of arranging his burial-place from William Pollexfen, his grandfather, who superintended 'the making of his tomb' (*A* 67).

85   *Drumcliff*: a village on the Bundoran Road to the north of Sligo lying under the slopes of Ben Bulben. Yeats died at Roquebrune on 28 January 1939. His body was brought to Ireland in 1948 and reinterred in Drumcliff Churchyard, 17 September 1948. Lines 92-4 of this poem are incised on his gravestone.

86   *An ancestor*: the Rev. John Yeats (1774-1848), Rector of Drumcliff parish in Co. Sligo (1811-46). See note on 'Introductory Rhymes' (*PNE* 112).

THREE SONGS TO THE ONE BURDEN   357

The date of composition is not known; the three songs first appeared in the   *371*
Spectator (26 May 1939).

I

9   *From mountain to mountain ride the fierce horsemen*: possibly a memory of the horsemen described by Mary Battle, the servant of George Pollexfen, Yeats's uncle who lived in Sligo. She described mysterious women as like 'the men one sees riding their horses in twos and threes on the slopes of the mountains with their swords swinging. There is no such race living now, none so finely proportioned' (*A* 266).

Yeats wrote to Ethel Mannin on 11 December 1936:

> As a young man I used to repeat to myself Blake's lines

'And he his seventy disciples sent
Against religion and government'

I hate more than you do, for my hatred can have no expression in action. I am a forerunner of that horde that will some day come down the mountains. (*L* 873)

10 *Manannan*: Manannan Mac Lir, the Gaelic god of the sea. Yeats probably drew upon H. d'Arbois Jubainville's *The Irish Mythological Cycle* and Lady Gregory's translation for his knowledge of Manannan Mac Lir.

19 *Crazy Jane*: an invented character, see notes on *Words for Music Perhaps* (*PNE* 268). Cf. also 'Crazy Jane on the Mountain' (*PNE* A123).

372 25 *likely couples*: Saul (*PYP* 168) draws attention to the philosophy of the Old Man in *Purgatory*: 'States are justified . . . by . . . the best born of the best' and the quotation from *The Anatomy of Melancholy* in *OTB*: '. . . it were happy for human kind, if only such parents as are sound of body and mind should be suffered to marry' (*E* 418).

II

372 1 *Henry Middleton*: a cousin of the poet, who became a recluse. Hone (*WBY* 21) remarks that he was the original of John Sherman in Yeats's novel *John Sherman*.

3 *A small forgotten house*: 'Elsinore' near Rosses Point, Co. Sligo. It still stands, and is reputed to have been a smuggler's house and haunted. See *McG* 45, who describes it as 'William' Middleton's summer residence; his other being Avena House in Sligo.

8 *keys to my old gate*: Hone (*WBY* 22) describes how Yeats and Mrs Yeats visited Henry Middleton in 1919. The gate was locked but Yeats climbed the wall and found his cousin dressed in a white suit in the sitting-room, which was littered with cheap novels and had a butter-churn in the middle of the floor. He said to Yeats, 'You see that I am too busy to see anyone.' In 1930 Michael and Anne Yeats climbed the wall but were turned away by the garden boy when they reached the hall door of the house.

20 *the Green Lands*: a desolate area of sandhills at Rosses Point, running inland from Deadman's Point.

III

373 2 *Nineteen-Sixteen*: the Easter Rising of 1916; see notes on 'Easter 1916' (*PNE* 193). The poem was originally entitled 'An Abbey Player – I meditate upon 1916'. This became 'An Abbey Player and his Song'.

5   *Post Office*: in the centre of Dublin, this building was occupied by the insurgents in 1916.

6   *City Hall*: south of the Liffey on Cork Hill, built by Thomas Cooley 1769–79 as the Royal Exchange; taken over by Dublin Corporation in 1850.

11   *the player Connolly*: this Connolly was an actor (hence 'player') shot in the fighting on Easter Monday, not to be confused with the labour leader James Connolly (see notes on 'Easter 1916' (*PNE* 193)) who was military commander at the Post Office and was shot after a Court-martial.

20   Pearse's writings, notably in *An Claidheamh Soluis (The Sword of Light)* which he edited, are full of the idea of the blood sacrifice, for instance: 'blood shed is a cleansing and a sacrificing thing'. See Ruth Dudley Edwards, *Patrick Pearse. The Triumph of Failure* (1977) for discussion of his political journalism.

24   *Pearse*: see notes on 'Easter 1916' (*PNE* 193). Yeats described him as   *374*
'preaching the blood sacrifice' and saying that blood must be shed in every generation. See 'Modern Ireland: an Address to American Audience 1932–1933', in *Irish Renaissance: a Gathering of Essays, Memoirs, and Letters from the Massachusetts Review* (1965).

THE BLACK TOWER   358

This is the last poem Yeats wrote; it is dated 21 January 1939 and first appeared   *396*
in *Last Poems and Two Plays* (1939).

1   *the old black tower*: this may derive from Browning, though there may also be a hint of Thoor Ballylee. See Patrick Diskin, 'O'Grady's Finn and his Companions. A Source for Yeats's ''The Black Tower'' ', *N & Q*, March 1961, 107–8.

6   *those banners*: these are the banners of political propaganda.

7   *the dead upright*: Henn (*LT* 251) connects this image with one of Charles Ricketts's illustrations to Oscar Wilde's *Sphinx*, called 'Rose up the Painted Swathéd Dead', though he thinks it may also refer to heroic burial on Knocknarea.
   Eoghan Bel, a king of Connaught killed at the Battle of Sligo (? 543/547), is said to have been buried upright on Knocknarea. *PNE* cites P. W. Joyce, *A Social History of Ancient Ireland* (1903) I, 551 for the custom of burying kings and chieftains upright in their armour facing their enemies' territory.

24   *the king's great horn*: W. J. Keith, in 'Yeats's Arthurian Black Tower',   *397*
Modern Language Notes, lxxv (Feb. 1960), suggests that this imagery derives from the Arthurian legend that Arthur, Guinevere, all his court and a pack of

hounds sleep in a vault beneath the Castle of Sewingshields in Northumberland. The king waits till someone blows the horn which lies on a table and cuts a garter laid beside it with a sword of stone. A farmer found the vault, cut the garter and Arthur woke, only to fall asleep again as the sword was sheathed with these words:

> O woe betide that evil day
> On which the witless wight was born
> Who drew the sword – the garter cut
> But never blew the bugle horn.

359 CUCHULAIN COMFORTED

395 This poem is dated 13 January 1939 in *CP*; it first appeared in *Last Poems and Two Plays* (1939). The poem is related to Yeats's play *The Death of Cuchulain*. It may be the poem for which Yeats wrote to Edith Shackleton Heald on 1 January 1939 that he was making 'a prose sketch for a poem – a kind of sequel – strange too, something new' (*L* 922). It is possible that it may also be the lyric arising out of the play mentioned in an earlier letter to her of December 1938. The prose draft, according to Mrs Yeats, was dictated on 7 January 1939. See *LT* 338.

Dorothy Wellesley gives an account of the prose version of the poem:

> On one of our visits to him at Cap Martin he read the prose theme of a poem he proposed to write in *terza rima*:
> A shade recently arrived went through a valley in the Country of the Dead; he had six mortal wounds, but had been a tall, strong, handsome man. Other shades looked at him from among the trees. Sometimes they went near to him and then went away quickly. At last he sat down, he seemed very tired. Gradually the shades gathered round him, and one of them who seemed to have some authority among the others laid a parcel of linen at his feet. One of the others said: 'I am not so afraid of him now that he is sitting still. It was the way his arms rattled.' Then another shade said: 'You would be much more comfortable if you would make a shroud and wear it instead of the arms. We have brought you some linen. If you make it yourself you will be much happier, but of course we will thread the needles. We do everything together, so everyone of us will thread the needles, so when we have laid them at your feet you will take whichever you like best.' The man with the six wounds saw that nobody had ever threaded needles so swiftly and so smoothly. He took the threaded needles and began to sew, and one of the shades said: 'We will sing to you while you sew; but you will like to know who we are. We are the people who run away from the battles. Some of us have been put to death as cowards, but others have hidden, and some even died without people knowing they were cowards.' Then they began to sing, and they did not sing like men and women, but like linnets that had been stood on a perch and taught by a good singing master. (*DWL* 193).

1 *a man . . . six . . . wounds*: Cuchulain. See note on 'Cuchulain's Fight with the Sea' (*PNE* 19). The six who gave him the fatal wounds were themselves killed by Conall Caernach. See Bjersby (*ICL* 53).

4   *shrouds*: *PNE* considers this reminiscent of Plato's myth of Er in the *Republic* (related to 'His Bargain' (*PNE* 281)); see notes where unborn souls have lots and samples of life put before them, and the soul which had been Orpheus chooses the life of a swan, out of enmity to the race of women, who had murdered him, while the soul which had been Thamyras chooses the life of a nightingale. (*Republic*, tr. Jowett (1875) III, 575–517.)

20   *our character*: the account of disincarnate state in *AV* (B) 223–5 may be   *396* germane to this poem. Yeats is there pondering upon the famous elemental of Leap Castle (for Leap Castle see note on 'Crazy Jane on God' (*PNE* 272)), and the transformation of the cowards into birds may echo his suggestions in that portion of *AV* about the spirit's relationship with the Celestial or the Passionate Body.

THREE MARCHING SONGS   360

These three poems were written between 3 November 1933 and 27 February   *377* 1934, and rewritten in December 1938. They first appeared in *Last Poems and Two Plays* (1939). They are later versions of 'Three Songs to the Same Tune' (*PNE* A101). See notes on them.

I
4   *Fled to far countries*: see note on 'Wild Geese' in 'September 1913' (*PNE* 115).

23–25   *. . . mock at O'Donnell,*   *378*
            Mock at the memory of both O'Neills,
            Mock Emmet, mock Parnell: see notes on 'Three Songs to the Same Tune' II (*PNE* A101).

II
4   *Troy . . . Helen*: see notes on 'The Rose of the World' (*PNE* 20).

9   *airy spot*: Yeats's note read: ' "Airy" may be an old pronunciation of   *379* "eerie" often heard in Galway and Sligo.' But it may be an echo of a line in Allingham's 'The Faeries': 'Up the airy mountain'.

21   *nothing up there at the top*: cf. notes (p. 502) on 'Three Songs to the Same Tune' III (*PNE* A101), and see note on 'Blood and the Moon' (*PNE* 243).

III
23   *the rope gave a jerk there*: cf. note on 'Three Songs to the Same Tune' I   *380* (*PNE* A101).

411

361   IN TARA'S HALLS

374   This poem was written in June 1938 and first appeared in *Last Poems and Two Plays* (1939).

1   *A man*: the MS. version had as first line 'A certain king in the great house at Tara'.

Tara's Halls: Tara, Co. Meath, was once the seat of the High Kings of Ireland. Recent excavations have revealed the site of a palace.

11   *The Sacred House*: the source of the image is uncertain.

362   THE STATUES

375   This poem was written on 9 April 1938 (but Curtis Bradford suggests April–June 1938), and first appeared in *LM* (March 1939) and *N* (15 April 1939).
    The prose draft of the poem reads:

I

They went out in noonday or under the new moon moving with - - - - - [indecipherable] only forms in marble, empty faces, measure Pythagorean perfection only that which is incapable of show is infinite in passion. Only passion sees God. Men were victors at Salamis, and Victory is nothing, now one up, then another, only their cold marble forms could drive back to the vague Asiatic norm. Only they could beat down Nature with their certainty. Weary of victory one went far from all his companions and sat so long in solitude that his body became soft and round, incapable of work or war, because his eyes were empty, more empty than skies at night . . . all men worshipped present deity. Apollo forgot Pythagoras and took the name of Buddha which was victorious Greece in the Asiatic mode. Others stayed away and were made - - - - - - [indecipherable] and conquer their sublime emptiness, and in a jungle nigh they saw - - - - - [indecipherable].

II

Where are you now? It is better that you shed the sunburn and become pale-white; did you appear in the Post Office in 1916? Is it true that Pearse called on you by the name of Cuchulain. Certainly we have need of you. The vague flood is at its. . . . For from all quarters is coming. . . . Come back with your Pythagorean numbers.

A passage in *OTB* gives the poem's meaning:

There are moments when I am certain that art must once again accept those Greek proportions which carry into plastic art the Pythagorean numbers, whose faces which are divine because all there is empty and measured. Europe was not born when Greek galleys defeated the Persian hordes at Salamis; but when the Doric studios sent out those broad-backed marble statues against the multiform, vague, expressive Asiatic sea, they gave to the sexual instinct of Europe its goal, its fixed type.   (*E* 451)

Last Poems

The poem has been discussed by Hazard Adams, 'Yeatsian art and Mathematic Form', *Centennial Review* (Winter 1960) 70-88; by Ellmann (*IY* 188-90); by V. Koch, *W. B. Yeats, The Tragic Phase* (1951) 57-75; by Unterecker (*RG* 278-81); by Peter Ure, ' "The Statues"; a note on the meaning of Yeats's Poem', *RES*, XV (1949) 254-7; by Wilson (*YI* 290-303); by E. Engelberg, *The Vast Design* (1964) 176-210. The last critic offers a view of Yeats's use of history in this poem and his account on pp. 196-7 and 202-3 is valuable.

1-2   *Pythagoras planned it. Why did the people stare?*
      His numbers: the Pythagorean doctrine of numbers paved the way for the art of the Greek sculptors who carved their statues by exact measurements. Cf. 'Under Ben Bulben' IV (*PNE* 356) lines 42-4 and note on 'The Delphic Oracle upon Plotinus' (*PNE* 292). For Pythagoras see note on 'Among School Children' (*PNE* 222).

3   *lacked character*: in *AV* Yeats gave his views of the development of Greek civilisation and pp. 268-72 of the 1937 edition are a key passage for the understanding of this poem:

> I imagine the annunciation that founded Greece as made to Leda, remembering that they showed in a Spartan temple, strung up to the roof as a holy relic, an unhatched egg of hers; and that from one of her eggs came Love and from the other War. But all things are from antithesis, and when in my ignorance I try to imagine what older civilisation that annunciation rejected I can but see bird and woman blotting out some corner of the Babylonian mathematical starlight.
>
> Was it because the older civilisation like the Jewish thought a long life a proof of Heavenly favour that the Greek races thought those whom the Gods love must die young, hurling upon some age of crowded comedy their tragic sense? Certainly their tribes, after a first multitudinous revelation – dominated each by its *Daimon* and oracle-driven – broke up a great Empire and established in its stead an intellectual anarchy. At some 1000 years before Christ I imagine their religious system complete and they themselves grown barbaric and Asiatic. Then came Homer, civil life, a desire for civil order dependent doubtless on some oracle, and then (Phase 10 of the new millennium) for independent civil life and thought. At, let me say, the sixth century BC (Phase 12) personality begins, but there is as yet no intellectual solitude. A man may rule his tribe or town but he cannot separate himself from the general mass. With the first discovery of solitude (Phases 13 and 14) comes, as I think, the visible art that interests us most today, for Phidian art, like the art of Raphael, has for the moment exhausted our attention. I recall a Nike at the Ashmolean Museum, with a natural unsystematised beauty like that before Raphael, and above all certain pots with strange half-supernatural horses dark on a light ground. Self-realisation attained will bring desire of power – systematisation for its instrument – but as yet clarity, meaning, elegance, all things separated from one another in luminous space, seem to exceed all other virtues. One compares this art with the thought of Greek philosophers before Anaxagoras, where one discovers the same phases, always more concerned with the truth than with its moral or political effects. One longs for the lost dramatists, the plays that were enacted before Aeschylus and Sophocles arose, both Phidian men.

413

But one must consider not the movement only from the beginning to the end of the ascending cone, but the gyres that touch its sides, the horizontal dance.

> Hands gripped in hands, toes close together,
> Hair spread on the wind they made;
> That lady and that golden king
> Could like a brace of blackbirds sing.

Side by side with Ionic elegance there come after the Persian wars a Doric vigour, and the light-limbed dandy of the potters, the Parisian-looking young woman of the sculptors, her hair elaborately curled, give place to the athlete. One suspects a deliberate turning away from all that is Eastern, or a moral propaganda like that which turned the poets out of Plato's Republic, and yet it may be that the preparation for the final systematisation had for its apparent cause the destruction, let us say, of Ionic studios by the Persian invaders, and that all came from the resistance of the *Body of Fate* to the growing solitude of the soul. Then in Phidias Ionic and Doric influence unite – one remembers Titian – and all is transformed by the full moon, and all abounds the flows. With Callimachus pure Ionic revives again, as Furtwängler has proved, and upon the only example of his work known to us, a marble chair, a Persian is represented, and may one not discover a Persian symbol in that bronze lamp, shaped like a palm, known to us by a description in Pausanias? But he was an archaistic workman, and those who set him to work brought back public life to an older form. One may see in masters and man a momentary dip into ebbing Asia.

Each age unwinds the thread another age had wound, and it amuses one to remember that before Phidias, and his westward-moving art, Persia fell, and that when full moon came round again, amid eastward-moving thought, and brought Byzantine glory, Rome fell; and that at the outset of our westward-moving Renaissance Byzantium fell; all things dying each other's life, living each other's death.

After Phidias the life of Greece, which being *antithetical* had moved slowly and richly through the *antithetical* phases, comes rapidly to an end. Some Greek or Roman writer whose name I forget will soon speak of the declining comeliness of the people, and in the arts all is systematised more and more, and the antagonist recedes. Aristophanes' passion-clouded eye falls before what one must believe, from Roman stage copies, an idler glance. (Phases 19, 20, 21). Aristotle and Plato end creative system – to die into the truth is still to die – and formula begins. Yet even the truth into which Plato dies is a form of death, for when he separates the Eternal Ideas from Nature and shows them self-sustained he prepares the Christian desert and the Stoic suicide.

I identify the conquest of Alexander and the break-up of his kingdom when Greek civilisation, formalised and codified, loses itself in Asia, with the beginning and end of the 22nd Phase, and his intention recorded by some historian to turn his arms westward shows that he is but a part of the impulse that creates Hellenised Rome and Asia. There are everywhere statues where every muscle has been measured, every position debated, and these statues represent man with nothing more to achieve, physical man finished and complacent, the women slightly tinted, but the men, it may be, who exercise naked in the open air, the colour of mahogany. Every discovery after the epoch of victory and defeat (Phase 22) which substitutes mechanics for power is an

414

elimination of intellect by delight in technical skill (Phase 23), by a sense of the past (Phase 24), by some dominant belief (Phase 25). After Plato and Aristotle, the mind is as exhausted as were the armies of Alexander at his death, but the Stoics can discover morals and turn philosophy into a rule for life. Among them doubtless – the first beneficiaries of Plato's hatred of imitation – we may discover the first benefactors of our modern individuality, sincerity of the trivial face, the mask torn away. Then, a Greece that Rome has conquered, and a Rome conquered by Greece, must, in the last three phases of the wheel, adore, desire being dead, physical or spiritual force. *(AV* (B) 268–72)

13 *not the banks of oars*: cf. the quotation from *OTB* above. Greek intellect rather than armies conquered the Persians. Salamis, the island which closes the bay of Eleusis on the south, and part of Athens from the time of Solon and Pisistratus, was the site of the battle (Sept., 480 BC) in which the Persian fleet was shatteringly defeated by the Athenians.

15 *Phidias*: see note on 'Under Ben Bulben' *(PNE* 356).

17 *One image*: Yeats wrote on 28 June 1938 to Edith Shackleton Heald, describing the effect of Alexander the Great's conquest of India (326 BC) on representations of the Buddha:

'In reading the third stanza remember the influence on modern sculpture and on the great seated Buddha of the sculptors who followed Alexander. Cuchulain is in the last stanza because Pearse and some of his followers had a cult of him. The Government has put a statue of Cuchulain in the rebuilt post office to commemorate this. *(L* 911)

'19 *No Hamlet thin from eating flies*: Ellmann *(IY* 189) remarks that Yeats branded Christianity as an Asian importation, the antithesis for Greece and, in the fourth stanza, Ireland: 'For Christianity has no Hamlets, full of their own selves, passionate for knowledge, but only monks with empty eyeballs, contemplating, like the Buddhists, nothingness.' The poem is complementary to a passage in 'Four Years 1887–1891':

Its [a portrait of William Morris by Watts] grave wide-open eyes, like the eyes of some dreaming beast, remind me of the open eyes of Titian's *Ariosto*, while the broad vigorous body suggests a mind that has no need of the intellect to remain sane, though it give itself to every fantasy: the dreamer of the Middle Ages. It is 'the fool of Faery . . . wide and wild as a hill', the resolute European image that yet half remembers Buddha's motionless meditation, and has no trait in common with the wavering, lean image of hungry speculation, that cannot but because of certain famous Hamlets of our stage fill the mind's eye. Shakespeare himself foreshadowed a symbolic change, that is, a change in the whole temperament of the world, for though he called his Hamlet 'fat' and even 'scant of breath', he thrust between his fingers agile rapier and dagger. *(A* 141–2)

The description of Hamlet thin with eating flies possibly suggested the introduction of Grimalkin (line 24) as it is a common supposition that cats grow thin through eating flies.

20   *Empty eyeballs knew*: cf. a passage in *AV* which culminates in this image:

> It is impossible to do more than select an arbitrary general date for the beginning of Roman decay (Phases 2 to 7, AD I to AD 250). Roman sculpture – sculpture made under Roman influence whatever the sculptor's blood – did not, for instance, reach its full vigour, if we consider what it had of Roman as distinct from Greek, until the Christian Era. It even made a discovery which affected all sculpture to come. The Greeks painted the eyes of marble statues and made out of enamel or glass or precious stones those of their bronze statues, but the Roman was the first to drill a round hole to represent the pupil, and because, as I think, of a preoccupation with the glance characteristic of a civilisation in its final phase. The colours must have already faded from the marbles of the great period, and a shadow and a spot of light, especially where there is much sunlight, are more vivid than paint, enamel, coloured glass or precious stone. They could now express in stone a perfect composure. The administrative mind, alert attention had driven out rhythm, exaltation of the body, uncommitted energy. May it not have been precisely a talent for this alert attention that had enabled Rome and not Greece to express those final *primary* phases? One sees on the pediments troops of marble Senators, officials serene and watchful as befits men who know that all the power of the world moves before their eyes, and needs, that it may not dash itself to pieces, their unhurried, unanxious, never-ceasing care. Those riders upon the Parthenon had all the world's power in their moving bodies, and in a movement that seemed, so were the hearts of man and beast set upon it, that of a dance; but presently all would change and measurement succeed to pleasure, the dancing-master outlive the dance. What need had those young lads for careful eyes? But in Rome of the first and second centuries, where the dancing-master himself has died, the delineation of character as shown in face and head, as with us of recent years, is all in all, and sculptors, seeking the custom of occupied officials, stock in their workshops toga'd marble bodies upon which can be screwed with the least possible delay heads modelled from the sitters with the most scrupulous realism. When I think of Rome I see always these heads with their world-considering eyes, and those bodies as conventional as the metaphors in a leading article, and compare in my imagination vague Grecian eyes gazing at nothing, Byzantine eyes of drilled ivory staring upon a vision, and those eyelids of China and of India, those veiled or half-veiled eyes weary of world and vision alike.   (*AV* (B) 275–7)

23   *gong and conch*: cf. the 'great cathedral gong' of 'Byzantium' (*PNE* 260).

24   *Grimalkin*: a cat (especially an old female cat); the word is made up of grey and malkin, an archaic dialect word for cat. See Shakespeare, *Macbeth* I, 1–9.

Buddha: see note on 'The Double Vision of Michael Robartes' (*PNE* 188).

25–6   *When Pearse summoned Cuchulain to his side,*
     What stalked through the Post office?: cf. note on line 17 above. Yeats sees Pearse (who was in the General Post Office in the Easter Rising of 1916) as summoning intellectual and aesthetic forces into being, as well as those skills of measuring and numbering, so that the Irish can return to the Pythagorean philosophy, cf. Ure, *RES* (1949) XV, 254–7 and Yeats (*E* 451) 'art must again

accept the Greek proportions'. See note on l. 17 above, and for Pearse, see note on 'Easter 1916' (*PNE* 193) and note on 'Three Songs to the One Burden' III (*PNE* 357).

NEWS FOR THE DELPHIC ORACLE   363

This poem's date of composition is uncertain; it was probably written during   *376*
1938 and first appeared in *LM* (March 1939) and *The New Republic* (22 March 1939).

1   *There all the golden codgers lay*: the 'codgers' are the immortals viewed ironically. The poem is closely related to Porphyry's account of the Delphic oracle on Plotinus. Yeats described MacKenna's translation of it as one of his favourite quotations (*E & I* 409) Cf. notes on 'The Delphic Oracle on Plotinus' (*PNE* 292) where the source material is given.

2   *silver dew*: Wilson (*Y & T* 219) thinks this refers to the nectar in the Greek oracle.

5-6   *Man-picker Niamh leant and sighed*
       By Oisin: Yeats introduced figures from Gaelic mythology into the Greek escatology. See note (p. 44) on Niamh, daughter of Aengus and Edain, 'The Hosting of the Sidhe' (*PNE* 40). Oisin, the son of Finn, lived with her for three hundred years. Niamh is described as 'man-picker' because she told Finn

                    . . . now I choose . . .
                    That I might have your son to kiss.

               ('The Wanderings of Oisin' (*PNE* 375))

8-9   *Pythagoras . . . Plotinus*: cf. notes (pp. 322-4) on 'The Delphic Oracle upon Plotinus' (*PNE* 292). See note on 'Among School Children' (*PNE* 222).

13   *a dolphin's back*: Yeats learned about the dolphins as conveyors of the soul after death from Mrs Strong's book *Apotheosis and the After Life* (cf. notes on 'Byzantium' (*PNE* 260)). In this poem he is also describing some pictures in Rome which include nymphs, satyrs and dolphins. These are the School of Raphael from the Papal Apartments at Castel S. Angelo, *Fregio e ricasco della volta con deita marine e grottesche* (ed. Alinari, 11895, 11896, and 11898).

15   *Those Innocents*: possibly the Holy Innocents (the male children under two whom Herod had killed in an attempt to kill Jesus Christ (see Matthew 2, 16-18)), as is suggested in a letter from Yeats to T. Sturge Moore (1870-1944) of 8 October 1930. See *W. B. Yeats and T. Sturge Moore: Their Correspondence, 1901-1937*, ed. Ursula Bridge (1953) 165. Yeats alludes to a statue by Raphael Santi (1483-1520) of the Dolphin carrying one of the Holy Innocents to Heaven. *PNE* suggests 'presumably' the immortals of the first stanza, but 'Innocents'

hardly matches those figures; 'Those' need not necessarily refer to them, nor 'That' in 'Sailing to Byzantium' (*PNE* 204).

22   *wades the choir of love*: cf. 'where . . . dwells . . . stately Pythagoras and all else that form the choir of Immortal Love, there where the heart is ever lifted in joyous festival' (*Plotinus* tr. MacKenna, I, 23)

25-6   *Slim adolescence that a nymph has stripped,*
        Peleus on Thetis stares: this relates to Poussin's 'The Marriage of Peleus and Thetis' which is in the National Gallery of Ireland. (It is now entitled 'Acis and Galatea'.) The painting is reproduced in *LT* 233. In Greek mythology Peleus, son of Aeacus and Endeis captured and married Thetis, a Nereid (daughter of Nereus and Doris). Their marriage was celebrated on Mount Pelion; their surviving son was Achilles.

31   *Pan's cavern*: Wilson (*Y & T* 222) regards the cavern as Porphyry's cave on the edge of heaven facing the foam of life, with one of its mouths in Porphyry facing on the fields of heaven, and regards Pan as its natural deity because it is a symbol of generation. He discusses the poem at length, pp. 216-23. In Greek mythology Pan was a fertility god, traditionally represented with small horns in his human head, with the legs, thighs, feet and tail of a goat. He invented the flute and delighted in caverns.

364   LONG-LEGGED FLY

381   This poem was written between November 1937 and April 1938. It was probably completed by 11 April 1938 (information from Mrs W. B. Yeats), and first appeared in *LM* (March 1939).

5   *Caesar*: see note on 'The Saint and the Hunchback' (*PNE* 185).

11   *topless towers*: of Troy, Marlowe's phrase in *The Tragical History of Dr Faustus* V, i, 94-5. See note on 'When Helen lived' (*PNE* 119).

15   *She thinks*: Maud Gonne. She is similarly described in 'Against Unworthy Praise' (*PNE* 98).

382   23   *the Pope's Chapel*: this stanza describes Michelangelo's paintings in the Sistine Chapel, Rome. See note on 'Under Ben Bulben' IV (*PNE* 356) and note on 'An Acre of Grass' (*PNE* 332).

365   A BRONZE HEAD

382   The date of composition of this poem is uncertain (probably 1937-8); it first appeared in *LM* (March 1939) and *The New Republic* (22 March 1937).

1   *right of the entrance*: of the Municipal Gallery of Modern Art, Dublin.

this bronze head: it is a plaster cast painted bronze by Lawrence Campbell, R.H.A., of Maud Gonne. It is illustrated in Hone, *WBY* 470. For their last meetings see *L* 909-10, and Maud Gonne, 'Yeats and Ireland', *Scattering Branches: Tributes to the Memory of W. B. Yeats* (1940) 25.

7   *Hysterica passio*: see notes on 'Parnell's Funeral' (*PNE* 304).

8   *No dark tomb-haunter*: the phrase may derive from Madame MacBride's habit of wearing long black flowing garments and a veil (widow's weeds) in the nineteen-twenties and thirties, as well as her attending funerals of republicans or laying wreaths on graves on political anniversaries – an activity in which she was frequently joined by Mrs Despard (see André Linklater, *An Unhusbanded Life. Charlotte Despard, Suffragette, Socialist and Sinn Feiner* (1980)). Yeats is contrasting Madame MacBride's gaunt appearance in old age with his memories of her youth, her potential for gentleness, even though he was then aware of her 'wildness'. This is part of her 'composite' nature.

13   *Profound McTaggart*: J. McT. E. McTaggart (1866-1925), author of *Studies in Hegelian Cosmology* (1901), which Yeats read in 1928. This poem, however, probably draws on his *[Human] Immortality and Pre-existence* (1915) which Yeats also read (information from Mrs W. B. Yeats):

> When science says that a material object – a planet or a human body – ceases to exist, what does it mean? It does not mean that anything is annihilated. It means that units, which were combined in a certain way, are now combined otherwise. The form has changed. But everything which was there before is there now.   (p. 63)

PNE cites his *The Nature of Existence* (1921) 138 and 142, where the compound nature of all substances is argued. The passages from *Human Immortality and Pre-existence* relates to the 'bronze head's' supernatural dimensions. Cf. Yeats's remarks in his Introduction to *The Resurrection*:

> All ancient nations believed in the re-birth of the soul and had probably empirical evidence like that Lafcadio Hearn found among the Japanese. In our time Schopenhauer believed it, and McTaggart thinks Hegel did, though lack of interest in the individual soul had kept him silent. It is the foundation of McTaggart's own philosophical system. . . . All our thought seems to lead by antithesis to some new affirmation of the supernatural.   (*E* 396-7)

A STICK OF INCENSE   366

The date of this poem's composition cannot be established (probably 1938); it   *383*
first appeared in *Last Poems and Two Plays* (1939).

2   *Virgin*: the Virgin Mary, mother of Jesus Christ, cf. a similar passage in 'Private Thoughts':

Among those our civilisation must reject, or leave unrewarded at some level below that co-ordination that modern civilisation finds essential, exist precious faculties. . . . I have noticed that clairvoyance, prevision, and allied gifts, rare among the educated classes, are common among peasants. Among those peasants there is much of Asia, where Hegel has said every civilisation begins. Yet we much hold to what we have that the next civilisation may be born, not from a virgin's womb, not a tomb without a body, not from a void, but of our own rich experience. *(E* 436-7)

3 *Saint Joseph*: the Virgin Mary's husband

367 HOUND VOICE

385 The date of this poem's composition is uncertain (probably Summer 1938); it first appeared in *LM* (Dec. 1938) and *N* (10 Dec. 1938).

The poem was written in a spirit of mockery.

368 JOHN KINSELLA'S LAMENT FOR MRS MARY MOORE

383 This poem was written on 21 or 29 July 1938 and first appeared in *LM* (Dec. 1938). It was originally entitled 'A Strong Farmer's complaint about Death'. John Kinsella and Mary Moore are invented characters.

384 11 *What shall I do*: Yeats wrote to Edith Shackleton Heald on 21 July 1938:

I have just thought of a chorus for a ballad. A strong farmer is mourning over the shortness of life and changing times, and every stanza ends 'What shall I do for pretty girls now my old bawd is dead?' I think it might do for a new *Broadside. (L* 912)

21 *a skin*: from the Irish phrase to put a skin on a story, to polish it, make it more effective.

26-7 *Adam's sin . . . Eden's garden*: see note on 'Adam's Curse' *(PNE* 83)

369 HIGH TALK

385 This poem was written between 29 July and August 1938 and first appeared in *LM* (Dec. 1938) and *N* (10 Dec. 1938).

1 *high stilts*: Yeats wrote of the 'nineties that (when they were over) 'we all got down off our stilts', and he may here be referring to his own creation of a poetic mythology, cf. line 3, 'no modern stalks upon higher', even though this was less exalted than that of his predecessors. In a letter to Dorothy Wellesley he wrote: 'I have now begun on the stollen [stolen] circus stilts' *(DWL* 182).

5 *piebald ponies*: the poem is reminiscent of some of Jack B. Yeats's pictures. *386*
Cf. 'The Circus Animals' Desertion' (*PNE* 373).

9 *Malachi Stilt-Jack*: Malachi was a minor Hebrew prophet, supposed author of
the last book of the Old Testament. Unterecker (*RG* 286) suggests that he may be
'tied to St Malachy, the twelfth-century saint [(1095–1148)] who assisted Yeats's
favourite Irish saint, Cellach'. But the figure is probably an invented one or a
memory of some figure in Yeats's youth in Sligo. The name Malachy is
occasionally used as a Christian name.

THE APPARITIONS   370

This poem was written in March and April 1938 and first appeared in *LM* Dec. *386*
1938).

Title   The Apparitions: these were a series of death dreams that occurred after
Yeats's illness in Majorca in January. Cf. Henn (*LT* 149), who remarks that
there were seven apparitions, not fifteen. But see next note.

8 *Fifteen apparitions*: cf. Yeats's letter to Mrs Shakespear of 11 November *387*
1933:

> Did I tell you that my apparition came a seventh time? As I awoke I saw a
> child's hand and arm and head – faintly self luminous – holding above – I was
> lying on my back – a five of diamonds or hearts I was [not] sure which. It was
> held as if the child was standing at the head of the bed. Is the meaning some
> fortune teller's meaning attached to the card or does it promise me five months
> or five years? Five years would be about long enough to finish my
> autobiography and bring out *A Vision*.

[In fact Yeats lived just a little over five years from November 1933.] Sheila
O'Sullivan (*YUIT* 277–8) links this poem to a story told to Lady Gregory by the
man in whose house the blind Irish poet Raftery died (*Poets and Dreamers* (1903)
26–7):

> I heard him telling my father one time that he was sick in Galway . . . and in
> the night he heard a noise . . . he put his hand out, and what he felt was the
> thinness of death, and his sight came to him, and he saw his wrapper [great
> coat] was hanging on the wall. . . . And in the morning his wife came in, and
> he asked where did she hang his wrapper the night before, and she told him it
> was in such a place, and that was the very place he saw it.

This passage is connected with the poem 'Raftery's Dialogue with Death' from
which Lady Gregory quoted the poet's description of death: 'His ribs were
bending like the bottoms of a riddle; his nose thin, his shoulders hard and sharp
. . . His poor bone without any kind of covering'. Sheila O'Sullivan thinks the
coat-hanger in Yeats's refrain takes the place of the sharp shoulders of death and
the coat, the place of Raftery's wrapper. There is also a parallel between the
child's hand in Yeats's dream and Raftery's hand.

8   *A coat upon a coat-hanger*: Curtis Bradford, 'Yeats's *Last Poems* Again', *Dolmen Press Yeats Centenary Papers* (1965) 274, quotes a sentence from a manuscript book Yeats was using at the time: 'The first apparition was the passage of a coat upon a coathanger slowly across room – it was extraordinarily terrifying.'

21   *increasing Night*: an image for death, cf. 'that great night' line 38, 'Man and the Echo' (*PNE* 372).

371   A NATIVITY

387   The date of this poem's composition was probably August 1936; it first appeared in *LM* (Dec. 1938).

1-2   *What woman hugs her infant there?*
       Another star . . .: cf. Yeats's notes on *WS* where he commented on 'The Mother of God' (*PNE* 261):

. . . the words 'a fallen flare through the hollow of an ear' are, I am told, obscure. I had in my memory Byzantine mosaic pictures of the Annunciation, which show a line drawn from a star to the ear of the Virgin. She conceived of the Word, and therefore through the ear a star fell and was born.

3-4   *What made the drapery glisten so?*
       Not a man but Delacroix: cf. 'Tomorrow's Revolution' (*OTB*)

We who are opposites of our times should for the most part work at our art and for good manners' sake be silent. What matter if our art or science lack hearty acquiescence, seem narrow and traditional? Horne built the smallest church in London, went to Italy and became the foremost authority upon Botticelli. Ricketts made pictures that suggest Delacroix by their colour and remind us by their theatrical composition that Talma once invoked the thunderbolt. . . . (*E* 417-18)

Mrs Yeats thought that Yeats included the French painter Ferdinand Victor Eugene Delacroix (1798-1863) for the rotunidity of his name. See *LT* 261.

388   6   *Landor's tarpaulin*: a draft version of the poem contained these lines:

> What brought that child and woman here?
> Landor's hammer on the roof
> What can brush the gnats aside?
> What can keep the rain aloof?

Yeats told his wife that he took great care to ensure [why?] that the insects in this poem were non-stinging.

The Landor image is obscure. Henn (*LT* 261) remarks on the structure of the poem (the last couplet returns to the Annunciation of the first) and states that both Landor and Delacroix knew Talma (line 10). Landor, physically violent, was calm in his writing. Henn suggests that the tarpaulin on the roof is faintly ridiculous, 'the temporary cover against popular ridicule'.

For Walter Savage Landor see note on 'To a Young Beauty' (*PNE* 152).

8   *Irving and his plume of pride*: Sir Henry Irving (1838–1905), famous actor, *né* Jonathan Henry Brodribb, whom Yeats had seen acting and had met in his teens with his father. Yeats admired his 'intellectual pride' (*Plays and Controversies*, 215, and *A* 125). He was particularly known for his Shakespearean roles.

10   *Talma*: François Joseph Talma (1763–1826), French tragic actor. Cf. passage from *OTB* quoted in note on lines 3–4.

11   *the woman*: this reverts to the annunciation of lines 1–2.

MAN AND THE ECHO   372

This poem was written in July 1938 and revised up to October 1938; it first   *393*
appeared in *Atlantic Monthly* and *LM* (Jan. 1939).

1   *that's christened Alt*: probably the glen, a rocky fissure on Knocknarea, mountain in Co. Sligo, perhaps chosen because of its rocky nature, as an Irish equivalent to Delphi. Cf. *Iliad*, IX, 406, where the rocky nature of Delphi is stressed: 'the stone threshold of the archer Phoebus Apollo encompasseth in *rocky* Pytho'.

11   *that play of mine: Cathleen ni Houlihan* (1902), which was performed in Dublin in April 1902 with Maud Gonne in the title role. Stephen Gwynn wrote in *Irish Literature and Drama in the English Language: a short History* (1936) 158:

> The effect of *Cathleen ni Houlihan* on me was that I went home asking myself if such plays should be produced unless one was prepared for people to go out to shoot and be shot. Yeats was not alone responsible; no doubt but Lady Gregory had helped him to get the peasant speech so perfect; but above all Miss Gonne's impersonation had stirred the audience as I have never seen another audience stirred.

12   *Certain men the English shot*: probably the leaders of the 1916 Rising, cf. 'Easter 1916' (*PNE* 193) (but it could also mean the total effect of the rebellion and 'troubles'). Cf. 'Sixteen Dead Men' (*PNE* 194) for 'talking at large' before the Rising, before the leaders were shot.

14   *that woman's reeling brain*: Margot (Collis's or) Ruddock's; see notes on 'Sweet Dancer' (*PNE* 324) and on 'A Crazed Girl' (*PNE* 335).

16   *a house lay wrecked*: Coole Park. Probably a reflection on the political movements which brought about the end of the 'great houses' in Ireland. The Wyndham Land Purchase Act of 1903 was the turning point in modern Irish history; through its provisions the large estates were broken up. The Gregory estate was already divided up before English rule in Ireland ended. Cf. notes on 'Upon a House shaken by the Land Agitation' (*PNE* 105). The house was sold to the Department of Forestry and sold by the Department to a contractor who demolished it in 1942.

394   22   *bodkin*: symbol of suicide. Cf. *Hamlet*, III, i: 'When he himself might his quietus make/with a bare bodkin'.

37   *Rocky Voice*: this voice is akin to the figure 'Old Rocky Face' of 'The Gyres' (*PNE* 321). See notes on that poem.

38   *great night*: see notes on 'increasing night' line 21, 'The Apparitions' (*PNE* 370).

373   THE CIRCUS ANIMALS' DESERTION

391   The date of this poem's composition is not certain (probably between November 1937 and September 1938. See Curtis Bradford, 'Yeats's *Last Poems* Again', *Dolmen Press Yeats Centenary Papers* (1965) 286): it first appeared in *Atlantic Monthly* and *LM* (Jan. 1939).

5   *Winter and summer*: circuses usually work a half-year season.

6   *My circus animals*: Yeats's early work. The idea of the circus may have come from Yeats's brother's drawings and paintings. Henn (*LT* 271) suggests the illustrations Jack Yeats made for the Cuala Press.

7   *Those stilted boys*: probably the Gaelic figures of Yeats's early poems and plays. Cf. his remark (probably written about the time he composed this poem) that he had given 'certain years to writing plays in Shakespearean blank verse about Irish kings for whom nobody cared a farthing' (*E* 418). Cf. also his remark that at the turn of the century everybody got down off their stilts.

that burnished chariot: probably Cuchulain's

8   *Lion and woman*: this may be a memory of 'Against Unworthy Praise' (*PNE* 98), a poem written about Maud Gonne, where she was described as 'Half lion, half child' and

> Enough if the work has seemed,
> So did she your strength renew,
> A dream that a lion had dreamed
> Till the wilderness cried aloud,
> A secret between you two, . . .

424

9   *old themes*: the chivalrous love poetry written by Yeats in the 'eighties (in particular, 'The Wanderings of Oisin' (1889)) before he met Maud Gonne in 1889.

10   *that sea-rider Oisin led by the nose*: because he was too chivalrous, and because Niamh fell in love with him and carried him off across the sea to faeryland with her on her horse. Cf. 'The Wanderings of Oisin' (*PNE* 375) and notes on 'News for the Delphic Oracle' (*PNE* 292).

11   *three enchanted islands*: Yeats wrote to Katharine Tynan on 6 February 1889, about *The Wanderings of Oisin*, telling her that 'There are three incompatible things which man is always seeking – infinite feeling, infinite battle, infinite repose – hence the three islands' (see *L* 111, and *LKT* 84).

allegorical dreams: Yeats had written to Katharine Tynan in September 1888, that in the second part of 'Oisin' he had

> said several things to which I only have the key. The romance is for my readers. They must not even know there is a symbol anywhere. They will not find out. If they did, it would spoil the art. Yet the whole poem is full of symbols – if it be full of aught but clouds. The early poems I know to be quite coherent, and at no time are there clouds in my details, for I hate the soft modern manner.   (*LKT* 68)

18   *The Countess Cathleen*: Yeats's play which he wrote for Maud Gonne, produced in Dublin on 8 May 1899 by the Irish Literary Theatre with Maud Gonne playing the part of the Countess Cathleen.

19-12   *She, pity-crazed, had given her soul away,*   392
        But masterful Heaven had intervened to save it.
        I thought my dear must her own soul destroy: the Countess was like Yeats's early interpretation of Maud Gonne's character. He told her that after they had met in London in 1891 (the year he first proposed marriage to her) he had come to understand the tale of a woman selling her soul to buy bread for her starving people as a symbol of all souls who lose their peace or fineness of soul or beauty of spirit in political service, but chiefly as a symbol of her soul that seemed to him incapable of rest. In the play two agents of the Devil come to Ireland in a time of famine (Maud Gonne had become ill through overstrain aiding in relief work among the peasants in Donegal who were threatened with famine) and take advantage of the starvation of the peasants to offer to buy their souls for gold. The Countess Cathleen sacrifices her goods to get money for food for her people. She is about to sell her soul when the poet Kevin (Aleel) tries to stop her, but in vain.

21   *my dear*: Maud Gonne

22   *fanaticism and hate*: cf. lines 57–64 'A Prayer for my Daughter' (*PNE* 201) with their terrible indictment of Maud Gonne's political hatred

25   *the Fool and Blind Man*: characters in Yeats's play *On Baile's Strand*

(1903) where the hero Cuchulain, having unwittingly killed his son, dies fighting the sea. *On Baile's Strand* was first performed in Dublin on 27 December 1904 by the Irish National Theatre Society.

Birgit Bjersby (*ICL* 79) remarks that the later Yeats 'admits or rather wants to tell us that *On Baile's Strand* is a drama in which the romantic dreams of his youth have found expression and in which he fights in desperation for his dream world against invading reality.' She quotes the conclusion of the 1905 version of the play (*ICL* 29-30) pointing out the stylistic repetitions in the closing speeches which culminate in the Blind Man's words:

> There will be nobody in the houses. Come this way; come quickly! The ovens will be full. We will put our hands into the ovens.

27-8   *Heart mysteries there, and yet when all is said*
       It was the dream itself: this may be a reference to Yeats's personal life after John MacBride married Maud Gonne in 1903. He took up the management of the Abbey Theatre from 1902 to 1910.

31   *Players and painted stage*: cf. 'The Fascination of What's Difficult' (*PNE* 99) with its 'theatre business, management of men'; 'At the Abbey Theatre' (*PNE* 106); and 'All Things can tempt Me' (*PNE* 110) for his views of his work in the Abbey Theatre at the time he was most deeply involved in its work.

374   POLITICS

392   This poem was written on 23 May 1938 and first appeared in *Atlantic Monthly* and *LM* (Jan. 1939).

A letter to Dorothy Wellesley of 24 May 1938 explains the poem's genesis in terms of the American poet Archibald MacLeish's (1892-1982) article, 'Public Speech and Private Speech in Poetry', *Yale Review* (Spring 1938):

> There has been an article upon my work in the *Yale Review*, which is the only article on the subject which has not bored me for years. It commends me above other modern poets because my language is 'public'. That word which I had not thought of myself is a word I want. Your language in 'Fire' is public, so is that of every good ballad. (I may send you the article because the criticism is important to us all.) It goes on to say that, owing to my age and my relation to Ireland, I was unable to use this 'public' language on what it evidently considered the right public material, politics. The enclosed little poem is my reply. It is not a real incident, but a moment of meditation. . . . P.S. In part my poem is a comment on ——'s panic-stricken conversation.
> No artesian well of the intellect can find the poetic theme. (*DWL* 163)

MacLeish's article also included the quotation from the German author Thomas Mann (1875-1955) which heads the poem.

NARRATIVE AND DRAMATIC

This heading covers the poems *The Wanderings of Oisin* (1889), *The Old Age of Queen Maeve* (1903), *Baile and Aillinn* (1903), *The Shadowy Waters* (1906) ('Introductory Lines'; 'The Harp of Aengus'; 'The Shadowy Waters'), *The Two Kings* (1914) and *The Gift of Harun Al-Rashid* (1923).

THIS poem was first published in *WO*; the first version seems to have been
finished in the autumn of 1887 (*LKT* 41). Yeats prepared it for the printer in the
early part of 1888. The poem has been extensively revised and *VE* 1-63 should
be consulted. A list of variant spellings is given on p. 1. The Gaelic sources are
Oisin i dTir na nOg and *Agallamh na Senorach*. See note on lines 139-45, and
Giles W. L. Telfer, *Yeats's Idea of the Gael* (1965). Yeats departed from the spirit
of the Gaelic originals; he believed that Irish legends and beliefs resembled those of
the east. See the discussion in *YCE* 45-51, and see also *Y: M & P*, 42-7 and F.
Shaw, 'The Celtic Element in the Poetry of W. B. Yeats', *Studies* (June 1934).
Yeats's note of 1912 (*CP*) reads:

> The poem is founded upon the Middle Irish dialogues of S. Patrick and Oisin
> and a certain Gaelic poem of the last century [by Michael Comyn: see note
> below]. The events it describes, like the events in most of the poems in this
> volume, are supposed to have taken place rather in the indefinite period, made
> up of many periods, described by the folk-tales, than in any particular century;
> it therefore, like the later Fenian stories themselves, mixes much that is
> mediaeval with much that is ancient. The Gaelic poems do not make Oisin go
> to more than one island, but a story in *Silva Gadelica* [see Standish Hayes
> O'Grady (1832-1915), *Silva Gadelica* (1892) II, 391-2] describes 'four
> paradises', an island to the north, an island to the west, an island to the south,
> and Adam's paradise in the east.

EPIGRAPH

Tulka: *PNE* suggests the Czech painter Josef Tulka (b. 1846) but does not link
him with the quotation (which may have been invented by Yeats). The name may
have been suggested by the Swedenborgian Charles Augustus Tulk (1786-1849)
whose father was an original member of the Theosophical Society (founded
1783). He wrote *The Record of Family Instruction* (1832), *Aphorisms* (1843),
various papers in the *New Church Advocat* and an unfinished *magnum opus,
Spiritual Christianity* (1846-7).

DEDICATION

Edwin J. Ellis (1848-1916) collaborated with Yeats in editing *The Works of
William Blake, Poetic, Symbolic and Critical* (3 vols, 1893). See accounts of him
in *M* 28-31, 32, 37 and in *A* 88, 159, 160, 162-5, 226, 241, 316 and 403.

BOOK I

1   *S. Patrick*: Saint Patrick (? 385–461), Ireland's patron saint, was largely responsible for introducing Christianity to Ireland.

5   *Oisin*: the son of Finn and Saeve (of the Sidhe). His name means 'the little fawn'. Yeats described him as the poet of the Fenian cycle of legend.

409   13   *Caoilte*: Caoilte Mac Ronain, see notes on 'The Secret Rose' (*PNE* 67). He was Finn's favourite warrior.

Conan: Conan Mail, a braggart Fenian warrior, whom Yeats called the Thersites of the Fenian cycle

Finn: Finn MacCumhail (MacCool) leader of the Fenians, and the main figure in the Fenian cycle of tales; he was Oisin's father.

15   *Bran, Sceolan and Lomair*: Bran and Sceolan were Finn's cousins, his aunt Uirne having been transformed while pregnant; Lomair was one of their three whelps.

16   *Firbolgs*: supposedly prehistoric invaders of Ireland, short and black-haired. Yeats commented, 'An early race who warred vainly upon the Fomorians, or Fomoroh, before the coming of the Tuath de Danaan. Certain Firbolg Kings, killed at Southern Moytura, are supposed to be buried at Ballisodare. It is by their graves that Usheen and his companions rode' (*P* (1895)). He also described them as 'a mythological race'. For the Fomorians, see note on 'The Madness of King Goll' (*PNE* 9) and for the Tuatha de Danaan see Yeats's note (quoted p. 42) in *WR*. The megalithic burial place is Carrowmore, Co. Sligo.

17–18   . . . *the cairn-heaped grassy hill*
         Where passionate Maeve is stony-still: Knocknarea, mountain in Co. Sligo, reputed burial place of Maeve. Cf. notes on 'Red Hanrahan's Song about Ireland' (*PNE* 84). Yeats commented that 'she is rumoured to be buried under the cairn on Knocknarea. Ferguson speaks [in Congal (1872). For Ferguson, see note on 'To Ireland in the Coming Times' (*PNE* 39)] of the "shell-heaped cairn of Maeve high up on haunted Knocknarea" but inaccurately for the cairn is of stones' (*P* (1895)). Maeve was 'a famous queen of the Red Branch cycle.' See Yeats's note on 'The Hosting of the Sidhe' (*PNE* 40) and note on 'The Ballad of Father O'Hart' (*PNE* 14). The Red Branch (or Ulster) is the major cycle of Irish Tales.

20   *A pearl-pale high-born lady*: Niamh, daughter of Aengus and Edain; her name means brightness or beauty. She was described as a child of the Shee (Sidhe) in a line of the version of the poem in *P* (1895). See note on the 'Hosting of the Sidhe' (*PNE* 40).

21   *findrinny*: *findruine*, an alloy. Yeats described it as a kind of red bronze

(*P* (1895)) and a kind of white bronze (*P* (1895; rev. 1899)). The latter is probably correct.

41   *Oscar's pencilled urn*: Oscar was Oisin's son. The lines borrow from Sir   *410* Samuel Ferguson's 'Aideen's Grave', the conclusion of which ran:

> A cup of bodkin pencill'd clay
> Holds Oscar; mighty heart and limb
> One handful now of ashes grey
> And she has died for him.
> (*Lays of the Western Gael*, II, 12–15)

43   *Gabhra*: the Fianna were almost wiped out in a battle here in 284 AD. The area is near Garristown, in north Co. Dublin. Yeats called it 'the great battle in which the power of the Fenians was broken' (*P*(1895)).

47   *Aengus and Edain*: Aengus was the Celtic god of love and beauty who lived in Tir na nOg, the country of the Young. See notes on 'Under the Moon' (*PNE* 86). Edain or Etain was 'a famous legendary queen who went away and lived among the Shee' (*P* (1895)); she 'was lured away by Meder (Midhir), King of the Shee' (*P* (1895; rev. 1899)). See 'The Two Kings' (*PNE* 381) which tells of her wooing by Midhir through King Eochaid's brother Ardan. The version in 'The Two Kings' departs from the Gaelic original. See *The Two Kings* (*PNE* 381) and an account in *PNE* of *Tochmarc Etaine* (the wooing of Etain) in which Aengus is foster-son to Midhir, for whom he obtains Etain as a wife. Midhir's previous wife Fuamnach turns Edain into a fly which takes refuge with Aengus.

48   *Niamh*: the name means brilliance. See Yeats's note in *WR* (quoted pp. 43–5) in note on 'The Hosting of the Sidhe' (*PNE* 40).

53   *the birds of Aengus*: the kisses of Aengus turned into birds and flew around his head. See P. Gurd, *The Early Poetry of William Butler Yeats* (1916), 55 and Yeats's footnote to *Baile and Aillinn* (*PNE* 377).

63   *Danaan*: Tuatha de Danaan, a magical race. See note on 'The White Birds'   *411* (*PNE* 29), and on 'The Hosting of the Sidhe' (*PNE* 40). Yeats remarked that Tuatha de Danaan means 'the race of the Gods of Dana, that Dana was the mother of all the ancient gods of Ireland' . . . and that they were the powers of light and life and warmth who battled with the Fomoroh, the powers of night and death and cold, and that the Tuatha, robbed of offerings and honour, have dwindled in the popular imagination until they have become the Faeries.' (*VE* 796)

71   *brazen bell*: cf. P. Gurd, *The Early Poetry of William Butler Yeats* (1916), 53, who describes as 'oblong and made of iron' the bells introduced into Ireland by St Patrick.

116   *Fenians*: Yeats's note in *P* describes them as the great military order of which Finn was chief.

413   139-145   *. . . now a hornless deer*
Passed by us, chased by a phantom hound
All pearly white, save one red ear;
And now a lady rode like the wind
With an apple of gold in her tossing hand;
And a beautiful young man followed behind
With quenchless gaze and fluttering hair: this passage owes much to Michael Comyn's 'The Lady of Oisin in the Land of Youth', translated by Brian O'Looney (see *Transactions of the Ossianic Society* IV (1859), 21-5, 117-18, 249, and David Comyn, *Gaelic Union Publications* (1880).

> We saw also, by our sides
> A hornless fawn leaping nimbly
> And a red-eared white dog,
> Urging it boldly in the chase.
> We beheld also, without fiction
> A young maid on a brown steed,
> A golden apple in her right hand,
> And she going on the top of the waves.
> We saw after her,
> A young rider on a white steed.

414   156   *Almhuin*: the Hill of Allen, Co. Kildare, where Finn brought Grainne after the death of Diarmuid on Ben Bulben.

416   218-20   *Where Aengus dreams . . . world be done*: cf. F. Shaw, 'The Celtic Element in the Poetry of W. B. Yeats', *Studies* (June 1934), 272-3, for a discussion of the 'very homely unmysterious Thir na n-Og' described in the original Gaelic poem

239   *this strange human bard*: Oisin's 'stories builded by his words' are earlier described as 'like coloured Asian birds/At evening in their rainless lands' (69-70). Originally, in *WO* (1887) Niamh remarks 'drops of honey are his words.'

421   383   *pale findrinny*: see note on line 21

BOOK II

423   The Second Book was thought to derive from the Glaucus episode in *Endymion* by Miss D. M. Hoare, *The Works of Morris and Yeats in Relation to Early Saga Literature* (1937), 114. The hall seemed to Horatio S. Krans, *William Butler Yeats and the Irish Literary Revival* (1904), 69, to come from *Hyperion*. P. Gurd, *The Early Poetry of William Butler Yeats* (1916), 59 suggested that 'the great fortress' was suggested by Shelley's 'Temple of the Spirit' in *The Revolt of Islam*. Saul (*PYP* 180) considers the 'chasm-like portals' called 'the enchanted towers of Carbonek' in Tennyson's 'The Holy Grail' may be echoed here.

1   *man of croziers*: St Patrick

10   *Druid*: for Druid see note on 'The Rose upon the Rood of Time' (*PNE* 17).

84   *Seven Hazel Trees*: P. Gurd, *The Early Poetry of William Butler Yeats*   *425*
(1916), 55, suggests that these are the same as the nine hazel trees of Wisdom of
the Tuatha de Danaan. Yeats's note reads:

> There was once a well overshadowed by seven sacred hazel trees in the midst of
> Ireland. A certain lady plucked their fruit, and seven rivers arose out of the land
> and swept her away. In my poems this is the source of all the waters of this
> world, which are therefore sevenfold.   (*P*(1895))

87   *Aed*: Aedh, Irish for Hugh. Aedh is a god of death: 'All who hear his harp
playing die. He was one of the two Gods who appeared to Cuhoollin before his
death, according to the bardic tale' (*P*(1895)). 'The source is Standish O'Grady,
History of Ireland' [(1878–80) II, 319] (*P*(1895; rev. 1899)).

95   *Heber*: Eber, a son of Milesius, who was supposed to rule over southern   *426*
Ireland after the Milesian invasion. Yeats commented that Heber and Heremon
were ancestors of the merely human inhabitants of Ireland (*P*(1895)).

120 *That woman*: the lady of II, line 69. She is 'That maiden' in *P*(1895).   *427*

128 *Ogham*: an ancient alphabet of twenty characters used in Ireland, usually
found in stone inscriptions, some dating back to the third century.

Manannan: Manannan Mac Lir, the god of the sea. Lear (*Lir* is the genitive), the
sea or ocean. Cf. 'Three Songs to the One Burden' (*PNE* 357).

134 *no milk-pale face*: Christ's

BOOK III

5   *Fenians, and Bran, Sceolan, Lomair*: see note on 1, line 15   *432*

49   *sleepers . . . the world began*: early editions read 'sleepers – no, neither in   *435*
house of a cann', cann being explained by Yeats as 'a kind of chieftain'

53   *bell-branch*: 'a legendary branch whose shaking cast all men into a gentle
sleep' (*P*(1895))

Sennachies: story-tellers

61   *king*: early editions read 'cann', a chieftain

80   *the name of the demon whose hammer*: Culann, a smith who made sword,   *437*

spear and shield for Conchubar, one of the major figures in the Red Branch (Ulster) cycle of Tales; see l. 89 below.

87   *kings of the Red Branch*: the Ulster cycle of tales

89   *Blanid*: She was the wife of the King of Munster and was in love with Cuchulain. Yeats's note reads 'The Heroine of a beautiful and sad story told by Keating' (*P* (1895)). Geoffrey Keating (*c.* 1570-*c.* 1650) wrote a *History of Ireland*; see the version in Irish Texts Society (1902-14) II, 224-26, which draws upon the Death of Cu-Roi Mac Daire. See R. I. Best's edition and translation of this, *Eriu* (1905) 2, 20-35. Curaoi, son of Daire, helped Cuchulain to sack Manainn, claimed the daughter of the lord of Manainn, Blanaid, as his prize, and when Cuchulain refused this, carried her off. Later she conspired with Cuchulain to kill Curaoi, whose harper Feircheirtne avenged his murder by killing her, by jumping off a high rock with her (killing himself in the act).

Mac Nessa: 'Concobar-Mac-Nessa, Concobar the son of Nessa' (*P* (1895)) Conchubar, King of Ulster

Fergus who feastward: see notes (p. 24) on 'Fergus and the Druid' (*PNE* 18). Fergus, Conchubar's stepfather, was under *Geasa* never to refuse an invitation to a feast, and though he was their safe-conduct, he left - though unwillingly - Deirdre and the sons of Usna (who were murdered by Conchubar's men), when Barach invited him (at Conchubar's order) to a feast. See note on 'The Rose of the World' (*PNE* 20).

90   *Cook Barach*: see previous note on line 89

438   91   *Dark Balor*: a Fomorian King, whom Yeats described as 'The Irish Chimaera, the leader of the hosts of darkness as the great battle of good and evil, life and death, light and darkness, which was fought out on the strands of Moytura, near Sligo' (*P* (1895)). The Chimaera was, in Greek mythology, a fire-breathing monster with the head of a lion, body of a goat, and tail of a serpent or dragon.

94   *Grania*:

'A beautiful woman, who fled with Dermot to escape from the love of aged Finn. She fled from place to place over Ireland, but at last Dermot was killed at Sligo upon the seaward point of Benbulben, and Finn won her love and brought her, leaning upon his neck, into the assembly of the Fenians, who burst into inextinguishable laughter.'   (*P* (1895))

This account was taken from Standish Hayes O'Grady's version of the story. See note on 'A Faery Song' (*PNE* 23).

104   *Bran, Sceolan, Lomair*: see note on Book I, 15.

439   116   *Conan's slanderous tongue*: see note on Book I, line 13.

152 *keened*: see note on line 22 'The Ballad of Father O'Hart' (*PNE* 14).   *442*

160 *Rachlin*: Rathlin, island off the coast of Co. Antrim

Bera of ships: possibly a place near Dunboy, but, more likely, Beare Island, Bantry Bay, Co. Cork named after a legendary Spanish princess, married to Eoghan Mor, king of Munster who forced Conn the Hundred Fighter to divide Ireland in two. Yeats is implying the length of Ireland by the phrase 'Rachlin to Bera'

163 *rath*: an Irish fort   *443*

167 *the straw-death*: death in bed

179 *Crevroe ... Knockfefin*: Padraic Colum has informed the editor that   *444*
Crevroe and Knockfefin are small townlands in Co. Sligo. See note on line 25 'The Man who dreamed of Faeryland' (*PNE* 33). *McG* 38 suggests Crevroe is Craobh ruadh (Red Branch), the building in which the Red Branch heroes lived at Emain Macha (Armagh). *PNE* suggests 'perhaps' Creeverow in Co. Antrim. *McG* 61–2, suggests Knockfefin may be Sliabh-na-mBan, the Mountain of the Women of Femen (*Feinhenn*), now known as Slievenamon, Co. Tipperary, a fairy palace named *Sid ar Femen*, the home of Bodb-Derg, son of Dagda, in which the Sidhe enchanted Finn MacCool.

184 *where Maeve lies*: Knocknarea, see note on Book I, lines 17–18.

198 *Hell*: Yeats wrote: *445*

In the older Irish books Hell is always cold, and this is probably because the Fomoroh, or evil powers, ruled over the north and the winter. Christianity adopted as far as possible the Pagan symbolism in Ireland as elsewhere, and Irish poets, when they became Christian, did not cease to speak of 'the cold flagstone of Hell.' The folk-tales, and Keating in his description of Hell, make use, however, of the ordinary fire symbolism.   (*P* (1895))

The mention of hell in Keating has not been traced. Two references, to 'cold hell' and the 'flag-stones of pain' in *Fenian Poems,* ed. John O'Daly, *Transactions of the Ossianic Society* (1859) IV, 15, 119 and 45 respectively, are given by *PNE*.

220 *a hay-cock out on the flood*: perhaps a memory of William Morris, 'The Haystack in the Floods'

The Old Age of Queen Maeve

449   The poem first appeared in *Fortnightly Review* (April 1903). Lines 1-8 were added in *CP*.

9   *Maeve*: Queen of Connaught, see note on 'The Ballad of Father O'Hart' (*PNE* 14).

451   11   *Cruachan*: Maeve's palace in Connaught

452   31   *praise another, praising her*: Yeats has been writing about Maud Gonne from 1-10. He addressed her in lines 130-41.

40   *Druid*: see note on 'To the Rose upon the Rood of Time' (*PNE* 17). See Yeats's note quoted on 'The Hosting of the Sidhe' (*PNE* 40).

453   58   *White-Horned Bull and the Brown Bull*: the story of the *Táin Bó Cualnge* concerns the cattle raid of Cooley, made by Maeve into Ulster because of a quarrel over these bulls. She was annoyed that her White-horned bull had gone to her husband's herds and she invaded Ulster to capture the brown bull of Cooley.

69   *Ailell*: Maeve's husband, see note on *l*. 41 above

71   *Fergus, Nessa's husband*: see notes on 'Fergus and the Druid' (*PNE* 18). Conchubar was Ness's son.

77   *Magh Ai*: Magh aoi, a plain in Co. Roscommon, dominated by Cruachan, ancestral lands of the Kings of Connaught (*McG* 68).

78   *of the Great Plain*: the central plain of Ireland or, perhaps, Magh Ai; or 'the Great Plain of the other world' (*PNE*); see Yeats's footnote (quoted on p. 438) on *Baile and Aillinn* (*PNE* 377).

84   *Aengus*: God of Love. See note on *WO* Book I, 47 (*PNE* 375).

454   92   *the children of the Maines*: Maeve had a son Maine, who was killed by Conchubar. He was married to Ferbe. Saul (*PYP* 96) mentions the tradition of seven Maines, outlawed sons of Maeve and Ailill, who joined in her fight against

Ulster and also helped Conaire Mor's foster brothers to raid Erin. There is also traditional authority for eight or nine Maines. See note on 'The Hour before Dawn' (*PNE* 125).

93   *Bual's hill*: Anbual's hill. He was Ethal Anbual, father of Caer; he was of the Connaught Sidhe. See *McG* 23.

101   *Aengus of the birds*: see note on line 53, *The Wanderings of Oisin* 1 (*PNE* 375).

130   *Friend*: Maud Gonne

141   *that great queen*: Maeve

455

457   YEATS was writing this 'half lyrical half narrative poem' in July 1901 (*L* 353)
and it was 'just finished' on 11 August 1901 (*Y & TSM* 2). It first appeared in
the *Monthly Review* (July 1902). Yeats wrote a footnote to the poem which ran:

> It is better, I think, to explain at once some of the allusions to mythological
> people and things, instead of breaking up the reader's attention with a series of
> foot-notes. What the 'long wars for the White Horn and the Brown Bull' were,
> and who 'Deirdre the harper's daughter' was, and why Cuchullain was called
> 'the hound of Ulad,' I shall not explain. The reader will find all that he need
> know about them, and about the story of Baile and Aillinn itself, in Lady
> Gregory's 'Cuchullain of Muirthemne', the most important book that has
> come out of Ireland in my time. 'The Great Plain' is the Land of the Dead and
> of the Happy; it is called also 'The Land of the Living Heart', and many
> beautiful names besides. And Findrias and Falias and Gorias and Murias were
> the four mysterious cities whence the Tuatha De Danaan, the divine race, came
> to Ireland, cities of learning out of sight of the world, where they found their
> four talismans, the spear, the stone, the cauldron, and the sword. The birds that
> flutter over the head of Aengus are four birds that he made out of his kisses; and
> when Baile and Aillinn take the shape of swans linked with a golden chain, they
> take the shape that other enchanted lovers took before them in the old stories.
> Midhir was a king of the Sidhe, or people of faery, and Etain his wife, when
> driven away by a jealous woman, took refuge once upon a time with Aengus in
> a house of glass, and there I have imagined her weaving harp-strings out of
> Aengus' hair. I have brought the harp-strings into 'The Shadowy Waters,'
> where I interpret the myth in my own way. (See also *CW* II, which includes
> *The Legendary and Mythological Foundation of the Plays and Poems*.)

The 'long wars' are of those described in the *Táin Bó Cualgne*, see note on *The
Old Age of Queen Maeve* (*PNE* 376). For Deirdre, see note on 'The Rose of the
World' (*PNE* 20). Cuchulain, originally called Setanta, killed the hound of the
smith Culann, and was then called the Hound of Culann, Cuchulain, after he
offered to take its place. Uladh is Ulster. See Lady Gregory *Cuchulain of
Muirthemne* (1902), 305-6, for the Baile and Aillinn story. For Tuatha de
Danaan, see Yeats's note on 'The Hosting of the Sidhe' (*PNE* 40). For Aengus
see note on *WO*, I, 47 (*PNE* 375). For Midhir see notes on 'The Harp of
Aengus' (*PNE* 379). For Etain see note below on *l.* 142. The 'house of glass' was
used by Aengus to carry Etain when she was in the shape of a fly. See John Rhys,
LCH, 145, who calls it a *Grianan*, a sun-bower. 'The Shadowy Waters' is in *PNE*
378-380. The original story, according to D. M. Hoare, *The Works of Morris
and Yeats in Relation to Early Literature,* 116-18, is in *Scél Baili Binn Bérlaig*,
but R. K. Alspach thinks that Yeats's immediate source was P. Kennedy,
Legendary Fictions of the Irish Celts (1866).

Title   Baile and Aillinn: Baile was the son of Buan and Aillinn the heir of   *459*
Lugaidh.

4   *Uladh*: Ulster

Buan's son: Buan, an Ulster goddess, the wife of Mesgedra the king. Sir Samuel
Ferguson, who wrote a poem 'Mesgedra', described the story: 'In the Conorian
cycle, the egg of Leda, so to speak, is the trophy taken from the dead Mesgedra by
Conoll Cornach under the circumstances which form the subject of this piece
[Mesgedra]', Ferguson, *Poems 1880*, 32. At Mesgedra's death, Buan 'lifted up
her cry of lamentation and even unto Tara and to Allen was her cry heard. . . .
On the roadside is her grave, even Coll Buana, ''the hazel of Buan'' from the
hazel that grows through the grave,' Eleanor Hull, *The Cuchullin Saga in Irish
Literature* (1898), 94.

7   *Aillinn, who was King Lugaidh's heir*: Lugaidh, the son of Curoi (Curaoi)
Mac Daire, a Munster king, who went to attack Cuchulain during the *Táin Bó
Cualgne* but, seeing Cuchulain was badly wounded after his fight with Ferdiad at
the Yellow Ford, refrained. Aillinn was Lugaidh's daughter. See note on *WO* III,
89 (*PNE* 375)

14-15   *the White Horn and the Brown Bull*: see note on line 58 'The Old Age
of Queen Maeve' (*PNE* 376).

16   *Honey-Mouth . . . Little-Land*: He was 'sweet-spoken', had little land and
was of the race of Rudraige. See Lady Gregory, *Cuchulain of Muirthemne* (1902)
305. See note on 'The Madness of King Goll' (*PNE* 9).

18   *Emain*: Emain Macha, Armagh, the capital of Ulster

21   *Muirthemne*: a plain in Co. Louth. It is called after Muirthemne, son of
Breogan, a Milesian leader. Cuchulain came from there, and it is the site of the
main fight in the *Táin Bó Cualgne.*

23   *there*: Rosnaree on the River Boyne, where they were to be married   *460*

25   *there*: Saul (*PYP* 184) glosses as Dundalk

73   *the Hound of Uladh*: Cuchulain, known as the Hound of Culann, and as the   *461*
Hound of Ulster. See gloss above, on Yeats's footnote.

76   *the harper's daughter and her friend*: Deirdre, daughter of Felimid
(Conchubar's story-teller), and Naoise, son of Usna, her lover

79   *betrayed*: see note on Fergus, line 89, *The Wanderings of Oisin* III (*PNE*
375).

91   *Deirdre and her man*: see note on line 76   *462*

439

463 117 *Ogham*: see note on line 128, *The Wanderings of Oisin* II (*PNE* 375).

123 *the Great Plain*: see Yeats's footnote quoted above

130 *the Hill Seat of Laighen*: a hill fort (*Irish* Dun Ailinne or Ailann) and seat of the Kings of Leinster on the Dublin–Kildare border in the Knockline Mountains, near Kilcullen. Leinster, Laighan, derives its name from spears called laigan used for the first time in the third century.

135 *Two swans*: the lovers Baile and Aillinn were changed by Aengus into swans.

139 *his changed body*: the old man of lines 25, 47, 100, 113 and 134 reveals himself as Aengus.

142 *Edain, Midhir's wife*: see Yeats's footnote quoted above and note on *WO*, I, 53 (*PNE* 375) and the poem 'The Harp of Aengus' (*PNE* 379).

464 153 *two sweet blossoming apple-boughs*: cf. 'Ribh at the Tomb of Baile and Aillinn' (*PNE* 309).

161-3 *Gorias . . . Findrias and Falias . . . And . . . Murias*: see Yeats's footnote quoted above

165 *Cauldron and spear and stone and sword*: Yeats's footnote explains that the Tuatha de Danaan found their talismans in these cities and he gives them as the spear, stone, cauldron and sword. The spear was Lugh's, the stone the *Lia Fail* or Stone of Destiny, brought to Scotland by fifth-century Irish invaders, then brought to England by Edward I and called the stone of Scone. (It is kept in Westminster Abbey and was removed by Scottish Nationalists in 1950, and spent some time in Scotland before it was brought back to Westminster Abbey by the police.) The cauldron was the Dagda's and the sword Lugh's.

176 *apples of the sun and moon*: cf. notes on 'The Man who dreamed of Faeryland' (*PNE* 33).

465 178 *Quiet's wild heart*: quiet is personified also in 'Maid Quiet' (*PNE* 68).

180 *glass boat*: see Gurd, *The Early Poetry of William Butler Yeats* (1916), 79 who cites Bonwick, *Irish Druids and Old Irish Religion* (1894), 293

188-93 *a yew tree . . . a wild apple . . . tablets of their board*: cf. notes on 'Ribh at the Tomb of Baile and Aillinn' (*PNE* 309).

194 *fighting at the ford*: between Cuchulain and Ferdiad in the *Táin Bó Cualnge*

200 *Beloved*: presumably Maud Gonne

The Shadowy Waters

YEATS probably finished work on *The Shadowy Waters* towards the end of 1899 (*L* 332). Lines 1–44 appeared in *S* (1 Dec. 1900). 'The Harp of Aengus' first appeared in the *North American Review* (May 1900), and the text of the play together with these two poems in *Poems 1899–1905* (1906). The text in *CP* is very different from the original version which is reprinted in *VE* 745 ff. There is a different version in *CPl*, an acting version used at the Abbey Theatre and published by Bullen in 1907. The 1900 version (Yeats wrongly calls it 1902 in notes to *CP*) was played by the Irish National Theatre Society at the Molesworth Hall, Dublin, in 1904 'with very unrealistic scenery before a very small audience of cultivated people'.

INTRODUCTORY LINES   378

1   *Coole*: see notes on 'The Wild Swans at Coole' (*PNE* 143).   *469*

2   *Shan-walla*: old wall (*Irish* Sean Bhalla). *PNE* suggests perhaps 'old road' (*Irish* Sean-bhealach).

4   *Kyle-dortha*: Kyle, coill, a wood; dortha, dorracha, dark, destroyed by fire

Kyle-na-no: (*Irish* Coill na gCno) the wood of the nuts

7   *Pairc-na-lee*: (*Irish* Pairc na Laoi) park or field of the calves

9   *Pairc-na-Carraig*: (*Irish* Pairc na Carraige) park or field of the rock, or, *PNE* suggests, (*Irish* Pairc na gCarraig), field of stones

11   *Pairc-na-tarav*: (*Irish* Pairc na dTarbh) park or field of the bulls

13   *Inchy wood*: either wood of the islands (see *McG*, 54) or (*Irish* [Coill na]n-Insi) of the water meadows (*McG* 96).

15   *Biddy Early*: a famous witch in Co. Clare. Cf. *A* 401.

22   *Forgael and Dectora*: the main characters in the *Shadowy Waters* (*PNE* 380).

441

379   THE HARP OF AENGUS

471   1-2   *Edain came out of Midhir's hill, and lay*
Beside young Aengus in his tower of glass: see Yeats's footnote to *Baile and Aillinn* (*PNE* 371) quoted in notes on that poem, and see note on 'The Host of the Air' (*PNE* 44). Midhir's hill is Sliabh Golry, near Ardagh, Co. Longford.

4   *Druid*: see note on 'To the Rose upon the Rood of Time' (*PNE* 17).

10   *Midhir's wife*: Fuamnach, the 'jealous woman' of Yeats's footnote, who turned Edain into a purple fly, carried by the wind to the house of Aengus, the tumulus of Newgrange, in the Boyne valley. Fuamnach found where Edain was hidden and called up a second wind by druid spells to blow her out of the house. Aengus killed Fuamnach. Edain was blown through Ireland for seven years, then she was drunk down in a glass of wine by Etar who bore her as a reincarnated Edain. The stories Yeats read first in 'poor translations', then in Lady Gregory's *Cuchulain of Muirthemne* (1902) and *Gods and Fighting Men* (1904).

380   THE SHADOWY WATERS

473   A Dramatic Poem

9   *Red Moll*: an invented character

33   *young man and girl*: Aengus and Edain: see notes (p. 534) on 'The Harp of Aengus' (*PNE* 379).

477   99   *man-headed birds* . . .: cf. lines 245-75, 525-31. Cf. also 'the cat-headed birds' in *The Dreaming of the Bones* (*CPl* 438) which Wilson (*YI* 230) associates with these man-headed birds. They are the spirits of the dead 'associated with many such apparitions in Celtic folklore and heroic myth'. The function of the image is 'purely atmospheric', creating an atmosphere of dark expectancy.

478   118   *All, all*: cf. note on line 137.

129   *Seaghan*: invented character

479   137   *all, all*: cf. note on line 21 'Broken Dreams' (*PNE* 167).

480   169   *hurley*: Irish game (resembling hockey) of some antiquity

490   386   *a wake*: see note on 'The Ballad of Father O'Hart' (*PNE* 14)

491   *Arthur*: see note on 'Towards Break of Day' (*PNE* 109).

410   *Iollan*: either Iollan, son of Fergus MacRoy, or Finn's uncle, Iollan

Eachtach, a chief of the Fianna, who left Uchtdealb of the Sidhe for Finn's aunt Tuiren, whom Uchtdealb then turned into a hound. On Iollan's promising to return to her, Uchtdealb turned Tuiren back into a human. *PNE* cites Nicholas O'Kearney, 'The Festivities at the House of Conan', *Transactions of the Ossianic Society* (1865) 2, 160–65 on this.

566   *Shape-changers*: see note on [May this Fire have Driven Out] (*PNE* A53).

597   *ancient worm*: probably change and decay. Cf. 'the old worm of the world'   499 in *The Countess Cathleen*.

The Two Kings

501   This poem was written in October 1912 and first appeared in *BR* and *P (Ch)* (Oct. 1913).

     The basic sources are in *The Yellow Book of Lecan* and *The Book of the Dun Cow.* There is a translation in D. M. Hoare, *The Works of Morris and Yeats in Relation to Early Saga Literature,* 124-7 and 151 ff. See also R. I. Best's translation of H. Arbois de Jubainville, *The Irish Mythological Cycle and Celtic Mythology* (1903). Saul (*PYP* 187) cites M. G. MacKimmie, *A Study of Yeats's 'the Two Kings'* (1951), an unpublished dissertation in the University of Connecticut.

503   *King Eochaid*: Eochaird the Ploughman (also spelt Echaid by Yeats, whose 1913 note gave the pronunciation as 'Yohee' (*VE* 276)), the High King of Ireland. Edain reborn (see note on 'The Harp of Aengus' (*PNE* 379)) married him. The right to embrace her was won by Midhir in a board game with Eochaid; she and Midhir flew away as birds to the mounds which Eochaid dug up to find her. He was gulled into accepting her identical daughter as his wife, and Edain stayed with Midhir. See note on 'The Host of the Air' (*PNE* 44).

     2   *Tara*: seat of the High King, in Co. Meath. See note on 'In the Seven Woods' (*PNE* 77).

     20   *Mountains of the Moon*: the Ruwenzori, a mountain range in Ruanda in Central Africa

505   61   *Edain*: Etain, Eochaid's Queen

       79   *Ardan*: Ailill Anguba in the original tale

       83   *Ogham*: see note on line 128, *The Wanderings of Oisin* II (*PNE* 375).

506   113   *Loughlan waters*: Norse or Scandinavian (*Irish lochlann*, Scandinavia); 'waters' was originally 'seas'.

507   148-9   *a man . . . unnatural majesty*: Midhir, King of the Sidhe

509   202   *Thrust him away*: in the original tale, Edain agrees to return to the land of Faery.

The Gift of Harun Al-Rashid

This poem was written in 1923 and first appeared in *English Life and The Illustrated Review* (Jan. 1924). It was included in *The Tower* (1928).

Yeats wrote a note which gives a flippant account of his marriage, in *The Cat and the Moon and Certain Poems* (1924) 38 ff. Harun al-Rashid has presented Kusta (who symbolises Yeats) with a new bride:

> According to one tradition of the desert, she had, to the great surprise of her friends, fallen in love with the elderly philosopher, but according to another Harun bought her from a passing merchant. Kusta, a Christian like the Caliph's own physician, had planned, one version of the story says, to end his days in a monastery at Nisibis [the Syrian residence of Armenian kings], while another story has it that he was deep in a violent love affair that he had arranged for himself. The only thing on which there is general agreement is that he was warned by a dream to accept the gift of the Caliph, and that his wife a few days after the marriage began to talk in her sleep, and that she told him all those things which he had searched for vainly all his life in the great library of the Caliph and in the conversation of wise men.

This refers to the automatic writing and the material of *AV*. Cf. *A Packet for Ezra Pound* (*AV* (B) 8–15), particularly the reference to his wife 'in the broken speech of some quite ordinary dream' (22) and the reference to 'an unnatural story of an Arabian traveller which I must amend and find a place for some day because I was fool enough to write half a dozen poems that are unintelligible without it' [*Michael Robartes and his Friends*] (*AV* (B) 19).

Title: Harun Al-Rashid (716–809), Caliph from 786–809

1   *Kusta Ben Luka*: a doctor and translator who lived from 820 to 892?. In his note Yeats writes that these stories seem a confused recollection of a 'little old box lost many years ago with Kusta-ben-Luka's longer box . . . . This little box was discovered . . . between the pages of a Greek book which had once been in the Caliph's library . . .'. He continues that he has elaborated in his poem but does not think it:

> too great a poetical licence to describe Kusta as hesitating between the poems of Sappho [Greek poetess (*c.* 612 BC) who lived in Lesbos] and the treatise of Parmenides as hiding places. Gibbon [Edward Gibbon (1737–94)] says the poems of Sappho were still extant in the twelfth century [Gibbon, *The History of the Decline and Fall of the Roman Empire*, ed. J. B. Bury (1909–14) VII,

445

111]. And it does not seem impossible that a great philosophical work of which we possess only fragments, may have found its way into an Arab library of the eighth century. Certainly there are passages of Parmenides that for instance numbered one hundred and thirty by Burkitt [Yeats read John Burnet, *Early Greek Philosophy* (1892) and *PNE* remarks that he marked in his copy, opposite the marginal number 130 (p. 188) this passage from Parmedides: 'The narrow circles are filled with unmixed fire and those surrounding them with night, and in the midst of these rushes their portion of fire. In the midst of these circles is the divinity that directs the course of all things; for she rules over all painful birth and all begetting, driving the female to the embrace of the male, and the male to that of the female. First of all the gods she contrived Eros'], and still more in his immediate predecessors which Kusta would have recognised as his own thought. This from Herakleitus [Heracleitus (*c* 535–475 BC) Greek philosopher who held that fire is the primordial substance and that all things are in perpetual flux] for instance, 'Mortals are immortals and immortals are Mortals, the one living the other's death and dying the other's life' (*VPl* 828–9). [(This passage was also marked in Yeats's copy of Burnet's *Early Greek Philosophy* p. 138).]

16   *Treatise of Parmenides*: Parmenides (b. 513 BC) founded the Eleatic School of Philosophy (after Elea in Italy) and rejected the theories of Heracleitus. He regarded the universe as an unchanging continuous indivisible whole.

514   32   *Vizir Jaffer*: He was vizier from 786 to 803, when he was imprisoned by the Caliph; perhaps from Jaffier in Otway's *Venice Preserv'd*.

517   128   *her sleeping form* . . .: this relates the experiences that went to the making of *AV*. See also notes on 'An Image from a Past Life' (*PNE* 191), which include the note Yeats wrote upon it.

519   *All, all those gyres and cubes and midnight things*: Yeats's footnote read 'This refers to the geometrical forms which Robartes describes the Judwali Arabs as making upon the sand for the instruction of their young people, and which, according to tradition, were drawn as described in sleep by the wife of Kusta-ben-Luka' (*The Dial* (June 1924)). For *All, all* see note on line 21 'Broken Dreams' (*PNE* 167). Yeats invented the Judwalis. See *AV* (A) xix and *AV* (B).

135   *Djinn*: a supernatural being

PART TWO

[ADDITIONAL POEMS]

Titles given in square brackets denote first lines of poems where Yeats gave no
title. They also denote untitled poems appearing in his prose, or as part of a play.

THE ISLAND OF STATUES   A1

This play described by Yeats as 'a poem called *The Island of Statues*, an Arcadian   *VE 644*
play in imitation of Edmund Spenser' (*A* 92) was first published in entire form in
DUR from April to July 1885. April contained Act I, Scene i, May Act I, Scenes
ii and iii, June Act II, Scenes i and ii, and July Act II, Scene iii. Act II, Scene iii was
included in *WO* as 'Island of Statues/A Fragment'. Act II, Scene iii, lines 1–15
and lines 248–263 had already been printed in *DUR*, March 1885. *P* (1895)
contained lines 1–15, entitled 'The Cloak, the Boat and the Shoes'.

sub-title Arcadian: Arcadia in the Peloponnesus (in southern Greece) was
regarded as a pastoral paradise.

ACT I

Scene i

9   *Dido*: the daughter of a Tyrian King, she was married to her uncle Sychaeus
who was murdered by her brother. She founded Carthage on the North African
coast. The Roman poet Virgil (70–19 BC) in his epic poem the *Aeneid* makes her
a contemporary of Aeneas, with whom she falls in love when he is shipwrecked on
the coast of Carthage. He leaves her, by order of the Gods, and she kills herself.

fire: Dido's funeral pyre

10   *the wanderer's ships*: those of Aeneas

12   *Argive Clytaemnestra*: see note on 'Leda and the Swan' (*PNE* 220).

13   *her lord's*: Agamemnon's

16   *steep*: Mount Ida, a mountain in Phrygia near Troy. From its summit the
gods watched the Trojan war.

17   *Oenone . . . Troia*: in Greek mythology Oenone was a nymph of Mount Ida
who fell in love with Paris (son of Priam, King of Troy) who was working as a
shepherd on Mount Ida. She prophesied the disasters ('the fires of Troia', or
Troy) that would happen when he went to Greece, and returned to Troy with
Helen, the wife of Menelaus, King of Sparta. When he was fatally wounded by
Philoctetes he had himself carried to her, but she refused to cure him. By the time
she had changed her mind and gone to Troy to help him he was dead and she then
took her own life.

109   *Arcadia's* and 166 *Arcadia*: see note on sub-title, above.

134–6   *Ida's mount . . . Oenone*: see note on lines 16–17 above.

Scene ii

60–83   *tree*: the Tree of Knowledge of good and evil in Eden, whose fruit was forbidden to Adam and Eve. After Eve ate the apple, at the serpent's prompting, they were expelled from Eden. See the Bible, Genesis 2, 16–17 and 3, 1–24.

Scene iii

2   *monk's-hood*: aconite

19   *Absolvo te*: (*Latin*) a phrase meaning 'I absolve you', said by Roman Catholic priests in the rite of penance, as a sign and enacting of the forgiveness of sins by God.

53–60   These lines show the Shelleyan influence to which Yeats referred: 'I soon chose Alastor for my chief of men and longed to share his melancholy, and maybe at last to disappear from everybody's sight as he disappeared drifting in a boat along some slow-moving river between great trees' (*A* 64). Cf. his remark that he had 'begun to write poetry in imitation of Shelley and of Edmund Spenser, play after play' (*A* 66).

77   *Pan*: see note on 'News for the Delphic Oracle' (*PNE* 363).

ACT II

Scene i

8   *carved on trees . . . sands*: the commonplace of lovers carving their beloveds' names on trees may not suit the oral tradition of pastoral poetry, with its emphasis on song, though Virgil, *Eclogue V*, has Mopsus write verses on a tree. The lover writing his beloved's name on the sand may derive from Spenser's sonnet *Amoretti* LXXV: 'One day I wrote her name upon the strand . . .'.

Scene ii

10–12 see note on II, i, 8 above

Scene iii

In *WO* Yeats gave this 'Summary of Previous Scenes':

Two shepherds at dawn meet before the door of the shepherdess Naschina and sing to her in rivalry. Their voices grow louder and louder as they try to sing each other down. At last she comes out, a little angry. An arrow flies across the scene. The two shepherds fly, being full of Arcadian timidity. Almintor, who is loved by Naschina, comes in, having shot the arrow at a heron. Naschina receives him angrily. 'No one in Arcadia is courageous,' she says. Others, to prove their love, go upon some far and dangerous quest. They but bring Arcadian gifts, small birds and beasts. She goes again angrily into her cottage. Almintor seeks the enchanted island, to find for her the mysterious flower, guarded there by the Enchantress and her spirits. He is led thither by a voice singing in a valley. The island is full of flowers and of people turned into stone. They chose the wrong flower. He also chooses wrong, and is turned into stone. Naschina resolves to seek him disguised as a shepherd. On her way she meets with the two shepherds of Scene I; they do not recognize her, but like to be near her. They tell her they love one maid; she answers, if that be so, they must clearly settle it by combat. She, not believing they will do so, passes on and comes to the edge of the lake in which is the enchanted island, and is carried over in a boat with wings. The shepherds also come to the edge of the lake. They fight fiercely, made courageous by love. One is killed. The scene quoted gives the adventures of Naschina on the island.   (*VP* 665)

267   *St Joseph's image*: Saint Joseph, husband of the Virgin Mary

287   *the Wanderer*: Aeneas. See note on I. i. 9, above.

296   *Arthur*: Arthur was the son of Uther Pendragon. See also note on 'Towards Break of Day' (*PNE* 198).

300   *Pan*: see note on I, iii, 77 above

310   *Achaians' tented chiefs*: the Achaians came from the Northern Peloponnese though the word in Homer means the Greeks (a word not used by Homer). Homer also called the people who fought against the Trojans Argives and Danaans.

LOVE AND DEATH   A2

This poem was published in *DUR*, May 1885.   *VE 680*

11   *Titan*: The sons and daughters, in Greek mythology, of Uranus (personification of the sky, the oldest Greek god, first ruler of the Universe) and Ge (the earth). They included Cronos (or Kronos, Saturn), Rhea, Oceanus, Tethys, and Hyperion. The Titans rose against Uranus and raised Cronos to the throne; subsequently Zeus rose against Cronos and the other Titans and hurled them from heaven with the aid of thunder and lightning.

31   *Mary's Garden*: presumably the Virgin Mary's

THE SEEKER   A3

This dramatic poem was first published in *DUR*, September 1885 and included in   *VE 681*
WO.

A4   LIFE

VE 686   This poem was first published in *DUR*, February 1886. Lines 1-4 and lines 17-20, form lines 1-4 and lines 17-20 in 'Quatrains and Aphorisims' in *WO*. See notes on 'Quatrains and Aphorisms' (*PNE* A23).

12   *Madonna*: (*Italian*) my lady. Generally, however, used of the Virgin Mary.

17   *Sophocles*: see note on 'Colonus' Praise' (*PNE* 223).

A5   THE TWO TITANS

VE 687   This poem was published in *DUR*, March 1886.

Title: see note on Titans, 'Love and Death' (*PNE* A2, *VE* 680).

29   *Genii*: nature spirits; in classical pagan belief, the guardians of a place, or the guiding spirit who attends a person from birth to death; in Arabic myth a demon or jinn.

41   *sybil's*: in Greek and Roman mythology any of a number of women believed to be oracles or prophetesses, the most famous being the sibyl of Cumae (who guarded Aeneas through the underworld in Virgil's *Aeneid*).

A6   ON MR NETTLESHIP'S PICTURE AT THE ROYAL HIBERNIAN ACADEMY

VE 688   This poem was first published in *DUR*, April 1886 and subsequently in *WO*.

Title: the painting was *Refuge* by J. T. Nettleship (1841-1902), an English artist and friend of Yeats's father John Butler Yeats.

2-3   *Lioness . . . funeral pyre*: The picture is of a forest fire, and is thus described in *Royal Hibernian Academy, 1886*, an illustrated art supplement of *DUR* March 1886:

Refuge 'In the midst of fire, and they have no hurt' J. T. Nettleship.—

> This is undoubtedly an impressive picture. On a rocky eminence, driven together into unexpected brotherhood by fear, we have a lion and a lioness and their cub; beside the lioness, and with the air of one that feels itself in security, an antelope is crouched. The lioness has forgotten her fear in maternal solicitude, and with touching intentness is licking her cub. The cub meantime has scented out the antelope, and divines its natural prey. There is something in the attitude of the cub which lets us know that the antelope has only just reached this doubtful asylum. Beyond the lioness a lynx watches, with pricked ears, the flutterings of a bird. All over dominates the central form of the king of

beasts. He stands with tail outstreched and head laid low, the saliva drops from his mouth, and he is roaring – not as when he shakes the forest – but a low musical roar at once of defiance and despair. Beyond the rolling fire and smoke we see a glimpse of a serene sky, in which is just visible the crescent moon in its first quarter. (p. 24)

MOSADA   A7

This verse play was first published in *DUR*, June 1886, and then separately in   *VE 689*
pamphlet form as *Mosada* (1886) and in *WO*. A privately printed edition was issued by the Cuala Press, Dublin, in 1943 based on 1889 text of *WO* 'with the manuscript corrections made by the author on his own copy'. The Frontispiece facsimile was from manuscript dated 7 June, 1886.

Quotation: source of fifteenth-century memoir not yet discovered

Scene i

sd   *Azubia*: *PNE* suggests possibly Zubia, near Granada, in Spain.

11   *Gomez*: presumably an invented character

24   *Azolar*: presumably an invented character

27   *Alpujarras*: mountains in Andalusia, southern Spain, where there has been much Moorish influence

32   *Cola*: presumably an imagined character

46   *Ebremar*: presumably an imagined character

102   *Ind*: India

103   sd *Inquisition*: The Inquisition was a judicial institution of the Roman Catholic Church (1232–1820) founded to discover and suppress heresy. In Spain it guarded the orthodoxy of Catholicism mainly by persecuting Jews and heretics (particularly Moors). It was established in 1478 and continued to function actively until the seventeenth century.

105   *Allah*: the principal muslim name for God, the one Supreme Being

Scene ii

sd   *Saint James*: Saint James the Great (d. 43 AD) one of the twelve apostles, brother of John the apostle. See the Bible, Matthew 4, 21. He is a saint particularly venerated in Spain

12   *Peter*: an invented character

19-20   *tale . . . saint of Munster*: *DU* and *Mosada* (1886) read

> is of a Russian tale
> Of Holy Peter of the Burning Gate
> A saint of Russia in a vision saw

which suggests Yeats may have invented this. Munster is the southern of the four provinces of Ireland.

21   *Peter*: Saint Peter, Keeper of Heaven's Gate

29   *Cock-a-doodle-doodle-do*: the stranger is reminding Peter that he denied Christ three times, as Christ foretold he would, before the cock crowed (see the Bible, Matthew 26, 34 and 69-75; Mark 14, 30 and 66-72; Luke 22, 34 and 56-62; and John 13, 38 and 18, 17, 25-27).

Scene iii

sd   *auto-da-fé*: a ceremony of the Spanish Inquisition, including the pronouncement and execution of sentences passed on heretics or sinners; it can also mean the burning to death of people condemned as heretics by the Inquisition.

13   *Hassan*: an invented character

A8   REMEMBRANCE

VE 704   This poem was published in *IM*, July 1886.

A9   A DAWN-SONG

VE 705-6   This poem was published in *The Irish Fireside*, 5 February 1887.

9   *ma cushla*: (*Irish*) my pulse. A term of endearment.

21   *rath*: fort (often a fairy fort, a raised mound) see note on *WO* III, 163 (*PNE* 375) 'the sacred cairn and rath'.

A10   THE FAIRY PEDANT

VE 706   This verse play was first published in *IM*, March 1887, then in *WO*. It was also included in 'A Celtic Christmas' (Christmas number of *The Irish Homestead*), December 1901 under the title 'A Solitary Fairy'.

sd   *Druidic*: see note on 'To the Rose upon the Rood of Time' (*PNE* 17).

HOW FERENCZ RENYI KEPT SILENT

A11

This poem was first published in *The Pilot* (Boston) on 6 August 1887. (It was sent by John O'Leary to the editor, John Boyle O'Reilly (1844-90), a Fenian sentenced to death in 1866, a sentence commuted to life imprisonment. He escaped from Dartmoor, was recaptured and then escaped from Australia in 1869.) Subsequently it was included in *WO* and in 'A Celtic Christmas' (Christmas number of *The Irish Homestead*), December 1900. *PNE* states that Ferencz Renyi is a fictitious character, but this is not certain, and Yeats probably thought him real, since when asked by Lajos Kropf for the source of the subject matter of the poem he told him that some circumstance, some report in a paper raked up the case, 'and it went all around the English press' (*Budapesti Szemle*, 1905, p. 315). Kropf discovered that Edith Nesbit also wrote about Renyi in September 1886, and had learned of his case in the *Pall Mall Gazette*; her poem, 'The Leaves of Splendid Silence', *The Leaves of Life* (1888), 100-107, is similar to Yeats's in many respects. The fate of Ferencz Renyi was described thus in the *Pall Mall Budget* 1886:

VE 709

A Hungarian Hero of '48

Hungarian papers announce the death of old Ferencz Rényi, a hero of one of the most terrible episodes of the Hungarian War of Independence in 1848. For thirty-six years Rényi has been a lunatic in a Buda-Pesth asylum, and the history of his sufferings is recorded after his death by the *Petit Parisien*. Ferencz Rényi was a young schoolmaster of twenty-seven years at the beginning of the war, proud, handsome, and full of buoyant life. His pupils adored him, and he was always welcome among the villagers, whether he came with his violin to play to their dances or whether his voice was heard among the patriots chanting the praise of their country. He lived with his mother and sister, and was engaged to a bright young Hungarian girl, when the Government, after proclaiming the independence of the country, called all good patriots to arms. Ferencz left his school and enlisted in the ranks. One day, after having fought valiantly at the head of a detachment of soliders, he was taken prisoner by the Austrians. Brought before General Haynau, Rényi refused to indicate the place where the rest of his regiment lay hidden. On learning that his home was in a neighbouring village the general sent for the mother and sister, and brought them into the room where the prisoner was kept. 'Now give me the information I require, if the lives of these two women are dear to you', said General Haynau to him. Rényi trembled, his eyes filled with tears, but he remained silent. 'Do not speak my son,' cried the old mother, 'do your duty, and think not of me, for at best I have only a few days to live.' 'If you betray your country,' added his sister, 'our name will be covered with shame, and what is life without honour? Do not speak Ferencz. Be calm; I shall know how to die.' Rényi remained silent, and a few minutes later the two women were dead. Another trial was to come. General Haynau sent for Rényi's future wife, who was weaker than his mother and sister. With wild cries the girl flung herself at her lover's feet, pleading: 'Speak, speak Ferencz. See, I am young. I love you; do not let me be killed. You will save yourself and me if you speak out. When you are free we will go far away and be happy. Speak, my Ferencz, and save your future wife.' She took his hands, clinging to him as a drowning man clings to his last support. The young Hungarian was choked with tears, but suddenly he pushed the girl aside and turned away. Once more she cried to him, but he did not heed her. Then the soldiers seized her. 'Be cursed', she shrieked; 'be cursed, you who let me die; you who will kill me; who are my assassin.' Rényi remained silent. The girl was shot, and the prisoner was taken back into his cell, but his reason was fled, and he was dismissed. Some friends found him and gave him a shelter; till after Hungary was once more suppressed and peace established, they obtained a place for him in the asylum in which he has recently died.

This is an abridged version of Jean Frollo's article 'Histoire d'un fou', *Le Petit Parisien*, 29 August 1886. There is a romantic ballad, 'Ferencz Renyi' by the Finnish author Kaarle Leopold Krohn, where the third victim of General Haynau is Renyi's wife. This poem appeared in *Joulukuusi* (Porvoo, 1888), 18–21, and in an anthology, *Kertovaisia Runoelmia. Alkuperäisiä* (Helsinki, 1890) 75–78. It remains popular, being included in Finnish anthologies and schoolbooks; the author said that it arose from a newspaper article. A Polish poet, Boleslaw Londynski, has also written on the subject; his poem 'Ferencz Renyi', appeared in his *Poezyje* (Warsaw, 1887) 235–38; he wrote in his introduction that Renyi died in September 1886. The question of whether Renyi existed at all has been discussed by Ferenc A. Molnar in an excellent article from which the preceding information has been extracted. 'The Legend of Ferenc Rényi, a Hungarian Hero of Freedom, in English, Finnish, Irish and Polish Literature', *Acta Litteraria Academiae Scientiarum Hungaricae*, 21 (1–2) 143–60; he has found that two brothers György Renyi (*d.* 1892) and Rudolf Renyi (*d.* 1899) took part in the Hungarian war of Independence, but has discovered no trace of Ferencz Renyi. His view is that the legend was made up by Jean Frollo who wrote the article in *Le Petit Parisien*. *PNE* suggests the possibility of Zigismond Perenyi, a nobleman tortured and executed by General Haynau in 1849, but in view of the *Pall Mall Budget*'s article and that of *Le Petit Parisien* this seems unlikely. The four non-Hungarian poets, however, who dealt with Renyi obviously considered the legend true. Michael Field's play on Renyi, *A Question of Memory*, which was produced at the Independent Theatre in London on 27 October 1893, was also founded on 'an old newspaper extract': it was published in a limited edition in 1893, and reissued in 1918.

subtitle: Hungary 1848: Yeats wrote a short commentary on his poem in *United Ireland* which shows his patriotic interest in Hungary's struggle against Austria, parallel to Ireland's against England.

5 *Hungary of the West*: Ireland

6–8 *the General . . . Haynau*: Baron Julius Jacob von Haynau (1786–1853), commander in chief of the Austrian forces from 1849.

SHE WHO DWELT AMONG THE SYCAMORES

A12

VE 715

This poem was first published in *IM*, September 1887, in *WO*, and in 'A Celtic Christmas' (Christmas number of *The Irish Homestead*), December 1902. In the last printing the title was 'She Dwelt Among the Sycamores'. See Yeats's letter of 12 December 1902 (*L* 390) to Lady Gregory about AE (George Russell) reprinting the poem in *The Irish Homestead*:

> No! I don't like that Sycamore poem, I think it perfectly detestable and always did and am going to write to Russell to say that the *Homestead* mustn't do this kind of thing anymore . . . . I wouldn't so much mind if they said they were early verses but they print them as if they were new work.

THE FAIRY DOCTOR

A13

VE 716

This poem was published in *The Irish Fireside*, 10 September, 1887 and in *WO*.

LOVE SONG

A14

VE 717

This poem was published in *Poems and Ballads of Young Ireland* (1888). It is based on a translation of an Irish song included in Edward Walsh's introduction to *Irish Popular Songs* (1883) 18.

> My hope, my love, we will proceed
> Into the woods, scattering the dews
> Where we will behold the salmon, and the ousel on its nest,
> The deer and the roe-buck calling,
> The sweetest bird on the branches warbling,
> The cuckoo on the summit of the green hill;
> And death shall never approach us
> In the bosom of the fragrant wood

(The stanza is from Eamon an Cnuic)

THE PHANTOM SHIP

A15

VE 718

This poem was first published in *The Providence Sunday Journal*, 27 May 1888 and then in *WO*.

17 *in stays*: the position of a sailing vessel relative to the wind so that the sails are luffing or aback.

31 *purgatory*: see note on 'The Pilgrim' (*PNE* 348).

A16   A LEGEND

VE 724   This poem first appeared in *The Vegetarian*, 22 December 1888 (illustrated by Jack B. Yeats (1871–1957), the poet's brother) and then in *WO*.

sub-title: *A drowned city*: This tradition is described in W. G. Wood-Martin, *History of Sligo, Country and Town* (1882–92) I, 51:

> . . . the original town stood on a plain, now overspread by the waters of Lough Gill, and . . . islets now studding the bosom of the lake are but the crests of verdant knolls which formerly adorned its green expanse. As proof, the remains of houses or buildings are said to be visible at the bottom of the lake on a sunshiny day.

4   *pitch and toss*: game (formerly frequently played at crossroads in Ireland) of skill and chance in which the player who pitches a coin nearest to a mark has the first chance to toss all the coins, winning those that land heads up.

A17   TIME AND THE WITCH VIVIEN

VE 720   This poem was included in *WO*

30   *Merlin*: a magician in Arthurian legend. Reference is made to the beguiling of Merlin by Nimiane (Nimue, or Vivien, two names arising from miscopying by successive scribes), who is called the Lady of the Lake in Malory's *Le Morte d'Arthur* In this, Nimiane, to get rid of him, inveigles him under a great stone (see line 47 below). Yeats presumably read *Merlin and Vivien*, one of Lord Tennyson's (1809–92) *Idylls of the King* (1859).

32   *Eve*: see note to *The Island of Statues* I, 61 (*PNE* A1).

A18   FULL MOODY IS MY LOVE AND SAD

VE 723   This poem was first published in *WO* (with the title 'Girl's Song') then included in the story 'Dhoya', in *John Sherman and Dhoya* (1891) and *CW* (V11).

A19   KANVA ON HIMSELF

VE 723   *title*: *Kanva*: this may be Kanva, the wise man who educates Sakuntala in the Sanskrit drama *Sakuntala*. See note on 'Anashuya and Vijaya' (*PNE* 4).

6   *Rajas and Maharajas*: (*Hindi*) rajahs or rajas are Indian rulers or landlords; superior to them are maharajahs or maharajas, Indian princes, especially rulers of the former native states

20 *As things were . . .*: an echo, possibly, of the *Gloria patri* in *The Book of Common Prayer*: 'as it was in the beginning, is now, and ever shall be, world without end'.

A LOVER'S QUARREL AMONG THE FAIRIES   **A20**

This poem was first published in *WO*   *VE 726*

sub-title: *leading a child*: cf. Yeats's notes on 'A Stolen Child' (*PNE* 10).

9 *banshee*: in Irish folklore the female spirit whose wailing warns of impending death (*Irish*, bean sidhe, woman of the fairies).

22 and 33 *Cranberry Fruit . . . Coltsfoot, Mousetail*: The names Yeats has given to the faeries are reminiscent of the names of the faeries in Shakespeare's *A Midsummer Night's Dream*: Peaseblossom, Cobweb, Moth and Mustardseed.

49 *her*: the child

THE PRIEST AND THE FAIRY   **A21**

This poem was first published in *WO*.   *VE 728*

13-14 *the only good*: cf. 'The Song of the Happy Shepherd (*PNE* 1) 'Words alone are certain good' (lines 10 and 43) and 'Then nowise worship dusty deeds' (line 22).

51 *Ave Maria*: 'Hail Mary', a prayer to the Virgin Mary in Roman Catholic ritual

STREET DANCERS   **A22**

This poem was first published in *WO* and subsequently in *The Leisure Hour*,   *VE 731*
April 1890.

28 *South Seas*: the Pacific

40 *Bedouin*: see note on 'Ego Dominus Tuus' (*PNE* 181)

QUATRAINS AND APHORISMS   **A23**

This poem was first published in this form in *WO*. Lines 21-24 and 5-8 appeared   *VE 734*
in *DUR*, January 1886, entitled 'In a Drawing Room', lines 1-4 and 17-20 in
DUR, February 1886, entitled 'Life'.

15   *Brahma*: see note on 'Anashuya and Vijaya' (*PNE* 4).

19   *Sophocles*: see note on 'Colonus' Praise' (*PNE* 223).

23   *Attic*: Attica, region in Greece including Athens

A24   IN CHURCH

VE 735   This poem was published in *The Girls' Own Paper*, 8 June 1889, 569.

A25   A SUMMER EVENING

VE 736   This poem was published in *The Girls' Own Paper*, 6 July 1889, 632.

A26   IN THE FIRELIGHT

VE 737   This poem was published in *The Leisure Hour*, March 1891.

8-9   *Fortune's wheel . . . rising . . . falling*: Fortune was often personified as a goddess (particularly in Roman literature) having for emblem a wheel symbolising vicissitude.

A27   MOURN – AND THEN ONWARD!

VE 737   This poem was published in *UI*, 10 October 1891 and the *Irish Weekly Independent*, 20 May 1893.

1   *Eri*: Erin, Eire, Ireland. See note on 'To the Rose upon the Rood of Time' (*PNE* 17).

The man: Charles Stewart Parnell, who died on 6 October 1891; see note on 'To a Shade' (*PNE* 118) and see Yeats's commentary quoted above on 'Parnell's Funeral' (*PNE* 304).

15   *tall pillar*: possibly an echo of the Bible, Exodus 13. 21-22:

> And the Lord went before them by day in a pillar of cloud, to lead them the way; and by night in a pillar of fire, to give them light; that they might go by day and by night; the pillar of cloud by day, and the pillar of fire by night, departed not from before the people.

WHEN YOU ARE SAD   **A28**

This poem was published in *CK*.   *VE 738*

12   *And . . . the whole world's trouble weeps with you*: an echo, perhaps, of Ella
Wheeler Wilcox's (pp. 855-1919) line in Solitude', *Poetical Works* (1917) 42.
'Laugh and the world laughs with you', though her concept in this poem was of
the solitude of sorrow. It may also echo the popular song's 'smile and the whole
world smiles with you'.

WHERE MY BOOKS GO   **A29**

This poem was published in W. B. Yeats, *Irish Fairy Tales* (The Children's   *VE 739*
Library) (1892).

THE BALLAD OF EARL PAUL   **A30**

This poem, dated 4 April (1893), was published in the *Irish Weekly Independent*,   *VE 739*
8 April 1893. Parts of it (lines 1-4, 9-12, 19-24, 37-44, 49-52, and 61-68)
were reprinted in an article by R. H., 'An Old Yeats Ballad', *DM*, April-June
1927.

Title   Earl Paul: The ballad is founded upon the legend of Sir John de Courcey
(*d.* 1217/19) who opposed King John (?1167-1216).

1   *Shield breaker*: Earl Paul

2   *John*: King John

3   *Own home*: in Kinsale, see lines 14 and 68

5-6   *bed of straw . . . stone*: Earl Paul was in prison in Kinsale

9   *Northumberland*: county in north-east England

10   *Isle of Wight*: island off the southern coast of England

14   *Kinsale*: Kinsale, seaport in County Cork, in the south of Ireland

59   *Thames*: England's most important river, which flows past Windsor Castle,
residence of the English monarchs, and through London, also the site of royal
palaces

66   *right hand*: place of honour

A31 THE DANAAN QUICKEN TREE

VE 742 This poem was published in *TB*, May 1893. For Yeats's note after the title see note on 'The Lake Isle of Innisfree' (*PNE* 24).

5 *Innisfree*: see notes on 'The Lake Isle of Innisfree' (*PNE* 24)

6 *Danaan quicken tree*: a fairy (mountain ash) tree.

9 *hurley*: see note on 'The Shadowy Waters' (*PNE* 380)

11 *berry*: berries were a food of the fairies

15-16 *ruddy fruit . . . poison to all men . . . meat to the Aslauga Shee*: Yeats comments in his note that the berries were poisonous to men in one legend, and, in another, able to endow them with superhuman power: both legends say they were the food of the Tuatha de Danaan. See note on 'The Madness of King Goll' (*PNE* 9). The story of the tree on Innisfree to which Yeats refers (in *A* 71-2) 'in the country history' is to be found in William Gregory Wood-Martin, *History of Sligo, County and Town* (1882-92) I, 63-64.

17 *Aslauga Shee*: (*Irish*) the host of the mound, the fairy host

28 *Dark Joan*: Yeats describes her in his note as going about the roads disguised as a clutch of chickens. She was regarded as bringing good luck to families among whom she appeared. *PNE* cites Nicholas O'Kearney, 'The Festivities at the House of Conan', *Transactions of the Ossianic Society* (1855), 2, 19, for Black Joanna of the Boyne who on Hallows-Eve would visit houses that were tidy and clean 'in the shape of a large black fowl of strange appearance'

29 *Niam*: see note on 'The Hosting of the Sidhe' (*PNE* 40) and on *The Wandering of Oisin* (*PNE* 375).

A32 WISDOM AND DREAMS

VE 743 This poem was published in *TB*, December 1893

A33 THE WIND BLOWS OUT OF THE GATES OF THE DAY

CPl 63 and 72 This is a song included in the play *The Land of Heart's Desire*, first published in 1894, first performed at the Avenue Theatre, Northumberland Avenue, London on 29 March 1894.

10 *Coolaney*: Colooney, a village near Sligo, Co. Sligo [*McG* uses the spelling Colloney]

[THE POET, OWEN HANRAHAN, UNDER A BUSH OF MAY]   A34

This poem was included in the story 'The Curse of Hanrahan the Red', first   M 243
published as 'The Curse of O'Sullivan the Red' in *NO*, 4 August 1894,
subsequently in *TSR*, and in 'Red Hanrahan's Curse', *Stories of Red Hanrahan*
(1904).

Title: Red Hanrahan: Yeats wrote in John Quinn's (1870–1924) copy of *Stories
of Red Hanrahan* (1904) that 'Red Hanrahan is an imaginary name – I saw it over
a shop, or rather a part of it over a shop in a Galway village – but there were many
poets like him in the eighteenth century in Ireland'. It is possible that Yeats had in
mind Owen O'Sullivan the Red (1748–84), whose name as 'O'Sullivan Rua' is
given to the poet hero in early versions of the stories published in periodicals. See
note on 'The Tower' (*PNE* 205). Details of O'Sullivan's life are given in *Reliques
of Jacobite Poetry* (1844, second edn 1866) ed. John O'Daly (1800–78) with
Edward Walsh's (1805–50) metrical versions. See also Daniel Corkery, *The
Hidden Ireland* (1924) ch. 8. Yeats, of course, claimed Hanrahan as his own
creation in 'The Tower': 'And I myself created Hanrahan'.

May: hawthorn

3   *Ballygawley Hill*: A hill five miles south of the town of Sligo, Slieve Daene
(Da-Ein), the Bird Mountain. See *McG* 19, for Ballydawley as correct name,
O'Daly's townland. See also *M* 241, 243 and *CPl* 68.

6   *Steep Place of the Strangers*: Lugnagall. See note on 'The Man who dreamed
of Faeryland' (*PNE* 33).

Gap of the Wind: see note on 'Running to Paradise' (*PNE* 124). Ireland has a
plethora of places called Windy Gap but here Yeats probably intends the gap in
the townland of Carrickhenry, opposite Carraroe Church, Co. Sligo, see *McG* 90.

7   *Castle Dargan*: this is near Ballygawley, Co. Sligo. See *A* 53–55; *M* 241,
243, 245; and *CPl* 640. See also *McG* 27.

9   *Paddy Bruen*: imagined character

Well of Bride: Bridget's Well, a townland in Co. Sligo, near Coloneey, named
after a holy well dedicated to Saint Bridget. See *M* 243.

11   *Peter Hart . . . Michael Gill*: imagined characters

13   *Shemus Cullinan*: imagined character

the Green Lands: an unfenced part of Rosses Point, in Co. Sligo, running from
Deadman's Point inland. See *M* 243; *PNE* 357.

15   *Paddy Doe*: another imagined character

463

A35   [OUT OF SIGHT IS OUT OF MIND]

M 166   This poem was included in the story 'The Wisdom of the King', which was first published under the title 'Wisdom' in *The New Review*, September 1895, and subsequently in *CW, TSR,* and *Stories of Red Hanrahan and the Secret Rose* (1927).

A36   [LIFT UP THE WHITE KNEE]

CPl 19   This is a song first published in the play *The Countess Cathleen* (1895) and included in subsequent editions of the play.

A37   [IMPETUOUS HEART BE STILL, BE STILL]

CPl 35   This is a song first published in the play *The Countess Cathleen* (1895) and included in subsequent editions of the play.

A38   A SONG OF THE ROSY-CROSS

TB   This poem was published in *The Bookman*, October 1895.

   Title: Rosy-Cross: the main symbol of the Rosicrucian Order. See Yeats's notes on 'The Mountain Tomb' (*PNE* 130)

A39   [SEVEN PATERS SEVEN TIMES]

M 315   This is from the story 'The Adoration of the Magi', published in *The Tables of the Law* & *The Adoration of the Magi*] (1897) and in *CW* (VII). Yeats's poem is prefaced by six lines of Irish (which are, according to *PNE*, an inaccurate text of an Irish poem by Domhall O'Fortharta, in *Siamsa an Gheimhridh* (1892), 29).
   The lines of Irish Yeats quoted run thus (he did not know any Irish himself so either adapted a literal translation for his own purposes, or had an inaccurate translation, or misremembered some version of the Irish poem):

> Seacht b-paidreacha fo seacht
> Chuir Muire faoi n-a Mal,
> Chuir Brighid faoi n-a brat,
> Chuir Dia faoi n-a neart,
> Eidir sinn 'san Sluagh Sidhe,
> Eidir sinn 'san Sluagh Gaoith

   1   *paters*: the Lord's Prayer, or the recital of it as an act of devotion (*Latin*, pater noster, Our father, the opening words of the prayer)

2   *Mary*: the Virgin Mary, mother of Jesus Christ

3   *Bridget*: Saint Brigid (*c.* 453–*c.* 523), a patron saint of Ireland who founded a monastery in County Kildare

THE GLOVE AND THE CLOAK   **A40**

This poem was published in *Roma* (Rome, 1897). It is perhaps not so far-fetched   *VE 744*
to see in this poem an allusion to Maud Gonne's dead child by the French
Boulangist Lucien Millevoye. Their second child Iseult was born in 1895. See
Yeats, *MS.* 132–3.

THE BLOOD BOND   **A41**

This song is from the three-act play *Diarmuid and Grania* written by Yeats and   *VPl 1200*
George Moore, and first published in *A Broad Sheet*, January 1902. The play,
performed on 21 October 1901, was first published in *DM*, April–June 1951.
See note on 'A Faery Song' (*PNE* 23) for Finn and Diarmuid.

SPINNING SONG   **A42**

This song is from the three-act play *Diarmuid and Grania* by Yeats and George   *AB*
Moore, published in *A Broad Sheet*, January 1902, and reprinted under the title
There are Seven that pull the thread with musical setting by Edward Elgar (1857–
1934), 1902. The play was performed on 21 October 1901; the 1951 text of the
play published in *DM*, April–June 1951, does not include this song.

[I AM COME TO CRY WITH YOU, WOMAN]   **A43**

This song is from the play *Cathleen ni Houlihan* (first published in 1902) and   *CPl 82*
included in subsequent editions of the play, which was first performed on 2 April
1902 in St Teresa's Hall, Dublin, with Maud Gonne as Cathleen. An
interpretation of *Cathleen ni Houlihan* by Yeats appeared in the *United Irishman*,
5 May 1902. In this he stated that he had put in the mouth of Cathleen ni
Houlihan verses 'about all those who have died or are about to die for her and
these verses are the key of the rest. She sings of one yellow-haired Donough in
stanzas that were suggested to me by some old Gaelic folk-song.' He then quotes
the song given in *PNE* but prefaces it with the lines

> I will go cry with the woman,
> For yellow-haired Donough is dead,
> With a hempen rope for a neck-cloth,
> And a white cloth on his head.   (*CPl* 82)

The folk-song to which Yeats referred is *Donnchadh Ban* or *Flaxen-haired Donough*. This is sometimes thought to have been composed by the blind Mayo poet and fiddler Anthony Raftery, see note on 'The Tower' (*PNE* 205). See also Myles Dillon, *Early Irish Literature* (1948) 185; Michael Yeats, 'W. B. Yeats and Irish folk-song', *Southern Folklore Quarterly* XXX, 2 June 1966, pp. 153–78; and A. Norman Jeffares and A. S. Knowland, *A Commentary on the Collected Plays of W. B. Yeats* (1975) 28–36 (*CPl* 73–82). A likely source is Lady Gregory 'West Irish Folk Ballads', *The Monthly Review*, October 1902. The revised version, in her *Poets and Dreamers* (1974 edn) 44–45 runs as follows:

In this simple lament, the type of a great many, only the first name of the young man it was made for is given: 'Fair-haired Donough.' It is likely the people of his own place know still to what family he belonged; but I have not heard it sung, and only know that he was 'some Connachtman that was hanged in Galway.' And it is clear it was for some political crime he was hanged, by the suggestion that if he had been tried nearer his own home, 'in the place he had a right to be,' the issue would have been different, and by the allusion to the Gall, the English:

It was bound fast here you saw him, and you wondered to see him,
Our fair-haired Donough, and he after being condemned;
There was a little white cap on him in place of a hat,
And a hempen rope in the place of a neckcloth.

I am after walking here all through the night,
Like a young lamb in a great flock of sheep;
My breast open, my hair loosened out,
And how did I find my brother but stretched before me!

The first place I cried my fill was at the top of the lake;
The second place was at the foot of the gallows;
The third place was at the head of your dead body
Among the Gall, and my own head as if cut in two.

If you were with me in the place you had a right to be,
Down in Sligo or down in Ballinrobe,
It is the gallows would be broken, it is the rope would be cut,
And fair-haired Donough going home by the path.

O fair-haired Donough, it is not the gallows was fit for you;
But to be going to the barn, to be threshing out the straw;
To be turning the plough to the right hand and to the left,
To be putting the red side of the soil uppermost.

O fair-haired Donough, O dear brother,
It is well I know who it was took you away from me;
Drinking from the cup, putting a light to the pipe,
And walking in the dew in the cover of the night.

O Michael Malley, O scourge of misfortune!
My brother was no calf of a vagabond cow;
But a well-shaped boy on a height or a hillside,
To knock a low pleasant sound out of a hurling-stick.

466

And fair-haired Donough, is not that the pity,
You that would carry well a spur or a boot;
I would put clothes in the fashion on you from cloth that would be lasting;
I would send you out like a gentleman's son.

O Michael Malley, may your sons never be in one another's company;
May your daughters never ask a marriage portion of you;
The two ends of the table are empty, the house is filled,
And fair-haired Donough, my brother, is stretched out.

There is a marriage portion coming home from Donough,
But it is not cattle nor sheep nor horses;
But tobacco and pipes and white candles,
And it will not be begrudged to them that will use it.

A very pathetic touch is given by the idea of the 'marriage portion,' the provision for the wake, being brought home for the dead boy.

3 *him*: yellow-haired Donough

8 *Enniscrone*: (*Irish* Inis Crabhann, the promontory of Crone) a seaside village in the west of Co. Sligo, five miles from Ballina. The poet's sister Lily Yeats was born there, at Moyle Lodge, where the Yeats family were staying on holiday.

[DO NOT MAKE A GREAT KEENING]   **A44**

This song is from the play *Cathleen ni Houlihan* (first published in 1902) and   *CPl* 82
included in subsequent editions of the play, which was first performed on 2 April
1902 in St. Teresa's Hall, Dublin with Maud Gonne as Cathleen. See note on [I
am come to cry with you, woman] (*PNE* A43).

1 *keening*: Irish form of mourning over the dead, raising the Keen (*Irish*
caoine); cf. 'The Ballad of Father O'Hart' (*PNE* 14).

15 *white-scarfed*: this can refer to white-robed priests at funerals, or else, as
suggested in *McG* 96, to young men in rural Ireland who wear white bands or
scarves 'in one shoulder across the breast and tied under the other arm with a
black ribbon, at funerals, usually those of young men and tragic deaths'.

6 *wakes*: watchings over the body, gatherings in honour of the dead

[THEY SHALL BE REMEMBERED FOR EVER]   **A45**

This song is from the play *Cathleen ni Houlihan* (first published in 1902) and   *CPl* 86
included in subsequent editions of the play, which was first performed on 2 April
1902 in St Teresa's Hall, Dublin, with Maud Gonne as Cathleen. See note on [I
am come to cry with you, Woman] (*PNE* A43).

A46 [O BIDDY DONAHOE]

VPl 1116   This is a song from the play *Where there is Nothing*, first published in 1902; this song is omitted from the 1903 printings.

A47 [THE SPOUSE OF NAOISE, ERIN'S WOE]

VPl 247   This is a song from the play *The Pot of Broth*, first published in *The Gael*, 1903, and included in subsequent editions of *The Hour Glass and other Plays* (1904); *The Hour Glass, Cathleen ni Houlihan, The Pot of Broth* (1904); and then, separately as *The Pot of Broth* (1905; 1911). See variant readings in *VPl*. This is not included in the version in *CPl*. The source is the blind Irish poet William Dall O'Heffernan's poem 'Eire's maid is she', the second stanza:

> The spouse of Naisi, Erin's woe
> The dame that laid proud Ilium low,
> Their charms would fade, their fame would flee
> Match'd with my fair *Beih Eirionn I*!

This version is from Edward Walsh, *Reliques of Irish Jacobite Poetry* (2nd edn 1866) 78-81.

1   *Naoise*: see note on 'Under the Moon' (*PNE* 86)

Erin: see note on 'To the Rose upon the Rood of Time' (*PNE* 17)

Helen: see note on 'A Woman Homer Sung' (*PNE* 92)

Venus: goddess of love and beauty in Roman mythology (Greek name Aphrodite)

4   *Mo ghradh*: (*Irish*), my love; *mo stor*: (*Irish*), my treasure; *mo chree*: mo chroí (*Irish*), my heart

8   *Granuaile*: Grania or Grace O'Málley (*c*. 1530–*c*. 1500), an Irish pirate queen who lived in several castles in the west of Ireland and visited Queen Elizabeth in London. Her name is used to personify Ireland in some Jacobite poetry.

A48 THERE'S BROTH IN THE POT FOR YOU, OLD MAN

CPl 93   This song is from the play *The Pot of Broth*, first published in *The Gael*, 1903, and included in subsequent editions: *The Hour Glass and Other Plays* (1904); *The Hour Glass, Cathleen ni Houlihan, The Pot of Broth* (1904); then separately as *The Pot of Broth* (1905; 1911). See variant readings in *VPl*. Yeats wrote in *The Hour Glass, Cathleen ni Houlihan, The Pot of Broth* (1904) that the words and the air of 'There's broth in the Pot' were 'taken down from an old woman known as Cracked Mary (the original of 'Crazy Jane'), who wanders about the plain of Aidhne, and who sometimes sees unearthly riders on white horses coming through stony fields to her hovel door at night time.'

5 *Jack the Journeyman*: see note on 'Crazy Jane and the Bishop' (*PNE* 268). As Lady Gregory used the name and both she and Yeats listened to Cracked Mary with interest and amusement it is possible that the name 'Jack the Journeyman' (used also in Crazy Jane and the Bishop) came from Cracked Mary. See note on *Words for Music Perhaps*. Richard J. Finneran, *Editing Yeats's Poems* (1984) suggests that 'Cracked Mary must have been familiar with' *Ancient and Modern Scottish Songs, Heroic Ballads, Etc* (1776), which includes 'I wish that you were dead, Goodman' (II, 207-08); he quotes the text:

> *I wish that you were dead, Goodman,*
> *And a green sod on your head, goodman,*
> *That I might ware my widowhood,*
> *Upon a ranting highlandman.*

> There's sax eggs in the pan, goodman,
> There's sax eggs in the pan, goodman,
> There's ane to you, and twa to me,
> And three to our JOHN HIGHLANDMAN,
> *I wish*, &c.

> There's beef into the pat, goodman,
> There's beef into the pat, goodman,
> The banes for you, and the brew for me,
> And the beef for our JOHN HIGHLANDMAN.
> *I wish*, &c.

> There's sax horse in the stable, goodman,
> There's sax horse in the stable, goodman,
> There's ane to you, and twa to me,
> And three to our JOHN HIGHLANDMAN.
> *I wish*, & c.

> There's sax ky in the byre, goodman,
> There's sax ky in the byre, goodman,
> There's nane o' them yours, but there's twa of them mine,
> And the lave is our JOHN HIGHLANDMAN'S
> *I wish*, &c.

[THERE'S NOBODY'LL CALL OUT FOR HIM]   A49

This song is from the play *The King's Threshold* first published in 1904 and first *CPl 120* performed in the Molesworth Hall, Dublin, on 7 October 1903 by the Irish National Theatre Society. The song was included in subsequent editions of the play. The five speeches according to the sd 'should be spoken in a rhythmical chant, or should rise into song'. They probably reflect Irish belief in the power of satire and the curse.

A50   [THE FOUR RIVERS THAT RUN THERE]

CPl 136   This song is from the play *The King's Threshold*; see note above on [There's nobody will call out for him] (*PNE* A49)

6   All the fowls of the air: possibly an echo of Cock Robin's

> All the birds of the air
> Fell a-sighing and a sobbing

or more likely, of Genesis 1, 26, 'the fowl of the air' (since Fedelm's next speech refers to 'Adam's paradise').

A51   ['WHY IS IT', QUEEN EDAIN SAID]

CPl 177   This is a song from the play *Deirdre*, which was first published under the title 'Queen Edaine', *McClure's Magazine*, September 1905. It was reprinted with an additional verse in *The Shanachie*, I, Spring 1966 where it was described by Yeats as:

> A Chorus from an unfinished play called 'The House of Usnach'. Deirdre is about to enter the house of the Red Branch. Three women, wandering musicians, sing these lines.   (*VE* 771)

In *Poems 1899-1905* (1906) it appeared under the title 'The Entrance of Deirdre/A Lyric Chorus' and here Yeats commented

> Two women are awaiting the entrance of Deirdre into the House of the Red Branch. They hear her coming and begin to sing. She comes into the house at the end of the second verse, and the women seeing her standing by Naoise and shrinking back from the house, not understanding that she is afraid of what is to come, think that it is love that has made her linger thus.   (*VE* 771-2)

It is included in *PW* I under the title 'Chorus for a Play'; and in *PW* I there is yet another explanation:

> It is sung at the entrance of Deirdre into the House of the Red Branch by certain wandering musicians. She comes to the threshold at the end of the second verse, and they, seeing her whispering to Naoise who is beside her, think that she is busy, with her love, not knowing that she is hesitating in fear.   (*VPl* 772)

It is included in *Poems: second series* (1906) under the title 'Songs from Deirdre', in *Deirdre* (1907) and in subsequent editions of the play. The play was first performed on 24 November 1906 at the Abbey Theatre, Dublin.

1   *Edain*: see notes on *WO* (*PNE* 375), on *Baile and Aillinn* (*PNE* 377), and on 'The Harp of Aengus' (*PNE* 379).

[COME RIDE AND RIDE TO THE GARDEN]   A52

This poem was, according to Lady Gregory (*Seven Short Plays* (1909) 201),   TS
owed to W. B. Yeats; it was included in her play *The˜ Travelling Man*, first
published in *The Shanachie*, Spring 1906

10   *Archangel Axel*: source not yet known. *PNE* draws attention to the
Confession of St Patrick, where the Angel Victor appears and urges him to go to
Ireland and suggests that Yeats may have found the reference in Douglas Hyde's
A Literary History of Ireland (1879) 143. The passage describes Patrick's
reaching his parents' home and their begging him to remain with them:

> But the angel Victor came in the guise of a man from Ireland, and gave him a
> letter, in which the voice of the Irish called him away, and the voices of those
> who dwell near the wood of Focluth called him to walk amongst them, and the
> spirit of God, too, urged him to return.

Hyde is here drawing upon the *Book of Armagh* (Bollandist edition), Folio 23,
66. See also *Liber Armandus The Book of Armagh*, ed. John Gwynn (1913) 39–
45.

[MAY THIS FIRE HAVE DRIVEN OUT]   A53

This is a song from the play *On Baile's Strand*. It was first published in *The*   CPl 262
Shanachie, Spring 1906, under the title 'Against Witchcraft'. It was first
included in the play in the edition of 1906 in *Poems 1899–1905* (1906), in *CW* II
and in subsequent editions. The play was first performed on 27 December 1904
by the Irish National Theatre Society.

2   *Shape-Changers*: a reference to the frequent changes of shape that occur in
Gaelic mythology. Cf. *The Shadowy Waters* (*PNE* 380) lines 566–7, where the
shape-changers are identified with 'the Ever-laughing Ones/The Immortal
Mockers'. See also *The Green Helmet* (*CPl* 226) line 4. D. E. S. Maxwell, 'The
Shape-Changers', *Yeats, Sligo and Ireland* (ed. Jeffares, 1976), 153–169,
discusses general implications of the idea.

23   *Emain's greatness*: Emain Macha, the seat of Conor MacNessa, King of
Ulster. See note on 'The Madness of King Goll' (*PNE* 9). Its greatest glory was in
the period of the Red Branch knights, and the heroic age in Ireland ends with the
destruction of Emain Macha by the Three Collas (*McG* 45–6).

[CUCHULAIN HAS KILLED KINGS]   A54

This is a song from the play *On Baile's Strand*; it was first published in the edition   CPl 254
of 1906, then in *Poems 1899–1905* (1906) and included in subsequent editions.

1   *Cuchulain*: see note on 'To the Rose upon the Rood of Time' (*PNE* 17) and
note on 'Cuchulain's Fight with the Sea' (*PNE* 19).

471

Banachas and Bonachas: T. P. Cross, *Motif Index of Early Irish Literature* (1952) 251, describes them as white-faced and puck-faced goblins respectively. *PNE* cites P. W. Joyce, *A Social History of Ireland* (1903), I, 269–70, who explains geniti-glinni as female apparitions of the valley, Bocanachs as male goblins, Bananachs as female. In some versions they are spelt Bananachs and Bocanachs or Bonochas, *VPl* 527. Yeats's source was probably Aubrey De Vere, *The Foray of Queen Meave* (1882) 178:

> While all along the circles of their shields,
> And all adown their swords, viewless for speed
> Ran, mad with rage, the demons of dark moors,
> And war-sprites of the valleys, Bocanachs
> And Banachas whose scream, so keen its edge
> Might shear the centuried forest as the scythe
> Shears meadow grass.

7   *Fomor*: See note on 'The Madness of King Goll' (*PNE* 9)

A55   [LOVE IS AN IMMODERATE THING]

CPl 191   This is a song in the play *Deirdre*, first published in 1907 and included in subsequent editions of the play. It was also included as a separate item, 'Songs from Deirdre/II', in *Poems: Second Series* (1909).

A56   [THEY ARE GONE, THEY ARE GONE, THE PROUD MAY LIE BY THE PROUD]

CPl 201   This is a song from the play *Deirdre* (first published in 1907) and included in subsequent editions of the play. It was also included as a separate item as 'Songs from Deirdre/III', in *Poems: Second Series* (1909).

A57   [I PUT UNDER THE POWER OF MY PRAYER]

CPl 344   This is a song from the play *The Unicorn from the Stars* (first published in 1908) and included in subsequent editions of the play. *The Unicorn from the Stars* is a reworking of an earlier play *Where There is Nothing*, written by Yeats, Lady Gregory and Douglas Hyde 'in a fortnight' as Yeats told the publisher A. H. Bullen, 'to keep George Moore from stealing the plot' (*L* 503). The earlier play was first published as a supplement to the *United Irishman*, 1 November 1902, and performed at the Royal Court Theatre, London, on 26 June 1904. Yeats withdrew it from circulation. It is reprinted in *VPl*. See Yeats's note to *PPV*. The first performance of *The Unicorn from the Stars* was given at the Abbey Theatre, Dublin, on 23 November 1907.

3–6   *Rafael ... Sathiel ... Hamiel ... Cassiel*: the angels of Wednesday,

Thursday, Friday and Saturday respectively. See *The Key of Solomon the King*, ed. S. Liddell MacGregor Mathers (1888), 8. For Mathers see note on 'All Souls' Night' (*PNE* 239).

[O COME ALL YE AIRY BACHELORS] A58

This is a song from the play *The Unicorn from the Stars* (first published in 1908) *CPl 354* and included in subsequent editions of the play

1 *O come all ye . . .*: the orthodox beginning to particular kinds of ballads and songs. The line echoes the opening of 'The Airy Bachelor': 'Come all you airy bachelors, a warning take by me'. Richard J. Finneran, *Editing Yeats's Poems* (1983), suggests that Yeats may have read it in the *Journal of the Irish Folk Song Society*, 2, 1–2 (1905), 33.

12 *Van Diemen's land*: Tasmania, the island south of Australia, named after Anton Van Diemen (1593–1645), and discovered by Abel Tasman (1603–*c*. 1659) the Dutch navigator who was sent in quest of the 'Great South Land' by Van Diemen, governor-general of Batavia. Much of Australia, including Tasmania, was used by Britain as a convict colony in the late eighteenth and early nineteenth centuries. The poem is probably based on the ballad 'Van Diemen's Land' or 'The Gallant Poachers'. Richard J. Finneran, *Editing Yeats's Poems* (1983) gives the following text, from the *Journal of the Folk-song Society*, I, 4 (1902) 142–3:

> Come all you gallant poachers, that ramble free from care,
> That walk out of a moon-light night with your dog, your gun, and snare;
> Where the lofty hare and pheasant you have at your command,
> Not thinking that your last career is on Van Diemen's Land.

> There was poor Tom Brown from Nottingham, Jack Williams and poor Joe
> Were three as daring poachers as the country well does know;
> At night they were trapannèd by the keeper's hideous hand,
> And for fourteen years transported were unto Van Diemen's Land.

> Oh! when we sailed from England we landed at the bay,
> We had rotten straw for bedding, we dared not to say nay;
> Our cots were fenced with fire, we slumber where we can,
> To drive away the wolves and tigers upon Van Diemen's Land.

> Oh! when that we were landed, upon that fatal shore,
> The planters they came flocking round full twenty score or more;
> They ranked us up like horses, and sold us out of hand,
> They yoked us to the plough, my boys, to plough Van Diemen's Land.

> There was one girl from England, Susan Summers was her name,
> For fourteen years transported was, we all well knew the same;
> Our planter bought her freedom, and he married her out of hand,
> Good usage then she gave to us, upon Van Diemen's Land.

Often, when I am slumbering, I have a pleasant dream,
With my sweet girl I am sitting, down by some purling stream,
Through England I am roaming, with her at my command,
Then waken, broken-hearted, upon Van Diemen's Land.

God bless our wives and families, likewise that happy shore,
That isle of sweet contentment, which we shall see no more;
As for our wretched females, see them we seldom can,
There are twenty to one woman upon Van Diemen's Land.

Come, all you gallant poachers, give ear unto my song,
It is a bit of good advice, although it is not long:
Lay by your dog and snare; to you I do speak plain,
If you knew the hardship we endure you ne'er would poach again.

A59   [O, JOHNNY GIBBONS, MY FIVE HUNDRED HEALTHS TO YOU]

CPl 355   This is a song from the play *The Unicorn from the Stars* (first published in 1908) and included in subsequent editions of the play. The poem is based upon a poem ascribed to Antony Raftery (*c.* 1784–1835) entitled 'The Whiteboys'. The fourth stanza runs:

O Johnny Gibbons, my five hundred farewells to you,
You are long from me away in Germany;
It was your heart, without deceitfulness, that was ever (given) to joyousness,
And now on this hill, above, we are weak of help.
It is told us from the mouth of the author
That the sloop whose crew was not baptized shall fire at us,
And unless you come for a relief to us in the time of hardship
We are a great pity, beneath the tops of valleys

The Whiteboys, an oath-bound secret society, first rose in 1761: they wore white shirts over their coats when on their nightly operations against local landlords, mainly in Cork, Waterford, Limerick and Tipperary. They levelled fences at night and were known also as levellers; after some time they began to commit cruel outrages.

1   *Johnny Gibbons*: PNE draws attention to Douglas Hyde's comments, *Songs Ascribed to Raftery* (1903) 197, n. 2, that Johnny Gibbons was a well-known outlaw living about the time of the 1798 Rebellion. See *CPl* 335, *l.* 217, 'Sure that man could not be Johnny Gibbons that was outlawed!'

A60   [O, THE LION SHALL LOSE HIS STRENGTH]

CPl 364   This is a song from the play *The Unicorn from the Stars* (first published in 1908) and included in subsequent editions of the play. It is based on an Irish poem translated by Lady Gregory. See her 'Boer Ballads in Ireland', *Poets and Dreamers* (1974 edn) 72:

When the lion shall lose its strength,
    And the bracket thistle begin to pine,
The Harp shall sound sweet, sweet, at length,
    Between the eight and the nine.

See also versions by Douglas Hyde in *Songs Ascribed to Raftery* (1903) 271 and
The Religious Songs of Connacht (1906) I, 261.

1   *lion*: symbol of England

2   *bracket-thistle*: symbol of Scotland. The 1908 editions give 'braket thistle';
CW III and *PPV* give 'braket-thistle'. Brake is fern or bracken.

3   *harp*: symbol of Ireland

[THREE THAT ARE WATCHING MY TIME TO RUN]   A61

This is a song from the play *The Unicorn from the Stars* (first published 1908)   *CPl 370*
included in subsequent editions of the play. It derives from 'The Worms, the
Children and the Devil' included in Douglas Hyde, *Religious Songs of Connacht*,
I, 51. Two versions of the first stanza of the poem are given by Hyde:

> Three there watching for my death
> Although they are even with me (?)
> Alas that they be not hanged with a Gad,
> The Devil, the children and the worm

and

> There be three – my heart, it saith –
> Wish the death of me infirm,
> Would that they were hanged on a tree,
> All three, Children, Devil, Worm.

[MY MAN IS THE BEST]   A62

This is a song from the play *The Golden Helmet* (1908). *The Golden Helmet* was   *VPl 444*
written in prose; the revised version in verse, *The Green Helmet* (1910), does not
include the song. For a study of the two versions see S. B. Bushrui, *YVP. The
Golden Helmet* was produced at the Abbey Theatre, Dublin on 19 March 1908,
The Green Helmet on 10 February 1910. The play is founded, Yeats
commented, upon 'an old Irish story, *The Feast of Bricriu*, given in Lady
Gregory's *Cuchulain of Muirthemne*' and is meant as an introduction to *On
Baile's Strand* (*CW* IV). The speakers are the wife of Laoghaire the victorious, the
wife of Conall Cearnach, and Emer, the wife of Cuchulain, and the play is built
upon a dispute between these three heroes of the Red Branch or Ulster cycle of

tales. In the play Emer is the only wife to sing, which gives her greater prominence (as befits Cuchulain's mate). The episode in *The feast of Bricriu* is usually known as 'The Word-War of the Women of Ulster'.

A63 [THE FRIENDS THAT HAVE IT I DO WRONG]

VE 778 This poem was published in *CW* II as *Preliminary Poem*.

3   *remake a song*: a reference to Yeats's habit of rewriting his poems, often altering them completely in the process. See G. D. P. Allt, 'Yeats and the revision of his early verse', *Hermathena, lxiv,* November 1944, and A. N. Jeffares, 'W. B. Yeats and his methods of writing verse', *The Nineteenth Century*, March 1946. See also note on 'rewording', *l.* 39 of 'The Song of the Happy Shepherd' (*PNE* 1)

4   *myself that I remake*: cf. 'An Acre of Grass' (*PNE* 332): 'Grant me an old man's frenzy,/ Myself must I remake . . .'.

A64 [I WAS GOING THE ROAD ONE DAY]

VPl 779 This is a song from the play *The Hour-Glass*. The first four lines were included in the play *The Hour-Glass*, in *The Unicorn from the Stars and Other Plays* (1908) and in *CW* IV. The play was first published in prose version in *The North American Review*, September 1903; this early version was first performed at the Molesworth Hall, Dublin on 14 March 1903. There was a drastic revision in 1912 and a 'new version' in prose and verse was performed at the Abbey Theatre, Dublin on 21 November 1912; this version was published by the English actor and stage designer Gordon Craig (1872-1966) in his magazine *The Mask* (Florence) April 1913, and in *The Hour-Glass* (1914). There was a revised text in *RPP*, one with minor revisions in *PPV*, substantially that given in *CP2*. For these revisions see S. B. Bushrui, 'The Hour-Glass: Yeats's Revisions 1903-1922', *YCE*. In an appendix to *CW* IV Yeats prefaced the first three stanzas with the remark that 'One sometimes has need of more lines of the little song, and I have put into English rhyme three of the many verses of a Gaelic ballad' (*VPl* 778). Lines 1-4 were not included after *CW* IV, but the three stanzas were included in Yeats's note to *PPV* with a more detailed preface: 'One sometimes has need of a few words for the pupils to sing at their first or second entrance.' *PNE* adds two stanzas. The source of the poem was a translation of an Irish folk song by Lady Gregory, 'The Noble Enchanter', *The Irish Homestead*, December 1901. The play was founded upon a story, 'The Priest's Soul', recorded by Lady Wilde, *Ancient Legends of Ireland* (1887) I, 60-67, which is reproduced in *CW* IV. Lady Gregory's translation runs as follows:

> I was going the road one fine day,
>   O, the brown and the yellow ale!
> And I met with a man that was no right man,
>   O, love of my heart.

He asked was the young woman with me my daughter, and I said she was my married wife.

He asked would I lend her for an hour or a day. 'Oh, I would not do that, but I would like to do what is fair. Let you take the upper path and I will go by the road, and whoever she will follow, let him belong to her forever.'

He took the upper path and I took the road, and she followed after him, he being in his youth.

She stayed walking there the length of three quarters, and she came home after, Mary without shame.

She asked me how was I in my health. 'As is good with my friends and bad with my enemies. And what would you do if I would die from you?' 'I would put a coffin of yellow gold on you.'

When myself heard those fine words, I lay down and died there. And there were two that went to the woods for timber, and they brought back a half board of holly and a half board of alder.

They put me into the boarded coffin, and four yards of the ugliest sack about me, and they lifted me up on their shoulders. 'Throw him now into the best hole in the street.'

'Oh, wait, wait, lay me down, till I tell you a little story about women; a little story today and a little story tomorrow, and a little story every day of the quarter.'

> And but that my own little mother was a woman,
> O, the brown and the yellow ale!
> I would tell you another little story about women,
> O, love of my heart!

[ACCURSED WHO BRINGS TO LIGHT OF DAY]　　　　　　　A65

This poem was published in *CW* VIII.　　　　　　　*VE 779*

[NOTHING THAT HE HAS DONE]　　　　　　　A66

This is a song from the play *The Green Helmet*, first published in the Abbey *CPl 239* theatre programme 10 February 1910, then in *The Green Helmet and Other Poems* (1910) and in subsequent editions of the play. The play was performed on 10 February 1910; the prose version *The Golden Helmet* on 19 March 1908: both productions were at the Abbey Theatre, Dublin. The poem is sung by Emer, Cuchulain's wife. Cf. [My man is the best] (*CPl* A62) and note on it. In *The Green Helmet* only Emer sings, not the other two wives.

[LAEGAIRE IS BEST]　　　　　　　A67

This is a song from *The Green Helmet*, first published in *The Green Helmet and* *CPl 233* *Other Poems* (1910) and included in subsequent editions of the play. It is sung by Laegaire.

1   *Laegaire*: see note on Laegaire on [My man is the best] (*PNE* A62)

4   *cat-heads*: Cf. Cairbre Cathead in *Diarmuid and Grania* (*VPl* 1208) 'who called the folk together and broke their [the forefathers of the Fianna] power for two hundred years.'

A68   [WHO STOLE YOUR WITS AWAY]

CPl 310   This is a song from *The Hour-Glass*; first published in *The Mask* (Florence), April 1913, it is included in subsequent editions of the play.

A69   [I HEAR THE WIND A-BLOW]

CPl 324   This is a song from the play *The Hour-Glass*, first published in *The Mask* (Florence), April 1913 and included in subsequent editions of the play

A70   [WERE I BUT CRAZY FOR LOVE'S SAKE]

CPl 8   This is a song from the play *The Countess Cathleen* (first published in 1913) and included in subsequent editions of the play; it first appeared in *P* (1895) and is sung by Aleel the poet. See M. J. Sidnell', 'Yeats's First Work for the Stage', *YCE*, 167ff.

A71   [THE MAN THAT I PRAISE]

CPl 219   This is the final song from the play *At the Hawk's Well* (first published 1917) and included in subsequent editions of the play. It is sung by the Three Musicians.

A72   [I CALL TO THE EYE OF THE MIND]

CPl 208   This is a song from the play *At the Hawk's Well* (first published 1917) and included in subsequent editions of the play. It is sung at the opening of the play by the Three Musicians.

A73   [THE BOUGHS OF THE HAZEL SHAKE]

CPl 209   This is a song from the play *At the Hawk's Well* (first published 1917) and included in subsequent editions of the play.

[O GOD, PROTECT ME] A74

This is a song from the play *At the Hawk's Well* (first published 1917) and *CPl 217* included in subsequent editions of the play. It is sung by the first Musician.

[HE HAS LOST WHAT MAY NOT BE FOUND] A75

This is a song from the play *At the Hawk's Well* (first published 1917) and *CPl 217* included in subsequent editions of the play. It is sung by the Three Musicians.

[COME TO ME, HUMAN FACES] A76

This is a song from the play *At the Hawk's Well* (first published 1917) and *CPl 219* included in subsequent editions of the play. It is sung by the Three Musicians. The final lyric is a summing up, in equivocal terms, of the equivocal themes of the play. Wilson (*YI* 59), supporting his view with the ending of the earliest draft:

> *Accursed the life of man, what he hopes for never comes.*
> *Between passion and emptiness, what he hopes for never comes.*

sees it in terms of 'consummate spiritual disillusion', a conclusion which in Nathan's view (*TD* 280) 'denies, in the face of reams of evidence, that Yeats cared anything about the subject of heroism'; Rajan (*YCI* 97), as the inevitability of failure, though he qualifies this view by suggesting that those who seek fulfilment will always seem fools by certain standards. Vendler (*YV* 215) comments: 'one finds one's own species of immortality at the well and tree. For Cuchulain it is battle and not the water, but he had to come to the well to find this out. The world counts praise of well and tree idiocy, and in those terms the last lyric criticizes Cuchulain – but such a criticism is actually praise.' She therefore disagrees with Bjersby's view (*ICL* 89) since it takes no account of Cuchulain's courage. For Peter Ure (*YTP* 70), it is precisely that courage 'without which there can be no heroic desire, but which is made the means to thwart it', that is the unifying theme of the play. Bloom (*Y* 296-7) also stresses the heroism, pointing out that Cuchulain shows no regret at the loss of his quest, only exultation at 'receiving his life's role, of incarnating the hero', in his true encounter, which is with Aoife – a view supported by Moore (*MLD* 204), who points out that 'Culchulain is in full possession of his *arete*. He goes out to face these supernatural women of the hills with joyous abandon, "*no longer as if in a dream*", but fully conscious of his capacity to live up to the heroic part his successful initiation has proved that destiny has assigned him'.

If the last two stanzas of the lyric are taken as an objective comment by a chorus that 'has no part in the action' ('Certain Noble Plays of Japan', *E & I* 226), and thus represents ordinary life, regarding any form of commitment, heroic or otherwise, as a kind of idiocy or folly, then their praise is highly ambiguous, issuing as it does from an empty well and a leafless tree. Moore (*MLD* 204) agrees, and adds a final comment: 'The heroes of the earlier plays were exhibited in all their tragic glamour. In this play Yeats has done an extremely difficult thing: he has shown the young Cuchulain at the start of his career, impulsive and valiant, convincingly innocent of any self-doubt; he has given us a devastating picture of the horrors of the heroic vocation; he has been ironic at the expense of both heroism and non-heroism, and at the same time he has managed to convey a weird sense of tranquil beauty.'

5   *unmoistened eyes*: cf. lines 16–18 (*CPl* 216):

> *She has felt your gaze and turned her eyes on us;*
> *I cannot bear her eyes, they are not of this world,*
> *Nor moist, nor faltering; they are no girl's eyes.*

6   *folly alone*: cf. lines 24 ff (*CPl* 212):

> *O, folly of youth,*
> *Why should that hollow place fill up for you,*
> *That will not fill for me?*

a mouthful of air: the phrase was used by Yeats to describe faeries, 'nations of gay creatures, having no souls; nothing in their bright bodies but a mouthful of sweet air' ('Tales from the Twilight', *SO* (1 March 1890)). See *IY* 325. The phrase was used in 'Ganconagh's' novel *John Sherman* (1891): for 'what have we in this life but a mouthful of air' (see *PYP* 72) and in this lyric as well as in the play *The King of the Great Clock Tower*, 'O, what is life but a mouthful of air?' (*CPl* 640). See Jeffares and Knowland, *A Commentary on the Collected Plays of W. B. Yeats* (1975) 263.

A77   [WHY DOES MY HEART BEAT SO]

CPl 433   This is a song from the play *The Dreaming of the Bones* (first published 1919) and included in subsequent editions of the play. It was published under the title 'Why does my Heart beat so?' in *Selected Poems* (1929). The stage direction reads: '*First Musician (or all three Musicians, singing)*'

14–16   *Like wine . . . cup of jade*: for a possible source of this image, see Yeats's account of *Nishikigi* (*PNE* 309). This is one of the binding or group metaphors of the play. For Nathan it implies sexual fulfilment or sexual power (*TD* 211), which 'is augmented by the repeated image of the red cock crowing in the potent and fulfilling month of March.' Clark (*YTDR* 52) sees it as a rather arbitrary sign for the coming of the spirits that 'fill waste mountains with the invisible tumult/Of the fantastic conscience', adducing the association of wine and the spirits of the dead in 'All Souls Night' (*PNE* 239):

> And it is All Soul's Night,
> And two long glasses brimmed with muscatel
> Bubble upon the table. A ghost may come;
> For it is a ghost's right,

His element is so fine
Being sharpened by his death,
To drink from the wine-breath
While our gross palates drink from the whole wine.

and 'A Drunken Man's Praise of Sobriety' (*PNE* 347):

A drunkard is a dead man,
And all dead men are drunk.

He suggests, however, that the filling of the cup is analogous to the direction the action takes as the characters climb to the summit of the mountain and to its climax.

[WHY SHOULD THE HEART TAKE FRIGHT]   A78

This is a song from the play *The Dreaming of the Bones* (first published 1919)   *CPl* 437
and included in subsequent editions of the play. It was published under the title, 'Why should the Heart take Fright?' in *Selected Poems* (1929). It is sung by the first musician. The 'cat-headed bird' which is mentioned between stanzas two and three in the play Wilson (*YI* 230–1) associates with the 'man-headed birds of *The Shadowy Waters*' which are the spirits of the dead and 'with many such apparitions in Celtic folk-lore and heroic myth'. The function of the image is 'purely atmospheric', to point the atmosphere of dark expectancy against which [the] action is played out'. See note on 'The Shadowy Waters' (*PNE* 380).

5 *Red bird of March:* for Wilson, *YI* 234–40, the red March cock is a 'clinching symbol, a device which will weld together aesthetically . . . Yeats's two themes of politics and ghosts'. He interprets it on several planes: its 'central function is to establish a simple day-night antithesis'; it is an 'emblem of consciousness and sanity' and also, being a cock of the springtime, 'a more powerful defence against the supernatural than any other'; it is also a reincarnation emblem; and 'the red symbolic bird of Mars, regent of war and in Yeats's system . . . of the first bloody phases of a new historical cycle. We know from many poems and plays that Yeats expected the "cycle of freedom" to begin with world-wide wars – involving among other things the liberation of Ireland – at a full moon in March, the month of Mars . . . the Easter Rising of 1916 came almost exactly at this time.' It is finally 'the symbol of heroic martial endeavour and of that universal anarchy that he thought would usher in the collapse of the present "objective" age; which the Dublin rebellion seemed to him at this time to presage.'

Clark (*YTDR* 56) substantially agrees, suggesting that dawn defeats the ghosts and releases the Young Man. 'The subjectivity of the ghosts has been presented through the darkness, the calls of night birds, the binding of clouds, the wind . . . blowing out the lantern, the dim path to the ruined abbey and on up to the ridge where the grave of the lovers is. All these are symbols of the dizzy dreams that spring from the dry bones of the dead, the consciousness of tragic guilt in the past.'

On the other hand, the Young Man's objectivity is presented 'through the dawn and sunlight, the crowing of the cocks and the panorama of the landscape ruined by civil war.'

Vendler (*YV* 186 ff), in spite of the overt political references in the play, both historical and contemporary, sees it in terms of 'mental travel' – an occasion in which the mind cannot cast out remorse for some reason or other, cannot come to terms with the events in its own memory – and interprets these lines as 'an impatient protest against the night and the powers that inhabit it, those powers that make us remember, relive and consider the past in all its mixed emotions. The musician cries out for a discarding of the past (as March always symbolizes a new phase) and urges the morning to break and dispel the ghosts.'

A79   [AT THE GREY ROUND OF THE HILL]

CPl 444   This is a song from the play *The Dreaming of the Bones* (first published 1919) and included in subsequent editions of the play. It was published under the title 'At the Grey Round of the Hill' in *Selected Poems* (1929). It is sung by the Musicians and concludes the play.

4   *Clare-Galway*: the townland of the plain (*Irish* Baile an Chlair), a townland in Co. Galway. See *McG* 31.

23   *Cat-headed bird*: see note on [Why should the heart take fright] (*PNE* A78).

26   *March birds*: cocks, see note on [Why should the heart take fright] (*PNE* A78).

A80   [A WOMAN'S BEAUTY IS LIKE A WHITE FRAIL BIRD]

CPl 281   This is a song from the play *The Only Jealousy of Emer* (first published 1919) and included in subsequent editions of the play. It was published under the title 'A Woman's Beauty is like a White Frail Bird' in *Selected Poems* (1929).

9   *toils of measurement*: cf. 'the Statues' with 'the lineaments of a plummet-measured face' and

> Pythagoras planned it. Why did the people stare?
> His numbers, though they moved or seemed to move
> In marble or in bronze, lacked character.
> But boys and girls, pale from the imagined love
> Of solitary beds, knew what they were,
> That passion could bring character enough,
> And pressed at midnight in some public place
> Live lips upon a plummet-measured face.

12   *Archimedes*: a Greek mathematician and inventor (*c.* 287–212 BC)

15–16   *A fragile, exquisite pale shell*
        That the vast troubled waters bring: cf. 'Ancestral Houses',
'Meditations in Time of Civil War,' I (*PNE* 206):

> though now it seems
> As if some marvellous empty sea-shell flung
> Out of the obscure dark of the rich streams,
> And not a fountain, were the symbol which
> Shadows the inherited play of the rich.

The image may derive from Shelley's *The Revolt of Islam* (Canto Fourth, I):

> Upon whose floor the spangling sands were strown
> And rarest sea-shells, which the eternal flood,
> Slave to the mother of the months, had thrown
> Within the walls of that grey tower.

23   *labyrinth of the mind*: cf. 'the labyrinth of her [Maud Gonne's] days' in
'Against Unworthy Praise' (*PNE* 98); 'the labyrinth of another's being' and 'a
great labyrinth' [of Maud Gonne's personality] in 'The Tower', II (*PNE* 205), 'to
die into the labyrinth of itself' in 'The Phases of the Moon' (*PNE* 183), 'the
labyrinth that he has made/In art and politics' in 'Nineteen Hundred and
Nineteen', III (*PNE* 213) and the 'labyrinth of the wind' in the same poem, VI;
and 'the unconquerable labyrinth of the birds' in 'Blood and the Moon', II (*PNE*
243).

[WHITE SHELL, WHITE WING]   A81

This is a song from the play *The Only Jealousy of Emer* (first published 1919)   *CPl 283*
and included in subsequent editions. It is sung by the First Musician.

                                                                            A82
[WHY DOES YOUR HEART BEAT THUS]
                                                                            CPl 295

This is the song which concludes the play *The Only Jealousy of Emer* (first
published 1919) and included in subsequent editions of the play. It was published
under the title 'Why does your Heart beat thus?' in *Selected Poems* (1929).

    Comments on this final lyric can be found in Nathan (*TD* 238–40), who
argues that earlier versions of the musicians' final song seemed merely an
extension of the concern with Fand's frustration that occupied the last half of the
play:

> With Fand's role cut so that Emer's part dominates the action, the last song
> can be seen for what it was meant to be, antistrophe, so to speak, to the play's
> opening song, which was devoted to introducing the beautiful Eithne Inguba,
> comparing her to a frail sea bird, useless product of untold suffering, cast upon

the shore of human life. As Eithne Inguba, one extreme form of woman, receives the musicians' first tribute, so Fand, the other extreme, receives their last. (238)

Helen Hennessy Vendler draws on a manuscript draft (at Harvard University) of the lyric to support her interpretation, which runs:

The final lyric shows Yeats at his most maddening, and here I must differ with Wilson, with whom I agree in general on *Emer*. The first two stanzas are common ground, but in the third, and on the refrain, we part company. Before I say more, I will print the lyric as I conceive it divided into voices:

Emer to Fand:	Why does your heart beat thus?
Emer to us:	Plain to be understood,
	I have met in a man's house
	A statue of solitude,
	Moving there and walking;
	Its strange heart beating fast
	For all our talking.
Emer to Fand:	O still that heart at last,
Emer to us:	O bitter reward
	Of many a tragic tomb!
	And we though astonished are dumb
	Or give but a sigh and a word,
	A passing word.
Emer to Fand:	Although the door be shut
	And all seem well enough,
	Although wide world hold not
	A man but will give you his love
	The moment he has looked at you,
	He that has loved the best
	May turn from a statue
	His too human breast.
Fand to us:	O bitter reward
	Of many a tragic tomb!
	And we though astonished are dumb
	Or give but a sigh and a word,
	A passing word.
Emer to Fand:	What makes your heart so beat?
	What man is at your side?
Fand to Emer:	When beauty is complete
	Your own thought will have died
	And danger not be diminished;
	Dimmed at three-quarter light,
	When moon's round is finished
	The stars are out of sight.
Emer to us:	O bitter reward, etc.

This arrangement of the poem is open to charges of over-ingenuity, but so is any other reading, given the inherent difficulty of the stanzas. It will be seen that in my reading Emer taunts Fand, then Fand taunts Emer, each claiming a victory of sorts. I am led to this reading partly by earlier versions of the closing lyric. In a manuscript draft at Harvard the play ends with a song bearing only a slight resemblance to the present lyric; in it, we can clearly see that Yeats's sympathies are equally divided between Fand and Emer:

> How may that woman find
> Being born to ill luck as it seems
> And groping her way half blind
> In labyrinths of his dreams
> A little friendship and love
> (For all the delight of the chase)
> (A passionate man [*unrecoverable word*] enough)
> (When he finds her not of his race)
> (A lover his courtship done)
> (Will weary likely enough)
> (Of the alien thing he has won)
> For all its chase and its jest
> Passion soon has enough
> Of an alien thing on its breast.
>
> O bitter reward
> Of many a tragic tomb!
> And we though astonished are dumb
> Or give but a look and a word
> A passing word.
>
> And how could I dream that this wife
> Busied at her hearthstone
> And a mere part of our life
> Could speak with a gentle tongue
> And give him the hand of a friend?
> Could she not see in (his) that eye
> That (she) it must endure to the end
> Reproach of jealousy?
>
> O bitter reward
> Of many a tragic tomb!
> And we though astonished are dumb
> Or give but a look or a word
> A passing word.

The first stanza is one of commiseration for Fand for the faithlessness of earthly lovers, and in reading it we must recall that in the early version which ends with this lyric Cuchulain eventually turns on Fand with recriminations: 'That face, though fine enough, is a fool's face.' He deserts Fand for Emer: not simply plucked back, he makes a deliberate choice against the alien, in favor of the familiar. And the refrain, too, seen in this light, is sympathetic to Fand: Cuchulain's tragic tomb has brought her only a bitter reward of momentary hope eventually frustrated. But the second stanza changes the perspective: Emer's unexpected nobility of behavior touches the narrator too. Far from being a mindless drudge, Emer has revealed depths of generosity and forgiveness: but she too has won bitter rewards from Cuchulain's sojourn among the dead – the loveless continuation of her marriage, reproaches for her jealousy. In short, the bewitchment has yielded only bitter fruit in all directions, and the play ends on a stalemate.

This is, I think, the mood in which the final version ends as well. We may glance for a moment at an intermediate draft. Dissatisfied with the version I have just quoted, Yeats wrote the lyric as we now have it, substantially the same except for the closing stanza:

> What makes (her) your heart so beat?
> Some one should stay at her side
> When beauty is complete
> Her own thoughts will have died
> And danger not be diminished;
> Dimmed at three-quarter light
> When moon's round is finished
> The stars are out of sight.

It is clear that the first question is addressed to Fand, whose beating heart is mentioned in the otherworld scene. We must then account for the woman in the second line, and it seems most probable that it is Emer, who will fade into insignificance beside the full moon. In her danger of extinction she needs a protector, a companion, a husband; powerless to help herself (because 'her own thoughts will have died') she should not be left alone. Fand, though to be pitied perhaps, is an inhuman creature hardly in need of a guardian or comforter.

We may now return to the final version of the lyric. The speaker of the first manuscript version is clearly a spectator whom for convenience we may call Yeats. The second version is less clearly objective, lacking as it does the reflective tone ('And how could I dream,' etc.) of the first. By the time we arrive at the final version, I am not sure whether any objective speaker is intended. The last stanza seems to be so clearly a dialogue of two warring positions that I am inclined to see the entire lyric in that way, but I may be mistaken.

To recapitulate: a speaker, sharing Emer's view, asks of Fand, 'Why does your heart beat thus?' implying that Fand's heartbeat is somehow strange or excited, being so close to the otherworld of death. Then the speaker explains the question by describing the unwonted appearance of 'a statue of solitude', as Fand is described, in Cuchulain's house. Emer's fear of the Sidhe is reflected in the speaker's language, and since Cuchulain's time among the Sidhe is a tragic death in Emer's eyes, the refrain embodies her reaction to the bitter reward of her renunciation – a loveless life. The impotence in the refrain echoes Emer's earlier speech of frustration, in which she says that after men are bewitched by the Sidhe their wives cannot penetrate their abstraction:

> Our men awake in ignorance of it all,
> But when we take them in our arms at night
> We cannot break their solitude.

'And we though astonished are dumb' – the reaction is Emer's.

In the second stanza, Emer momentarily asserts her victory over the 'statue of solitude'; though Fand may have supreme beauty, and can lure whom she will, still men may find themselves too human to be permanently happy with a Woman of the Sidhe. This is not true, and Emer knows it: Cuchulain did not return of his own accord – he was plucked away. But it is the perennial human hope, and it is Emer's dramatic function to voice the claims of human attachment. Her refrain, however, once again repeated, immediately negates her vaunted power. Fand replies victoriously in the third stanza, comparing humanly beautiful women like Emer and Eithne to stars which vanish in the light of a full moon. Cuchulain has no choice, she says: all human attraction is eclipsed when the Muse displays her sovereignty. Though human beauty may have temporary victories, in reality these are ephemeral, and the danger of losing Cuchulain to the otherworld is not diminished by this temporary setback. The hapless human residue doomed to extinction at Phase 15 ('your own thought will have died', says Fand) can only look on and sigh, murmuring perhaps a protest which is unheard and vanishes as soon as it is uttered. Officially, Emer has Cuchulain back; officially, Eithne has his love; but we notice that Yeats has not given Cuchulain the drink of forgetfulness mentioned in the source. His Cuchulain will not forget the Woman of the Sidhe. (*YV* 230-4).

Harold Bloom remarks (*Y* 298-306) that the play ends with a difficult song that expresses Fand's bitter grief and Yeats's acute sense of his vision's limitation:

Fand, the woman of the Sidhe, is the 'statue of solitude,/Moving there and walking,' a phantom with a beating heart, like the Christ of *The Resurrection*. That heart cannot be stilled at last, despite the bitter reward it has received, which is the loss of Cuchulain. For the Muse's lovers are faithless: 'He that has loved the best/May turn from a statue/His too human breast.' Cuchulain too was human, all too human; the forerunner is not always a Zarathustra. We are asked to attend to the suffering of the bereft Muse, and while it is difficult to feel sympathy for an occult grief, Yeats is unique enough among the poets almost to compel it in us. Even the Sidhe may be betrayed; the Belle Dame wither, in spite of her beauty, on the cold hill's side. (*Y* 305-6)

[MOTIONLESS UNDER THE MOON-BEAM]   A83

This is a song from the play *Calvary* (first published 1921) and included in   *CPl* 449
subsequent editions of the play.

3   *the white heron*: The heron is a type of subjectivity as is made clear in the note Yeats appended to the play in *Four Plays for Dancers* (1921):

I have written the little songs of the chorus to please myself, confident that singer and composer, when the time came for performance, would certainly make it impossible for the audience to know what the words were. I used to think that singers should sing a recipe for a good dish, or a list of local trains, or something else they want to get by heart, but I have changed my mind and now I prefer to give him some mystery or secret. A reader can always solve the mystery and learn the secret by turning to a note, which need not be as long as those Dante put to several of the Odes in the *Convito*. I use birds as symbols of subjective life, and my reason for this, and for certain other things, cannot be explained fully till I have published some part at any rate of those papers of Michael Robartes, over which I have now spent several years. The following passage in a letter written by Robartes to Aherne in the spring of 1917 must suffice. 'At present I rather pride myself on believing all the superstitions of the Judwalis, or rather in believing that there is not one amongst them that may not be true, but at first my West European mind rebelled. Once in the early morning, when I was living in a horse-hair tent among other similar tents, a young Arab woke me and told me to come with him if I would see a great wonder. He brought me to a level place in the sand, just outside the tent of a certain Arab, who had arrived the night before and had, as I knew, a reputation as a wonder-worker, and showed me certain marks on the sand. I said they were the marks of a jackal, but he would not have this. When he had passed by a little after sunrise there was not a mark, and a few minutes later the marks were there. No beast could have come and gone unseen. When I asked his explanation he said they were made by the wonder-worker's 'Daimon' or 'Angel'. 'What', I said, 'has it a beast's form?' 'He goes much about the world,' he said; 'he has been in Persia and Afghanistan, and as far west as Tripoli. He is interested in things, in places, he likes to be with many people, and that is why his Daimon has the form of a beast, but your Daimon would have a bird's shape because you are a solitary man.' Later on, when I mastered their philosophy, I came to learn that the boy had but classified the wonder-worker and myself according to their division of all mankind into those who are dominated by objects and those who are dominated by the self or *Zat*, or, as we would say, into objective and subjective natures. Certain birds, especially as I see things, such lonely birds as the heron, hawk, eagle, and swan, are the natural symbols of subjectivity, especially when floating upon the wind alone or alighting upon some pool or river, while the beasts that run upon the ground, especially those that run in packs, are the natural symbols of objective man. Objective men, however personally alone, are never alone in their thought, which is always developed in agreement or in conflict with the thought of others and always seeks the welfare of some cause or institution, while subjective men are the more lonely the more they are true to type, seeking always that which is unique or personal.

I have used my bird-symbolism in these songs to increase the objective loneliness of Christ by contrasting it with a loneliness, opposite in kind, that unlike His can be, whether joyous or sorrowful, sufficient to itself. I have surrounded Him with the images of those He cannot save, not only with the birds, who have served neither God nor Caesar, and await for none or for a different saviour, but with Lazarus and Judas and the Roman soldiers for whom He has died in vain. 'Christ', writes Robartes, 'only pitied those whose suffering is rooted in death, in poverty, or in sickness, or in sin, in some shape of the common lot, and he came especially to the poor who are most subject to exterior vicissitude'. I have therefore represented in Lazarus and Judas types of that intellectual despair that lay beyond His sympathy, while in the Roman soldiers I suggest a form of objectivity that lay beyond His help . . .'

11-14   *But that . . . soon*: Christ's birth, at Phase 15, the full moon, initiates the objective Christian age, which supplants the previous subjective one, and only the certainty of the renewal of the cycle can support the subjective heron. His only salvation is his self-absorption.

A84   [O, BUT THE MOCKERS' CRY]

CPl 451 . This is a song from the play *Calvary* (first published 1921) and included in subsequent editions of the play

1-6   *O but the ... played*: Vendler (*YV* 174) compares the flute music in the play *The Herne's Egg* played to summon Attrecta, which announces a new dispensation.

[TAKE BUT HIS LOVE AWAY]   A85

This is a song from the play *Calvary* (first published 1921) and included in   *CPl 453*
subsequent editions of the play

1-7   *Take but ... at the full*: When the objective era is over, at Christ's death, and the subjective returns, deprived of His [Christ's] love which gives meaning to their lives, they would become mere fragments of subjectivity

3   *eagle, swan or gull*: see Yeats's note above on [Motionless under the Moon-Beam] (*PNE* 83).

[LONELY THE SEA-BIRD LIES AT HER REST]   A86

This is a song from the play *Calvary* (first published 1921) and included in   *CPl 457*
subsequent editions of the play.

7   *In blue deep ... air*: Wilson (*YI* 173) traces this back to the early story *The Tables of the Law*. See *M* 299.

12-13   *But where ... empty*: cf. the closing stanza of 'The Wild Swans at Coole' (*PNE* 143). An early draft read:

> Where have last year's cygnets gone?
> Coole lake's empty.

[THE HERO, THE GIRL, AND THE FOOL]   A87

This poem was first published in *SPF* under the title 'Cuchulain, The Girl and   *SPF, PY*
The Fool'; it was included in *The Tower* (1928; 1929) but only the last twelve lines (18-29) were included under the title 'The Fool by the Roadside' in *CP*; the poem in this form was published in *AV* (A). The longer version appears in *The Poems of W. B. Yeats* (1949). See note on 'The Fool by the Roadside' (*PNE* 225).

1   *rage at my own image*: cf. the parrot of 'The Indian to his Love' (*PNE* 6) 'raging at his own image in the enamelled sea'

16   *only God has loved us for ourselves*: cf. 'For Anne Gregory' (*PNE* 255):

> . . . only God, my dear
> Could love you for yourself alone . . .

A88   [SHALL I FANCY BEAST OR FOWL]

CPl 416   This is a song from the play *The Player Queen* (first published in 1922) and included in subsequent editions of the play. It is sung by Decima, a character in the play. Yeats was working on *The Player Queen* in September 1908 and had almost finished it by September 1914. He continued to work on it in 1916 and was revising it a year later. It began as a verse tragedy, he wrote in *PPV*, but the thought of *PASL* (see, in particular, *M* 333–4) was coming into his head and this poetical play had 'neither simplicity nor life.' He decided that he could 'get rid of the play' if he turned it into a farce 'and never did I do anything so easily, for I think that I wrote the present play in about a month'. *The Player Queen* was first performed by the Stage Society on 25 May 1919 at the King's Hall, Covent Garden, and later the same year at the Abbey Theatre, Dublin.

2   *Queen Pasiphae*: in mythology the daughter of Helios, married to Minos of Crete who, in order to receive the throne, prayed to Poseidon to send him a bull from the sea to sacrifice. The bull was so beautiful that Minos would not kill it, whereupon Pasiphae fell in love with it, disguised herself as a cow, and bore the Minotaur, half-man, half-bull, which lived in the labyrinth of Crete.

3   *Leda*: the mother of the Dioscuri (Castor and Pollux), Helen and Clytaemnestra. Zeus raped her in the shape of a swan and begat Helen (see note on 'Leda and the Swan' (*PNE* 220).
      These myths are used by Yeats to express the notion that the destruction of the old dispensation and the birth of the new are generated at the point of union of the temporal and the extra-temporal, the divine and the bestial. Hence Septimus's next speech. As yet, however, the Unicorn is not coupled to its opposite.

A89   [UPON THE ROUND BLUE EYE I RAIL]

CPl 417   This is a song from the play *The Player Queen* (first published 1922) and included in subsequent editions of the play.

2   *milk-white horn*: the poem is about a unicorn. The unicorn never appears in the play, but seems to have different significations for different characters. To the Tapster and the mob, incapable of vision, it is a real animal and its coupling with the Queen an act of bestialism; to the romantic poet Septimus it is an image of nobility, beauty and chastity; to the Queen an image of her own self-mortification, timidity and prudery.
      In a letter to his sister Elizabeth, Yeats said that the unicorn was 'a private

490

symbol belonging to my mystical order' and that it was the soul (*L* 662), Cf., however, *CPl* 338, lines 14-16. Melchiori, in his discussion of the Unicorn image (*WMA* 35-71), points out that this explanation is only partial. In *Where There is Nothing* Paul Ruttledge, the prototype of Martin Hearne, has a vision of an apocalyptic beast 'with iron teeth and brazen claws that can root up spires and towers', defined as 'Laughter, the mightiest of the enemies of God.' But this symbol is uneasily combined with another for the same concept – 'white angels on white unicorns'. The visual origins of the unicorn symbol can be found in Gustave Moreau's painting *Ladies and Unicorns*, and in the design drawn by U. L. Brockman for the endpapers of the magazine *The Dome*, to which Yeats contributed regularly between 1897 and 1900. This depicted a unicorn, rampant, on a mosaic background, its head encircled by a solar disc.

The visual impact of the unicorn image, already confirmed in *The King's Threshold* (see 112, lines 19-20) and in *Deirdre* (175, line 16), was reinforced for him by its symbolic significance. The title for the third grade of the Order of the Golden Dawn, which Yeats held for some time in the early nineties, was that of *Monocris* (or *Monoceros*) *de Astris*, the Unicorn from the Stars.

In *The Unicorn from the Stars* Martin takes over from the earlier play the image of the unicorn as the Apocalyptic Beast, reinforced now by Biblical associations from the Book of Revelations and Isaiah, though all references to the image of the wild beast of laughter are discarded.

The spiritual significance is also a development of Paul Ruttledge's transformation of the physical revolution on to the mental plane: 'We cannot destroy the world with armies, it is inside our minds that it must be destroyed, it must be consumed in a moment inside our minds.' The unicorn becomes, in effect, a symbol for a divine force working within the soul and manifested in the moment of inspiration, of joyous vision, that will bring renewal with destruction.

[SONG OF THE DRUNKARD]   A90

This song is included only in the version of the play *The Resurrection* published   *VPl 914*
in *The Adelphi*, June 1927. The next version of the play was published in *Stories of Michael Robartes and his Friends* (1931).
Title: *drunkard*: He is a drunken priest, a worshipper of Dionysus, the Greek god.

3   *drum and rattle . . . drunken god*: cf. the text of the play in *The Adelphi* (*VPl* 910 and 912):

> *The Hebrew*: There is that noise again. I can see them
>   now. They
>   are women and some carry on their shoulder a bier
>   with a dead man, while others shake rattles or beat
>   upon
>   drums. Some of the crowd are angry but the Roman
>   soldiers keep them back.

The Egyptian: Are you certain that they are
women and not men in women's clothes with rouged
faces?

The Hebrew: They are passing at the end of the
street and the crowd obstructs the view. Now I can
see. I think you are right – they walk like men and
their cheeks and lips are vermilion – an impossible
vermilion.

The Egyptian: Nor is that a dead man, but a
painted wooden image of a dead man. I have seen them
in Alexandria – they are new arrivals here. They
worship a drunken God called among the Greeks
Diony-
sus, and at the first full moon in March they gather in
some field outside the town, one of them with a live
kid in his arms. The others stand in a circle and he
throws the kid into the midst of them and they fall
upon it tumbling over one another and seize it with
their teeth and their hands, and tear it asunder, and eat
the raw flesh, their heads and garments all spotted with
blood. And all the while they keep crying out upon
the God Dionysus whose flesh they eat and whose
blood they drink.

The Hebrew: Horrible – only a Greek could have
such thoughts.

The Egyptian: Then they go into the town and
march hither and thither, some with a painted
image of
a dead man upon their shoulders, some dancing and
rending their clothes and calling upon their God to rise
from the dead.

A91   [WHAT MESSAGE COMES TO FAMOUS THEBES FROM THE GOLDEN HOUSE]

CPl 479   This is a chorus from Yeats's *Sophocles' King Oedipus* (first published 1928) and
included in subsequent editions of the play. See note on 'Colonus' Praise' (*PNE*
223) for Yeats's treatment of the Oedipus legend and the translations he used.

chorus: The Chorus consisted of Theban elders, men of noble birth.

1   *the Golden House*: Delphi was wealthy in its dedicated adornments, and also
because the treasury of the temple acted as a bank in which gold and silver could
be deposited.

2   *Zeus*: because Zeus is speaking by the mouth of his son Apollo. Cf. Paul
Masqueray's note in his translation, p. 146. 'Tous les oracles sont inspirés par
Zeus et Loxias, en particulier, est l'interprète de son père.'

6   *the Delian God's reply*: Delos is a small island in the Cylades, in the Aegean Sea, sacred to Apollo (whose birthplace it was in legend) who was honoured by a festival held there as early as the eighth century BC.

7   *the God of Death*: in the original Ares, who is not merely a war god in Sophocles but a destroyer – here connected with the plague, because he 'bears no rattling shield and yet consumes this form with pain'.

11   *that God-trodden western shore*: cf. Jebb's version: '. . . grant that . . . may turn his back in speedy flight . . . borne by a fair wind to the great deep of Amphitrite, or to those waters in which none find haven, even to the Thracian wave' and Masqueray's 'qu'il tourne le does, soit vers le lit immense d'Amphitrite, soit vers le flot inhospitalier de la mer de Thrace'. The 'great deep' of Amphitrite was the Atlantic.

16   *Master of the thunder-cloud*: Zeus, the only certain Greek god of Indo-European origin. The word means sky; his residence was on Mount Olympus. The title of 'Father' was not due to his begetting gods and men but was to be understood in the sense of a protector and ruler of a family. He stood for the maintenance of laws, such as a respect for guests: he was a God of the household. Zeus dethroned Kronos and fought against the Titans (possibly pre-Greek gods) with the Olympian gods, Kronos himself having dethroned his father Uranus.

19   *God-hated God*: probably taken from the end of the chorus and a rendering of ἀπότιμου, without honour. Jebb renders this 'the God unhonoured among Gods' (p. 41).

20   *Artemis*: Apollo's sister, a daughter of Zeus, and a virgin huntress who also brought fertility to man and beast, and was a helper of women in childbirth.

21   *Maenads*: women inspired to frenzy by Dionysus. They celebrated his power in song, dance and music, and had superhuman force, uprooting trees, killing wild animals and eating their raw flesh. The women of Thebes followed Dionysus, became Maenads and destroyed his enemies, Pentheus and Orpheus. See note on [Song of the drunkard] (*PNE* A90).

22   *Lysian King*: Apollo as God of light (λύξ) or, more likely, if *Lycian* is intended, Apollo as chief deity of Lycia, a country in south-west Asia Minor.

23   *Bacchus' wine ensanguined face*: Bacchus was another name for Dionysus (a Lydian word), and was probably the god, primarily of vegetation, in Asia Minor.

A92   [THE DELPHIAN ROCK HAS SPOKEN OUT, NOW MUST A WICKED MIND]

CPl 488   This is a chorus from Yeats's *Sophocles' King Oedipus* (first published 1928) and included in subsequent editions of the play.

1   *The Delphian Rock*: see note on [What message comes to famous Thebes from the Golden House] (*PNE* A91). Delphi's town and temple stood in an amphitheatre-like recess on a high platform of rock, sloping out from the south face of the cliff. Delphi was the chief oracular shrine of Phoebus Apollo, a prophetic god from the earliest times (his other functions covered music, archery, medicine and the care of flocks and herds). His oracles were regarded as the supreme authority in matters of purification. At Delphi the medium (the Sibyl) was filled with the God or his inspiration. Apollo was a latecomer to the site; his priestess was called the Pythia.

4   *Cloudy Parnassus*: Snowy is the adjective used by Sophocles, and so translated by Jebb and Masqueray. See note (p. 255) on Yeats's use of the latter's translation.

the Fates: the avenging spirits, the Κῆρες

5-7   *That sacred crossing-place . . . That navel*: the omphalos (a white stone having the shape of a navel) in the temple at Delphi, hence the oracle. It was regarded as the centre of the earth, hence the 'crossing-place'.

A93   [FOR THIS ONE THING ABOVE ALL I WOULD BE PRAISED AS A MAN]

CPl 499   This is a chorus from Yeats's *Sophocles' King Oedipus* (first published 1928) and included in subsequent editions of the play

3   *Olympian Zeus . . . Empyrean*: Zeus was the greatest of the Olympian gods. For Empyrean see note on 'From the "Antigone"' (*PNE* 303).

12   *Delphian Sibyl*: see note on [The Delphian Rock has spoken out, now must a wicked mind] (*PNE* A92).

13   *navel-stone*: see note on [The Delphian Rock has spoken out, now must a wicked mind] (*PNE* A92)

A94   [OEDIPUS' NURSE, MOUNTAIN OF MANY A HIDDEN GLEN]

CPl 506   This is a chorus from Yeats's translation *Sophocles' King Oedipus* (first published 1928) and included in subsequent editions of the play.

1   *Oedipus' nurse, mountain*: Mount Cithaeron. Oedipus was abandoned on it when an infant.

494

5   *the hidden glen*: Jebb describes it as having 'winding glens' and he comments that the phrase 'becomes vivid to anyone who traverses Cithaeron by the road ascending from Elusis and winding upwards to the pass of Dryoscephalae whence it descends into the plain of Thebes' (p. 136)

6   *Helicon*: see note on 'The Leaders of the Crowd' (*PNE* 197)

7   *Lord Pan* or *Lord Apollo* or *the mountain Lord*: For Pan, see note on 'News for the Delphic Oracle' (*PNE* 363); for Apollo, see note on [The Delphian Rock has spoken out, now must a wicked mind] (*PNE* A92); the mountain Lord is Dionysus. For him see note on 'Two Songs from a Play' (*PNE* 218)

Bacchantes: the maenads, women inspired to ecstatic frenzy by Dionysus. The classic description is in the Athenian dramatist Euripides' (480–406 BC) tragedy, *The Bacchae*. See also 'Astrea's holy child' (*PNE* A98).

[WHAT CAN THE SHADOW-LIKE GENERATIONS OF MAN ATTAIN]   A95

This is a chorus from Yeats's *Sophocles' King Oedipus* (first published 1928) and   *CPl 510*
included in subsequent editions of the play.

4   *the woman-breasted fate*: the sphinx, a mythological monster with lion body and human head: in Greek literature it was female. In an early version of the legend the Sphinx was sent to Thebes by the goddess Hera, and asked the Thebans the riddle about the three ages of man. They failed to solve it and after each attempt of theirs the Sphinx carried off one of them. Finally Oedipus solved the riddle. The Sphinx then committed suicide or was killed by Oedipus. According to Apollodorus she threw herself from a rock when her riddle was solved.

6   *Thebes*: see note on [What message comes to famous Thebes from the Golden House] (*PNE* A98)

7   *the bed of his birth*: in ignorance he married his mother Jocasta, who hanged herself when the secret of their relationship was revealed.

8   *his father*: Laius

10   *Begetter*: he had four children by Jocasta, Eteocles and Polynices, Antigone and Ismene.

[MAKE WAY FOR OEDIPUS. ALL PEOPLE SAID]   A96

This is the final chorus concluding Yeats's translation *Sophocles' King Oedipus*   *CPl 517*
(first published 1928) and included in subsequent editions.

A97   [HUDDON, DUDDON AND DANIEL O'LEARY]

VE 787   This poem was first published in *Stories of Michael Robartes and His Friends* (1931). In Yeats's note, in this volume, he states that as a child he pronounced O'Leary as though it rhymed with 'dairy'. It was subsequently included in *AV* (B) where these characters are Peter Huddon, John Duddon and Daniel O'Leary. See note on 'Tom the Lunatic' (*PNE* 289) for a reference to 'Hudden and Dudden and Donald O'Neary'.

A98   [ASTREA'S HOLY CHILD]

CPl 586   This is a song from the play *Resurrection*, first published in *Stories of Michael Robartes and His Friends* (1931) and included in subsequent editions of the play.

Title: Astrea's holy child: Astrea was a daughter of Zeus who aided humans on earth in the Golden Age. She was a goddess of Justice and sometimes was regarded as a daughter of Astraeus the Titan by Eos. In her heavenly transformation she was Virgo. Here her child is Dionysus. See notes on 'Two Songs from a Play' (*PNE* 218).

13   *The murderous Titans*: see note on 'Love and Death' (*PNE* A2).

wandering women: the Maenads, followers of Dionysus, see note on 'Bacchantes' in [Oedipus' nurse, mountain of many a hidden Glen] (*PNE* A94).

A99   [MOVE UPON NEWTON'S TOWN]

W & B 77   This poem was first published in the 'Introduction to *Fighting the Waves*', *DM*, April–June 1932. It was subsequently included in *W & B*.

1   *Newton's*: Sir Isaac Newton (1642–1727), English scientist and mathematician. Cf. 'At Algeciras – A Meditation on Death' (*PNE* 257)

2   *Hobbes ... Locke*: Thomas Hobbes (1588–1679), English empiricist and rationalist philosopher, author of *Leviathan* (1651). John Locke (1632–1704), English philosopher, founder of Liberalism and English Empiricism, author of *Essay Concerning Human Understanding* (1690) which argued that all knowledge is founded on and ultimately derives itself from sense ... or sensation'. Yeats thought science had driven out 'legends, stories, superstitions that protected the immature and the ignorant with symbol; and now that the flower has crossed our rooms, science must take their place and demonstrate as philosophy has in all ages, that states are justified, not by multiplying or, as it would seem, comforting those that are inherently miserable but because sustained

by those for whom the hour seems ''awful'', and by those born out of themselves, the best born of the best' (*W & B* 76-7). See note on 'Fragments' (*PNE* 219) and Yeats's note on 'Leda and the Swan' (*PNE* 220).

[SHOULD H. G. WELLS AFFLICT YOU]   A100

This poem was first published in the 'Introduction to *Fighting the Waves*', *DM*,   *W & B* 79
April-June 1932, and subsequently included in *W & B*

1   *H. G. Wells*: Wells (1866-1946), an English author of scientific romances, preoccupied with Utopian ideas, originally thought the onward march of science would bring about a millennium and put this view in such works as *The Work, Wealth and Happiness of Mankind* (1932). (He later became pessimistic on realising science could work for evil.) Yeats placed the four lines of the poem after these remarks:

> Yet it may be that our science, our modern philosophy, keep a subconscious knowledge that their raft, roped together at the end of the seventeenth century, must, if they so much as glance at that slow moving flower [see note on 'Move upon Newton's Town' (*PNE* A100)] part and abandon on us to the storm or it may be, as Professor Richet [Charles Robert Richet (1850-1935), a French physiologist awarded the Nobel Prize in 1913] suggests at the end of his long survey of psychical research from the first experiments of Sir William Crookes [(1832-1919), the English chemist and physicist] to the present moment, that all it can do is, after a shady scrutiny, to prove the poverty of the human intellect, that we are lost amid alien intellects, near but incomprehensible, more incomprehensible than the most distant stars. We may, whether it scrutinise or not, lacking its convenient happy explanations, plunge as Rome did in the fourth century according to some philosopher of that day into 'a fabulous formless darkness'. (*W & B* 77-8)

Science - opium of the suburbs: This echoes the well known phrase of Karl Marx (1818-1883) that 'religion . . . is the opium of the people' in his *Zur Kritik der Hegelschen Rechtsphilosophie* (1844).

THREE SONGS TO THE SAME TUNE   A101

These poems were written between 30 November 1933 and February 1934: they   *CP 320*
first appeared in the *Spectator* (23 Feb. 1934) then in *P* (*Ch*) 1934, next in *KGCT* and *FMM*. They were revised as 'Three Marching Songs' in *Last Poems and Two Plays* (1939). See note on them.

Yeats's note after the title in *The Spectator* (23 February 1934) read:

> In politics I have but one passion and one thought, rancour against all who, except under the most dire necessity, disturb public order, a conviction that public order cannot long persist without the rule of educated and able men. That order was everywhere their work, is still as much a part of their tradition

as the *Iliad* or the Republic of Plato; their rule once gone, it lies an empty shell for the passing fool to kick in pieces. Some months ago that passion laid hold upon me with the violence which unfits the poet for all politics but his own. While the mood lasted, it seemed that our growing disorder, the fanaticism that inflamed it like some old bullet imbedded in the flesh, was about to turn our noble history into an ignoble farce. For the first time in my life I wanted to write what some crowd in the street might understand and sing; I asked my friends for a tune; they recommended that old march, 'O'Donnell Abu.' I first got my chorus, 'Down the fanatic, down the clown,' then the rest of the first song. But I soon tired of its rhetorical vehemence, thought that others would tire of it unless I found some gay playing upon its theme, some half-serious exaggeration and defence of its rancorous chorus, and therefore I made the second version. Then I put into a simple song a commendation of the rule of the able and educated, man's old delight in submission; I wrote round the line 'The soldier takes pride in saluting his captain,' thinking the while of a Gaelic poet's lament for his lost masters: 'My fathers served their fathers before Christ was crucified.' [Egan O'Rahilly (1670–1726); Yeats substituted 'served' for the 'followed' of Frank O'Connor's translation, included in his *The Wild Bird's Nest: Poems from the Irish* (1932) 23.] I read my songs to friends, they talked to others, those others talked, and now companies march to the words 'Blueshirt Abu,' and a song that is all about shamrocks and harps or seems all about them, because its words have the particular variation upon the cadence of 'Yankee Doodle' [a folk song, origin unknown] Young Ireland [Irish political movement founded in 1842 by Thomas Davis and his friends] reserved for that theme. I did not write that song; I could not if I tried. Here are my songs. Anybody may sing them, choosing 'clown' and 'fanatic' for himself, if they are singable – musicians say they are, but may flatter – and worth singing.

The note he appended as 'Commentary on Three Songs' in *P(Ch)* (Dec. 1934) and in *KGCT* read:

For thirty years I have been a director of the Abbey Theatre. It is a famous theatre, known to students of dramatic literature all over the world, but company and building are small, it often turns many away from its cheaper seats. It holds some five hundred persons; that five hundred, or whatever moiety of it is there on any particular evening, is mainly boys and girls out of the shops and factories. They come again and again to a favourite play, all others are casual or uncertain, except some old adherents who have lasted out the thirty years, and a few students from the National University [University College, Dublin, a constituent college of the National University of Ireland]. If it were in Poland, in Sweden, in some Balkan State, it would have four or five times as many in company, in audience, draw into that audience those that were highly educated or highly placed, have behind it for moments of emergency ample Government support. It would be expected to send its best players now and again to foreign countries that it might raise the prestige of its nation as do the bronze replicas of the Roman wolf, a master-piece of Etruscan art, the Italian Government has set up in America wherever Italian emigrants are numerous. When I was a foolish lad I hoped for something of the kind. When I founded the Irish Literary Society, the National Literary Society, barred from the Chair politicians and Lord Mayors that literature might live its own sincere life, I hoped for a literature Ireland would honour as Poland honours its literature. Synge, Lady Gregory, A.E. came first; then many novelists and dramatists; Moore and Shaw turned their thoughts to Ireland; nobody could have hoped for so much genius. But most of these writers are better known in other countries, even our novelists who describe in simple vivid speech the circumstance and history of their country, find most of their readers among the Irish in America, and in England; more perhaps among Englishmen and Americans, without Irish blood, than in Ireland. Sometimes I receive a little propagandist paper issued by the Polish Government, written in French, and find there pictures of the noble eighteenth century palace where the Polish Academy of Letters meets [*Pologne Litteraire*, 87, 15 December 1933]. Our not less distinguished Academy meets in a room hired for five shillings a night. The explanation is that our upper class cares nothing for Ireland except as a place for sport, that the rest of the population is drowned in religious and political fanaticism. Poland is a Catholic nation and some ten years ago inflicted upon the national enemy an overwhelming, world-famous defeat, but its fanaticism, if it has any, thwarts neither science, nor art, nor letters. Sometimes as the representative of the Abbey Theatre I have called upon some member of Mr Cosgrave's or Mr de Valera's government to explain some fanatical attack - we are a State Theatre though our small subsidy has been lately reduced [it was £850 in 1925-6; £1,000 up to 1933 when it was reduced to £750] - once as a member of the Irish Academy to complain of the illegal suppression of a book, and upon each occasion I came away with the conviction that the Minister felt exactly as I felt but was helpless: the mob reigned. If that reign is not broken our public life will move from violence to violence, or from violence to apathy; our [apathy, our (*KGCT*)] Parliament disgrace and debauch those that enter it; our men of letters live like outlaws in their own country. It will be broken when some government seeks unity of culture not less than economic unity, welding to the purpose, museum, school, university, learned institution. A nation should be like an audience in some great theatre - 'In the theatre,' said Victor Hugo, 'the mob becomes a people' [*PNE* suggests Victor Hugo, *Intellectual Autobiography*, ed. L. O'Rourke (1907) 369-70] - watching the sacred drama of its own history; every spectator finding self and neighbour there, finding all the world there, as we find the sun in the bright spot under the burning glass. We know the world through abstractions, statistics, time tables, through images that refuse to compose themselves into a clear design. Such knowledge thins the blood. To know it in the concrete we must know it near at hand; religion itself during our first impressionable years in the dramatis personae of our own narrow stage; I think of those centuries before the great schism had divided the East and West accepted by Catholic and Protestant alike. [See Yeats's note, quoted (p. 350) above.] Into the drama must enter all that have lived with precision and energy; Major Sirr, picture lover, children lover, hateful oppressor [Henry Charles Sirr (1764-1841), Town Major of Dublin (equivalent of head of police). He took part in the capture of Lord Edward Fitzgerald and organised the capture of Robert Emmet and other Irish leaders. He relied greatly on informers], should he strike some creative fancy, not less than Emmet and Fitzgerald; the Ascendency, considering its numbers as fruitful of will and intellect as any stock on earth, not less than those Wild Geese, those Catholic gentlemen who, in the words of Swift, carried into foreign service 'a valour' above 'that of all nations.' [See note on 'September 1913' (*PNE* 115). Swift's letter (July-2 August 1732) was written to Charles (the Chevalier) Wogan (1698-1754) a Jacobite soldier of fortune.]

If any Government or party undertake this work it will need force, marching men (the logic of fanaticism, whether in a woman or a mob is drawn from a premise protected by ignorance and therefore irrefutable); it will promise not this or that measure but a discipline, a way of life; that sacred drama must to all native eyes and ears become the greatest of the parables. There is no such government or party today; should either appear I offer it these trivial songs and what remains to me of life.

April, 1934

P.S. Because a friend [Captain Dermot MacManus] belonging to a political party wherewith I had once some loose associations, told me that it had, or was about to have, or might be persuaded to have, some such aim as mine, I wrote these songs. Finding that it neither would nor could, I increased their fantasy, their extravagance, their obscurity, that no party might sing them.

August 1934
(*VE* 835-8)

I

10 *the tune of O'Donnell Abu*: Michael Joseph McCann (?1824-83), a Young Irelander, wrote 'O Domhnaill Abu'. The song (which later became 'Parnell Abu') was meant to be sung to the tune 'Roderick Vick Alpine Dhu', the 'Boat Song' in Sir Walter Scott's *Lady of the Lake*, but it became famous with another tune composed by Joseph Haliday (1775-1846). This information is from Georges-Denis Zimmermann, *Irish Political Street Ballads and Rebel Songs 1780-1900* (Geneva, 1966), 64, 79, 113, who cites *Irish Book Lover*, XXVI, 85, for some of his material.

25-6 Saul suggests a comparison to 'The Night before Larry was stretched', an eighteenth-century ballad: 'He kicked too – but that was all pride.'

II

7 *'Drown all the dogs,' said the fierce young woman*: see an anecdote quoted in *Y:M & P* 279:

Here is our most recent event.... Blueshirts are upholders of law, incarnations of public spirit, rioters in the cause of peace and George hates Blueshirts. She was delighted when she caught their [local Blueshirt family] collie-dog in our hen-house and missed a white hen. I was going into town and she said 'I will write and complain; if they do nothing I will go to the police'. When I returned in the evening she was plunged in gloom. Her letter sent by the gardener had been replied to at once in these words 'Sorry, have done away with collie-dog' – note the Hitler touch – a little later came the gardener and in his presence . . . [four dogs had been drowned]. . . . A fifth had revived when taken out of the water, and (as it was not their dog) but a stray——had hunted it down the road with a tin can tied to its tail. There was a sixth dog, —— said, but as it had been with her for some time she would take time to think whether to send it to the dogs' home or drown it. I tried to console George . . . after all she was only responsible for the death of the collie and so on – but there was something wrong and at last it came out. The white hen had returned. Was she to write and say so? I said 'You feel a multimurderess and if you write —— will too.' 'But she will see the hen.' 'Put it in the pot.' 'But it's my best layer.' However I insisted and the white hen went into the pot.

500

Frank O'Connor tells the story in a more stylised form:

> . . . as a fascist he was the least fanatical of men. Mrs Yeats was on the opposite side, as I was, and one evening he told me a little moral tale to illustrate the virtues of fascism. 'You see, O'Connor, the people next door are Blueshirts. The Blueshirts keep a dog. George is a De Valeraite and George keeps hens. The fascist dog worries the democratic hens. Today her favourite hen disappeared, and George said, "It's that damn fascist dog!" so she wrote to the neighbours to complain. But you see, O'Connor, to Blueshirts the idea of order is sacred and back comes a note that reads, "Dear Madam, Dog Destroyed." And now George, who is English and very fond of animals, is filled with remorse.'
>
> The following week when we met he began to chuckle. 'O'Connor, remember the fascist dog? Remember the democratic hen? The democratic hen has come home! Now, George is full of guilt and insists on apologising. I won't hear of it. I say, "George, nothing you can do will bring the fascist dog back to life." '
>
> I enjoyed the story, but once more what interests me is the monologue, that telephone conversation of which one hears only part. Could the fascist dog and the democratic hen be the source of the dog and goose of one of his deplorable fascist marching songs – the dog of law drowned by the fierceness of humanitarian sentiments. (*The Backward Look* 181-2)

23 *mock at*: cf. 'Nineteen Hundred and Nineteen' v (*PNE* 213).

O'Donnell: Two O'Donnell brothers are possible. The first (and most likely) Red Hugh O'Donnell (*c*. 1571-1602), chief of the O'Donnells, shared victory of the Yellow Ford (1598) with Hugh O'Neill: he went to Spain after the Battle of Kinsale (1601) for help, and died there, reputedly poisoned in 1602. The second younger brother Rory O'Donnell (1575-1665) succeeded him. Rory visited James I at Hampton Court and was created an Earl, 1603. He attempted to rouse the Catholic Lords to rebel but on discovery of the plot fled to Rome with the Earl of Tyrone, eldest son of the first Earl of Tyrone.

24 *both O'Neills*: possibly Shane O'Neill 'the Proud' (*c*. 1530-1567), who was elected 'the O'Neill' in 1559, made his submission to Elizabeth in London 1562; he destroyed Scottish settlements in Antrim, but supported Mary Queen of Scots; he invaded the Pale and burned Armagh 1566; he defeated the MacDonnells at Ballycastle but was killed by them at Cushendun in 1567. But probably Hugh O'Neill, the second Earl of Tyrone (b. *c*. 1540). He succeeded to the title in 1585, married Mabel Bagenal 1591 and when her brother refused to hand over her dowry he captured Blackwater fort and ravaged Co. Louth. He was proclaimed a traitor and elected the O'Neill in 1591. He beat Bagenal at the Yellow Ford in 1598. Munster rose and O'Neill marched to receive the Spanish force at Kinsale. But his territory was largely taken by English forces when he returned. He was offered reasonable terms by Elizabeth and submitted. James I received him at Hampton Court. After he returned a law suit was referred to the King, and he was informed that this was a plot to trap him, so he and Hugh Roe O'Donnell left Rathmullen in 1607 and settled in Rome. This was known as the

'Flight of the Earls'. His overtures for a return were repulsed and he died – of melancholia – in 1616.

There is a remote possibility that Owen Roe O'Neill (*c.* 1590–1649) may be intended as one of the two O'Neills. A nephew of Hugh, he defeated the Scottish parliamentarians at Benburb, Co. Tyrone in 1646.

25   *Emmet*: see notes on 'Introductory Rhymes' (*PNE* 112) and on 'September 1913' (*PNE* 115)

Parnell: see notes on 'To a Shade' (*PNE* 118)

III

4   *Troy backed its Helen*: line 4 in the first printed version read:

'What's equality? – Muck in the yard.'

Cf. for the present version 'When Helen lived' (*PNE* 119). Cf. also notes on 'The Rose of the World' (*PNE* 20).

7   The refrain originally ran as in the first of these songs:

'*Those fanatics*' etc.

11   *Empty up there at the top*: cf. 'Blood and the Moon' (*PNE* 243) with its 'time/Half dead at the top' and the query in 'Blood and the Moon' IV (*PNE* 243)

Is every modern nation like the tower,
Half dead at the top?

The idea of this line and line 12 may derive from Swift. See the Introduction to *WWP* and notes on 'bitter wisdom' line 12 'Parnell's Funeral' II (*PNE* 304). See also 'Three Marching Songs' II (*PNE* 360): 'What if there's nothing up there at the top?'

A102   [LET IMAGES OF BASALT, BLACK, IMMOVABLE]

W & B 35   This poem was first published in the Introduction to *WWP*, included in *W & B*. It follows upon this passage of prose:

The Indian ascetic passing into his death-like trance knows that if his mind is not pure, if there is anything there but the symbol of his God, some passion, ambition, desire, or phantasy will confer upon him its shape or purpose, for he is entering upon a state where thought and existence are the same. One remembers those witches described by Glanvil who course the field in the likeness of hares while their bodies lie at home, and certain mediumistic phenomena. The ascetic would say, did we question him, that the unpurified dead are subject to transformations that would be similar were it not that in their case no physical body remains in cave or bed or chair, all is transformed. They examine their past if undisturbed by our importunity, tracing events to their source, and as they take the form their thought suggests, seem to live

502

backward through time; or if incapable of such examination, creatures not of thought but of feeling, renew as shades certain detached events of their past lives, taking the greater excitements first. When Achilles came to the edge of the blood-pool (an ancient substitute for the medium) he was such a shade. Tradition affirms that, deprived of the living present by death, they can create nothing, or, in the Indian phrase, can originate no new Karma. Their aim, like that of the ascetic in meditation, is to enter at last into their own archetype, or into all being: into that which is there always. They are not, however, the personalities which haunt the séance-room: these when they speak from, or imply, supernormal knowledge, when they are more than transformations of the medium, are, as it were, new beings begotten by spirit upon medium to live short but veritable lives, whereas the secondary personalities resemble those eggs brought forth without the assistance of the male bird. They, within their narrow limits, create; they speak truth when they repeat some message suggested by the past lives of the spirit, remembered like some pre-natal memory, or when, though such instances must be few, begotten by some spirit obedient to its source, or, as we might say, blessed; but when they neither repeat such message nor were so begotten they may justify passages in Swedenborg that denounce them as the newspapers denounce cheating mediums, seeing that they find but little check in their fragmentary knowledge or vague conscience.

Brancusi's hand: Constantin Brancusi (1871–1957) a Rumanian sculptor

[THEY DANCE ALL DAY THAT DANCE IN TIR-NAN-OGE]   A103

This is a song from the play *KGCT*, first published in *Life and Letters*, October   *CPl 633*
1934, then as *KGCT* (1934) and included in subsequent editions.

1 *Tir-nan-oge*: the Land of the Young, in Irish mythology, timeless elysium of the gods and the dead

2–8 *Every lover . . . bound and wound*: for perfect love as the timeless interpenetration of opposites see 'Chosen' (*PNE* 298):

> If questioned on
> My utmost pleasure with a man
> By some new-married bride, I take
> That stillness for a theme
> Where his heart my heart did seem
> And both adrift on the miraculous stream
> Where – wrote a learned astrologer –
> The Zodiac is changed into a sphere.

Yeats's explanation of the Thirteenth Cycle or Thirteenth Cone runs as follows:

It is that cycle which may deliver us from the twelve cycles of time and space. The cone which intersects ours is a cone in so far as we think of it as the antithesis to our thesis, but if the time has come for our deliverance it is the phaseless sphere, sometimes called the Thirteenth Sphere, for every lesser cycle contains within itself a sphere that is, as it were, the reflection or messenger of the final deliverance. Within it live all souls that have been set free and every *Daimon* and *Ghostly Self*; our expanding cone seems to cut through its gyre; spiritual influx is from its circumference, animate life from its centre. 'Eternity also', says Hermes in the Aeslepius dialogue, 'though motionless itself, appears to be in motion.' When Shelley's Demogorgon – eternity – comes from the centre of the earth it may so come because Shelley substituted the earth for such a sphere.* (*AV* (B) 210–11).

He also commented on it as follows:

The *Thirteenth Cone* is a sphere because sufficient to itself; but as seen by Man it is a cone. It becomes even conscious of itself as so seen, like some great dancer, the perfect flower of modern culture, dancing some primitive dance and conscious of his or her own life and of the dance. There is a mediaeval story of a man persecuted by his Guardian Angel because it was jealous of his sweetheart, and such stories seem closer to reality than our abstract theology. All imaginable relations may arise between a man and his God. I only speak of the *Thirteenth Cone* as a sphere and yet I might say that the gyre or cone of the *Principles* is in reality a sphere, though to Man bound to birth and death, it can never seem so, and that it is the antinomies that force us to find it a cone. Only one symbol exists, though the reflecting mirrors make many appear and all different. (*AV* (B) 240)

speech of birds: Vendler (*YV* 142) associates with the Shrouds of 'Cuchulain Comforted' (*PNE* 359) who sing with the throats of birds.

For there the hound . . . bell: an echo of a passage from *The Wanderings of Oisin*:

We galloped; now a hornless deer
Passed by us, chased by a phantom hound
All pearly white, save one red ear;
And now a lady rode like the wind
With an apple of gold in her tossing hand,
And a beautiful young man followed behind
With quenchless gaze and fluttering hair. (*PNE* 375)

The source for the image is probably Brian O'Looney's translation of Michael Comyn's *The Lay of Oisin in the Land of Youth* (the Gaelic poem of the last century mentioned in Yeats's notes):

We saw also, by our sides
A hornless fawn leaping nimbly,
And a red-eared white dog
Urging it boldly in the Chase

(See Russell K. Alspach, 'Some Sources of Yeats's ''The Wanderings of Oisin''', *PMLA*, September 1943.) Cf. also 'He Mourns for the change . . .' (*PNE* 52):

Do you not hear me calling, white deer with no horns?
I have been changed to a hound with one red ear . . .

* Shelley, who had more philosophy than men thought when I was young, probably knew that Parmenides represented reality as a motionless sphere. Mrs Shelley speaks of the 'mystic meanings' of *Prometheus Unbound* as only intelligible to a 'mind as subtle as his own'.

In the original version the following note was printed after the title:

In the old Irish story of Usheen's journey to the Islands of the Young, Usheen sees amid the waters a hound with one red ear, following a deer with no horns; and other persons in other old Celtic stories see the like images of the desire of the man, and of the desire of the woman 'which is for the desire of the man', and of all desires that are as these. The man with the wand of hazel may well have been Angus, Master of Love; and the boar without bristles is the ancient Celtic image of the darkness which will at last destroy the world, as it destroys the sun at nightfall in the west.

A fuller note in *WR* read:

My deer and hound are properly related to the deer and hound that flicker in and out of various tellings of the Arthurian legends, leading different knights upon adventures, and to the hounds and to the hornless deer at the beginning of, I think, all tellings of Oisin's journey to the country of the young. The hound is certainly related to the Hounds of Annwvyn or of Hades, who are white, and have red ears, and were heard, and are, perhaps, still heard by Welsh peasants, following some flying thing in the night winds; and is probably related to the hounds that Irish country people believe will awake and seize the souls of the dead if you lament them too loudly or too soon. An old woman told a friend and myself that she saw what she thought were white birds, flying over an enchanted place, but found, when she got near, that they had dogs' heads; and I do not doubt that my hound and these dog-headed birds are of the same family. I got my hound and deer out of a last-century Gaelic poem about Oisin's journey to the country of the young. After the hunting of the hornless deer, that leads him to the seashore, and while he is riding over the sea with Niamh, he sees amid the waters – I have not the Gaelic poem by me, and describe it from memory – a young man following a girl who has a golden apple, and afterwards a hound with one red ear following a deer with no horns. This hound and this deer seem plain images of the desire of the man 'which is for the woman', and 'the desire of the woman which is for the desire of the man', and of all desires that are as these. I have read them in this way in *The Wanderings of Oisin*, and have made my lover sigh because he has seen in their faces 'the immortal desire of immortals'.

The man in my poem who has a hazel wand may have been Aengus, Master of Love; and I have made the boar without bristles come out of the West, because the place of sunset was in Ireland, as in other countries, a place of symbolic darkness and death. – 1899. (*CW* 1)

16   *a bell*: an echo of the 'brazen bell' of *The Wanderings of Oisin*: This is the bell which is said to strike at midnight 'when the old year dies' (*CPl* 637). It is referred to in the song of the First Attendant as Head, 639, and it strikes as the Queen dances, 640, *SD*. It is also, of course, the bell of time and history – see Yeats's Commentary on 'Parnell's Funeral' (*PNE* 304) reprinted above 332 *ff*, with its view of history divided by Four Bells:

When lecturing in America I spoke of Four Bells, four deep tragic notes, equally divided in time, so symbolising the war that ended in the Flight of the Earls; the Battle of the Boyne; the coming of French influence among our peasants; the beginning of our own age; events that closed the sixteenth, seventeenth, eighteenth and nineteenth centuries. My historical knowledge, such as it is, begins with the Second Bell. *(KGCT)*

The notion of eternity threatened by time is clearer in an earlier version of the opening song given in a letter to Olivia Shakespear:

First musician (singing)
I wait until the tower gives forth the chime;
And dream of ghosts that have the speech of birds;
Because they have no thoughts they have no words;
No thought because no past or future; Time
Comes from the torture of our flesh, and these,
Cast out by death and tethered there by love,
Touch nerve to nerve throughout the sacred grove
And seem a single creature when they please.

Second musician (singing)
I call to mind the iron of the bell
And get from that my harsher imagery,
All love is shackled to mortality,
Love's image is a man-at-arms in steel;
Love's image is a woman made of stone;
It dreams of the unborn; all else is nought;
To-morrow and to-morrow fills its thought;
All tenderness reserves for that alone.

The letter continues: 'The inner ideas in these lines are taken up later. One might say the love of the beloved seeks eternity, that of the child seeks time.' (*L* 817)

A104 [O WHAT MAY COME]

CPl 638 This is a song from the play *KGCT*, first published in *Life and Letters*, October 1934, then as *KCGT* (1934), and included in subsequent editions of the play.

A105 [O, BUT I SAW A SOLEMN SIGHT]

CPl 640. This is a song from the play *KGCT*, first published in *Life and Letters,* October 1934, then as *KGCT* (1934) and included in subsequent editions. It was published separately under the title 'The Wicked Hawthorn Tree' in *A Broadside*, February 1935.

3 *Castle Dargan's ruin*: see note on [The Poet, Owen Hanrahan, under a bush of may] (*PNE* A34). See also *A* 54, 55, for Yeats's liking the place for the romance of the two ruined castles facing each other across a lake (the other was Castle Fury), and for his fishing for pike at Castle Dargan as a boy.

Additional Poems

[TO GARRET OR CELLAR A WHEEL I SEND]   **A106**

This poem was first published in *W & B*   *VE 787*

1 Garret or Cellar: In the Introduction to the play *The Words upon the Window-Pane* (*W & B* 5-6) Yeats wrote:

> Somebody said the other night that Dublin was full of clubs – he himself knew four – that met in cellars and garrets and had for their object our general improvement. He was scornful, said that they had all begun by drawing up a programme and passing a resolution against the censorship and would never do anything else. When I began my public life Dublin was full of such clubs that passed resolutions and drew up programmes, and though the majority did nothing else some helped to find an audience for a school of writers. The fall of Parnell had freed imagination from practical politics, from agrarian grievance and political enmity, and turned it to imaginative nationalism, to Gaelic, to the ancient stories, and at last to lyrical poetry and to drama. Political failure and political success have had the same result except that to-day imagination is turning full of uncertainty to something it thinks European, and whether that something will be 'arty' and provincial, or a form of life, is as yet undiscoverable. Hitherto we have walked the road, but now we have shut the door and turned up the lamp. What shall occupy our imagination? We must, I think, decide among these three ideas of national life: that of Swift; that of a great Italian of his day; that of modern England. If the Garrets and the Cellars listen I may throw light upon the matter, and I hope if all the time I seem thinking of something else I shall be forgiven. I must speak of things that come out of the common consciousness, where every thought is like a bell with many echoes.

[THE BRAVEST FROM THE GODS BUT ASK]   **A107**

This poem was published in *W & B*.   *VE 788*

[DECLINE OF DAY]   **A108**

This poem was published in *W & B*, in the Introduction to the play *The Cat and the Moon*   *W & B 137*

Nineveh: see note on 'Fragments' II (*PNE* 219).

[WOULD I WERE THERE WHEN THEY TURN AND THEBAN ROBBERS FACE]   **A109**

This is a chorus from Yeats's translation *Sophocles' Oedipus at Colonus*, first published in *CPl* (1934) and included in subsequent editions.   *CPl 556*

507

1   *Theban robbers*: for note on Thebes see on [What Message comes to famous Thebes from the Golden House] (*PNE* A91).

2   *Colonus*: the men, the warriors of Colonus. Colonus was Colonus of the Horses, an Attic deme or district, the birthplace of Sophocles (495-606 BC), a hill little more than a mile north of Athens

3   *Pythian Strand*: the shore of the bay of Eleusis just beyond the pass of Daphne, about six miles from Colonus. Pythian (see Jebb, *Sophocles* II, 167) alludes to the Ionic temple of Apollo in the highest, narrowest part of the pass of Daphne. 'Further away to the West' refers to the temple of Eleusis, sacred to the 'immortal spirits', Demeter and Persephone

4-5   *the life of the blessed ... living man ... none living know*: the Greek means those who have been initiated by the Eumolpid hierophant at Eleusis (the temple of Demeter and Persephone) and bound by him to secrecy. These Eleusinian mysteries offered some prospect of bliss after death.

6   *Oea's ... snow*: probably on Mount Aegaleos

8   *Theseus*: King of Athens. The son of Aethra (daughter of Pittheus, the King of Troezen) Theseus grew up not knowing his father was Aegeus, king of Athens. He was acknowledged as the heir of Aegeus after he arrived in Athens and killed the sons of his uncle Pallas who were intriguing against his father. He is a character in Sophocles' *Oedipus at Colonus*.

14   *Son of Rhea*: Poseidon, a son of Kronos and Rhea; he was Hippios, god of the horses and god of the sea. Rhea, daughter of Uranus and Gaia, was the mother of the gods. See Jebb (*Sophocles* II, 171) who remarks that 'the cult was that of the Phrygian Mother Cybele; in Attica it was connected with the Eleusinian cult of Demeter'

15-20   *Goddess Pallas Athene ... God's daughter Pallas Athene*: Athene was the daughter of Zeus. See note on 'A Thought from Propertius' (*PNE* 166).

23-24   *the deer ... Apollo and Artemis*: here in their guise of hunting god and goddess, Artemis being 'a smiter of deer'. They were the twin children of Zeus and Leto.

A110   [WHAT IS THIS PORTENT? WHAT DOES IT SHADOW FORTH?]

CPl 567   This is a chorus from Yeats's *Sophocles' Oedipus at Colonus*, first published in *CPl* (1934) and included in subsequent editions.

4   *blind ... beggar-man*: Oedipus. He killed his father Laius, not knowing his

identity, then married the king's widow Jocasta, his own mother. He blinded himself when his relationship with Jocasta was revealed. See notes on 'Colonus' Praise' (*PNE* 223).

19   *King of Athens*: Theseus, see note on [Would I were there when they turn and Theban robbers face] (*PNE* A109)

20   *Poseidon's altars*: see note on 'Son of Rhea' in the poem [Would I were there when they turn and Theban robbers face] (*PNE* A109)

[I CALL UPON PERSEPHONE, QUEEN OF THE DEAD]   A111

This is a chorus from Yeats's *Sophocles' Oedipus at Colonus,* first published in   *CPl* 571
CPl (1934) and included in subsequent editions

1-2   *Persephone . . . Hades*: In Greek mythology Persephone (Proserpine), the daughter of Zeus and Demeter, was the queen of the dead; she was married to Hades, a son of Kronos, lord of the lower world.

3   *the Furies*: the Erinyes; see note on 'To Dorothy Wellesley' (PNE 332).

4   *Stygian hell*: the Styx was the main river in Hades, the lower world of Greek mythology.

7   *hundred headed dog*: Cerberus, a monstrous dog who guarded the entrance to the lower world; he is variously described as having three or fifty or a hundred heads.

8   *daughter of Earth and Tartarus*: Jebb's version of the play, *Sophocles, The Plays and Fragments* II (3rd edn 1900), gives 'son'; Masqueray's *Sophocle* II (1924) 216 gives 'daughter' (*fille*). The daughter of Earth (Ge) and (her son) Tartarus was Echidna; their other child was Typhoeus. Echidna was half woman, half serpent; by Typhoeus she was the mother of Cerberus.

[HE HAD FAMISHED IN A WILDERNESS]   A112

This song was first published under the title 'The Singing Head and the Lady',   *CPl* 627
The Spectator, 7 December 1934. It was included, without a title, in the Commentary *KGCT*; and, without a title, in *FMM* and included in subsequent editions.
    The lyric is prefaced in *A Full Moon in March* by a dialogue between the First and Second Attendants:

Second Attendant: What do we sing?
First Attendant: An ancient Irish Queen
                     That stuck a head upon a stake

Second Attendant: Her lover's head
                    But that's a different queen, a different story.

The First Attendant then sings the song. The ancient Irish Queen to whom they refer is part of the legend of Aodh and Dectira which Yeats wrote about in his early story 'The Binding of the Hair', first published in *The Savoy*, 1896, and again in the 1897 edition of *TSR*. In this, Aodh, a strolling minstrel, comes to Queen Dectira's court and falls in love with her while she is binding up her hair. He kneels before her and is about to sing her his love when he is interrupted by a disturbance in the hall. The Queen's enemies have invaded her territories and in the ensuing battle he is killed. Queen Dectira goes out at dawn to search for him but finds only a head hanging from a bush by its dark hair. The head sings the lyric 'He Gives His Beloved Certain Rhymes' (*PNE* 57).

13   *Innkeeper's daughter*: Theophano, the Empress of Byzantium, married by Romanus II, *c.* 956 AD. For Byzantium see notes on 'Sailing to Byzantium' (*PNE* 204) and 'Byzantium' (*PNE* 260)

14   *burned great cities down*: a reference to Helen of Troy. Cf. 'No Second Troy' (*PNE* 94) and note on 'The Rose of the World' (*PNE* 20)

A113   [EVERY LOUTISH LAD IN LOVE]

CPl 622   This song is from the play *FMM*, first published in *P(Ch)*, March 1935, and is included in subsequent editions of the play.

Pythagoras : see note on 'Among School Children' (*PNE* 222). Pythagoras, the sixth-century Greek philosopher, thought the universe had a mathematical basis. He believed in the Orphic doctrine of metempsychosis, the purificatory or punishing process in which souls transmigrated from man to man, or man to animal, or animal to man. Pythagoras and every loutish lad are antithetical opposites. Perfected love, the interpenetration of opposites, makes the lout wise and the philosopher foolish.

A114   [CHILD AND DARLING, HEAR MY SONG]

CPl 628   This song is from the play *FMM*, first published in *P(Ch)*, March 1935, and is included in subsequent editions of the play.

1–8   *Child ... cruelty*: Helen Hennessy Vendler (*YV* 155–6) considers this lyric as explaining the cruelty of the previous song, commenting that 'the havoc wreaked by the Muse on her devotees is a proof of her love: whom she loves she chastens, since all knowledge and power arise . . . from obstruction and terror'.

3   *not from me/But my virgin cruelty*: in thus distinguishing herself from her

cruelty the Queen does not, in the play, see herself as an entity: that has to wait for the climactic dance.

5   *Great my love*: this either refers back to the sexual symbolism earlier in the play – 'Some man has come, some terrifying man, / For I have yawned and stretched myself three times' – or it implies that the whole process of the interpenetration of the Queen and Swineherd is preordained in the inevitable movement of the cycles of change.

6   *loved in shame*: this may refer back to the incident in the play where the Queen drops her veil, an act that prepares for her defilement, but is still accompanied by a sense of shame, symbolised by her standing with her back to the audience. In the play's final dance her defilement, her union with the severed head of the swineherd, is frontal and shameless.

[I SING A SONG OF JACK AND JILL]   A115

This song is from the play *FMM*, first published in *P(Ch)*, March 1935 and   *CPl 628* included in subsequent editions of the play.

Title: Jack and Jill: It is 'a' song of Jack and Jill, not the orthodox and well-known nursery rhyme. Yeats used the Jack and Jill imagery earlier in 'To a Young Beauty' (*PNE* 152); here he uses it somewhat in the manner of the Grimm brothers' tales.

11   *in the sky*: in the play *FMM* the Swineherd's heart is resurrected as a star, on one level 'the artifact itself' (Whitaker, *S&S* 290) or, as Vendler (*YV* 156) comments: 'the lesser ecstasy of love is sacrificed for the greater ecstasy of art . . . To achieve song . . . experience must be immolated. In being made into a poem, life is detached, made into something external and public, and sacrificed on the altar of form.'

SD   She dances: 'Woman craves for, is obsessed by, the sexual act. Her dance before the severed head ends as she takes it to her breast . . . Woman is eternally seeking this ravishment, within her very being; because of the ''craving in her bones'' '; Henn (*LT* 288), who also connects the image of the severed head with the Second Coming, quoting *AV*(B) 273:

> When I think of the moment before revelation I think of Salome . . . dancing before Herod and receiving the Prophet's head in her indifferent hands, and wonder if what seems to us decadence was not in reality the exaltation of the muscular flesh and of civilization perfectly achieved.

An earlier MS. version (see Curtis Bradford, *YW* 288) is more explicit:

> He laughs again. The dance expresses refusal. She takes up the head and lays it upon the ground. She dances before it. Her dance is a dance of invitation. She takes up the head and dances with the head to drum taps which grow quicker

and quicker. Her dance expresses the sexual act. She kisses the head. Her body shivers. She sinks slowly down, holding the head against her breast. Song of the closing of the curtain or the unfolding and folding of the cloth. The song at the end of 'Clock Tower' with the line 'Their desecration and the lover's night'.

A116   [WHY MUST THOSE HOLY, HAUGHTY FEET DESCEND]

CPl 629   This is a song from the play *FMM* first published in *P(Ch)*, March 1935 and included in subsequent editions of the play.

A117   [CLIP AND LIP AND LONG FOR MORE]

CPl 639   This song is from the play *KGTB*, first published in *FMM*.

2   *abstracts*: mere shadows of supernatural union

9   *nuptial bed of man*: cf. 'The marriage bed is the symbol of the solved antinomy, and were more than symbol could a man there lose and keep his identity but he falls asleep. That sleep is the same as the sleep to Death.' (*AV*(B) 52)

18   *sacred Virgil*: This view of the Roman poet Virgil (70–19 BC) is based on the medieval interpretation of his Fourth Eclogue which seemed to have the force of a divine prophecy. For the association between Virgil and the ushering in of a new cycle, see notes on 'Two songs from a Play' (*PNE* 218) and Yeats's play *The Resurrection* (*CPl* 590).

20   *a stone upon my tongue*: the same image is used at the end of the first section of 'A Dialogue of Self and Soul' (*PNE* 242) when the Soul declares its inability to describe the mystical union of Is and Ought, Knower and Known – thought and its object:

> . . . intellect no longer knows
> *Is* from the *Ought*, or *Knower* from the *Known* –
> That is to say, ascends to Heaven;
> Only the dead can be forgiven;
> But when I think of that my tongue's a stone.

A118   DEDICATION

VE 790   This poem was published in *A Speech and Two Poems* (privately printed, Dublin, 1937). The other poem was 'The Municipal Gallery Revisited' (*PNE* 354).

1   *MacCartan*: Patrick McCartan (1878–1963), an Irish-American admirer of

Yeats who was organiser of an American 'Testimonial Committee for W. B. Yeats' in 1937; the fifty members of the committee established a fund to give Yeats a sufficient income for the rest of his life. On 17 August 1937 Yeats, who had decided that he would use the money for spending his winters in warmer climates, made the matter public at a banquet of the Irish Academy of Letters. He received £600 in 1937 and £400 in June 1938.

5   *Farrell, steel king*: James A. Farrell (1863-1943), President of the US Steel Corporation from 1911 to 1932, was chairman of the Testimonial Committeee.

7   *Dudley Digges*: Dudley Digges (1879-1947), an Irish actor who resigned and moved to the United States in 1904, having refused to play in the first production of Synge's *In the Shadow of the Glen*.

[THIS THEY NAILED UPON A POST]   A119

This song was first published in the play *The Herne's Egg* (1938) and included in   *CPl 651*
subsequent editions of the play.

3   *herne*: heron

[WHEN I TAKE A BEAST TO MY JOYFUL BREAST]   A120

This song was first published in the play *The Herne's Egg* (1938) and included in   *CPl 664*
subsequent editions of the play.

[WHEN BEAK AND CLAW THEIR WORK BEGAN]   A121

This song was first published in the play *The Herne's Egg* and included in   *CPl 673*
subsequent editions of the play.

WHY SHOULD NOT OLD MEN BE MAD?   A122

This poem was written in January 1936, and first appeared in *OTB*.   *CP 388*

4   *a drunken journalist*: not identified, but R. M. Smylie (1894-1954), son of a former editor of the *Sligo Times*, and himself an editor of the *Irish Times* from 1934, has been suggested. He held court in the Palace Bar, Fleet Street, Dublin, and wrote under the pen name 'Nichevo'.

5   *a girl that knew all Dante once*: Iseult Gonne. For Dante see note on 'Ego Dominus Tuus' (*PNE 181*).

6 *a dunce*: Francis Stuart (b. 1902), the novelist and poet, who married Iseult Gonne in 1920. He subsequently married Gertrude Meiszner. His autobiography, *Things to live for*, was published in 1936. Yeats's views on him changed from time to time. Cf. a letter to Mrs Shakespear of 25 July 1932:

> Read *The Coloured Dome* by Francis Stuart. It is strange and exciting in theme and perhaps more personally and beautifully written than any book of our generation; it makes you understand the strange Ireland that is rising up here. What an inexplicable thing sexual selection is. Iseult picked this young man, by what seemed half chance, half a mere desire to escape from an impossible life, and when he seemed almost imbecile to his own relations. Now he is her very self made active and visible, her nobility walking and singing. If luck comes to his aid he will be our great writer. (*L* 799-80)

See also his comment in 'Modern Ireland', *Massachusetts Review* (Winter 1964) 266-7, in which he described him as possessing:

> a style full of intellectual passion and music. . . . He himself is typical of the new Ireland. . . . Shortly after I first met him he spent fifteen months in jail as a political prisoner; then he was [in] trouble with his Church as one of the editors of a weekly review called in half-a-dozen Catholic papers infamous, immoral, blasphemous. A little later [he] was spending his life under the influence of St John of the Cross in meditation [and] prayer. A little [later] still he owned a racehorse and was betting at the Curragh.

7 *A Helen of social welfare dream*: probably Maud Gonne (though he may have had Constance Markievicz in mind also). The comma after 'dream' was not in the original MS. Cf. *WBY* 210 for the screaming upon a waggonette, where Hone records how Miss Horniman told Yeats 'the greatest poet is always helpless beside a beautiful woman screaming from a cart'. Cf. note on 'The Rose of the World' (*PNE* 20)

A123   CRAZY JANE ON THE MOUNTAIN

CP 390   This poem was written in July 1938 and first appeared in *OTB*.

1-2   *the Bishop* (*Said Crazy Jane*): cf. the earlier poems about Crazy Jane and notes on *Words for Music Perhaps* (*CP* 290). Yeats wrote to Dorothy Wellesley on 13 July 1938 that he was writing a new Crazy Jane poem – 'a wild affair' (*L* 912).

7   *A King had some beautiful cousins*: a reference to the brutal killing of the last Tsar of Russia, Nicholas II (1886-1918), and his family, by Commissar Yurovsky and ten Lettish soldiers at Ekaterinburg in July 1918. (See E. M. Almedingen, *The Romanovs* (1966).) Yeats wrote:

> I have been told that King George V [1865-1936] asked that the Russian royal family should be brought to England. The English Prime Minister refused, fearing the effect upon the English working classes. That story may be no more

true than other stories spoken by word of mouth, but it will serve for an example. The average Englishman would think King George's submission, his abandonment of his relations to a fate already foreseen, if proved, a necessary, even a noble sacrifice. It was indeed his submission, his correctness as a constitutional sovereign that made his popularity so unbounded that he became a part of the English educational system. Some thousands of examination papers were distributed to schoolchildren in a Northern industrial district with the question, 'Who was the best man who ever lived?' The vast majority answered, 'King George the Fifth'. Christ was runner-up. (*E* 442–3)

Cf. Dorothy Wellesley's comment on Yeats's visit to her in July 1938:

I discovered later that he considers George V should have abdicated as a protest when his cousin the Czar was dethroned. 'My God!' he said, 'in ancient Ireland such conduct as that of George V would have been an impossibility,' adding that 'the English should have declared war upon their ally Russia in 1917'. About all this Yeats was intensely serious. (*DWL* 171)

'Cracked Mary's Vision', an unpublished poem of 1929 (see Ellmann *IY* (101–2)) also attacked George V (contrasted with a King of the 'great troop' of the 'Long-haired Tuatha de Danaan'). Each of the poem's three stanzas ends 'May the devil take King George.' For the King's attitude to the Russian royal family see Kenneth Rose, *King George V* (1983).

15 *Great-bladdered Emer*: a footnote in *OTB* reads:

In a fragment from some early version of *The Courting of Emer*, Emer is chosen for the strength and volume of her bladder. This strength and volume were certainly considered signs of vigour. A woman of divine origin was murdered by jealous rivals because she made the deepest hole in the snow with her urine. (*E* 433)

No reference in this connection to Emer has been found. *PNE* cites 'The Deaths of Lugaid and Derbforgaill', *Eriu* 5 (1911) 201–218. Derbforgaill, daughter of the King of Norway, married Lugaid of the Red Stripes, and was killed by jealous women after winning a contest in which women made pillars of snow and urinated on them. Cuchulain had arranged that Derbforgaill, whom he had intended to marry (but of whom he had become a blood relative by sucking a wound of hers) should marry Lugaid instead.

Dorothy Wellesley's comment has a touch of the unintentionally ludicrous:

When he had read the poem I said, 'What could be better?' I attempted, however, to point out that 'great-bladdered' would prove a stumbling-block to any reader not versed in Irish folklore and suggested 'great bellied' instead, saying that this would equally well give the same eugenic meaning without altogether losing the coarseness so necessary to the poem. 'No, I must have bladder!' he exclaimed. I think he is right. He went on to tell how in the Irish legend all other women were jealous of the Queen's power of retention due to the size of her bladder. This was of great importance as seeming a mark of vigour; also how the Queen was able to make a larger hole in the snow than the other women, so that they were jealous, and set upon her and killed her. I suggested he should write a short separate poem on this legend alone, saying that the snow gave the theme its poetry. 'She made a deeper golden hole in the snow' I said. 'Yes', he replied, with intensity. 'Perhaps to-morrow I shall write the poem.' (*DWL* 171–2)

17   *Cuchulain*: see note on 'To the Rose upon the Rood of Time' (*PNE* 17).

A124   A STATESMAN'S HOLIDAY

CP 389   This poem was completed in April 1938 and first appeared in *OTB*.

A passage in *OTB* explains the mood of the poem (which [untitled] followed this prose passage):

> In my savage youth I was accustomed to say that no man should be permitted to open his mouth in Parliament until he had sung or written his *Utopia*, for lacking that we could not know where he was taking us, and I still think that artists of all kinds should once again praise or represent great or happy people. Here in Monte Carlo, where I am writing, somebody talked of a man with a monkey and some kind of stringed instrument, and it has pleased me to imagine him a great politician. I will make him sing to the sort of tune that goes well with my early sentimental poems.   (*E* 451–2)

5   *Oscar*: possibly Oscar Wilde, but Saul (*PYP* 173) writes 'presumably Oscar (Tschirky) of the Waldorf (NY)'. But cf. *A* 139 where Yeats remarked '. . . the dinner-table was Wilde's event and made him the greatest talker of his time, and his plays and dialogues have what merit they possess from being now an imitation, now a record, of his talk'.

13   *grass-green Avalon*: the original MS. of the poem contained as refrain 'But a Burne-Jones boat and the grass-green island of Avalon'. Cf. notes on 'Under the Moon' (*PNE* 86). Yeats may have had in mind the Burne-Jones designs for Stannon Hall, (these, executed by Morris's company, included the 'Ship of the Knights') or possibly the picture of Arthur in Avalon (1880). Another water-colour was entitled 'The Boat'.

14   *a great Lord Chancellor*: Torchiana (*Y & GI* 356) suggests F. E. Smith (1872–1930), who became Lord Birkenhead. He had been government prosecutor at Casement's trial, had guaranteed the authenticity of Casement's Diaries. Earlier he had worked with Carson to keep Ulster out of any Home Rule settlement. He was Lord Chancellor from 1912 to 1922, known for his oratory as well as his legal acumen. But Torchiana considers that Yeats may have had Lord Glenavy in mind. He points out that Churchill's name appeared in an early MS. of the poem.

15   *the Sack*: a large square bag of wool covered with cloth without back or arms on which the Lord Chancellor sits in the House of Lords

16   *Commanding officer*: Torchiana (*Y & GI* 355) suggests Sir Hubert Gough [1870–1963], loyal to Ulster, who refused to take up defensive positions in

Belfast (he commanded the Third Cavalry Brigade at the Curragh Camp) in March 1914, resigned, was dismissed and reinstated. This Curragh 'mutiny' accelerated the progress of events that led to the 1916 Rising.

18   *de Valéra*: see notes on 'Parnell's Funeral' (*PNE* 304).

19   *the King of Greece*: George II (1890-1947), who returned to Greece in 1935 and appointed General Metaxas as head of the government.

20   *the man that made the motors*: probably William Morris (1887-1963), who became Lord Nuffield. The Morris car factories were situated at Cowley, Oxford, and at the time Yeats lived there produced cars known as Morris Oxfords and Morris Cowleys. Yeats mentions Morris (*OTB*) as a self-made man whose benefactions would substitute applied science for ancient wisdom in Oxford (*E* 423). Saul (*PYP* 173) suggests Ford as possible.

34   *a strutting turkey walk*: possibly a parody of Yeats's own style of walking. Cf. Torchiana, ' "Among School Children" and the Education of the Irish Spirit', *IER* 123.

[THE HARLOT SANG TO THE BEGGARMAN]   A125

This song concludes the play *The Death of Cuchulain*, first published in the Cuala   *CPl* 704-5
Press edition of *Last Poems and Two Plays* (1939) and is included in subsequent editions.

1   *The harlot*: this symbol is discussed in Wilson, *Y & T* 176-85

3   *Conall, Cuchulain, Usna's boys*: for Conall and Cuchulain see note on [My Man is the Best] (*PNE* A62). In the play Cuchulain was given six mortal wounds; those who gave them were themselves killed by Conall Cearnach. See Birgit Bjersby's comment:

> When he [Cuchulain] was dead a man called Lugaid cut his head off, but Conall Cearnach enacted a terrible vengeance on behalf of Cuchulain; according to one version he returned to the Ulster men with Lugaid's head. According to another he brought the heads of all the chief men taking part in this last fight against Cuchulain. On his return he showed Emer (Cuchulain's wife) the heads telling her of his exploits.   (*ICL* 53)

Usna's Sons were Naoise, and Ainle and Ardan, who accompanied Naoise to Scotland when he ran away with Deirdre, King Conchubar's intended bride. See note on 'The Rose of the World' (*PNE* 20).

5   *Maeve*: see Yeats's note on 'The Hosting of the Sidhe' (*PNE* 40)

7   *can get/No grip on their thighs*: Wilson (*Y & T* 116) refers to the

'intractability of the ethereal body to mortal touch', and comments that the harlot cannot make love with the Sidhe, quoting Plutarch upon the subject.

9–10   *long pale faces . . . great horses*: cf. 'Under Ben Bulben' (*PNE* 356):

> Swear by those horsemen, by those women
> Complexion and form prove superhuman,
> That pale long-visaged company
> That air in immortality
> Completeness of their passions won;
> Now they ride the wintry dawn
> Where Ben Bulben sets the scene

16   *adore and loathe*: cf. 'The Lady's First Song' (*PNE* 326)

> I am in love
> And that is my shame.
> What hurts the soul
> My soul adores,
> No better than a beast
> Upon all fours

Cf. also 'Crazy Jane Grown Old Looks at the Dancers' (*PNE* 274) where the dancing youth winds the girl's coal-black hair 'As though to strangle her' and the dancing girl 'Drew a knife to strike him dead'. Yeats wrote about this poem in a letter to Mrs Shakespear of 2 March 1929:

> Last night I saw in a dream strange ragged excited people singing in a crowd. The most visible were a man and woman who were I think dancing. The man was swinging around his head a weight at the end of a rope or leather thong and I knew that he did not know whether he would strike her dead or not, and both had their eyes fixed on each other, and both sang their love for one another. I suppose it was Blake's old thought 'sexual love is founded on spiritual hate' (*L* 758).

See also 'Anima Hominis' where the warfare of man and demon is imagined in love (*M* 336–7).

19   *the Post Office*: see note on 'Three Songs to the One Burden' (*PNE* 357) where the Easter Rising of 1916 is the subject.

21   *Pearse and Connolly*: see notes on 'Easter 1916' (*PNE* 193). Pearse is celebrated in the third stanza, but a different Connolly, the actor, in the second stanza of 'Three Songs to the One Burden' (*PNE* 357).

22–23   *men first shed their blood?/Who thought Cuchulain*: Yeats is probably thinking here of Pearse's cult of sacrifice. He

> had said
> That in every generation
> Must Ireland's blood be shed

See notes on 'The Rose Tree' (*PNE* 195) and note (p. 194) on 'Sixteen Dead

Men' (*PNE* 194). The theme linking Pearse (who was fighting in the General Post Offfice, Dublin, in 1916) with Cuchulain also appears in the fourth stanza of 'The Statues' (*PNE* 362):

> When Pearse summoned Cuchulain to his side
> What stalked through the Post Office? What intellect
> What calculation, number, measurement replied?

In this poem Yeats saw Pearse summoning intellectual and aesthetic forces into being (through becoming part of the process of mythology).

29 *A statue's there*: Yeats wrote on 28 June 1938 to Edith Shackleton Heald that 'Pearse and some of his followers had a cult of him [Cuchulain]. The government has put a statue of Cuchulain in the rebuilt Post Office to commemorate this'

30 *Oliver Sheppard*: The Irish sculptor Oliver Sheppard (1865–1941) whose statue *The Death of Cuchulain* (executed *c*. 1911–12) is situated in the General Post Office, Dublin, a memorial to the 1916 Rebellion.

Gaelic Names

YEATS commented that when he wrote most of the poems in *P* (1895; rev. 1899) he had hardly considered seriously the question of the pronunciation of the Irish words. He had copied at times somebody's perhaps fanciful spelling, and at times the ancient spelling as he found it in some literal translation, pronouncing the words as they were spelt. In 1899 he supposed he would not at any time have defended this system, but he did not then know what system to adopt. He added:

> The modern pronunciation, which is usually followed by those who spell the words phonetically, is certainly unlike the pronunciation of the time when classical Irish literature was written, and, as far as I know, no Irish scholar who writes in English or French has made that minute examination of the way the names come into the rhythms and measures of the old poems which can alone discover the old pronunciation. A French Celtic scholar gave me the pronunciation of a few names, and told me that Mr Whitley Stokes had written something about the subject in German, but I am ignorant of German. If I ever learn the old pronunciation, I will revise all these poems, but at present I can only affirm that I have not treated my Irish names as badly as the mediaeval writers of the stories of King Arthur treated their Welsh names.

In his note of 1892 he reversed the correct pronunciation of the long and short vowels in Cuchulain, saying Cuchulain was pronounced Cuhoolin; it should have been Coo-hullin. In a glossary he gave the old spelling in parentheses wherever he had adopted somebody's phonetic spelling in the poems. Information from this is supplied in this edition. In *CP* he adopted Lady Gregory's spelling of Gaelic names with two exceptions.

> The 'd' of Edain ran too well in my verse for me to adopt her perhaps more correct Etain, and for some reason unknown to me I have always preferred 'Aengus' to her 'Angus'. In her *Gods and Fighting Men* and *Cuchulain of Muirthemne* she went as close to the Gaelic spelling as she could without making the names unpronounceable to the average reader.

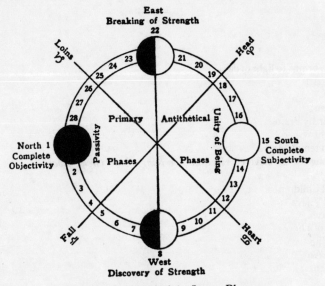

The Great Wheel of the Lunar Phases

Index to Titles

522

Index to first lines

533

535

542